THE ENCYCLOPEDIA OF
MILITARY AIRCRAFT

THE ENCYCLOPEDIA OF
MILITARY AIRCRAFT

ROBERT JACKSON

p

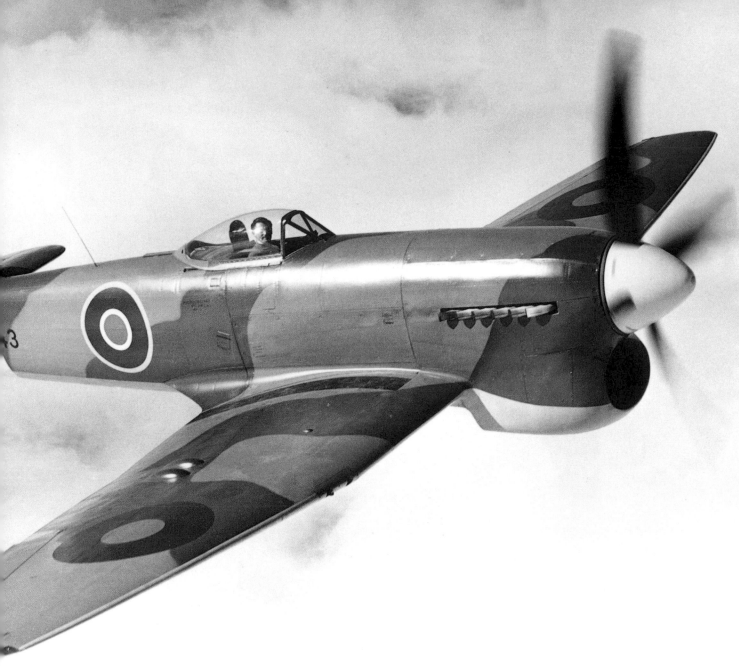

Contents

❙INTRODUCTION

▲ *The Grumman F-14 Tomcat has seen action in the Gulf War, the Balkans, and Afghanistan, and in the 1980s was involved in several clashes over Libya.*

On January 19, 1910, Lieutenant Paul Beck of the US Army released sandbags, representing bombs, over Los Angeles from an airplane flown by pioneer aviator Louis Paulhan, and on June 30, Glenn H. Curtiss dropped dummy bombs from a height of 50ft (15m) in an area representing the shape of a battleship, marked by buoys on Lake Keuka. The feasibility of discharging firearms from an aircraft was also demonstrated on August 20, 1910, when US Army Lieutenant Jacob Earl Fickel fired a 0.30-in (7.62-mm) caliber rifle at a ground target at Sheepshead Bay, New York.

Such were the humble beginnings of military aviation, the first steps on the path that would lead to the stealth bombers, the air superiority fighters, and the vertical takeoff combat aircraft of today, with all their awesome striking power.

By 1910, the air arms of the world's major powers were beginning to take shape. When Europe became embroiled in war four years later, the value of the aircraft as an instrument of reconnaissance was soon established, and it was the need to deny this vital element of air reconnaissance to the enemy that led directly to the birth of the fighting airplane, armed with one or more machine guns. Warfare breeds new technology, and the single most important technological development in the air war of 1914–18 was the development, in 1915, of the synchronized machine gun, enabling the weapon to fire forward through the propeller disk. With this new-

▶ *The Avro Lancaster was one of the most successful bombers of WWII. These aircraft of No. 50 Squadron were pictured in August 1942.*

found ability to use the whole aircraft as an aiming platform came a scientific approach to aerial fighting; experienced pilots began to formulate tactics and combat maneuvers that formed the principles on which future air combat would be based. Such were the technological strides made during four years of war that the aircraft evolved from a flimsy, unreliable machine barely capable of crossing the English Channel into a heavy bomber capable of attacking the German capital, Berlin, from bases in eastern England.

Progress followed several diverse paths of air warfare; by 1918 the world's first strategic bombing forces were operational, and the fighting airplane had gone to sea on the first custom-made aircraft carrier. By the time hostilities ended in November 1918, air power had become a major factor in the

military machine of every major nation, and there were few who doubted that it would play a decisive part in the wars of the future.

After a period of stagnation following the "war to end all wars," the limited conflicts of the 1930s, in Spain and elsewhere, gave renewed impetus to the development of the aircraft as a fighting machine, and World War II saw the evolution of specialized roles such as tactical fighter-bomber, night fighter, antishipping strike aircraft, and so on. In the wake of WWII, the destructive power of nuclear weapons was to dominate air power doctrine for the next half century, to such an extent that many of the tactical air power lessons, learned the hard way during World War II, were forgotten. Yet the war that erupted in Korea in June 1950 required the use of tactical air power on a scale not seen since the Battle of Normandy, for it was the United Nations' only means of blunting the North Korean offensive during the crucial early weeks of the conflict. The Korean War had a dramatic effect on the organisation and equipment of both the USAF and the Soviet Air Force. On both sides of the Iron Curtain, three years of jet combat experience over the Yalu was woven into the designs of new air interceptors. In the United States, the agile brain of Lockheed's Clarence Johnson and his design team gave birth to the revolutionary F-104 Starfighter, while Russia's answer was the MiG-21. All-weather fighters, too, assumed high priority; in 1955 the USAF received the first examples of the Convair F-102 Delta Dagger, the outcome of a USAF requirement dating back to 1950, and in the following year Soviet air defense squadrons received the Yakovlev Yak-25 Flashlight. The lessons of Korea were also absorbed by the British, who accelerated deployment of their nuclear deterrent force (the V-force) and ordered fighter types like the Hawker Hunter and Gloster Javelin into "super-priority" production. Both, eventually, would be replaced by the Mach 2 English Electric Lightning interceptor. The French, too, pushed ahead with the development of their Dassault Mirage family of advanced combat aircraft.

This time, the tactical air power lessons learned in Korea would not be forgotten. A huge emphasis was placed on the development of advanced multirole naval strike aircraft, assuring the application of tactical air support in areas outside the range of land-based aircraft; so were born the A-4 Skyhawk and the potent, multirole F-4 Phantom. The war in Vietnam, with its attendant huge losses of tactical aircraft, produced a requirement for an aircraft capable of penetrating sophisticated air defense systems, hitting its targets with pinpoint accuracy, and surviving to fight another day; and so the concept of the "stealth" combat aircraft was formulated, coming to fruition in the F-117A and the B-2.

The air war over Vietnam produced two other main requirements, one for a close support aircraft that could

▲ *The Sea Harrier FRS Mk I proved itself in combat during the Falklands conflict in 1982, operating from HMS Hermes and HMS Invincible.*

operate from primitive sites close to the front line, and the other for an agile combat aircraft. The first was met by the British Harrier V/STOL aircraft, which was further developed by McDonnell Douglas for the US Marine Corps, while the second produced the USAF's McDonnell Douglas F-15 and the Navy's Grumman F-14 Tomcat. In 1991, the F-15 proved its value as an air superiority fighter over Iraq, where its principal adversary was its Russian-built equivalent, the MiG-29.

In other areas, too, the conflicts in Korea and Vietnam produced urgent military aircraft requirements, and one of the most important was in the tactical transportation field. Korea had shown the need for a transportation aircraft with a large load-carrying capacity that could operate from rough airstrips, and again it was Lockheed that came up with the answer in the C-130 Hercules, the most versatile transportation aircraft ever designed.

The aircraft mentioned above represent just a few of the hundreds of types, from the very earliest to the very latest, assembled in this profusely illustrated book, each with its own specification. Here, in one volume, is the story of military aviation at a glance, in a panorama of development spanning two centuries.

▮ AEG C.IV

The AEG (Allgemeine Elektritzitäts Gesellschaft) C-type armed two-seaters were developed from the company's B-type unarmed reconnaissance and training biplanes. The principal type was the C.IV, an effective and versatile design, which entered service in the spring of 1916 and which served on all fronts almost until the end of World War I. A night bomber version capable of carrying six 110-lb (50-kg) bombs, the C.IVN, was also developed at the end of 1916.

SPECIFICATION: Type general-purpose biplane • Crew 2 • Powerplant one 160hp Mercedes D.III water-cooled in-line • Max speed 98mph (158km/h) at sea level • Service ceiling 16,404ft (5,000m) • Endurance 3hrs • Wingspan 44ft 2in (13.46m) • Length 23ft 5in (7.15m) • Height 11ft (3.35m) • Weight 2,469lb (1,120kg) loaded • Armament two machine guns; 220lb (100kg) of bombs

▲ AEG produced a total of 658 "C'" types, the majority being the C.IV which gave useful service with German front-line combat units.

▮ AEG G.IV

The AEG G.IV was the most widely used member of a family of the company's G-series of medium bombers, built between 1915 and 1918. Entering service in late 1916, of mixed wood and steel tubing construction, the G.IV incorporated all the best features of its predecessors, the G.I, G.II, and G.III. Because of its limited range and fairly low operational ceiling, the G.IV was used mainly for tactical bombing. In 1917 the units equipped with the type deployed to the southern front and began night bombing attacks on Italian towns, the main targets being Venice, Padua, Verona, and Treviso. Returning to the Western Front in 1918, the G.IVs flew night bombing missions until the end of the war.

SPECIFICATION: Type medium bomber • Crew 3 • Powerplant two 260hp Mercedes D.IVa 6-cylinder liquid-cooled in-lines • Max speed 103mph (165km/h) • Service ceiling 14,760ft (4,500m) • Endurance 4hrs 30mins • Wingspan 60ft 4in (18.4m) • Length 31ft 10in (9.7m) • Height 12ft 9in (3.9m) • Weight 8,002lb (3,630kg) loaded • Armament two machine guns; 882lb (400kg) of bombs

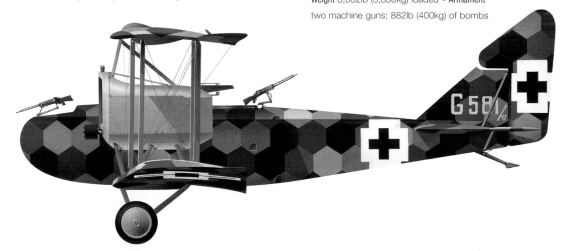

▮ Aeritalia G.222

A versatile medium transport that can operate effectively from short, rough airstrips, the Aeritalia G.222 flew in prototype form on July 18, 1970. The first of 50 production aircraft was delivered at the end of 1978, replacing the Fairchild C-119 in the Italian Air Force's transport units. A prototype ECM version, equipped with extensive electronic installations and with accommodation for 10 systems operators, was also produced in 1978. The transport type had some export success, customers including Argentina (3), Dubai (1), Libya (20), Nigeria (4), Somalia (4), USA (10), and Venezuela (8).

SPECIFICATION: Type tactical transportation • Crew 3 • Powerplant two 3,400hp General Electric T64-GE-P4D turboprops • Max speed 336mph (540km/h) at 15,000ft (4,575m) • Service ceiling 25,000ft (7,620m) • Max range 2,832 miles (4,558km) • Wingspan 131ft 3in (40.0m) • Length 106ft 3in (32.40m) • Height 38ft 5in (11.65m) • Weight 35,270lb (16,000kg) loaded • Armament none

▶ The Aeritalia G.222 demonstration aircraft, I-MARD, pictured over the Egyptian desert.

❙ Aermacchi MB.326 ITALY

One of the most important light attack and training aircraft to emerge during the Cold War era, the Aermacchi MB.326 first flew on December 10, 1957. Numerous variants were

▲ Australia's MB.326Hs are used for fighter support, including attack lead-in training.

produced during the aircraft's lengthy career, depending on the customer's requirements. The most noteworthy version was the MB.326K single-seater of 1970, which, although designed as an operational trainer, could also be used in a tactical support role. In its various guises the MB.326 has been used by the air forces of Argentina, Australia, Dubai, Ghana, South Africa, Tunisia, Zaire, and Zambia.

SPECIFICATION: Type light ground-attack aircraft (data MB.326K) • Crew 1 • Powerplant one 4,000-lb (1,814-kg) thrust Rolls-Royce Viper 632-42 turbojet • Max speed 553mph (890km/h) at 5,000ft (1,525m) • Service ceiling 41,000ft (12,500m) • Max range 680 miles (1,090km) • Wingspan 35ft 7in (10.85m) including tip tanks • Length 35ft (10.67m) • Height 12ft 2in (3.72m) • Weight 13,000lb (5,895kg) loaded • Armament two 1.19-in (30-mm) DEFA cannon; six underwing points with provision for up to 4,000lb (1,814kg) of external ordnance

❙ Aermacchi MB.339 ITALY

The Aermacchi MB.339 was developed from the MB.326 to replace this aircraft and the Fiat G.91T in the advanced jet training and close support roles, the new aircraft being produced in single-seat and two-seat configurations. Customers for the two-seat trainer-attack version have included Argentina, Dubai, Ghana, Italy, Malaysia, Nigeria, and Peru.

SPECIFICATION: Type combat trainer/strike aircraft (data MB.339K) • Crew 1 • Powerplant one 4,450-lb (2,018-kg) thrust Piaggio-built RR Viper 680-43 turbojet • Max speed 508mph (815km/h) at 30,000ft (9,150m) • Service ceiling 46,700ft (14,240m) • Combat radius 230 miles (371km), low level with max payload • Wingspan 36ft 10in (11.22m) • Length 36ft 11in (11.24m) • Height 13ft 1in (3.99m) • Weight 14,000lb (6,350kg) • Armament two 1.19-in (30-mm) DEFA cannon; six underwing points with provision for up to 4,000lb (1,814kg) of external ordnance

▲ The prototype Aermacchi MB.339A two-seat light attack aircraft pictured against an Alpine background.

■ Aero A.11

CZECHOSLOVAKIA

First flown in 1923, the versatile Aero A.11 general-purpose biplane superseded the early Letov aircraft that had been built soon after the inauguration of the Czech aircraft industry during 1918–19. The aircraft proved so successful in Czech Army Air Force service that 440 were built in over 20 different models. As well as the day and night reconnaissance versions, there were the Ab.11 and Ab.11N day and night bomber variants, the A.21, A.24, and A.25 trainers, and the

A.29 target tug. The latter was also fitted with floats, and was the first seaplane built in Czechoslovakia.

SPECIFICATION: Type reconnaissance biplane • Crew 2 • Powerplant one 240hp Walter W.IV 8-cylinder liquid-cooled engine • Max speed 133mph (214km/h) at 8,200ft (2,500m) • Service ceiling 23,600ft (7,200m) • Max range 466 miles (750km) • Wingspan 41ft 11in (12.77m) • Length 26ft 11in (8.20m) • Height 10ft 2in (3.10m) • Weight 3,260lb (1,480kg) empty • Armament one 0.303-in (7.62-mm) machine gun

▲ *In 1926 an Aero Ab.11 completed a 9,320-mile (15,000-km) publicity tour of 23 countries.*

■ Aero L-29 Delfin

CZECHOSLOVAKIA

▲ *The most successful Czech-built aircraft ever, the L-29 saw combat in a number of conflicts.*

A two-seat basic and advanced trainer, the Aero L-29 first flew in April 1959 and in 1961 it was selected as standard training equipment for the Soviet Air Force, which accepted more than 2,000 of the 3,600 aircraft built.

The type subsequently served with all the Warsaw Pact air forces and with many other Soviet-aligned air arms. First deliveries were made in 1963 and the L-29 remained in production for 11 years.

SPECIFICATION: Type jet trainer • Crew 2 • Powerplant one 1960-lb (890-kg) thrust Motorlet M701 VC-150 turbojet • Max speed 407mph (655km/h) at 16,400ft (5,000m) • Service ceiling 36,100ft (11,000m) • Normal range 397 miles (640km) • Wingspan 33ft 8in (10.29m) • Length 35ft 5in (10.81m) • Height 10ft 3in (3.13m) • Weights 5,027lb (2,280kg) empty; 7231lb (3,280kg) loaded • Armament none

■ Aero L-39

CZECHOSLOVAKIA

SPECIFICATION: Type trainer/light attack aircraft • Crew 1/2 • Powerplant one 3,792-lb (1,720-kg) thrust Ivchenko AI-25TL turbofan • Max speed 391mph (630km/h) at 16,404ft (5,000m) • Service ceiling 29,525ft (9,000m) • Max range 1,087 miles (1,750km) • Wingspan 31ft (9.46m) • Length 40ft 5in (12.32m) • Height 15ft 5in (4.72m) • Weights 7,341lb (3,330kg) empty; 11,618lb (5,270kg) loaded • Armament one 0.9-in (23-mm) GSh-23L twin-barrel cannon; AA-2 Atoll AAMs; rocket pods (57 or 130mm); bombs up to 1,102lb (500kg)

The L-39 Albatros was designed to succeed the L-29 as the standard jet trainer in the air forces of Czechoslovakia, the USSR, and East Germany. Fitted with a turbofan engine, it was much more powerful than its predecessor and was developed into a light attack aircraft. Two versions of this were produced, the L-39ZO single-seater, with reinforced wings for the carriage of underwing stores, and the L-39ZA, which retained the two-seat configuration of the trainer.

▲ *The Aero L-39 was produced in four variants, the most numerous of which was the L-39C trainer model.*

∎ AGO C.II

▲ *Two examples of the C.II-W floatplane were evaluated by the Imperial German navy, but no orders were placed.*

One of the best reconnaissance aircraft of World War I, the AGO (Aerowerke Gustav Otto) C.II of 1915 was unusual in that it was a pusher-type design, with twin tail booms. A fast, maneuverable aircraft with a respectable range, it remained in service for about a year before being replaced by more modern types.

SPECIFICATION: Type reconnaissance biplane • Crew 2 • Powerplant one 220hp Benz IV 6-cylinder liquid-cooled in-line • Max speed 86mph (137km/h) • Service ceiling 14,764ft (4,500m) • Max range 360 miles (580km) • Wingspan 47ft 7in (14.5m) • Length 32ft 3in (9.84m) • Height 10ft 5in (3.17m) • Weight 4,290lb (1,946kg) • Armament one machine gun

∎ Aichi B7A Ryusei "Grace"

JAPAN

The Aichi B7A Ryusei (Shooting Star) torpedo bomber, developed in response to a 1941 Japanese Navy requirement, first flew in May 1942, but the principal variant, the B7A-2, did not enter service until 1944, production having been delayed by engine difficulties and then by an earthquake. By the time the type became operational the Imperial Japanese

Navy no longer had any aircraft carriers, and the 114 aircraft that were built saw limited service with land-based units.

SPECIFICATION: Type torpedo-bomber • Crew 2 • Powerplant one 2,000hp Nakajima NK9C Homare 12 18-cylinder radial • Max speed 352mph (566km/h) at sea level • Service ceiling 36,910ft (11,250m) • Max range 1,888 miles (3,038km) • Wingspan 47ft 3in (14.40m) • Length 37ft 8in (11.49m) • Height 13ft 4in (4.07m) • Weight 14,330lb (6,500kg) loaded • Armament two fixed forward-firing 0.79-in (20-mm) cannon in wing leading edges and one 0.51-in (13-mm) machine gun in rear cockpit; one 1,764-lb (800-kg) Long Lance torpedo

▲ *The Ryusei, here illustrated in B7A-1 form, was destined never to fly from an operational Imperial Japanese Navy aircraft carrier.*

▌Aichi D3A "Val"

The Aichi D3A, which featured prominently in the attack on Pearl Harbor and the Japanese conquests in Southeast Asia, first flew in January 1938, and between December 1939 and August 1945, 1,495 were built in two principal variants. The first was the D3A-1, which entered service in 1940; the second was the D3A-2, which had the more powerful 1,000hp Kinsei engine and increased fuel capacity. This was the major production version, 1,016 being built. By 1943 the type was obsolete and many were adapted as D3A2-K trainers. Many more were expended in Kamikaze attacks at Leyte and Okinawa.

SPECIFICATION: Type naval dive-bomber • Crew 2 • Powerplant one 1,300hp Mitsubishi Kinsei 54 14-cylinder radial • Max speed 267mph (430km/h) at 9,845ft (3,000m) • Service ceiling 34,450ft (10,500m) • Max range 840 miles (1,352km) • Wingspan 47ft 2in (14.37m) • Length 33ft 5in (10.20m) • Height 12ft 7in (3.80m) • Weight 9,100lb (4,122kg) • Armament two 0.303-in (7.7-mm) machine guns in upper forward fuselage and one in rear cockpit; external bomb load of 816lb (370kg)

▲ The Aichi D3A was Japan's principal carrier-based dive-bomber for the first two years of the Pacific War.

▌Aichi E13A "Jake"

▲ The E13A was numerically the most important of all Japanese float seaplanes of World War II, and had a remarkable range and endurance.

The Aichi E13A was the Japanese Navy's leading ship-borne reconnaissance aircraft and saw widespread service in the Pacific war. The aircraft flew in prototype form in 1940 and entered production in the second half of 1941, its first combat mission being to scout ahead of the Japanese carrier task force heading for Pearl Harbor.

SPECIFICATION: Type naval reconnaissance floatplane • Crew 3 • Powerplant one 1,080hp Mitsubishi Kinsei 43 14-cylinder radial • Max speed 234mph (377km) at 9,845ft (3,000m) • Service ceiling 28,640ft (8,730m) • Max range 1,298 miles (2,089km) • Wingspan 47ft 7in (14.50m) • Length 37ft 1in (11.30m) • Height 15ft 5in (4.70m) • Weight 8,818lb (4,000kg) loaded • Armament one 0.79-in (20-mm) downward-firing cannon in ventral position and one 0.303-in (7.7-mm) machine gun in rear cockpit; external bomb load of 551lb (250kg)

Aichi E16A Zuiun "Paul"

JAPAN

Designed as a successor to the E13A-1 Jake, the E16A Zuiun (Auspicious Cloud) reconnaissance floatplane was also used as a dive-bomber. The prototype flew in August 1943 and the type entered service in the following year. Only one version, the E16A-1, was used by the Imperial Japanese Navy, 256 examples being built.

SPECIFICATION: Type reconnaissance/dive-bomber floatplane ● Crew 2 ● Powerplant one Mitsubishi MK8D Kinsei 54 14-cylinder radial ● Max speed 273mph (439km/h) at 18,040ft (5,500m) ● Service ceiling 32,810ft (10,000m) ● Max range 1,491 miles (2,400km) ● Wingspan 42ft (12.81m) ● Length 35ft 6in (10.83m) ● Height 15ft 8in (4.79m) ● Weight 10,052lb (4,560kg) loaded ● Armament two forward-firing 0.79-in (20-mm) cannon in wings and one 0.303-in (7.7-mm) machine gun in rear cockpit

▲ The Aichi E16A-1 was an excellent reconnaissance floatplane, which entered service only after the Allies had achieved total air superiority.

Aichi M6A-1 Seiran

JAPAN

▲ Originally known as the M6A1-K Seiran Kai, the trainer derivative of the submarine-based Seiran was never to reach production status.

The Aichi M6A-1 Seiran (Mountain Haze) was designed to be carried in the Japanese Navy's I-400 class super-submarine, the aircraft being housed in watertight cylindrical hangars. Four submarines and 10 Seirans would have formed the nucleus of the 1st Japanese Submarine Fleet, which was preparing to attack the Panama Canal when the atomic bombs brought an end to the Pacific war. Twenty-eight Seirans were built.

SPECIFICATION: Type attack floatplane ● Crew 1 ● Powerplant one 1,400hp Atsuta 32 in-line engine ● Max speed not known ● Service ceiling not known ● Max range 712 miles (1,146km) ● Wingspan not known ● Length not known ● Height not known ● Weight not known ● Armament one 500-lb (226-kg) bomb

AIDC AT-3A

TAIWAN

The AT-3A twin-turbofan military trainer was developed by the Taiwanese Aero Industry Development Center in collaboration with Northrop. The first prototype flew in September 1980 and 60 production aircraft were built. The aircraft proved to be a very effective advanced trainer, being exceptionally agile and able to carry a wide variety of ordnance.

SPECIFICATION: Type advanced flying and weapons trainer ● Crew 2 ● Powerplant two 3,500lb (1,588kg) thrust Garrett TFE731-1-2L turbofans ● Max speed 562mph (904km/h) at 36,090ft (11,000m) ● Service ceiling 48,065ft (14,650m) ● Max range 1,417 miles (2,280km) ● Wingspan 34ft 3in (10.46m) ● Length 42ft 4in (12.9m) ● Height 14ft 3in (4.36m) ● Weight 17,505lb (7,940kg) ● Armament provision for two 0.50-in (12.7-mm) guns in ventral pack; wingtip rails for Sidewinder AAMs; up to 5,998lb (2,720kg) of stores on five hardpoints

▲ An AT-3B radar-equipped two-seater. The AT-3 replaced the Lockheed T-33 in Republic of China Air Force service.

▌AIDC Ching-Kuo

The Ching-Kuo, Taiwan's indigenous air defense fighter, was developed with much assistance from a number of US companies, including General Dynamics, and resembles a heavily modified F-16. The prototype flew for the first time on May 28, 1989, and was damaged in a landing accident some months later; the second prototype crashed in July 1989,

killing its pilot. The program went ahead, however, and the first Ching-Kuo was delivered to the Chinese Nationalist Air Force in 1994, although the lifting of restrictions on the sale of US military aircraft to Taiwan (which was why the Ching-Kuo was developed in the first place) resulted in the original requirement for 250 aircraft being reduced to 130.

SPECIFICATION: Type air defense fighter • Crew 1 • Powerplant two 9,460-lb (4,291-kg) thrust ITEC TFE1042-70 turbofans • Max speed 792mph (1,275km/h) at 36,000ft (10,975m) • Service ceiling 55,000ft (16,760m) • Max range classified • Wingspan 29ft 6in (9.00m) • Length 47ft 6in (14.48m) • Height 15ft 3in (4.65m) • Weight 20,000lb (9,072kg) • Armament one 0.79-in (20-mm) M61A1 Vulcan rotary six-barrel cannon; six external pylons for AAMs, AASMs, and various combinations of rocket or gun pods

▲ *The Ching-Kuo is undoubtedly a formidable air-defense weapon.*

▌Airco DH.2

Designed by Geoffrey de Havilland, the DH.2 was a single-seat pusher type whose prototype had been sent to France in July 1915 for operational trials; unfortunately, it was brought down in enemy territory on August 9. The DH.2 was powered by a 100hp Monosoupape engine and was armed with a single Lewis gun mounted on a pivot in the prow, enabling it to be traversed from left to right or elevated upward and downward. In practice, pilots found this arrangement too wobbly and secured the gun in a fixed forward-firing position. Rugged and highly maneuverable, the DH.2 was to achieve more success in action against the Fokkers than any other Allied fighter type. No. 24 Squadron was commanded by Major L. G. Hawker, who on July 25, 1916, while flying a Bristol Scout of No. 5 Squadron, had been awarded the

Victoria Cross for engaging three enemy aircraft in quick succession and shooting one down. No. 24 squadron gained its first victory on April 2, 1916 and claimed its first Fokker on the 25th of that month, and from then on its tally rose steadily. In June 1916 its pilots destroyed 17 enemy aircraft, followed by 23 in July, 15 in August, 15 in September, and 10 in November. On November 23, however, Major Hawker was shot down by an up-and-coming German pilot named Manfred von Richthofen.

SPECIFICATION: Type scouting biplane • Crew 1 • Powerplant one 100hp Gnome Monosoupape piston or 110hp Le Rhone rotary engine • Max speed 93mph (150km/h) • Service ceiling 4,265ft (1,300m) • Endurance 2hrs 45mins • Wingspan 28ft 3in (8.61m) • Length 25ft 2in (7.68m) • Height 9ft 6in (2.91m) • Weight 1,421lb (645kg) loaded • Armament one forward-firing 0.303-in (7.62-mm) Lewis gun on flexible mounting

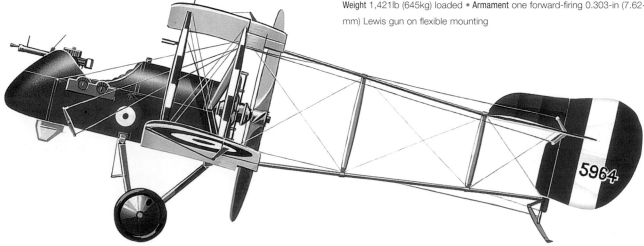

▌Airco DH.4

The Airco DH.4 was designed by Geoffrey de Havilland in response to a War Office requirement for a new day bomber and was without doubt the best and most versatile aircraft in its class in World War I, comparable in its day to

de Havilland's most outstanding creation of World War II, the Mosquito.

The 1,449 British-built aircraft were manufactured by various subcontractors. By the spring of 1918 the DH.4 equipped nine RFC squadrons and was also in service with the RNAS (the two Services were to amalgamate on April 1, 1918 to form the Royal Air Force). The DH.4 was originally designed around the 200hp BHP (Beardmore-Halford-Pullinger) engine, but development of this was delayed and so seven different engine types were fitted to production aircraft.

The bulk of DH.4 production took place in the US, where 4,846 aircraft were built by three companies. Many were powered by the 400hp Liberty 12 engine. As well as serving with the US Army Air Service, DH.4s were also widely used for civilian roles, such as crop dusting and aerial survey.

SPECIFICATION: **Type** day bomber biplane • **Crew** 2 • **Powerplant** various, but typically one 250hp Rolls-Royce Eagle VI in-line engine • **Max speed** 143mph (230km/h) • **Service ceiling** 22,000ft (6,705m) • **Endurance** 3hrs 45mins • **Wingspan** 42ft 4in (12.92m) • **Length** 30ft 8in (9.35m) • **Height** 11ft (3.35m) • **Weight** 3,472lb (1,575kg) • **Armament** two fixed forward-firing 0.303-in (7.62-m) Vickers machine guns and two in rear cockpit; provision for 460lb (209kg) of bombs on external pylons

◀ *The Airco DH.4 was an extremely successful light bomber, and was more effective than its successor, the DH.9.*

▌Airco DH.5

The Airco DH.5 was the least successful of de Havilland's designs, and was operational for only eight months. It was an attempt to combine the excellent all-round view of the DH.2 with the higher performance of a tractor biplane layout, to which end de Havilland gave the wings a backward stagger in order to seat the pilot forward of the leading edge of the upper wing. Six squadrons were armed with the type from May 1917. Its poor performance in inexperienced hands, allied with the fact that its pilots had convinced themselves

that it was dangerous to fly (mainly because of its unconventional appearance) resulted in its withdrawal from first-line units in January 1918.

▲ *With an airframe of considerable strength, the DH.5 was fully aerobatic, although its unusual layout caused some pilots to distrust it.*

SPECIFICATION: **Type** scouting biplane • **Crew** 1 • **Powerplant** one 110hp Le Rhone 9 rotary • **Max speed** 102mph (164km/h) at 10,000ft (3,048m) • **Service ceiling** 16,000ft (4,877m) • **Endurance** 2hrs 45mins • **Wingspan** 25ft 8in (7.82m) • **Length** 22ft (6.71m) • **Height** 9ft 1in (2.78m) • **Weight** 1,492lb (677kg) loaded • **Armament** two fixed forward-firing 0.303-in (7.62-mm) Vickers machine guns

■ Airco DH.9/9A

Derived from the DH.4, the DH.9 first entered service with No. 103 Squadron at Old Sarum, Wiltshire, in December 1917, and first went into action with No. 6 Squadron in France the following March. Crews soon discovered that the DH.9 had a disappointing performance, mainly because its BHP engine and derivatives yielded only 230hp instead of the anticipated 300. With a full bomb load the DH.9 could barely climb to 15,000ft (4,575m), which was 7,000ft (2,135m) lower than the ceiling of the DH.4, which it was supposed to replace. In addition, fuel consumption above 10,000ft (3,050m) was appallingly high at 15 gallons per hour, and engine failures were rife; of 12 DH.9s which set out to bomb the railroad triangle at Metz-Sablon on May 29, for example, six were forced to turn back with engine trouble.

Despite its shortcomings, the DH.9 was an adequate fighting airplane once freed of its bomb load; this was partly due to the fact that the pilot and observer were seated back to back, which made for better communication than in the

DH.4, where the cockpits were separated. By August 1918 RAF DH.9 squadrons in France were rearming with the Packard Liberty-powered DH.9A. This greatly improved the aircraft's performance, and the DH.9A went on to perform an important policing role in British-controlled territories in the Middle East and India throughout the 1920s.

▶ *D.H.9As belonging to No. 39 Squadron are seen in close formation during a training flight in 1923.*

SPECIFICATION: **Type** bomber biplane (data DH.9A) • **Crew** 2 • **Powerplant** one 420hp Packard Liberty 12 V-type engine • **Max speed** 123mph (198km/h) • **Service ceiling** 16,750ft (5,105m) • **Endurance** 5hrs 15mins • **Wingspan** 45ft 11in (14.01m) • **Length** 30ft 3in (9.22m) • **Height** 11ft 4in (3.45m) • **Weight** 4,645lb (2,107kg) loaded • **Armament** one fixed forward-firing 0.303-in (7.62-mm) Vickers MG and one or two 0.303-in (7.62-mm) Lewis machine guns in rear cockpit; provision for 660lb (299kg) of bombs on external pylons

■ Airspeed Oxford

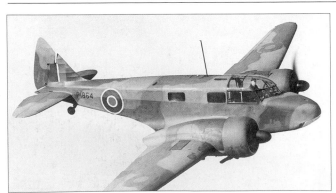

▲ *In RAF service Oxfords fulfilled a number of roles, most numerous of which was serving as navigational or radio-operational trainers.*

Many thousands of British and Commonwealth aircrew trained on the Airspeed Oxford during World War II. The Oxford I was a bombing and gunnery trainer, while the Oxford II was equipped for radio and navigational training. The Mks III and V (the Mk IV being a one-shot test bed) had different engines but performed similar functions.

SPECIFICATION: **Type** crew trainer • **Crew** 3 • **Powerplant** two 350hp Armstrong Siddeley Cheetah IX 70cylinder radials • **Max speed** 182mph (298km/h) • **Service ceiling** 19,200ft (5,852m) • **Max range** 910 miles (1,464km) • **Wingspan** 53ft 4in (16.25m) • **Length** 34ft 6in(10.51m) • **Height** 11ft 1in (3.38m) • **Weight** 7,600lb (3,447kg) loaded • **Armament** none

▌Albatros B.II

Designed by Ernst Heinkel, the Albatros B.II of 1914 was the progenitor of a line of fighting airplanes whose names were to become synonymous with the air war over the Western Front. At the very start of its career, the B.II showed its prowess by establishing an altitude record of 14,765ft (4,500m). Deployed on a very large scale, the B.II was withdrawn from first-line duties in 1915. It remained in service as a trainer for the rest of the war, and was still in use in 1919 with the Royal Swedish Air Force.

▲ *The Albatros B.II established the Albatros Flugzeugwerke GmbH as a respected name in the aircraft industry.*

SPECIFICATION: Type reconnaissance biplane • Crew 2 • Powerplant one 100hp Mercedes 6-cylinder liquid-cooled in-line • Max speed 66mph (105km/h) at sea level • Service ceiling 9,840ft (3,000m) • Endurance 4hrs • Wingspan 42ft (12.8m) • Length 25ft (7.63m) • Height 10ft 4in (3.15m) • Weight 2,361lb (1,071kg) loaded • Armament none

▌Albatros C.I

The most widely used reconnaissance aircraft of World War I, the Albatros C-series biplanes were developed from the unarmed B.II of 1914. The C.I, which made its appearance in 1915, had excellent flight characteristics and an engine that was more powerful than almost any used by its adversaries. Armed with a ring-mounted LMG 14 Parabellum machine gun, it was a formidable opponent. The positions of the observer and gunner were reversed from the B.II—the observer/gunner now sat in the rear seat, providing him with a broader field of fire. Many of Germany's future air aces, including Oswald Boelcke and Manfred von Richthofen, flew their first missions in C.Is.

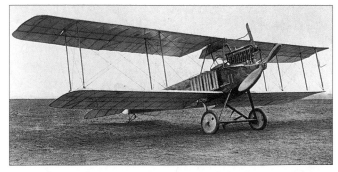

▲ *Both the tall exhaust pipe and fuselage-mounted radiators are clearly illustrated by this C.I.*

SPECIFICATION: Type reconnaissance biplane • Crew 2 • Powerplant one 160hp Mercedes D.III liquid-cooled in-line • Max speed 87mph(140km/h) • Service ceiling 9,843ft (3,000m) • Endurance 2hrs 30mins • Wingspan 42ft 4in (12.90m) • Length 25ft 9in (7.85m) • Height 10ft 4in (3.14m) • Weight 2,624lb (1,190kg) loaded • Armament one 0.30-in (7.5-mm) Parabellum machine gun

▌Albatros C.III

Successful as the Albatros C.I was, the C.III, which entered service with the Flieger Abteilungen (flight sections) of the German Army early in 1915, was even more so. In general, the C.III resembled the Albatros B.III (a variant of the B.II) of 1914, from which its was derived.

Faster and more maneuverable than the C.I, the C.III was built in greater numbers than any other C-type Albatros and remained in first-line service for about a year, carrying out observation, photo-reconnaissance, and light bombing missions, until being relegated to the training role.

SPECIFICATION: **Type** reconnaissance biplane • **Crew** 2 • **Powerplant** one 160hp Mercedes D.III liquid-cooled in-line • **Max speed** 87mph (140km/h) • **Service ceiling** 11,155ft (3,400m) • **Endurance** 4hrs • **Wingspan** 38ft 4in (11.70m) • **Length** 26ft 3in (8m) • **Height** 10ft 2in (3.10m) • **Weight** 2,983lb (1,353kg) loaded • **Armament** one or two 0.30-in (7.5-mm) Parabellum machine guns

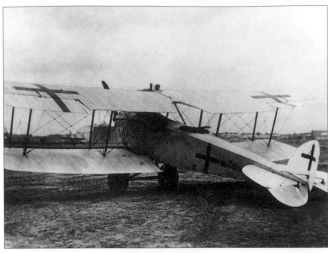

▲ *The Albatros C.III was a natural progression in the Albatros series of general purpose biplanes, and was the company's most prolific two-seater.*

▌Albatros C.V

▲ *This specially decorated C.V, photographed in 1917, was the 2,500th Albatros aircraft to be built.*

The Albatros C.V, which also made its appearance early in 1916, was slightly larger than the C.III, with a new, more powerful engine, and was almost completely redesigned. Despite being aerodynamically clean, the C.V was not a success because of its 8-cylinder in-line engine, which gave constant trouble and resulted in many accidents. Despite this, about 400 aircraft were built before the type was replaced in mid-1916 by the Albatros C.VII. This machine, although a compromise design, served in substantial numbers before it was replaced in 1917.

SPECIFICATION: **Type** reconnaissance biplane • **Crew** 2 • **Powerplant** one 220hp Mercedes D.IV 8-cylinder liquid-cooled in-line • **Max speed** 106mph (170km/h) • **Service ceiling** 16,405ft (5,000m) • **Endurance** 3hrs 15mins • **Wingspan** 41ft 11in (12.78m) • **Length** 29ft 4in (8.95m) • **Height** 11ft 8in (3.56m) • **Weight** 3,494lb (1,585kg) loaded • **Armament** two 0.30-in (7.5-mm) Parabellum machine guns; 220lb (100kg) of bombs

▌Albatros C.X

The Albatros C.X, which appeared at the front in the summer of 1917, was a far more effective aircraft than its predecessors. Great care had been taken to ensure that it was as aerodynamically refined as possible, and the new 260hp Mercedes D.IVa engine gave it a much-improved performance and payload-carrying capacity. The Albatros C.X continued to serve on all fronts until the summer of 1918, when it was supplanted by the final variant, the C.XII. The best of all the C-series armed reconnaissance aircraft, the C.XII remained in service until the end of the war.

◀ *Considerable care was taken to ensure that the C.X was as aerodynamically refined as possible, resulting in good performance and range.*

SPECIFICATION: **Type** reconnaissance biplane • **Crew** 2 • **Powerplant** one Mercedes D.IVa 6-cylinder liquid-cooled in-line • **Max speed** 109mph (175km/h) at sea level • **Service ceiling** 16,405ft (5,000m) • **Endurance** 3hrs 20mins • **Wingspan** 47ft 11in (14.36m) • **Length** 30ft (9.15m) • **Height** 11ft 2in (3.40m) • **Weight** 3,677lb (1,668kg) • **Armament** two 0.30-in (7.5-mm) Parabellum machine guns, plus light bomb load

■ Albatros D.II

GERMANY

The Albatros D.II was the successor to the Albatros D.I. It appeared on the Western Front in September 1916 and formed the equipment of Jagdstaffeln 2 and 11, commanded respectively by Oswald Boelcke and Manfred von Richthofen. It soon established an ascendency over Allied fighters, Boelcke shooting down 11 machines in 16 days. The

D.II was similar, but had N-shaped struts between the fuselage and upper wing, and fuselage-side air intakes.

▲ *Manfred von Richthofen, the "Red Baron" scored his first confirmed victory while flying this D.II on 17 September 1916.*

SPECIFICATION: **Type** scout • **Crew** 1 • **Powerplant** one 160hp Mercedes D.III 6-cylinder liquid-cooled in-line • **Max speed** 109mph (175km/h) • **Service ceiling** 17,060ft (5,200m) • **Endurance** 1hr 30mins • **Wingspan** 27ft 10in (8.5m) • **Length** 24ft 3in (7.4m) • **Height** 9ft 8in (2.95m) • **Weight** 1,957lb (888kg) loaded • **Armament** two 0.31-in (7.92-mm) LMG 08/15 machine guns

■ Albatros D.III

GERMANY

The first of the Albatros "V-strutters," the Albatros D.III was the most effective of all the Albatros fighter designs produced during World War I. The type was a development of the D.II, fitted with a high-compression version of the Mercedes D.III engine to give good high-altitude performance and with the lower wings much narrower in chord that the upper mainplane. The D.II was issued to the Jagdstaffeln from January 1917, and within a few weeks all 37 Jastas on the Western Front were armed with Albatros fighters. The D.III remained in service throughout the year, 446 being delivered in total. Albatros D.IIIs also operated with the German Air Service in

Palestine and Macedonia, and equipped some squadrons of the Austro-Hungarian Air Arm. Some D.IIIs were supplied to the newly established Polish Air Force in 1919.

▲ *The D.III reached a peak strength of 446 machines during November 1917, even though it was already being superseded by the D.V.*

SPECIFICATION: **Type** scout • **Crew** 1 • **Powerplant** one 175hp Mercedes D.IIIa 6-cylinder liquid-cooled in-line • **Max speed** 109mph (175km/h) at 3281ft (1,000m) • **Service ceiling** 18,044ft (5,500m) • **Endurance** 2hrs • **Wingspan** 29ft 8in (9.05m) • **Length** 24ft (7.33m) • **Height** 9ft 9in (2.98m) • **Weight** 1,953lb (886kg) loaded • **Armament** two fixed forward-firing 0.31-in (7.92-mm) LMG 08/15 machine guns

▌Albatros D.Va

Chronologically, the next aircraft in line after the Albatros D.III was the D.IV, but this experienced many problems with its experimental Mercedes D.III engine and never entered production. The D.V was therefore the next production version, entering service in May 1917. This was quickly followed by the D.Va, which differed only in minor detail such as a revised aileron control system. By May 1918, a total of 1,512 D.Vs and Vas were in service on the Western Front, but by this time they were outclassed by the latest Allied fighter aircraft. Heavy losses were also incurred due to a structural defect in the lower wing. Total production of the two variants was in excess of 3,000 machines.

◀ *The Albatros D.V/Va, latest in a long line of Albatros scouts, was developed in response to advances made in Allied fighter aircraft.*

SPECIFICATION: Type scout • Crew 1 • Powerplant one 180hp Mercedes D.IIIa 6-cylinder liquid-cooled in-line • Max speed 116mph (186km/h) • Service ceiling 18,700ft (5,700m) • Endurance 2hrs • Wingspan 29ft 8in (9.05m) • Length 24ft (7.33m) • Height 8ft 10in (2.70m) • Weight 2,066lb (937kg) loaded • Armament two fixed forward-firing 0.31-in (7.92-mm) LMG 08/15 machine guns

▌Amiot 143

SPECIFICATION: Type bomber • Crew 4-6 • Powerplant two 870hp Gnome-Rhone Kirs 14-cylinder radial engines • Max speed 193mph (310km/h) • Service ceiling 25,920ft (7,900m) • Max range 1,243 miles (2,000km) • Wingspan 80ft 5in (24.53m) • Length 59ft 11in (18.26m) • Height 18ft 7in (5.68m) • Weights 13,448lb (6,100kg) empty; 21,385lb (9,700kg) loaded • Armament four 0.30-in (7.5-mm) MAC 1934 machine guns, one each in nose and dorsal turrets and fore and aft in ventral gondola; internal and external bomb load of up to 3,527lb (1,600kg)

First flown in April 1935, the Amiot 143 was a reengined version of the Amiot 140 of 1931. On May 10, 1940, when Germany invaded France and the Low Countries, four Groupes de Bombardement (GB I/34, II/34, I/38, and II/38) were still equipped with this obsolescent type. They flew many bombing missions against the advancing enemy columns, suffering heavy losses. Fifty Amiot 143s remained in service at the time of France's surrender, and subsequently formed part of the Vichy Air Force.

▲ *Slow and cumbersome, the Amiot 143 suffered terrible losses during daylight bombing operations in the Battle of France and was restricted to night bombing.*

Amiot 354

The graceful Amiot 354 was a direct descendant of the Amiot 370 mailplane, which captured several world speed records in 1938. The first military production aircraft, designated Amiot 351, was rolled out in January 1940, by which time orders had risen to 249 aircraft. The principal difference between the Amiot 351 and 354 was that the former had twin fins; the tail units of both derivatives were interchangeable.

SPECIFICATION: Type reconnaissance bomber • Crew 4 • Powerplant two 1,060hp Gnome-Rhone 14N 14-cylinder radial engines • Max speed 298mph (480km/h) at 13,100ft (4,000m) • Service ceiling 32,808ft (10,000m) • Max range 2,175 miles (3,500km) with an 1,764lb (800kg) bomb load • Wingspan 74ft 10in (22.83m) • Length 47ft 6in (14.50m) • Height 13ft 4in (4.08m) • Weights 10,417lb (4,725kg) empty; 24,912lb (11,300kg) loaded • Armament one 0.79-in (20-mm) cannon and two 0.30-in (7.5-mm) machine guns; internal bomb load of 2,646lb (1,200kg)

About 60 Amiot 351/354s were delivered before the Franco-German armistice, some of these served with the Vichy Air Force. At least two flew on special duties operations with the Luftwaffe.

▲ The most graceful of all France's piston-engined bombers, the Amiot 354 came too late to be of use in the Battle of France.

AMX International

The AMX International is the product of collaboration between the Italian companies Aeritalia and Aermacchi on the one hand, and the Brazilian EMBRAER company on the other, to produce a new lightweight tactical fighter bomber to replace the Italian Air Force's Fiat G.91s and Lockheed F-104Gs and the Brazilian Air Force's AT-26s. The selected powerplant was the Rolls-Royce Spey turbofan, built under license by an Italian consortium. The first prototype AMX flew in May 1984 and by 1990 seven development aircraft had amassed more than 2,500 hours. The aircraft entered service with the Italian Air Force in 1990, and deliveries to the Brazilian Air Force began a year later.

◀ The AMX was initially plagued by problems, many relating to US unwillingness to supply high-tech avionics systems.

SPECIFICATION: Type multirole combat aircraft • Crew 1 • Powerplant one 11,030-lb (5,003-kg) thrust license-built Rolls-Royce Spey Mk 807 turbofan • Max speed 651mph (1,047km/h) at sea level • Service ceiling 42,650ft (13,000m) • Combat radius 345 miles (556km) lo-lo • Wingspan 29ft 1in (8.87m) • Length 43ft 5in (13.23m) • Height 14ft 11in (4.55m) • Weight 28,660lb (13,000kg) loaded • Armament one 0.79-in (20-mm) M61A1 cannon or two 1.19-in (30-mm) DEFA cannon (Brazilian aircraft); five external hardpoints for up to 8,377lb (3,800kg) of ordnance; wingtip rails for AAMs

Ansaldo A.1 Balilla

During World War I, Italy's Corpo Aeronautica Militare had relied heavily on French-designed combat aircraft, with the exception of bombers and naval types. The first Italian-designed fighter, the Ansaldo A1 Balilla (Hunter), did not enter service until 1918, and only a small number of the 108 aircraft built reached the front-line squadrons. It was exported to several countries, including Russia and Poland, resulting in its use on both sides of the Russo-Polish war of 1920.

◄ *With its 400-hp (298-kW) Curtis K-12 engine driving a four-bladed propeller, the modified Balilla racer achieved some success in the US.*

SPECIFICATION: **Type** scouting biplane • **Crew** 1 • **Powerplant** one 220hp SPA 6A 6-cylinder liquid-cooled in-line • **Max speed** 137mph (220km/h) • **Service ceiling** 16,400ft (5,000m) • **Endurance** 1hr 30mins • **Wingspan** 25ft 2in (7.68m) • **Length** 22ft 5in (6.84m) • **Height** 8ft 3in (2.53m) • **Weight** 1,951lb (885kg) loaded • **Armament** two 0.30-in (7.62-mm) machine guns

▌Antonov An-12 "Cub"   USSR

Faced with the problem of providing an efficient logistics service for its huge army, over distances extending from eastern Europe to Kamchatka on the Pacific coast, the Soviet government placed very heavy demands on designers and manufacturers to provide large numbers of heavy freighters. One designer in particular, Oleg Antonov, specialized in this type of aircraft, and his solution was to develop a cargo

version of his An-10A turboprop passenger design. Most examples of the new aircraft, the An-12, were for military use. Military An-12s were widely exported to "friendly foreign" countries, including India, which received 41. The An-12 entered production in the People's Republic of China in 1980 under the designation Shaanxi Y-8, having made its first evaluation flights there some six years earlier. It is used in a wide variety of roles, including that of flight refueling tanker, airborne early warning (AEW), and drone launcher. A maritime surveillance version, designated Y-8X and equipped with a Litton Canada APS-504 search radar in a chin radome, as well as a Litton inertial and Omega navigation systems, entered service with the Chinese Navy in 1986.

▲ *In standard military transport form, the An-12 is more or less equivalent to the West's C-130 Hercules.*

SPECIFICATION: **Type** military transportation • **Crew** 4 • **Powerplant** four 4,000hp Ivchenko AI-20K turboprops • **Max speed** 360mph (580km/h) • **Service ceiling** 33,465ft (10,200m) • **Max range** 2,110 miles (3,400km) • **Wingspan** 124ft 8in (38m) • **Length** 108ft 7in (33.10m) • **Height** 34ft 6in (10.53m) • **Weight** 134,482lb (61,000kg) • **Armament** none

▌Antonov An-22 "Cock"   USSR

First revealed at the Paris Air Show in June 1965, the huge An-22 heavy transport entered service with both Aeroflot and the Soviet Air Force, which used it to transport large loads such as missiles on tracked launchers and dismantled aircraft. When it made its debut the An-22 was the heaviest aircraft ever built. Fifty aircraft were completed up to 1974, when production ended.

SPECIFICATION: **Type** heavy lift transport • **Crew** 5-6 • **Powerplant** four 15,000hp Kuznetsov NK-12MA turboprops • **Max speed** 460mph (740km/h) at sea level • **Service ceiling** not known • **Max range** 6,800 miles (10,950km) • **Wingspan** 211ft 4in (64.4m) • **Length** 1,89ft 7in (57.8m) • **Height** 41ft 1in (12.53m) • **Weight** 551,160lb (250,000kg) loaded • **Armament** none

▲ *The An-22, the heaviest aircraft ever built when it entered service, was intended to transport bulky loads such as missiles.*

∎ Antonov An-24/An-26 "Coke" and "Curl"   USSR

▲ *Hungary's No. 1 "Camel" Transport Squadron maintains a fleet of nine of the versatile Antonov An-26 freighters.*

Designed as a feeder-liner, the An-24 was used in some numbers in the military transportation role by the Soviet Air Force and Soviet-aligned air arms around the world, some being equipped as airborne command posts. One version of the An-24 was the An-24RT, which was intended for freight or mixed transport and which had an under-fuselage loading ramp. Antonov used the An-24RT as the basis for the An-26, a more sophisticated transport capable of loading and unloading light, jeep-type vehicles via its underfuselage ramp, which could be slid forward on railed tracks for direct loading. The aircraft could also be used for air-dropping operations and could be quickly adapted for passenger, paratroop, or transportation duties. The An-26 was flight tested in 1968 and deliveries to the first customers began a year later. A further development was the An-32 which had twice the power of the An-24.

SPECIFICATION: **Type** military transportation (data An-26) • **Crew** 3 • **Powerplant** two 2,820hp Ivchenko AI-24T turboprops • **Max speed** 335mph (539km/h) at 11,500ft (3,500m) • **Service ceiling** 27,900ft (8,500m) • **Range** 807 miles (1,300km) • **Wingspan** 95ft 7in (29.20m) • **Length** 77ft 2in (23.50m) • **Height** 27ft 4in (8.32m) • **Weight** 52,911lb (24,000kg) loaded • **Armament** none

∎ Antonov An-72 "Coaler"   USSR

Featuring engines mounted above the wing, designed with exhaust over-wing trailing edge devices to increase lift at low airspeeds, the An-72 tactical transport was intended for rough-field operations. Two prototypes were built, the first flying on August 31, 1977. The An-74 was a development with uprated turbofan engines, developed for use in the Arctic and Antarctic. An airborne warning version of the An-74 was code-named Madcap by NATO.

SPECIFICATION: **Type** tactical transportation (data An-72 Coaler-C) • **Crew** 3 • **Powerplant** two 14,330-lb (6,500-kg) thrust Lotarev D-36 turbofans • **Max speed** 438mph (705km/h) at 32,810ft (10,000m) • **Service ceiling** 38,715ft (11,800m) • **Max range** 497 miles (800km) with max payload • **Wingspan** 104ft 7in (31.9m) • **Length** 92ft 2in (28.7m) • **Height** 28ft 4in (8.65m) • **Weight** 76,072lb (34,500kg) loaded • **Armament** none

▲ *In addition to its STOL capabilities, the An-72 also displays a remarkable degree of maneuverability.*

▌Arado Ar 68

Sharing with the Heinkel He 51 and its immediate ancestor, the Arado Ar 65, the distinction of being one of the first single-seat fighters to serve in the still-secret Luftwaffe, the prototype Arado Ar 68V-1 first flew in 1934, powered by a 660hp BMW VI engine, and entered production in the same

year. The main production models were the Ar 68E with the 610hp Junkers Jumo 210B, the Ar 68F with the 675 hp BMW VI, and the Ar 68G with a 750hp BMW VI. The Ar 68H was a one-shot experimental version with an enclosed cockpit and a BMW 132 air-cooled radial engine. The Ar 68 was of wood and steel tube construction with fabric covering, and was a single-bay biplane with N-type interplane struts and a spatted cantilever undercarriage. The type entered service in 1935, but had been relegated to the fighter training role by September 1939.

▲ A Jumo 210Da engine, complete with two-stage supercharger, powered the Ar 68E.

SPECIFICATION: Type fighter biplane • Crew 1 • Powerplant one 750hp BMW VI liquid-cooled V-type • Max speed 190mph (305km/h) • Service ceiling 26,575ft (8,100m) • Max range 258 miles (415km) • Wingspan 36ft (11m) • Length 31ft 2in (9.5m) • Height 10ft 9in (3.28m) • Weight 5,457lb (2,475kg) loaded • Armament two fixed forward-firing 0.31-in (7.92-mm) MG 17 machine guns

▌Arado Ar 95

Similar in many respects to the radial engined Arado Ar 68H, the Arado Ar 95 was designed as a two-seat torpedo-bomber and reconnaissance biplane for service aboard the German Navy's planned aircraft carriers. A two-seat single-bay staggered biplane with a light metal monocoque fuselage, the aircraft had aft-folding wings. The prototype Ar 95V-1 flew for the first time in the fall of 1936, fitted with twin light metal floats. A few aircraft were sent to Spain for evaluation during the civil war and the type saw limited Luftwaffe service.

SPECIFICATION: Type maritime reconnaissance aircraft • Crew 2 • Powerplant one 880hp BMW 132De 9-cylinder radial • Max speed 193mph (310km/h) • Service ceiling 23,945ft (7,300m) • Max range 683 miles (1,100km) • Wingspan 41ft ⅛in (12.50m) • Length 36ft 5in (11.1m) • Height 11ft 9in (3.6m) • Weight 7,848lb (3,560kg) loaded • Armament one fixed forward-firing 0.31-in) 7.92-mm) MG 17 machine gun and one flexible 7.92 MG in rear cockpit; under-fuselage rack with provision for an 1764-lb (800-kg) torpedo or 1,102lb (500kg) of bombs

▲ Official German interest in the Ar 95 was limited, since it was expected to be obsolete by the time Germany could commission the first of its aircraft carriers.

Arado Ar 96

GERMANY

The Arado Ar 96 was by far the most important advanced trainer used by the Luftwaffe. Of all-metal light alloy construction, the aircraft had a wide track with inward-retracting gear, to enable easier handling by student pilots on the ground. The first of a small batch of Ar 96A-1 production aircraft flew in 1938, but the main production series was the Ar 96B, ordered in 1940. Very few Ar 96s were built by Arado; until mid-1941 production was undertaken by the Ago

▶ *Pictured in a somewhat sorry state on a training airfield in Austria at the end of World War II, these Ar 96s are now fit only for scrap.*

SPECIFICATION: **Type** advanced trainer • **Crew** 2 • **Powerplant** one 450hp Argus As.410 12-cylinder air-cooled V-type • **Max speed** 211mph (340km/h) at 9,840ft (3,000m) • **Service ceiling** 23,295ft (7,100m) • **Max range** 615 miles (990km) • **Wingspan** 36ft 1in (11m) • **Length** 29ft 11in (9.13m) • **Height** 8ft 6in (2.6m) • **Weight** 3,736lb (1,695kg) loaded • **Armament** none

Flugzeugwerke, but most were built by the Czechoslovak Avia Company and Letov of Prague. By the end of the war no less than 11,546 aircraft had been completed. Czech production of the aircraft continued until 1948.

Arado Ar 196

GERMANY

The Arado Ar 196 was designed as a successor to the Heinkel He 50, a catapult-launched spotter biplane carried by German warships in the 1930s. The twin-float Ar 196 first flew in the summer of 1938 and 536 Ar 196A production aircraft were

▲ *A very versatile aircraft, the Ar 196 floatplane operated from German Navy shore bases as well as from capital ships such as the* Bismarck *and* Tirpitz.

built, entering service shortly before the outbreak of World War II. The major production model was the Ar 196A-3. One of these became famous on May 5, 1940 by accepting the surrender of HM submarine *Seal*, which had been forced to the surface in the Kattegat with mine damage. The Ar 196 was widely used in the North Atlantic, where it operated from major surface units like the *Bismarck*, and the Mediterranean and Adriatic, where it operated from shore bases.

SPECIFICATION: **Type** reconnaissance floatplane • **Crew** 2 • **Powerplant** one 970hp BMW 132K 9-cylinder radial • **Max speed** 199mph (320km/h) • **Service ceiling** 22,960ft (7,000m) • **Max range** 665 miles (1,070km) • **Wingspan** 40ft 8in (12.40m) • **Length** 36ft (11m) • **Height** 14ft 7in (4.45m) • **Weight** 8,223lb (3,730kg) loaded • **Armament** two 0.79-in (20-mm) fixed forward-firing cannon in wing; one 0.31-in (7.92-mm) machine gun in starboard side of forward fuselage, and one 0.31-in (7.92-mm) in rear cockpit, plus external bomb load of 220lb (100kg)

Arado Ar 232

GERMANY

The Ar 232 military freighter, which flew early in 1941, was produced in two versions, the Ar 232A with two 1,595hp BMW 801A or 801L engines, and the Ar 232B with four 1,000hp Bramo Fafnir 323 engines. One of the Ar 232's

unusual features was its multiwheel static undercarriage. On the Ar 232A this comprised 11 pairs of small wheels with low pressure tires and independently sprung suspension on which the whole airplane was lowered for loading or discharging freight; the Ar 232B had 10 pairs of these small wheels. The boxcar fuselage was of all-metal semimonocoque construc-

▲ *In service, the Ar 232 was nicknamed "Tausendfüssler" (millipede) due to its multi-unit undercarriage.*

tion, and the all-metal wing used a rudimentary form of boundary layer control over the flaps and ailerons. Only 22 aircraft were built, these being issued to Transport-geschwader TG5 and the transportation squadron of I/KG200, the Luftwaffe's special duties unit, for clandestine operations behind enemy lines on the Russian Front.

SPECIFICATION: Type medium transportation • Crew 4 • Powerplant four 1,200hp Bramo 323-R Fafnir 9-cylinder radials • Max speed 211mph (340km/h) • Service ceiling 22,640ft (6,900m) • Max range 830 miles (1,335km) • Wingspan 109ft 10in (33.50m) • Length 77ft 2in (23.52m) • Height 18ft 8in (5.70m) • Weight 46,649lb (21,160kg) loaded • Armament one 0.79-in (20-mm) cannon in dorsal turret, one 0.51-in (13-mm) machine gun in nose position, and one or two 0.51-in (13-mm) machine gun in rear of fuselage pod

▌Arado Ar 234   GERMANY

The Ar 234 Blitz (Lightning) was the world's first opera-tional jet bomber. The origins of the type can be traced to a 1940 requirement issued by the German Air Ministry for a fast, turbojet-powered reconnaissance aircraft. The proto-type Ar 234V-1, which flew for the first time on June 15, 1953, and the next seven aircraft (Ar 234V-2 to V-8) all used the trolley-and-skid arrangement. The second prototype, the Ar 234V-2, was similar to the first machine, but the Ar 234V-3 was fitted with an ejection seat and rocket-assisted takeoff equipment, the rocket pods being installed under the wings.

Although the launching trolley and landing skid arrange-ment had functioned well, it was realized that the aircraft's immobility on landing would be a severe disadvantage when

SPECIFICATION: Type jet bomber (Ar 234B-2) • Crew 1 • Powerplant two 1,764lb (800kg) thrust BMW 003A-1 turbojets • Max speed 461mph (742km/h) at 19,685ft (6,000m) • Service ceiling 32,808ft (10,000m) • Max range 1,013 miles (1,630km) • Wingspan 46ft 3in (14.11m) • Length 41ft 5in (12.64m) • Height 14ft 1in (4.30m) • Weight 21,715lb (9,850kg) loaded • Armament two fixed rearward-firing 0.79-in (20-mm) MG.151 cannon in underside of rear fuselage; external bomb load of 3,307lb (1,500kg)

it came to operational deployment, so it was decided to abandon this configuration and with it the Ar 234A-1, as the initial production version was to have been designated, and fit the aircraft with a conventional wheeled undercarriage. The fuselage was slightly widened to accommodate two mainwheels midway along its length, and a nosewheel was mounted under the pilot's cockpit. In this guise the aircraft was designated Ar 234B, of which 210 were built. Only two versions were used operationally; these were the Ar 234B-1 unarmed reconnaissance variant, and the Ar 234B-2 bomber. It was planned to replace the B series in production by the C series, but only 19 had been completed when the war ended.

The first operational Ar 234 sorties were flown by the V-5 and V-7 prototypes, which were delivered to I/Versuchsverband.Ob.d.L (Luftwaffe High Command Trials Unit) at Juvincourt, near Reims, in July 1944. Both aircraft were fitted with Walter rocket-assisted takeoff units and made their first reconnaissance sorties on July 20, photographing harbors on the south coast of England from an altitude of 29,530ft (9,000m). Several more sorties were made over

▲ *The Ar 234 was used extensively in the last months of the war in the reconnaissance and fast attack roles, beginning operations in July 1944.*

the UK before the unit was transferred to Rheine in September. Other reconnaissance trials units received the Ar 234, and in January 1945 these were amalgamated into

I/F.100 and I/F.123 at Rheine, and I/F.33 at Stavanger, Norway. The latter unit flew reconnaissance sorties over the British naval base at Scapa Flow, in the Orkneys, until mid-April 1945.

The bomber version of the Ar 234 equipped KG 76 from October 1944, flying its first operational missions during the Ardennes offensive in December. The jet bombers were very active in the early weeks of 1945, one of their most notable missions being the ten-day series of attacks on the Ludendorff bridge at Remagen, captured by the Americans in March 1945. Very few Ar 234 sorties were flown after the end of March, although an experimental Ar 234 night fighter unit, the Kommando Bonow, equipped with two Ar 234s converted to carry upward-firing cannon, continued to operate until the end of the war.

■ Armstrong Whitworth Albemarle

GREAT BRITAIN

Designed to Specification B.18/38, which called for a twin-engined medium bomber of mixed wood and metal construction, the prototype Armstrong Whitworth Albermarle flew on March 20, 1939. In the event, the aircraft never served in its intended role, being employed as a transport and glider

tug. Large numbers of Albemarles took part in the Allied invasions of Sicily and Normandy, and in the air drop at Arnhem. Production totaled 600 aircraft.

▲ *Adorned with D-Day stripes, this No. 297 Sqn Albemarle GT.Mk V demonstrates the glider-towing apparatus seen trailing behind the aircraft.*

SPECIFICATION: Type transport and glider tug • Crew 4 • Powerplant two 1590hp Bristol Hercules XI radial engines • Max speed 265mph (426km/h) at 10,500ft (3,200m) • Service ceiling 18,000ft (5,486m) • Max range 1,300 miles (2,092km) • Wingspan 77ft (23.47m) • Length 59ft 11in (18.26m) • Height 15ft 7in (4.75m) • Weight 36,500lb (16,556kg) loaded • Armament four 0.303-in (7.62-mm) machine guns in dorsal turret

■ Armstrong Whitworth Atlas

GREAT BRITAIN

The Armstrong Whitworth Atlas was one of the most versatile army cooperation aircraft of the 1920s, and was the first

aircraft designed specifically for that role to serve with the RAF. The prototype Atlas flew for the first time on May 10, 1925, and the first units became operational in October 1927. The type equipped six RAF squadrons and 449 aircraft were built, including 146 trainers, before production ended in 1933.

▲ *A message hook beneath the fuselage, forward-firing machine-gun and Scarff ring around the rear cockpit were features of all army co-op Atlases.*

SPECIFICATION: Type army cooperation biplane • Crew 2 • Powerplant one 450hp Armstrong Siddeley Jaguar IVC radial • Max speed 142mph (228km/h) • Service ceiling 16,800ft (5,120m) • Max range 480 miles (770km) • Wingspan 39ft 6in (12.04m) • Length 28ft 6in (8.68m) • Height 10ft 6in (3.20m) • Weight 4,018lb (1,823kg) loaded • Armament one fixed forward-firing Vickers machine gun and one Lewis machine gun in rear cockpit, both 0.303-in (7.62-mm); four 112-lb (50-kg) bombs on underwing racks

▌Armstrong Whitworth Siskin III

The Siskin fighter of the 1920s had its origin in the Siddeley SR.2, which was named Siskin and flown in 1919, powered by a 320hp ABC Dragonfly radial engine. It was later reengined with the 300hp Armstrong Siddeley Jaguar radial. Two civilian Siskin IIs were built, one a two-seater, and this aircraft won the 1923 King's Cup Air Race at an average speed of 149mph (240km/h). The single-seat Siskin II served as a prototype fighter. The first production version was the Siskin III, which entered service with No. 41 Squadron at Northolt in May 1924. Only two squadrons used the Siskin III (the other being No. 111), nine more being equipped with the Siskin IIIA, which had a supercharged 425hp Jaguar IVS

SPECIFICATION: Type fighter • Crew 1 • Powerplant one 425hp Armstrong Siddeley Jaguar IVS 14-cylinder radial • Max speed 156mph (251km/h) at sea level • Service ceiling 27,000ft (8,230m) • Max range 280 miles (450km) • Wingspan 33ft 2in (10.11m) • Length 25ft 4in (7.72m) • Height 10ft 2in (3.10m) • Weight 3,012lb (1,366kg) loaded • Armament two 0.303-in (7.62-mm) Vickers machine guns in front fuselage; provision for four 20-lb (9-kg) bombs under lower wing

engine. Altogether, 70 Siskin IIIs and 382 Siskin IIIAs were built between 1927 and 1931. The Siskin IIIA was also adopted by the RCAF, which retained the type until 1929.

▲ A superb aerobatic aircraft, this Armstrong Whitworth Siskin IIIA is in the colors of No. 43 Squadron of the Royal Air Force, pictured in 1929.

▌Armstrong Whitworth Whitley

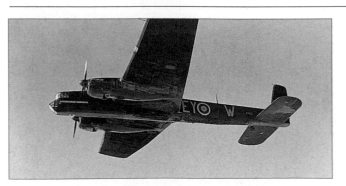

Designed to Specification B.3/34, the prototype Whitley flew on March 17, 1936 and was followed by a production batch of 34 Whitley Mk Is, first deliveries being made to No. 10 Squadron in March 1937. These aircraft were powered by Armstrong Siddeley Tiger radial engines, as were 46 Mk IIs and 80 Mk IIIs, but the Mks IV (33 built) and IVA (7 built) were completed with Rolls-Royce Merlin IV and X in-line

◀ At the beginning of World War II, the Whitley was the RAF's primary long-range bomber. This Mk V of No. 78 Sqn carries an array of mission symbols.

SPECIFICATION: Type heavy bomber • Crew 5 • Powerplant two 1,075hp Rolls-Royce Merlin X V-type in-line engines • Max speed 230mph (370km/h) at 16,400ft (5,000m) • Service ceiling 26,000ft (7,925m) • Max range 2,400 miles (3,862km) • Wingspan 84ft (25.60m) • Length 70ft 6in (21.49m) • Height 15ft (4.57m) • Weight 33,500lb (15,195kg) • Armament one 0.303-in (7.62-mm) Vickers machine gun in nose and four 0.303-in (7.62-mm) Browning machine guns in tail turret; up to 7,000lb (3,175kg) of bombs internally

engines respectively. The main wartime version was the Mk V, of which 1,466 were produced, and together with the Vickers Wellington and Handley Page Hampden the type

sustained RAF Bomber Command's strategic bombing offensive during the early part of World War II. The RAF had 207 Whitleys on strength at the outbreak of war. A general reconnaissance version, the Whitley VII (146 built) was produced for RAF Coastal Command, this variant having increased range and carrying ASV radar for antishipping patrols. Bomber Command's Whitleys carried out some notable long-range missions, including the first raid on Italy in June 1940. The type was also used for special operations, some being modified for dropping paratroops and agents. Withdrawn from first-line service in 1942, Whitleys continued in use as troop and freight transporters and as glider tugs.

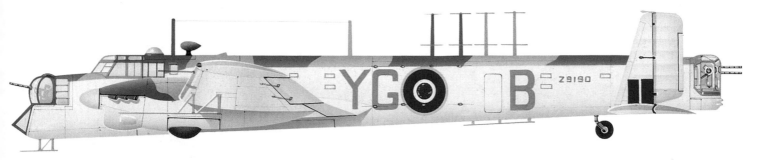

▌Armstrong Whitworth FK.8

GREAT BRITAIN

Designed by the talented Dutchman Frederick Koolhoven, who joined Armstrong Whitworth of Coventry in 1914, the FK.8 army cooperation aircraft—known to its crews as the "Big AW" or "Big Ack" – was a larger, sturdier, and more powerful version of his earlier FK.3. It first flew in May 1916 and eventually equipped nine RFC squadrons at home and overseas. About 1,400 were built in total, serving in the reconnais-

sance, patrol, day and night bombing, and ground-attack roles throughout 1917 and 1918. The FK.8 was well liked by its crews, and definitely superior to its contemporary, the RE.8.

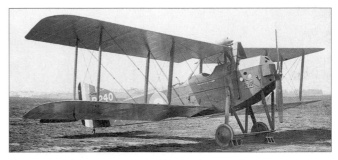

▲ This view of an early-production FK.8 demonstrates the unorthodox undercarriage structure, with a single main strut.

SPECIFICATION: Type army cooperation biplane • Crew 2 • Powerplant one 160hp Beardmore in-line engine • Max speed 95mph (153km/h) • Service ceiling 12,106ft (3,690m) • Endurance 3hrs • Wingspan 43ft 6in (13.26m) • Length 31ft 5in (9.58m) • Height 10ft 11in (3.33m) • Weight 2,811lb (1,275kg) • Armament one fixed forward-firing 0.303-in (7.62-mm) Vickers machine gun; one 0.303-in (7.62-mm) Lewis machine gun in rear cockpit

▌Atlas Cheetah

SOUTH AFRICA

Resembling Israel's IAI Kfir, the Atlas Cheetah was a direct result of the UN arms embargo imposed on South Africa in 1977. Anxious to upgrade its fleet of aging Mirage III aircraft, the SAAF embarked on a major modification program that involved the rebuilding of some 50 percent of the original Mirage airframe, incorporating modifications that included the addition of intake-mounted canards and dogtooth lead-

SPECIFICATION: Type combat and training aircraft • Crew 1-2 • Powerplant one 15,873lb (7,200kg) thrust SNECMA Atar 9K-50 turbojet • Max speed 1,452mph (2,337km) at altitude • Service ceiling 55,775ft (17,000m) • Combat radius 745 miles (1,200km) • Wingspan 26ft 11in (8.22m) • Length 50ft 6in (15.40m) • Height 13ft 11in (4.25m) • Weight classified • Armament two 1.19-in (30-mm) DEFA cannon; external stores

ing edges. Named Cheetah, the modified aircraft also featured new navigation and weapon systems. The first aircraft, modified from a Mirage IIID2, was declared operational in July 1987, and 30 aircraft were eventually returned to service in their new guise.

◀ To mark the 75th anniversary of the SAAF in 1995, No. 2 Squadron applied this extravagant color scheme to one of its Cheetah Cs.

▌ Auster Mks 3-9

The Auster AOP (Air Observation Post) aircraft were army cooperation versions of the famous high-wing light aircraft developed after World War II by Auster Aircraft. The AOP.6 saw extensive service with British forces in Korea (1950–53). In action in Malaya from 1955, the Mk.9, which featured a considerably more powerful engine combined with a larger wing, served in large numbers with the Army Air Corps, being widely exported abroad. The type proved to operate well on rough airstrips and could operate from plowed fields and mud airstrips.

▲ Auster Mk.6 artillery observation aircraft seen over Korea in 1952. Austers operated in support of the British Commonwealth forces.

SPECIFICATION: Type army cooperation monoplane (data AOP.9) • Crew 2–3 • Powerplant one 180hp Blackburn Cirrus Bombardier in-line • Max speed 127mph (204km/h) • Service ceiling 18,500ft (5,640m) • Max range 246 miles (395km) • Wingspan 36ft 5in (11.10m) • Length 23ft 8in (7.21m) • Height 8ft 5in (2.56m) • Weight 2130lb (966kg) loaded • Armament none

▌ Avia B.534

Probably the finest fighter biplane ever built, and one of the last mass-produced biplane fighters, the Avia B.534 first flew in August 1933, and an initial order for 100 machines was placed by the Czech Army Air Force. Early B.534s had an open cockpit, but a sliding hood was introduced on later aircraft. First deliveries were made in the second half of 1935. A B.534 that took part in the International Air Meeting at Zurich in 1937 outflew everything except the Messerschmitt Bf 109, and even then it was only 7mph (11km/h) slower than the German fighter. Production totalled 445 aircraft, the B.534 becoming the standard fighter equipment of the Czech fighter squadrons, and also serving with Bulgaria and the Luftwaffe.

In 1939, after the German occupation of Bohemia and Moravia, large numbers of B.534s were acquired by the Slovak Air Force, which later used them against the Russians.

▲ Like the Fiat CR.42 and Gloster Gladiator, the B.534 was one of the last mass-produced biplane fighters.

SPECIFICATION: Type fighter • Crew 1 • Powerplant one 850hp Hispano-Suiza HS 12Y in-line engine • Max speed 245mph (394km/h) • Service ceiling 34,777ft (10,600m) • Max range 360 miles (580km) • Wingspan 30ft 10in (9.40m) • Length 26ft 10in (8.20m) • Height 10ft 2in (3.10m) • Weights 3,219lb (1,460kg) empty; 4,674lb (2,120kg) loaded • Armament four fixed forward-firing 0.303-in (7.7-mm) Model 30 machine guns; underwing racks for up to six 44-lb (20-kg) bombs

Aviatik B.I

GERMANY

The early products of the Automobil und Aviatik AG were copies of French designs, but as it gained experience the company embarked on designs of its own. The B.I two-seat reconnaissance aircraft that entered service in 1914 was developed from a 1913 design for a racing biplane, the observer being seated in the front cockpit. The B.I was followed into service by the B.II, which had a more powerful Mercedes engine.

▲ *The Aviatik B.I seated its observer forwards and pilot to the rear – less than ideal in combat.*

SPECIFICATION: Type reconnaissance biplane • Crew 2 • Powerplant one 100hp Mercedes 6-cylinder liquid-cooled in-line • Max speed 62mph (100km/h) • Service ceiling not known • Endurance 4hrs • Wingspan 45ft 10in (13.97m) • Length 26ft 2in (7.97m) • Height 10ft 10in (3.30m) • Weight 2,400lb (1,088kg) loaded • Armament none

Aviatik C.I

GERMANY

SPECIFICATION: Type reconnaissance biplane • Crew 2 • Powerplant one 120hp Mercedes D.II 6-cylinder in-line • Max speed 89mph (142km/h) • Service ceiling 11,480ft (3,500m) • Endurance 3hrs • Wingspan 41ft (12.50m) • Length 26ft (7.92m) • Height 9ft 8in (2.95m) • Weight 2,954lb (1,340kg) loaded • Armament one 0.31-in (7.92-mm) Parabellum machine gun on flexible mount in rear cockpit

The C.I was the first Aviatik aircraft designed from the outset for military use. Early production aircraft had the observer in the front cockpit, but provided with a machine gun, although his field of fire was badly restricted, so he was moved to the rear cockpit. With this arrangement the aircraft was designated C.Ia, but production soon switched to the C.II, with a more powerful Benz engine.

▲ *The first Aviatik aircraft designed for military use from the outset was the C.I. Construction was of wood and fabric.*

▌Avro Anson

Originally intended to be a light transport, the Avro Anson was adapted to the coastal reconnaissance role to meet an Air Ministry requirement of May 1934. The prototype flew in March 1935, and the aircraft entered service as the Anson Mk.I a year later. By the outbreak of war the RAF had 760 serviceable Anson Is, equipping 10 squadrons of Coastal Command and 16 of Bomber Command (in which it served as an interim aircraft until types such as the Whitley became available). In Coastal Command it was soon replaced by the Lockheed Hudson, although some continued to serve in the

SPECIFICATION: Type coastal reconnaissance aircraft/light bomber (Anson Mk.I) • Crew 3-5 • Powerplant two 335hp Armstrong Siddeley Cheetah IX radials • Max speed 188mph (302km/h) • Service ceiling 19,000ft (5,790m) • Max range 790 miles (1,271km) • Wingspan 56ft 6in (17.22m) • Length 42ft 3in (12.88m) • Height 13ft 1in (3.99m) • Weight 9,300lb (4,218kg) loaded • Armament up to four 0.303-in (7.62-mm) machine guns on cabin mountings (or in dorsal turret); bomb load of 500lb (227kg)

air-sea rescue role. It was as a crew trainer and light transport, however, that the Anson excelled. By the time production ended in 1952 8,138 Ansons (including 6,704 Mk Is) had been built in Britain, with a further 2,882 built in Canada.

▼ *The Anson T.Mk. 20 bomb aimer/navigator trainer featured a transparent nosecone for the bomb aimer and racks for 16 dummy bombs.*

▌Avro Bison

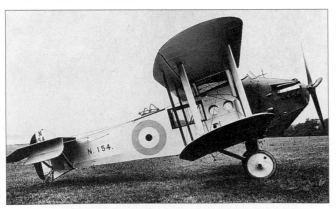

▲ *The second Bison prototype, shown here, had its wing raised 1ft 3in (0.38m) above the fuselage.*

The Avro Bison was designed to Admiralty Specification 3/11, calling for a carrier-based fleet spotter and reconnaissance aircraft. The Royal Navy took delivery of 53 aircraft, which were retired in 1929 and replaced by the Fairey IIIF. The Bison, which first flew in 1921, had a deep fuselage housing an internal cabin for the observer/navigator and radio operator.

SPECIFICATION: Type fleet spotter biplane • Crew 3-4 • Powerplant one 450hp Napier Lion in-line engine • Max speed 110mph (177km/h) • Service ceiling 14,000ft (4,265m) • Max range 340 miles (547km) • Wingspan 46ft (14.02m) • Length 36ft (10.97m) • Height 13ft 10in (4.22m) • Weight 5,800lb (2,631kg) loaded • Armament one 0.303-in (7.62-mm) Lewis machine gun on flexible mount in rear cockpit

Avro Lancaster

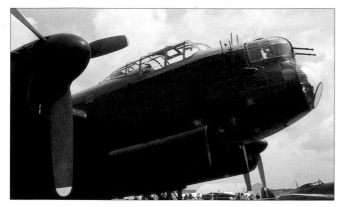

▲ Close-up of the nose of a Lancaster, showing the bomb-aimer's perspex "blister" and the nose turret with its two machine guns.

SPECIFICATION: Type heavy bomber (data Lancaster Mk III) • Crew 7 • Powerplant four 1,640hp Rolls-Royce Merlin 28 or 38 12-cylinder V-type engines • Max speed 287mph (462km/h) • Service ceiling 19,000ft (5,790m) • Max range 1,730 miles (2,784km) with a 12,000-lb (5,443-kg) bomb load • Wingspan 102ft (31.09m) • Length 69ft 6in (21.18m) • Height 20ft 6in (6.25m) • Weight 65,000lb (29,484kg) loaded • Armament two 0.303-in (7.7-mm) machine guns in nose turret, two 0.303-in (7.7-mm) machine guns in dorsal turret, and four 0.303-in (7.7-mm) machine guns in tail turret. Maximum internal bomb load 18,000lb (8,165kg)

One of the most famous bomber aircraft of all time, the Avro Lancaster was developed from the Avro Manchester, a design that suffered from the unreliability of its two Rolls-Royce Vulture engines. While production of the Manchester was in progress one airframe, BT308, was designated a "four-engined Manchester" and fitted with four Rolls-Royce Merlin XX engines. This was the first prototype Lancaster, which first flew on January 9, 1941 with triple fins and without ventral or dorsal turrets. (A ventral turret was to have been a feature of the Lancaster, but was eliminated to provide extra bomb bay space.) Before the full test program was initiated, the aircraft was fitted with twin fins on a tailplane spanning 33ft (10m), which improved flight characteristics considerably. The first Lancaster, BT308, was delivered to No. 44 (Rhodesia) Squadron at Waddington, Lincolnshire in September 1941 for familiarization, and by January 1942 the squadron had begun to replace its Handley Page Hampdens with the type. First operational sortie with Lancasters was on March 3, 1942, when four aircraft laid mines in the Heligoland Bight.

As an insurance against possible interruption in supplies of Merlins, it was decided to equip some Lancasters with four 1,650hp Bristol Hercules 6 (or 16) radials in place of the Merlin XX, these aircraft becoming the Lancaster Mk II, 300 of which were built. Little modification was made during its life to the basic Lancaster airframe, a testimonial to its sturdi-

ness and reliability, and so very little extra work was necessary when the Mk III with Packard-built Merlin engines superseded the Mk 1 on the production lines. Deployment of the Lancaster III enabled Bomber Command to use first the 8,000-lb (3,624-kg) bomb, then the 12,000-lb (5,436-kg) Tallboy, and finally the 22,000lb (9,966kg) Grand Slam, recessed in the doorless bomb bay. Specially modified Lancasters of No. 617 Squadron RAF also carried out the famous attack on the Mohne, Eder, and Sorpe dams in May 1943. The last Lancaster raid of the war was made against an SS barracks at Berchtesgaden on April 25, 1945. During the war Lancasters flew 156,192 sorties, dropping 608,612 tons of bombs. Losses in action were 3,431 aircraft, a further 246 being destroyed in operational accidents. At its peak strength in August 1944 no fewer than 42 Bomber Command squadrons were armed with the Lancaster.

The much-modified Lancasters IV and V became the Lincoln Mks I and II. The Mk VI, nine of which were converted from Mks I and III, was equipped for electronic countermeasures. The last production Lancaster was the Mk VII, 180 of which were built by Austin Motors. Lancasters remained in service with RAF Bomber Command for some time after WWII until replaced by the Avro Lincoln, and RAF Coastal Command used the GR.3 maritime patrol version until this was replaced by the Avro Shackleton. Avro refurbished 54 Mk 1s and VIIs and converted them to the maritime patrol role for use by France's Aéronavale, and other Mk 1s were converted for photographic survey work as the PR.Mk.1. Total Lancaster production, all variants, was 7,374 aircraft.

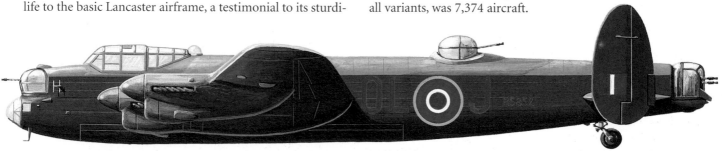

▌Avro Lincoln

▲ *Although it continued to serve in RAF Bomber Command until the early 1950s, the Avro Lincoln was completely outclassed by that time.*

Designed to Specification B.14/43 to meet a requirement for a Lancaster replacement, the prototype Avro Lincoln flew for the first time on June 9, 1944. Deliveries to the RAF began in

SPECIFICATION: Type heavy bomber (data Lincoln B.1) • Crew 7 • Powerplant four Rolls-Royce Merlin 85 V-12 in-line engines • Max speed 319mph (513km/h) at 18,500ft (5,640m) • Service ceiling 30,500ft (9,300m) • Max range 1,470 miles (2,365km) • Wingspan 120ft (36.57m) • Length 78ft 3in (23.85m) • Height 17ft 3in (5.25m) • Weight 75,000lb (34,020kg) loaded • Armament twin 0.50-in (12.7-mm) remotely controlled Browning machine guns in nose turret and two in tail turret; twin 0.79-in (20-mm) Hispano Mk 4/5 cannon in dorsal turret (later deleted)

the spring of 1945. The Lincoln became operational too late to see active service in World War II, although plans had been made to send several squadrons to the Far East as part of "Tiger Force" for operations against Japan. Lincolns did, however, see action against communist terrorists during the Malayan Emergency of the 1950s. The RAAF operated the type as the Lincoln B.30; five aircraft were assembled from British-built components, and a further 68 built under license. The Lincoln was retired from RAF Bomber Command at the end of 1955, being replaced by the Canberra jet bomber. The last air arm to operate the type as a bomber was the Argentine Air Force, which received 12 Lincoln B.1s and used them until 1963.

▌Avro Manchester

Designed (as was the Handley Page Halifax) to meet the requirements of Specification 13/36, which called for a twin-engined heavy bomber, the Manchester was powered by two 1760 Rolls-Royce Vulture engines which, in service, were to give constant trouble. The prototype Manchester (L7246) flew on July 25, 1939, being followed by a second aircraft on

▶ *Dogged throughout its career by troublesome engines, the Avro Manchester was developed into the classic Lancaster bomber.*

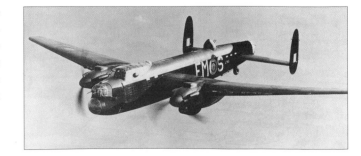

SPECIFICATION: Type heavy bomber • Crew 7 • Powerplant two 1,760hp Rolls-Royce Vulture 24-cylinder X-type engines • Max speed 265mph(426km/h) • Service ceiling 19,200ft (5,850m) • Max range 1,630 miles (2,623km) • Wingspan 90ft 1in (27.46m) • Length 69ft 4in (21.14m) • Height 19ft 6in (5.94m) • Weight 56,000lb (25,402kg) loaded • Armament two 0.303-in (7.62-mm) machine guns in nose turret, two in ventral turret (later replaced by dorsal turret), and four in tail turret, plus internal bomb load of 10,350lb (4,695kg)

May 26, 1940. The Manchester Mk I, which featured a central tail fin as well as twin fins and rudders, became operational with No. 207 Squadron in November 1940, the first 20 being followed by 200 Manchester IAs with the central fin removed. The Manchester was withdrawn from operations in 1942, its unreliable engines having cost the lives of many aircrew, and the Manchester Mk III, modified to take four Rolls-Royce Merlin engines, became the prototype Avro Lancaster.

▌Avro Shackleton

Designed in 1946 to meet a requirement for a Liberator replacement in RAF Coastal Command, the Avro Type 696 Shackleton (originally designated Lincoln ASR.3) flew for the first time on March 9, 1949, powered by four Rolls-Royce Griffon engines. It was the first British four-engined aircraft with contrarotating propellers. The first of 77 production Shackleton MR.1s entered service with No. 120 Squadron at Kinloss, Scotland, in April 1951. The Shackleton MR.2 had modifications that

▲ Avro Shackleton AEW.8 airborne early warning aircraft, a Mk.2 conversion.

SPECIFICATION: Type long-range maritime patrol aircraft (data MR.3) • Crew 10-13 • Powerplant four Rolls-Royce Griffon 57A V-12 liquid-cooled engines • Max speed 302mph (486km/h) • Service ceiling 20,000ft (6,100m) • Max range 4,215 miles (6,780km) • Wingspan 119ft 10in (36.53m) • Length 87ft 4in (26.62m) • Height 23ft 4in (7.11m) • Weight 100,000lb (45,360kg) loaded • Armament two 0.79-in (20-mm) cannon; various internal loads

included a ventral ASV radome, while the MR.3 incorporated some radical design changes, with an altered wing shape, wingtip tanks, and a tricycle undercarriage. The MR.3 was later fitted with Armstrong Siddeley Viper turbojets in the outboard engine nacelles, being designated Mr.3 Phase 3. The last RAF squadron to operate the Shackleton was No. 8, which reformed at Kinloss in 1972 in the early warning role with Shackleton AEW Mk 2s (converted MR.2s). Shackletons were also supplied to the South African Air Force.

▌Avro Tutor

The Avro Tutor elementary trainer was designed to replace the Avro 504N in the RAF's flying training schools. Having all the excellent handling characteristics of its predecessor, it was selected for production in 1930, the first of an eventual 395 aircraft (from the production total of 795) being delivered in 1933. The Tutor was also exported in small numbers to Canada, Eire, Greece, Denmark, and China, and was built under license in South Africa.

SPECIFICATION: Type elementary trainer • Crew 2 • Powerplant one 240hp Armstrong Siddeley Lynx IVC radial engine • Max speed 122mph (196km/h) • Service ceiling 16,200ft (4,940m) • Max range 250 miles (402km) • Wingspan 34ft (10.36m) • Length 26ft 6in (8.08m) • Height 9ft 7in (2.92m) • Weight 2,458lb (1,115kg) loaded • Armament none

▲ This Type 621 Tutor was part of the penultimate Tutor batch delivered to the RAF.

■ Avro Vulcan

SPECIFICATION: Type strategic bomber (data: B.2) • Crew 5 • Powerplant four 20,000lb (9,072kg) thrust Bristol Siddeley Olympus Mk.301 turbojets • Max speed 645mph (1,038km/h) at high altitude • Service ceiling 65,000ft (19,810m) • Max range 4,600 miles (7,403km) • Wingspan 111ft (33.83m) • Length 99ft 11in (30.45m) • Height 27ft 2in (8.28m) • Weight 250,000lb (113,398kg) loaded • Armament 21x1,000-lb (453-kg) HE bombs; Yellow Sun Mk.2 or WE.177B nuclear weapons; Blue Steel ASM with Red Snow nuclear warhead (Vulcan B.2BS)

◀ *The giant wing of the Vulcan is shown to great effect by this B.Mk.2 MRR at low level.*

The first bomber in the world to employ the delta wing planform, the Avro Type 698 Vulcan prototype (VX770) flew for the first time on August 30, 1952, and the first production Vulcan B.Mk.1 was delivered in July 1956. Production of the B.Mk.1 was terminated with the 45th aircraft, the remaining Vulcans on order being completed to B.Mk.2 standard with flight refueling equipment. Having relinquished the QRA (Quick Reaction Alert) role for which it was designed to the Royal Navy's Polaris-armed submarines, the RAF's Vulcan force was assigned to NATO and CENTO in the free-fall

bombing role. In May 1982, Vulcans operating from Ascension Island in the Atlantic carried out attacks on the Falkland Islands in support of British operations to recapture these from Argentina. Total Vulcan production was 136 aircraft, including the two prototypes and 89 B.Mk.2s.

▶ *This early production Vulcan Mk.I was pictured during tests at Woodford, Cheshire in September 1955.*

■ Avro York

SPECIFICATION: Type transportation aircraft • Crew 5 + 24 passengers • Powerplant 1,280hp four Rolls-Royce Merlin XX in-line engines • Max speed 298mph (480km/h) at 21,000ft (6,400m) • Service ceiling 21,300ft (6,500m) • Max range 2,700 miles (4,345km) • Wingspan 102ft (31.09m) • Length 78ft 6in (23.93m) • Height 17ft 10in (5.43m) • Weight 68,507lb (31,075kg) loaded • Armament none

Derived from the Lancaster bomber in 1942, the Avro York was initially produced only in small numbers, but it went into mass production in 1944 and 257 were built, approximately 50 of which were civil transports. The York equipped nine squadrons of RAF Transport Command and was the mainstay of the RAF contribution to the Berlin Airlift in 1948–49. It was replaced by the Handley Page Hastings in the early 1950s.

Avro 504

The Avro 504, which first flew at Brooklands in July 1913, was a straightforward development of the Type E, which was already on order for the Royal Flying Corps. In a production life spanning well over a decade more than 10,000 Avro 504s

▲ *A pair of Avro 504Ns cavort at low level. The Type 504 remained in RAF service into the early 1930s.*

were built, serving as bomber, reconnaissance, fighter, and training aircraft during World War I. It is as a trainer that the Avro 504 is best remembered; thousands of British and Commonwealth pilots learned to fly in it, and after the war surplus 504s were snapped up for commercial use, being used for joyriding, "barnstorming," and for training civilian pilots. The Avro 504N, was the peacetime production aircraft, being converted from the standard Avro 504K RAF trainer and having a different engine and undercarriage. Series production totaled 598 examples, the last being completed in 1932. The Avro 504 was then progressively replaced by the Avro Tutor.

SPECIFICATION: Type scouting biplane • Crew 1 • Powerplant one 100hp Gnome Monosoupape piston or 110hp Le Rhone rotary engine • Max speed 93mph (150km/h) • Service ceiling 4,265ft(1,300m) • Endurance 2hrs 45mins • Weight 1,421lb (645kg) loaded • Wingspan 28ft 3in (8.61m) • Length 25ft 2in (7.68m) • Height 9ft 6in (2.91m) • Armament one forward-firing 0.303-in (7.62-mm) Lewis gun on flexible mounting

Avro Canada CF-100

Canada, forming the first line of defense against the threat of bombers attacking the North American continent across the great wastes of the Arctic, was quick to identify the need for a long-range night and all-weather interceptor during the early postwar years. In response to this requirement, Avro Canada designed the CF-100, at that time the largest fighter aircraft in the world. The prototype CF-100 Mk1 flew on January 19, 1950, powered by two Rolls-Royce Avon RA3 turbojets; production aircraft were fitted with the Avro Orenda. In September 1950 an order was placed with Avro Canada for 124 CF-100 Mk3s for the RCAF.

The first production Mk4A flew on October 24, 1953 and

▶ *A CF-100 makes a rocket-assisted take-off. The CF-100 was the largest and heaviest interceptor in the world when it first flew.*

SPECIFICATION: Type all-weather interceptor • Crew 2 • Powerplant two Avro Orenda turbojets each rated at 7,264lb (3,295kg) thrust • Max speed 650mph (1,046km/h) at 10,000ft (3,050m) • Service ceiling 54,000ft (16,470m) • Max range 2,000 miles (3,218km) • Wingspan 60ft 8in (18.54m) • Length 54ft 2in (16.53m) • Height 14ft 5in (4.42m) • Weights 23,070lb (10,464kg) empty; 33,554lb (15,220kg) loaded • Armament 52 2.95-in (75-mm) HVAR rockets in wingtip pods

the aircraft entered service with No. 445 Squadron in the following year. In all, 510 Mk4As and 4Bs (the latter with Orenda 11 engines) were built. By the end of 1957 nine RCAF squadrons were operating the type, providing round-the-clock air defense coverage of Canada's far north. Four CF-100 squadrons also served in Germany as part of Canada's NATO commitment, and 53 examples of the last production version, the Mk5, were delivered to Belgium.

▌BAC (Vickers) VC-10

▲ No. 101 Sqn, RAF, operates four K.Mk.3s, based on the the long-fuselage Super VC-10.

Designated VC-10 C.Mk.I, 14 examples of this four-jet long-haul airliner were delivered to No. 10 Squadron, RAF Air Support Command, between 1966 and 1968. Four standard VC-10s and five Super VC-10s were later converted as flight refueling tankers and delivered to the RAF in 1984 and 1985 as VC-10 K.Mk.2s and VC-10 K.Mk.3s. A final batch of five ex-British Airways Super VC-10s, converted in the early 1990s, received the designation VC-10 K.Mk.4. No 101 Squadron's VC-10s saw intensive action during Operation Desert Storm, refueling RAF and US Navy aircraft.

SPECIFICATION: Type jet tanker (data VC-10 K-3) • Crew 4 • Powerplant four 21,800lb (9,905kg) thrust Rolls-Royce Conway 301 turbofans • Max speed 580mph (935km/h) • Service ceiling 38,000ft (11,600m) • Max range 4,725 miles (7,600km) • Wingspan 182ft 5in (55.60m) • Length 171ft 9in (52.30m) • Height 39ft 6in (12m) • Weight 335,000lb (152,000kg) • Armament none

▌Beechcraft C-45 Expediter

Several developed versions of Beechcraft's 1938 Model 18 feederliner saw military service during World War II in a variety of roles. Transport and general purpose versions were produced in large numbers for the USAAF (C-45 Expediter and UC-45 Traveler) and the USN (JRB). The Expediter I was also supplied to the RAF under the Lend-Lease scheme. The AT-7 and AT-11 were respectively navigation and bombing/gunnery trainer versions, and the F-2 was a photographic reconnaissance variant. Civil variations of the Model 18 design remained in production for a record 32 years.

SPECIFICATION: Type light transportation • Crew 2, plus 6-8 passengers • Powerplant two 450hp Pratt & Whitney R-985 AN-1 9-cylinder radials • Max speed 215mph (345km/h) • Service ceiling 20,000ft (6,100m) • Max range 700 miles (1,130km) • Wingspan 47ft 8in (14.53m) • Length 34ft 3in (10.44m) • Height 9ft 8in (2.95m) • Weight 8,727lb (3,960kg) loaded • Armament none

▲ A specialized bomb-aimer trainer, the AT-11 featured a glazed nose. The type was unofficially named Kansan.

▌Beechcraft T-34 Mentor

First flown in December 1948, the Beechcraft T-34 Mentor was developed from the civilian Beechcraft Bonanza, differing primarily by having tandem seating for pupil and instructor. The Mentor was built in large numbers, serving with the US services and with many countries within the US

sphere of influence. Variants were the T-34A for the USAF (450), T-34B for the USN, and T-34C, which had a PTRA turboprop in place of the earlier Continental piston engine (300 built). Export T-34C-1s could be equipped to carry out light attack missions.

SPECIFICATION: Type trainer (data T-34C) • Crew 2 • Powerplant one 400hp Pratt & Whitney PT6A-25 turboprop • Max speed 288mph (464km/h) at sea level • Service ceiling 30,000ft (9,145m) • Max range 748 miles (1,205km) • Wingspan 33ft 3in (10.16m) • Length 28ft 8in (8.75m) • Height 9ft 7in (3.02m) • Weight 4,360lb (1,978kg) loaded • Armament none

◀ *Beech beat off rival proposals from Temco and Ryan to win a USN order for the T-34B. The type served into the late 1970s.*

Beechcraft T-44A

UNITED STATES

The Beechcraft T-44A was another aircraft derived from one of the company's commercial designs, in this case the twin-turboprop King Air 90. The first converted model flew in 1976 and the type entered service with the US Navy in the following year. The T-44A is used to train Navy pilots to fly multiengined aircraft.

SPECIFICATION: Type trainer • Crew 2 • Powerplant two 550hp Pratt & Whitney PT6A-34B turboprops • Max speed 276mph (447km/h) at 15,000ft (4,570m) • Service ceiling 29,500ft (8,990m) • Max range 1,456 miles (2,344km) • Wingspan 50ft 2in (15.32m) • Length 35ft 4in (10.82m) • Height 14ft 2in (4.33m) • Weight 9,650lb (4,377kg) loaded • Armament none

Bell P-39 Airacobra

UNITED STATES

The design of the Bell P-39 Airacrobra was unusual in that its Allison in-line engine was installed below and behind the pilot's seat, driving the propeller via an extension shaft coupled to a gearbox in the nose of the aircraft. The XP-39 prototype flew in April 1939, and although no orders were immediately forthcoming from the US military, France placed an order for 100 aircraft. Some of these were taken over by the RAF in 1941, but the type fell far short of British expectations and only one squadron (No. 601) was issued with it for a short time.

The first model to serve with the USAAF was the P-39C, which was followed by the P-39D with self-sealing fuel tanks. The Airacobra went into action with the 8th Pursuit Group in northern Australia early in 1942, subsequently deploying its aircraft to forward airstrips in New Guinea. Shortly afterward the unit's designation was changed to the 8th Fighter Group and it was joined by the 35th Fighter Group, also with P-39s. The

▲ *The P-39 Airacobra was outclassed in combat with the Japanese Zero, but was very popular with Soviet pilots, who made extensive use of it.*

SPECIFICATION: Type fighter (data P-39N) • Crew 1 • Powerplant one 1,200hp Allison V-1710-85 12-cylinder V-type • Max speed 399mph (642km/h) at 9,700ft (2,955m) • Service ceiling 38,500ft (11,735m) • Max range 750 miles (1,207km) • Wingspan 34ft (10.36m) • Length 30ft 2in (9.19m) • Height 12ft 5in (3.78m) • Weight 8,200lb (3,720kg) loaded • Armament one hub-firing 1.46-in (37-mm) gun; two 0.50-in (12.7-mm) machine guns in upper forward fuselage, and four 0.30-in (7.62-mm) machine guns in the wings; provision for one 500-lb (227-kg) bomb under the fuselage

fighters were a mixture of P-39Ds and Airacobra Mk Is, drawn from the canceled British order. P-39s were also used by the 347th Fighter Group in New Caledonia, with detachments being deployed to Guadalcanal for air defense. Other P-39 variants were the P-39F, -J, -K, -L, -M, -N, and -Q, all with progressively uprated engines but few other design changes.

As well as the Pacific, P-39s saw action in Tunisia and during the invasion of southern France, where they were used by Free French squadrons. The biggest operator, however, was the Soviet Union, which was supplied with 4,773 under Lend-Lease and used them to very good effect. Total P-39 production was 9,558.

∎ Bell P-59 Airacomet

America's first jet fighter was the Bell P-59 Airacomet, the prototype of which flew on October 1, 1942 under the power of two General Electric I-A turbojets, derived from the Whittle W.2B engine. A higher-powered engine, the 1400-lb (635-kg) thrust I-16, was installed in the 13 trials aircraft which followed. The US Navy evaluated two of these, and a third was sent to the United Kingdom in exchange for a Gloster Meteor Mk 1. The Airacomet proved to be underpowered and its performance fell far below expectations, so the original order for 100 aircraft was reduced. Twenty P-59As were built with J31-GE-3 engines, and 30 P-59Bs with J31-GE-5s. Although the Airacomet did not serve operationally in World War II, it provided the Americans with invaluable experience in the operation of jet aircraft.

SPECIFICATION: Type fighter-bomber (data P-59A) • Crew 1 • Powerplant two General Electric J31-GE-3 turbojets • Max speed 413mph (664km/h) at 20,000ft (6,100m) • Service ceiling 46,200ft (14,080m) • Max range 520 miles (837km) • Wingspan 45ft 6in (13.87m) • Length 38ft 1in (11.62m) • Height 12ft (3.66m) • Weight 13,700lb (6,214kg) loaded • Armament one 1.46-in (37-mm) gun, three 0.50-in (12.7-mm) machine guns in the nose; external bomb or rocket load of 2,000lb (907kg)

▲ *Plagued by engine problems, the XP-59A (illustrated) reached an altitude of just 25ft (7.62m) on its first flight.*

∎ Bell P-63 Kingcobra

The Bell P-63 Kingcobra design was based on a modified Airacobra, the XP-39E. Two XP-63 prototypes were built; the first of which flew on December 7, 1942. Intended to succeed the P-39 in the fighter and fighter-bomber roles, only 332 examples were in fact delivered to the USAAF and used as gunnery targets. Of the 1,725 P-63A and 1,227 P-63C Kingcobras built, 2,421 were supplied to the USSR under Lend-Lease, proving to be excellent ground-attack aircraft, and 300 were allocated to the Free French Air Force.

SPECIFICATION: Type fighter-bomber (data P-63A) • Crew 1 • Powerplant one 1,325hp Allison V-1710-95 V-type • Max speed 408mph (657km/h) at 24,450ft (7,452m) • Service ceiling 43,000ft (13,105m) • Max range 450 miles (724km) • Wingspan 38ft 4in (11.68m) • Length 32ft 8in (9.96m) • Height 12ft 7in (3.84m) • Weight 8,800lb (3,992kg) loaded • Armament one hub-firing 1.46-in (37-mm) gun; two 0.50-in (12.7-mm) machine guns in upper forward fuselage, and one in each wing; provision for one 500-lb (227-kg) bomb under the fuselage and one under each wing

∎ Beriev Be-6 "Madge"

The USSR continued to develop flying boats after the end of World War II, and in 1945 the Georgi M. Beriev bureau, based at Taganrog on the Azov Sea, designed the Be-6, the most advanced flying boat so far constructed in the Soviet Union. Flight testing was completed in 1947 and the type was ordered into production for the Soviet Navy, the first production aircraft flying early in 1949. The Be-6 formed the mainstay of the Morskaya Aviatsiya's maritime patrol squadrons during the 1950s, being used as a transport and fishery protection aircraft in addition to its primary role.

▶ *This early Be-6 is pictured with an Ilyushin gun barbette in the tail.*

SPECIFICATION: **Type** maritime patrol flying boat • **Crew** 7 • **Powerplant** two 2,300hp Shvetsov ASh-73TKs 18-cylinder radials • **Max speed** 258mph (415km/h) at 7,875ft (2,400m) • **Service ceiling** 20,000ft (6,100m) • **Max range** 3,045 miles (4,900km) • **Wingspan** 108ft 4in (33m) • **Length** 77ft 3in (23.55m) • **Height** 24ft 7in (7.48m) • **Weight** 61,976lb (28,112kg) loaded • **Armament** five 0.9-in (23-mm) cannon; 8,820lb (4,000kg) of bombs or depth charges

▌Beriev Be-12 "Mail"

USSR

▲ *A Be-12 amphibian makes its approach to land at a naval air base in Arctic Russia. The Mail was a very effective maritime patrol aircraft.*

First seen publicly in 1961, the turboprop-powered Beriev Be-12 amphibian was the type selected to replace the Be-6. The prototype flew in 1960 and service deployment was rapid. The Be-12 featured a sharply cranked, high-set wing similar to the Be-6's, a configuration dictated by the need to raise the engines well clear of the water. The single-step hull had a high length-to-beam ratio and was fitted with two long strakes to keep spray away from the engines on takeoff. There was a glazed observation position in the nose, surmounted by a long thimble-type radome, and a "stinger" tail housed Magnetic Anomaly Detection (MAD) equipment. During its service career, the Be-12 established numerous records for turboprop-powered amphibians.

SPECIFICATION: **Type** maritime patrol flying boat • **Crew** 5-6 • **Powerplant** two 4,000hp Ivchenko AI-20D turboprops • **Max speed** 379mph (610km/h) at 5,000ft (1,525m) • **Service ceiling** 40,000ft (12,185m) • **Max range** 2,485 miles (4,000km) • **Wingspan** 108ft (32.91m) • **Length** 95ft 9in (29.18m) • **Height** 21ft 11in (6.68m) • **Weight** 65,035lb (29,500kg) loaded • **Armament** up to 22,250lb (10,092kg) of bombs and depth charges; no defensive armament

▌Beriev KOR-1/KOR-2

USSR

In the mid-1930s a pressing need for a catapult-launched floatplane prompted Beriev to design the KOR-1 (Be-2), which entered service in 1938. During the early days of the German attack on Russia some were fitted with a fixed under-carriage and used as light bombers against Romanian forces. The KOR-2 (Be-4) was developed in conjunction and featured an inverted-gull parasol wing with a pylon-mounted engine. The KOR-2 flew in 1940, but relatively few were completed.

SPECIFICATION: **Type** reconnaissance seaplane (data KOR-2) • **Crew** 2 • **Powerplant** one 900hp Shvetsov M-62 radial • **Max speed** 223mph (360km/h) at sea level • **Service ceiling** 26,575ft (8,100m) • **Max range** 590 miles (950km) • **Wingspan** 39ft 4in (12m) • **Length** 34ft (10.5m) • **Height** 13ft 3in (4.05m) • **Weight** 6,085lb (2,760kg) • **Armament** one 0.30-in (7.62-mm) machine gun in rear cockpit; up to 661lb (300kg) of bombs on underwing racks

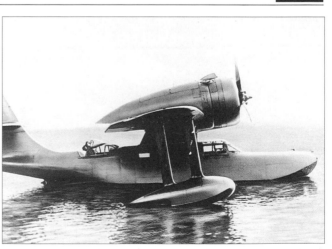

▲ *Representing a major advance over the KOR-1, the duties of the KOR-2 included flying as a catapult flying boat from Soviet warships.*

▌Beriev MBR-2 "Mote"

The MBR-2 was Georgi Beriev's first flying boat design, and it went on to achieve great success. Deliveries to the Soviet Navy began in 1934 and the definitive version was the MBR-2AM-34, which had a fully enclosed cockpit, glazed midship gunner's position, and a redesigned fin and rudder. Around 1,300 were built and saw considerable service with all four Soviet fleets from the Winter War of 1939–40 to the last actions in 1945. After the war the MBR-2 served on fishery protection duties for nearly a decade, hence the NATO reporting name allocated to it.

◀ The MBR-2 saw considerable operational service. The AM-34 engine drove a pusher-propeller.

SPECIFICATION: Type maritime patrol flying boat • Crew 4-5 • Powerplant one 680hp M-17 12-cylinder in-line engine • Max speed 124mph (200km/h) at sea level • Service ceiling 14,435ft (4,400m) • Max range 404 miles (650km) • Wingspan 62ft 4in (19m) • Length 44ft 3in (13.5m) • Height 16ft 5in (5m) • Weight 9,039lb (4,100kg) • Armament one 0.30-in (7.62-mm) ShKAS machine gun on ring mount in bow position and one in midship position; up to 1,102lb (500kg) of bombs on underwing racks

▌Blackburn Baffin

The Baffin two-seat torpedo bomber was developed by Blackburn as a private venture, the company marrying what was already a well-proven airframe design to a Bristol Pegasus radial engine. The two Baffin prototypes appeared in 1932 and 1933, and production began in September of the latter year. Only 29 Baffins were built, but 60 Blackburn Ripons were also reengined with the Pegasus and converted into Baffins.

SPECIFICATION: Type torpedo bomber biplane • Crew 2 • Powerplant one 565hp Bristol Pegasus 1.M3 radial engine • Max speed 136mph (219km/h) • Service ceiling 15,000ft (4,570m) • Max range 540 miles (869km) • Wingspan 45ft 6in (13.88m) • Length 38ft 3in (11.68m) • Height 12ft 10in (3.91m) • Weight 7,610lb (3,452kg) loaded • Armament one fixed forward-firing 0.303-in (7.7-mm) Vickers machine gun; one 0.303-in (7.7-mm) gun on flexible mounting in rear cockpit; under-fuselage rack for one torpedo or up to 2,000lb (907kg) of bombs

▲ K3589 was one of two pre-production Baffins. It was delivered for test work in 1933 and retained until sold for scrap in 1937.

▌Blackburn Beverley

Developed from the Blackburn and General Aircraft Universal Freighter, the Beverley C.1 military transport entered service with RAF Transport Command in April 1956 and equipped three squadrons until replaced by the Lockheed Hercules a decade later. The Beverley could carry 94 fully equipped troops or a payload of 45,000lb (20,142kg).

▲ Massive and ponderous, the Blackburn Beverley served RAF Transport Command well in the 1950s and '60s until replaced by the C-130.

SPECIFICATION: Type transportation aircraft • Crew 4 • Powerplant four 2,850 Bristol Centaurus 273 18-cylinder radials • Max speed 238mph (383km/h) at 5,700ft (1,740m) • Service ceiling 16,000ft (4,880m) • Max range 1,300 miles (2,090km) • Wingspan 162ft (49.38m) • Length 99ft 5in (30.30m) • Height 38ft 9in (11.81m) • Weight 143,00lb (64,865kg) loaded • Armament none

▌Blackburn Botha

GREAT BRITAIN

Designed to meet a 1935 requirement for a twin-engined reconnaissance bomber with a bomb bay large enough to accommodate an 18-in (457-mm) torpedo, the Blackburn Botha turned out to be a spectacular failure. Despite being seriously underpowered, the type was ordered into production, 580 being built. The Botha entered service in October 1939, but proved so inadequate operationally that only one squadron (No. 608) was armed with it. Its front-line career lasted less than a year, after which it was relegated to second-line duties as a navigation and gunnery trainer.

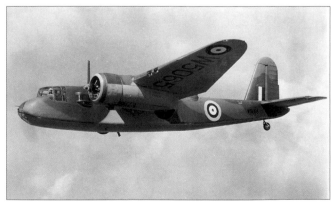

SPECIFICATION: Type reconnaissance and torpedo bomber • Crew 4 • Powerplant two 930hp Bristol Perseus XA 9-cylinder radials • Max speed 249mph (401km/h) • Service ceiling 18,400ft (5,610m) • Max range 1,270 miles (2,044km) • Wingspan 59ft (17.98m) • Length 51ft (15.56m) • Height 14ft 7in (4.46m) • Weight 18,450lb (8,369kg) • Armament one 0.303-in (7.7-mm) machine gun in nose and two in dorsal turret; internal bomb and torpedo load of 2,000lb (907kg)

▲ Although produced in some numbers, the Botha was a failure and was withdrawn from service in late 1944.

■ Blackburn Dart

▲ *A Blackburn Dart being manhandled on a carrier deck in 1932.*

The Blackburn Dart was a development of the Swift torpedo-bomber of 1919, the only production versions of which went for export. The Dart entered service with the Fleet Air Arm in 1923 and 120 were built, remaining first-line equipment until 1933. On July 1, 1926 a Dart made the first night landing on an aircraft carrier, HMS *Furious*. A twin-float version of the Dart was named the Velos. Darts in Fleet Air Arm service were eventually replaced by the Blackburn Ripon.

SPECIFICATION: Type torpedo-bomber biplane • Crew 1 • Powerplant one 450hp Napier Lion IIB 12-cylinder V-type engine • Max speed 107mph (172km/h) • Service ceiling 12,700ft (3,870m) • Max range 285 miles (460km) • Wingspan 45ft 6in (13.86m) • Length 35ft 4in (10.77m) • Height 12ft 11in (3.94m) • Weight 6,382lb (2,895kg) loaded • Armament one 1,650-lb (750-kg) torpedo

■ Blackburn Firebrand

In the summer of 1940, the British Admiralty issued a requirement for an interceptor designed around the most powerful piston engine then available, the 2,300hp Napier

SPECIFICATION: Type naval strike fighter (data TF.Mk.5) • Crew 1 • Powerplant one 2,500hp Bristol Centaurus IX 18-cylinder radial • Max speed 350mph (563km/h) • Service ceiling 28,500ft (8,690m) • Max range 746 miles (1,200km) • Wingspan 51ft 3in (15.62m) • Length 38ft 11in (11.86m) • Height 14ft 11in (4.55m) • Weight 17,500lb (7,938kg) loaded • Armament four 0.79-in (20-mm) Hispano cannon; one 1,850-lb (839-kg) torpedo or two 1,000-lb (453-kg) bombs

Sabre III. Blackburn Aircraft Ltd. submitted their design, the Type B37, and the first of three prototypes flew on February 27, 1942. As a result of preservice trials, the Admiralty decided to redevelop the aircraft as a torpedo-fighter, designated Firebrand TF.Mk.2. Because of a shortage of Sabre engines it was then decided to reengine the aircraft with a Bristol Centaurus radial, the new model emerging as the Firebrand TF.Mk.3. The modified aircraft entered service with No. 813 Squadron as TF.Mk.4 in September 1945, too late to see action in WWII. Only Nos. 813 and 827 Squadrons were armed with the Firebrand, 225 of which were built.

▲ *Too late to see service in World War II, the Blackburn Firebrand had a short career with the Royal Navy's Fleet Air Arm.*

Blackburn Iris

Designed in response to Specification R.14/24 for a long-range maritime reconnaissance flying boat. The wooden-hulled prototype, designated R.B.I (R.B. being the initials of Robert Blackburn) first flew in June 1926. Four aircraft were ordered under the designation R.B.IB Iris Mk III. The aircraft

undertook some spectacular long-distance flights during their careers. Three were refitted with Rolls-Royce Buzzard engines and continued to serve as Iris Mk Vs until 1934.

SPECIFICATION: Type maritime reconnaissance flying boat • Crew 5 • Powerplant three 675hp Rolls-Royce Condor 12-cylinder in-line engines • Max speed 118mph (190km/h) • Service ceiling 10,000ft (3,050m) • Max range 470 miles (756km) • Wingspan 97ft (29.57m) • Length 67ft 5in (20.54m) • Height 25ft 6in (7.77m) • Weight 29,000lb (13,154kg) loaded • Armament three 0.303-in (7.7-mm) machine guns; 2,000lb (907kg) of bombs

▲ In addition to its revised powerplant, the Mk V Iris introduced larger-diameter propellers and aluminum rather than steel fuel tanks.

Blackburn Kangaroo

The Blackburn Kangaroo was one of the last heavy bombers to be built in Britain before the end of World War I. Twenty-four Kangaroos were built, and 10 of these were issued to No. 246 Squadron (the only unit to operate the type) at Seaton Carew, on the Durham coast, from January 1918.

Operational flying began on May 1, the Kangaroos flying more than 600 hours on antisubmarine patrols over the North Sea between then and November 11. During that time they were credited with the shared destruction of UC 70 with the destroyer HMS *Ouse*.

▲ Only one RAF squadron operated the Blackburn Kangaroo during WWI.

SPECIFICATION: Type heavy bomber/maritime patrol aircraft • Crew 4 • Powerplant two 255hp Rolls-Royce Falcon II 12-cylinder in-line engines • Max speed 100mph (161km/h) • Service ceiling 10,500ft (3,200m) • Endurance 8hrs • Wingspan 74ft 10in (22.82m) • Length 46ft (14.02m) • Height 16ft 10in (5.13m) • Weight 8,017lb (3,636kg) • Armament two 0.303-in (7.7-mm) machine guns; up to 1,000lb (453kg) of bombs

Blackburn Ripon

The Blackburn Ripon torpedo-bomber, the prototype of which flew on April 17, 1926, was a more powerful and versatile development of the Dart, which it replaced in Fleet Air Arm service from 1929. The type was produced in three principal variants, the Mk.II, Mk.IIA, and Mk.IIC, the lat-

ter having an all-metal wing structure, and production continued until 1933, with 91 aircraft built for British military service.

SPECIFICATION: Type torpedo-bomber and reconnaissance biplane • Crew 2 • Powerplant one 570hp Napier Lion 12-cylinder liquid-cooled V-type • Max speed 126mph (203km/h) • Service ceiling 10,000ft (3,050m) • Max range 815 miles (1,310km) • Wingspan 44ft 10in (13.66m) • Length 36ft (10.97m) • Height 13ft 4in (4.06m) • Weight 7,405lb (3,359kg) • Armament one forward-firing 0.303-in (7.7-mm) Vickers machine gun and one Lewis gun in rear cockpit. One Mk VIII or Mk X torpedo, or up to 1,653lb (750kg) of other ordnance

▲ Designed from the outset as a torpedo-bomber, the Ripon, as exemplified by this Mk.IIC, could deliver a standard 18in (457mm) torpedo.

▌Blackburn Shark

The Baffin's successor on the Royal Navy's aircraft carriers was the Blackburn Shark, which first flew on August 24, 1933. A contract was signed covering an initial batch of 16 aircraft, the first Shark Mk.I entering service in May 1935. A month later a new contract was signed for three aircraft of the second series (Mk.II), and further orders in 1935 and 1936 brought the eventual total built to 126. The final version was the Shark Mk.III, which had a glazed cockpit canopy. The Shark was progressively replaced by the Fairey Swordfish from 1938. A seaplane variant was used for reconnaissance and gunnery spotting on board the battleship *Warspite* and the battlecruiser *Repulse*. Seventeen Mk IIIs were built under license in Canada for the RCAF, while six Shark IIAs were exported to Portugal.

▲ *Apart from its narrow-chord cowling, the Shark prototype (illustrated) was similar to the production Mk.I.*

SPECIFICATION: Type torpedo-bomber and reconnaissance aircraft (data Mk III) • Crew 2-3 • Powerplant one 760hp Armstrong Siddeley Tiger VI 14-cylinder radial engine • Max speed 152mph (245km/h) at 6,500ft (1,980m) • Service ceiling 16,400ft (5,000m) • Max range 625 miles (1,005km) • Wingspan 46ft (14.02m) • Length 35ft 2in (10.72m) • Height 12ft 1in (3.68m) • Weight 8,050lb (3,651kg) loaded • Armament one forward-firing 0.303-in (7.7-mm) Vickers machine gun and one Lewis gun in rear cockpit. One Mk VIII or Mk X torpedo, or up to 1,576lb (715kg) of other ordnance

▌Blackburn Skua

The Blackburn Skua two-seat naval dive-bomber was designed to meet the requirements of Specification O.27/34, and the prototype flew in 1937. The Skua was the first monoplane to be adopted by the Royal Navy, and it saw more action as a fighter than it did in its intended role. Skuas shot down the first German aircraft to fall victim to British fighters in World War II, and in operations off Norway in April-May 1940 they dive-bombed and sank the steamer *Bahrenfels* and the light cruiser *Königsberg*. Skuas operated in the North Sea, Atlantic, and Mediterranean, being replaced by Fairey Fulmars and Hawker Sea Hurricanes in 1941. The Blackburn Roc was a fighter variant with a dorsal power-operated turret mounting four 0.303-in (7.7-mm) Browning machine guns.

SPECIFICATION: Type naval dive-bomber/fleet protection fighter • Crew 2 • Powerplant one 890hp Bristol Perseus XII 9-cylinder radial engine • Max speed 225mph (363km/h) at 6,500ft (2,000m) • Service ceiling 19,100ft (5,820m) • Max range 758 miles (1,220km) • Wingspan 46ft 2in (14.07m) • Length 35ft 7in (10.85m) • Height 12ft 6in (3.81m) • Weight 8,216lb (3,727kg) • Armament five forward-firing 0.303-in (7.7-mm) Browning machine guns; 740lb (335kg) of bombs

▲ *The Skua was withdrawn from operational service in 1941, having proved moderately successful.*

▌Blériot XI

The Blériot XI monoplane was the deceptively flimsy-looking aircraft made famous by pioneer aviator Louis Blériot's flight across the English Channel on July 25, 1909. In the months that followed this historic occasion, the basic design underwent a number of alterations, making it suitable for military use. In 1910 it was adopted by France's Aviation Militaire, then by Italy's Military Aviation Service in 1911, and finally by Britain's Royal Flying Corps (RFC) in 1912. The Blériot XI was produced in five basic variants, 132 aircraft being built in total. The XI Militaire and XI Artillerie were single-seaters with 50hp Gnome rotary engines, the XI-2 Artillerie and XI-2 Génie were two-seaters with 70hp Gnome engines, while the CI-3 was a three-seater with a 140hp Gnome.

◄ *The Blériot XI-3 seated three people in tandem and featured a more powerful engine than the XI.*

SPECIFICATION: **Type** reconnaissance monoplane • **Crew** 1-3 • **Powerplant** one 50hp, 70hp, or 140hp Gnome rotary engine • **Max speed** 66mph (106km/h) • **Service ceiling** 3,280ft (1,000m) • **Endurance** 3hrs 30mins • **Wingspan** 33ft 11in (10.33m) • **Length** 27ft 10in (8.48m) • **Height** 8ft 5in (2.65m) • **Weight** 1,838lb (834kg) loaded (Bleriot XI-2) • **Armament** none

▌Blériot-Spad 51

FRANCE

A fast and attractive biplane fighter, the Blériot-Spad 51 was designed by Andre Herbemont within France's rearmament program of 1924. The prototype flew on June 16 that year, and although the type was not adopted by the Armée de l'Air, 50 examples were exported to Poland in 1925–26, serving with the legendary 11th (Kosciusko) squadron. Ten more aircraft were built but only two were exported, one to Turkey and the other to the Soviet Union.

SPECIFICATION: **Type** fighter biplane • **Crew** 1 • **Powerplant** one 380hp Gnome-Rhone Jupiter 9-cylinder radial engine • **Max speed** 143mph (231km/h) at 16,400ft (5,000m) • **Service ceiling** 29,530ft (9,000m) • **Max range** not known • **Wingspan** 31ft 1in (9.47m) • **Length** 21ft 2in (6.45m) • **Height** 10ft 2in (3.10m) • **Weight** 3,595lb (1,631kg) loaded • **Armament** two 0.30-in (7.5-mm) machine guns

▌Blériot-Spad 510

FRANCE

The Blériot-Spad 510 was the last biplane to serve with the Armée de l'Air and had one of the shortest careers of any combat aircraft. Developed from the experimental S.91 to meet an air ministry requirement for a single-seat fighter, it entered service in July 1937 and was withdrawn from first-line units in August, being relegated to second-line duties. The prototype flew for the first time on January 6, 1933 and 60 aircraft were built. The design suffered from a weak undercarriage, and the aircraft was plagued by continual engine troubles.

SPECIFICATION: **Type** fighter • **Crew** 1 • **Powerplant** one 690hp Hispano-Suiza 12xbrs 12-cylinder liquid-cooled V-type engine • **Max speed** 231mph (372km/h) at 9,840ft (3,000m) • **Service ceiling** 32,645ft (9,950m) • **Max range** 435 miles (700km) • **Wingspan** 29ft(8.84m) • **Length** 23ft 4in (7.10m) • **Height** 11ft 2in (3.41m) • **Weight** 3,957lb (1,795kg) loaded • **Armament** four 0.30-in (7.5-mm) machine guns

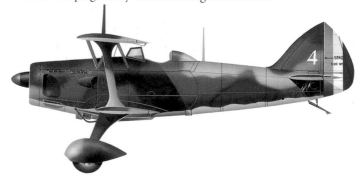

▌Bloch MB.131

▲ *Seven French air groups were flying the MB.131 at the start of WWII. The type was easily outclassed by the Messerschmitt Bf 109 and British fighters.*

The Bloch MB.131, conceived originally as a multirole aircraft, flew for the first time in its definitive form in August 1936, 142 aircraft being subsequently built. In the spring of 1939 the type equipped seven general reconnaissance squadrons, but by the outbreak of World War II many had been relegated to second-line duties. About 50 aircraft were still available for operations, and several were lost to enemy action. Fifty-three Bloch 131s remained in southern France after the armistice, the survivors were scrapped by the Germans at the end of 1942.

SPECIFICATION: Type reconnaissance bomber • Crew 4 • Powerplant two 950hp Gnome-Rhone 14N 14-cylinder radial engines • Max speed 217mph (349km/h) at 12,300ft (3,750m) • Service ceiling 23,785ft (7,250m) • Max range 808 miles (1,300km) • Wingspan 66ft 6in (20.27m) • Length 58ft 7in (17.88m) • Height 13ft 5in (4.10m) • Weight 18,960lb (8,590kg) loaded • Armament three 0.30-in (7.5-mm) machine guns; 1,941lb (88kg) of bombs

▌Bloch MB.151/152

First flown in August 1938, the Bloch MB.151 fighter was derived from the MB.150-01; this aircraft had a checkered career, twice failing to leave the ground on its attempted maiden flight. After substantial redesign it emerged as the MB.151; the Armée de l'Air was to have received over 200 by April 1, 1939, but in fact only one had been delivered by that date and the eventual production total was 140 machines. The Bloch MB.152, derived from the 151, used the same airframe but had a more powerful engine; it flew for the first time on December 15, 1938 and 482 were delivered to the Armée de l'Air and the Aéronavale before the armistice. In action with nine Groupes

SPECIFICATION: Type fighter • Crew 1 • Powerplant one 1,080hp Gnome-Rhone 14N-25 14-cylinder radial engine (MB.152) • Max speed 316mph (509km/h) • Service ceiling 32,808ft (10,000m) • Max range 335 miles (540km) • Wingspan 34ft 7in (10.54m) • Length 29ft 10in (9.10m) • Height 9ft 11in (3.03m) • Weights 4,758lb (2,158kg) empty; 6,173lb (2,800kg) loaded • Armament four 0.30-in (7.5-mm) fixed forward-firing machine guns, or two 0.79-in (20-mm) cannon and two 0.30-in (7.5-mm) machine guns

de Chasse and two naval Escadrilles, the MB.152s claimed 146 kills and 34 probables, losing 86 of their own number.

▲ *Bloch MB.152 fighters seen in the red and yellow identification markings of Vichy France after the armistice with Germany.*

▌Bloch MB.174

In 1938, the SNCA du Sud-Ouest produced the prototype of a fast three-seat reconnaissance aircraft powered by two 870hp GnomeRhone 14N radial engines, the Bloch MB.170. No production of this aircraft was undertaken, as a development of the basic design, the MB.174, was considered superior and was ordered instead. The Armée de l'Air received two versions, the MB.174A-3 reconnaissance aircraft and the MB.174B-3 light bomber. The MB.174's first operational mission was carried out on March 29, 1940 by an aircraft of GR II/33 flown by Capitaine Antoine de Saint-Exupery, the famous author and philosopher. About 49 Bloch MB.174s (both variants) were used on operations.

SPECIFICATION: Type reconnaissance bomber • Crew 3 • Powerplant two 1,140hp Gnome-Rhone 14N 14-cylinder radial engines • Max speed 329mph (530km/h) • Service ceiling 36,090ft (11,000m) • Max range 798 miles (1,285km) with a 882-lb (400-kg) bomb load • Wingspan 58ft 8in (17.90m) • Length 40ft 2in (12.25m) • Height 11ft 7in (3.55m) • Weights 12.346lb (5,600kg) empty; 15,784lb (7,160kg) loaded • Armament three to seven MAC 1934 0.30-in (7.5-mm) machine guns; max internal bomb load of 882lb (400kg)

▼ An MB.174A-3 of the Groupe de Reconnaissance II/33 of the Vichy-controlled Armée de l'Air based at Tunis-El Aouina.

▌Bloch MB.200

Developed to a specification first issued in 1932, the Bloch 200 first flew in 1934, and 12 Escadres de Bombardement were equipped with the type by the end of 1935. At the outbreak of war in September 1939 92 Bloch 200s were still in first-line service, some seeing action on the Lorraine Front in the first weeks of the war. The aircraft was assigned to secondary duties in the winter of 1939–40; some captured MB.200s were later used for training by the Luftwaffe.

SPECIFICATION: Type bomber • Crew 4-5 • Powerplant two 870hp Gnome-Rhone 14Kirs 14-cylinder radial engines • Max speed 176mph (283km/h) at 14,000ft (4,270m) • Service ceiling 26,245ft (8,000m) • Max range 621 miles (1,000km) • Wingspan 73ft 7in (22.45m) • Length 51ft 10in (15.80m) • Height 12ft 10in (3.92m) • Weights 9,480lb (4,300kg) empty; 16,490lb (7,480kg) loaded • Armament one 0.30-in (7.5-mm) machine gun each in nose and dorsal turrets and ventral gondola; external bomb load of 2,646lb (1,200kg)

▲ These MB.200s of 2e Escadrille GB I/23 demonstrate the type's ungainly appearance.

▌Bloch MB.210

SPECIFICATION: Type medium bomber • Crew 5 • Powerplant two 950hp Gnome-Rhone 14N 14-cylinder radial engines • Max speed 200mph (322km/h) at 11,480ft (3,500m) • Service ceiling 32,480ft (9,900m) • Max range 808 miles (1,300km) • Wingspan 74ft 10in (22.80m) • Length 61ft 9in (18.82m) • Height 22ft (6.70m) • Weight 22,465lb (10,190kg) loaded • Armament three 0.30-in (7.5-mm) machine guns; 3,527lb (1,600kg) of bombs

A low-wing, retractable-undercarriage development of the MB.200, first flown on November 23, 1934, the MB.210 was numerically the most important bomber in service with the Armée de l'Air in September 1939, 238 aircraft equipping 10 bomber groups in metropolitan France and two in North Africa. At the outbreak of war the MB.210 Groupes were withdrawn for re-equipment with LeO 451 and Amiot 354s, but in May 1940 the situation was so desperate that GB I/21, II/21, and I/23, which had not yet received their new aircraft, were ordered to carry out night operations. Between May 19 and June 13 seven MB.210s were lost in action. At the armistice about 100 MB.210s still survived in France.

▲ The Bloch MB.210 was obsolete by the outbreak of WWII, and became easy prey for the the more advanced fighter aircraft of the Luftwaffe.

▌Blohm und Voss Bv 138

The Blohm und Voss Bv 138 reconnaissance flying boat was designed in 1936–37 and three prototypes flew in 1938. They were fitted with 600hp Junkers Jumo 205C engines, and the planned initial production version, the Bv 138A, was to have been similarly powered. However, extensive modifications were made before the aircraft was accepted for service use. The circular tail booms were replaced by booms of rectangular section, and the rear section of the hull and the vertical

SPECIFICATION: Type maritime reconnaissance flying boat • Crew 5 • Powerplant three 1,000hp Junkers Jumo 205D 12-cylinder Diesel engines • Max speed 177mph (285km/h) • Service ceiling 16,405ft (5,000m) • Max range 2,672 miles (4,300km) • Wingspan 88ft 4in (26.94m) • Length 65ft 1in (19.85m) • Height 19ft 4in (5.90m) • Weight 38,912lb (17,650kg) loaded • Armament one 0.79-in (20-mm) trainable cannon in bow turret and one in rear hull turret; one 0.50-in (13-mm) trainable rearward-firing machine gun behind central engine nacelle; one trainable 0.31-in (7.92-mm) lateral-firing machine gun in starboard hull position; bomb load of 661lb (300kg)

tail surfaces were also redesigned. With these modifications and the addition of 700hp Jumo 205D engines, the aircraft entered production in 1939 as the Bv 138A-1, initial deliveries being made in 1940. The 25 A-1s were followed by six Bv 138B-0 and 14 B-1s, but the definitive version was the Bv 138C-1, of which 227 were built. The Bv 138 saw widespread service in Norway and the North Atlantic area, where one of its tasks was to cooperate with U-boats.

▲ The distinctive fuselage shape of the Bv 138 led to the popular nickname "Die fliegende Holzschuh" (the flying clog).

▌ Blohm und Voss Bv 141

GERMANY

Designed as a tactical reconnaissance aircraft, the Bv 141 had a very unusual asymmetric layout, with the fully glazed crew nacelle offset to starboard of the centerline and a boom, carrying the engine at the front and the tail unit at the rear, offset to port. The first of three prototypes flew in February 1938, and flight trials led to the strengthening of the structure and a revised tail unit. In its new form the aircraft was redesignated Bv 141B, but the aircraft was not considered a success and only a dozen or so were built, some of these undergoing operational trials on the Eastern Front.

SPECIFICATION: Type reconnaissance aircraft • Crew 3 • Powerplant one 1,560hp BMW 801A 14-cylinder radial • Max speed 272mph (438km/h) • Service ceiling 32,810ft (10,000m) • Max range 1,181 miles (1,900km) • Wingspan 57ft 3in (17.46m) • Length 45ft 9in (13.95m) • Height 11ft 9in (3.60m) • Weight 13,448lb (6,100kg) loaded • Armament two 0.31-in (7.92-mm) fixed forward-firing machine guns in crew nacelle, one in the dorsal position, and another in the rotating tail cone position, plus external bomb load of 441lb (200kg)

▲ *Prototype V9 was the first Bv 141B-0 machine. It differed from the A-0 aircraft by having its tailplane offset to port.*

▌ Blohm und Voss Bv 222

GERMANY

The largest flying boat to see operational service in WWII, the Blohm und Voss Bv 222 Wiking (Viking) started life as a 1937 project for a 24-passenger flying boat airliner to operate between Berlin and New York. The Bv 222 was revamped as a long-range maritime patrol aircraft. The first prototype, the Bv 222V-1, flew for the first time on September 7, 1940 and there were eight prototypes in total. As the defunct civil airliner had carried the designation Bv 222B, the military variant was given the designation Bv 222C, of which only four Bv 222C-0 pre-production examples were completed.

SPECIFICATION: Type long-range maritime patrol aircraft • Crew 11 • Powerplant six 1,000hp Junkers Jumo 207C 12-cylinder Diesels • Max speed 242mph (390km/h) • Service ceiling 23,950ft (7,300m) • Max range 3,790 miles (6,100km) • Wingspan 150ft 11in (46.00m) • Length 121ft 4in (37.00m) • Height 35ft 9in (10.90m) • Weight 108,025lb (49,000kg) loaded • Armament one 0.79-in (20-mm) trainable cannon in the dorsal turret and each of the two power-operated wing turrets; 0.50-in (13-mm) machine guns in the bow position and each of the four lateral hull positions

▲ *Entering Luftwaffe service in autumn 1942, Bv 222V-8 had been shot down by the end of the year. It was the last of the Bv 222A aircraft.*

▌ Boeing B-9

UNITED STATES

In January 1930, as a private venture, designer John Sanders began work on a bomber project using the Boeing Monomail fast mail-carrier design as his basis. The result was a twin-engined aircraft bearing the Company designation Model 215. The Air Corps encouraged the project, although no funds were made available, and the aircraft flew for the first time on April 29, 1931 with the military designation YB-9. An aerodynamically very clean low-wing monoplane, the

▶ *The USAAC's first all-metal cantilever bomber (Y1B-9A, foreground) and first production monoplane fighter (Boeing XP-936) formate.*

SPECIFICATION: Type bomber • Crew 4 • Powerplant two 600hp Pratt & Whitney R-1831-13 radials • Max speed 186mph (299km/h) • Service ceiling 22,500ft (6,862m) • Max range 990 miles (1,593km) • Wingspan 76ft 10in (23.4m) • Length 51ft 6in (15.7m) • Height 12ft (3.66m) • Weight not known • Armament one flexible 0.30-in (7.62-mm) machine gun in nose and one in upper rear fuselage position; up to 2,200lb (996kg) of bombs internally and on underwing racks

YB-9 was powered by two Pratt & Whitney R-1831-13 engines producing 600-hp at 6,000ft (1,830m). The YB-9 prototype achieved a speed of 163mph (262km/h).

Testing revealed some shortcomings, including excessive engine vibration and a tendency of the long fuselage to twist in flight, and after various improvements, when its designation was changed to Y1B-9A, the top speed was raised to 186mph (299km/h), which made it faster than any of its contemporaries and most of the fighter aircraft of the time. Disappointingly for Boeing, the Air Corps ordered only six production B-9s, plus the prototype; the big contract went to the Glenn L. Martin Company's B-10 bomber, which was to be the backbone of the Air Corps' bomber arm for a decade to come.

▍Boeing B-17 Flying Fortress

UNITED STATES

▲ *A Boeing B-17G pictured at the moment of take-off. The later Flying Fortress models carried as many as 14 machine guns for self-defense.*

The B-17 Flying Fortress was designed in response to a United States Army Air Corps requirement, issued in 1934, for a long-range, high-altitude daylight bomber. The prototype, bearing the company designation Boeing Model 299, was powered by four 750hp Pratt & Whitney Hornet engines and flew for the first time on July 28, 1935. Although the prototype was later destroyed in an accident, the cause was attributed to human error and the project went ahead. Thirteen Y1B-17s and one Y1B-17A were ordered for evaluation, and after the trials period these were designated B-17 and B-17A respectively. The first production batch of 39 B-17Bs, featuring a modified nose, enlarged rudder, and various other modifications, were all delivered by the end of March 1940; meanwhile a further order had been placed for 38 B-17Cs, which were powered by four Wright 1,200hp Cyclone engines and featured some minor changes. Twenty of these were supplied to the RAF as the Fortress I in 1941, but after sustaining several losses on bombing operations the remainder were diverted to Coastal Command or the Middle East.

By the time the Pacific war began the B-17D, 42 of which had been ordered in 1940, was in service. This was generally similar to the C model, and the Cs in service were subsequently modified to D standard. About half the early-model B-17s in the Pacific Theater were destroyed by Japanese air attack in the first days of the Far Eastern war. A new tail design, the main recognition feature of all subsequent Fortresses, was introduced with the B-17E, together with improved armament, which for the first time included a tail gun position. The B-17E was the first version of the Flying Fortress to see combat in the European Theater of Operations, operating initially with the 97th Bombardment

SPECIFICATION: Type medium/heavy bomber (data B-17G) • Crew 10 • Powerplant four 1,200hp Wright Cyclone R-1820-97 radial engines • Max speed 302mph (486km/h) • Service ceiling 35,600ft (10,850m) • Max range 2,000 miles (3,220km) with 6,000-lb (2,722-kg) bomb load • Wingspan 103ft 9in (31.62m) • Length 74ft 9in (22.78m) • Height 19ft 1in (5.82m) • Weight 72,000lb (32,660kg) loaded • Armament twin 0.50-in (12.7-mm) machine guns under nose, aft of cockpit, under center fuselage and in tail, and single-gun mountings in side of nose, in radio operator's hatch, and waist positions; maximum bomb load 17,600lb (7,983kg)

Group. All B-17s in the Pacific Theater were eventually transferred to Europe to reinforce the British-based US Eighth Army Air Force. The RAF received 42 B-17Es in 1942 under the designation Fortress IIA. A total of 512 B-17Es was produced, this variant being followed into service by the further refined B-17F, which entered production in April 1942. Total production of the B-17F was 3,400, including 61 examples that were converted to the long-range reconnaissance role as the F-9. Another 19 were delivered to RAF Coastal Command as the Fortress II.

The last 86 B-17Fs were fitted with a chin-mounted power-operated Bendix turret mounting a pair of 0.50-in (12.7-mm) guns, which proved invaluable as the Luftwaffe increasingly adopted frontal fighter attacks. This became standard on the B-17G, the major production model, which mounted 13 0.50-in (12.7-mm) machine guns. The RAF

▶ *During the B-17G production run, Boeing built 4,035 aircraft, Douglas added another 2,395 and Lockheed Vega completed 2,250 examples.*

received 85 B-17Gs as the Fortress III, some of these being used for electronic countermeasures. Ten B-17Gs were converted for reconnaissance as the F-9C, while the US Navy and Coast Guard used 24 PB-1Ws and 16 PB-1Gs for maritime surveillance and aerial survey. About 130 were modified for air-sea rescue duties as the B-17H or TB-17H, with a lifeboat carried under the fuselage and other rescue equipment.

During World War II B-17s flew 291,508 sorties over Europe, dropping 640,036 tons (650,000 tonnes) of bombs.

Boeing B-29 Superfortress

The Boeing B-29 Superfortress was the outcome of design studies that started in 1937. Three prototypes were ordered in that year, the first XB-29 flying on September 21, 1942. By that time orders for 1,500 aircraft had already been placed, the B29 program having been given maximum priority following the Japanese attack on Pearl Harbor. The first YB-29 evaluation aircraft were delivered to the 58th Bombardment Wing in July 1943, B-29-BW production aircraft following three months later. The other main versions of the B-29 that made their appearance during the war were the B-29A-BN with a four-gun forward upper turret and increased Wingspan, and the B-29B-BA with a reduced gun armament and increased bomb load. A reconnaissance version was designated F-13A (later RB-29). The B-29 had many technical innovations, including the installation of remotely controlled gun turrets, periscopically sighted by gunners seated within the fuselage.

At the end of 1943 the decision was taken to use the B-29 exclusively in the Pacific theater, two bombardment wings, the 58th and 73rd, being assigned to XX Bomber Command.

SPECIFICATION: **Type** strategic heavy bomber • **Crew** 10 • **Powerplant** four 2,200hp Wright R-3350-57 radial engines • **Max speed** 358mph (576km/h) at 25,000ft (7,620m) • **Service ceiling** 31,800ft (9,695m) • **Max range** 4,100 miles (6,598km) • **Wingspan** 142ft 3in (43.36m) • **Length** 99ft 0in (30.18m) • **Height** 29ft 7in (9.01m) • **Weight** 141,100lb (64,003kg) loaded • **Armament** four-gun turret over nose, two-gun turrets under nose, over and under rear fuselage, all with guns of 0.50-in (12.7-mm) caliber, and one 0.79-in (20-mm) and two 0.50-in (12.7-mm) guns in tail. Up to 20,000lb (9,072kg) of bombs.

The first units to be equipped with the B-29 were deployed to bases in India and Southwest China in the spring of 1944, the first combat mission being flown on June 5 against Bangkok in Japanese-held Thailand before attacks on the Japanese mainland were initiated ten days later. The establishment of five operational bases in the Marianas in March 1944 brought the B-29s much closer to Japan, and five bombardment wings were redeployed there from their bases

▲ *The B-29 introduced a new era in complex and expensive warplanes, but it will always be best remembered for its atomic missions against Japan.*

followed by a complete revision of tactics, the B-29s now carrying out large-scale night incendiary area attacks on Japan's principal cities, with devastating results; for example, on the night of March 9/10, 1945 279 B-29s dropped 1,667 tons (1,693 tonnes) of incendiaries on Tokyo, killing more than 80,000 people.

The B-29s that dropped the atomic bombs on Hiroshima and Nagasaki on August 6 and 9, 1945, "Enola Gay" and "Bock's Car," belonged to the 509th Bombardment Wing (Provisional), which was to become the principal US nuclear weapons trials unit. The B-29 continued to be the mainstay of the USAF Strategic Air Command for several years after 1945, and saw almost continual action during the three years of the Korean war, suffering considerable losses. The basic B-29 design underwent several modifications. These included the SB-29 (search and rescue), TB-29 (trainer), WB-29 (weather reconnaissance), and KB-29 (tanker).

in India and China, coming under the control of XXI Bomber Command, with its HQ on Guam. The move was

▌Boeing B-47 Stratojet

UNITED STATES

In September 1945 the Boeing aircraft company commenced design of a strategic jet bomber project designated Model 450. The aircraft, which was a radical departure from conventional design, featured a thin, flexible wing—based on wartime research data—with 35 degrees of sweep and carrying six turbojets in underwing pods, the main undercarriage being housed in the fuselage. Basic design studies were completed in June 1946, and the first of two XB-47 Stratojet prototypes flew on December 17, 1947, powered by six Allison J35 turbojets. Later, the J35s were replaced by General Electric J47-GE-3 turbojets, the XB-47 flying with these in October 1949. Meanwhile, Boeing had received a contract for ten B-47A Stratojets in November 1948, and the first of this preproduction batch flew on June 25, 1950. The B-47A was used for trials and evaluation and, to some extent, for crew

SPECIFICATION: Type strategic medium bomber (data B-47E) • Crew 3 • Powerplant four 6,000lb (2,721kg) thrust General Electric J47-GE-25 turbojets • Max speed 606mph (975km/h) at 16,300ft (4,968m) • Service ceiling 40,500ft (12,345m) • Max range 4,000 miles (6,435km) • Wingspan 116ft (35.35m) • Length 109ft 10in (33.47m) • Height 27ft 11in (8.50m) • Weight 206,700lb (93,759kg) loaded • Armament two 0.79-in (20-mm) cannon in tail position; 20,000lb (9,072kg) of conventional bombs; Mk.15/39 or Mk.28 nuclear stores

conversion. The first production model was the B-47B, which was powered by J47-GE23 engines and which featured a number of structural modifications, including a strengthened wing. It carried underwing fuel tanks, and was fitted with eighteen JATO solid fuel rockets to give an emergency

▲ *An RB-47H of the 55th Strategic Reconnaissance Wing pictured at Upper Heyford, Oxfordshire. The aircraft is carrying an ALD-4 jammer pod.*

takeoff thrust of up to 20,000lb (9,060kg). The most numerous version of the Stratojet was the B-47E, which first flew on January 30, 1953; 1359 were built. Variants included the RB-47E reconnaissance aircraft, the QB-47E radio-controlled drone, and the ETB-47 crew trainer. Further variants were the RB-47H and RB-47K, which were modified for electronic intelligence gathering and had a pressurized compartment containing three signals specialists in the bomb bay. At the peak of its deployment in the mid-1950s the Stratojet equipped 27 Strategic Air Command medium bombardment wings. About 1,800 B-47s of all variants were built between 1946 and 1957.

▲ A grand total of more than 1,800 Stratojets was completed, at one time equipping 28 SAC wings.

Boeing B-50

UNITED STATES

The B-50 was a straightforward development of the B-29, but with improvements that included more powerful engines and a taller fin and rudder. It originated as the B-29D and was in fact 75 percent a new aircraft, with a new aluminum wing structure some 16 percent stronger and 26 percent more efficient than that of the B-29 while weighing 650lb (294kg) less. The vertical tail surfaces were five feet higher than those of the B-29, and were hinged to fold horizontally over the starboard tailplane to enable the B-50 to be housed in existing hangars. Strategic Air Command took delivery of the first of 79 B-50As in 1947, followed by 45 B-50Bs in 1949. The major production version was the

B-50D, which had increased fuel capacity and flight refueling capability; 222 were built. B-50 variants included the RB-50 photo-reconnaissance aircraft, the TB-50H trainer, and the KB-50 tanker.

▲ The B-50, an improved model of the B-29 with far greater range and payload, gave the USAF Strategic Air Command a true nuclear capability.

SPECIFICATION: Type strategic heavy bomber (data B-50D) • Crew 10 • Powerplant four 3,500hp Pratt & Whitney R-4360-35 Wasp Major 28-cylinder radials • Max speed 380mph (611km/h) at 25,000ft (7,620m) • Service ceiling 36,700ft (11,190m) • Max range 4,900 miles (7,880km) • Wingspan 14ft 5in (43.1m) • Length 100ft (30.48m) • Height 34ft 7in (10.54m) • Weight 173,000lb (78,472kg) loaded • Armament 12 0.50-in (12.7-mm) machine guns and one 0.79-in (20-mm) cannon in remotely controlled barbettes; up to 20,000lb (9,072kg) of bombs

Boeing B-52 Stratofortress

UNITED STATES

The B-52 was the product of a USAAF requirement, issued in April 1946, for a new jet heavy bomber to replace the Convair B-36 in Strategic Air Command. Two prototypes were ordered in September 1949, the YB-52 flying for the first time on April 15, 1952 powered by eight Pratt & Whitney J57-P-3 turbojets. On October 2, 1952 the XB-52 also made its first

◄ Sensors in the turrets on the underside of this B-52G's nose allow the crew to fly low-level missions in zero visibility.

flight, both aircraft having the same powerplant. The two B-52 prototypes were followed by three B-52As, the first of which flew on August 5, 1954. These aircraft featured a number of modifications and were used for trials, which were still in progress when the first production B-52B was accepted by SAC's 93rd Bomb Wing at Castle AFB, California. Fifty examples were produced for SAC (including 10 of the 13 B-52As originally ordered, which were converted to B-52B standard) and it was followed on the production line by the B-52C, 35 of which were built. The focus of B-52 production then shifted to Wichita with the appearance of the B-52D, the first of which flew on May 14, 1956; 170 were eventually built. Following the B-52E (100 built) and the B-52F (89) came the major production variant, the B-52G, which car-

ried the AGM-28 Hound Dog ASM; 193 examples were produced, 173 of these being converted in the 1980s to carry 12 Boeing AGM-86B Air Launched Cruise Missiles. The last version was the B-52H, which had been intended to carry the canceled Skybolt IRBM but was modified to carry four Hound Dogs instead. The B-52 was the mainstay of the West's airborne nuclear deterrent forces for three decades, but it was in a conventional role that it went to war, first over Vietnam, then in the Gulf War of 1991, and more latterly in support of NATO operations in the former Yugoslavia.

SPECIFICATION: Type long-range strategic bomber (data B-52G) • Crew 6 • Powerplant eight 13,750lb (6,238kg) thrust Pratt & Whitney J57 P-43W turbojets • Max speed 630mph (1,014km/h) at 24,000ft (7,315m) • Service ceiling 55,000ft (16,765m) • Max range 8,500 miles (13,680km) • Wingspan 185ft (56.40m) • Length 157ft 7in (48.00m) • Height 40ft 8in (12.40m) • Weight 488,000lb (221,500kg) loaded • Armament remotely controlled tail barbette with four 0.50-in (12.7-mm) machine guns; up to 27,000lb (12,247kg) of conventional bombs; Mk.28 or Mk.43 nuclear free-falling weapons; two North American AGM-28B Hound Dog strategic stand-off missiles on underwing pylons

▲ A B-52G approaching its KC-135 tanker aircraft to take on fuel. During the cold war, part of the B-52 force was always airborne.

▪ Boeing FB-1 Series

In early 1925, the US Navy placed an order for 16 examples of the Boeing PW-9 fighter, which were delivered later that year under the designation FB-1. These aircraft were not adapted for carrier use and were deployed to US Marine Corps units operating in China. With the installation of

arrester gear on two more aircraft, for carrier trials on the USS *Langley*, the designation was changed to FB-2; the FB-3 and FB-4 were modifications leading to the major production version, the FB-5. This variant flew for the first time in October 1926 and 27 examples were built. The last variant, the FB-6, was based on the FB-4 prototype and was fitted with a Pratt & Whitney Wasp radial engine.

▲ The 27 Boeing FB-5s ordered by the US Navy became the first fighters for that service intended from the outset for carrier operations.

SPECIFICATION: Type naval fighter (data Boeing FB-5) • Crew 1 • Powerplant one 520hp Packard 2A-1,500 12-cylinder V-type • Max speed 159mph (256km/h) • Service ceiling 18,925ft (5,770m) • Max range 390 miles (628km) • Wingspan 32ft (9.75m) • Length 23ft 5in (7.14m) • Height 8ft 2in (2.49m) • Weight 2,835lb (1,286kg) • Armament one 0.50-in (12.7-mm); one 0.30-in (7.62-mm) fixed forward-firing machine guns

▪ Boeing F3B/F4B Series

In February 1928, the prototype of a new fighter, developed jointly by the USN and Boeing in the course of the preceding year, made its appearance. This was the F3B-1, 74 of which

were delivered from 1929 for service on board the USS *Langley, Lexington*, and *Saratoga*. It was followed by the F4B (the fighter that was ordered by the USAAC as the P-12); the

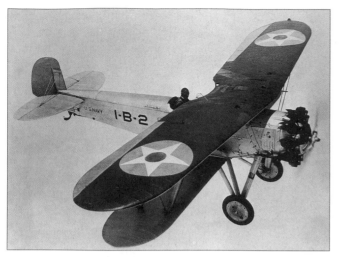

▲ *The US Navy operated the F3B-1 in the fighter-bomber role for four years.*

Navy ordered an initial batch of 27 F4B-1s for service on board the USS *Langley* and *Lexington*, with a follow-up order for 41 F4B-2s in June 1930 to equip the fighter element of the air groups on *Lexington* and *Yorktown*. In April 1931 a further order was placed for 21 F4B-3s, with metal fuselages, and this was followed in January 1932 by an order for 92 F4B-4s, which had modified tailplanes. This final version remained in first-line service until 1937.

SPECIFICATION: Type fighter (data F3B-1) • Crew 1 • Powerplant one 415hp Pratt & Whitney Wasp 9-cylinder radial • Max speed 157mph (253km/h) • Service ceiling 21,500ft (6,550m) • Max range 340 miles (547km) • Wingspan 33ft (10.06m) • Length 24ft 10in (7.57m) • Height 9ft 2in (2.79m) • Weight 2,945lb (1,336kg) loaded • Armament one 0.50-in (12.7-mm); one 0.30-in (7.62-mm) fixed forward-firing machine guns

▌Boeing C-97

The Boeing C-97 military transport had its origins in a requirement issued during World War II by the USAAF for a long-range cargo variant of the B-29 Superfortress bomber. In response, Boeing produced the Model 367, or YC-97, which featured a fully pressurized two-deck fuselage and which used the same wing, engines, landing gear, and tail assembly as the B-29. The military variants were the C-97 Stratofreighter and the KC-97 tanker, nearly 900 of which were produced. In 1948 the first of the YC-97As flew at an

average daily utilization of between nine and 12 hours on the Berlin Airlift. The C-97 was the mainstay of the USAF's air transportation service throughout the 1950s.

▲ *The chin radome of the C-97A housed an AN/APS-42 search radar.*

SPECIFICATION: Type military transport • Crew 4, plus 100 passengers • Powerplant four 3,500hp Pratt & Whitney R-4360 Wasp Major 28-cylinder radials • Cruising speed 340mph(550km/h) at 25,000ft (7,620m) • Service ceiling 32,000ft (9,755m) • Range 4,200 miles(6,760km) • Wingspan 141ft (43.00m) • Length 110ft (33.60m) • Height 38ft (11.65m) • Weight 148,500lb (66,135kg) loaded • Armament none

▌Boeing KC-97G

The KC-97G tanker variant of the C-97 was developed to support Strategic Air Command's B-47 Stratojet strategic bomber force. Normal interior equipment provided for 96 equipped troops or 69 stretcher cases, without the need to remove transfer tanks and the boom operator's station. One of many variants, the KC-97L was fitted with J47-GE25A booster jet pods in place of the original long-range under-wing tanks. The pods were taken from the KC-97's predecessor in the flying tanker role, the Boeing KB-50, and gave the KC-97L a much-needed speed and altitude boost to enable it

to operate more effectively with its receiver aircraft, the Boeing B-47 Stratojet.

SPECIFICATION: Type flight refueling tanker (data KC-97G) • Crew 5, plus 96 passengers • Powerplant four 3,500hp Pratt & Whitney R-4360 Wasp Major 28-cylinder radials • Cruising speed 340mph (550km/h) at 25,000ft (7,620m) • Service ceiling 32,000ft (9,755m) • Range 4,200 miles (6,760km) • Wingspan 141ft (43.00m) • Length 110ft (33.60m) • Height 38ft (11.65m) • Weight 148,500lb (66,135kg) • Armament none

▲ *The Boeing KC-97G was developed as an aerial tanker to support Strategic Air Command's B-47 Stratojet fleet.*

▌Boeing KC-135

UNITED STATES

In 1954, the USAF announced its intention to purchase a development of the Boeing 367-80 (the prototype Boeing 707) jet airliner for use as a tanker-transport. The military version flew

▲ *McDonnell Douglas F-15C Eagle fighters tanking from a Boeing KC-135. Flight refueling was a vital aspect of the 1991 Gulf War with Iraq.*

for the first time on August 31, 1956 with the designation KC-135A and 724 production aircraft were built between then and 1965.

In the 1970s the KC-135 fleet was subjected to a major overhaul designed to keep it viable into the 21st century, in parallel with the B-52 force, which it had been designed to support in the first place. France and Israel also use the KC-135. Other military developments of the Boeing 707 airliner include the RC-135 electronic surveillance and E-3 airborne warning and control aircraft, the latter commonly known as the AWACS.

SPECIFICATION: Type tanker/transport • Crew 5 • Powerplant four 18,000lb (8,165kg) thrust Pratt & Whitney TF33-P-S turbofans • Cruising speed 530mph (853km/h) at 40,000ft (12,200m) • Service ceiling 40,600ft (12,375m) • Max range 2,875 miles (4,627km) • Wingspan 130ft 10in (39.88m) • Length 136ft 3in (41.53m) • Height 41ft 8in (12.70m) • Weight 322,500lb (146,284kg) loaded • Armament none

▌Boeing PW-9

UNITED STATES

One of the first post-World War I American fighter aircraft to enter service was the Boeing PW-9 (the designation signifying Pursuit, Water-cooled engine), a small and maneuverable machine powered by a 435hp Curtiss V-12 engine. Boeing developed the PW-9, originally designated the Model 15, as a private venture after gaining experience building fighter aircraft under contract to other manufacturers. The prototype flew for the first time on April 29, 1923 and was evaluated by

the USAAC, which placed its first production orders, totaling 30 aircraft in 1924. Deliveries of these aircraft to USAAC units in Hawaii and the Philippines began in October 1925. Twenty-five more fighters, incorporating minor modifications, were ordered as PW-9As; these were followed by 15 PW-9Bs, which were actually completed as part of a batch of 40 PW-9Cs and 16 PW-9Ds, which featured refinements such as wheel brakes and an increased rudder area.

SPECIFICATION: Type fighter • Crew 1 • Powerplant one 435hp Curtiss D-12D 12-cylinder V-type • Max speed 165mph (265km/h) • Service ceiling 20,175ft (6,150m) • Endurance 2hrs 35mins • Wingspan 32ft (9.75m) • Length 23ft 1in (7.04m) • Height 8ft 8in (2.64m) • Weight 3,170lb (1,438kg) loaded • Armament one 0.50-in (12.7-mm) and one 0.30-in (7.62-mm) fixed forward-firing machine guns

▶ Minor refinements left the PW-9A indistinguishable from the PW-9.

▋Boeing P-12

In 1928, Boeing offered the USAAC a military version of its F4B biplane fighter, developed for the US Navy. This was at first rejected, but the Navy's reports on the performance of

▲ At least one P-12B has been restored and is flown in the markings of the 95th Attack Squadron of the 17th Attack Group, USAAC.

the F4B were so glowing that the Army ordered nine examples under the designation P-12, plus a tenth aircraft, the XP-12A, which had a modified undercarriage and ailerons. In all, the USAAC took delivery of 90 P-12Bs, 96 P-12Cs, and 110 P-12Es, which entered service in 1931 with more powerful engines and a metal fuselage; and 25 P-12Fs, which also had uprated engines. The service life of the P-12/F-4B series covered the most dangerous years of the interwar period; but those years also marked the end of the biplane fighter's era.

SPECIFICATION: Type fighter • Crew 1 • Powerplant one 450hp Pratt & Whitney R-1340-9 9-cylinder radial • Max speed 178mph (286km/h) • Service ceiling 26,200ft (7,991m) • Max range 675 miles (1,086km) • Wingspan 30ft 1in (9.18m) • Length 20ft 1in (6.13m) • Height 8ft 10in (2.68m) • Weight 2,623lb (1,190kg) loaded • Armament one 0.50-in (12.7-mm) and one 0.30-in (7.62-mm) fixed forward-firing machine guns

▋Boeing P-26

The United States took its first step on the road of all-metal monoplane fighter design with the Boeing P-26, which first flew in March 1932. Deliveries of production P-26As to the USAAC began at the end of 1933, and despite its dangerously high landing speed pilots soon gave the little fighter the affectionate nickname "Peashooter." The P-26 became standard pursuit equipment in Hawaii and the Panama Canal area, and was one of the aircraft ranged against the Japanese during the attack on Pearl Harbor.

SPECIFICATION: Type fighter • Crew 1 • Powerplant one 600hp Pratt & Whitney Wasp 9-cylinder radial • Max speed 234mph (377km/h) • Service ceiling 27,230ft (8,300m) • Max range 621 miles (1,000km) • Wingspan 27ft 11in (8.52m) • Length 23ft 7in (7.18m) • Height 10ft 1in (3.05m) • Weight 2,955lb (1,340kg) loaded • Armament two 0.50-in(12.7-mm) or 0.30-in (7.62-mm) fixed forward-firing machine guns

In 1940 surplus American P-26s were used to form the Philippine Army Air Force. Production for the AAC totaled 111 P-26As and 25 P-26Bs, the latter with a more powerful engine. A further 11 P-26s (P-26Bs) were supplied to China. These saw action against the Japanese in Manchuria in 1937.

▲ The first all-metal monoplane fighter produced in the USA, the Boeing P-26 saw combat against Japanese forces invading Manchuria in 1937.

▮ Boeing-Stearman PT-17 Kaydet

UNITED STATES

One of the most widely used basic trainers of World War II, the Boeing-Stearman Kaydet was produced in several versions, differing in powerplant and equipment. The PT-13 of 1935 had a Lycoming engine, while the PT-17 of 1940 and the PT-18 had Continental and Jacobs engines respectively. The PT-27, with different instrumentation and an enclosed cockpit, was built for Canada. In US Navy service the Kaydet was designated N2S. Production totaled 10,346 aircraft.

SPECIFICATION: Type trainer (data PT-17) • Crew 2 • Powerplant one 220hp continental R-670-5 7-cylinder radial • Max speed 124mph (199km/h) • Service ceiling 11,200ft (3,415m) • Max range 505 miles (812km) • Wingspan 32ft 2in (9.8m) • Length 25ft (7.63m) • Height 9ft 2in (2.79m) • Weight 2,716lb (1,232kg) • Armament none

▼ Many PT-17s, like this one, are still flying in the 21st century, lovingly maintained by private owners. The type was built in massive numbers.

▮ Boulton Paul Defiant

GREAT BRITAIN

In March 1937, Boulton Paul received a contract for 87 production examples of its design for a two-seat fighter armed with a four-gun power-operated turret, the P82, and the name Defiant was adopted. The first Defiant squadron, No. 264, began to rearm with the new type at Martlesham Heath on December 8, 1939. As a day fighter the Defiant was a disaster, suffering heavy losses in day combat, but it went on to enjoy considerable success in the night fighter/intruder role.

SPECIFICATION: Type fighter • Crew 2 • Powerplant one 1,030hp Rolls-Royce Merlin III 12-cylinder V-type • Max speed 304mph (489km/h) • Service ceiling 30,350ft (9,250m) • Max range 465 miles (748km) • Wingspan 39ft 4in (11.99m) • Length 35ft 4in (10.77m) • Height 14ft 5in (4.39m) • Weight 8,350lb (3,788kg) loaded • Armament four 0.303-in (7.7-mm) Browning machine guns in power-operated dorsal turret

▲ *Defiants of No. 264 Squadron. The two Defiant squadrons suffered serious casualties when used as day fighters in the Battle of Britain.*

▌Boulton Paul Sidestrand/Overstrand

GREAT BRITAIN

The Boulton and Paul Sidestrand I medium bomber, designed to Specification 9/24, flew for the first time in 1926. Only 18 Sidestrands were built, these being issued to No. 101 Squadron. The principal variants were the Mk II and Mk III, which had different engines. The Overstrand was a modified version with a power-operated nose turret, enclosed cockpit, and a heating system for the crew; 27 were built, and were used by No. 101 Squadron until late 1938. Despite their ugly and ungainly appearance, both proved to be excellent bombers.

SPECIFICATION: Type medium bomber (data Overstrand) • Crew 5 • Powerplant two 580hp Bristol Pegasus radial engines • Max speed 153mph (246km/h) • Service ceiling 22,500ft (6,860m) • Max range 545 miles (877km) • Wingspan 72ft (21.95m) • Length 46ft (14.02m) • Height 15ft 6in (4.72m) • Weight 12,000lb (5,443kg) • Armament one 0.303-in (7.7-mm) Lewis machine gun in nose turret and one each in the dorsal and ventral positions; up to 1,600lb (726kg) of bombs internally

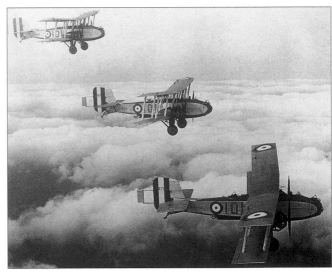

▲ *Despite proving to be an excellent aircraft for bombing and gunnery, only one RAF squadron was equipped with the Sidestrand.*

▌Breda Ba.19

ITALY

A great many top Italian aerobatic pilots of the interwar years learned their trade in the Breda Ba.19 aerobatic trainer. Extremely maneuverable, it was widely used by the Regia Aeronautica's aerobatic teams during the 1930s until the debut of the Fiat CR.30. 41 production aircraft were delivered in 1931–2, as well as a handful of two-seat trainers.

SPECIFICATION: Type aerobatic training biplane • Crew 1 • Powerplant one 200hp Alfa Romeo Lynx 7-cylinder radial • Max speed 130mph (210km/h) • Service ceiling 22,965ft (7,000m) • Max range 522 miles (840km) • Wingspan 29ft 6in (9m) • Length 21ft 8in (6.60m) • Height 7ft 3in (2.20m) • Weight 1,995lb (905kg) loaded • Armament none

■ Breda Ba.25

The equivalent of Britain's famous Tiger Moth, the Breda Ba.25 was the most widely used Italian basic trainer of the 1930s. It was built in numerous versions, differing from one another mainly in the type of engine that was installed. The pilot and instructor were usually seated in tandem open cockpits, although a single-bay type was also built. The Ba.25, which was joined in service by a more powerful version, the Ba.28, was exported to China, Ethiopia, and Paraguay. Total production for Italy's Regia Aeronautica totaled 719 machines, while many others were sold to private owners.

SPECIFICATION: Type basic trainer • Crew 2 • Powerplant one 220hp Alfa Romeo Lynx 7-cylinder radial • Max speed 127mph (205km/h) • Service ceiling 16,075ft (4,900m) • Max range 248 miles (400km) • Wingspan 32ft 10in (10m) • Length 26ft 3in (8.00m) • Height 9ft 6in (2.90m) • Weight 2,204lb (1,000kg) • Armament none

▲ *Thousands of Italian airmen learned to fly in the Breda 25 basic trainer, which was built in numerous versions during the 1930s.*

■ Breda Ba.65

A low-wing monoplane with a fully enclosed glazed cockpit,

SPECIFICATION: Type ground attack aircraft (data single-seat version) • Crew 1 • Powerplant one 1030hp Fiat A.80 RC41 18-cylinder radial • Max speed 267mph (430km/h) • Service ceiling 27,230ft (8300m) • Max range 342 miles (550km) • Wingspan 39ft 8in (12.10m) • Length 31ft 6in (9.60m) • Height 10ft 6in (3.20m) • Weight 7695lb (3490kg) (loaded) • Armament four 0.30in (7.62mm) machine guns; 2200lb (1000kg) of bombs

the Breda Ba.65 of 1935 was designed specifically as a ground attack aircraft, and made its operational debut in the Spanish Civil War. About 150 were still in first-line service when Italy entered World War II in June 1940; most were deployed in North Africa and suffered heavily at the hands of British fighters, lacking maneuverability and power. Many of the Ba.65 units operated two-seat versions, with an observer/gunner manning a turret or a single 0.303in (7.7mm) machine gun.

▲ The Breda Ba.65 was Italy's first single-engined combat aircraft with a low monoplane wing to enter quantity production.

▌Breda Ba.88

ITALY

SPECIFICATION: Type tactical bomber • Crew 2 • Powerplant two 1,000hp Piaggio P.XI RC40 14-cylinder radials • Max speed 304mph (490km/h) • Service ceiling 26,245ft (8,000m) • Max range 1,020 miles (1,640km) • Wingspan 51ft 2in (15.60m) • Length 35ft 5in (10.79m) • Height 10ft 2in (3.10m) • Weight 14,881lb (6,750kg) loaded • Armament three 0.50-in (12.7-mm) fixed forward-firing machine guns and one in rear cockpit; internal bomb load of 2,205lb (1,000kg)

First flown in October 1936, the Breda Ba.88 Lince (Lynx) tactical bomber appeared to be a promising concept, but in practice proved to be operationally useless. One hundred were built and some were used in the early phase of the Italian campaign in North Africa in 1940, but the few survivors were soon withdrawn and used as decoy aircraft on Italian airfields.

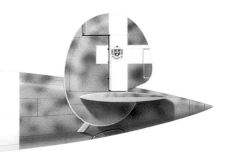

▌ Breguet Br.XIV

Louis Breguet established his aircraft manufacturing company at Douai in 1900, but was forced to relocate to Villacoublay in 1914 in front of the rapid German advance. In the late summer of 1916 his Chief Engineer, Louis Vullierme, began the design of Breguet's most successful wartime product, the Br.XIV. The prototype of this two-seat reconnaissance/light bomber aircraft made its first flight barely two months later, on November 21, and the first Br.14A-2 production aircraft entered service with the Aéronautique Militaire in the following spring. The Br.XIV quickly established a reputation for toughness and reliability, and by the end of World War I orders for nearly 5,500 aircraft had been placed, a total that would reach 8,000 by the time the production lines shut down in 1926. The Br.XIVB-2 bomber variant was the principal aircraft to serve with France's strategic bombing force, carrying out many attacks

SPECIFICATION: Type reconnaissance/light bomber • Crew 2 • Powerplant one 300hp Renault 12F in-line engine • Max speed 114mph (184km/h) • Service ceiling 19,690ft (6,000m) • Endurance 2hrs 45mins • Wingspan 47ft 1in (14.36m) • Length 29ft 1in (8.87m) • Height 10ft 10in (3.3m) • Weights 2,271lb (1,030kg) empty; 3,450lb (1,565kg) loaded • Armament one fixed forward-firing 0.303-in (7.7-mm) machine gun; twin 0.303-in (7.7-mm) Lewis machine guns on mounting in rear cockpit; underwing racks for up to 88lb (40kg) of bombs

▲ *Seen here in civilian markings, the Br.XIV was France's outstanding light bomber design of WWI. Many were used by civil concerns post-war.*

on targets in the Saar region in the closing months of WWI. The Br.XIV also equipped the bomber squadrons of the American Expeditionary Force. The type served in a number of roles, including that of air ambulance, and pioneered mail routes in Africa in the postwar years.

▌ Breguet Alizé

▲ *A contemporary of the Royal Navy's Fairey Gannet, the Breguet Alizé gave sterling service to the French Navy for many years.*

In 1948 Breguet Aviation received a contract from the French Navy for two prototypes of a carrier-based strike aircraft, the Br960 Vultur. The first of these flew on August 3, 1951, powered by a 980hp Armstrong Siddeley Mamba turboprop and Hispano-Suiza Nene 101 turbojet, and was followed on September 15, 1952 by the second aircraft and a Nene 104. This second machine was modified to serve as an aerodynamic test bed for an improved ASW design, which emerged as the Br1050 Alizé (Tradewind). The prototype Alizé flew on October 6, 1956 and the type was ordered into production for the Aéronavale, some 75 aircraft eventually being delivered for sea service on the aircraft carriers Foch, Clemenceau, and Arromanches and ashore at various establishments. With modifications to extend their service life, these venerable aircraft are still in service with the Aéronavale today. Twelve Alizés were also supplied to the Indian Navy.

SPECIFICATION: Type antisubmarine warfare aircraft • Crew 3 • Powerplant one 2,100hp Rolls-Royce Dart RDa21 turboprop engine • Max speed 285mph (458km/h) at sea level • Service ceiling 20,000ft (6,100m) • Max range 1,785 miles (2,872km) • Wingspan 51ft 2in (15.6m) • Length 45ft 6in (13.87m) • Height 15ft 7in (4.76m) • Weights 12,548lb (5,692kg) empty; 18,100lb (8,199kg) loaded • Armament three depth charges or one torpedo internally; two depth charges and six RPs or two ASMs underwing

▌Breguet 521 Bizerte

The Breguet Br 521 Bizerte was a long-range maritime reconnaissance flying boat, the prototype of which flew in September 1933. An all-metal biplane with three radial engines, the Bizerte was a military version of the Breguet Br 530 Saigon commercial aircraft, which in turn was developed from the British Short Calcutta. Thirty Bizertes were built and served with five squadrons of the French Navy from 1935 until their disbandment in June 1940. Some were taken over by the Germans and used for air-sea rescue work.

▲ *The Breguet Bizerte served with five squadrons of the French Navy.*

SPECIFICATION: Type long-range maritime reconnaissance aircraft • Crew 8 • Powerplant three 900hp Gnome-Rhone 14Kirs 14-cylinder radial engines • Max speed 151mph (243km/h) • Service ceiling 19,685ft (6,000m) • Max range 1,305 miles (2,100km) • Wingspan 115ft 4in (35.18m) • Length 67ft 2in (20.48m) • Height 24ft 6in (7.50m) • Weights 20,878lb (9,470kg) empty; 36,597lb (16,600kg) loaded • Armament five 0.30-in (7.5-mm) machine guns; 660lb (300kg) of bombs

▌Breguet Br 693

The Breguet 690 series of combat aircraft stemmed from a 1934 specification for a three-seat heavy fighter. In June 1938 Breguet received an order for 100 production Br 691s for service as light-attack bombers, but only 78 were completed. One of them became the prototype for the next production model, the Br 693, which flew for the first time on October 25, 1939. French Air Force units were just beginning to equip with the type on May 10, 1940, when the Germans invaded,

and the two fully equipped Groupes—GBA I/54 and II/54— bore the brunt of the action, suffering heavy losses.

In all, the Br 693s flew some 500 sorties, losing 47 aircraft of the 106 delivered. Total production was 224. The final production version was the Br 695. This was virtually identical apart from the installation a foreign-manufactured engine, the Pratt & Whitney Twin Wasp Junior radial. 50 were built and 33 delivered before France's collapse.

SPECIFICATION: Type light attack bomber • Crew 2 • Powerplant two 700hp Gnome-Rhone 14M Mars 14-cylinder radial engines • Max speed 295mph (475km/h) • Service ceiling 27,885ft (8,500m) • Max range 839 miles (1,350km) • Wingspan 50ft 5in (15.36m) • Length 31ft 8in (9.67m) • Height 10ft 5in (3.19m) • Weights 6,636lb (3,010kg) empty; 12,125lb (5,500kg) loaded • Armament one 0.79-in (20-mm) cannon and two 0.30-in (7.5-mm) fixed forward-firing machine guns; three 0.30-in (7.5-mm) machine guns fixed and obliquely rearward-firing, plus one trainable; internal bomb load of 882lb (400kg)

Breguet Atlantic

INTERNATIONAL

The Breguet 1150 Atlantic, developed in response to a NATO Armaments Committee requirement for a new maritime patrol aircraft to replace the Lockheed P-2 Neptune in service with NATO's European air forces, was a truly interna-

SPECIFICATION: Type long-range maritime patrol aircraft (data Breguet 1150) • Crew 12 • Powerplant two 6,105hp Rolls-Royce Tyne RTy.20 Mk 21 turboprops • Max speed 409mph (658km/h) • Service ceiling 32,800ft (10,000m) • Max range 5,590 miles (9,000km) • Wingspan 119ft 1in (36.3m) • Length 104ft 2in (31.75m) • Height 37ft 2in (11.33m) • Weight 95,900lb (43,500kg) loaded • Armament Mk 43 Brush or LK4 homing torpedoes; standard NATO bombs, HVAR rockets, underwing ASMs, or 385-lb (175-kg) depth charges

tional project, about a third of the development work being borne by the United States and the work shared between France, West Germany, the Netherlands, and Belgium, with Britain contributing the Rolls-Royce Tyne engines and de Havilland propellers (both built under license by a European consortium). The prototype Atlantic flew on October 21, 1961 and first deliveries to the French Navy were made in December 1965. France ordered 40, Germany 20, Italy 18, and the Netherlands 6. A much-modified and upgraded version, the Dassault-Breguet "Nouvelle Generation" Atlantique ATL.2, was developed for the French Navy, the first of 42 planned aircraft entering service in October 1989.

▲ *Developed by an international consortium to meet a NATO requirement, the Atlantic is seen here in its ANG (Atlantic Nouvelle Generation) guise.*

▌ Brewster SB2A Buccaneer

The Brewster SB2A Buccaneer was designed as a shipboard reconnaissance and dive-bomber, a land-based variant, the A-34, being developed in parallel for the USAAC. The British Purchasing Commission also placed substantial orders for the type in 1940 and the first examples arrived in Britain in 1942, receiving the name Bermuda. Of the 750 aircraft completed, 450 were allocated to the RAF, but no operational use

could be found for the type and most were relegated to training and target towing. In the meantime, the USAAC had canceled its entire order, because the Buccaneer's performance fell far short of expectations, and only a few examples of the SB2A-1 reached the USN before production was abandoned.

SPECIFICATION: Type reconnaissance/dive-bomber • Crew 3 • Powerplant one 1,600hp Wright R-2600-19 Double Cyclone radial • Max speed 284mph (457km/h) • Service ceiling 23,000ft (7,015m) • Max range 695 miles (1,118km) • Wingspan 47ft 8in (14.56m) • Length 39ft 2in (11.94m) • Height 15ft 3in (4.65m) • Weight 12,239lb (5,552kg) loaded • Armament four wing-mounted 0.50-in (12.7-mm) and two manually operated 0.30-in (7.62-mm) machine guns in rear cockpit; bomb load of 1,000lb (453kg)

▲ *Supplied to the RAF under Lend-Lease, the Buccaneer was identified in the UK as the Bermuda Mk I.*

▌ Brewster Buffalo

The prototype Brewster Model 139, or XF2A-1, flew for the first time in 1938, and as the F2A-1 single-seat carrier fighter entered service with the US Navy in the following year. This model was underpowered and soon declared surplus to requirements, 44 being sold to Finland in 1940. The F2A-2

(Model 339) and F2A-3 (Model 439) saw limited service with the USN, 21 fighters of the latter type forming the bulk of the air defense of Midway Island when the Japanese attacked it in June 1942. Meanwhile, the British Purchasing Commission placed a contract for 170 Model 339 fighters, the type being named Buffalo by the RAF, who also took over an additional 38 aircraft ordered by Belgium. The Netherlands Government also ordered 72 Model 339 and 439 fighters for service in the East Indies. The RAF rejected the Buffalo for operational service in Europe, but deemed it suitable for service in the Far East, where it was hopelessly outclassed by Japanese fighters in Malaya, Singapore, and Burma.

▲ *This F2A-3 was photographed in August 1942, by which time all US Navy Buffalos had been passed to the Marine Corps.*

SPECIFICATION: Type fighter (data F2A-3) • Crew 1 • Powerplant one 1,200hp Wright R-1820-40 Cyclone 9-cylinder radial • Max speed 321mph (517km/h) • Service ceiling 33,200ft (10,120m) • Max range 965 miles (1,553km) • Wingspan 35ft (10.67m) • Length 26ft 4in (8.03m) • Height 12ft 1in (3.68m) • Weight 7,159lb (3,247kg) • Armament four 0.50-in (12.7-mm) machine guns, two in upper forward fuselage and two in wing

▌ Bristol Beaufighter

In October 1938, the Bristol Aeroplane Company submitted a proposal for a twin-engined night fighter, heavily armed and equipped with AI radar, to the RAF Air Staff. Specification F.17/39 was written around the proposal and

an order placed for 300 Beaufighters, as the aircraft would be named. The first of four Beaufighter prototypes (R2052) flew for the first time on July 17, 1939, powered by two Bristol Hercules I-SM engines (forerunners of the Hercules III). By

SPECIFICATION: Type night fighter (Mks I, II, and VI); antiship strike aircraft (TF Mk X) • Crew 2 (Mks I, II, and VI); 2-3 (TF Mk X) • Powerplant two 1,636hp Bristol Hercules VI 14-cylinder radials (Mk VI); two 1,770hp Hercules XVII 14-cylinder radials (TF Mk X) • Max speed Mk VI, 333mph (536km/h); TF Mk X, 318mph (512km/h) • Service ceiling Mk VI, 26,500ft (8,075m); TF Mk X, 15,000ft (4,572m) • Normal range Mk V, 1,480 miles (2,382km); TF Mk X, 1,470 miles (2,366km) • Wingspan 57ft 10in (17.63m) • Length 41ft 8in (12.70m) • Height 15ft 10in (4.82m) • Weights Mk VI 21,600lb (9,798kg) loaded; TF Mk X 25,200lb (11,431kg) loaded • Armament Mk VI four Hispano 0.79-in (20-mm) fixed forward-firing cannon in underside of forward fuselage; six 0.303-in (7.7-mm) machine guns in leading edges of wing (two to port and four to starboard). TF Mk X four 0.79-in (20-mm) fixed forward-firing cannon in underside of forward fuselage and one trainable rearward-firing 0.303-in (7.7-mm) machine gun in dorsal position; one 1,600-lb (748-kg) or 2,127-lb (965-kg) torpedo, two 500-lb (227-kg) bombs, eight 3-in (76.2-mm) rocket projectiles.

▶ *The Bristol Beaufighter proved itself outstanding in combat, serving in all theaters of war as a night fighter and anti-shipping aircraft.*

mid-1940 Bristol had received a second contract, for 918 Beaufighters. Two variants were now to be produced, the Mk I with Hercules III engines and the Mk II with Rolls-Royce Merlins, the Hercules being in short supply. Delays in the production of AI Mk IV radar equipment prevented the full complement of five Beaufighter squadrons from becoming operational until the spring of 1941, but despite early teething troubles those that were operational enjoyed some success. The first AI-assisted Beaufighter kill was claimed on the night of November 19/20, 1940, when Flt.Lt. John

Cunningham and Sgt. Phillipson of No. 604 Squadron were credited with the destruction of a Junkers 88. Thirteen more Beaufighter squadrons were assigned to the night defense of Great Britain in 1941–42, and many of the RAF's night fighter aces scored their early kills while flying the heavy twin-engined fighter. Total Mk I production was 914 aircraft, while 450 Mk IIs were built.

The Beaufighter Mk IC, 300 of which were produced, was a long-range strike fighter variant for RAF Coastal Command, and was also used equally as effectively as a ground attack aircraft in the Western Desert. It was supplanted by the Mk VI (the Mks III, IV, and V being experimental aircraft); Mk VIs for Fighter Command were designated Mk VIF (879 aircraft), and those for Coastal Command Mk VIC (693 aircraft). Sixty Mk VIs on the production line were completed as Interim Torpedo Fighters, but two new variants for Coastal Command soon appeared. These were the TF Mk X torpedo bomber and the Mk XIC, which was not equipped to carry torpedoes. Both were fitted with 1,770hp Hercules XVII engines and had a dorsal cupola containing a rearward-firing 0.303-in (7.7-mm) machine gun. Production of the TF Mk X, which was the most important British antishipping aircraft from 1944 to the end of the war, totaled 2,205 aircraft, while 163 aircraft were completed to Mk XIC standard. The Beaufighter TF Mk X was also built in Australia as the TF Mk 21 (364 examples), the RAAF using it to good effect in the Southwest Pacific.

◀ *This Beaufighter wears the blue and white roundels of South-East Asia Command, the red deleted for fear of confusion with the Japanese insignia.*

Bristol Beaufort

The fast, twin-engined Bristol Beaufort was the RAF's standard torpedo-bomber from 1940 to 1943. Design work on the aircraft began in 1935 and the prototype made its first flight on October 15, 1938. The Beaufort Mk I went into service in 1939 and took part in some notable actions, including an attack on the German battlecruiser *Gneisenau* in Brest harbor on April 6, 1941, resulting in serious damage to the warship and the posthumous award of the VC to Flying Officer Kenneth Campbell of No. 22 Squadron. The Beauforts operated mainly in the North Sea and Atlantic areas, but some squadrons were deployed to Malta in 1942 and caused great destruction to Axis supply convoys crossing to North Africa. Seven hundred Beauforts were built in

SPECIFICATION: Type torpedo-bomber (data Mk I) • Crew 4 • Powerplant two 1130 Bristol Taurus VI 14-cylinder radials • Max speed 265mph (426km/h) • Service ceiling 16,500ft (5,050m) • Max range 1,600 miles (2,575km) • Wingspan 57ft 10in (17.62m) • Length 44ft 7in (13.59m) • Height 12ft 5in (3.79m) • Weight 21,228lb (9,630kg) • Armament two 0.303-in (7.7-mm) Vickers K guns in dorsal turret and one in port wing, plus one rearward-firing 0.303-in (7.7-mm) Browning machine gun under nose; up to 1,000lb (453kg) of bombs internally and 500lb (227kg) externally, or one 1,605-lb (728-kg) torpedo semirecessed

Australia (Mks V–VIII), serving with the RAAF in the Solomons, Timor, New Guinea, and other Pacific battle areas. Some were converted to Mk IX troop transports.

▲ The standard torpedo-bomber in service with Bomber Command during 1940–43, the Beaufort acquitted itself well until superseded by the Beaufighter.

Bristol Blenheim

In August 1935 the Air Ministry issued Specification B28/35, covering the conversion of the Bristol Type 142, a fast eight-seat passenger aircraft developed as a private venture, to the bomber role under the designation Type 142M. Some major modifications were necessary, including raising the wing from the low- to mid-wing position to make room for an internal bomb bay, and widening the nose section to accommodate both pilot and observer/bomb aimer. Defensive armament comprised a single 0.303-in (7.7-mm) Lewis machine gun in a power-operated dorsal turret; the thinking was that the aircraft was fast enough to outrun any contemporary fighter. A Browning 0.303-in (7.7-mm) was also installed in the port wing leading edge and fired by the pilot.

In September 1935 the Air Ministry placed an initial order for 150 aircraft under the service designation Blenheim Mk I, a second order for 434 aircraft following on completion of the trials program in December 1936. The first Blenheims were delivered to No. 114 Squadron in March 1937; 1,280 Mk Is were built in total, and of these 1,007 were

▲ A Blenheim Mk IV of No. 139 Squadron over Belgium during the "Phoney War" of 1939–40. Blenheims suffered terrible losses in the Battle of France.

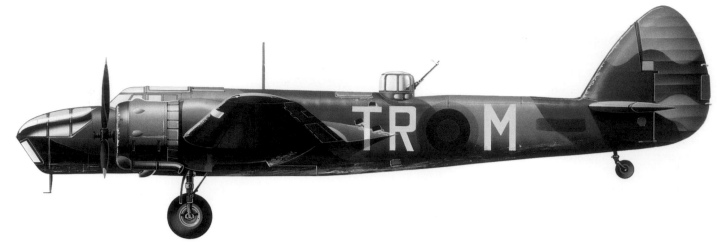

SPECIFICATION: **Type** light bomber (data Mk IV) • **Crew** 3 • **Powerplant** two 920hp Bristol Mercury XV radial engines • **Max speed** 266mph (428km/h) at 11,800ft (3,595m) • **Service ceiling** 22,000ft (6,705m) • **Max range** 1,460 miles (2,340km) • **Wingspan** 56ft 4in (17.7m) • **Length** 42ft 7in (12.98m) • **Height** 9ft 10in (2.99m) • **Weight** 14,400lb (6,537kg) loaded • **Armament** one 0.303-in (7.7-mm) Browning machine gun in leading edge of port wing, two 0.303-in(7.7-mm) Browning machine guns in dorsal turret, two 0.303-in (7.7-mm) rearward-firing blister position under nose; max internal bomb load of 1,000lb (454kg)

on RAF charge at the outbreak of World War II in September 1939. These included 147 completed as Mk IF fighters, fitted with a ventral gun pack containing four Browning machine guns; some of these were later equipped with AI radar and served as interim night fighters in the fall of 1940. By the time war broke out, however, most of the Mk I bombers were serving in the Middle and Far East, the home-based squadrons having rearmed with the improved Blenheim Mk IV. Twelve Blenheims were supplied to Finland (which built an additional 55 between 1941 and 1944), 13 to Romania, and 22 to Yugoslavia, where a further 48 were built under license.

The Blenheim Mk IV was basically a Mk I airframe with two 995hp Mercury XV radials driving de Havilland three-

blade variable pitch propellers, extra fuel tankage, and a much redesigned, lengthened nose. By September 3, 1939 the RAF had 197 Blenheim IVs on strength, and on the second day of the war aircraft of Nos. 107 and 110 Squadrons from Marham, Norfolk, carried out the RAF's first offensive operation when they unsuccessfully attacked units of the German Navy in the Elbe Estuary. The inadequacy of the Blenheim's defensive armament became apparent in the battles of Norway and France, when Blenheims engaged in antishipping operations in the North Sea suffered appalling losses. The armament was subsequently increased to five machine guns. In 1941 most of the RAF's home-based Blenheim IVs were under the control of No. 2 Group, based in East Anglia, from where they carried out ongoing antishipping patrols (Operation Channel Stop) and attacks on targets in France and the Low Countries. The Blenheims were eventually replaced in No. 2 Group by the Douglas Boston and the de Havilland Mosquito. In all, 1930 Mk IVs were built. The final British-built version of the Blenheim was the Mk V, of which 942 were produced, mostly the VD tropical version for service in North Africa. Combat losses were very heavy and the type was soon replaced by US Baltimores and Venturas. In Canada, Fairchild built 676 Blenheims for the RCAF, by whom they were designated Bolingbroke Mks I to IV.

∎ Bristol Bombay   GREAT BRITAIN

First flown in June 1935, the Bristol Bombay stemmed from

SPECIFICATION: **Type** bomber/transport • **Crew** 3-6 • **Powerplant** two 1010 Bristol Pegasus XXII 9-cylinder radials • **Max speed** 192mph (309km/h) • **Service ceiling** 25,000ft (7,620m) • **Max range** 2,230 miles (3,589km) • **Wingspan** 95ft 9in (29.18m) • **Length** 69ft 3in (21.11m) • **Height** 19ft 6in (5.94m) • **Weight** 20,000lb (9,072kg) loaded • **Armament** one 0.303-in (7.7-mm) machine gun in nose and one in tail turret; two more optionally in beam positions

a 1931 requirement for a bomber/transport, optimized for service in Africa, the Middle East, and India. The first of 50 production aircraft entered service in March 1939, by which time the type was already practically obsolete. Nevertheless, the Bombay rendered invaluable service as a transportation and casualty-evacuation aircraft in the UK and North Africa for much of World War II, and also helped successfully evacuate the Greek royal family from Crete to Egypt in 1940. The type was retired in 1944.

▌Bristol Brigand

Tracing its ancestry to the Bristol Beaufighter, the Bristol Type 167 Brigand was originally developed as a torpedo-bomber, the first of four TF.1 prototypes flying on December 4, 1944. The war's end, however, brought about a change in requirements and only 11 TF.1s were built, production being switched to the B.Mk.1 light bomber variant. This served with Nos. 8, 45, and 84 Squadrons in the Middle East and Malaya. The Met Mk 3 was an unarmed weather reconnaissance variant, and the T. Mk 4 was used for radar training.

▲ *The Brigand was not particularly successful as a light bomber, and its early career was plagued by accidents caused by structural failure.*

SPECIFICATION: **Type** light bomber • **Crew** 3 • **Powerplant** two 2,470hp Bristol Centaurus 57 radial engines • **Max speed** 358mph (576km/h) at 16,000ft (4,880m) • **Service ceiling** 26,000ft (7,925m) • **Max range** 1,980 miles (3,168km) • **Wingspan** 72ft 4in (22.04m) • **Length** 46ft 5in (5.33m) • **Height** 17ft 6in (5.33m) • **Weight** 39,000lb (17,690kg) loaded • **Armament** four fixed 0.79-in (20-mm) Hispano cannon in nose; 3,000lb (1,361kg) of bombs or rocket projectiles

▌Bristol Bulldog

In September 1926 the Air Ministry issued a requirement for a new single-seat day and night fighter to be powered by a radial air-cooled engine and armed with two Vickers machine guns. Bristol was the successful manufacturer and its prototype flew for the first time on May 17, 1927 as the Bulldog I. After some structural modifications the type re-emerged as the Bulldog Mk II, and 25 production aircraft were ordered to equip Nos. 3 and 17 Squadrons. The Bulldog eventually equipped 10 RAF home defense squadrons, the main version being the Mk IIA. The Bulldog also served in small numbers with the air forces of Denmark, Estonia, Finland, Latvia, Siam, and Sweden, 456 being built in total.

SPECIFICATION: **Type** fighter biplane (data Mk IIA) • **Crew** 1 • **Powerplant** one 490hp Bristol Jupiter VIIF radial engine • **Max speed** 174mph (280km/h) • **Service ceiling** 29,300ft (8,940m) • **Max range** 300 miles (482km) • **Wingspan** 33ft 10in (10.30m) • **Length** 25ft 2in (7.70m) • **Height** 8ft 9in (2.70m) • **Weight** 3,490lb (1,583kg) loaded • **Armament** two fixed forward-firing 0.303-in (7.7-mm) Vickers machine guns; up to four 20-lb (9-kg) bombs on underwing racks

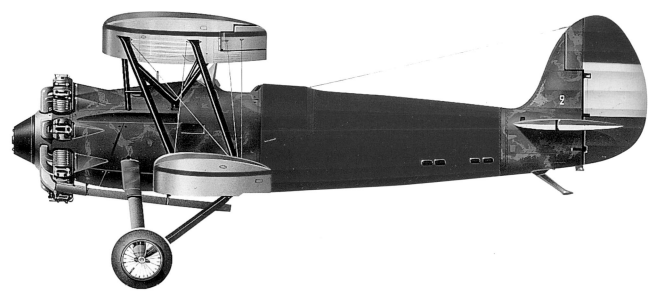

▮Bristol F.2B Fighter

The two-seat Bristol F.2A Fighter made its operational debut during the Allied spring offensive of 1917. Fifty F.2As were built, powered by a 190hp Rolls-Royce Falcon engine giving a top speed of around 115mph (185km/h) and armed with a centrally mounted forward-firing Vickers gun and a single Lewis mounted in the rear cockpit. The first examples arrived in France with No. 48 Squadron toward the end of March and were rushed into action before their pilots had time to get used to them or to develop proper tactics. At first they were flown like earlier two-seaters, oriented around the observer's gun as the primary weapon, and losses were heavy. When flown offensively, in the same way as a single-seat fighter, the Bristol Fighter proved to be a superb weapon and went on to log a formidable record of success in action. Several hundred Bristol Fighters were ordered in 1917, these being the F.2B version with a 220hp Falcon II or 275hp Falcon III engine, wide-span tailplanes, modified lower wing center sections, and an improved view from the front cockpit. The F.2B eventually served with six RFC squadrons on the Western Front, four in the UK, and one in Italy. As well as the RAF, which did not retire the last of its F.2Bs until 1932, the type was operated by Australia, Belgium, Canada, Eire, Greece, Mexico, New Zealand, Norway, Peru, and Spain. Total production reached 5,308 aircraft.

SPECIFICATION: Type fighter biplane • Crew 2 • Powerplant one 275hp Rolls-Royce Falcon III in-line engine • Max speed 123mph (198km/h) • Service ceiling 18,000ft (5,485m) • Endurance 3hrs • Wingspan 39ft 3in (11.96m) • Length 25ft 10in (7.87m) • Height 9ft 9in (2.97m) • Weight 3,250lb (1,474kg) • Armament one fixed forward-firing 0.303-in (7.7-mm) Vickers machine gun, plus one or two 0.303-in (7.7-mm) Lewis guns on flexible mounting in rear cockpit; up to 20lb (12.9kg) bombs on underwing racks

▲ The Bristol F.2B "Fighter" proved to be a superlative combat aircraft when used aggressively. It served for many years after WWI.

▮Bristol M1C Bullet

The Bristol Bullet was potentially a superb fighter rejected for large-scale production on the grounds that its landing speed was too high. The real reason was that it was a monoplane, a format against which there was much prejudice in the RFC. The result was that only 125 M1Cs were built, some being issued to squadrons in the Middle East and the Balkans in 1917 and others to training units.

SPECIFICATION: Type scouting monoplane • Crew 1 • Powerplant one 110hp Le Rhone 9J rotary engine • Max speed 130mph (209km/h) at sea level • Service ceiling 20,000ft (6,096m) • Endurance 1hr 45mins • Wingspan 30ft 9in (9.37m) • Length 20ft 5in (6.24m) • Height 7ft 9in (2.37m) • Weight 1,348lb (611kg) • Armament one fixed forward-firing 0.303-in (7.7-mm) Vickers machine gun

▮Bristol Scout

One of the first types to deploy to France with the RFC in August 1914, the Bristol Scout had all the attributes of a good fighting machine, but was not kept in production because of the company's preoccupation with the F.2A/B. The Scout was produced in four versions (A, B, C, and D) and was the first British aircraft to be fitted with a synchronized machine gun. Production of all variants was 373. Most Scouts had been withdrawn from first-line service by mid-1916.

▶ *The Bristol Scout had most of the attributes of a good fighting machine – with a more effective armament it could have been a great one.*

SPECIFICATION: **Type** scouting biplane • **Crew** 1 • **Powerplant** one 80hp Gnome rotary engine • **Max speed** 93mph (149km/h) • **Service ceiling** 15,500ft (4,724m) • **Endurance** 2hrs 30mins • **Wingspan** 24ft 7in (7.49m) • **Length** 20ft 8in (6.30m) • **Height** 8ft 6in (2.59m) • **Weight** 1,200lb (544kg) loaded • **Armament** one fixed forward-firing 0.303-in (7.7-mm) Vickers synchronized machine gun

▮ British Aerospace (Blackburn/Hawker Siddeley) Buccaneer

GREAT BRITAIN

Designed in 1954 to meet a Royal Navy requirement for a high-speed strike aircraft capable of operating from existing carriers and having sufficient firepower to destroy major Soviet surface units, the Blackburn B103 Buccaneer flew for the first time on April 30, 1958.

Forty production Buccaneer S.Mk.1 aircraft, with Bristol Siddeley Gyron Junior turbojets, were delivered from July 1962, and were followed by 84 more powerful S.Mk.2s with Rolls-Royce Spey turbofans. Sixteen S.2s were also supplied to the South African Air Force, these being fitted with an auxiliary rocket motor to improve "hot and high" takeoff.

The Royal Navy's surviving S.2s were transferred to the RAF from 1969, undergoing substantial refurbishment and modification for the low-level strike role, in which they replaced the Canberra and filled the gap created by the cancelation of TSR-2. The ex-RN Buccaneers were designated S.2A, a further 43 new aircraft being equipped to carry the Martel antiradar missile and designated S.2B. The Buccaneer was progressively replaced by the Panavia Tornado GR.1.

SPECIFICATION: **Type** strike aircraft • **Crew** 2 • **Powerplant** two 11,255-lb (5,105-kg) thrust Rolls-Royce Spey Mk 101 turbofans • **Max speed** 646mph (1,040km/h) at 200ft (60m) • **Service ceiling** 40,000ft (12,190m) • **Max range** 2,300 miles (3,700km) • **Wingspan** 44ft (13.41m) • **Length** 63ft 5in (19.33m) • **Height** 16ft 3in (4.97m) • **Weight** 62,000lb (28,123kg) loaded • **Armament** four 1000-lb (454-kg) bombs on inside of rotary bomb door; up to 12,000lb (5,443kg) of bombs or missiles on underwing pylons

▲ *A Buccaneer of the Lossiemouth Strike Wing takes on fuel from a Victor tanker during Operation Desert Storm in 1991.*

■ British Aerospace (English Electric/BAC) Canberra

▲ *IF1029 was one of 10 refurbished RAF B.Mk 15/16 airframes delivered to the Indian Air Force as Canberra B(I).Mk 66 aircraft in 1970–71.*

SPECIFICATION: Type jet bomber (data B.2) • Crew 2 • Powerplant two 6,500-lb (2,948-kg) thrust Rolls Royce Avon Mk 101 turbojets • Max speed 570mph (917km/h) at 40,000ft (12,192m) • Service ceiling 48,000ft (14,630m) • Max range 2,656 miles (4,274km) • Wingspan 63ft 11in (19.20m) • Length 65ft 6in (19.96m) • Height 15ft 8in (4.78m) • Weight 54,950lb (24,925kg) loaded • Armament up to 6,000lb (2,727kg) of bombs internally, with provision for 2,000lb (909kg) of external stores on underwing pylons. (Note B.15/16 armed with "Red Beard" 15-kiloton 1,750-lb (792-kg) nuclear bomb; B(I)8 with US Mk 7/43)

Originally designed for the radar bombing role, the English Electric Canberra was the greatest success story of Britain's postwar aviation industry. The first prototype Canberra B.1 flew on May 13, 1949, and after the nose was redesigned with a visual bombing station the aircraft became the B.2, which entered service with No. 101 Squadron of RAF Bomber Command in May 1951. A photoreconnaissance version, the PR.3 was issued to No. 540 Squadron in 1953; the PR.7 and PR.9 were two subsequent reconnaisance variants. The next variant was the T.4 dual-control trainer, which appeared in 1954; this was followed by the B.5, a converted PR.3 intended for target marking, but only a few examples were built before it was superseded by the B.6, a more powerful version with Rolls-Royce Avon 109 engines. The B(I)6 was an interim night interdictor version, superseded by the B(I)8; the latter featured some radical modifications, the most notable being an entirely redesigned fuselage nose and offset fighter-type cockpit. The Canberra T.11 was a version for training AI observers, while the B.15, designed for service in the Near and Far East, was a modified B.6 with underwing hard points for bombs or rocket packs. The B.16, for service in Germany, was similar, but retained many of the B.6's radar aids. Other Canberra variants included the U.Mk.10 target drone (modified B.2), the T.17 ECM trainer, the E.15 electronic reconnaissance variant, the TT.18 target tug, the T.19 target facilities aircraft, and the T.22 trainer for the Royal Navy.

The Canberra was built under license in the US as the Martin B.57, and in Australia as the B.20 and T.21. India was a major export customer, while refurbished Canberras were sold to Argentina (two being lost in the 1982 Falklands war), Chile, Ecuador, France, Peru, Rhodesia/Zimbabwe, South Africa, Sweden, Venezuela, and West Germany.

■ British Aerospace/McDonnell Douglas Harrier

The Harrier II traces its lineage back to 1957, when Hawker Siddeley Aircraft Ltd. launched the concept of the P.1127 V/STOL aircraft. The P.1127 was designed around the Bristol BE.53 vectored-thrust engine, the forerunner of the Rolls-Royce Pegasus. In this revolutionary turbofan, air from the fan and the low-pressure compressor is diverted to the front pair of vectoring nozzles, while the remaining engine thrust is directed through the rear pair of rotating nozzles. A development of the P.1127, the Kestrel, was evaluated in 1965 by pilots of the RAF, US Air Force, US Navy, US Army, and the Federal German Luftwaffe. The aircraft was selected by the RAF and, named Harrier GR.1, entered service on April 1, 1969. This, the world's first operational V/STOL aircraft, was followed by the GR.1A and GR.3, the latter having a nose-mounted laser

SPECIFICATION: Type V/STOL close support aircraft • Crew 1 • Powerplant one 21,750-lb (9,866-kg) thrust Rolls Royce Mk 105 Pegasus vectored-thrust turbofan • Max speed 661mph (1,065km/h) at sea level • Service ceiling 50,000ft (15,240m) • Combat radius 172 miles (277km) with 6,000lb (2,722kg) bomb load • Wingspan 30ft 4in (9.25m) • Length 47ft 1in (14.36m) • Height 11ft 7in (3.55m) • Weight 31,000lb (14,061kg) loaded • Armament two 1-in (25-mm) Aden cannon; external hardpoints with provision for up to 9,000lb (4,082kg) of stores (short takeoff) or 7,000lb (3,175kg) of stores (vertical takeoff). Stores include AAMs, ASM, free-fall or guided bombs, cluster bombs, dispenser weapons, napalm tanks, rocket launchers, and ECM pods

▲ *The developed version of the Hawker Siddeley P.1127, known as the Kestrel, was evaluated at RAF West Raynham.*

rangefinder and uprated Pegasus Mk 103 engine. In 1966 six Kestrels were sent to the US for triservice trials on land and sea under the designation XV-6A, and in 1969 the US Marine Corps received approval to buy the first of 102 aircraft, with the designation AV-8A. American funding had played a key role in the development of the Harrier, and it was Vietnam, a land war requiring timely, fixed-wing close air support, that finally influenced the purchase decision.

▲ *The BAe Harrier has enjoyed a truly astonishing development history, made possible mainly because of American funding.*

British Aerospace (Hawker Siddeley) Hawk

GREAT BRITAIN

Designed as a Gnat and Hunter replacement in the advanced training and strike roles, the Hawker Siddeley Hawk prototype flew in August 1974 and the first two operational Hawk T.Mk.1s (out of an eventual total of 175) were handed over in November 1976. The Hawk T.Mk.1A is a tactical weapons trainer with three pylons, the one on the centerline normally occupied by a 1.19-in (30-mm)

SPECIFICATION: Type advanced jet trainer • Crew 2 • Powerplant one 5,200-lb (2,359-kg) thrust Rolls Royce/Turbomeca Adour Mk 151 turbofan • Max speed 645mph (1,038km/h) • Service ceiling 50,000ft (15,240m) • Endurance 4hrs • Wingspan 30ft 9in (9.39m) • Length 36ft 7in (11.17m) • Height 13ft 1in (3.99m) • Weight 17,085lb (7,750kg) loaded • Armament under-fuselage/wing hardpoints for up to 5,660lb (2,567kg) of stores

▲ A trio of Hawk T.1s bearing the distinctive colors of the RAF display team, the Red Arrows, pictured on take-off.

Aden gun pack. The Hawk Series 60 and Series 100 are two-seat export versions, while the Hawk 200 is a single-seat dedicated ground attack variant. Hawks have been exported to some 20 countries. Hawks also serve with the RAF's Red Arrows aerobatic display team, based at RAF Scampton in Lincolnshire.

▊British Aerospace (English Electric/BAC) Lightning

GREAT BRITAIN

Only the RAF, of all the world's air forces, made the jump from subsonic to Mach 2.0 fighter with no Mach 1.0 plus intermediary, replacing the Hawker Hunter day fighter and the Gloster Javelin all-weather fighter with the Mach 2 English Electric (later BAC) Lightning. The Lightning had its origin in a Ministry of Supply specification that was issued in 1947 and called for a manned supersonic research aircraft. English Electric's design, the P.1, submitted in 1949, was quickly seen to have an operational application, and development of the aircraft for research and military purposes continued in parallel. The first P.1A research prototype flew on August 4, 1954, powered by two Bristol Siddeley Sapphires, and three operational prototypes, designated P.1B, were also built. The first of these flew on April 4, 1957, powered by two Rolls-Royce Avons, and exceeded Mach 1.0 on its first flight.

▲ A Lightning F.2A bearing the blue-and-white check insignia of No. 19 Squadron, which used the type on air defense duties in Germany.

On November 25, 1958 it became the first British aircraft to reach Mach 2.0, which it did in level flight. By this time the P.1B had been given the name Lightning and ordered into

production for RAF Fighter Command. The first production Lightning F.Mk.1 flew on October 29, 1959, and fully combat-equipped Lightnings began entering RAF service in July 1960. The Lightning, which had an initial climb rate of 50,000ft (15,240m) per minute, was constantly improved during its career, culminating in the F6 version. This had a revised wing leading edge designed to reduce subsonic drag and improve range, and was fitted with a large ventral fuel pack with more than double the capacity of earlier packs. The first Lightning F6 flew in April 1964 and entered service in the following year. It was the last jet fighter of purely British design, and it was to serve the RAF well in the front line of NATO's air defenses until its eventual retirement in 1988.

◀ *The Lightning was the last jet fighter to be solely designed in the UK.*

SPECIFICATION: **Type** interceptor (data F.6) • **Crew** 1 • **Powerplant** two 15,680-lb (7,112-kg) thrust Rolls-Royce Avon 302 turbojets • **Max speed** 1,500mph (2,415km/h) at 40,000ft (12,190m) • **Service ceiling** 62,000ft (18,920m) • **Max range** 800 miles (1,287km) • **Wingspan** 34ft 10in (10.61m) • **Length** 5ft 3in (16.84m) • **Height** 19ft 7in (5.97m) • **Weight** 50,000lb (22,680kg) • **Armament** two 1.19-in (30-mm) Aden guns in ventral pack; two Firestreak or Red Top AAMs

▌British Aerospace (Hawker Siddeley) Nimrod

GREAT BRITAIN

SPECIFICATION: **Type** long-range maritime patrol and SW aircraft • **Crew** 13 • **Powerplant** four 12,140lb (5,507kg) thrust Rolls Royce Spey Mk 250 turbofan engines • **Max speed** 575mph (925km/h) • **Service ceiling** 42,000ft (12,800m) • **Max range** 5,755 miles (9,262km) • **Wingspan** 114ft 10in (35m) • **Length** 129ft 1in (39.34m) • **Height** 29ft 9in (9.08m) • **Weight** 192,000lb (87,090kg) • **Armament** internal bay with provision for 13,500lb (6,123kg) of stores, including nine torpedoes and/or depth charges; underwing pylons for Harpoon antiship missiles or pairs of Sidewinder AAMs

Derived from the Comet 4C airliner, the Hawker Siddeley Nimrod was designed to replace the Shackleton as the RAF's standard long-range maritime patrol aircraft. The prototype flew for the first time on May 23, 1967, and deliveries of production Nimrod MR.Mk.1 aircraft began in October 1969. The first 38 Nimrods were delivered between 1969 and 1972, equipping five squadrons and No. 236 OCU; another eight were delivered in 1975, while three, designated Nimrod R.1, were converted to the electronic intelligence role. From 1979

▼ *A British Aerospace Nimrod MR.2 in the "hemp" overall camouflage scheme. Note the Sidewinder air-to-air missiles under the wings.*

the Nimrod fleet was significantly upgraded to MR.2 standard, with improved avionics and weapon systems. Flight refueling equipment was added at the time of the 1982 Falklands war. All Nimrods are scheduled to be rebuilt between 2003 and 2008, retaining only the fuselage shell of existing aircraft. The new aircraft, designated Nimrod MRA.4, will have new wings and undercarriage and BMW/Rolls Royce fuel-efficient engines.

▌ British Aerospace Sea Harrier

GREAT BRITAIN

▲ *A Sea Harrier FRS.1 of No. 800 Naval Air Squadron at the hover over the flight deck of the carrier USS* Dwight D. Eisenhower *during an exercise.*

The Sea Harrier FRS.1 was ordered to equip the Royal Navy's three Invincible-class aircraft carriers. The nose was lengthened to accommodate the Blue Fox AI radar, and the cockpit was raised to permit the installation of a more substantial avionics suite and to provide the pilot with a better all-round view. Armed with Sidewinder AAMs, the Sea Harrier FRS.1 distinguished itself in the 1982 Falklands war. At the height of the campaign, on May 21, 1982, Sea Harriers were being launched on combat air patrols at the rate of one pair every 20 minutes. The Sea Harrier force was later upgraded to FA.2 standard, the forward fuselage being redesigned to accommodate the Ferranti Blue Vixen pulse-Doppler radar. The avionics suite was wholly upgraded and the aircraft armed with the AIM-120 AMRAAM medium-range air-to-air missile, enabling it to engage multiple targets beyond visual range.

SPECIFICATION: Type multirole combat aircraft (data FA.2) • Crew 1 • Powerplant one 21,500-lb (9,752-kg) thrust Rolls Royce Pegasus Mk 106 vectored thrust turbofan • Max speed 736mph (1,185km/h) at sea level • Service ceiling 51,000ft (15,545m) • Combat radius 115 miles (185km) on high-level CAP with 90-minute loiter on station • Wingspan 25ft 3in (7.70m) • Length 46ft 6in (14.17m) • Height 12ft 2in (3.71m) • Weight 26,200lb (11,884kg) loaded • Armament two 1-in (25-mm) Aden cannon; five external pylons with provision for AIM-9 Sidewinder, AIM-120 AMRAAM; two Harpoon or Sea Eagle antiship missiles, up to a total of 8,000lb (3,629kg)

▲ *The Sea Harrier FA.Mk 2 combines the Blue Vixen radar and AMRAAM missiles, producing a much more potent interceptor than the earlier FRS.Mk 1.*

■ Canadair CL.28 Argus

In April 1954 Canadair received a development contract for a long-range maritime patrol aircraft design based on the Bristol Britannia airliner, the new aircraft retaining the Britannia's wings, tail, landing gear, and flying controls. A completely new unpressurized fuselage was designed with provision for a weapons bay and new internal installations, and the Britannia's turboprop engines were replaced by Wright Cyclone turbo-compounds. The prototype Cl-28 Argus flew on March 28, 1957 and the first fully operational Argus Mk I was delivered to No. 405 Squadron RCAF in May 1958.

SPECIFICATION: Type long-range maritime patrol and ASW aircraft • Crew 15 • Powerplant four 3,400hp Wright Cyclone R-3350-EA1 turbo-compound engines • Max speed 288mph (464km/h) at sea level • Service ceiling 25,700ft (7,838m) • Max range 4,000 miles (6,436km) • Wing span 142ft 3in (43.38m) • Length 125ft 5in (38.26m) • Height 36ft 8in (11.20m) • Weights 81,000lb (36,693kg) empty; 157,000lb (71,121kg) loaded • Armament up to 8,000lb (3,624kg) of offensive maritime stores

▼ *Canadair completely redesigned the Britannia fuselage so that, although it resembled the airliner, the Argus was in fact a very different machine.*

■ CANT Z.501

First flown in 1934, the CANT (Cantieri Riuniti dell'Adriatico) Z.501 Gabbiano (Seagull) flying boat was the standard equipment of Italy's maritime reconnaissance squadrons at the outbreak of World War II, and 202 were in service in 15 squadrons when Italy entered the conflict on June 10, 1940. On May 19, 1934, the prototype established a world seaplane distance record of 2,566 miles (4,130km), flying from Monfalcone to Massawa in Eritrea in 26 hours 35 minutes. Some Z.501s were supplied to Nationalist Spain and Romania.

SPECIFICATION: Type maritime reconnaissance flying boat • Crew 5 • Powerplant one 900hp Isotta-Fraschini XI R2C 15-cylinder radial • Max speed 171mph (275km/h) at sea level • Service ceiling 22,965ft (7,000m) • Max range 1,491 miles (2,400km) • Wing span 73ft 9in (22.50m) • Length 46ft 11in (14.30m) • Height 14ft 6in (4.40m) • Weight 15,542lb (7,050kg) loaded • Armament three 0.303-in (7.7-mm) machine guns, one each in bow, engine nacelle turret, and dorsal turret; external bomb load of 1,411lb (640kg)

▲ *The Cant Z.501 was widely used in the maritime reconnaissance role when Italy entered the war, serving with 15 squadrons.*

■ CANT Z.506B

Derived from the civilian CANT Z.506, the CANT Z.506B Erone (Heron) maritime reconnaissance seaplane entered service in 1938 and 324 aircraft were subsequently built, 95 being operational at the time of Italy's entry into the war. The type was initially used in the bomber role, but was later fitted with heavier defensive armament and operated as a maritime reconnaissance, convoy escort, and antisubmarine air-craft. Some were converted to the air-sea rescue role as the Z.506S, remaining in service until 1959.

SPECIFICATION: Type maritime reconnaissance and bomber floatplane • Crew 5 • Powerplant three 750hp Alfa Romeo 126 RC.34 nine-cylinder radials • Max speed 217mph (350km/h) at sea level • Service ceiling 26,245ft (8,000m) • Max range 1,705 miles (2,745km) • Wingspan 86ft 11in (26.50m) • Length 63ft 1in (19.24m) • Height 24ft 5in (7.45m) • Weight 28,008lb (12,705kg) loaded • Armament one 0.50-in (12.7-mm) machine gun in dorsal turret; one rearward-firing 0.303-in (7.7-mm) machine gun in ventral gondola, and one each in beam positions; internal bomb load of 2,646lb (1,200kg)

▶ *The CANT Z.506, seen here taxying off Gibraltar after Italy's surrender, was widely used in the Mediterranean and Aegean during World War II.*

▋CANT Z.1007

SPECIFICATION: Type medium bomber (data Z.1007bis) • Crew 5 • Powerplant three 1,000hp Oiaggio P.XI R2C.40 14-cylinder radials • Max speed 290mph (466km/h) • Service ceiling 26,900ft (8,200m) • Max range 1,087 miles (1,750km) • Wingspan 81ft 4in (24.80m) • Length 60ft 2in (18.35m) • Height 17ft 5in (5.22m) • Weight 30,029lb (13,621kg) loaded • Armament one 0.50-in (12.7-mm) machine gun in dorsal turret and one in ventral position; one 0.303-in (7.7-mm) machine gun in each of two beam positions; internal bomb load of 2,646lb (1,200kg)

Designed by Filippo Zapatta, the CANT Z.1007 Alcione (Kingfisher) first flew in March 1937 and entered service late in 1938. The type was produced in three versions, the Z.1007 (35 built), the Z.1007bis, and the Z.1007ter (526 built), the last two featuring a larger airframe, better defensive armament, and uprated engines. The Z.1107 was widely used by the Regia Aeronautica throughout the Balkans and the Mediterranean. The aircraft was produced in both single- and twin-finned configurations. A twin-engined version, the potentially excel-lent CANT Z.1008, never went into production.

▋Caproni Ca.30 Series

The name of Caproni, together with that of Russia's Igor Sikorsky, was to be synonymous with the design and pro-duction of the world's first heavy bombers. The twin-boom Caproni Ca.30, progenitor of a long line of multiengined warplanes, flew in 1913 and featured three 80hp Gnome-

Rhone engines fitted inside the fuselage nacelle, one driving a pusher propeller and the others driving tractor propellers on the tail booms via driveshafts. This arrangement proved too cumbersome, so in 1914 Caproni produced the Ca.31, which had engines mounted on the front of the twin booms; it went into production as the Ca.1. Only 162 examples of this aircraft were produced before production switched to the Ca.2 (Ca.32), which had three in-line engines, and the Ca.3 (Ca.33), which had more powerful engines, a better performance, and a greater bomb load; in total 164 Ca.2s and 269 Ca.3s were built.

Caproni Ca.2s carried out the first Italian bombing raid of World War I, on August 25, 1914. Caproni Ca.33s also equipped the Italian Naval Air Arm's first torpedo-

bomber squadrons, as well as two squadrons of France's Aviation Militaire.

SPECIFICATION: Type heavy bomber (data Ca.3) • Crew 4 • Powerplant three 150hp Isotta-Fraschini V.4B in-line engines • Max speed 87mph (140km/h) • Service ceiling 13,450ft (4,100m) • Max range 280 miles (450km) • Wingspan 72ft 10in (22.2m) • Length 35ft 9in (10.9m) • Height 12ft 2in (3.7m) • Weight 7,302lb (3,312kg) • Armament two or four 0.303-in (7.7-mm) Revelli machine guns in cockpit positions; up to 992lb (450kg) of bombs

Caproni Ca.40 series

The Caproni Ca.40 series of bombers made its appearance in the last year of the war. The Caproni C.40, C.41, and C.42 were triplane versions of the basic design and carried the military designation C.4; only three Ca.40s were built before production switched to the Ca.41 and Ca.42. Thirty-two of the latter were built, six being loaned to the Royal Naval Air Service. The Ca.44, Ca.45, and Ca.46 biplanes were produced under the military designation Ca.5; 225 were built.

SPECIFICATION: Type heavy bomber (data Ca.42) • Crew 4 • Powerplant three 270hp Isotta-Fraschini V 6-cylinder in-line engines • Max speed 78mph (126km/h) at sea level • Service ceiling 9,842ft (3,000m) • Endurance 7hrs • Wingspan 98ft 1in (29.9m) • Length 42ft 11in (13.1m) • Height 20ft 8in (6.30m) • Weight 14,793lb (6,710kg) • Armament four 0.303-in (7.7-mm) machine guns; 3,197lb (1,450kg) of bombs

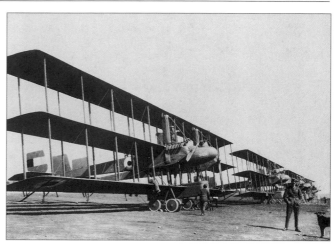

▲ Given the serials N526 to N531, the six Caproni Ca.41 bombers bought for Britain's Royal Naval Air Service were never used operationally.

Caproni Ca.101 series

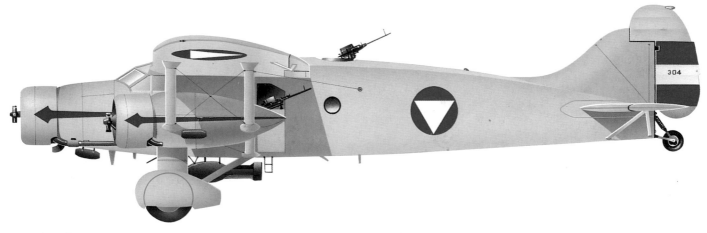

During the interwar years Caproni ceased building large bomber types and instead concentrated on smaller, multipurpose aircraft. The two principal types in this new series were the Ca.101 and Ca.133. The Ca.101 was produced in single-,

twin-, and three-engined versions, and served mainly as a medium bomber in Italy's African colonies, as well as being used for reconnaissance and casualty evacuation work. The three-engined Ca.133 was a stronger and more aerodynamic

SPECIFICATION: Type medium bomber (data Ca.101) • Crew 3 • Powerplant three Alfa Romeo D-2 9-cylinder radial engines • Max speed 124mph (200km/h) • Service ceiling 20,000ft (6,100m) • Max range 620 miles (1,000km) • Wingspan 64ft 6in (19.68m) • Length 50ft 8in (15.47m) • Height 13ft 1in (4.0m) • Weight 11,317lb (5,133kg) loaded • Armament two to three 0.303-in (7.7-mm) machine guns; up to 1,100lb (500kg) of bombs

version, which saw wide service with the Regia Aeronautica during the Italian campaign in Abyssinia in the 1930s. It could carry 18 fully equipped troops and was armed with four 0.303-in (7.7-mm) machine guns, one firing from the door in the port side, and the others in dorsal turret and ventral positions. The last variant was the Ca.148, of which 106 were built, which was used both as for civil and military transportation.

▌Caproni Ca.135

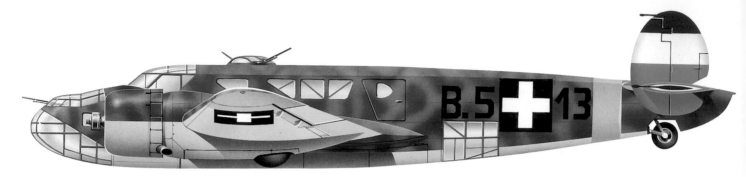

SPECIFICATION: Type medium bomber • Crew 4 • Powerplant two 1,000hp Piaggio P.XI RC.40 14-cylinder radials • Max speed 273mph (440km/h) • Service ceiling 21,325ft (6,500m) • Max range 746 miles (1,200km) • Wingspan 61ft 8in (18.80m) • Length 47ft 2in (14.40m) • Height 11ft 1in (3.40m) • Weight 21,050lb (9,550kg) loaded • Armament one 0.5-in (12.7-mm) machine gun in nose turret, one in dorsal turret, and one in ventral position; internal bomb load of 3527lb (1,600kg)

Intended as a fast, modern medium bomber, the Ca.135 first flew in April 1935 and was produced exclusively for export, 32 being supplied to Peru and 180 to Hungary, the latter being used in tactical operations against the Soviet Union. Unfortunately for those countries which had decided to purchase the aircraft, the Ca.135 proved disappointing in almost every respect, and by mid-1942 it had been relegated to the training role.

▌Caproni Ca.310

▲ The Caproni Ca.310 was one of the major success stories of Italy's aviation industry during the 1930s, despite its disappointing performance.

The most prolific general-purpose light twin-engined aircraft family ever manufactured by the Italian aircraft industry was the Caproni Ca.309-Ca.314 family. The two principal types in this series were the Ca.309 Ghibli (Desert Wind) and the Ca.310 Libeccio (South-West Wind). The Ca.310, which appeared in 1937, was a refined version of the Ca.309, with a retractable undercarriage and modernized airframe. This aircraft was widely used by reconnaissance units of the Regia Aeronautica, despite having a somewhat disappointing performance, and it was also used by Hungary, Norway, Peru, and Yugoslavia.

SPECIFICATION: Type light reconnaissance bomber • Crew 3 • Powerplant two 470hp Piaggio P.VII C.35 7-cylinder radials • Max speed 227mph (365km/h) • Service ceiling 22,965ft (7,000m) • Max range 746 miles (1,200km) • Wingspan 53ft 1in (16.20m) • Length 40ft (12.20m) • Height 11ft 6in (3.52m) • Weight 10,251lb (4,650kg) • Armament two 0.303-in (7.7-mm) machine guns in leading edges of the wing and one in the dorsal turret; internal bomb load of 882lb (400kg)

CASA C-101 Aviojet

SPAIN

SPECIFICATION: Type advanced flying/weapons trainer • Crew 2 • Powerplant one 3,500-lb (1,588-kg) thrust Garrett AiResearch TFE731 turbofan • Max speed 501mph (806km/h) at 20,000ft(6,095m) • Service ceiling 42,000ft (12,800m) • Endurance 7hrs • Wingspan 34ft 9in (10.6m) • Length 41ft (12.5m) • Height 13ft 11in (4.25m) • Weight 10,692lb (4,850kg) • Armament one 1.19-in (30-mm) DEFA cannon; up to 4,410lb (2,000kg) of external stores on six hardpoints

The C-101 was developed by the Spanish CASA company as a replacement for the Hispano HA.200 jet trainer. The type made its first flight in June 1977, and deliveries of the 92 production aircraft on order for the Spanish Air Force began in 1980. More than two decades later the aircraft is still in service. The C-101's weapons system was upgraded in the 1990s and the improved aircraft was the subject of limited export orders from Chile, Honduras, and Jordan.

▲ Seen here in the markings of the Spanish Air Force, the CASA C-101 Aviojet was also exported to Chile, Honduras and Jordan.

▌Caudron G.4

The Caudron G.4 bomber, which flew for the first time in March 1915, was a twin-engined biplane developed from the single-engined G.3 reconnaissance aircraft of 1914. Although its defensive armament was poor, the G.4 had a good performance and was very reliable. The G.4 was widely used by the Aviation Militaire, the Italian Flying Corps, the Royal Flying Corps, and the Royal Naval Air Service, the British aircraft being used to attack seaplane and airship bases in Belgium.

SPECIFICATION: Type bomber/reconnaissance • Crew 2 • Powerplant two 80hp Le Rhone 9-cylinder rotary engines • Max speed 82mph (132km/h) • Service ceiling 14,110ft (4,300m) • Endurance 3hrs 30mins • Wingspan 56ft 5in (17.20m) • Length 23ft 6in (7.16m) • Height 8ft 5in (2.60m) • Weight 2,932lb (1,330kg) loaded • Armament one 0.30-in (7.5-mm) machine gun; 249lb (113kg) of bombs

▲ *The G.4's short crew nacelle had an observer/ gunner's cockpit in the nose, although the field of fire was limited by the proximity of the engines.*

▌Caudron R.11

One of the last French bombers of World War I, the Caudron R.11 was also the last model of the R series bombers designed by RenE Caudron from 1915 onward. The R.11 was intended to replace the R.4, whose performance and payload capacity had fallen short of expectations. The smaller and lighter R.11 went into service in April 1918, initially as a night bomber, but later had its armament increased and was assigned to bomber escort duties.

SPECIFICATION: Type bomber/escort • Crew 3 • Powerplant two 220hp Hispano-Suiza 8B liquid-cooled in-line engines • Max speed 114mph (183km/h) • Service ceiling 19,520ft (5,950m) • Endurance 3hrs • Wingspan 38ft 9in (11.8m) • Length 27ft 8in (8.5m) • Height 9ft 5in (2.9m) • Weight 4,773lb (2,165kg) loaded • Armament five 0.30-in (7.5-mm) machine guns; 265lb (120kg) of bombs

▌Cessna A-37B Dragonfly

SPECIFICATION: Type light attack aircraft (data A-37B) • Crew 1 • Powerplant two 2,850-lb (1,293-kg) General Electric J85-GE-17A turbojets • Max speed 507mph (816km/h) at 16,000ft (4,875m) • Service ceiling 41,765ft (12,730m) • Max range 460 miles (740km) with 4,100lb (1,860kg) load • Wingspan 35ft 10in (10.93m) • Length 28ft 3in (8.62m) • Height 8ft 10in (2.70m) • Weight 14,000lb (6,350kg) • Armament one 0.30-in (7.62-mm) GAU-2 Minigun six-barrel machine gun; eight underwing hardpoints for 5,000lb (2,268kg) of stores

◀ *The A-37B Dragonfly light-attack aircraft could carry a substantial load of underwing ordnance, as is shown in this photograph.*

The Cessna A-37B light-attack aircraft, developed from the T-37, the USAF's first jet built specifically for training pilots, appeared in 1954. The war in Vietnam produced a requirement for an attack version, and 39 T-37s were converted as A-37As in 1966, being fitted with eight underwing hard-points, wingtip fuel tanks, and more powerful engines.

The A-37B version had a reinforced structure, increased fuel capacity, and provision for in-flight refueling. Over a 10-year period from 1967 577 A-37Bs were built, many being exported to Latin American countries.

▮ Cessna AT-17

UNITED STATES

Based on the prewar T-50 commercial cabin monoplane, the Cessna AT-17 twin-engine trainer entered service in 1942, 450 being built. This initial variant was followed by the AT-17A with metal propellers (223 built), the AT-17B (466), and AT-17C (60), the latter having updated equipment. A light transportation version, the UC-78 Bobcat, was also developed, and proved highly successful; over 3,000 were built for the USAAF and the US Navy, where it was designated JRC-1.

SPECIFICATION: Type trainer (data AT-17) • Crew 2, plus 4 passengers • Powerplant two 225hp Jacobs R-775-9 7-cylinder radials • Max speed 195mph (314km/h) • Service ceiling 22,000ft (6,700m) • Max range 750 miles (1,200km) • Wingspan 41ft 11in (12.78m) • Length 32ft 9in (9.98m) • Height 9ft 11in (3.02m) • Weight 5,730lb (2,600kg) loaded • Armament none

▲ JRC-1s served with the US Navy. As with all members of the T-50 family, the JRC-1 had electrically actuated retractable landing gear and flaps.

▮ Cessna L-19 Bird Dog

UNITED STATES

▲ The Cessna L-19 Bird Dog served the US well in Korea, standing up to the most rugged and inhospitable conditions, and remained in service for many years.

SPECIFICATION: Type observation and liaison aircraft (data L-19A) • Crew 2 • Powerplant one 213hp Continental C-470 4-cylinder horizontally opposed air-cooled • Max speed 151mph (243km/h) at sea level • Service ceiling 18,500ft (5,640m) • Max range 530 miles (850km) • Wingspan 36ft (10.97m) • Length 25ft 9in (7.85m) • Height 7ft 3in (2.21m) • Weight 2,400lb (1,088kg) • Armament none

The Cessna L-19 observation and liaison aircraft, developed from the commercial Cessna 170, was one of the USAF's most widely used light aircraft. The initial production aircraft, the L-19A, was mass-produced to the extent of 2,500 aircraft ordered by October 1954, those built under the earlier contracts seeing extensive service in Korea. The TL-19D, ordered in 1956, was a trainer (310 built), while the last version was the L-19E of 1957 (376 built).

▮ Chance Vought F4U Corsair

UNITED STATES

SPECIFICATION: Type naval fighter (data F4U-1) • Crew 1 • Powerplant one 2,000hp Pratt & Whitney R-2800-8 radial engine • Max speed 417mph (671km/h) at 19,900ft (6,066m) • Service ceiling 36,900ft (11,247m) • Max range 1,015 miles (1,633km) • Wingspan 41ft (12.50m) • Length 33ft 4in (10.17m) • Height 16ft 1in (4.90m) • Weight 14,000lb (6,350kg) loaded • Armament six 0.50-in (12.7-mm) machine guns in wings

▲ In production longer than any other US fighter of World War II, the Corsair was credited with a 11:1 ratio of kills against the Japanese.

The prototype XF4U-1 flew for the first time on May 29, 1940, and on April 2, 1941 Vought received a contract for 584 aircraft, the type to be named Corsair in US Navy service. Because of many essential modifications, however, the first production aircraft did not fly until June 25, 1942. The Brewster and Goodyear companies were designated associated constructors; the former subsequently built 735 aircraft under the designation F3A-1 (its contract was canceled in 1944 because of shoddy working practices) and the latter 3,808, designated FG-1. The first Vought-built F4U-1 was delivered to the USN on July 31, 1944. Carrier trials began in September 1942 and the first Corsair unit, Marine Fighting Squadron VMF-214, was declared combat-ready in December, deploying to Guadalcanal in February 1943. After trials with VF-12, the Corsair became operational with Navy Fighting Squadron VF-17 in April 1943, deploying to a land base in New Georgia in September.

Of the 12,681 Corsairs built during World War II, 2,012 were supplied to the Royal Navy, equipping 19 squadrons of the Fleet Air Arm; some of these aircraft were diverted to equip three squadrons of the Royal New Zealand Air Force, operating in the Solomons. The first RN squadron to arm with the Corsair I (F4U-1) was No. 1830, on June 1, 1943. RN Corsair squadrons provided cover for Fleet Air Arm attacks on the German battleship *Tirpitz* in 1944, and subsequently deployed to the Pacific with a British carrier task force in

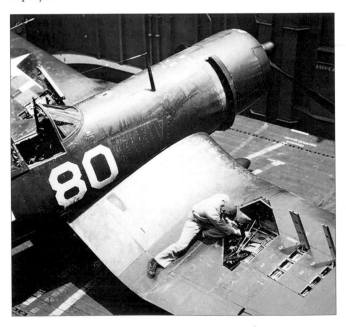

▲ A maintenance crew member services the 0.5in (12.7mm) machine guns on an F4U Corsair during the Pacific war.

1945, taking part in the final offensives against Japan. Corsair variants used by the RN were the Corsair II (F4U-1A), Corsair III (F3A-1), and Corsair IV (FG-1).

Variants of the Corsair included the F4U-1C cannon-armed fighter, F4U-1D fighter-bomber, F4U-2 night fighter, F4U-3 high altitude research version, and F4U-4 fighter.

Postwar developments included the F4U-5 fighter-bomber, F4U-5N night fighter, and F4U-5P photo reconnaissance aircraft, all of which gave tremendous service during the Korean War of 1950–53, the F4U-6 (later A-1) attack aircraft, and the F4U-7, also supplied to the French Navy. French Corsairs saw combat during the Anglo-French Suez operation of 1956.

Chance Vought F6U Pirate

 UNITED STATES

One of the earliest American shipboard jet fighters, the first of three prototype XF6U-1 Pirates flew on October 2, 1946. A production batch of 30 aircraft was ordered under the designation F6U-1, the first of these flying in July 1949. After evaluation, the Pirate was withdrawn from service and the remaining 35 on order were canceled.

◀ *The US Navy accepted the first of 30 production model F6U-1s in 1949. The F6U Pirate was the first jet aircraft designed by Vought.*

SPECIFICATION: **Type** naval fighter • **Crew** 1 • **Powerplant** one 4,200-lb (1,902-kg) thrust Westinghouse WE-30A turbojet • **Max speed** 555mph (894km/h) • **Service ceiling** 41,000ft (12,505m) • **Max range** 750 miles (1,206km) • **Wingspan** 32ft 10in (9.98m) • **Length** 37ft 7in (11.43m) • **Height** 12ft 11in (3.90m) • **Weight** 11,300lb (5,119kg) loaded • **Armament** four 0.79-in (20-mm) cannon

Chance Vought F7U Cutlass

 UNITED STATES

The radical Chance Vought F7U Cutlass, first flown on September 29, 1948, had several claims to fame. It was the first production naval aircraft to achieve supersonic flight; the first to release bombs at supersonic speed; and, in its day, it was the heaviest single-seat carrier fighter in service. Its unorthodox design featured a 38-degree swept wing carrying wide-span powered elevons, air brakes, and full-span leading edge slats. Twin vertical tails were mounted at one-third span. These features were very advanced for the time, as was the use of afterburning engines, an automatic stabilization system, and controls with artificial feedback. The performance of the F7U-1 fell short of USN requirements and production was halted after 14 aircraft so that major

modifications could be made. The much-redesigned aircraft emerged as the F7U-3, which entered service in April 1954. The F7U-3M was armed with four Sparrow AAMs, while the F7U-3P was a photoreconnaissance version.

▲ *The Chance Vought Cutlass was the most radical fighter ever to see operational service with the US Navy.*

SPECIFICATION: **Type** naval fighter-bomber (data F7U-1) • **Crew** 1 • **Powerplant** two 4,200-lb (1,905-kg) Westinghouse J34-32 turbojets • **Max speed** 665mph (1,070km/h) at sea level • **Service ceiling** 41,000ft (12,500m) • **Combat radius** 600 miles (966km) • **Wingspan** 38ft 8in (11.78m) • **Length** 39ft 7in (12.07m) • **Height** 9ft 10in (3m) • **Weight** 16,760lb (7,604kg) • **Armament** four 0.79-in (20-mm) M-2 cannon

Commonwealth CA-12 Boomerang

Produced as a stopgap fighter following the Japanese offensives in the Pacific, the Commonwealth CA-12 Boomerang prototype was completed in only five months and flew for the first time on May 29, 1942. The type entered service with No. 2 OTU in October 1942 and was first used operationally by

No. 84 Squadron in New Guinea in April 1943. The Boomerang proved to be a robust and maneuverable aircraft with an excellent rate of climb. Production totaled 250 aircraft.

SPECIFICATION: Type fighter/ground attack aircraft • Crew 1 • Powerplant one 1,200hp Pratt & Whitney R-1830-S3C4 Twin Wasp radial • Max speed 305mph (491km/h) • Service ceiling 34,000ft (10,363m) • Max range 930 miles (1,497km) • Wingspan 36ft (10.97m) • Length 26ft 7in (8.15m) • Height 13ft (3.96m) • Weight 7,700lb (3,492kg) loaded • Armament two 0.79-in (20-mm) cannon, four 0.303-in (7.62-mm) machine guns; 500lb (227kg) of bombs

▲ *Above: Named* Sinbad II, *this CA-13 was flown by Flt Lt A. W. Clarke with the RAAF's No. 5 Sqn in March 1944.*

Consolidated B-24 Liberator

The Consolidated B-24 Liberator was built in larger numbers than any other US warplane of World War II, 18,431 being produced in total, and was delivered in greater quantities than any other bomber in aviation history. A contract for one prototype, designated XB-24, was approved on March 30, 1939, and this aircraft took off on its maiden flight from Lindberg Field, California, on December 29, 1939. It was followed by seven YB-24 service evaluation aircraft, and while these were under construction a number of changes were made to the XB-24, including the replacement of the original 1200hp Pratt & Whitney R-1830-33 engines with R-1830-41s, which were equipped with General Electric B-2 turbo superchargers for high altitude flight. The tail span was also increased by 2ft (0.6m). With these and other modifications the aircraft was redesignated XB-24B.

The production model for the USAAC was the B-24A, the first of nine were delivered in May 1941. A further development batch of nine B24Cs was also delivered, leading to the first major production models, the B-24D (2738 aircraft), the generally similar B-24E (791 aircraft), and B-24G (430 aircraft) with a power-operated nose turret. Further developments of

SPECIFICATION: Type long-range heavy bomber (data: B-24J) • Crew 8-10 • Powerplant four 1,200hp Pratt & Whitney R-1830-65 radial engines • Max speed 290mph (467km/h) • Service ceiling 28,000ft (8,535m) • Max range 2,000 miles (3,220km) with a 8,800lb (3,992kg) bomb load • Wingspan 110ft (33.53m) • Length 67ft 2in (20.47m) • Height 18ft (5.49m) • Weight 65,000lb (29,484kg) loaded • Armament two gun turrets in nose, tail, upper fuselage aft of cockpit, and under center fuselage, and single manual guns in waist (beam) positions, totaling 10 0.5-in (12.7-mm) machine guns, plus a normal bomb load of 8,800lb (3,992kg)

the Liberator were the B-24H, 738 of which were built by Consolidated with a Consolidated nose turret, and 2,362 of which were produced by Douglas and Ford with an Emerson turret; the B-24J, an improved B-24H with an autopilot and other operational upgrades, including a more effective bomb sight (6,678 built by Consolidated, Douglas, Ford, and North American); the B-24L with two manually operated tail guns rather than a turret (1,667 aircraft from Consolidated and Ford); and the B-24M, an improved version of the B-24J (2,593 aircraft from Consolidated and Ford).

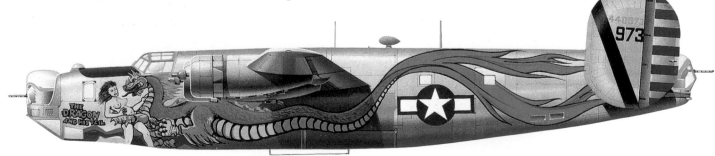

Other Liberator variants included the C-87 and RY transport, AT-22 trainer, F-7 long-range photoreconnaissance, and PB4Y-1 maritime reconnaissance versions.

Six unarmed LB-30 Liberators, originally intended for France but diverted to the RAF, were soon followed by armed variants, beginning with 20 Liberator Mk I aircraft that were equivalents of the B-24A. Some of these were used for maritime reconnaissance, equipped with ASV radar and a ventral gun tray. These were in turn followed, from August 1941, by

◄ *This early Liberator Mk III shows off the glazed nose of this variant. All bomber Liberators up to the earliest B-24Gs had this shorter forward fuselage.*

139 Liberator Mk II and 260 Liberator Mk III aircraft, also for the maritime reconnaissance role, and 112 B-24Gs for service as Liberator B MK V bombers and GR Mk V maritime reconnaissance aircraft. The numbers of later Liberator variants delivered to the RAF and Commonwealth air forces were 1302 B-24J, 437 B-24L, and 47 B-24M aircraft. The B-24J machines served as Liberator B Mk VI bombers with a ball turret or as Liberator GR Mk VI long-range maritime reconnaissance aircraft, with ASV radar replacing the ball turret, while the equivalent marks based on the B-24L and B-24M were the Liberator B Mk VIII and the Liberator GR Mk VIII. The Liberator bombers served mainly in Southeast Asia, where they equipped 14 squadrons, while their maritime reconnaissance counterparts succeeded in closing the "mid-Atlantic gap" where air cover for the vital Atlantic convoys had hitherto been absent. Also delivered to the RAF were 24 Liberators C Mk VII based on the C-87 transportation derivative of the B-24D.

■ Consolidated PBY Catalina

On February 28, 1928, the US Navy issued a contract for a prototype flying boat, the XPY-1, to the Consolidated Aircraft Corporation. This aircraft, which was designed for an alternative installation of two or three engines, was the first large monoplane flying boat procured by the USN, and was the initial configuration that eventually evolved into the most outstanding parasol monoplane flying boat of all time, the PBY Catalina. A contract for the construction of the prototype PBY, then known as the XP3Y-1, was issued to Consolidated on October 28, 1933. The aircraft flew for the first time on March 21, 1935, operational deliveries being made to Patrol Squadron VP-11F in October 1936. The initial version, the PBY-1, demonstrated its long-range capability when 12 aircraft of Patrol Squadron VP-3 flew from San Diego to Coco Solo in the Panama Canal Zone, a distance of 3,292 miles (5,297km) in 27hrs 58mins.

The PBY-1 was fitted with 850hp Pratt & Whitney R-1830-64 engines, and was followed into service in 1937 by 50 PBY-2s, with 1,000hp Pratt & Whitney engines. Three examples of the next variant, the PBY-3, were delivered to the USSR in 1938, along with a manufacturing license. The Soviet version, designated GST and powered by Russian-built 950hp M87 engines, was used in the transportation role.

The PBY-4, which appeared in 1938, featured the large midships "blister" observation and gun positions that were to become a well-known characteristic of the PBY. In April 1939 the US Navy ordered an amphibious version, and this

▲ *The prototype XPBY-5A, the amphibious version produced for service in northern waters. The observation blisters have not yet been fitted.*

became the prototype for the PBY-5A, which was to be widely used in World War II. In July 1939 the RAF received a PBY for evaluation, and this resulted in an order for 50 aircraft similar to the USN's PBY-5. The RAF named them Catalina Mk I; the US Navy subsequently adopted the name Catalina. The RAF doubled its original order during 1940, and orders also began to flow in from other countries; Australia ordered 18, Canada 50, France 30, and the Netherlands East Indies 36. The variant that fulfilled these initial orders, and ongoing orders for the US Navy, was the PBY-5, with 1,200hp R-1830-92 radials. The last 33 aircraft of an order for 200 PBY-5s were completed as amphibians to PBY-5A standard. Total

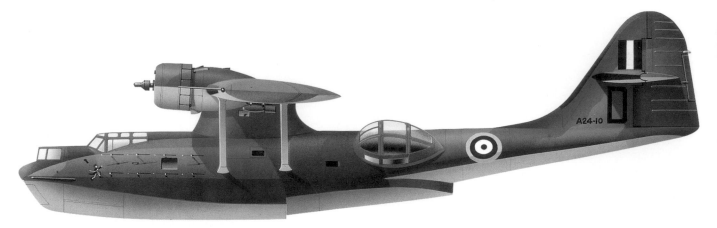

production of the PBY-5 was 750, followed by 794 PBY-5As, 56 of which went to the USAF as OA-10s.

Lend-Lease Agreement supplies to Britain included 225 PBY-5Bs (Catalina IA) and 97 Catalina IVAs, the latter fitted with ASV radar. Further development of the Catalina resulted in the PBY-6A (235 aircraft) with revised armament, an enlarged tail, and a search radar scanner mounted over the cockpit, and the Naval Aircraft Factory PBN-1 Nomad (156 aircraft), built to PBY-5A standard but featuring improvements such as a larger tail unit, greater fuel capacity, and better armament. Most of these were shipped to the USSR. The PBY-5A was also built in Canada as the Canadian Vickers PVB-1A. Production of the Catalina, which ended in April 1945, included 2,398 by Consolidated and 892 by other manufacturers, plus an unknown number built in the USSR as the GST.

▲ *This photograph shows one of the Catalina's large observation blisters to good effect.*

SPECIFICATION: **Type** maritime reconnaissance amphibious flying boat (data PBY-5) • **Crew** 7-9 • **Powerplant** two 1,200hp Pratt & Whitney R-1830-92 Twin Wasp 14-cylinder radial engines • **Max speed** 179mph (288km/h) at 7,000ft (2,135m) • **Service ceiling** 14,700ft (4,480m) • **Max range** 2,545 miles (4,095km) • **Wingspan** 104ft (31.70m) • **Length** 63ft 10in (19.45m) • **Height** 20ft 2in (6.15m) • **Weight** 35,420lb (16,067kg) loaded • **Armament** two 0.5-in (12.7-mm) machine guns in bow turret and one in each beam blister; one 0.30-in (7.62-mm) machine gun in ventral tunnel; plus a war load of up to 4,000lb (1,814kg) of bombs, mines, or depth charges, or two torpedoes

▌ Consolidated PB2Y Coronado

UNITED STATES

The Consolidated PB2Y Coronado was developed to replace the PBY Catalina, which it never succeeded in doing. It was used mainly in the transport role.

SPECIFICATION: **Type** reconnaissance bomber (data PB2Y-3) • **Crew** 10 • **Powerplant** four 1,200hp Pratt & Whitney R-1830-88 Twin Wasp 14-cylinder radials • **Max speed** 213mph (343km/h) at 20,000ft (6,100m) • **Service ceiling** 21,000ft (6,400m) • **Max range** 1,370 miles (2,200km) • **Wingspan** 115ft (35.05m) • **Length** 79ft 3in (24.16) • **Height** 27ft 6in (8.30m) • **Weight** 68,000lb (30,845kg) loaded • **Armament** 10 0.50-in (12.5-mm) machine guns; up to 12,000lb (5,443kg) of bombs

Developed in 1935 to succeed the Catalina, the Consolidated Coronado never managed to equal the PBY's exceptional operational qualities. The XPB2Y-1 prototype flew on September 17, 1937 and the first PB2Y-2 production aircraft entered service in 1940. The main version was the PB2Y-3, of which 210 were ordered in November 1940. The PB2Y-3R was a passenger/cargo adaptation; the PB2Y-5 fulfilled a similar role, with uprated engines; and the PB2Y-5H was an air ambulance with provision for 25 stretcher cases. Ten Coronados operated with RAF Transport Command in 1944.

▮ Consolidated PB4Y-2 Privateer

UNITED STATES

Developed from the US Navy's PB4Y-1 antisubmarine version of the B-24, the PB4Y Privateer fulfilled a pressing need for a very long-range strategic reconnaissance aircraft. The first of three prototypes flew on September 20, 1943 and the aircraft entered production as the PB4Y-2, 1,370 being ordered in two separate batches. In the event, only 736 Privateers were delivered before the end of the war. The Privateer was not widely used, but saw service as an electronic intelligence aircraft and as a maritime patrol aircraft during the Korean War.

▲ *The USN used its PB4Ys on patrol duties and also as Elint platforms, in which role one became the first Cold War shoot-down victim.*

SPECIFICATION: Type long-range strategic reconnaissance aircraft • Crew 11 • Powerplant four 1,350hp Pratt & Whitney R-1830-94 Twin Wasp 14-cylinder radials • Max speed 237mph (381km/h) • Service ceiling 20,700ft (6,300m) • Max range 2,800 miles (4,500km) • Wingspan 110ft (33.53m) • Length 74ft 7in (22.73m) • Height 30ft 1in (9.17m) • Weight 65,000lb (29,485kg) loaded • Armament 12 0.50-in (12.5-mm) machine guns; up to 12,800lb (5,800kg) of bombs

▮ Consolidated PT Series

UNITED STATES

Consolidated's PT series of trainers, beginning with the PT-1 of 1925 (225 built), were designed to replace the famous Curtiss JN-4 "Jenny." Variants included the PT-3 of 1928 (130 produced) and PT-4 of 1929 (100 delivered). Naval equivalent were the NY-1, NY-2, and NY-3. The Consolidated trainers remained in service until 1939.

▲ *The US Army Air Corps received just 10 PT-12 biplane trainers.*

SPECIFICATION: Type trainer (data PT-3) • Crew 2 • Powerplant one 220hp Wright R-790 9-cylinder radial • Max speed 98mph (157km/h) • Service ceiling 15,200ft (4,630m) • Max range 300 miles (482km) • Wingspan 34ft 6in (10.52m) • Length 27ft 11in (8.50m) • Height 9ft 10in (3m) • Weight 2,627lb (1,192kg) loaded • Armament none

▌Convair B-36

◀ *The massive size of the Convair B-36 becomes apparent when pictured adjacent to its predecessor in SAC service, the Boeing B-29.*

The first bomber with a truly global strategic capability to serve with any air force, the B-36 flew for the first time on August 8, 1946, powered by six Pratt & Whitney R-4630-25 "pusher" engines developing 3,000hp each. Two more prototypes, the YB-36 and the YB-36A, both of which flew in 1947, followed the first XB-36. Unlike the two earlier aircraft, which had conventional undercarriages, the YB-36A had a bogie-type assembly and a modified cockpit, the canopy being raised above the line of the fuselage to improve visibility. An initial production batch of 22 B-36As was built, the first being delivered to Strategic Air Command in the summer of 1947. These aircraft were unarmed, and were used for crew training. The second production model, the B-36B, was powered by six Pratt & Whitney R-4630-41 engines with water injection, and was fully combat equipped with 12 0.79-in (20-mm) KM24A1 cannon in the six remotely controlled turrets, together with nose and tail armament. Seventy-three were built the first flying on July 8, 1948. Thirty-five B-36A/B models had been delivered to SAC by the end of 1948. The most important production version was the B-36D, which had four J47 turbojets as well as its six radial engines; 22 aircraft were built and 64 earlier models brought up to B-36D standard. It was followed by the B-36F (28 built), B-36H (81), and B-36J (33). Reconnaissance variants were the RB-36D, RB-36E, and RB-36H. The last B-36 was delivered to SAC in August 1954.

SPECIFICATION: Type strategic heavy bomber (data B-36H) • Crew 15 • Powerplant six 3,800hp Pratt & Whitney R-4360-53 Wasp Major 28-cylinder radials, plus four 5,200-lb (2,358-kg) thrust General Electric J47-GE-19 turbojets • Max speed 411mph (661km/h) at 36,400ft (11,094m) • Service ceiling 39,900ft (12,160m) • Max range 6,800 miles (10,940km) • Wingspan 230ft (70.1m) • Length 162ft 1in (49.4m) • Height 46ft 8in (14.22m) • Weight 410,000lb (185,976kg) loaded • Armament one 10,000lb (4,530kg) Mk 7 nuclear store; up to 84,000lb (38,052kg) of conventional bombs

▼ *The massive Convair B-36 gave the USAF Strategic Air Command the ability to deliver nuclear weapons to a target anywhere in the world.*

Convair B-58 Hustler

SPECIFICATION: Type strategic bomber • Crew 3 • Powerplant four 15,600-lb (7,075-kg) thrust General Electric J79-GE-5 turbojets • Max speed 1,385mph (2,228km/h) at 40,000ft (12,190m) • Service ceiling 64,000ft (19,500m) • Max range 5125 miles (8248km) • Wingspan 56ft 10in (17.32m) • Length 96ft 9in (29.49m) • Height 31ft 5in (9.58m) • Weight 160,000lb (72,576kg) loaded • Armament one 0.79-in (V) Vulcan six-barrel cannon; 19,450lb (8,820kg) of nuclear or conventional stores

The first supersonic bomber to enter service with the USAF, the Convair B-58 prototype flew on November 11, 1956. It was anticipated that the type would replace the B-47, but in the event only two Bomb Wings, the 43rd and 305th, were equipped with it. The B-58 was a bold departure from conventional design, having a delta wing with conical-cambered leading edge, an area-ruled fuselage, and four podded turbojets. The three-man crew occupied tandem cockpits, and the B-58 was the first aircraft in the world in which the crew had individual escape capsules for use at supersonic speeds. Weapons and extra fuel were carried

in a large, jettisonable under-fuselage pod. The only production version was the B-58A; 103 were built, eight being converted as TB-58 trainers. During an operational career lasting 10 years, from 1960 to 1970, the B-58 established several records.

▼ The B-58 Hustler was designed to penetrate Soviet SAM defences with a supersonic "dash" over the target.

Convair F-102/F-106

In 1950, the USAF formulated a requirement for a night and all-weather interceptor incorporating the latest fire control system. This was eventually to emerge as the Convair F-102, whose design was based on experience gained during flight testing of the XF-92 delta-wing research aircraft. Two prototype YF-102s were built, the first flying on October 24, 1953. This aircraft was damaged beyond repair only a week later, but testing resumed with the second machine in January 1954. Eight more YF-102s were built for evaluation, and it soon became apparent that the aircraft's performance fell short of expectations. After substantial airframe redesign the machine reemerged in December 1954 as the YF-102A, and the type was ordered into full production. The first F-102A

Delta Dagger was handed over to Air Defense Command in June 1955, but it was another year before the type was issued to squadrons. In all, 875 were delivered.

A more advanced design, the F-102B, had an electronic weapons control system and eventually entered service in 1959 as the F-106 Delta Dart after a protracted development history.

▼ A sleek and purposeful-looking aircraft, the F-102 was, in fact, something of a disappointment in service.

SPECIFICATION: Type all-weather interceptor (data F-102A) • Crew 1 • Powerplant one 17,200lb (7,802kg) thrust Pratt & Whitney J57-P-23 turbojet • Max speed 825mph (1,328km/h) at 36,000ft (10,970m) • Service ceiling 54,000ft (16,460m) • Max range 1,350 miles (2,172km) • Wingspan 38ft 1in (11.62m) • Length 68ft 4in (20.84m) • Height 21ft 2in (6.46m) • Weight 31,500lb (14,288kg) loaded • Armament up to six AAMs; 12 folding-fin aircraft rockets

▲ *A Convair F-106 seen at Edwards Air Force Base, the US Air Force's flight test centre, in May 1967.*

▌Curtiss A-12 Shrike

▲ *Ugly in design, the Curtiss Shrike was typical of the combat aircraft produced by the US aircraft industry in the early 1930s.*

A clumsy, low-wing monoplane and a contemporary of the Boeing P-26 fighter, the Curtiss A-12 Shrike was a typical USAAC assault aircraft of the 1930s and was designed to replace the Curtiss Falcon biplane. The prototype flew in 1931 and was followed by 13 preseries and 46 production aircraft. The type gave long service with the US army's attack groups, and some nine aircraft were still operational when the Japanese attacked Pearl Harbor in December 1941.

SPECIFICATION: Type assault aircraft • Crew 2 • Powerplant one 690hp Wright Cyclone 9-cylinder radial • Max speed 175mph (282km/h) • Service ceiling 15,150ft (4,620m) • Endurance 3hrs 30mins • Wingspan 44ft (13.41m) • Length 32ft 3in (9.83m) • Height 9ft 4in (2.84m) • Weight 5,900lb (2,670kg) loaded • Armament four 0.303-in (7.7-mm) fixed forward-firing machine guns and one in rear cockpit; 400lb (180kg) of bombs

▌Curtiss BF2C Goshawk

Although built only in small numbers, the Curtiss Goshawk biplane dive-bombers were well known in the 1930s. Two prototypes were ordered in 1932 and 28 examples of the production BF2C were delivered to the US Navy in 1933. These

were followed by 27 aircraft of a second production model, the BF2C-1, which had a different engine and was fitted with a manually operated retractable undercarriage. Structural faults limited the BF2C-1's service life to only a few months.

◀ The metal-framed wing of the BF2C-1 offered greater strength for the dive-bombing role, but was more prone to vibration in flight.

SPECIFICATION: Type naval dive-bomber (data BF2C-1) • Crew 1 • Powerplant one 700hp Wright R-1820-04 Cyclone 9-cylinder radial • Max speed 285mph (459km/h) • Service ceiling 27,000ft (8,230m) • Max range 570 miles (719km) • Wingspan 31ft 6in (9.60m) • Length 23ft (7.01m) • Height 10ft 10in (3.3m) • Weight 5,086lb (2,307kg) loaded • Armament two fixed forward-firing 0.303-in (7.7-mm) machine guns; 474lb (215kg) of bombs

▌Curtiss C-46 Commando

UNITED STATES

▲ Although it performed a magnificent task in the Pacific Theater, the C-46 was overshadowed by its contemporary, the Douglas C-47.

The Curtiss C-46 Commando was a true workhorse of the USAAF, especially in the Pacific Theater. The type flew for

SPECIFICATION: Type transport (data C-46A) • Crew 4 • Powerplant two 2,000hp Pratt & Whitney R-2800-51 Double Wasp 18-cylinder radials • Max speed 269mph (433km/h) at 15,000ft (4,570m) • Service ceiling 27,600ft (8,400m) • Max range 1,200 miles (1,930km) • Wingspan 78ft 6in (23.94m) • Length 76ft 4in (23.27m) • Height 21ft 9in (6.63m) • Weight 56,000lb (25,400kg) loaded • Armament none

the first time on March 26, 1940. A preliminary batch of 25 C-46 passenger transports was followed by 1,491 C-46A freighters with a single large cargo door, and by 1,410 C-46Ds with double doors and a modified nose. The single-door C-46E (17 built) and the double-door C-46F (234 built) used different powerplants, while 160 aircraft were completed as R5C-1s for the US Marine Corps. Although it had a distinguished career in the Pacific and China-Burma-India theaters, the Commando did not appear in Europe until March 1945, when it took part in the airborne assault on the Rhine.

▌Curtiss F9C Sparrowhawk

Originally intended for carrier-based operations, the Curtiss F9C was modified as a parasite fighter to be launched and retrieved in flight by the airships USS *Akron* and Macon. The first experiment was carried out on October 27, 1931 with the prototype XF9C-1 and further trials took place with the improved XF9C-2, the aircraft being hooked to the mother ship on a trapeze. Six production F9C-2 aircraft were ordered for service with the *Akron*, being transferred to the *Macon*

when the *Akron* was destroyed in April 1933. Experiments ended when the *Macon* was also lost in February 1935.

▲ *This F9C-2 was photographed as it hung from Macon's trapeze prior to launching.*

SPECIFICATION: **Type** parasite fighter • **Crew** 1 • **Powerplant** one 420hp Wright Whirlwind 9-cylinder radial • **Max speed** 177mph (284km/h) at 4,000ft (1,220m) • **Service ceiling** 19,200ft (5,800m) • **Max range** 360 miles (590km) • **Wingspan** 25ft 6in (7.77m) • **Length** 20ft 1in (6.13m) • **Height** 7ft 1in (2.16m) • **Weight** 2,752lb (1,248kg) loaded • **Armament** two 0.303-in (7.7-mm) fixed forward-firing machine guns

▌Curtiss H.16

The Curtiss H.16, whose prototype appeared at the end of 1917, was the largest and most effective American flying boat

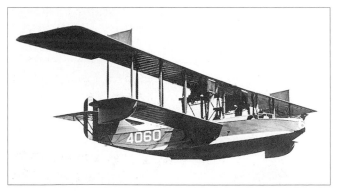

▲ *This photograph of an H.16 illustrates the attachment of its wingtip floats directly beneath the outer surfaces of the lower wing.*

of World War I. Heavily armed, and with a useful bomb load, it was produced in substantial numbers; 150 were built by the Naval Aircraft Factory at Philadelphia, 77 of them for the US Navy with 40hp Liberty 12 engines. A further 125 H.16s were ordered for the RNAS, but 50 were canceled and another 50 placed in storage in the United Kingdom. The remaining 25, delivered beginning in March 1918, saw service from British coastal bases during the closing months of the war.

SPECIFICATION: **Type** maritime reconnaissance flying boat • **Crew** 4 • **Powerplant** two 400hp Liberty 12-cylinder V-type • **Max speed** 95mph (153km/h) at sea level • **Service ceiling** 9,950ft (3,033m) • **Max range** 378 miles (608km) • **Wingspan** 95ft (28.98m) • **Length** 46ft 1in (14.06m) • **Height** 17ft 8in (5.4m) • **Weight** 10,900lb (4,944kg) • **Armament** five-six 0.303-in (7.7-mm) machine guns; up to 920lb (417kg) of bombs

▌Curtiss JN-4

Built in its thousands, the famous Curtiss JN-4 "Jenny" was the

SPECIFICATION: **Type** trainer (data JN-4) • **Crew** 2 • **Powerplant** one 90hp Curtiss OX-5 8-cylinder V-type • **Max speed** 75mph (121km/h) at sea level • **Service ceiling** 11,000ft (3,353m) • **Endurance** 2hrs 15mins • **Wingspan** 43ft 7in (13.28m) • **Length** 27ft 4in (8.33m) • **Height** 9ft 10in (3m) • **Weight** 2,130lb (966kg) loaded • **Armament** none

result of a US Army specification of 1914, calling for a biplane trainer with a tractor engine. By the end of World War I 7,471 examples had been built; these included 2,041 of the basic JN-4, 781 JN-4As, 25765 JN-4Ds, 929 JN-4Hs, and 1,035 examples of the last variant, the JN-6H. By the time production ceased, the engine power of the little trainer had virtually doubled. During the "barnstorming" era of the 1920s thousands of "Jennys" were flown at traveling aerial pageants throughout the US.

▲ *The Curtiss JN-4 "Jenny" was the most widely used US aircraft of World War I, and was built in massive quantities for service at home and overseas.*

∎ Curtiss P-1/P-6 Hawk

The Curtiss P-1 stemmed from the PW-8, 25 of which were built for the USAAS and which was a contemporary of the Boeing PW-9. On June 23, 1924, Lt. Russell Maughan of the USAAS made a dawn-to-dusk transcontinental flight across the US in one of these machines. Fifteen P-1s were ordered initially, their design being based on the XPW-8B, which had tapered upper and lower wings. The P-1 was the first of the famous Curtiss Hawk series of fighters, the USAAC acquir-

▶ *The P-5 designation was applied to five examples of the type for evaluation in the high-altitude role.*

SPECIFICATION: Type fighter (data P-6E) • Crew 1 • Powerplant one 600hp Curtiss V-1570-23 Conqueror in-line engine • Max speed 198mph (319km/h) at sea level • Service ceiling 24,700ft (7,530m) • Max range 570 miles (917km) • Wingspan 31ft 6in (9.6m) • Length 23ft 2in (7.06m) • Height 8ft 11in (2.72m) • Weight 3,392lb (1,539kg) loaded • Armament two fixed forward-firing 0.30-in (7.62-mm) machine guns

ing 25 P-1As, 25 P-1Bs, and 33 P-1Cs from 1924. In 1928, two Curtiss P-1 aircraft were modified and, designated XP-6 and XP-6A, took part in the National Air Races, the winner registering 201mph (323km/h). This achievement led the US Army to order 18 examples of a fighter variant (nine YP-6s and nine P-6As). Successive modifications produced the P-6D and the final Hawk variant, the P-6E, 46 of which were delivered in 1932.

∎ Curtiss P-36

Although not particularly a success story, the Curtiss P-36 had the distinction of being the USAAC's first "modern" monoplane fighter. Designed as a private venture, the proto-

type first flew in May 1935. Three YP-36 aircraft were ordered for evaluation, these being followed by 178 P-36A fighters, which entered service in 1938, and 31 P-36C fighters

▲ *Deliveries of the P-36 to the US Army Air Corps began in April 1938, and a number saw action against the Japanese at Pearl Harbor on 7 December 1941.*

with two additional wing-mounted 0.30-in (7.62-mm) machine guns.

SPECIFICATION: Type fighter (data P-36C) • Crew 1 • Powerplant one 1,200hp Pratt & Whitney R-1830-17 14-cylinder radial • Max speed 311mph (500km/h) at 15,000ft (4,570m) • Service ceiling 33,700ft (10,270m) • Max range 820 miles (1,320km) • Wingspan 37ft 3in (11.37m) • Length 28ft 10in (8.79m) • Height 9ft 3in (2.82m) • Weight 6,010lb (2,726kg) • Armament one 0.50-in (12.7-mm) and one 0.30-in (7.62-mm) machine guns in upper forward fuselage; two wing-mounted 0.30-in (7.62-mm) machine guns

The type was exported as the Curtiss Hawk 75, 112 of which were delivered to the Chinese Air Force in 1938 as Hawk 75Ms. A further 25 generally similar Hawk 75Ns were produced for Thailand, and 30 Hawk 75Os for Argentina. The Hawk 75A, also built for export, featured a retractable undercarriage and other improvements; this version was ordered by France, which placed orders totaling 730, but deliveries were still incomplete when France was invaded in May 1940, and the remaining aircraft were diverted to the RAF, in whose service the aircraft was known as the Mohawk. The Hawk fought with GC I/5 in the Battle of France and performed well against the Bf 109 and 110.

Curtiss P-40

UNITED STATES

The P-40 originated as a development of the radial-engined Curtiss P-36A Hawk. In July 1937 the USAAC ordered the prototype of a possible variant, designated XP-40 and pow-

ered by the new liquid-cooled Allison V-1710 12-cylinder Vee-type engine. The tenth production P-36A was fitted with the new powerplant on the assembly line, and this aircraft flew for the first time in October 1938. On April 27, 1939 the USAAC awarded Curtiss-Wright a contract for 524 production P-40s, the largest order ever placed for an American fighter up to that time; this was subsequently scaled down to 200, all of which were delivered to the Air Corps by September 1940. France's Armée de l'Air—which during the "phoney war" period of 1939–40 was already operating the nimble Curtiss Hawk 75A (P-36A)—placed an order for 140 P-40s, these being given the export designation Hawk 81A-1. Before the first Hawk 81A-1 could be delivered, however, France fell, and the full order was taken over by the British Purchasing Commission on behalf of the RAF. Although considered unsuitable for operational use by Fighter Command, the P-40s were fitted with four wing-mounted Browning

◄ *This Curtiss P-40E Kittyhawk bears the shark's mouth markings of No. 112 Squadron RAF, which was very successful in the Western Desert campaign.*

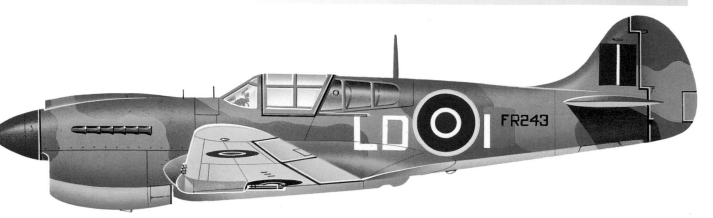

0.303-in (7.7-mm) machine guns and allocated to Army Cooperation Command as the Tomahawk I, for use in the tactical reconnaissance role. They served until 1942, when they were replaced by another American type, the North American Mustang I.

Deliveries of P-40s to the USAAC resumed in February 1941, the armament now having been brought up to the standard of the batch intended for France by the addition of four 0.303-in (7.7-mm) machine guns in the wings. An armored windshield and armor plating for the pilot were also fitted. The modified aircraft was designated P-40B and 130 were delivered to the USAAC, together with 110 identical aircraft which went to the RAF as the Hawk 81A-2, to be known as the Tomahawk IIA in RAF service. The next P-40 variant was the P-40C, which was fitted with larger, self-sealing fuel tanks and two more wing guns; 193 went to the USAAF (as the USAAC

had now become) and 930 to the RAF as the Tomahawk IIB, although 146 of these were diverted to the Soviet Union following the German invasion of June 1941 and another 100 to the American Volunteer Group (AVG), operating in China. In all, 2,430 P-40s were allocated to the Soviet Union in World War II, of which 2,097 were actually delivered; many were lost in transit. The RAF's Tomahawk IIBs had the fuselage-mounted armament deleted, retaining only the four wing guns. The P-40D was substantially redesigned, its four wing guns being upgraded to 0.50-in (12.7-mm) caliber and the nose armament removed. Provision was also made for the carriage of bombs under the wings or fuselage. Only 22 P-40Ds went to the USAAF as the Hawk 87A Warhawk, but 560 were allocated to the RAF, which gave them the new name Kittyhawk I. The USAAF preferred the P-40E, with six wing guns; it ordered 820 of this model, and another 1,500 became Kittyhawk IAs. Installation of the much superior Packard-Merlin engine produced the P-40F, of which 1,311 were built, some being supplied to the USSR and others to the Free French Air Force. The RAF received 21 P-40Ks and 600 P-40Ms (Kittyhawk III) and 586 P-40Ns (Kittyhawk IV). US production, which included 1,300 P-40Ks, with increased fin area, 700 P-40Ls (with only four guns), and 4,219 P-40Ns, the latter having a 1,360hp V-1710-81 engine, ended in December 1944 after 13,738 aircraft had been built.

SPECIFICATION: Type fighter/fighter-bomber • Crew 1 • Powerplant one 1,360hp Allison V-1710-81 V-12 engine • Max speed 378mph (609km/h) at 10,500ft (3,200m) • Service ceiling 38,000ft (11,580m) • Max range 240 miles (386km) • Wingspan 37ft 4in (11.38m) • Length 33ft 4in (10.16m) • Height 12ft 4in (3.76m) • Weight 11,400lb (5,171kg) loaded • Armament six 0.50-in (12.7-mm) machine guns in the wings, plus a bomb load of up to three 500lb (227kg) bombs

▌Curtiss SBC Helldiver

UNITED STATES

The Curtiss SBC was the second US naval aircraft to bear the name Helldiver; the first was the F8C dive-bomber of 1928, 110 of which were produced for the USN and USMC as the F8C-1, F8C-3, F8C-4, and F8C-5, these being delivered from 1931. The SBC originated as a high-wing monoplane design of 1933, the XF12C-1, and ended by becoming the last combat biplane to be built in the United States.

A second prototype was built in biplane configuration, and this was flown on December 9, 1935. Orders for 83 SBC-3 and 174 SBC-4s followed, and 50 of 90 aircraft pro-

duced to meet a French requirement were actually on their way to Europe when France was overrun, being abandoned

SPECIFICATION: Type reconnaissance/dive-bomber (data SBC-4) • Crew 2 • Powerplant one 950hp Wright R-1820-34 Cyclone 9-cylinder radial • Max speed 237mph (381km/h) at 15,200ft (4,635m) • Service ceiling 27,300ft (8,320m) • Max range 590 miles (950km) • Wingspan 34ft (10.36m) • Length 28ft 4in (8.63m) • Height 12ft 7in (3.83m) • Weight 7,632lb (3,462kg) loaded • Armament two 0.30-in (7.62-mm) machine guns; 1,000lb (454kg) of bombs

◀ *In RAF service, the Cleveland Mk.I had a very limited flying career. Note the gun sight protruding from the windscreen.*

at Martinique and later entering USN service. Five of the remaining aircraft were recovered for RAF use, for use as trainers under the designation Cleveland Mk.I.

By the time the US entered the war the SBC Helldiver was obsolete on the front line and was quickly relegated to secondary duties, although the type remained in service with the USMC until 1943.

▌Curtiss SB2C Helldiver

UNITED STATES

The SB2C Helldiver was designed as a replacement for the SBD Dauntless; in fact it never was, for the Douglas dive-bomber continued in operational service until the end of the war. Because of delays following the crash of the prototype, the first production Helldiver did not fly until June 1942 and the type made its operational debut on November 11, 1943 in an attack on the Japanese-held island of Rabaul. The SB2C-1 (978 built) was followed in production by the SB2C-3 (1112), featuring an uprated engine (the SB2C-2 being an abandoned floatplane version) and the SB2C-4

(2,045), which had underwing bomb or rocket attachments and perforated landing flaps. The SB2C-5 (970 aircraft) had extra fuel tankage, while the USAAF took delivery of 900 examples of a ground attack version, the A-25A.

▲ *The Curtiss Helldiver was not an easy aircraft to fly, and was generally unpopular with its crews. Continual problems delayed its entry into service.*

SPECIFICATION: Type naval reconnaissance/dive-bomber (data SB2C-1C) • Crew 2 • Powerplant one 1,700hp Wright R-2600-8 Cyclone 14-cylinder radial • Max speed 281mph (452km/h) at 10,000ft (3,050m) • Service ceiling 24,200ft (7,375m) • Max range 1,375 miles (2,213km) • Wingspan 49ft 8in (15.15m) • Length 36ft 8in (11.18m) • Height 13ft 1in (4m) • Weight 16,812lb (7,626kg) • Armament two wing-mounted 0.79-in (20-mm) cannon, plus two 0.30-in (7.62-mm) machine guns in rear cockpit

▌Curtiss SC-1 Seahawk

UNITED STATES

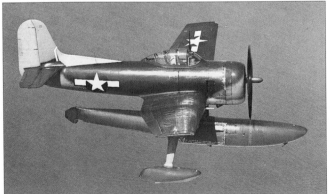

▲ *Curtiss developed the Seahawk as a single-seater, the development of ASV radar and other sensors making the observer dispensable.*

The Curtiss SC-1 Seahawk was the last US reconnaissance aircraft produced during WWII for use on board capital ships. The prototype flew on February 16, 1944 and was followed by 566 production aircraft, although the type did not see action until June 1945, shortly before the Allied invasion of Borneo.

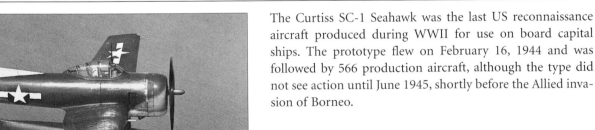

SPECIFICATION: Type naval reconnaissance aircraft • Crew 1 • Powerplant one 1,350hp Wright R-1820-62 Cyclone 9-cylinder radial • Max speed 313mph (504km/h) at 28,600ft (8,720m) • Service ceiling 37,400ft (11,400m) • Max range 1,090 miles (1,750km) • Wingspan 41ft (12.50m) • Length 36ft 4in (11.07m) • Height 18ft (5.48m) • Weight 9,000lb (4,082kg) loaded • Armament two 12.5-mm (0.50-in) machine guns; 750lb (340kg) of bombs

▌Curtiss SO3C Seamew

Originally named Seagull, the SO3C Seamew was not a particularly successful design, but 800 were built by Curtiss and by Ryan, as the SOR-1. The XSO3C-1 prototype flew in 1940 and the type remained in service until it was withdrawn early in 1944. One hundred SO3C-2s were delivered to the Royal Navy, whose name Seamew was adopted by the US Navy. The SO3C was produced in both landplane and floatplane versions.

SPECIFICATION: Type naval reconnaissance aircraft • Crew 2 • Powerplant one 600hp Ranger V-770-6 12-cylinder in-line • Max speed 168mph (269km/h) at 11,800ft (3,600m) • Service ceiling 16,500m (5,030m) • Max range 640 miles (1,030km) • Wingspan 38ft (11.58m) • Length 34ft 9in (10.5m) • Height 14ft 2in (4.31m) • Weight 7,105lb (3,223kg) loaded • Armament two 0.30-in (7.62-mm) machine guns; 650lb (295kg) of bombs

▲ This photograph shows the landplane version of the Seamew. Some aircraft, delivered to the Royal Navy, were modified for use as target drones.

▌Curtiss-Wright CW-21 Demon

Based on an earlier design, the CW-19R, the Curtiss-Wright CW-21 was developed in 1938 as a lightweight interceptor, intended mainly for export. The prototype flew in January 1939 and three production CW-21Bs were ordered for evaluation by the Chinese Air Force, but all three crashed due to faulty fuel on the final stage of their delivery flight and no further order was forthcoming. The Netherlands, however,

took delivery of 25 aircraft for service in the East Indies, and these saw action against the invading Japanese in February 1942.

SPECIFICATION: Type fighter • Crew 1 • Powerplant one 1,000hp Wright R-1820-G5 9-cylinder radial • Max speed 314mph (505km/h) at 12,200ft (3,719m) • Service ceiling 34,300ft (10,455m) • Max range 630 miles (1,014km) • Wingspan 35ft (10.67m) • Length 27ft 2in (8.28m) • Height 8ft 11in (2.72m) • Weight 4,500lb (2,041kg) loaded • Armament two 0.50-in (12.5-mm) and two 0.30-in (7.62-mm) machine guns in upper front fuselage

▲ In combat, the Dutch CW-21Bs often became embroiled in dogfights, a type of air combat for which they had not been intended.

▌Dassault Etendard/Super Etendard

FRANCE

Originally designed to meet the requirements of a mid-1950s tactical strike fighter contest—which it lost to the Fiat G.91— the Dassault Etendard (Standard) showed such outstanding qualities that a development contract was awarded on behalf

SPECIFICATION: Type carrier-borne strike and interceptor aircraft • Crew 1 • Powerplant one 11,023-lb (5,000-kg) thrust SNECMA Atar 8K-50 turbojet (Super Etendard) • Max speed 733mph (1,180km/h) at low level • Service ceiling 44,950ft (13,700m) • Combat radius 528 miles (850km) hi-lo-hi with one Exocet and two external tanks • Wingspan 31ft 6in (9.60m) • Length 46ft 11in (14.31m) • Height 12ft 8in (3.86m) • Weights 14,330lb (6,500kg) empty; 26,455lb (12,000kg) loaded • Armament two 1.19-in (30-mm) DEFA cannon; provision for up to 4,630lb (2,100kg) of external stores; two Exocet ASMs; MATRA Magic AAMs

of the French Navy, which at that time was looking for a strike aircraft capable also of high-altitude interception. The navalized prototype Etendard IVM-01 flew on May 21, 1958, powered by a SNECMA Atar 8B turbojet. The first of 69 production Etendard IVMs was delivered to the Aéronavale on January 18, 1962, being followed into service by the Etendard IVP, an unarmed reconnaissance/tanker variant. The Dassault Super Etendard, which first flew on October 3, 1975, was fitted with a SNECMA Atar 8K-50 turbojet and was intended for the low-level attack role, primarily against shipping. Fourteen Super Etendards were supplied to Argentina starting in 1981, and the five that had been delivered at the time of the Falklands War of May–June 1982, armed with the Exocet ASM, proved highly effective against British vessels.

▲ *A fine naval combat aircraft, the Dassault Etendard made headlines during the 1982 Falklands War, when its Exocet missiles sank British ships.*

▌Dassault Mirage III

FRANCE

One of the biggest success stories in the field of post-1945 combat aircraft design, the Dassault Mirage III owed its origin to the Dassault Mk550 Mirage I of 1954, which, together with the SE Durandal and the SO Trident, was a contender in a French Air Force competition for a high-altitude interceptor. The Mirage I proved too small to carry an effective war load and its twin Viper turbojets lacked the necessary power, so the airframe was substantially redesigned and enlarged and fitted with a single SNECMA Atar G1 engine. Designated Mirage III-

001, the new aircraft made its first flight on November 17, 1956 and exceeded Mach 1.5 in level flight on January 30, 1957.

The French government instructed Dassault to proceed with a multimission version, the Mirage IIIA, the prototype of which (Mirage IIIA-01) flew on May 12, 1958. The Mirage IIIC, which flew on October 9, 1960, was the first production version and was identical to the IIIA, with an Atar 09 B3 turbojet and a SEPR 841 or 844 auxiliary rocket motor. One hundred Mirage IIICs were ordered by the Armée de l'Air.

▲ *Dassault Mirage IIIS aircraft for the Swiss Air Force were fitted with canard foreplanes to provide extra maneuverability on take-off in mountainous terrain.*

Seventy-two similar aircraft, without rocket motors or missiles, were supplied to the Israeli Air Force, first deliveries being made to No. 101 Squadron in 1963. These aircraft were designated Mirage IIICJ and saw considerable action during the subsequent Arab-Israeli wars. Sixteen more aircraft of the IIIC series were supplied to South Africa as the Mirage IIICZ; the SAAF also took delivery of three Mirage IIIBZ two-seaters, which carried the same armament as the IIIC. The Mirage IIIE was a long-range tactical strike variant, 453 examples being produced for the Armée de l'Air and further aircraft for export. A version of the IIIE, the IIIO, was manufactured under license in Australia, while the Mirage IIIP for Pakistan saw action in the 1971 conflict with India. Another version of the Mirage IIIE was the IIIS, delivered to the Swiss Air Force. The Mirage IIIR was the reconnaissance version of the IIIE, equipped with a battery of five OMERA Type 31 cameras in place of the nose radar.

▶ *The Mirage III provided the French Air Force with its first true multi-role combat aircraft, and proved to have a remarkable development potential.*

SPECIFICATION: Type tactical strike aircraft (Mirage IIIE) • Crew 1 • Powerplant one 13,668-lb (6,200-kg) thrust SNECMA Atar 9C turbojet • Max speed 863mph (1,390km/h) at sea level • Service ceiling 55,775ft (17,000m) • Combat radius 745 miles (1,200km) at low level with 2,000-lb (907-kg) payload • Wingspan 26ft 11in (8.22m) • Length 54ft (16.50m) • Height 14ft 9in (4.50m) • Weights 15,540lb (7,050kg) empty; 29,760lb (13,500kg) loaded • Armament two 1.19-in (30-mm) DEFA cannon; provision for up to 6,614lb (3,000kg) of external stores, including special (i.e. nuclear) weapons

▌Dassault Mirage IV

 FRANCE

In 1956, the French Air Ministry issued a draft specification for a new supersonic bomber to carry France's first atomic bomb, the AN22 free-fall weapon with a 60 kiloton warhead. Avions Marcel Dassault proposed a scaled-up version of the Mirage III, which was accepted. Designated Mirage IVA in its definitive form, the prototype Mirage IV-01 flew for the first time in June 1959, and the first production aircraft entered service with the 91e Escadre de Bombardement in 1964. The

SPECIFICATION: Type supersonic strategic bomber • Crew 2 • Powerplant two 15,432-lb (7,000-kg) thrust SNECMA Atar 9K turbojets • Max speed 1,454mph (2,340km/h) at 40,000ft (12,190m) • Service ceiling 65,600ft (20,000m) • Max range 770 miles (1,240km) • Wingspan 38ft 10in (11.84m) • Length 76ft 10in (23.41m) • Height 17ft 8in (5.46m) • Weight 69,665lb (31,600kg) loaded • Armament up to 16,000lb (7,257kg) of conventional or nuclear stores

▲ *The Mirage IV, seen here taking off with rocket assistance, was the core of France's nuclear deterrent forces for many years.*

Mirage IV was a two-seater; the navigator/systems operator sat in a virtually unglazed cabin behind the pilot's cockpit. Sixty aircraft subsequently equipped three escadres, dispersed on airfields throughout metropolitan France and served by 12 Boeing KC-135F tankers. Later, a much-reduced Mirage IV force was stressed for the low-level role and was armed with the Aérospatiale ASMP nuclear-tipped ASM, the aircraft being designated Mirage IVP. The Mirage IV was withdrawn in the 1990s, the last few aircraft being converted to a reconnaissance/electronic intelligence role.

▌Dassault Mirage V   FRANCE

The Mirage V and 50 fighter-bombers, both intended for export, were the final developments in the long-running Mirage III series. Three versions (attack, reconnaissance, and training) were built under license in Belgium. Many ex-Belgian aircraft were sold to Chile; other French-built aircraft were exported to Abu Dhabi, Colombia, Libya, and Pakistan. Fifty of the Mirage Vs sold to foreign air forces had been ordered by Israel in 1966, but were never supplied because of an arms embargo. The Mirage 50, sold to Chile and Venezuela, retained the same basic airframe as the Mirage III and V, but was fitted with the uprated Atar 9K-50 turbojet. Improvements taken up by export operators include an inflight refueling probe, improved avionics and foreplane canards to improve maneuverability.

SPECIFICATION: Type fighter-bomber • Crew 1 • Powerplant one 13,668lb (6,200kg) SNECMA Atar 9C turbojet • Max speed 1,188mph (1,912km/h) at altitude • Service ceiling 55,775ft (17,000m) • Combat radius 404 miles (650km) with a 2,000-lb (907-kg) bomb load • Wingspan 26ft 11in (8.22m) • Length 51ft (15.55m) • Height 14ft 9in (4.50m) • Weights 14,550lb (6,600kg) empty; 30,203lb (13,700kg) loaded • Armament two DEFA 552A cannon; provision for up to 8,818lb (4,000kg) of external stores

Dassault Mirage F.1

The Mirage F.1 single-seat strike fighter was developed as a private venture. Powered by a SNECMA Atar 09K, the prototype flew for the first time on December 23, 1966 and the first production aircraft entered service with the 30e Escadre at Reims early in 1974. Variants produced included the F.1A

▶ *Originally developed as a private venture, the Mirage F.1 has proved to be a major success story, and is widely used by Middle East air forces.*

SPECIFICATION: Type multirole fighter/attack aircraft • Crew 1 • Powerplant one 15,873-lb (7,200-kg) thrust SNECMA Atar 9K-50 turbojet • Max speed 1,460mph (2,350km/h) at high altitude • Service ceiling 65,615ft (20,000m) • Max range 560 miles (900km) with maximum load • Wingspan 27ft 6in (8.40m) • Length 49ft 2in (15m) • Height 14ft 9in (4.50m) • Weights 16,314lb (7,400kg) empty; 33,510lb (15,200kg) loaded • Armament two 1.19-in (30-mm) DEFA 553 cannon; up to 13,889lb (6,300kg) of external stores

ground attack aircraft, the F.1C interceptor, and the F.1B two-seat trainer. The Mirage F.1 was the subject of large overseas export orders, notably to countries in the Middle East.

Dassault Mirage 2000

SPECIFICATION: Type air superiority and attack fighter • Crew 1 • Powerplant one 21,384lb (9,700kg) thrust SNECMA M53-P2 turbofan • Max speed 1,453mph (2,338km/h) at high altitude • Service ceiling 59,055ft (18,000m) • Max range 920 miles (1,480km) with 2,205-lb (1,000-kg) payload • Wingspan 29ft 11in (9.13m) • Length 47ft 1in (14.36m) • Height 17ft (5.20m) • Weights 16,534lb (7,500kg) empty; 37,480lb (17,000kg) loaded • Armament two DEFA 554 cannon; provision for up to 13,885lb (6,300kg) external stores

Five prototypes were built—the first flying on March 10, 1978. A two-seat version, the Mirage 2000B (the fifth prototype) flew on October 11, 1980. The first unit to become operational with the Mirage 2000C-1 was Escadre de Chasse 1/2 "Cigognes" at Dijon on July 2, 1984. The Mirage 2000N, first flown on February 2, 1983, was developed as a replacement for the Mirage IIIE and is armed with the ASMP medium-range nuclear missile. Like its predecessors, the Mirage 2000 has been the subject of substantial export orders from Abu Dhabi, Egypt, Greece, India, and Peru. In Indian Air Force service the aircraft is known as the Varya (Thunderstreak).

The Mirage 2000, the first of the Mirage family to take advantage of "fly-by-wire" technology, was designed as an interceptor to replace the Mirage F.1. The type was formally adopted by the French Government on December 18, 1975 as the primary French Air Force combat aircraft from the mid-1980s.

▌ Dassault Mystère IIC

The Dassault MD452 Mystère IIC, which flew for the first time on February 23, 1951, was a straightforward swept-wing version of the Ouragan. Some 150 Mystère IIcs served with the French Air Force, and Israel had plans to purchase some in 1954–55, but in view of the type's poor service record—several of the earlier French machines having been lost through structural failure—it was decided to buy the far more promising Mystère IV instead.

▶ *The Dassault Mystère IIC, France's first operational swept-wing jet, was dogged by many problems and had a poor serviceability record.*

SPECIFICATION: Type fighter • Crew 1 • Powerplant one 6,613-lb (3,000-kg) thrust SNECMA Atar 101D3 turbojet • Max speed 658mph (1,060km/h) • Service ceiling 42,650ft (13,000m) • Max range 745 miles (1,200km) • Wingspan 42ft 9in (13.10m) • Length 38ft 6in (11.70m) • Height 13ft 11in (4.25m) • Weights 11,574lb (5,250kg) empty; 16,424lb (7,450kg) loaded • Armament two 1.19-in (30-mm) Hispano 603 cannon

▌ Dassault Mystère IVA

SPECIFICATION: Type fighter-bomber • Crew 1 • Powerplant one 6,283-lb (2,850-kg) thrust Hispano Suiza Tay 250A turbojet • Max speed 696mph (1,120km/h) • Service ceiling 45,000ft (13,750m) • Max range 820 miles (1,320km) • Wingspan 36ft 5in (11.10m) • Length 42ft 2in (12.90m) • Height 14ft 5in (4.40m) • Weights 12,952lb (5,875kg) empty; 20,950lb (9,500kg) loaded • Armament two 1.19-in (30-mm) DEFA 551 cannon; up to 2,000lb (907kg) of stores

The Dassault Mystère IV was unquestionably one of the finest combat aircraft of its era. Although developed from the Mystère IIC, it was in fact a completely new design. The prototype Mystère IVa flew for the first time on September 28, 1952, and early trials proved so promising that the French Government placed an order for 325 production aircraft six months later in April 1953. The fighter was also delivered to India, and Israel acquired the first of 60 in April 1956, the type replacing the Gloster Meteor F.8 in Israeli Air Force service. Production of the Mystère IVA was completed in 1958, with the 421st aircraft. A one-shot variant of the Mystère IV, the Mystère IVB, was fitted with an afterburning Rolls-Royce RA7R turbojet and became the first French aircraft to exceed the speed of sound in level flight. It served as a test bed for the next Dassault fighter, the Super Mystère B.2.

▌Dassault Ouragan

For the first few years of its post-World War II existence the French Air Force had no alternative but to rely on foreign jet aircraft, like the de Havilland Vampire, for its first-line equipment. However, on February 28, 1949 Avions Marcel Dassault flew the prototype of a straightforward, no-frills jet fighter that had begun as a private venture in November 1947. Powered by a Rolls-Royce Nene 102 turbojet, built under license by Hispano-Suiza, the Dassault MD.450 Ouragan (Hurricane) became the first jet fighter of French design to be ordered in quantity, some 350 production aircraft being delivered to the French Air Force starting in 1952. The Ouragan was exported to India, where it was known as the Toofani (Whirlwind), and to Israel, which received 75 examples. Although the Ouragan was inferior to

the MiG-15, the principal jet fighter type equipping the Egyptian Air Force at that time, it performed well in the ground attack role, leaving another French-built type—the Mystère IVA—to tackle the MiGs.

▼ *The Dassault Ouragan was France's first indigenous jet fighter, and was also exported to India and Israel. It performed well in the ground attack role.*

SPECIFICATION: Type fighter-bomber • Crew 1 • Powerplant one 5,070-lb (2,300-kg) Hispano-Suiza Nene 104B turbojet • Max speed 584mph (940km/h) • Service ceiling 49,210ft (15,000m) • Max range 620 miles (1,000km) • Wingspan 43ft 2in (13.20m) including tip tanks • Length 35ft 3in (10.74m) • Height 13ft 7in (4.15m) • Weights 9,150lb (4,150kg) empty; 16,755lb (7,600kg) loaded • Armament four 0.79-in (20-mm) Hispano 404 cannon; two 1,000-lb (434-kg) bombs, or 16 4.1-in (105-mm) rockets, or eight rockets and two 101-Imp gal (458-liter) napalm tanks

▌Dassault Rafale

France, originally a member of the European consortium that was set up to develop Eurofighter, decided to withdraw at an early stage and develop a smaller and lighter agile combat aircraft for the 21st century. The result was the Dassault Rafale (Squall). As with Eurofighter, a technology demonstrator was built; known as Rafale-A, this flew for the first time on July 4, 1986. Powered by two SNECMA M88-2 augmented turbofans, each rated at 16,424lb

(7,450kg) thrust with reheat, Rafale is a single-seat aircraft with a compound sweep delta wing, all-moving canard, single fin, and semivented intakes. It incorporates digital fly-by-wire,

▶ *Developed at huge cost, the Dassault Rafale is the result of France's "go it alone" policy, and is designed for both land- and carrier-based service.*

SPECIFICATION: Type multirole combat aircraft • Crew 1/2 • Powerplant two 16,424-lb (7,450-kg) SNECMA M88-2 turbofans • Max speed 1,324mph (2,130km/h) at high level • Service ceiling 55,000ft (16,765m) • Combat radius 1,152 miles (1,854km) air-air mission • Wingspan 35ft 9in (10.90m) • Length 50ft 2in (15.30m) • Height 17ft 6in (5.34m) • Weight 42,990lb (19,500kg) loaded • Armament one 1.19-in (30-mm) DEFA 791B cannon, up to 13,228lb (6,000kg) of external stores

relaxed stability, and electronic cockpit with voice command. Composites and aluminum-lithium will comprise over 50 percent of the production aircraft's airframe weight, resulting in a seven to eight percent weight saving.

In the strike role, Rafale can carry one Aerospatiale ASMP standoff nuclear bomb; in the interception role, armament is up to eight AAMs with either IR or active homing; and in the air-to-ground role, a typical load is 16 500-lb (227-kg) bombs, two AAMs, and two external fuel tanks. The aircraft is compatible with the full NATO arsenal of air-air and air-ground weaponry. Built-in armament comprises one 1.19-in (30-mm) DEFA cannon in the side

of the starboard engine duct. The aircraft has a maximum level speed of 2.0M at altitude and 864mph (1,390km/h) at low level. France, which plans to have 140 Rafales in air force service by 2015, sees the aircraft as vital to the defense of her territory. Low-level penetration combat radius with 12 550-lb (250-kg) bombs, four AAMs, and three external fuel tanks is 570 miles (1,055km).

The naval version, Rafale M, will equip France's carriers, while the Armée de l'Air will be equipped with 212 Rafale D (Discret, meaning stealthy). This variant features radar-absorbent paint, and a reprofiled fin-fuselage junction.

The first production Rafales were delivered in mid-2002.

▌Dassault Super Mystère B2

 FRANCE

This transonic successor to the Mystère IVA featured a thinner, more sharply swept wing, an improved intake, and modified cockpit. It flew for the first time on March 2, 1955, powered by the Avon RA7R, and on its fourth flight it exceeded Mach 1 on the level, becoming the first production aircraft of European design to do so. Super Mystère production totaled 180 aircraft, equipping two French Air Force escadres de chasse and two interceptor squadrons of the Israeli Air Force.

▶ *The Dassault Super Mystère B2 was the first French combat aircraft capable of exceeding Mach One in level flight.*

SPECIFICATION: Type fighter-bomber ● Crew 1 ● Powerplant one 9,833-lb (4,460-kg) thrust SNECMA Atar G-2/3 Turbojet ● Max speed 743mph (1,195km/h) at 39,370ft (12,000m) ● Service ceiling 55,775ft (17,000m) ● Max range 540 miles (870km) ● **Wingspan** 34ft 6in (10.52m) ● **Length** 46ft 4in (14.13m) ● Height 14ft 11in (4.55m) ● **Weight** 15,282lb (6,932kg) ● Armament two 1.19-in (30-mm) DEFA 551 cannon; internal Matra launcher for 35 SNEB 2.7-in (68-mm) rockets; up to 2,000lb (907kg) of external stores

▌Dassault/Dornier Alpha Jet

INTERNATIONAL

The Franco-German Alpha Jet was produced in two major versions, the Alpha Jet A (A for Appui, or support) light attack aircraft, and the Alpha Jet E (E for Ecole, or School) basic and advanced trainer. The E model, which also has a light attack capability, was produced for the French Air Force and a number of foreign customers, while deliveries of the A model to the Federal German Luftwaffe began in 1979. The French Air Force took delivery of 176 aircraft between 1978 and 1985, and export customers include Belgium, Cameroon, Cote d'Ivoire, Egypt, Morocco, Qatar, and Togo.

▲ *Produced jointly by France and Germany, the Alpha Jet has been in service since 1978, and has been the subject of several foreign orders.*

SPECIFICATION: Type light strike and reconnaissance aircraft (data Alpha Jet A) • Crew 2 • Powerplant two 2,976-lb (1,350-kg) Turbomeca Larzac 04 turbofans • Max speed 576mph (927km/h) • Service ceiling 45,930ft (14,000m) • Max range 363 miles (583km) hi-lo-hi • Wingspan 29ft 10in (9.11m) • Length 43ft 5in (13.23m) • Height 13ft 9in (4.19m) • Weight 17,637lb (8,000kg) loaded • Armament one 1-in (27-mm) IWKA Mauser cannon; up to 5,511lb (2,500kg) of ordnance on five fuselage hardpoints

▌de Havilland (Hawker Siddeley) Dominie T.Mk.1

GREAT BRITAIN

In 1963 the Royal Air Force ordered 20 Hawker Siddeley 125s (de Havilland having been absorbed into the Hawker Siddeley Group, although the "DH" prefix continued to be used for some time in US sales campaigns. The aircraft were Series 2s, similar to the 1B but with lower powered Viper 520 engines. Known in RAF service as the Dominie T.Mk.1, the aircraft were used as navigational trainers and operated by No. 6 Flying Training School at RAF Finningley near Doncaster, Yorkshire, replacing piston-engined Varsities. Starting in October 1973, Finningley was responsible for all nonpilot aircrew training in the RAF. Twelve Dominies (CC-1 to CC-3) were also purchased for fast communications duties.

SPECIFICATION: **Type** training and communications aircraft • **Crew** 2 •
Powerplant two Rolls-Royce Bristol Viper turbojets of 3,360lb (1,525kg)
thrust each • **Max speed** 450mph (724km/h) at 37,000ft (11,300m) • **Service
ceiling** 41,000ft (12,500m) • **Max range** 1,940 miles (3,120km) • **Wingspan** 47ft
(14.33m) • **Length** 47ft 5in (14.45m) • **Height** 16ft 6in (5.03m) • **Weight**
23,300lb (10,568kg) loaded • **Armament** none

▶ *The de Havilland Dominie provided RAF navigators and air electronics
officers with jet training experience.*

de Havilland Hornet and Sea Hornet

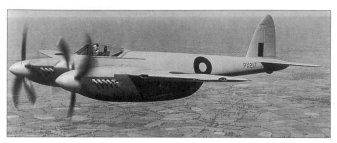

▲ *De Havilland's Hornet, especially in the F.Mk 1 form illustrated, was a
much lighter and more streamlined aircraft than the Mosquito.*

The de Havilland Hornet was the fastest twin piston-engined
fighter in the world, and perhaps the ultimate in British piston-engined fighter design. It began life as a private venture
in 1942 to meet the need for a long-range escort fighter for
service in the Far East, but major orders for the Hornet F.1
were canceled at the end of the war and only 60 were built,
entering RAF service in 1946. These were followed by 132

Hornet F.3s, which served with four first-line RAF air defense
squadrons until they were withdrawn in 1941. Many were
subsequently sent to the Far East, where they were used in the
ground attack role against communist terrorists in Malaya.
The naval version was the Sea Hornet F.Mk.20, 79 being
built, and the NF.MK.21 was a naval night fighter variant.
The last Hornet variant was the PR.Mk.22, with a battery of
cameras in place of armament. Total Sea Hornet production
was 187 aircraft, including prototypes.

SPECIFICATION: **Type** fighter (data Hornet F.3) **Crew** 1 **Powerplant** two 2,030hp
Rolls-Royce Merlin 130/131 liquid-cooled V-12 engines **Max speed** 466mph
(750km/h) at 22,000ft (6,705m) **Service ceiling** 37,500ft (11,430m) **Max range**
2,500 miles (4,022km) **Wing span** 45ft (13.71m) **Length** 36ft 8in (11.17m)
Height 14ft 2in (4.32m) **Weight** 16,100lb (7,303kg) loaded **Armament** four
0.79-in (20-mm) Hispano cannon; 2,000lb (907kg) of bombs or eight 60-lb
(27-kg) RPs

de Havilland Mosquito

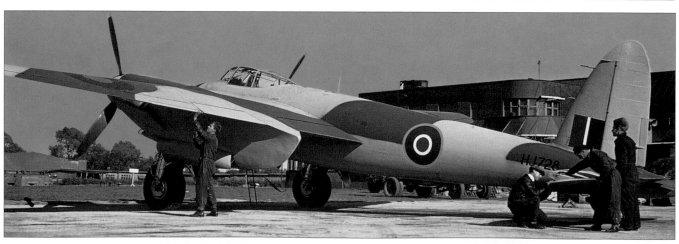

▲ *Produced in over 30 variants, the DH Mosquito was one of the most versatile aircraft of all time, remaining in service into the 1950s.*

▲ *A fine wartime color photograph of a Mosquito of No. 105 Squadron RAF, the first operational Mosquito bomber unit.*

Begun as a private venture, the first prototype of Geoffrey de Havilland's famous all-wood Mosquito, completed in bomber configuration, flew for the first time on November 25, 1940. The second prototype was completed as a photoreconnaissance aircraft and flew on June 10, 1941, while the third was equipped as a night fighter and made its first flight a few weeks earlier, on May 15, 1941.

The PR Mosquito was the first into service, being issued to No. 1 Photographic Reconnaissance Unit at RAF Benson, Oxfordshire in September 1941. The first operational sortie was flown on September 20th. The first Mosquito B.IV bombers went to No. 105 Squadron at Marham, Norfolk, in May 1942, and made their first operational sortie on the 31st. Five aircraft were sent to Cologne to photograph the damage caused by the previous night's 1,000-bomber raid and to drop a few bombs. One Mosquito was hit by flak and crashed in the North Sea. Total production of the B.IV, which eventually equipped 12 squadrons, was 273 aircraft.

The Mosquito NF.II night fighter prototype was completed with AI Mk IV radar in a "solid" nose and a powerful armament of four 0.79-in (20-mm) cannon and four machine guns. The first Mosquito fighter squadron, No. 157, formed at Debden in Essex on December 13, 1941. Seventeen squadrons were eventually armed with the NF.II, 466 of which were built. Ninety-seven Mk IIs were later converted to NF.Mk.XII standard with AI.Mk.VIII with centimetric radar; they were followed by 270 NF.Mk.XIIIs, the production counterpart of the Mk.XII. These and subsequent night fighter Mosquitoes retained only the 0.79-in (20-mm) cannon armament. Other specialist night fighter Mosquitoes were the Mks XV and XVII, 100 of which were converted from Mk IIs, and the NF.Mk.XIX. The latter aircraft, and the Mk XVII, were equipped with the US-made AI.Mk.X.

It was the Mosquito NF.Mk.II that provided the basis for the major production version, the FB.Mk.VI fighter-bomber, of which 2,718 were built during and after the war. The first Mk VI was a converted Mk II, and this flew for the first time in February 1943. The Mk.VI, armed with bombs and RPs, equipped some of Coastal Command's strike wings and also some squadrons of No. 2 Group, specializing in low-level precision attacks.

The Mosquito FB.Mk.XVIII (27 built) carried eight rockets and two 500-lb (227-kg) bombs, and was armed with a single 6-pdr (57-mm) gun in the nose. Known as the Mosquito "Tsetse," this variant was used by 248 and 254 squadrons. The first high-altitude bomber version was the B.IX (54 built), and this was followed by 387 examples of the B.XVI, fitted with a pressurized cabin. Its successor was the B.35, which did not become operational before the end of the war. The photoreconnaissance equivalents were the PR.IX, XVI, and 34. The last night fighter variant was the NF.30, which was similar to the Mk XIX, but with improved Merlins. Canadian Mosquito production, which ran to 1,134 aircraft, powered by Packard-built Merlins, included the Mks XX and 25 bombers, Mk 26 fighter-bomber, and Mks 22 and 27 trainers. Forty Canadian-built reconnaissance Mosquitoes were supplied to the USAAF as the F.8. Total Mosquito production reached 7,781 aircraft, 6,710 of which were built during the war years.

SPECIFICATION: Type fighter-bomber (data Mk.VI) • Crew 2 • Powerplant two 1,480hp Rolls-Royce Merlin 21 or 23 12-cylinder V-type engines • Max speed 370mph (595km/h) • Service ceiling 34,500ft (10,515m) • Max range 1,705 miles (2,744km) • Wingspan 54ft 2in (16.51m) • Length 42ft 11in (13.08m) • Height 17ft 5in (5.31m) • Weight 20,000lb (9,072kg) loaded • Armament four 0.79-in (20-mm) fixed forward-firing cannon and four 0.303-in (7.7-mm) fixed forward-firing machine guns in the nose, plus an internal and external load of bombs, RPs, or drop tanks of up to 2,000lb (907kg)

de Havilland Sea Vixen

The de Havilland Sea Vixen had its origin in the DH.110, which had competed with the Gloster Javelin for the RAF's all-weather fighter requirement. Carrier trials were carried out in 1956, a seminavalized DH.110 preproduction aircraft making the first full-stop arrested landing on board HMS Ark Royal on April 5, and the first fully navalized machine, equipped with folding wings and Rolls-Royce Avon 208 engines, flew on March 20, 1957. Known initially by the des-ignation FAW.20, the aircraft was officially named Sea Vixen later that year and redesignated FAW.1, the type being issued to three squadrons. In 1961, two FAW.1s were modified by the installation of additional fuel tanks in forward extensions of the tail booms, and these aircraft served as the prototypes for the FAW.2 variant, which was issued to operational squadrons in 1965. In 1968 an aerobatic team, known as Simon's Sircus, was formed with five Sea Vixen FAW.Mk 2s from No. 892 Squadron.

Total production of the Sea Vixen, which was retired in 1971, came to 120 Mk 1s and 30 Mk 2s, 67 Mk 1s being brought up to Mk 2 standard.

◀ *A de Havilland Sea Vixen pictured at the moment of launch from an aircraft carrier. The Sea Vixen was developed from the ill-fated DH.110.*

SPECIFICATION: Type all-weather strike fighter • Crew 2 • Powerplant two 11,230-lb (5,094-kg) thrust Rolls-Royce Avon 208 turbojets • Max speed 690mph (1,110km/h) at sea level • Service ceiling 48,000ft (14,640m) • Max range 600 miles (965km) FAW.1; 800 miles (1,287km) FAW.2 • **Wingspan** 51ft (15.54m) • Length 55ft 7in (17.02m) • Height 10ft 9in (3.28m) • Weight 41,575lb (18,858kg) loaded • Armament four Firestreak or Red Top AAMs, Bullpup ASMs on under-wing pylons

de Havilland Tiger Moth

Probably the most famous, and one of the most attractive, basic training aircraft of all time, the DH.82A Tiger Moth flew for the first time on October 26, 1931 and went into large-scale production almost immediately, mostly for the Royal Air Force. The majority of Tiger Moths were built to Air Ministry Specification T.26/33 as Tiger Moth Mk IIs, with a rear fuselage decking in plywood rather than fabric and stringers, and provision for an instrument training hood over the rear cockpit. By the end of World War II, 7,290 Tiger Moths had been produced, and large numbers of aircraft were sold on the civil market as war-surplus stock. A much-loved aircraft among hobby flyers, the Tiger Moth remains a common sight in the 21st century—a tribute to the type's durability and strength.

▶ *This Tiger Moth Mk II formation hailed from the Oxford University Air Squadron and was photographed in 1947.*

SPECIFICATION: Type training aircraft • Crew 2 • Powerplant one 130hp de Havilland Gipsy Major in-line engine • Max speed 104mph (167km/h) • Service ceiling 13,600ft (4,145m) • Max range 300 miles (483km) • **Wingspan** 29ft 4in (8.94m) • Length 23ft 11in (7.29m) • Height 8ft 10in (2.69m) • Weight 1,825lb (828kg) loaded • Armament none

de Havilland Vampire

▲ *This Vampire FB.Mk 5 demonstrates the type's distinctive twin-boom layout to good effect.*

Design work on the DH.100 Vampire, Britain's second jet fighter, began in May 1942, the prototype flying on September 20, 1943, and in the spring of 1944 it became the first Allied jet aircraft capable of sustained speeds of over 500mph (804km/h) over a wide altitude range. The first production Vampire flew in April 1945 and the Vampire F.1 was delivered to Nos. 247, 54, and 72 Squadrons in 1946 and 70 aircraft were delivered to Sweden. The Vampire Mk 2 was a Mk 1 airframe fitted with a Rolls-Royce Nene turbojet and did not enter service, only three being built. It was followed by the Vampire F.3, a long-range version with extra internal fuel, underwing tanks, and a de Havilland Goblin 2 turbojet; 85 were supplied to the RCAF, four to Norway, and 12 to

SPECIFICATION: Type fighter-bomber (data Vampire FB.5) • Crew 1 • Powerplant one 3,130-lb (1,420-kg) thrust de Havilland Goblin 2 turbojet • Max speed 548mph (882km/h) at 30,000ft (9,145m) • Service ceiling 44,000ft (13,410m) • Max range 1,220 miles (1,960km) • **Wingspan** 38ft (11.58m) • Length 30ft 9in (9.37m) • Height 8ft 10in (2.69m) • Weight 12,390lb (5,620kg) loaded • Armament four 0.79-in (20-mm) British Hispano cannon; up to 2,000lb (907kg) of bombs or RPs

Mexico, and the type was built under license in India.

The Nene-engined F.Mk.4 was to have been the production version of the Mk 2 and was developed into the F.30/31 built under license for the RAAF. The Vampire FB.5 was a ground attack version and was widely exported as the FB.52, being supplied to Egypt, Finland, Italy, New Zealand, Norway, South Africa, Sweden, and Venezuela. The FB.6 had an up-rated Goblin turbojet and was license-produced in Switzerland. The Vampire FB.9 was a tropicalized version of the FB.5, with an air-conditioned cockpit, and was used by the RAF, RNZAF, SAAF, RRAF, and India. The Vampire NF.10 was a night fighter, the T.11 a two-seat trainer, while the F.20 and F.21 were navalized versions. One of the biggest overseas Vampire users was France, which built the Nene-engined Vampire Mk 53 as the Mistral.

The number of Vampires produced in the UK totaled 1,900 when production ceased in 1953.

▲ *DH Vampire FB.5s lined up on an RAF airfield in the 1940s. The Vampire was easy to fly and was popular with pilots and ground crews alike.*

de Havilland Venom

The prototype de Havilland Venom, developed from the twin-boom Vampire and originally known as the Vampire FB.Mk 8, first flew on September 2, 1949 and series production began with the FB.1, of which 373 were built. The definitive version was the FB.4, which flew in December 1953; 150 were supplied to the RAF, 250 were license-built in Switzerland and others were exported to Iraq and Venezuela. The Swiss-built aircraft per-

formed remarkably well in the mountain valleys, and were not retired until 1983.

Two night fighter variants, the NF.2 and NF.3, appeared in

SPECIFICATION: Type fighter-bomber (data Venom FB.4) • Crew 1 • Powerplant one 5,150-lb (2,336-kg) (de Havilland Ghost 105 turbojet) • Max speed 640mph (1,030km/h) • Service ceiling 48,000ft (14,630m) • Max range 1,075 miles (1,730km) • Wingspan 41ft 8in (12.70m) including tip tanks • Length 31ft 10in (9.71m) • Height 6ft 2in (1.88m) • Weight 15,310lb (6,945kg) loaded • Armament four 0.79-in (20-mm) British Hispano cannon; two 1,000-lb (454-kg) bombs or eight 60-lb (27.2-kg) RPs

1950 and 1953 respectively. Sweden acquired 62 NF.51s between 1952 and 1957, these being designated J.33 in Swedish AF service. The type was produced for the Royal Navy as the Sea Venom FAW 20, FAW 21, and FAW 22, 256 being built; Sea Venoms were also built under license in France as the Aquilon (North Wind). RAF and Royal Navy Venoms and Sea Venoms saw action during the Suez campaign of 1956.

de Havilland (Canada) DHC-5 Buffalo

▲ Buffalos fly on with No. 442 Sqn, Canadian Armed Forces, where their STOL performance is utilized during SAR operations in British Columbia.

Developed in response to a US Army requirement for a tactical transport, the DHC-5 Buffalo was an enlarged version of the Caribou, the prototype flying in April 1964. Designated CC-115 in the Canadian Armed Forces and C-8A in US Army service, the aircraft was used extensively in Vietnam. Examples were also supplied to Brazil and Peru.

SPECIFICATION: Type tactical transport • Crew 3 (plus 41 passengers) • Powerplant two 3,133hp General Electric CT64-820-4 turboprops • Max speed 290mph (467km/h) at 10,000ft (3,050m) • Service ceiling 31,000ft (9,450m) • Max range 691 miles (1,112km) • Wingspan 96ft (29.26m) • Length 79ft (24.08m) • Height 28ft 8in (8.73m) • Weights 24,190lb (10,972kg) empty; 49,200lb (22,316kg) loaded • Armament none

Dewoitine D.27

Although the French designer Emile Dewoitine went on to produce some fine fighter aircraft in the 1930s, business was so poor in the years after World War I that he was forced to close down his business in France and move to Switzerland in 1927. In the following year he produced the D.27 parasol monoplane fighter, 66 of which were built for the Swiss Army starting in 1931. The D27 was also license-built in Romania

and Yugoslavia. A strengthened version, the D53, was tested in France, and seven were used experimentally by naval Escadrille 7C1, operating from the carrier Béarn.

▲ This reconditioned D.27 shows to good effect the type's parasol layout and retractable undernose radiator installation.

SPECIFICATION: Type fighter • Crew 1 • Powerplant one 500hp Hispano-Suiza 12Mc 12-cylinder liquid-cooled V-type • Max speed 194mph (312km/h) • Service ceiling 30,185ft (9,200m) • Max range 373 miles (600km) • Wingspan 32ft 2in (9.80m) • Length 21ft 4in (6.50m) • Height 9ft 2in (2.79m) • Weight 3,046lb (1,382kg) • Armament two 0.30-in (7.5-mm) fixed forward-firing machine guns

Dewoitine D.500/510

France's first cantilever low-wing monoplanes were those of the handsome, all-metal Dewoitine D.500 series. The prototype D.500 flew on June 18, 1932, and development culmi-

nated in the D.510, which flew in August 1934. The D.510 in particular enjoyed considerable success; in addition to serving with the Armée de l'Air it was widely exported, and

Chinese D.510s saw action against the Japanese in the summer of 1938. France received 99 D.500s, 143 D.501s (which differed only from the D.500 in having no propeller spinner), and 88 D.510s. The D.510 was an upgraded version with a more powerful Vee engine, which allowed a machine gun to fire through the hollow propeller shaft. The last unit to fly the Dewoitine was Escadrille I/6 at Dakar, West Africa, which relinquished its six D.501s in 1941.

SPECIFICATION: Type fighter • Crew 1 • Powerplant one 690hp Hispano-Suiza 12Kbrs 12-cylinder liquid-cooled V-type • Max speed 223mph (359km/h) • Service ceiling 33,465ft (10,200m) • Max range 535 miles (860km) • Wingspan 39ft 4in (12m) • Length 25ft 5in (7.74m) • Weight 3,770lb (1,710kg) loaded • Armament four 0.30-in (7.5-mm) MAC 1934 machine guns (D.500/501); one engine-mounted 0.79-in (20-mm) HS9 cannon and two wing-mounted 0.30-in (7.5-mm) machine guns (D.510)

▲ The Dewoitine D.510 was one of France's inter-war success stories, being widely exported as well as equipping the bulk of the Armée de l'Air's fighter squadrons.

∎ Dewoitine D.520

FRANCE

◀ The D.520 was the best fighter produced by France before her defeat in June 1940, and also saw action during the 1941 Syrian campaign.

Design of the D.520 fighter began in 1936 as a private venture, the first prototype flying on October 2, 1938. An initial order for 200 was placed in April 1939, and the eventual total on order up to April 1940 was 2,200 for the Armée de l'Air and 120 for the Aéronavale. When the Germans struck in the west on May 10, 1940 only 36 D.520s had been delivered, and these were operational with GC I/3. Four more groupes de chasse and three naval escadrilles rearmed with the type before France's surrender, but only GC I/3, II/7, II/6, and the naval AC 1 saw any action. The D.520 groupes claimed 114 victories and 39 probables; 85 D.520s were lost. 165 D.520s were evacuated to North Africa and a further 180 machines were built after the armistice, bringing the production total to 905.

SPECIFICATION: Type fighter • Crew 1 • Powerplant one 930hp Hispano-Suiza 12Y-45 12-cylinder V-type • Max speed 336mph (540km/h) • Service ceiling 36,090ft (11,000m) • Max range 957 miles (1,540km) • Wingspan 33ft 5in (10.20m) • Length 28ft 8in (8.76m) • Height 8ft 5in (2.56m) • Weights 4,685lb (2,125kg) empty; 6,151lb (2,790kg) loaded • Armament one HS 404 0.79-in (20-mm) fixed forward-firing cannon in the nose; four 0.30-in (7.5-mm) machine guns in wing leading edges

∎ DFW B.I

GERMANY

The DFW (Deutsche Flugzeugwerke) B.I was one of the earliest German biplanes to see service in World War I, and although it was a biplane its wing planform reflected that of the Etrich Taube monoplane, a design dating back to 1910. The DFW B.I flew very well and was popular with its pilots, the type remaining in first-line service until 1915.

SPECIFICATION: Type reconnaissance biplane • Crew 2 • Powerplant one 100hp Mercedes 6-cylinder in-line engine • Max speed 75mph (120km/h) • Service ceiling 9,840ft (3,000m) • Endurance 4hrs • Wingspan 45ft 11in (14m) • Length 27ft 6in (8.40m) • Height 9ft 10in (3m) • Weight 2,333lb (1,015kg) loaded • Armament none

■ DFW C.V

GERMANY

▲ *The DFW C.V was widely used for ground attack as well as reconnaissance, and was able to defend itself against Allied fighters.*

SPECIFICATION: **Type** reconnaissance biplane • **Crew** 2 • **Powerplant** one 200hp Benz Bz IV 6-cylinder liquid-cooled in-line • **Max speed** 97mph (155km/h) • **Service ceiling** 16,405ft (5,000m) • **Endurance** 3hrs 30mins • **Wingspan** 43ft 6in (13.27m) • **Length** 25ft 10in (7.87m) • **Height** 10ft 8in (3.25m) • **Weight** 3,146lb (1,430kg) loaded • **Armament** two 0.30-in (7.5-mm) Parabellum machine guns in observer's cockpit

The highly successful DFW C.V, which appeared in the summer of 1916, was the most numerous aircraft built in Germany during World War I. Over 1,000 examples were produced, and it remained in operational use up to the first months of 1918. Derived from, and faster than, the preceding C.IV, it had very good flight characteristics, being able to out-maneuver even the most modern Allied fighters in the hands of a skilled pilot, and as a result it was extremely popular with its crews.

■ Dornier Do 17

GERMANY

▲ *The Dornier Do 17Z could easily be distinguished from earlier versions of the bomber by its extensively glazed cockpit and "beetle eye" glazed nose.*

Designed as a fast mailplane for Deutsche Lufthansa and first flown in 1934, the Dornier Do 17 was not adopted for this task after three single-finned aircraft had been evaluated. It was then developed as a high-speed bomber with twin fins, 12 prototypes being built and tested. The first military examples, the Do 17E-1 and Do 17F-1, entered service in 1939 and were intended for the high-speed bomber and long-range

reconnaissance roles respectively, the latter having extra fuel tankage and two bomb-bay cameras. These aircraft were powered by two BMW VI 12-cylinder V-type engines and were evaluated in combat during the Spanish Civil War.

Development of the Do 17E/F led to the Do 17M/P medium bomber/reconnaissance types with Bramo 323 radial engines. These were followed by 18 Do 17S/U preproduction types, which preceded the introduction of the definitive radial-engined variant, the Do 17Z with its glazed nose and cockpit, over 500 of which were built. Although faster than most contemporary fighters when it entered service, the Do 17 quickly became obsolescent and suffered heavy losses in the battles of France and Britain.

SPECIFICATION: **Type** medium bomber (Do 17Z) • **Crew** 4–5 • **Powerplant** two 1,000hp BMW Bramo 323P Fafnir 9-cylinder radials • **Max speed** 255mph (410km/h) • **Service ceiling** 26,905ft (8,200m) • **Max range** 932 miles (1,500km) • **Wingspan** 59ft (18m) • **Length** 51ft 10in (15.80m) • **Height** 15ft 1in (4.60m) • **Weight** 18,937lb (8,590kg) loaded • **Armament** one or two 7.92-mm (0.31-in) trainable machine guns in the windscreen, nose, dorsal, and ventral positions; internal bomb load of 2,205lb (1,000kg)

■ Dornier Do 18

The Do 18 was designed to fulfill the dual role of medium-range maritime reconnaissance aircraft to replace the Dornier Wal, and as a mailplane flying boat for service with Deutsche Lufthansa. The first of four prototypes flew in March 1935 and only six civilian boats were completed, most of the 148 production aircraft being assigned to military service from 1938. The principal military variants were the Do 18D (75 aircraft) with 600hp Junkers Jumo 205D Diesel engines; the Do 18G, which was an improved Do 18D with revised armaments and provision for rocket-assisted takeoff; and the Do 18H trainer. Production of the Do 18G and Do 18H ran to 71 aircraft, and many Do 18Gs were converted to Do 18N standard for service in the air-sea rescue role. The

Do 18 played a part in all the early skirmishes between the Royal Navy and the Kriegsmarine in the North Sea area during the early months of World War II.

SPECIFICATION: Type maritime reconnaissance flying boat • Crew 4 • Powerplant two 880hp Junkers Jumo 205D six-cylinder horizontally opposed Diesel engines • Max speed 166mph (267km/h) • Service ceiling 13,780ft (4,200m) • Max range 2,175 miles (3,500km) • Wingspan 77ft 9in (23.70m) • Length 63ft 7in (19.37m) • Height 17ft 5in (5.32m) • Weight 23,809lb (10,800kg) loaded • Armament one 0.79-in (20-mm) trainable rearward-firing cannon in dorsal turret, and one 0.50-in (13-mm) forward-firing machine gun in the bow position; external bomb load of 220lb (100kg)

■ Dornier Do 22

The Dornier Do 22 reconnaissance bomber and torpedo-carrying floatplane was developed in 1934 by the Swiss subsidiary of the Dornier-Werke at Altenheim, where two prototypes were built. The type was not ordered by the Luftwaffe, and production aircraft were built for export only, being purchased by Latvia, Greece, and Yugoslavia. A landplane variant was also developed. Twelve Do 22 floatplanes were supplied to the Royal Yugoslav Naval Air Service, and four of these escaped to Egypt in April 1941, continuing operations with Allied forces in the Mediterranean.

SPECIFICATION: Type reconnaissance bomber and torpedo floatplane • Crew 3 • Powerplant one 860hp Hispano-Suiza 12Ybrs in-line engine • Max speed 217mph (350km/h) at 9,840ft (3,000m) • Service ceiling 29,520ft (9,000m) • Max range 1,428 miles (2,300km) • Wingspan 53ft 1in (16.20m) • Length 43ft (13.12m) • Height 15ft 10in (4.80m) • Weight 8,820lb (4,000kg) loaded • Armament four 0.31-in (7.9-mm) machine guns; one torpedo or equivalent bomb load

▲ The Do 22's rear cockpit housed a gunner and a radio operator, whose position in the front half of this cockpit was protected by a glazed canopy.

▌Dornier Do 24

The Dornier Do 24 flying boat was designed in 1935 to fulfill a requirement of the Royal Netherlands Naval Air Service. Three prototypes were begun and the first flight was made on July 3, 1937 by the Do 24V-3 D-ADLR. The Netherlands Navy

SPECIFICATION: Type maritime reconnaissance and air-sea rescue flying boat ● Crew 4-5 ● Powerplant three 1,000hp BMW-Bramo Fafnir radials (BMW 301R) ● Max speed 211mph (340km/h) at 9,840ft (3,000m) ● Service ceiling 19,352ft (5,900m) ● Max range 1,801 miles (2,900km) ● Wingspan 88ft 7in (27m) ● Length 72ft 2in (22m) ● Height 18ft 10in (5.75m) ● Weight 39,249lb (17,800kg) loaded ● Armament one 0.79-in (20-mm) trainable cannon in dorsal turret; one 0.31-in (7.9-mm) trainable machine gun in bow turret and one in tail turret

received eleven Do 24Ks built in Germany and another 25 aircraft built under license in Holland. In 1940 the invading German forces used some of the Dutch-built aircraft for air-sea rescue duties under the designation Do 24N, and in 1941 production of the Do 24T transport and reconnaissance version resumed. To supply more flying boats by the Luftwaffe, the Chantiers Aero-Maritimes de la Seine (CAMS) factory at Sartrouville, France, began production of the Do 24T, producing about 50 complete and partially complete aircraft up to liberation. All the Do 24Ts were eventually completed, and those that did not go to the Luftwaffe were used by the French Navy until 1953. The Dutch Do 24s saw action in the Far East in 1941, and 12 ex-German Do 24T-3s were used for many years by the Spanish Navy's air-sea rescue group.

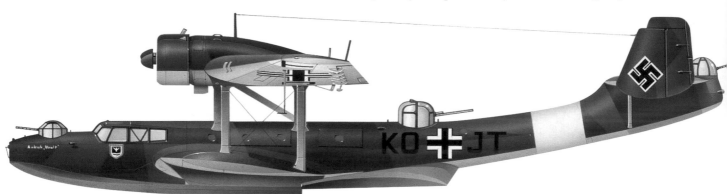

▌Dornier Do 217

Although the Dornier Do 217 was a redesign, it was in essence a larger and more powerful version of its predecessor, the Dornier Do 17. The first production series was produced in several variants, the first being the Do 217E-1, which appeared at the end of 1940. It was followed by the E-2 and E-3, which differed in their defensive armament and were intended for dive-bombing. Other subvariants included E-2/R-4 torpedo

SPECIFICATION: Type bomber (Do 217E-2) ● Crew 4 ● Powerplant two 1,580hp BMW 801ML 14-cylinder radials ● Max speed 320mph (515km/h) ● Service ceiling 29,530ft (9,000m) ● Range 1,740 miles (2,800km) ● Wingspan 62ft 4in (19m) ● Length 59ft 8in (18.20m) ● Height 16ft 6in (5.03m) ● Weight 36,299lb (16,465kg) loaded ● Armament one 0.59-in (15-mm) cannon in lower port side of nose, one 0.50-in (13-mm) MG in dorsal turret, and one in ventral step position, one 0.31-in (7.92-mm) machine gun in nose and one in each cockpit side window; bomb load of 8,818lb (4,000kg)

▼ *First of the truly effective Do 217 night fighters, the Do 217J-2 featured radar and a powerful nose-mounted armament.*

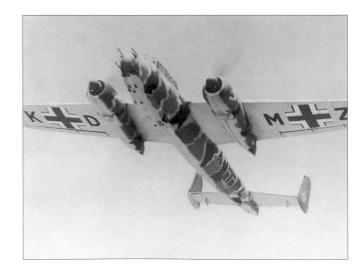

bomber, the E-2/R10 maritime patrol aircraft, and the E-5, which was capable of carrying radio-guided air-to-surface missiles. Other variants produced after 1941 were the Do 217J and N night fighters; the Do 217K, which had a redesigned nose and a heavier defensive armament; and Do 217M, which like the N was fitted with Daimler-Benz in-line engines.

▮Dornier Do 335

GERMANY

▲ The unorthodox Dornier Do 335 was a formidable combat aircraft, but like other German types came too late to influence the outcome of the air war.

The Dornier Do 335 heavy fighter was one of the more unconventional designs to emerge from World War II, and

SPECIFICATION: Type heavy fighter • Crew 1 • Powerplant one 1,750hp DB 603A-2 in-line engine in the nose and one in the tail • Max speed 474mph (763km/h) at 21,000ft (6,400m) • Service ceiling 37,400ft (11,400m) • Max range 858 miles (1,380km) • Wingspan 45ft 3in (13.80m) • Length 45ft 5in (13.85m) • Height 16ft 4in (95m) • Weight 21,186lb (9,610kg) loaded • Armament one 1.19-in (30-mm) MK 103 cannon firing through the spinner and two 15-mm MG 151/15 cannon mounted above the front engine; provision for one 1,102-lb (500-kg) bomb in internal bay aft of the cockpit

was in production when the war ended. It was powered by two DB 603 engines mounted in tandem, one forward and one aft with the cockpit in between. Armed with 1.19-in (30-mm) cannon, the Do 335 was capable of 470mph (760km/h), and would have presented the Allies with a formidable challenge had it been available in quantity some months earlier.

The prototype Do 335V-1 flew for the first time in September 1943 and the first Do 335A-1 production aircraft were delivered for operational evaluation early in 1945. Some of the prototypes were completed as two-seat night fighters.

▮Douglas AD Skyraider

UNITED STATES

Designed in 1944 and intended as a potent carrier-borne attack aircraft for use in the projected invasion of Japan, the prototype XBT2D-1 Skyraider flew for the first time on March 18, 1945 and an order was placed for 548 AD-1 production aircraft, this being reduced to 277 after VJ-Day. The last 36 AD-1s were completed as AD-1Q radar countermeasures aircraft. A much improved model, the AD-2, appeared in 1948; 156 were delivered, together with 22 AD-2Q countermeasures aircraft. Further modifications resulted in the AD-3; total production was 194 aircraft, including 125 basic AD-3s, 23 AD-3Qs, 15 AD-3Ns for night attack, and 31 AD-3W early warning aircraft. By mid-1949 the AD-3 had

▲ A Skyraider of Navy Attack Squadron VA-728 preparing to take off for an attack on a target in North Korea in 1950.

been replaced on the production line by the AD4, which was equipped with APS-19A radar and a P-1 autopilot. By the time AD-4 production ended in 1953, 1,032 aircraft had been delivered. Forty AD-4W early warning aircraft were supplied to the Royal Navy as the Skyraider AEW.1. A further variant

SPECIFICATION: Type naval attack aircraft (data AD-6) • Crew 1 • Powerplant one 2,700hp Wright R-3350-26W Cyclone 18-cylinder radial • Max speed 322mph (518km/h) • Service ceiling 28,500ft (8,690m) • Max range 1,143 miles (1,840km) • Wingspan 50ft (15.24m) • Length 38ft 10in (11.83m) • Height 15ft 8in (4.77m) • Weight 25,000lb (11,340kg) loaded • Armament four wing-mounted 0.79-in (20-mm) cannon; 8,000lb (3,628kg) of bombs

of the basic AD-4 was the AD-4B, which had four wing-mounted 0.79-in (20-mm) cannon and which could carry nuclear weapons. The Skyraider played a prominent part in the Korean War, going into action for the first time on July 3, 1950 from the USS *Valley Forge*.

The AD-5 multirole version of the Skyraider (670 built) was followed by the AD-6, which was specially equipped for low-level attack, and the AD-7, which had an improved engine and further structural strengthening. Deliveries ended in February 1957 after 713 AD-6s and 72 AD-7s had been built. A much-modified version of the Skyraider, the A-1, was widely used in the ground attack role during the Vietnam War.

▌Douglas A3D Skywarrior

SPECIFICATION: Type carrier-borne strategic bomber (data A3D-2) • Crew 3 • Powerplant two 12,400-lb (5,635-kg) Pratt & Whitney J57-P-10 turbojets • Max speed 610mph (982km/h) at 10,000ft (3,050m) • Service ceiling 43,000ft (13,110m) • Max range 2,000 miles (3,220km) • Wingspan 72ft 6in (22.10m) • Length 76ft 4in (23.30m) • Height 23ft 6in (7.16m) • Weight 82,000lb (37,195kg) loaded • Armament two remotely controlled 0.79-in (20-mm) cannon in tail turret, plus provision for 12,000lb (5,443kg) of conventional or nuclear weapons in internal bomb bay

▲ *EA-3Bs of VQ-1 flew electronic reconnaissance and Comint missions during the Vietnam War.*

First flown on October 28, 1952, the Douglas A3D (later A-3) Skywarrior was the first carrier-borne bomber designed for strategic nuclear strike, and was intended to operate from the US Navy's Forrestal-class carriers. Deliveries of production

A3D-1s began in the latter half of 1954, this version being replaced by the structurally strengthened A3D-2, which entered service with the US Pacific Fleet early in 1957. Variants were the A3D-2P photoreconnaissance aircraft, the A3D-2Q ELINT aircraft, and the A3D-2T trainer. The Skywarrior—its variants redesignated A-3A, A-3B, RA-3B, EA-3B, and TA-3B in 1962—remained in first-line service until the late 1960s.

▌Douglas A-4 Skyhawk

The prototype XA4D-1 Skyhawk flew on June 22, 1954, and the first of 165 production A4D-1 Skyhawks were delivered to Attack Squadron VA-27 on September 27, 1956. They were replaced on the production line by the A4D-2, production of which ran to 542 examples. The next Skyhawk to appear was the A4D-2N, which had a lengthened nose to accommodate terrain clearance radar. The variant also featured a rocket-boosted low-level ejection seat. Deliveries to the USN began in 1959 and ended in 1962 after 638 aircraft had been built. In July 1961 another variant, the A4D-5 (later redesignated

▲ *One of the most versatile combat aircraft ever built, the A-4 Skyhawk gave remarkable service over Vietnam, and could absorb incredible battle damage.*

▲ *Two-seat Skyhawks provided carrier-capable training facilities for USN/USMC aircrew from 1966 until their retirement in 1999.*

A-4E) made its appearance, with an up-rated engine, greater offensive load and a 27 percent range increase. Five hundred were built. The next variant, the A-4F, was an attack bomber with a J52-P-8A turbojet, heavily armored cockpit, and updated avionics housed in a "hump" aft of the cockpit. Production was completed in 1968 after 146 machines had been built. The TA-4F was a tandem two-seat trainer, and the A-4G and TA-4G were similar aircraft supplied to the Royal Australian Navy. The A-4H was a variant supplied to Israel, the TA-4J was a simplified version of the TA-4F, the A-4K was a variant for the RNZAF, and the A-4M was developed for the USMC. During the 1960s the Skyhawk equipped some 40 USN and USMC squadrons, and saw extensive action during the Vietnam War. About 40 percent of Israel's Skyhawks were lost during the Yom Kippur war of 1973, but this attrition was made good by the delivery of A-4N Skyhawk IIs, a light attack version. The A-4Y was an updated A-4M for the USMC. The 2,900th Skyhawk was delivered in 1977. Skyhawks were supplied to Singapore and Argentina, which used them during the Falklands war of 1982.

SPECIFICATION: Type carrier-borne attack bomber (data A-4E) • Crew 1 • Powerplant one 8,500-lb (3,855-kg) thrust Pratt & Whitney J52-P-6 turbojet • Max speed 685mph (1,102km/h) at sea level • Service ceiling 49,000ft (14,935m) • Max range 920 miles (1,480km) • Wingspan 27ft 6in (8.38m) • Length 40ft 1in (12.21m) • Height 15ft 2in (4.62m) • Weight 24,500lb (11,113kg) loaded • Armament two 0.79-in (20-mm) cannon; 8,200lb (3,719kg) of external ordnance

▌Douglas A-17/DB-8

UNITED STATES

The Douglas A-17 originated in the Northrop YA-13 attack bomber of 1934. The YA-13 became the YA-16 and ultimately the YA-17; 110 production A-17s for the USAAC were followed by 129 A-17As, which featured a retractable main undercarriage. In August 1937 the Northrop Corporation became the El Segundo Division of the Douglas company, so although the A-17 and A-17A attack aircraft used by the US Army retained the Northrop name, the export version of the aircraft was designated Douglas DB-8A. The fixed-undercarriage DB-8A-1 was built under license in Sweden; the similar

DB-8A-2 was supplied to Argentina; and the DB-8A-3, with a retractable undercarriage, was supplied to the Netherlands Army Air Corps. DB-8A variants were also supplied to Iraq, Norway, and Peru, while 61 A-17As were supplied to the RAF, who passed them on to South Africa. France received 32 examples before she was overrun.

▲ *In its production form the A-17 featured cutaway spats for its main undercarriage, the undercarriage legs themselves being faired with large "trousers".*

SPECIFICATION: Type attack bomber (data A-17A) • Crew 3 • Powerplant one 825hp Pratt & Whitney R-1535-13 engine • Max speed 206mph (331km/h) • Service ceiling 20,700ft (6,313m) • Max range 800 miles (1,287km) • Wingspan 47ft 9in (14.56m) • Length 31ft 8in (9.65m) • Height 12ft (3.66m) • Weight 7,550lb (3,425kg) loaded • Armament four wing-mounted 0.30-in (7.62-mm) machine guns and one in rear cockpit; bomb load of up to 1,200lb (544kg)

▎Douglas DB-7 Series

The Douglas DB-7 attack bomber series began with the Model 7A, submitted in response to a USAAC requirement of 1938. The first prototype, designated Model 7B and featuring a tricycle undercarriage, flew on October 26, 1939; 100 examples were ordered by France in February 1940 and 186, designated A-20 and A-20A, by the USAAC three months later. These, with the manufacturer's designation DB-7, had a narrower and deeper fuselage than the original model. The French order was subsequently increased to 270 DB-7s and 100 DB-7As, the latter having 1,600hp Wright Cyclone engines. France fell after 115 aircraft had been delivered, 95 of these surviving in North Africa; the rest were diverted to Britain, where they were converted into Havoc night fight-

SPECIFICATION: Type light attack bomber (data A-20G) • Crew 3 • Powerplant two 1,700hp Wright R-2600-13 14-cylinder radials • Max speed 339mph (546km/h) at 10,000ft (3,050m) • Service ceiling 23,700ft (7,225m) • Max range 2,100 miles (3,380km) • Wingspan 61ft 4in (18.69m) • Length 47ft 11in (14.63m) • Height 17ft 7in (5.36m) • Weight 27,200lb (12,338kg) • Armament six 0.50-in (12.7-mm) machine guns in the nose, two in dorsal position, and one in ventral position; bomb load of 4,000lb (1,814kg)

ers/intruders with "solid" noses mounting up to 12 0.303-in (7.7-mm) machine guns. The USAAC also converted 60 A-20s into P-70 "stopgap" night fighters. The RAF ultimately received 781 aircraft, named Boston III, while 808 similar aircraft were produced for the USAAC/USAAF as the A-20C. Of these, 202 went to the RAF as the Boston IIIA. Next major variant was the A-20G, 2850 being built with the "solid" nose of the fighter variants and an increased bomb-carrying capacity. Later variants were the A-20J (450 built) and A-20K (413), which had a molded plastic transparent nose; these were designated Boston IV and V in RAF service. Total production of the DB-7 series, including the fighter variants, was 7,385, almost half of this output going to the Soviet Union.

◀ *Havoc Mk I (Turbinlite) aircraft were fitted with a 2,700-million candlepower spotlight in the nose.*

▎Douglas A-26 Invader

First flown in July 1942, the A-26 Invader was ordered in three variants: the A-26 three-seat attack bomber, the A-26A two-seat night fighter and intruder, and the A-26B three-seat heavy assault aircraft with a battery of machine guns in a solid nose. The A-26B, of which 1,355 were built, was the fastest US bomber of WWII and entered combat in both European and Pacific theaters in November 1944. The other production model of the A-26 to see service in WWII was the A-26C, of which 1,091 were delivered. The redesignated B-26B and

SPECIFICATION: Type three-seat light attack bomber (data A-26B) • Crew 3 • Powerplant two 2,000hp Pratt & Whitney R-2800-27 18-cylinder radials • Max speed 355mph (571km/h) at 10,000ft (3,050m) • Service ceiling 22,100ft (6,735m) • Max range 1,300 miles (2,092km) • Wingspan 70ft (21.34m) • Length 50ft 7in (15.42m) • Height 18ft 6in (5.64m) • Weight 28,423lb (12,893kg) • Armament six 0.50-in (12.7-mm) machine guns mounted in nose; two in dorsal barbette; two in ventral barbette (optional); bomb load of 6,000lb (2,722kg)

B-26C both saw extensive service as night intruders during the Korean War. Some were supplied to France and were used in Indo-China postwar, while 70 were converted to B-26K standard for counterinsurgency operations over Vietnam.

▲ *A battle-damaged B-26 making an emergency landing at an airstrip in Korea. B-26 intruders carried out fierce night attacks on enemy convoys.*

Douglas B-18

USA

SPECIFICATION: Type medium-heavy bomber (data B-18A) • Crew 5 •
Powerplant two 1,000hp Wright R-1820-53 Cyclone 9-cylinder radials • Max
speed 215mph (346km/h) at 10,000ft (3,050m) • Service ceiling 23,900ft
(7,285m) • Max range 1,200 miles (1,931km) • Wingspan 89ft 6in (27.28m) •
Length 57ft 10in (17.63m) • Height 15ft 2in (4.62m) • Weight 27,673lb
(12,552kg) loaded • Armament one 0.30-in (7.62-mm) machine gun in nose,
dorsal, and ventral positions; up to 6,500lb (2,948kg) of bombs

The Douglas B-18 (DB-1) was a medium-heavy bomber
evolved from the DC-3 commercial transport and winner of
the 1936 USAAC bomber competition. A total of 133 B-18s
and 217 improved B-18As were produced. Twenty were
transferred to the Royal Canadian Air Force, in whose service
the type was known as the Digby I. In 1939–40 122 B-18As
were converted to B-18B standard by the installation of specialist radio equipment for maritime patrols, two aircraft
being transferred to the Brazilian Air Force. The B-18 ended
its career as a paratroop trainer.

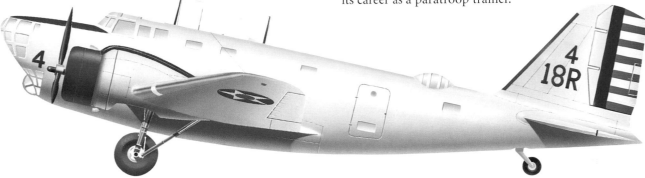

Douglas B-23 Dragon

USA

The Douglas B-23 Dragon medium bomber was first projected in November 1938 to supersede the B-22, which in
effect was to have been an up-rated B-18A. Featuring a greatly improved aerodynamic form and the latest American ideas
on bomber defensive armament, the B-23 was the first

American bomber to carry a tail gunner. There was no prototype, and the first of 38 production B-23s flew on July 27,
1939, by which time they were already obsolete. Twelve were
converted to UC-67 transport configuration, and the rest
were relegated to glider towing and training.

▶ *Born out of an effort to reverse the B-18's failure to compete effectively
with the B-17, the B-23 failed to show any improvement in performance.*

SPECIFICATION: Type medium bomber • Crew 6 • Powerplant two 1,600hp Wright
2600-3 Cyclone radials • Max speed 282mph (454km/h) at 10,000ft (3,050m) •
• Service ceiling 31,600ft (9,638m) • Max range 1,455 miles (2,341km) •
Wingspan 92ft (28.06m) • Length 58ft 4in (17.79m) • Height 18ft 6in (5.64m) •
Weight 30,437lb (13,806kg) loaded • Armament one 0.30-in (7.62-mm)
machine gun in each of nose, ventral, and dorsal positions, and one 0.50-in
(12.7-mm) machine gun in tail; up to 4,000lb (1,812kg) of bombs

Douglas B-66

USA

In 1953, Douglas received an order from the USAF to modi-
fy the A3D as a land-based reconnaissance and bomber aircraft, and five RB-66As were produced for service evaluation

in 1954. These were followed by the first production version,
the B-66B (72 built), which began to replace the Martin B-57
Canberra in the USAF's tactical bomber wings starting in

March 1956. It was preceded slightly by the RB-66B reconnaissance aircraft, of which 145 examples were built; this being followed by the RB-66C and the WB-66D (77 built of both subtypes), the latter a specialized weather reconnaissance version. The RB-66C equipped two tactical reconnais-

sance wings. Many existing B-66/RB-66 aircraft were modified for the electronic warfare role as EB-66s and saw action in the Vietnam War.

SPECIFICATION: Type tactical reconnaissance aircraft (data RB-66B) • Crew 3 • Powerplant two 10,200-lb (4,627-kg) thrust Allison J71-A-11 turbojets • Max speed 631mph (1,015km/h) at 36,000ft (10,973m) • Service ceiling 38,900ft (11,855m) • Max range 2,000 miles (3,220km) • Wingspan 72ft 6in (22.10m) • Length 75ft 2in (22.90m) • Height 23ft 7in (7.19m) • Weight 83,000lb (37,648kg) • Armament two remotely controlled 0.79-in (20-mm) cannon in tail barbette

▲ *An early RB-66B-DT demonstrates the contemporary "natural metal" finish and buzz-number.*

▍Douglas C-47

Without question, the transportation workhorse of the Allies in World War II was the Douglas C-47, the military version of the immortal DC-3. In fact, the first Douglas commercial transports to be acquired by the US services were a number of DC-2s, designated C-32A and C-34 by the Army and R2D-1 by the Navy, followed by 35 C-39s; these were hybrids, with DC-2 fuselages and DC-3 tail units and outer wing panels. The first 953 C-47s were troop or cargo transports; these were followed by 4,991 C-47As and 3,108 C-47Bs, deliveries beginning in 1942. A specialized troop transport version, of

◀ *In South Africa, the Dakota served on as a transport and even as a maritime patrol aircraft into the 1990s.*

which 277 were built between 1941 and 1943, was designated C-53 Skytrooper. More than 1,200 C-47s were supplied under Lend-Lease to the RAF, where they were known as the Dakota Mks I to IV. Total wartime production of the C-47 series amounted to 10,123 aircraft. In addition, 700 were delivered to the Soviet Union, where around 2,000 examples were license-built as the Lisunov Li-2; these had Soviet-built engines and were fitted with a dorsal gun position. The type was also license-built in Japan for the Imperial Japanese Navy, being allocated the Allied code-name Tabby.

The rugged C-47 was renowned in every theater of war; but it is best remembered for its part in the Allied airborne operations in Europe in September 1944, culminating in the gallant failure of the British 1st Airborne Division at Arnhem.

SPECIFICATION: Type transport • Crew 3 • Powerplant two 1,200hp Pratt & Whitney R-1830-92 14-cylinder radials • Max speed 230mph (370km/h) at 10,000ft (3,050m) • Service ceiling 24,000ft (7,315m) • Max range 1,600 miles (2,575km) • Wingspan 95ft (28.90m) • Length 64ft 5in (19.63m) • Height 16ft 11in (5.20m) • Weight 31,000lb (14,061kg) loaded • Armament none

▲ *The C-47 was used in all major Allied airborne operations of WWII, and was the workhorse of the air transport forces.*

▮Douglas C-54 Skymaster

▲ *This aircraft was the first C-54D to be built. It was later converted by Convair to the SC-54D standard illustrated.*

SPECIFICATION: Type long-range transportation (data C-54A) • Crew 6 • Powerplant four 1,290hp Pratt & Whitney R-2000-7 Twin Wasp radials • Max speed 265mph (426km/h) • Service ceiling 22,000ft (6,700m) • Max range 3,900 miles (6,275km) • Wingspan 117ft 6in (35.81m) • Length 93ft 10in (28.60m) • Height 27ft 6in (8.38m) • Weight 62,000lb (28,125kg) loaded • Armament none

The Douglas C-54 was another of Douglas Aircraft's major success stories. It was derived from the DC-4 commercial airliner, which had been designed in 1935 and which, after a protracted development career, had finally appeared in prototype form in 1942. The aircraft appeared so promising that that first orders placed by US airlines were directed to be completed for military use, and more than 100 C-54s subsequently served with the Air Transport Command. One aircraft, nicknamed "Sacred Cow," was President Roosevelt's personal transportation during the war. The C-54 remained in USAF service long after WWII and was prominent in the Berlin Airlift, augmented by the Douglas C-118.

▮Douglas C-124 Globemaster II

SPECIFICATION: Type heavy-lift transportation (data C-124C) • Crew 8 • Powerplant four 3,800hp Pratt & Whitney R-4360-63A Wasp Major 28-cylinder radials • Max speed 230mph (370km/h) at 10,000ft (3,050m) • Service ceiling 18,400ft (5,600m) • Max range 4,030 miles (6,480km) • Wingspan 174ft 2in (53.08m) • Length 130ft (39.62m) • Height 48ft 4in (14.73m) • Weight 194,500lb (88,225kg) loaded • Armament none

The C-124 was an extensively modified version of the C-74 Globemaster I. The C-124 was the largest heavy cargo and troop transport in production in the early 1950s, being able to carry 200 fully equipped troops, and despite problems with its engines it was rushed into service on airlift operations during the Korean war. The two production versions were the C-124A and C-124C, the latter having more powerful engines; 445 were built.

▲ *The C-124 heavy-lift transport aircraft was rushed into service during the Korean War, despite constant engine problems.*

▌Douglas C-133 Cargomaster

First flown on April 23, 1956, the giant C-133 entered service with the USAF Military Air Transport Service in 1957 and subsequently equipped the 1st and 84th Air Transport Squadrons. The type was produced in two variants; the C-133A and -B. Most C-133s were configured to transport Atlas, Titan, and Minuteman ICBMs.

SPECIFICATION: Type heavy lift transportation • Crew 10 • Powerplant four 6,500hp Pratt & Whitney T34-P-7WA turboprops • Max speed 355mph (571km/h) • Service ceiling 19,400ft (5,915m) • Max range 3,975 miles (6,395km) • Wingspan 179ft 8in (54.76m) • Length 157ft 6in (48m) • Height 39ft 3in (11.98m) • Weight 316,600lb (143,600kg) loaded • Armament none

◀ *The Cargomaster was conceptually similar to the Lockheed Hercules, but was a much larger aircraft of far greater capacity.*

▌Douglas F3D Skynight

SPECIFICATION: Type all-weather fighter (data F3D-2) • Crew 2 • Powerplant two 3,400-lb (1,542-kg) thrust Westinghouse J34-WE-36 turbojets • Max speed 600mph (965km/h) at 20,000ft (6,096m) • Service ceiling 40,000ft (12,190m) • Max range 1,200 miles (1,930km) • Wingspan 50ft (15.24m) • Length 45ft 6in (13.86m) • Height 16ft (4.87m) • Weight 26,850lb (12,179kg) • Armament four 0.79-in (20-mm) cannon

Developed in response to a 1946 US Navy specification calling for an all-weather jet fighter, the prototype F3D Skynight (the type was originally called Skyknight, but the second "k" was dropped through common lack of usage) flew for the first time on March 28, 1948, and after evaluation 28 examples were ordered of the first production series, the F3D-1. The improved F3D-2 appeared in February 1951, and this variant accounted for 237 aircraft out of a total of 268 built. Used

▲ *A US Marine Corps F3D seen over the mountainous terrain of Korea. The Skynight was used in the night bomber support role.*

solely by the US Marine Corps, starting in November 1952 the Skynight provided effective night bomber support for USAF B-29 and B-26 aircraft operating over North Korea. Some aircraft were converted to the electronic warfare role with the designation EF-10B and saw service in the early months of the Vietnam War, supporting strikes against SAM sites.

▌Douglas F4D Skyray

The design of the Douglas F4D Skyray owed much to the wartime work of Dr. Alexander Lippisch, whose delta-wing designs had made an impression on the US Navy's Bureau of Aeronautics. In 1947, the Douglas Aircraft Company was asked to investigate the feasibility of incorporating a delta wing into the design of a short-range naval interceptor capable of climbing to 50,000ft (15,250m) in just over three minutes and intercepting bombers traveling at 600mph (965km/h). The result was the XF4D-1 Skyray, which first flew on January 23, 1951. When the first production F4D-1 exceeded Mach One in level flight on June 5, 1954, it seemed probable that the aircraft would soon enter service, but serious problems—including a dangerous high speed stall at altitude—had to be overcome before the aircraft could be deployed operationally in 1956. Production of the Skyray ended in 1958 with the 419th aircraft, but the type remained in first-line service until well into the 1960s. During its operational career the Skyray established five new time-to-height records; on one attempt, it reached over 49,000ft (14,945m) in little more than two and a half minutes. A proposed supersonic Skyray successor, the F5D Skylancer, never went into production, although four examples were evaluated.

▶ *It was the US Navy's desire to experiment with the delta-wing layout that led to the Skyray. In service, the type proved something of a disappointment.*

SPECIFICATION: **Type** naval fighter (data F4D-1) • **Crew** 1 • **Powerplant** one 10,200lb (4,626kg) thrust Pratt & Whitney J57-P-8A turbojet • **Max speed** 695mph (1,118km/h) at 36,000ft (10,975m) • **Service ceiling** 55,000ft (16,765m) • **Max range** 1,200 miles (1,931km) • **Wingspan** 33ft 6in (10.21m) • **Length** 45ft 8in (13.93m) • **Height** 13ft (3.96m) • **Weight** 25,000lb (11,340kg) • **Armament** four 0.79-in (20-mm) cannon; up to 4,000lb (1,814kg) of ordnance, including Sidewinder AAMs, on six underwing hardpoints

▌Douglas SBD Dauntless

The evolution of the Douglas SBD Dauntless began in November 1934, when a Northrop design team based a proposal for a new navy dive-bomber on the Northrop A-17 light attack bomber. A prototype was ordered and flew in July 1935 with the designation XBT-1. In February 1936 an order was placed for 54 production BT-1s with 825hp Wright R-1535-94 engines. The last aircraft of this batch was fitted with a 1,000hp R-1820-32 engine and completed as the XBT-2. Further modifications were carried out and when the Northrop Corporation became a division of Douglas on August 31, 1937 the aircraft was redesignated XSBD-1.

Delivery of 57SBD-1s to the US Marine Corps began in mid-1940, the aircraft now having been fitted with the large, perforated dive flaps that were a distinctive feature of the Dauntless. At the same time, the US Navy ordered 87 SBD-2s with extra fuel tankage, protective armor and autopilots. The SBD-2 was followed into service by the SBD-3; delivery of the first 174 SBD-3s began in March 1941, the US Navy subsequently receiving a further 410. The Dauntless formed the attack element of the Navy's carrier air groups at the time of the Japanese strike on Pearl Harbor, and in the early months of 1942 the SBDs, operating from the carriers *Lexington* and *Yorktown*, carried out a number of offensive operations against enemy shore installations and shipping. In May 1942, during the Battle of the Coral Sea, SBDs joined with TBD Devastator torpedo aircraft to sink the Japanese light carrier *Shoho* and damage the fleet carrier *Shokaku*, forcing the Japanese to abandon plans to occupy Port Moresby, New Guinea. In June 1942, during the Battle of Midway, the two aircraft types again joined forces to make coordinated dive-bombing and torpedo attacks on units of

▮ Fairchild C-82/C-119

The Fairchild Corporation's first post-World War II operational transportation design, the C-82 Packet, soon gave way to a much modified version, the C-119 Boxcar. Over 1,300 were subsequently built, and the C-119 saw widespread service with the USAF, the US Navy (as the R4Q), and the air forces of Belgium, Brazil, Canada, Nationalist China, France, India, Italy, Morocco, and Norway. Some USAF C-119s were specially modified for satellite recovery. The C-119 was very active in the Korean War, dropping both airborne forces and supplies, and was used by the French in Indo-China.

SPECIFICATION: Type transportation • Crew 4 (plus 40 paratroops) • Powerplant two 3,500hp Wright R-3350-89 Cyclone 18-cylinder radials • Max speed 218mph (350km/h) at 10,000ft (3,050m) • Service ceiling 23,900ft (7,285m) • Max range 1,770 miles (2,850km) • Wingspan 109ft 4in (33.32m) • Length 86ft 6in (26.36m) • Height 26ft 3in (8m) • Weight 85,000lb (38,556kg) loaded • Armament none

▲ *A distinctly longer nose ahead of the cockpit was a key recognition feature of the C-82. Production aircraft were equipped for glider-towing.*

▮ Fairchild C-123 Provider

The C-123 was developed from the experimental Chase XG-20 transportation glider, two examples of which were built in 1948. One was fitted with Pratt & Whitney R-2800 engines and became the XC-123 Avitruc; the other was fitted with four J47 turbojets and became the sole C-123A. The aircraft entered production as the C-123B and 302 were built between 1954 and 1958. Of these, six went to Saudi Arabia, 18 to Venezuela, and others to Thailand and South Vietnam. C-123Bs were used by the 315th Air Command Group in Vietnam, mostly in connection with defoliation programs.

◄ *This C-123 flew with the 63rd TAS, 439 TAW, Air Force Reserve from Westover AFB, Massachusetts after 1974. It wears SEA theatre camouflage.*

SPECIFICATION: Type transportation • Crew 2 (plus 61 passengers) • Powerplant four 2,300hp Pratt & Whitney R-2800-99W Double Wasp 18-cylinder radials • Max speed 205mph (330km/h) • Service ceiling 29,000ft (8,840m) • Max range 1,470 miles (2,365km) • Wingspan 110ft (33.53m) • Length 75ft 9in (23.08m) • Height 34ft 1in (10.38m) • Weight 60,000lb (27,000kg) loaded • Armament none

▮ Fairchild Republic A-10 Thunderbolt II

In December 1970 Fairchild Republic and Northrop were each selected to build a prototype of a new close support aircraft for evaluation under the USAF's A-X program, and in January 1973 it was announced that Fairchild Republic's contender, the YA-10, had been selected. Fairchild met the armor requirement by seating the pilot in what was virtually a titanium "bathtub," resistant to most firepower except a direct hit from a heavy-caliber shell, and added to this a so-called redundant structure policy whereby the pilot could retain control even if the aircraft lost large portions of its airframe, including one of the two rear-mounted engines. The core of the A-10's built-in firepower was its massive GAU-8/A seven-barrel 1.19-in (30-mm) rotary cannon, which was mounted on the centerline under the forward fuselage. The A-10 was designed to operate from short, unprepared strips less than 1,500ft (457m) long. Deliveries began in March

SPECIFICATION: Type close support and assault aircraft • Crew 1 • Powerplant two 9,065-lb (4,112-kg) thrust General Electric TF34-GE-100 turbofans • Max speed 439mph (706km/h) at sea level • Service ceiling 25,000ft (7,625m) • Combat radius 250 miles (402km) • Wingspan 57ft 6in (17.53m) • Length 53ft 4in (16.26m) • Height 14ft 8in (4.47m) • Weight 50,000lb (22,680kg) • Armament one 1.19-in (30-mm) GAU-8/A rotary cannon with 1,350 rounds; 11 hardpoints for up to 16,000lb (7,248kg) of ordnance, including Rockeye cluster bombs, Maverick ASMs, and SUU-23 0.79-in (20-mm) cannon pods

▲ This AFRES A-10A demonstrates the gray scheme that was adopted later in the type's career.

1977; in all, the USAF took delivery of 727 aircraft for service with its tactical fighter wings, the emphasis being on European operations. The A-10 had a combat radius of 250 miles (402km), enough to reach a target area on the East German border from a Forward Operating Location (FOL) in central Germany and then move onto another target area in northern Germany. The aircraft had a three and a half hour loiter endurance, although operational war sorties in Europe would probably have lasted between one and two hours. In general, operations by the A-10s envisaged co-operation with US Army helicopters; the latter would hit the mobile SAM and AAA systems accompanying a Soviet armored thrust, and with the enemy's defenses at lest temporarily stunned or degraded, the A-10s would be free to concentrate their fire on the tanks. These tactics were used to deadly effect in the 1991 Gulf War.

▲ Known as the "Warthog", the A-10 Thunderbolt II is one of the ugliest aircraft ever designed, and also one of the most deadly in its intended role.

▌Fairey Albacore

SPECIFICATION: Type naval torpedo-bomber and reconnaissance biplane • Crew 3 • Powerplant one 1,130hp Bristol Taurus XII 14-cylinder radial • Max speed 161mph (257km/h) • Service ceiling 20,700ft (6,310m) • Max range 930 miles (1,497km) • Wingspan 49ft 11in (15.23m) • Length 39ft 11in (12.18m) • Height 12ft 6in (3.81m) • Weight 12,500lb (5,670kg) loaded • Armament one 0.303-in (7.7-mm) machine gun in starboard lower wing, plus one or two mounted in rear cockpit; external torpedo or bomb load of 2,000lb (907kg)

Resulting from a 1936 requirement, the Fairey Albacore was in effect a modernized and improved development of the Fairey Swordfish, with an enclosed cockpit, an up-rated engine, hydraulically operated flaps, and a number of aero-dynamic refinements. The prototype Albacore flew in December 1938 and the first of 798 production Albacore Mk Is entered service in March 1940. The type eventually equipped 15 Fleet Air Arm squadrons, taking part in some notable fleet actions. It was retired in 1944, a year before the Swordfish, which it had been intended to replace.

▌Fairey Barracuda

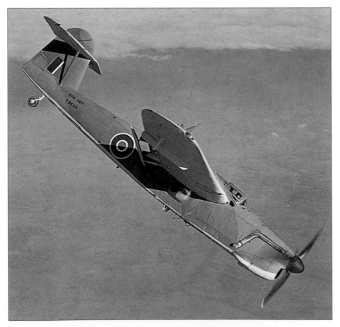

▲ The Fairey Barracuda first saw action during the Salerno landings in Italy in September 1943, and made a successful attack on the battleship Tirpitz in the following year.

SPECIFICATION: Type torpedo- and dive-bomber (data Barracuda II) • Crew 3 • Powerplant one 1,640hp Rolls-Royce Merlin 432 V-12 • Max speed 228mph (367km/h) at 1,750ft (533m) • Service ceiling 16,600ft (5,060m) • Max range 1,150 miles (1,851km) • Wingspan 49ft 2in (14.99m) • Length 39ft 9in (12.12m) • Height 15ft 1in (4.60m) • Weight 14,100lb (6,396kg) • Armament two 0.303-in (7.7-mm) Vickers "K" machine guns in rear cockpit; one 1,620lb (735kg) torpedo or one 1000-lb (454-kg) bomb beneath fuselage, or four 450-lb (204-kg) or six 250-lb (113-kg) bombs under wings

The Fairey Barracuda was designed to Specification S.24/37 and was the first British carrier-based monoplane torpedo bomber of all-metal construction. The Barracuda's entry into service was delayed when its intended engine, the Rolls-Royce Exe, was abandoned, and when the prototype eventually flew on December 7, 1940 it was under the power of a Rolls-Royce Merlin 30. The first of 30 Barracuda Is flew in May 1942, this batch being followed by 1,688 Barracuda IIs with uprated Merlin 32s. Dogged by weight problems throughout its life, the Barracuda saw only limited service in home waters, its most successful operation being an attack on the German battleship Tirpitz in April 1944.

▌Fairey Battle

▲ *Fairey Battles of No. 88 Squadron RAF seen in formation with Curtiss Hawks of the French Air Force's GC I/5 during the "phoney war" period.*

The Rolls-Royce Merlin-engined Fairey Battle light bomber, one of the types chosen for large-scale production, was designed to Specification P.23/35, first deliveries being made to No. 63 Squadron in May 1937. On September 2, 1939 10 Battle squadrons of the Advanced Air Striking Force deployed to France, and in May 1940 they suffered appalling losses in attempts to bomb enemy columns and bridges over the Meuse.

Due to its inability to defend itself from enemy fire the Battle was soon assigned to second-line duties, although in the autumn of 1940 squadrons based in England carried out many night attacks on concentrations of invasion barges in the German-occupied Channel ports.

SPECIFICATION: Type light bomber • Crew 3 • Powerplant one Rolls-Royce Merlin II 12-cylinder V-type • Max speed 252mph (406km/h) • Service ceiling 26,000ft (7,925m) • Max range 1,200 miles (1,931km) • Wingspan 54ft (16.45m) • Length 42ft 5in (12.93m) • Height 15ft (4.57m) • Weight 11,700lb (5,307kg) loaded • Armament one 0.303-in (7.7-mm) machine gun in leading edge of starboard wing and one in rear cockpit; internal and external bomb load of 1,500lb (680kg)

▌Fairey Campania

The Fairey Campania was the first-ever airplane to be designed for operation from an aircraft carrier. The first prototype flew for the first time on February 16, 1917 and the aircraft appeared in two main variants, the F.17 and F.22. At the end of World War I there were 42 Campanias on RAF charge, 26 of them with Rolls-Royce Eagle engines. Campanias served on the seaplane carriers *Campania*, *Nairana*, and *Pegasus*.

SPECIFICATION: Type general-purpose seaplane • Crew 2 • Powerplant one 345hp Rolls-Royce Eagle VIII 12-cylinder V-type • Max speed 80mph (129km/h) • Service ceiling 5,500ft (1,676m) • Endurance 3hrs • Wingspan 61ft 7in (18.78m) • Length 43ft 5in (13.12m) • Height 15ft 1in (4.60m) • Weight 5,657lb (2,566kg) • Armament one 0.303-in (7.7-mm) Lewis machine gun in rear cockpit; light bomb load

▲ *The Campania prototype, which first flew on February 16, 1917.*

Fairey Firefly

GREAT BRITAIN

▲ With an S-51 helicopter hovering in the background, a Firefly of No. 825 Sqn prepares for launch from the carrier HMS Ocean during the Korean War.

The prototype Fairey Firefly two-seat naval fighter first flew on December 22, 1941, production getting under way toward the end of the following year. It became operational in October 1943 on board the carrier HMS *Indefatigable*. Fireflies provided fighter cover during the series of Fleet Air Arm attacks on the battleship *Tirpitz* in the summer of 1944, and in January 1945, while deploying to the Pacific, they took part in the destruction of Japanese-held oil refineries in Sumatra. In the Pacific theater the Firefly proved to be a very versatile aircraft, operating as day and night fighter, fighter-bomber and reconnaissance aircraft. The first major post-

war variant was the Firefly Mk 4, which in turn was replaced by the Mk 5. Operating from light carriers, Fireflies carried out many strikes during the Korean War.

SPECIFICATION: Type naval fighter (data Mk I) • Crew 2 • Powerplant one 1,730hp Rolls-Royce Griffon IIB 12-cylinder V type • Max speed 316mph (508km/h) at 14,000ft (4,250m) • Service ceiling 28,000ft (8,500m) • Max range 1,300 miles (2,100km) • Wingspan 44ft 6in (13.56m) • Length 37ft 7in (11.46m) • Height 13ft 7in (4.14m) • Weight 14,020lb (6,350kg) loaded • Armament four 0.79-in (20-mm) Hispano cannon

Fairey Flycatcher

GREAT BRITAIN

The RN's first post-World War I fighter was the Gloster Nightjar, one of a series of aircraft derived from the Nighthawk. Twenty-two were built, and were replaced in 1923

SPECIFICATION: Type naval fighter biplane • Crew 1 • Powerplant one 40hp Armstrong Siddeley Jaguar III 14-cylinder radial • Max speed 134mph (215km/h) at 5,000ft (1,500m) • Service ceiling 20,350ft (6,200m) • Max range 260 miles (420km) • Wingspan 29ft (8.84m) • Length 23ft (7.01m) • Height 12ft (3.65m) • Weight 3,028lb (1,373kg) loaded • Armament two 0.303-in (7.7-mm) machine guns; 80lb (36kg) of bombs

▲ The Fairey Flycatcher served on every British aircraft carrier during the 1920s, and was the first Fleet Air Arm aircraft fitted with wheel brakes.

by the Fairey Flycatcher, a highly popular little aircraft that was to remain in service for 11 years. Although the initial production order was for only nine aircraft, subsequent contracts brought the final number produced to 193. Flycatchers were delivered to eight fighter flights, serving aboard the aircraft carriers *Argus*, *Courageous*, *Eagle*, *Furious*, and *Hermes* in many parts of the world, as well as on shore stations. An unusual feature of the Flycatcher was that its airframe was designed to be dismantled easily for transportation by sea. No section of the airframe was more than 13ft 6in (4.11m) long.

Fairey Fox

The Fairey Fox light bomber was designed around the US Curtiss V-12 engine. The prototype flew on January 3, 1925 and proved to be a good 30mph (48km/h) faster than any contemporary RAF fighter. Enough aircraft (28) were ordered to equip one RAF squadron, No. 12, but despite the promise shown by the Fox it was not issued to other units. Production was undertaken by Avions Fairey in Belgium, who built 178 examples, including the all-metal Fox VI.

SPECIFICATION: Type light bomber biplane • Crew 2 • Powerplant one 480hp Fairey Felix (Curtiss V-12 V-type) • Max speed 156mph (251km/h) • Service ceiling 17,000ft (5,180m) • Max range 650 miles (1,046km) • Wingspan 38ft (11.58m) • Length 31ft 2in (9.50m) • Height 10ft 8in (3.25m) • Weight 4,117lb (1,867kg) • Armament one fixed forward-firing 0.303-in (7.7-mm) Vickers machine gun and one on flexible mount in rear cockpit

▲ *Later Fox production was of the Fox IA, with the Kestrel IIA engine. J9026 was among the final batch of four Foxes completed.*

Fairey Fulmar

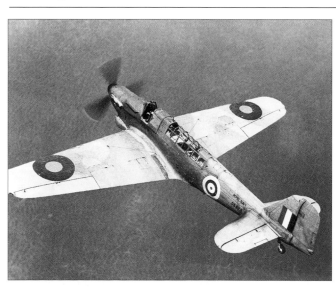

The prototype Fairey Fulmar two-seat naval fighter first flew on January 4, 1940, and the type was quickly ordered into production, with 250 Fulmar Mk Is being built. The Mk 1

SPECIFICATION: Type naval fighter (data Fulmar Mk I) • Crew 2 • Powerplant one 1,080hp Rolls-Royce Merlin VIII 12-cylinder V-type • Max speed 280mph (450km/h) • Service ceiling 26,000ft (7,925m) • Max range 800 miles (1,290km) • Wingspan 46ft 4in (14.13m) • Length 40ft 3in (12.26m) • Height 14ft (4.26m) • Weight 9,800lb (4,440kg) loaded • Armament eight 0.303-in (7.7-mm) Browning machine guns

◄ *This Fulmar Mk II was fitted with the later Merlin Mk 30 engine and tropical equipment. Note the extensive glazing of the observer's cockpit.*

was replaced on the production lines by the Mk II (350 built) with a more powerful Merlin 30 engine, and by mid-1942 14 Fleet Air Arm squadrons were armed with the fighter. The Fulmar first went into action with No. 806 Squadron on board HMS *Illustrious* in the Mediterranean in August 1940, and was to play an important part in defending the vital Malta convoys. Although the Fulmar had a poor maximum speed and ceiling, and a slow rate of climb, it was well armed and maneuverable.

▌Fairey Gannet

▲ *A Fairey Gannet T4 in bright training colours pictured at an air display at RAF Odiham, Hampshire, in September 1966.*

The Fairey Gannet, its portly outline a familiar sight in many parts of the world during the late 1950s, originated in an Admiralty requirement, issued in 1945, for a new antisubmarine aircraft. Fairey Aviation selected the Armstrong Siddeley Mamba turboprop and suggested coupling two of these engines together, driving a coaxial propeller. The result was the Double Mamba. Each half of the powerplant could be controlled separately, giving the pilot the option of shutting down one half and feathering the propeller to extend cruise range and lengthen search time. The Gannet prototype flew on September 19, and the aircraft was ordered into production as the Gannet AS.1, the first operational squadron, No. 826, forming in January 1955. The 170th production AS.1 received a more powerful Double Mamba

SPECIFICATION: Type antisubmarine warfare aircraft (data Gannet AS.4) • Crew 3 • Powerplant 3,035hp one Armstrong Siddeley Double Mamba 101 coupled turboprop • Max speed 299mph (481km/h) at sea level • Service ceiling 25,000ft (7,629m) • Max range 940 miles (1,510km) • Wingspan 54ft 4in (16.56m) • Length 43ft (13.10m) • Height 13ft 8in (4.16m) • Weight 22,505lb (10,208kg) loaded • Armament 2,000lb (907kg) of torpedoes, mines, depth charges etc.

ping the Royal Navy's ASW squadrons until 1960, when it began to be replaced by ASW helicopters. The Mks T2 and T4 were trainers. The last version of the Gannet was the AEW.3 early warning aircraft, which equipped four flights of No. 849 Squadron.

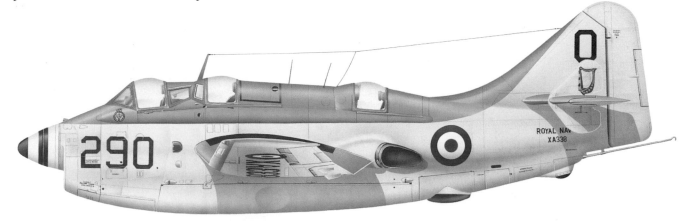

▌Fairey Gordon

▲ *Optional floats enabled the naval version of the Gordon, the Fairey Seal, to be deployed on warships in its catapult-launched floatplane configuration.*

SPECIFICATION: **Type** general purpose biplane (data Gordon Mk I) • **Crew** 2 • **Powerplant** one 525hp Armstrong Siddeley Panther IIA 14-cylinder radial • **Max speed** 145mph (233km/h) at 3,000ft (914m) • **Service ceiling** 22,000ft (6,700m) • **Max range** 600 miles (965km) • **Wingspan** 45ft 9in (13.94m) • **Length** 36ft 8in (11.17m) • **Height** 14ft 2in (4.31m) • **Weight** 5,900lb (2,675kg) loaded • **Armament** two 0.303-in (7.7-mm) machine guns; 460lb (208kg) of bombs

The Fairey Gordon light bomber and general-purpose aircraft, in service from 1931–38, was the eventual derivative of the Fairey III of 1917, and in fact was originally known as the IIIF Mk V. Production total was 176 aircraft (Mks I and II), but many Fairey IIIFs were brought up to Gordon standard. A naval version was named the Seal, of which 90 were built.

▌Fairey Hendon

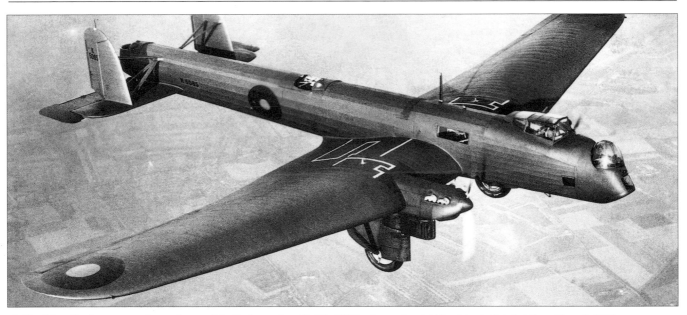

▲ *The Fairey Hendon was an advanced concept for its day, and enabled the RAF to pioneer the night bombing tactics that it would use in WWII.*

The Hendon night bomber was built in 1930 to meet the requirements of Specification B.19/27. Originally intended to

SPECIFICATION: **Type** heavy bomber • **Crew** 5 • **Powerplant** two 600hp Rolls-Royce Kestrel VI in-line engines • **Max speed** 156mph (251km/h) at 15,000ft (4,575m) • **Service ceiling** 21,500ft (6,557m) • **Max range** 1,360 miles (2,188km) • **Wingspan** 101ft 9in (31.03m) • **Length** 60ft 9in (18.53m) • **Height** not known • **Weight** 20,000lb (9,060kg) • **Armament** three 0.303-in (7.7-mm) Lewis guns in nose, dorsal, and tail positions; up to 1,660lb (752kg) of bombs carried internally, or alternatively 15–20 troops

have Bristol Mercury V radials, the prototype was powered by two Jupiter VIII engines. The first low-wing bomber monoplane to be built in Britain, and the first to equip the RAF, the Hendon was an advanced concept, designed to carry its bomb load internally in the wings. The prototype was rebuilt after a crash and, fitted with Kestrel IIIS engines, was known as the Hendon I. Due to delays production emphasis was placed on the competing Handley Page Heyford, only fourteen more aircraft, fitted with Kestrel VIs and designated Hendon IIs, were issued to No. 38 (B) Squadron in 1938. These were replaced by Vickers Wellingtons just before the outbreak of World War II.

▌Fairey Swordfish

SPECIFICATION: **Type** torpedo/ASW/reconnaissance aircraft • **Crew** 3 •
Powerplant one 820hp Bristol Pegasus XXX radial engine • **Max speed**
138mph (222km/h) • **Service ceiling** 19,250ft (5,867m) • **Max range** 546 miles
(879km) • **Wingspan** 45ft 6in (13.86m) • **Length** 35ft 8in (10.87m) • **Height** 12ft
4in (3.76m) • **Weight** 7,510lb (3,406kg) loaded • **Armament** one fixed forward-
firing 0.303-in (7.7-mm) machine gun and one trainable 0.303-in (7.7-mm)
gun in rear cockpit, plus an offensive load of one 18-in (457-mm) torpedo
or eight 60-lb (27.2-kg) rocket projectiles

▲ *Despite its antiquated appearance, the Swordfish carried out its wartime
roles with great efficiency, and remained in service throughout WWII.*

The Swordfish was derived from the private-venture Fairey
TSR 1, the prototype of which was lost in an accident in
September 1933. Undeterred, the Fairey Aviation
Company's design team followed up with a slightly larger
development, the TSR II (Torpedo-Spotter-Reconnaissance
II). The prototype, K4190, flew for the first time on April
17, 1934 and a contract for 86 production Swordfish Mk I
aircraft was placed in April 1935, the aircraft entering service with No. 825 Squadron of the Fleet Air Arm in July
1936. By the outbreak of World War II 689 Swordfish had
been delivered or were on order. Thirteen squadrons were
equipped with the type, and a further 12 were formed during the war years.

It was in the Mediterranean Theater that the Swordfish
really proved its worth. Swordfish inflicted considerable
damage on Italian shipping, culminating in the spectacular
night attack on the Italian fleet at Taranto on November 11,
1940 by 21 Swordfish of Nos. 815 and 819 Squadrons from
HMS *Illustrious*. At one stroke, the Italian battle fleet was
reduced from six to three capital ships at a crucial period of
the war, and for the loss of only two Swordfish.

Other notable Swordfish actions included the Battle of
Cape Matapan in March 1941, the crippling of the German
battleship *Bismarck* in May, and the gallant action against the
Scharnhorst, *Gneisenau*, and *Prinz Eugen* during the famous
"Channel Dash" of February 1942, when all six Swordfish of
No. 825 Squadron involved were shot down.

The Swordfish Mk II, which appeared in 1943, had metal-
covered lower wings, enabling it to carry rocket projectiles.
The Swordfish Mk III carried ASV radar in a housing
between the main landing gear legs. All three Swordfish variants were converted as Mk IVs for service with the Royal
Canadian Air Force, and many Mk Is were converted as twin-
float seaplanes. Swordfish production ended on August 18,
1944, by which time 2,391 aircraft had been built.

▌Fairey Seafox

The Fairey Seafox, one of the most widely used British aircraft during the early part of World War II, was designed to be catapult-launched from the Royal Navy's capital ships. The prototype of this little biplane flew on May 27, 1936 and production ended in 1938, by which time 31 aircraft had

been built. One of the most important actions in which the Seafox participated was the pursuit and destruction of the German battleship *Admiral Graf Spee* in December 1939.

▲ *The Fairey Seafox, designed to be launched from capital ships, played a key role in hunting down the German battleship* Admiral Graf Spee.

SPECIFICATION: Type reconnaissance biplane • Crew 2 • Powerplant one 395hp Napier Rapier radial engine • Max speed 124mph (200km/h) at 5,860ft (1,785m) • Service ceiling 11,000ft (3,350m) • Max range 440 miles (708km) • Wingspan 40ft (12.19m) • Length 35ft 5in (10.80m) • Height 12ft 1in (3.68m) • Weight 11,000ft (3,350m) • Armament one rear-mounted 0.303-in (7.7-mm) Lewis machine gun

▌Fairey III Series

The prototype Fairey IIIA was a twin-float seaplane converted to landplane configuration. The IIIA was followed by the IIIB naval bomber with an increased span and the same 260 Sunbeam Maori II engine as the IIIA; of the 30 ordered, the last six were completed to IIIC standard with the Rolls-Royce Eagle VIII engine, as were 30 further aircraft. Some of these

saw active service as part of the Allied Intervention Force in North Russia in 1919. The second most numerous variant was the Fairey IIID, of which 207 were produced. In March/April 1926, four RAF Fairey IIIDs carried out a spectacular long-distance formation flight from Northolt to Cape Town, returning to Lee-on-Solent via Greece, Italy, and France in June. No serious problems were encountered on the 13,900-mile (22,366-km) round trip. The final and most numerous variant of this versatile aircraft was the IIIF, production of which totaled 597 aircraft.

▲ *Originally referred to as the "IIIC (Improved)", the Fairey IIID was available in Mk I and Mk II forms. The latter – illustrated – had Lion V and VA engines.*

SPECIFICATION: Type general-purpose biplane (data Fairey IIID) • Crew 3 • Powerplant one 450hp Napier Lion IIB 12-cylinder V-type • Max speed 105mph(171km/h) • Service ceiling 17,000ft (5,180m) • Max range 550 miles (885km) • Wingspan 46.1ft (14.05m) • Length 37ft (11.28m) • Height 11ft 4in (3.45m) • Weight 4,918lb (2,231kg) • Armament one 0.303-in (7.7-mm) Vickers machine gun in front fuselage and one 0.303-in (7.7-mm) Lewis gun in rear cockpit; provision for small bombs under lower wing

▌Farman MF.7

▶ *The MF.7's two long, upward-curving elevator supports gave it the nickname "Longhorn".*

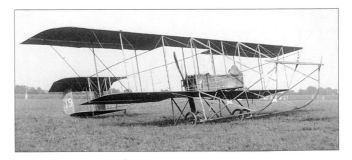

SPECIFICATION: Type reconnaissance biplane • Crew 2 • Powerplant one 70hp Renault 8-cylinder air-cooled in-line engine • Max speed 59mph (95km/h) at sea level • Service ceiling 13,123ft (4,000m) • Endurance 3hrs 30mins • Wingspan 50ft 5in (15.40m) • Length 37ft 2in (11.35m) • Height 11ft 4in (3.45m) • Weight 1,885lb (855kg) loaded • Armament none

Developed in the years before World War I, the Maurice Farman MF.7, despite its rather antiquated appearance, gave excellent service in the early months of the conflict. It served with both the French and British flying services from 1913 in the observation role, being relegated to training duties after May 1915.

▌Farman HF.20

The Henri Farman Series 20 biplanes, which were employed in a reconnaissance role with all the Allied air forces in the first year of World War I, proved to be seriously underpowered and were barely capable of sustaining the extra weight of a defensive machine gun. The HF.27 variant had a steel-tube airframe in place of the earlier wooden one.

▶ *The Farman Series 20 biplanes, although employed in considerable numbers, were generally unsuccessful, being badly underpowered.*

SPECIFICATION: **Type** reconnaissance biplane • **Crew** 2 • **Powerplant** one 80hp Gnome 7A 7-cylinder air-cooled rotary • **Max speed** 65mph (100km/h) • **Service ceiling** 9,022ft (2,750m) • **Endurance** 3hrs 20mins • **Wingspan** 51ft (15.54m) • **Length** 28ft 9in (8.79m) • **Height** 10ft (3.10m) • **Weight** 1,565lb (710kg) loaded • **Armament** one 0.30-in (7.5-mm) machine gun

▌Farman MF.11

▲ *This restored MF.11 was photographed while overflying the 1937 RAF display at Hendon.*

In May 1915 the MF.7 was replaced by the improved and more powerful MF.11, designed in 1914. Aerodynamically and structurally improved, this aircraft was equipped with a machine gun for the observer. On December 21, 1914, a Farman MF.11 of the Royal Naval Air Service carried out the first night bombing mission of the war, attacking Ostend harbor. In Italy the MF.11 was built under license by SIA, equipping 24 squadrons of the Italian Air Service.

SPECIFICATION: **Type** reconnaissance bomber • **Crew** 2 • **Powerplant** one 100hp Renault 8-cylinder air-cooled in-line V-type • **Max speed** 66mph (106km/h) at sea level • **Service ceiling** 12,467ft (3,800m) • **Endurance** 3hrs 45mins • **Wingspan** 53ft (16.15m) • **Length** 31ft (9.45m) • **Height** 10ft 5in (3.18m) • **Weight** 2,045lb (928kg) loaded • **Armament** one 0.30-in (7.5-mm) machine gun; 288lb (130kg) of bombs

▌Farman F.40

After working independently of each other in the prewar years, the brothers Henri and Maurice Farman joined forces in 1914 to produce a new biplane that incorporated the best features of their earlier models. This was the Farman F.40, which made its appearance in 1915. Used as a general-purpose aircraft, it was not particularly effective in action, mainly because of its inadequate armament. It was later relegated to the role of night bomber and then training aircraft.

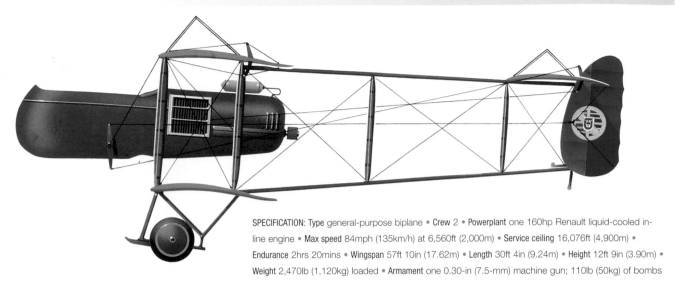

SPECIFICATION: Type general-purpose biplane • Crew 2 • Powerplant one 160hp Renault liquid-cooled in-line engine • Max speed 84mph (135km/h) at 6,560ft (2,000m) • Service ceiling 16,076ft (4,900m) • Endurance 2hrs 20mins • Wingspan 57ft 10in (17.62m) • Length 30ft 4in (9.24m) • Height 12ft 9in (3.90m) • Weight 2,470lb (1,120kg) loaded • Armament one 0.30-in (7.5-mm) machine gun; 110lb (50kg) of bombs

▌Farman F.221/222

 FRANCE

Designed to meet a requirement for a five-seat night bomber issued in 1929, the Farman 221 was the first four-engined bomber to enter service with the Armée de l'Air. From December 1939 Farman 221s and 222s (the latter having a retractable undercarriage) carried out leaflet-dropping operations, switching to night bombing in May 1940. They undertook several notable missions, including an attack on the BMW factory in Munich. Most of the Farmans were converted to the transportation role and evacuated to North Africa, where they were destroyed by Allied air attack in November 1942.

▲ *A Farman F.222 being prepared for a sortie. They were the only four-engined heavy bombers in service at the start of World War II.*

SPECIFICATION: Type heavy night bomber • Crew 5 • Powerplant four 970hp Gnome-Rhone 14N-11/15 radial engines • Max speed 199mph (320km/h) • Service ceiling 26,245ft (8,000m) • Max range 1,243 miles (2,000km) with a 5,511-lb (2,500-kg) bomb load • Wingspan 118ft 1in (36m) • Length 70ft 4in (21.45m) • Height 17ft (5.19m) • Weights 23,148lb (10,500kg) empty; 41,226lb (18,700kg) loaded • Armament three 0.30-in (7.5-mm) machine guns, one each in nose, dorsal, and ventral positions; internal bomb load of 9,259lb (4,200kg)

▌Felixstowe F.2A

 GREAT BRITAIN

Derived from the Curtiss H-12 flying boat, 50 of which were supplied to the Royal Navy in 1917, the Felixstowe F.2A set the pattern for all British maritime aircraft up to the 1920s. Named after the Royal Naval Air Station where it was developed, the F.2A was a first-class aircraft, and was widely used with great success on long North Sea patrols.

SPECIFICATION: Type maritime patrol flying boat • Crew 4 • Powerplant two 345hp Rolls-Royce Eagle VIII V-type engines • Max speed 84mph (135km/h) at 2,000ft (610m) • Service ceiling 9,600ft (2,930m) • Endurance 6hrs • Wingspan 95ft 7in (29.15m) • Length 46ft 3in (14.10m) • Height 17ft 6in (5.33m) • Weight 10,978lb (4,980kg) • Armament four–seven 0.303-in (7.7-mm) machine guns; 460lb (208kg) of bombs

▲ *Just under 100 examples of the F.2A were built, the type remaining in operational use until the end of World War I in 1918.*

FFVS J-22

SPECIFICATION: Type fighter • Crew 1 • Powerplant one 1,065hp Pratt & Whitney Twin Wasp 14-cylinder radial • Max speed 358mph (576km/h) • Service ceiling 30,500ft (9,300m) • Max range 780 miles (1,250km) • Wingspan 32ft 10in (10m) • Length 25ft 7in (7.80m) • Height 9ft 2in (2.79m) • Weight 6,280lb (2,850kg) loaded • Armament four 0.303-in (7.7-mm) machine guns

In 1940, alarmed by the possible threat to its neutrality, the Swedish government authorized the production of an indigenous fighter aircraft, the FFVS J-22. The prototype flew in September 1942, followed by the first production aircraft in September 1943. Deliveries of production machines, 198 in all, began two months later.

Fiat BR.20

ITALY

The Fiat BR.20 medium bomber was modern and technically advanced when the prototype flew in February 1936, but it was already obsolescent by the time Italy entered World War II in 1940. Nevertheless, 580 examples were built before production ceased in the summer of 1942, 85 of these being delivered to Japan, which used the aircraft as an interim bomber during its operations in Manchuria. About half the total production involved the BR.20M, an improved model with better streamlining, heavier defensive armament, and

SPECIFICATION: Type medium bomber • Crew 5 • Powerplant two 1,030hp Fiat A.80 • Max speed 267mph (430km/h) • Service ceiling 23,620ft (7,200m) • Max range 770 miles (1,240km) • Wingspan 70ft 8in (21.56m) • Length 53ft (16.17m) • Height 14ft 1in (4.30m) • Weight 22,795lb (10,340kg) • Armament one 0.303-in (7.7-mm) machine gun in nose turret, two in dorsal turret, and one in ventral position; internal bomb load of 3,527lb (1,600kg)

more armor. The BR.20 was used in the Spanish Civil War and saw service on all fronts in World War II, taking part in night attacks on the British Isles in October and November 1940. It was used extensively against Malta in the early months of the Axis offensive against the island. The BR.20bis was the final and much improved variant, but only 15 examples were produced before the armistice.

◀ The Fiat BR.20 bomber saw service on all war fronts, and took part in the Regia Aeronautica's assault on the island of Malta in 1940–41.

Fiat CR.1

ITALY

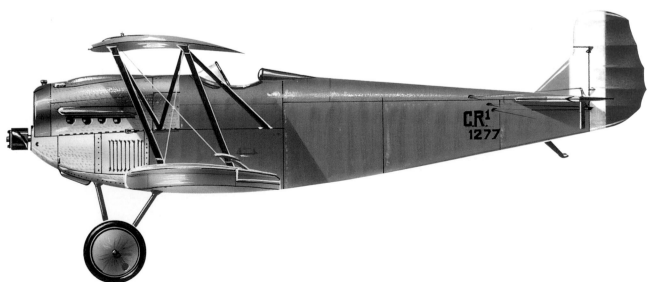

The first standard fighter of Italian design to enter service after World War I was the Fiat CR.1, the initials being those of its designer, Celestino Rosatelli. About 100 CR.1s were built, and these began to enter service in 1924–25 with units of the 1st Fighter Group, based in Italy. In all 240 CR.1s were ordered, and by 1926 12 fighter squadrons were armed with the type. A distinctive feature of the CR.1 was that its lower wing had a greater span than the upper.

SPECIFICATION: Type fighter • Crew 1 • Powerplant one 320hp Isotta-Fraschini Asso 8-cylinder V-type • Max speed 168mph (270km/h) • Service ceiling 24,440ft (7,450m) • Max range 405 miles (650km) • Wingspan 29ft 4in (8.95m) • Length 20ft 6in (6.24m) • Height 7ft 10in (2.40m) • Weight 2,546lb (1,155kg) • Armament two fixed forward-firing 0.303-in (7.7-mm) machine guns

Fiat CR.20   ITALY

Celestino Rosatelli followed up the CR.1 with the CR.20, which flew in June 1926 and had improved reliability, maneu-

▲ *In ICR.20 form, the type was deeply unpopular. The floats made for vicious handling inadequacies, including a tendency to fall out of loops.*

verability, and structural strength. It had a lengthy career, more than 670 aircraft being produced over a seven-year period. The CR.20 was Fiat's first all-metal fighter; in the tactical role it saw action against dissident tribesmen in Libya and, toward the end of its career, it was used in support of Italy's invasion of Abyssinia (Ethiopia) in 1935–36. The CR.20bis was an improved model with a redesigned undercarriage. The CR.20/20bis was exported in some numbers to Austria, Hungary, Lithuania, Paraguay, Poland, and the Soviet Union.

SPECIFICATION: Type fighter • Crew 1 • Powerplant one 410hp Fiat A.20 12-cylinder V-type • Max speed 161mph (260km/h) • Service ceiling 27,885ft (8,500m) • Max range 466 miles (750km) • Wingspan 32ft 1in (9.80m) • Length 22ft (6.71m) • Height 9ft 1in (2.79m) • Weight 3,064lb (1,390kg) loaded • Armament two fixed forward-firing 0.303-in (7.62-mm) Vickers machine guns

Fiat CR.32   ITALY

SPECIFICATION: Type fighter (data Fiat CR.32quater) • Crew 1 • Powerplant one 600hp Fiat A.30 RAbis 12-cylinder V-type • Max speed 233mph (375km/h) • Service ceiling 28,870ft (8,800m) • Max range 422 miles (680km) • Wingspan 31ft 2in (9.50m) • Length 24ft 5in (7.45m) • Height 8ft 7in (2.63m) • Weight 4,079lb (1,850kg) loaded • Armament two fixed forward-firing 0.303-in (7.62-mm) Breda-SAFAT machine guns

◀ *The Fiat CR.32 fighter was used extensively in the Spanish Civil War, and was flown by the leading Spanish Nationalist air ace, Joaquin Garcia Morato, who had 36 victories.*

The CR.20's successor was the Fiat CR.30, which first flew on March 5, 1932 and which was designed in response to a requirement issued by the Italian Air Minister, Italo Balbo, for a "super fighter." The first of 121 CR.30s was delivered in the spring of 1934, but the type was soon superseded by the more refined CR.32, which made its appearance in 1933. It was considerably faster than the CR.30 and more maneuverable. Delivery of the first series (383 aircraft) began in 1935, this being followed by 328 examples of the improved CR.32bis. Two more variants, the CR.32ter (100 aircraft) and CR.32quater (401) were produced, these differing in armament and airframe detail. Total production of the CR.32 consequently amounted to 1,212 aircraft, making it numerically the most important biplane of its era. It was used extensively in the Spanish Civil War and in the early months of World War II, being used in Greece and East Africa.

▌Fiat CR.42 Falco

ITALY

▲ *The Fiat CR.42 took part in attacks on the British Isles towards the end of the Battle of Britain, suffering heavy losses to the RAF's Spitfires and Hurricanes.*

SPECIFICATION: Type fighter • Crew 1 • Powerplant one 840hp Fiat A.74 R1C 14-cylinder radial engine • Max speed 293mph (472km/h) • Service ceiling 32,265ft (9,835m) • Max range 416 miles (670km) • Wingspan 35ft 11in (10.96m) • Length 25ft 6in (7.79m) • Height 9ft 8in (2.96m) • Weight 5,324lb (2,415kg) loaded • Armament two 0.50-in (12.7-mm) Breda-SAFAT fixed forward-firing machine guns in upper forward fuselage

Although most fighter aircraft designers had switched to the monoplane configuration by the mid-1930s, Fiat's Celestino Rosatelli persisted with the open-cockpit, fabric-covered fighter biplane concept and developed the Fiat CR.41, a variant of the CR.32 with a radial engine and modified tail surfaces. This was further developed into the CR.42 Falco

(Falcon), the last of Italy's fighting biplanes. The Fiat CR.42 has been called a contemporary of the Gloster Gladiator, but in fact there was a four-year gap between the first flights of their respective prototypes, the first Gladiator flying in September 1934 and the CR.42 in May 1938. Like the Gladiator, the CR.42 was the subject of substantial export orders, serving with the air arms of Hungary, Belgium, and Sweden; but unlike the Gladiator, which was phased out of first-line service in 1941, the Italian fighter remained in full production from February 1939 until late in 1942. Some 272 were in service at the time of Italy's entry into the war in June 1940. Fifty CR.42s operated alongside Luftwaffe units in the Battle of Britain, suffering heavy losses. Production totaled 1,781 aircraft.

▌Fiat G.12T

ITALY

The Fiat G.12T was one of a number of three-engined transports used by the Regia Aeronautica during World War II. Developed from the commercial G.12C of 1937, the type was militarized in 1941 and small numbers continued to serve after the armistice with both the Co-Belligerent Air Force and the fas-

cist Aviazione della RSI. Later versions, which served with the postwar Italian Air Force, included the G.12LA and the G.12LP.

▲ *The G.12T had a beautifully contoured fuselage. The landing gear was of the retractable tailwheel type, and power was provided by three Fiat engines.*

SPECIFICATION: Type transportation • Crew 4 • Powerplant three 800hp Fiat A.74 RC42 14-cylinder radials • Max speed 242mph (390km/h) at 16,400ft (4,998m) • Service ceiling 27,900ft (8,500m) • Max range 1,430 miles (2,300km) • Wingspan 93ft 10in (28.60m) • Length 65ft 11in (20.10m) • Height 16ft 1in (4.90m) • Weight 33,100lb (15,000kg) • Armament two 0.303-in (7.62-mm) machine guns

▌Fiat G.50 Freccia

ITALY

Designed by Giuseppe Gabrielli, the Fiat G.50 Freccia (Arrow) was Italy's first monoplane fighter, flying for the first time on February 26, 1937. Although markedly inferior to the Macchi MC.200, the G.50 was ordered into production, and 783 examples were built in total. Two fighter groups were

armed with the type at the time of Italy's entry into the war in June 1940, these taking part in the short campaign against an already defeated France. Fiat G.50 units served on the Russian Front and in North Africa. Although the basic design of the G.50 was sound, it suffered from being underpowered.

◀ *This G.50 carries the markings of 352ª Stormo, 20° Gruppo while it was serving with the CAI (Corpo Aereo Italiano) in Belgium in 1940–41.*

SPECIFICATION: Type fighter • Crew 1 • Powerplant one 840hp Fiat A.74 RC38 14-cylinder radial • Max speed 294mph (473km/h) at 19,685ft (6,000m) • Service ceiling 35,100ft (10,700m) • Max range 420 miles (675km) • Wingspan 36ft (10.98m) • Length 25ft 7in (7.80m) • Height 9ft 8in (2.95m) • Weight 5,280lb (2,395kg) loaded • Armament two 0.50-in (12.7-mm) Breda-SAFAT machine guns

▌Fiat G.55 Centauro
ITALY

The basic soundness of the Fiat G.50's design was revealed by the aircraft that was developed as its successor, the G.55 Centauro. Fitted with a DB.605A engine and featuring an enclosed cockpit, the G.55 was the best fighter produced in Italy during World War II, but it did not enter production until 1943, with the result that only a few had been delivered before the Armistice. Production continued, however, and most of the 130 or so aircraft that were completed served with the pro-German Aviazione della RSI, performing well against Allied fighter types such as the Spitfire and Mustang.

SPECIFICATION: Type fighter • Crew 1 • Powerplant one 1,475hp Daimler-Benz DB 605A 12-cylinder V-type • Max speed 385mph (620km/h) at 24,300ft (7,400m) • Service ceiling 41,700ft (12,700m) • Max range 1,025 miles (1,650km) • Wingspan 38ft 10in (11.85m) • Length 30ft 9in (9.37m) • Height 12ft 4in (3.77m) • Weight 8,201lb (3,720kg) loaded • Armament two 0.50-in (12.7-mm) machine guns and three 0.79-in (20-mm) cannon

▲ *The Fiat G.55 was Italy's best fighter of World War II, but did not enter service until shortly before the armistice.*

▌Fiat G.59
ITALY

A product of the immediate postwar years, the unusually powerful and aerobatic Fiat G.59 trainer was derived from the G.55 Centauro and was produced in single- and two-seat versions as the G.59A and G.59B. The single-seater was developed in response to an order for a combat version from Syria, which took delivery of 26 aircraft armed with four 0.79-in (20-mm) cannon.

The last variants were the single-seat G.59-4A single-seater and the G.59-4B two-seater; these appeared in 1951 and were fitted with a bubble canopy.

▲ *Close-up of the Rolls-Royce Merlin-engined G.59. In all, 188 G.59s were built, with export examples going to Argentina and Syria.*

SPECIFICATION: Type combat trainer (data G.59-4A) • Crew 1 • Powerplant one 1,420hp Rolls-Royce Merlin 500/20 V-12 V-type • Max speed 368mph (593km/h) at 20,340ft (6,200m) • Service ceiling 37,730ft (11,500m) • Max range 620 miles (1,000km) • Wingspan 36ft 6in (11.12m) • Length 31ft 1in (9.47m) • Height 12ft 1in (3.78m) • Weight 7,630lb (3,460kg) loaded • Armament two 0.50-in (12.7-mm) machine guns

▌Fiat G.82

The Fiat G.82 was developed from the Fiat G.80, the first jet aircraft to be built in postwar Italy, which first flew in December 1951 powered by a de Havilland Goblin turbojet. The G.82, fitted with a Rolls-Royce Nene engine, failed to secure a NATO jet trainer order and only five were serving with the Italian Air Force until 1956. Two were later transferred to an experimental unit, where they remained until 1959.

SPECIFICATION: Type jet trainer • Crew 2 • Powerplant one 5,000lb (2,270kg) thrust Rolls-Royce Nene 2/21 turbojet • Max speed 565mph (910km/h) at 9,850ft (3,000m) • Service ceiling 41,000ft (12,500m) • Max range 1,000 miles (1,600km) • Wingspan 38ft 9in (11.80m) • Length 42ft 5in (12.93m) • Height 13ft 4in (4.07m) • Weight 13,780lb (6,250kg) loaded • Armament two 0.50-in (12.7-mm) machine guns or two 0.79-in (20-mm) cannon

▲ The Fiat G.82 was built in response to a NATO jet trainer competition, but failed to meet the necessary requirements. Only a few were built.

▌Fiat G.91

The Fiat G.91 lightweight ground attack fighter was designed in response to a NATO requirement issued in 1954, Fiat being awarded a contract for three prototypes and 27 pre-production aircraft. Total procurement of all G.91 variants

from 1956 to 1977 was 756. The initial version, the G.91R, was built in four subseries the R-1 and R-1B for the Italian Air Force (90); the R-3 for the Federal German Luftwaffe (50 built in Italy and 294 in Germany); and the

▲ A two-seat Fiat G.91T trainer of the Italian Air Force. The versatile G.91 was the winner of a 1954 NATO light fighter contest.

SPECIFICATION: Type single-seat tactical reconnaissance aircraft (data G.91R-3) • Crew 1 • Powerplant one 5,000-lb (2,268-kg) thrust Fiat-built Bristol Siddeley Orpheus 803 turbojet • Max speed 675mph (1,086km/h) at 5,000ft (1,520m) • Service ceiling 42,978ft (13,100m) • Combat radius 200 miles (320km) • Wingspan 28ft 1in (8.56m) • Length 33ft 9in (10.30m) • Height 13ft 1in (4m) • Weight 12,125lb (5,500kg) • Armament two 1.19-in (30-mm) DEFA cannon; four underwing pylons for various ordnance; three Vinten cameras

R-4 (50), originally intended for Turkey and Greece but in the event delivered to Germany. The second basic version was the G.91T two-seat trainer, 99 being built for Italy and 66 for Germany. Forty-two ex-Luftwaffe G.91R-3/4s and eight G.91Ts were also operated by the Portuguese Air Force. The last G.91 variant was the G.91Y, which was substantially redesigned and had two General Electric J85 turbojets to allow a greater tactical load.

Fiat R.2

Designed by Celestino Rosatelli, the R.2 reconnaissance aircraft of 1918 was one of the first machines to carry the Fiat name. It was intended to be an improvement on another aircraft, the SIA (Societa Italiana Aviazione) 7B2, after that concern had been taken over by Fiat. Some 500 R.2s were ordered, but most were canceled with the end of World War I and only 129 were built, some remaining in service until 1925.

SPECIFICATION: Type reconnaissance biplane • Crew 2 • Powerplant one 300hp Fiat A12bis 6-cylinder in-line engine • Max speed 108mph (175km/h) at sea level • Service ceiling 15,750ft (4,800m) • Max range 340 miles (550km) • Wingspan 40ft 4in (12.30m) • Length 28ft 10in (8.80m) • Height 10ft 10in (3.30m) • Weight 3,792lb (1,720kg) loaded • Armament two–three machine guns

Fiat RS.14

Conceived in 1938 as a land-based bomber and later adapted, the Fiat RS.14 maritime reconnaissance seaplane had a troubled development phase, and did not enter service until 1942. It served in the Mediterranean and Aegean throughout the final year of Italy's war. Almost all of the 152 aircraft delivered were destroyed.

SPECIFICATION: Type torpedo-bomber and reconnaissance floatplane • Crew 4–5 • Powerplant two 840hp Fiat A.74 RC38 14-cylinder radial engines • Max speed 242mph (390km/h) at 15,400ft (4,693m) • Service ceiling 16,400ft (5,000m) • Max range 1,550 miles (2,500km) • Wingspan 64ft 1in (19.54m) • Length 46ft 3in (14.10m) • Height 18ft 6in (5.63m) • Weight 18,700lb (8,470kg) loaded • Armament three 0.50-in (12.7-mm) machine guns; up to 880lb (400kg) of bombs

▲ In a bombing role the RS.14 could carry a long ventral gondola to accommodate various combinations of anti-submarine bombs.

Fieseler Fi 156 Störch

A remarkable aircraft, the Fi 156 Störch (Stork) was fitted with powerful high-lift devices that permitted it to take off in only 70 yards (65m), land in 20 yards (18m), and virtually hover in a 25mph (40km/h) headwind without any loss of control. The result of a 1935 requirement for an army co-operation, casualty evacuation, and liaison aircraft, the Fi 156 first flew in the spring and entered service in 1937. Production totaled about 2,900 aircraft, the main variants being the unarmed Fi 156A model, the Fi 156C armed model

SPECIFICATION: Type army cooperation, liaison, and casualty evacuation aircraft • Crew 3 (Fi 156C) • Powerplant one 240hp Argus As10C-3 8-cylinder inverted-V type • Max speed 109mph (175km/h) • Service ceiling 17,060ft (5,200m) • Max range 631 miles (1,015km) • Wingspan 46ft 9in (14.25m) • Length 32ft 5in (9.90m) • Height 10ft (3.05m) • Weight 2,910lb (1,320kg) loaded • Armament one 0.31-in (7.92-mm) trainable machine gun in rear of cockpit

in four subvariants, and the Fi 156D air ambulance model in two subvariants. The Störch was widely used on all fronts, and was noted for its part in the daring rescue by German commandos of the Italian dictator, Mussolini, from a tiny plateau on the Gran Sasso in 1943.

◄ *This lovingly restored Fieseler Störch, bearing the British registration G-AZMH, was pictured at Duxford in 1975.*

▌Fieseler Fi 167

GERMANY

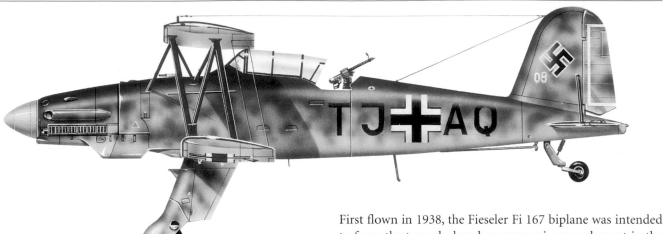

SPECIFICATION: **Type** torpedo-bomber and reconnaissance biplane • **Crew** 2 • **Powerplant** one 1,100hp Daimler-Benz DB 601B 12-cylinder inverted-Vee type • **Max speed** 202mph (325km/h) at sea level • **Service ceiling** 26,905ft (8,200m) • **Max range** 932 miles (1,500km) • **Wingspan** 44ft 3in (13.50m) • **Length** 37ft 4in (11.40m) • **Height** 15ft 9in (4.80m) • **Weight** 10,692lb (4,850kg) loaded • **Armament** one 0.31-in (7.92-mm) fixed forward-firing machine gun in starboard side of forward fuselage, one trainable 0.31-in (7.92-mm) in rear cockpit, plus an external bomb and torpedo load of 2,205lb (1,000kg)

First flown in 1938, the Fieseler Fi 167 biplane was intended to form the torpedo-bomber-reconnaissance element in the air group assigned to the *Graf Zeppelin*, Germany's proposed aircraft carrier. The aircraft handled well and had several innovations, including full-span automatic slots on the leading edges of both wings and large flaps on both wings that gave the aircraft exceptional low-speed characteristics and permitted near-vertical descents. Twelve preproduction Fi 167A-0s were ordered and were ready for evaluation by the summer of 1940, but work on the *Graf Zeppelin* was halted and the aircraft were withdrawn, all but three being sold to Romania for coastal patrol over the Black Sea.

▌FMA IAe.58 Pucara

ARGENTINA

▶ *Still remaining in front-line service with Argentina, the Pucará is undoubtedly a capable type, but was unsuited to operations in the Falklands War.*

SPECIFICATION: **Type** assault aircraft • **Crew** 2 • **Powerplant** two 1,022hp Turboméca Astazou XVIG turboprops • **Max speed** 310mph (500km/h) at 9,842ft (3,000m) • **Service ceiling** 32,808ft (10,000m) • **Max range** 1,890 miles (3,042km) • **Wingspan** 47ft 6in (14.50m) • **Length** 46ft 7in (14.25m) • **Height** 17ft 6in (5.36m) • **Weights** 7,815lb (3,545kg) empty; 7,936lb (3,600kg) loaded • **Armament** two 0.79-in (20-mm) cannon and four 0.303-in (7.62-mm) machine guns; up to 3,571lb (1,620kg) external stores

Originally known as the Delfin, the IAe.58 Pucara twin-turboprop assault aircraft flew for the first time on August 20, 1969 powered by two AirResearch TPW331 engines. Intended primarily for counterinsurgency work, the type entered service with the Argentine Air Force's 11th Escuadron de Exploration y Ataque in June 1978. The Pucara presented a serious threat to British forces during the Falklands campaign of 1982. About one hundred were delivered.

Focke-Wulf Fw 56   GERMANY

The Focke-Wulf Fw 56 Stösser (Falcon Hawk) was designed by Kurt Tank and built in 1934, subsequently being built in large numbers for the civil flying clubs, for export and for the Luftwaffe. The Fw 56 was supplied to the Austrian and Hungarian Air Forces as well as to the Luftwaffe. The aircraft had excellent high-speed diving characteristics, and was used by Ernst Udet to demonstrate dive-bombing techniques to the German General Staff, leading to their official adoption.

SPECIFICATION: Type single-seat advanced trainer • Crew 2 • Powerplant one 240hp Argus As 10C8-cylinder inverted-Vee air-cooled engine • Max speed 173mph (278km/h) at sea level • Service ceiling 20,336ft (6,200m) • Max range 250 miles (400km) • Wingspan 34ft 5in (10.50m) • Length 25ft 3in (7.60m) • Height 11ft 7in (3.52m) • Weight 2,196lb (996kg) loaded • Armament none

▲ This, the first of the pre-production aircraft, incorporated a number of changes compared to the earlier machines. These included a revised exhaust arrangement to prevent noxious gases from entering the cockpit.

Focke-Wulf Fw 58 Weihe   GERMANY

First flown in 1935, the Focke-Wulf Fw 58 Weihe (Kite) light transport was built in large numbers and was widely exported. The Fw 58B, was used by the Luftwaffe as a pilot, radio, and navigational and gunnery trainer, this model normally having a glazed nose section with a single 3.1-in (7.9-mm) gun and an open gun position aft. A twin-float version of the Fw 58B was known as the Fw 58W. The principal wartime production version of the Weihe was the Fw 58C.

▲ The Focke-Wulf Fw 58 was one of the Luftwaffe's "workhorse" aircraft during World War II, serving in a variety of training and transport roles.

SPECIFICATION: Type general-purpose transportation • Crew 2 • Powerplant two 240hp Argus As10C 8-cylinder inverted-Vee air cooled engines • Max speed 150mph (242km/h) • Service ceiling 18,372ft (5,600m) • Max range 497 miles (800km) • Wingspan 68ft 10in (21m) • Length 45ft 11in (14m) • Height 13ft 9in (4.19m) • Weight 7,936lb (3,600kg) loaded • Armament one 0.31-in (7.9-mm) machine gun in nose and one in dorsal position

Focke-Wulf Fw 187   GERMANY

A high-performance twin-engined heavy fighter, the Fw 187 Falke (Falcon) first flew in the summer of 1937 and, although considerably underpowered, attained a maximum speed of 326mph (525km/h). Its handling characteristics were superb,

▶ Though the Fw 187 demonstrated excellent performance, the RLM refused to proceed with the type, ordering only three pre-production models.

SPECIFICATION: Type heavy escort fighter • Crew 2 • Powerplant two 700hp
Junkers Jumo 210Ga 12-cylinder inverted-Vee engines • Max speed 329mph
(529km/h) at 13,124ft (4,000m) • Service ceiling 32,810ft (10,000m) • Max range
not known • Wingspan 50ft 2in (15.30m) • Length 36ft 5in (11.10m) • Height 12ft
7in (3.85m) • Weight 11,023lb (5,000kg) loaded • Armament two fixed 0.79-in
(20-mm) cannon and four 0.31-in (7.92-mm) machine guns in nose

its turn radius being superior to that of many contemporary single-engined fighters. Orders for seven further Fw 187A-0 aircraft were placed, but despite being superior to the Bf 110 in most respects the type was not adopted. After brief trials with JG 77in Norway the Fw 187A-0s were assigned to the defense of the Focke-Wulf aircraft factory at Bremen.

■ Focke-Wulf Fw 189

GERMANY

The Fw 189 Uhu (Owl) short-range reconnaissance aircraft first flew in July 1938 and entered service in 1940. An unorthodox design, it featured two tail bombs, each bearing an engine, on either side of a heavily glazed central nacelle. Production totaled 848, excluding 16 prototype and preproduction aircraft. Subvariants of the basic Fw 189A included the Fw 189A-2, with heavier defensive armament, the Fw 189A-3 dual-control trainer, and the Fw 189A-4 tactical support model with ventral armor and 0.79-in (20-mm) can-

non. The Fw 189 saw extensive service on the Eastern Front in WWII, where it enjoyed considerable success. About 30 aircraft were operated as night fighters against Soviet Po-2 biplanes carrying out "nuisance" attacks.

SPECIFICATION: Type tactical reconnaissance aircraft • Crew 3 • Powerplant two
465hp Argus As 410A-1 12-cylinder engines • Max speed 217mph
(350km/h) • Service ceiling 23,950ft (7,300m) • Max range 416 miles (670km)
• Wingspan 60ft 4in (18.40m) • Length 39ft 5in (12.03m) • Height 10ft 2in
(3.10m) • Weight 9,193lb (4,170kg) loaded • Armament two fixed 0.31-in
(7.92-mm) forward-firing machine guns in wing roots, one 0.31-in (7.92-
mm) twin-barrel machine guns in dorsal position and one in the tail cone
turret, plus a bomb load of 441lb (200kg)

▲ *The Fw 189 was widely used in the tactical reconnaissance role on the Russian front, and some were operated as night fighters.*

■ Focke-Wulf Fw 190

GERMANY

The Focke-Wulf Fw 190 stemmed from a suggestion by the German Air Ministry in 1937 that the company should develop an interceptor fighter to complement the Bf 109. Instead of opting for the Daimler Benz DB601 in-line engine,

already in production for the Bf 109, Kurt Tank, Focke-Wulf's technical director, chose the BMW type 139 18-cylinder radial, which was still in the development stage. Three prototypes were built, the first of which flew on June 1, 1939. Apart from some engine overheating problems the flight tests went very well, and construction of the other prototypes was accelerated. The fifth Fw 190 was reengined with the new 1,660hp BMW 14-cylinder 801C-0 engine, and this met all the Luftwaffe requirements. Its success led to the construction of 30 preproduction aircraft designated Fw 190A-0, these being followed by the Fw 190A-1, which went into service with JG26 at Le Bourget, Paris, in August 1941.

The Fw 190A-1 was followed into production by the A-2 (426 built), with a longer span and heavier armament, and

◀ *One of the most versatile combat aircraft of World War II, the Fw 190 was used on all fronts. Seen here is the Fw 190A-8/U1 two-seat trainer.*

509 A-3 fighter-bombers. Both JG 2 and JG 26 rearmed with the A-3 in June 1942 and began attacks on targets on the south coast of England. The next variant, the Fw 190A-4, of which 494 were built, had a methanol-water power boost system. The A-5 was a development of the A-4 with the engine relocated 5.9in (0.15m) farther forward; 723 aircraft were delivered, and undertook a variety of roles including assault, night fighting, torpedo-bomber, and bomber destroyer. Some A-5s were modified as two-seat Fw 190S-5 trainers, the S denoting Schulflugzeug (training aircraft). The Fw 190A-6, of which 569 were built, was a version of the Fw 190A-5/U10 fighter with a lightened wing structure and a fixed armament of four 0.79-in (20-mm) cannon.

The Fw 190A-7, which entered production in December 1943, had a revised armament of two 0.79-in (20-mm) cannon in the wing roots and two 0.50-in (12.7-mm) machine guns in the forward fuselage. Only 80 aircraft were built before it was supplanted by the Fw 190A-8, the last new-build variant of the Fw 190A series. Total production was 1,334 aircraft. The A-8 was fitted with a nitrous oxide power boost system and an extra fuel tank in the rear fuselage. Some were converted to the training role with the designation Fw 190S-8.

Although designed as a fighter, the Fw 190 proved readily adaptable to the ground attack role, and 1942 saw the emergence of the Fw 190G long-range attack variant. This interim aircraft was followed, out of sequence, by the Fw 190F, which was basically a Fw 190A-5 airframe with strengthened landing gear, more armor protection, and a combination of one ETC 501 bomb rack under the fuselage and four ETC 50 bomb racks under the wings. A batch of 30 Fw 190F-1 aircraft was followed by 271 Fw 190F-2s with an improved canopy, about 250 Fw 190F-3s with a revised wing structure, 385 Fw 190F-7s based on the Fw 190A-7, and an unknown number of Fw 190F-9s with the powerful 2270hp BMW 801TS/TH turbocharged engine.

SPECIFICATION: Type fighter (Fw 190A-8) • Crew 1 • Powerplant one 2,100hp BMW 801D-2 radial engine with water-methanol boost • Max speed 406mph (654km/h) at 19,685ft (6,000m) • Service ceiling 37,402ft (11,400m) • Max range 915 miles (1,470km) • Wingspan 34ft 5in (10.50m) • Length 29ft (8.84m) • Height 13ft (3.96m) • Weight 10,802lb (4,900kg) loaded • Armament two 0.31-in (7.92-mm) machine guns in nose and up to four 0.79-in (20-mm) cannon in wings, plus provision for wide range of under-fuselage and underwing bombs and RPs

Focke-Wulf Fw 190D-9

GERMANY

The final, and much altered, version of the Fw 190 was the Fw 190D. In this model, the BMW radial engine that had powered earlier versions was discarded and replaced by the 1776hp Junkers Jumo 213A-1 engine, a liquid-cooled powerplant whose annular radiator duct gave the new variant a radial-engined appearance.

The major production model was the D-9, which, characterized by its long, newly contoured engine cowling, entered service with III/JG 54 in the fall of 1944, followed by I/JG 26. Both Gruppen were given the task of defending the air bases used by the Messerschmitt 262 jet fighter. Early in 1945 II/JG 26 also rearmed with the type, as did JG 2, JG 6, and JG 301. The Fw 190D-9 was a pure interceptor; other variants,

equipped for ground attack, included the D-11 with two wing-mounted 1.19-in (30-mm) MK108 cannon, and the D-12 and D-13, powered by a Jumo 213F engine and armed respectively with a single nose-mounted MK 108 or MK103.

SPECIFICATION: Type fighter • Crew 1 • Powerplant one 1,776hp Junkers Jumo 213A-1 liquid-cooled engine • Max speed 426mph (685km/h) at 19,685ft (6,000m) • Service ceiling 39,372ft (12,000m) • Max range 520 miles (837km) • Wingspan 34ft 5in (10.50m) • Length 33ft 5in (10.24m) • Height 11ft (3.35m) • Weight 10,670lb (4,850kg) loaded • Armament two wing-mounted machine guns 151/20 0.79-in (20-mm) cannon; two 0.31-in (7.92-mm) machine guns mounted above the engine

▲ *An early model "long nose" Fw 190D, fitted with a BMW radial engine, in the markings of a Luftwaffe trials unit, Erprobungskommando 16.*

▍Focke-Wulf Fw 200 Condor

GERMANY

Early in 1939 the Focke-Wulf design team started work on a bomber version of the Fw 200 civil airliner, originally to fulfill a Japanese order, the converted aircraft being designated Fw 200C. By the time the first Fw 200C had been completed World War II had begun, and the Condor was taken on by the Luftwaffe, the aircraft being ordered into production for the maritime reconnaissance role. The first unit to receive the maritime reconnaissance Condor was the Luftwaffe's Long-Range Reconnaissance Squadron (Fernaufklärungsstaffel), which began operations in April 1940 and was redesignated I/KG 40 later in the month. Production of the Fw 200C-1 continued throughout 1940, 36 aircraft being produced in the course of the year, and in 1941 Focke-Wulf turned out 58 Fw 200C-2s, which differed from the C-1 in having two bomb racks of improved design under each wing. While the initial production version of the Condor was operationally successful, it suffered from a serious structural weakness of the rear fuselage, and some aircraft were destroyed when they literally broke in half on landing. To remedy the problem a structurally strengthened version, the Fw 200C-3, was placed in production by mid-1941, and this variant of the Condor was produced in greater numbers than its predecessors. Normal endurance was 9 hours and 45 minutes, but with internal long-range tanks fitted the aircraft could remain airborne for as long as 18 hours. KG 40's Condors presented a far more serious threat than submarines to Allied shipping in

▼ *The Focke-Wulf Fw 200 Condor presented a major threat to Allied shipping in the Atlantic and North Sea during 1940–41.*

the Atlantic and North Sea in 1940–41. Between August 1940 and February 1941 they claimed 363,000 tons (368,826 tonnes) sunk; most of this loss occurred in April 1941, when 116 ships totaling 323,000 tons (328,185 tonnes) were sunk. The final operational version of the Condor was the Fw 200C-6, developed from the C-3 to carry a Henschel Hs 293B

SPECIFICATION: Type long-range maritime patrol aircraft • Crew 6 • Powerplant four 1,200hp BMW-Bramo 323R-2 Fafnir nine-cylinder radial engines (FW 200C-3/U4) • Max speed 224mph (360km/h) at 15,420ft (4,700m) • Service ceiling 19,685ft (6,000m) • Max range 2,759 miles (4,440km) • Wingspan 107ft 8in (32.84m) • Length 76ft 11in (23.32m) • Height 20ft 8in (6.30m) • Weight 50,044lb (22,700kg) loaded • Armament one 0.31-in (7.92-mm) gun in forward dorsal turret, one 0.50-in (13-mm) gun in rear dorsal position, two 0.50-in (13-mm) guns in beam positions, one 0.79-in (20-mm) gun in forward position of ventral gondola and one 0.31-in (7.92-mm) gun in aft ventral position; maximum bomb load of 4,630lb (2,100kg)

air-to-surface missile under each outer engine nacelle, the underwing bomb racks being removed. The combination of Hs 293 and Fw 200 was first used operationally on December 28, 1943.

The total number of Condors produced during the war years was 252 aircraft. Many were relegated to transportation duties in 1942, nine being lost in attempts to resupply the German garrison at Stalingrad.

▼ *Known as the "Scourge of the Atlantic", the Condor was notorious in Britain as one of Germany's most potent anti-shipping weapons.*

▌Focke-Wulf Ta 152

GERMANY

The Focke-Wulf Ta 152, bearing the prefix that denoted the name of its designer, Kurt Tank, was a long-span version of the Fw 190D-9 and was intended for high altitude interception. The first production model was the Ta 152H, whose

▲ *Kurt Tank's successful Fw 190 design gave him the right to use the first letters of his surname to prefix all subsequent Focke-Wulf designs.*

speed at high altitude was greater than any Allied fighter. The prototype flew toward the end of 1944 and production, which started in January 1945, reached a total of 150 aircraft, some of which were delivered to Erprobungskommando 152 at Rechlin and to JG 301, which was assigned to the defense of the Me 262 bases.

A second production version, the Ta 152C, made its appearance early in 1945.

SPECIFICATION: Type high-altitude interceptor • Crew 1 • Powerplant one 1,750hp Junkers Jumo 213E-3 12-cylinder liquid cooled V-type • Max speed 472mph (759km/h) at 41,000ft (12,500m) • Service ceiling 48,550ft (14,800m) • Max range 755 miles (1,215km) • Wingspan 47ft 4in (14.43m) • Length 35ft 2in (10.71m) • Height 11ft (3.35m) • Weight 10,472lb (4,744kg) loaded • Armament two wing-mounted 0.79-in (20-mm) MG151/20 cannon; one engine-mounted MK108 1.19-in (30-mm) cannon

▌Focke-Wulf Ta 154

GERMANY

The Focke-Wulf Ta 154 Moskito was a promising night fighter design that was plagued by structural problems. Designed to be of wooden construction throughout, in order to utilize the skills of trained woodworkers and cut down on the use of scarce metals, the Moskito featured a tricycle undercarriage

with large-diameter tires to facilitate takeoffs from unprepared strips. Powered by two Junkers Jumo 211F engines, the Ta 154 carried a crew of two (pilot and radio/radar operator). Armament comprised two forward-firing 1.19-in (30-mm) and two 0.79-in (20-mm) cannon, with a single 1.19-in (30-

▲ *This aircraft was the first "Moskito" to be fitted with radar equipment and became the prototype for the Ta 154A-0/U-1 night fighter.*

SPECIFICATION: Type night fighter • Crew 2 • Powerplant two Junkers Jumo 211F 12-cylinder inverted-Vee liquid-cooled engines • Max speed 395mph (635km/h) at 20,000ft (6,100m) • Service ceiling 34,440ft (10,500m) • Endurance 2hrs 45mins • Wingspan 52ft 6in (16m) • Length 39ft 8in (12.10m) • Height 11ft 5in (3.50m) • Weight 18,191lb (8,250kg) loaded • Armament two 1.19-in (30-mm) MK108 cannon and two 0.79-in (20-mm) MG151 cannon in fuselage sides; one obliquely mounted 1.19-in (30-mm) MK108 cannon in upper rear fuselage

mm) cannon mounted obliquely in the rear fuselage. The prototype Ta 154V-1 flew in July 1943 and the type was ordered into production in November, but there were continual delays and in June 1944 the first two production Ta 154A-1s were accidentally destroyed—one when it fell apart because faulty glue had been used in its assembly and the other when its flaps broke away on a landing approach—and as a result the production order was canceled. Seven more production Ta 154A-1s were completed, however, and these were used operationally for a while by I/NJG3 at Stade and by NJGr10. There is no record of their combat achievements, if indeed there were any.

∎ Fokker C.V

NETHERLANDS

The Fokker C.V was undoubtedly one of the most successful aircraft designed in the years between the two world wars. Versatile and easy to maintain, an added bonus was that the wings and engine could be readily interchanged, depending on the customer's requirements, and that these changes could be carried out within an hour.

The prototype C.V flew in May 1924 and was followed

SPECIFICATION: Type general-purpose biplane (data Fokker C.VD) • Crew 2 • Powerplant one 450hp Bristol Jupiter 9-cylinder radial • Max speed 200mph (320km/h) • Service ceiling 19,680ft (6,000m) • Max range 740 miles (1,200km) • Wingspan 41ft (12.50m) • Length 31ft 4in (9.55m) • Height 11ft 6in (3.50m) • Weight 4,222lb(1,915kg) loaded • Armament two 0.30-in (7.62-mm) machine guns

by three early versions, the C.VA, C.VB, and C.VC, which were fitted with liquid-cooled in-line engines. The next two variants, the C.VD and C.VE, differed in that they could be fitted with radial engines, and also had a modified wing platform. Apart from serving with the Royal Netherlands Air Force, the Fokker C.V in its several versions was either sold to or license-built in Denmark, Hungary, Italy (where it was manufactured by IMAM as the Ro.1), Norway, Sweden, and Switzerland. Many C.Vs were still in Dutch service in 1940. Captured Danish aircraft were used by the Luftwaffe for night operations on the Eastern Front in the summer of 1944.

Fokker C.X

NETHERLANDS

▲ The Fokker C.X was the last in the line of Antony Fokker's graceful biplane light bomber designs, and was produced only in small numbers.

The Fokker C.X reconnaissance/bomber biplane was produced in 1933 to succeed the C.V, but in the event it was built only in small numbers. Of the 30 aircraft acquired by the Netherlands Army Air Service, 10 were shipped to the Dutch East Indies. A further 35 aircraft, powered by the Bristol Mercury radial engine, were license-built in Finland.

SPECIFICATION: Type reconnaissance/bomber biplane • Crew 2 • Powerplant one 650hp Rolls-Royce Kestrel V in-line engine • Max speed 212mph (341km/h) at 10,000ft (3,050m) • Service ceiling 27,400ft (8,357m) • Max range 520 miles (837km) • Wingspan 39ft 4in (12m) • Length 30ft 2in (9.21m) • Height 10ft 10in (3.29m) • Weight 4,960lb (2,247kg) loaded • Armament two 0.30-in (7.62-mm) machine guns; 877lb (398kg) of bombs

Fokker Dr.I

GERMANY

Made famous as the red-painted mount of Baron Manfred von Richthofen at the time of his death, the rotary-engined Dr.I triplane was introduced into service in October 1917, but although it was a supremely maneuverable fighter it was already being outclassed by a new generation of fighting scouts. Its early career was marred by a series of fatal crashes. The fact that it received many accolades—at which Anthony Fokker himself expressed surprise—was due in the main to the skilled men who flew it, such as Richthofen and Werner Voss. It was never used in very large numbers.

SPECIFICATION: Type scouting triplane • Crew 1 • Powerplant one 110hp Oberursel Ur11 9-cylinder rotary • Max speed 115mph (185km/h) • Service ceiling 20,000ft (6,100m) • Endurance 1hr 30mins • Wingspan 23ft 7in (7.19m) • Length 18ft 11in (5.77m) • Height 9ft 8in (2.95m) • Weight 1291lb (586kg) loaded • Armament two fixed forward-firing 0.31-in (7.92-mm) LMF 08/51 machine guns

▲ Although it was outclassed by the end of 1917, the Fokker Dr.I remained the preferred mount of pilots such as Manfred von Richthofen.

Fokker D.VII

GERMANY

Without doubt the best fighter of World War I to be produced in any numbers, the Fokker D.VII had its origins late in 1917, at a time when the German Flying Corps was beginning to lose the ascendency and technical superiority it had enjoyed

▲ *The best German fighter aircraft to serve in quantity during WWI, the Fokker D.VII was much prized as war booty by the Allies.*

for nearly three years. The German High Command considered the situation to be so serious that it ordered German aircraft manufacturers to give top priority to the development of new fighters; the prototypes of the various designs would take part in a competitive fly-off. The Fokker D.VII proved to be by far the best all-round contender and won by a handsome margin, Fokker receiving an initial contract for 400 aircraft. (Up to that time, the largest order Fokker had received for any of his fighter designs had been for 60 Dr.I triplanes.) The first

examples were delivered to JG 1, and about 1,000 had been completed by the time of the Armistice in November 1918.

SPECIFICATION: **Type** scouting biplane • **Crew** 1 • **Powerplant** one 185hp BMW III 6-cylinder in-line engine • **Max speed** 124mph (200km/h) • **Service ceiling** 22,965ft (7,000m) • **Endurance** 1hr 30mins • **Wingspan** 29ft 2in (8.90m) • **Length** 22ft 9in (6.95m) • **Height** 9ft (2.75m) • **Weight** 1,940lb (880kg) loaded • **Armament** two fixed forward-firing 0.31in (7.92mm) LMG 08/15 machine guns

▌Fokker D.VIII

GERMANY

Another Fokker design of 1918 that at first appeared to show much promise was the E.V. A very simple design, it had a one-piece cantilever parasol wing and twin Spandau machine guns mounted immediately in front of the cock-

▶ *A parasol monoplane design, the Fokker D.VIII was well liked by the pilots who flew it and in some respects was better than the D.VII.*

SPECIFICATION: **Type** scouting monoplane • **Crew** 1 • **Powerplant** one 110hp Oberursel UR.11 rotary engine • **Max speed** 115mph (185km/h) • **Service ceiling** 20,669ft (6,300m) • **Endurance** 1hr 30mins • **Wingspan** 27ft 6in (8.40m) • **Length** 19ft 2in (5.86m) • **Height** 9ft 3in (2.82m) • **Weight** 1,238lb (562kg) loaded • **Armament** two fixed forward-firing 0.31-in (7.92-mm) LMG 08/15 machine guns

pit. Production E.Vs were delivered to the German Flying Corps from July 1918, but in August Jasta 6, one of the first

units to receive the type, experienced three serious crashes due to wing structural failure. Imperfect timber and faulty manufacturing methods were found to have been the cause, but 60 aircraft were immobilized in the factory while investigations were carried out and it was not until September that production was started again, the type now bearing the designation Fokker D.VIII. It was more maneuverable than the D.VII biplane and had a better operational ceiling, although it was slightly slower. Only about 90 had been delivered by the end of the war and, although its pilots reported that it handled well, it had little chance to prove itself in action.

Fokker D.XI–D.XVII

NETHERLANDS

Returning to his native Holland after World War I, Anthony Fokker soon began building military aircraft again, at first only for export. His first successful Dutch-built design was the D.XI of 1923; 126 examples were purchased by the Soviet

▲ The Fokker D.XIII gained four world air speed records in 1925; about 50 examples were supplied to the USSR to train German pilots.

government, which assigned them to the secret training of German pilots. Further purchases by Argentina, Romania, Spain, Switzerland, and the US brought the total built to 178. The Fokker D.XII, which was not a success, was developed into the D.XIII fighter; fast, with an excellent all-round performance, it too was purchased by the USSR, 50 examples being built. In 1929 Fokker received an order from the Royal Netherlands Army Air Service for 15 examples of a new fighter, the D.XVI, followed by 11 D.XVIIs. The latter remained in service until 1940, although only in a training role.

SPECIFICATION: Type fighter (data Fokker D.XIII) • Crew 1 • Powerplant one 450hp Napier Lion XI 12-cylinder V-type • Max speed 164mph (265km/h) • Service ceiling 26,246ft (8,000m) • Max range 373 miles (600km) • Wingspan 36ft 1in (11m) • Length 25ft 11in (7.90m) • Height 9ft 6in (2.90m) • Weight 3,549lb (1,610kg) loaded • Armament two fixed forward-firing 0.30-in (7.62-mm) machine guns

Fokker D.XXI

NETHERLANDS

Designed in 1935, the D.XXI was originally intended for the Royal Netherlands East Indies Army Air Service, but instead 36 examples were ordered for the home air force. Seven Dutch-built D.XXIs were supplied to Finland, which built 93 more under license. The Dutch aircraft fought against hopeless odds during the German invasion of May 1940, while the Finnish D.XXIs were prominent in the "Winter War" against the USSR in 1939–40.

▶ Although it retained anachronistic fixed main undercarriage units, the D.XXI gave a reasonably good account of itself, especially in Finnish hands.

SPECIFICATION: Type fighter • Crew 1 • Powerplant one 830hp Bristol Mercury VIII 9-cylinder radial • Max speed 286mph (460km/h) • Service ceiling 36,090ft (11,000m) • Max range 578 miles (930km) • Wingspan 36ft 1in (11m) • Length 26ft 10in (8.20m) • Height 9ft 8in (2.95m) • Weight 4,519lb (2,050kg) • Armament four 0.31-in (7.92-mm) machine guns, two in upper forward fuselage and two in wings

▌Fokker D.XXIII

SPECIFICATION: Type fighter • Crew 1 • Powerplant two 540hp Walter Sagitta I-SR 12-cylinder in-lines • Max speed 326mph (524km/h) • Service ceiling 29,520ft (9,000m) • Max range 560 miles (900km) • Wingspan 37ft 9in (11.50m) • Length 35ft 1in (10.70m) • Height 10ft 11in (3.34m) • Weight 6,600lb (2,990kg) loaded • Armament four 0.31-in (7.92-mm) machine guns

▲ *The Fokker D.XXIII had many innovations, including the use of a tractor and a pusher engine, with the pilot's cockpit mounted in between.*

Although it never entered production, the Fokker D.XXIII was noteworthy as one of the most interesting and innova-tive fighters of the late 1930s. Designed in 1938, it was a twin-boom, twin-engine monoplane with a tricycle undercarriage, the engines—one tractor, one pusher—being mounted on a central nacelle with the pilot's cockpit in between. The sole prototype flew for the first time in May 1939, but was destroyed by German bombing in 1940.

▌Fokker E.I–E.III

▲ *A Fokker Monoplane pictured with its pilot, Feldwebel Prehn, and his mechanics. The E.III wrested air superiority from the Allies in 1915.*

Early in 1915, the Dutch designer Anthony Fokker, who had been shown early French attempts to produce a device to enable a machine gun to be fired through an aircraft's pro-peller arc, set about designing a simple engine-driven system that operated the mechanism of a Parabellum machine gun once during each revolution of the propeller while the pilot depressed the trigger. The mechanism was successfully demonstrated on a Fokker M5K monoplane; this was given the military designation E.I (the "E" signifying Eindecker, or monoplane), and so became the first German aircraft dedi-cated to the pursuit and destruction of enemy aircraft.

The "Fokker Scourge," as it came to be known, began on July 1, 1915, when Lieutenant Kurt Wintgens of Feldflieger Abteilung 6b, flying the Fokker M5K, shot down a French Morane monoplane. The production Fokker E.I had begun to reach the front-line German units in June, and the small number of machines available, in the hands of pilots whose names would soon become legendary, began to make their presence felt. Foremost among them were Lieutenants Max Immelmann and Oswald Boelcke, both of Feldflieger Abteilung 62.

The E.I was superseded by a refined and strengthened

▼ *A Fokker Monoplane being inspected by French personnel after being brought down during the Battle of the Marne in 1915.*

version, the E.II. The definitive version of the Fokker Monoplane was the E.III, some of which were armed with twin Spandau machine guns. Abteilung 62 rearmed with the new type at the end of 1915. The Fokker Monoplane was the first dedicated fighter aircraft to see operational service, and for months it made Allied reconnaissance flights into German territory virtual suicide missions.

SPECIFICATION: Type scouting monoplane • Crew 1 • Powerplant one 100hp Oberursel U.1 9-cylinder rotary engine • Max speed 83mph (134km/h) • Service ceiling 11,500ft (3,500m) • Endurance 2hr 45 mins • Wingspan 31ft 3in (9.52m) • Length 23ft 11in (7.30m) • Height 9ft 6in (2.89m) • Weight 1,400lb (635kg) loaded • Armament one fixed forward-firing 0.31-in (7.92-mm) Spandau machine gun

▌Fokker G.I   NETHERLANDS

SPECIFICATION: Type heavy fighter and assault aircraft (data G.IA) • Crew 2–3 • Powerplant two 830hp Bristol Mercury VIII 9-cylinder radials • Max speed 295mph (475km/h) • Service ceiling 30,510ft (9,300m) • Max range 932 miles (1,500km) • Wingspan 56ft 3in (17.16m) • Length 35ft 8in (10.87m) • Height 12ft 5in (3.80m) • Weight 11,023lb (5,000kg) • Armament nine 0.31-in (7.92-mm) machine guns, eight in a nose battery, and one in the nacelle tail cone; external bomb load of 882lb (400kg)

Developed as a private venture and first flown on March 16, 1937 at Eindhoven, the Fokker G.I heavy fighter was ordered by the Royal Netherlands Army Air Service in 1937, with

▲ The Fokker G.1 heavy fighter was a very advanced design by the standards of the time, but never had the chance to prove itself in combat.

deliveries of an initial batch of 36 G.IA production aircraft to the 3rd and 4th Fighter Groups beginning in 1938. A small number of the 23 surviving aircraft saw limited action during the German invasion of Holland, most being destroyed on the ground. The type had been offered for export as the G.IB and orders had been placed by Denmark (18), Estonia (9), Finland (26), Sweden (18), and Spain, but these were never fulfilled and 14 of the Finnish aircraft were taken over by the Germans for use as trainers.

▌Fokker S.14   NETHERLANDS

◀ This machine, either the second or third production Mach-Trainer, shows off the type's simple but eminently functional lines.

SPECIFICATION: Type jet trainer • Crew 2 • Powerplant one 3,470-lb (1,574-kg) thrust Rolls-Royce Derwent turbojet • Max speed 445mph (716km/h) at 20,000ft (6,100m) • Service ceiling 36,500ft (11,125m) • Max range 560 miles (900km) • Wingspan 39ft (11.89m) • Length 43ft 8in (13.30m) • Height 15ft 4in (4.67m) • Weight 12,196lb (5,532kg) loaded • Armament none

The first jet aircraft designed and built in Holland, the S.14 flew for the first time on May 20, 1951, powered by a Rolls-Royce Derwent turbojet. It was the first jet aircraft anywhere in the world to be designed specifically for the training role. Twenty S.14s served with the RNAF into the 1960s as conversion trainers. Production ceased in 1955.

▌Fokker T.V

NETHERLANDS

The Fokker T.V was designed to a Netherlands Army Air Service specification that originally called for a dual-role medium bomber and long-range fighter, and for this reason a relatively heavy armament was installed. Rather unstable and a handful to fly, sixteen aircraft were delivered in 1938. The nine that were still serviceable at the time of the German invasion of May 1940 succeeded in destroying almost 30 enemy aircraft on the ground, but all but one were eventually lost in a series of gallant but hopeless attacks on the advancing enemy.

▲ The Netherlands Army Air Service's lumbering Fokker T.V bombers were thrown into action against the advancing Germans in May 1940, nearly all being destroyed.

SPECIFICATION: **Type** medium bomber • **Crew** 5 • **Powerplant** two 925hp Bristol Pegasus XXVI 18-cylinder radials • **Max speed** 280mph (450km/h) • **Service ceiling** 25,260ft (7,704m) • **Max range** 1,012 miles (1,628km) • **Wingspan** 68ft 10in (20.98m) • **Length** 52ft 6in (16.01m) • **Height** 16ft 5in (5.03m) • **Weight** 15,928lb (7,225kg) • **Armament** one nose-mounted 0.79-in (20-mm) cannon and four trainable 0.31-in (7.9-mm) machine guns firing from dorsal, lateral, and ventral positions and the tail cone; bomb load of up to 2200lb (1,000kg)

▌Fokker T.VIII

NETHERLANDS

Designed in response to a Dutch Naval Air Service requirement for a modern torpedo-bomber and reconnaissance floatplane suitable for home and in the Dutch East Indies, the Fokker T.VIII first flew in 1938 and about 30 VIII-W production aircraft had been delivered, or were about to be delivered, at the time of the German invasion in 1940. Nine escaped to the UK and equipped No. 320 (Dutch) Squadron at Pembroke Dock. When three of the aircraft were lost the remaining aircraft could not be operated due to lack of spares, and so were flown to Felixstowe for storage.

The T.VIIIs seized by the Germans were used for coastal patrol work in the Mediterranean. The T.VIII-L was a landplane version built for Finland, only the prototype of which was completed.

▲ The Fokker T.VIII naval torpedo bomber and reconnaissance aircraft was used by both sides after the Germans overran Holland.

SPECIFICATION: **Type** maritime reconnaissance and torpedo-bomber floatplane • **Crew** 3 • **Powerplant** two 450hp Wright R-975-E3 Whirlwind 9-cylinder radials • **Max speed** 177mph (285km/h) at 9,845ft (3,000m) • **Service ceiling** 22,310ft (6,800m) • **Max range** 1,709 miles (2,750km) • **Wingspan** 59ft (18m) • **Length** 42ft 7in (13m) • **Height** 16ft 4in (5m) • **Weight** 11,023lb (5,000kg) • **Armament** two 0.31-in (7.92-mm) machine guns, one in port side of forward fuselage and one in rear of cockpit; internal bomb or torpedo load of 1,323lb (600kg)

▌Fouga Magister

FRANCE

Famous as the equipment of the French "Patrouille de France" and the Belgian "Diables Rouges" aerobatic teams, the Fouga CM.170 Magister was one of the most successful jet trainers ever developed, seeing widespread service with the French and several other air forces. It was the first jet trainer to enter service anywhere in the world, and was also notable for its distinctive butterfly tail.

In the light ground attack role, the Magister distinguished

▲ *Fouga Magister jet trainers of the French Air Force pictured at the Salon de Provence air show in March 1978.*

itself in the Arab–Israeli war of 1967, carrying out devastating rocket attacks against Egyptian armor in Sinai. The CM.170 Magister prototype flew on July 23, 1952 and production aircraft were progressively upgraded with more powerful engines and other equipment. Over 900 Magisters were built, of which 400 went to the French AF and 250 to the Luftwaffe. A version for the French Navy was the CM.175 Zephyr; 45 were delivered. A small number of Magisters remain operational with the Force Aérienne Belge, undertaking communications duties.

SPECIFICATION: Type training/light attack aircraft • Crew 2 • Powerplant two 880-lb (400-kg) thrust Turboméca Marboré turbojets • Max speed 403mph (650km/h) at sea level • Service ceiling 36,090ft (11,000m) • Max range 575 miles (925km) at 20,000ft (6,096m) • Wingspan 37ft 5in (11.40m) • Length 33ft (10.06m) • Height 14ft 4in (4.38m) • Weights 4,740lb (2,150kg) empty; 7,055lb (3,200kg) loaded • Armament two 0.30-in (7.5-mm) or 0.303-in (7.62-mm) machine guns in nose; rocket projectiles, bombs or wire-guided missiles under wings

▌ Friedrichshafen G.III

GERMANY

▲ *Together with the Gotha G.V, the Friedrichshafen G.III formed the backbone of the German night bomber force during 1917–18.*

SPECIFICATION: Type night bomber • Crew 3 • Powerplant two 260hp Mercedes D.IVa 6-cylinder liquid-cooled in-line engines driving "pusher" propellers • Max speed 85mph (135km/h) • Service ceiling 14,765ft (4,500m) • Endurance 5hrs • Wingspan 77ft 9in (23.70m) • Length 42ft (12.80m) • Height 12ft (3.66m) • Weight 8,664lb (3,930kg) loaded • Armament two 0.31-in (7.9-mm) machine guns in front and rear cockpits; up to 3,307lb (1,500kg) of bombs

Entering service in February 1917, the Friedrichshafen G.III twin-engined night bomber was developed from the G.I and G.II, the last of which went into limited production. The G.III partnered the Gotha G V in constituting the main German bombing strength up to the end of World War I, operating mainly against targets in France and Macedonia but occasionally taking part in attacks on southeastern England. Later versions were the G.IV and G.V, both of which were short-nosed variants without a front gun position and with tractor instead of pusher propellers.

▌General Dynamics F-16 Fighting Falcon

USA

SPECIFICATION: Type air superiority and strike fighter (data F-16C) • Crew 1 • Powerplant either one 23,770-lb (10,800-kg) Pratt & Whitney F100-PW-200 or one 28,984-lb (13,150-kg) General Electric F110-GE-100 turbofan • Max speed 1,320mph (2,142km/h) at altitude • Service ceiling 50,000ft (15,240m) • Combat radius 575 miles (925km) • Wingspan 31ft (9.45m) • Length 49ft 6in (15.09m) • Height 16ft 8in (5.09m) • Weight 35,400lb (16,057kg) • Armament one General Electric M61A1 multibarrelled cannon; seven external hardpoints for up to 20,450lb (9,276kg) of ordnance

▲ As the primary USAF tactical warplane, the F-16 is provided with the latest weaponry. This F-16C is dropping a JDAM test round.

The F-16, designed and built by General Dynamics, had its origin in a USAF requirement of 1972 for a lightweight fighter and first flew on February 2, 1974. In service with many air arms other than the USAF, it carries an advanced GEC-Marconi HUDWACS (HUD and Weapon Aiming Computer System) in which target designation cues are shown on the head-up display as well as flight symbols. The HUDWAC computer is used to direct the weapons to the target, as designated on the HUD. The F-16 HUDWAC shows horizontal and vertical speed, altitude, heading, climb and roll bars, and range-to-go information for flight reference. There are five ground attack modes and four air combat modes. In air combat, the "snapshoot" mode lets the pilot aim at crossing targets by drawing a continuously computed impact line (CCIL) on the HUD. The lead-computing off sight (LCOS) mode follows a designated target; the dogfight mode combines snapshoot and LCOS; and there is also an air-to-air missile mode. The F-16's underwing hardpoints are stressed for maneuveres up to 9g, enabling the F-16 to dogfight while still carrying weaponry. The F-16B and -D are two-seat versions, while the F-16C, delivered from 1988, featured numerous improvements in avionics and was available with a choice of engine. F-16s have seen action in the Lebanon (with the Israeli Air Force), in the Gulf War, and the Balkans.

▲ The F-16B, seen here, is a two-seat version of the Fighting Falcon. The F-16 has been a major success story.

A typical stores load might include two wingtip-mounted Sidewinders, with four more on the outer underwing stations; a podded GPU-5/A 1.19-in (30-mm) cannon on the centerline; drop tanks on the inboard underwing and fuselage stations; a Pave Penny laser spot tracker pod along the starboard side of the nacelle; and bombs, ASMs, and flare pods on the four inner underwing stations. The aircraft can carry advanced beyond-visual-range missiles, Maverick ASMs, HARM, and Shrike antiradar missiles, and a weapons dispenser carrying various types of submunition. The F-16 has been constantly upgraded to extend its life well into the 21st century.

▋ General Dynamics F-111

 USA

The development history of the F-111 began in 1962, when the General Dynamics Corporation, in association with Grumman Aircraft, was selected to develop a variable-geometry tactical fighter to meet the requirements of the USAF's TFX program. An initial contract was placed for twenty-three development aircraft, including eighteen F111As for the USAF and five F-111Bs for the US Navy (in the event, the Navy canceled the F-111 order). Powered by two Pratt & Whitney TF30-P-1 turbofan engines, the prototype F-111A flew for the first time on December 21, 1964, and during the second flight on January 6, 1965 the aircraft's wings were swept through the full range from 16° to 72.5°.

One hundred and sixty production F-111As were built, the first examples entering service with the 4,480th Tactical Fighter Wing at Nellis AFB, Nevada, in October 1967. On March 17th the following year six aircraft from this unit flew to Takhli AFB in Thailand for operational evaluation in Vietnam, making their first sorties on March 25th. The operation ended unhappily when three of the aircraft were lost as a result of metal fatigue in a control rod, but the problem was rectified and in September 1972 the F-111As of the 429th and 430th Tactical Fighter Squadrons deployed to Takhli and performed very effective service in the closing air offensive of the war, attacking targets in the Hanoi area at night and in all weathers through the heaviest antiaircraft concentrations in the history of air warfare.

Years ahead of its time in technological terms, the F-111 incorporated many novel design features, such as a zero-speed, zero-altitude emergency escape module. The F-111E variant, which superseded the F-111A in service, featured modified air intakes to improve performance above 2.2M. Reequipment of the 20th TFW (55th, 77th, and 79th TFS) with its full complement of 72 aircraft was completed in the summer of 1971 and the unit, which became fully operational in November that year, was assigned the war role of interdicting targets such as airfields, railroad marshalling yards and junctions, vehicle parks, and storage depots deep inside hostile territory as part of NATO's 2nd Allied Tactical Air Force.

The F-111F was a fighter bomber variant, combining the best features of the F-111E and FB-111A (a strategic bomber variant for Strategic Air Command, 76 built), while the F-111C (24 built) was a strike version for the RAAF. The F-111D (96 built) was optimized for tactical support. Total production of the F-111, all variants, was 562 aircraft, including 23 development aircraft.

SPECIFICATION: Type interdictor (data F-111E) • Crew 2 • Powerplant two 25,100-lb (11,385-kg) Pratt & Whitney TF-30-P100 turbofans • Max speed 1,650mph (2,655km/h) at altitude • Service ceiling 59,000ft (17,985m) • Max range 2,925 miles (4,707km) • Wingspan 63ft (19.20m) unswept; 31ft 11in (9.74m) swept • Length 73ft 6in (22.40m) • Height 17ft 1in (5.22m) • Weight 100,000lb (45,359kg) loaded • Armament one 0.79-in (20-mm) M61A-1 multibarreled cannon and one 750-lb (340-kg) B43 nuclear store, or two B43s in internal bay; provision for up to 31,000lb (14,290kg) of ordnance on eight underwing hardpoints

▲ *An echelon formation of three F-111E Aardvarks and an EF-111A Raven flies at low level along the snowy coast of northern Scotland.*

▌Gloster Gamecock

GREAT BRITAIN

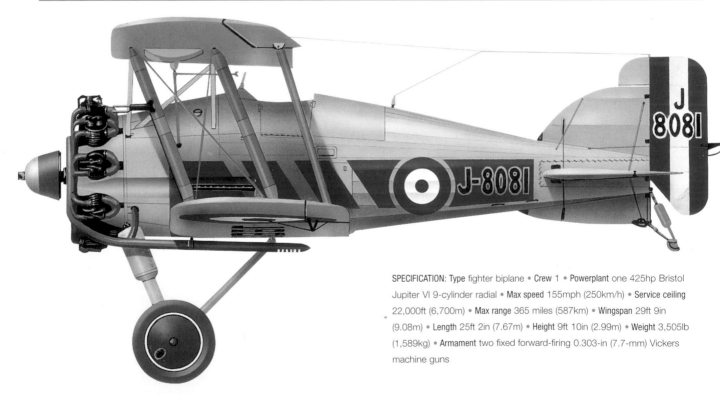

SPECIFICATION: Type fighter biplane • Crew 1 • Powerplant one 425hp Bristol Jupiter VI 9-cylinder radial • Max speed 155mph (250km/h) • Service ceiling 22,000ft (6,700m) • Max range 365 miles (587km) • Wingspan 29ft 9in (9.08m) • Length 25ft 2in (7.67m) • Height 9ft 10in (2.99m) • Weight 3,505lb (1,589kg) • Armament two fixed forward-firing 0.303-in (7.7-mm) Vickers machine guns

The Gloster Gamecock prototype, the last wooden biplane fighter designed for the RAF, first flew in February 1925, and the type equipped five RAF squadrons from May 1926. The Gamecock's service life was relatively short-lived. This was partly because of an abnormally high accident rate; of the 90 Gamecocks built, 22 were lost in spinning or landing accidents. The Gamecock I's shortcomings were to some extent cured in the Gamecock II, which had a longer-span top wing, a revised vertical tail unit, and other improvements. Fifteen were built under license in Finland as the Kukko.

Gloster Gauntlet

The Bristol Bulldog was replaced in RAF service by the Gloster Gauntlet, the last of the RAF's open-cockpit fighter biplanes. It was an ironic state of affairs, because the prototype Gauntlet, which had first flown in 1928, had shown an inferior performance to the Bulldog and another contender, the Hawker Hawfinch, and the Bulldog had been chosen in preference. Glosters, however, had proceeded with the development of the Gauntlet as a private venture, refitting it with a 640hp Bristol Mercury engine, and this gave it a top speed of 230mph (370km/h), well in excess of the Bulldog's. A production order for 24 aircraft was placed, and the Gauntlet Mk I entered service with No. 19 Squadron in May 1935. The Gauntlet Mk II, with an uprated Mercury engine, began to enter service a year later, and at the peak of its service in the spring of 1937 it equipped 14 home-based fighter squadrons. Gauntlet Mk II production was 204 aircraft. Ex-RAF Gauntlet Mk IIs were supplied to Australia, Finland, Rhodesia, and South Africa.

SPECIFICATION: Type fighter biplane (data Gauntlet Mk II) • Crew 1 • Powerplant one 640hp Bristol Merrcury VI 9-cylinder radial • Max speed 230mph (370km/h) • Service ceiling 33,200ft (10,120m) • Max range 460 miles (740km) • Wingspan 32ft 9in (9.99m) • Length 26ft 5in (8.05m) • Height 10ft 3in (3.12m) • Weight 3,970lb (1,801kg) loaded • Armament two fixed forward-firing 0.303-in (7.7-mm) Vickers machine guns

▲ The Gloster SS.19B, J9125, which became the prototype Gauntlet. The aircraft underwent repeated modification in armament and engine.

Gloster Gladiator

The Gloster Gladiator was designed to be a refined private venture successor to the Gauntlet, developed to Air Ministry Specification F7/30. Designated SS.37, the prototype was flown in September 1934 and evaluated by the Air Ministry in the following year, the trials resulting in a production order for 23 machines, followed by two further orders for 100 and 28 aircraft. These were powered by 840hp Mercury IXS engines and were armed with four Vickers machine guns; they were given the RAF name Gladiator. First deliveries were made to No. 27 Squadron at Tangmere in February 1937, and the type went on to equip eight squadrons of Fighter Command. The Gladiator II was developed to fulfill foreign orders, 147 being produced for this purpose, and 252 were also built for the RAF. The Gladiator, the last of the

▲ *The Gloster Gladiator was the last of the RAF's biplane fighters. It performed valiantly against the Italians in Greece and North Africa.*

RAF's biplane fighters, although outclassed by German and Italian monoplane fighters, was to render gallant service during the early months of the war in both Europe and the Middle East. The naval equivalent, the Sea Gladiator, was an adaptation of the Mk II, and equipped seven Fleet Air Arm squadrons from 1939.

SPECIFICATION: Type fighter biplane (data Gladiator Mk II) • Crew 1 • Powerplant one 830hp Bristol Mercury VIIIA 9-cylinder radial • Max speed 257mph (414km/h) • Service ceiling 33,200ft (10,120m) • Max range 440 miles (708km) • Wingspan 32ft 3in (9.83m) • Length 27ft 5in (8.36m) • Height 11ft 7in (3.53m) • Weight 4,864lb (2,206kg) loaded • Armament four fixed forward-firing 0.303-in (7.7-mm) Colt-Browning machine guns

▌Gloster Grebe

GREAT BRITAIN

The first post-World War I British fighter design, the Gloster Grebe was the brainchild of Harry Folland, Chief Designer of the Gloucestershire Aircraft Company. Folland had previously worked for the Nieuport and General Aircraft Co., which had been set up in Britain late in 1916 to license-build French fighters. In 1917 the British-based firm began to design its own aircraft, the first of which was the Nighthawk, the first British fighter to be powered by a stationary radial engine instead of the more common rotary type. The Grebe prototype was originally ordered as a Nighthawk; it made its first public appearance in June 1923 and entered RAF service

with No. 111 Squadron in October that year, subsequently equipping five more RAF fighter squadrons. One of them, No. 25 Squadron, subsequently became famous for its spectacular aerobatic displays in the mid-1920s. Despite some early problems, the Grebe was a maneuverable and robust aircraft, and was the first British machine to survive a terminal velocity dive, reaching 240mph (386km/h). Grebes also took part in some interesting experiments, one of which involved the release of a pair of aircraft from beneath the airship R.33 in October 1926. The production Grebe, of which 129 were built, was designated Mk II.

SPECIFICATION: Type fighter biplane • Crew 1 • Powerplant one 400hp Armstrong Siddeley Jaguar IV 14-cylinder radial engine • Max speed 151mph (243km/h) • Service ceiling 23,000ft (7,010m) • Endurance 2hrs 45mins • Wingspan 29ft 4in (8.94m) • Length 20ft 3in (6.17m) • Height 9ft 3in (2.82m) • Weight 2,622lb (1,189kg) • Armament two fixed forward-firing 0.303-in (7.7-mm) Vickers machine guns

Gloster Javelin

GREAT BRITAIN

Developed as a replacement for the night fighter versions of the Meteor, Vampire, and Venom, the Gloster GA.5 Javelin prototype—the world's first twin-jet delta and an extremely radical design for its day—flew for the first time on November 26, 1951, powered by two Armstrong Siddeley Sapphires. The maiden flight was attended by a serious snag in the shape of rudder buffeting, and further flight testing was delayed while modifications were carried out. Then, on June 29, 1952, the prototype lost both elevators and was destroyed in a crash landing at Boscombe Down. There were further delays, including the loss of a second prototype, before the Javelin FAW.1 was ordered into "super-priority" production for the RAF. The first production aircraft flew on July 22, 1954 and deliveries began to No. 46 Squadron at RAF

▲ *Primary armament for later variants of the Javelin, including this FAW.Mk 7, was the de Havilland Firestreak infra-red heat-seeking AAM.*

Odiham in February 1956.

The Javelin FAW.2 differed from the FAW.1 only in its use of the American-designed AI22 (APQ43) radar, while the FAW.4, featured an all-moving tailplane. Several further variants of the Javelin were produced, featuring either aerodynamic refinements or different avionics; the last production model was the FAW.8, the final aircraft being completed in June 1960, but a number of Javelin FAW7s were brought up to FAW8 standard (although with British AI radar) and designated FAW9. The T.3 was a trainer version.

SPECIFICATION: Type all-weather interceptor (data FAW.8) • Crew 2 • Powerplant two 11,000-lb (4,990-kg) thrust Armstrong Siddeley Sapphire Sa.7R turbojets with limited reheat • Max speed 700mph (1,130km/h) at sea level • Service ceiling 52,000ft (15,849m) • Max range 1,200 miles (1,930km) • Wingspan 52ft (15.80m) • Length 56ft 3in (17.10m) • Height 16ft (4.80m) • Weight 42,510lb (19,282kg) loaded • Armament four fixed 1.19-in (30-mm) Aden cannon in outer mainplanes; provision for four Firestreak AAMs

Gloster Meteor

GREAT BRITAIN

The Gloster Meteor, the RAF's first operational jet fighter, traced its lineage to the first British experimental jet, the Gloster E.28/39, which flew for the first time on May 15, 1941 under the power of a single Whittle W.2/7000 turbojet. The Meteor was Gloster's answer to Air Ministry specification F.9/40, calling for a single-seat interceptor powered by gas turbine engines. The low thrust output of the engines available at the time dictated a twin-engine configuration, but apart from the radical nature of its form of propulsion the Meteor was entirely conventional in design. Twelve prototypes were ordered and eight were completed, the first flying on March 5, 1943. The aircraft was powered by two 1,500-lb (680-kg) thrust Halford H.1 turbojets, but the first 20 production aircraft were fitted with the 1,700-lb (771-kg) Rolls-Royce Welland. Twelve of these were issued to No. 616 Squadron, which deployed to Manston and flew its first "Dive" (anti V-1) patrol on July 27th.

The Meteor destroyed only 13 V-1s, but it came very late to the battle and it was underpowered. The next variant, the Meteor F.3, was a much better proposition, using the 2,000-lb (906-kg) thrust Rolls-Royce Derwent I engine; but deliveries

▲ *This Meteor Mk 3, EE387, carried out deck-landing trials on the aircraft carriers HMS* Eagle *and HMS* Illustrious *in 1951.*

to No. 616 Squadron did not begin until December 1944. The Mk 3 version, which eventually equipped 15 squadrons of RAF Fighter Command in the immediate postwar years, and which had been operationally tested in a ground attack role in Belgium with Nos. 616 and 514 Squadrons in the closing weeks of the war, was followed into service by the Meteor

F.Mk.4. Powered by two Rolls-Royce Derwent 5s, the F.Mk.4 first flew in April 1945 and subsequently, in November, set up a new world air speed record of 606mph (975km/h). It was the first Meteor mark to be exported, being supplied to Argentina (100), Holland (65), Belgium (48), and Denmark (20). The most prolific of the Meteor variants was the F.Mk.8, which equipped 32 regular and 11 RAuxAF squadrons in the early 1950s. This version was also the subject of major export orders, going to Egypt (8), Belgium (23, plus 67 license-built), Denmark (20), Syria (19), Holland (5, plus 155 license-built), Brazil (60), and Israel (11). The F.8 also equipped No. 77 Squadron RAAF, which saw action in Korea.

The Meteor FR.9 was a fighter-reconnaissance variant,

SPECIFICATION: Type fighter (data Meteor F.Mk.8) • Crew 1 • Powerplant two 3,500lb (1,587kg) thrust Rolls-Royce Derwent 8 turbojets • Max speed 598mph (962km/h) at 33,000ft (10,000m) • Service ceiling 43,000ft (13,106m) • Max range 980 miles (1,580km) • Wingspan 37ft 2in (11.32m) • Length 44ft 7in (13.58m) • Height 13ft (3.96m) • Weight 19,100lb (8,664kg) • Armament four 0.79-in (20-mm) Hispano cannon

while the PR.10 was an unarmed photoreconnaissance aircraft. NF.11, NF.12, NF.13, and NF.14 were night fighters; the U.15-U.21 were target drones; the TT.20 was a target tug; and the T.7 was a two-seat trainer. Meteor production, all variants, totaled 3,545 aircraft.

▲ The Meteor Mk 7 was the tandem two-seat trainer version of the Gloster fighter. It had an appalling accident rate.

▌Grigorovitch I-6 Series

USSR

In 1932 the Russian designer Dmitri Grigorovitch, having collaborated with fellow designer Polikarpov for some time, produced a design of his own, the I-6 single-seat biplane, a very light and maneuverable fighter with a maximum speed of 200mph (322km/h). He then produced a two-seat biplane fighter, the DI-3, characterized by its twin fins and rudders;

SPECIFICATION: Type fighter (data DI-3) • Crew 2 • Powerplant one 600hp M-17 in-line engine • Max speed 170mph (272km/h) at sea level • Service ceiling 20,660ft (6,300m) • Max range 490 miles (790km) • Wingspan 38ft 9in (11.80m) • Length 25ft 7in (7.80m) • Height not known • Weight 4,080lb (1,850kg) loaded • Armament two fixed forward-firing 0.30-in (7.62-mm) machine guns and one in rear cockpit

it was fitted with a 600hp M-17 engine and three 0.30-in (7.62-mm) machine guns.

The I-7, which appeared shortly afterward, was a landplane version of a proposed floatplane fighter for the Soviet Naval Aviation, which in fact was not built. The top speed of the I-7 was 210mph (338km/h), and the aircraft was armed with four 0.30-in (7.62-mm) machine guns. The years 1930–33 saw the appearance of three more fighter designs that never left the drawing board. These were the twin-engined I-9, which was to have been fitted with two 480hp M-22 engines, giving it an estimated maximum speed of 130mph (215km/h); and the I-10 single-seat gull-wing monoplane with a 625hp M-25 radial engine and an estimated top speed of 220mph (354km/h).

Grumman AF-2 Guardian

USA

Originally designed as a torpedo-bomber, the prototype Grumman XTB3F-1 Guardian flew for the first time on December 1, 1945 with a composite powerplant comprising one Pratt & Whitney R-2800-34W radial engine and one Westinghouse 19XB-2B turbojet, the latter mounted in the rear fuselage. The turbojet was subsequently removed, and after considerable redesign two new prototypes made their appearance in 1948–49, bearing the designations XTB3F-1S and XTB3F-2S, the former being equipped as a submarine "hunter" and the latter as a "killer." Both types were ordered into production for the US Navy as the AF-1S and AF-2S, but the former was soon changed to AF-2W. The aircraft were intended to operate in conjunction, the -2W carrying out the search and directing the attacking -2S to its underwater target. The first Guardians were delivered to Navy squadron VS-25 in October 1950 and the type remained in service until August 1955. Total production was 389 aircraft, including prototypes.

SPECIFICATION: Type antisubmarine aircraft (data AF-2S) • Crew 2 • Powerplant one 2,400hp Pratt & Whitney R-2800-48W radial • Max speed 317mph (510km/h) at 16,000ft (4,880m) • Service ceiling 32,500ft (9,900m) • Max range 1,500 miles (2,410km) • Wingspan 60ft 8in (18.49m) • Length 43ft 4in (13.20m) • Height 16ft 2in (4.92m) • Weight 25,500lb (11,567kg) loaded • Armament two 2,000-lb (907-kg) torpedoes or 4,000lb (1,814kg) of bombs

▶ The Grumman AF-2W Guardian, seen here, was designed to hunt submarines in conjunction with its "killer" partner, the AF-2S.

Grumman A-6 Intruder

USA

Designed specifically as a carrier-based low-level attack bomber with the ability to deliver both nuclear and conventional warloads with pinpoint accuracy in all weathers, the Grumman A-6 was the winner in a 1957 US Navy design contest. The A-6A prototype flew on April 19, 1960 and the first operational aircraft entered service with Attack Squadron VA-42 on February 1, 1963. The last delivery took place in December 1969, by which time 488 had been built. The A-6A saw extensive action over Vietnam and also participated in later actions, such as the strike on Libya in April 1986. The next variant was the EA-6A electronic warfare aircraft, 27 examples of which were produced for the US Marine Corps; this was followed by the EA-6B Prowler, with advanced avionics and a longer nose section. Only 77

Prowlers were built, but the fleet was substantially updated in the 1990s. The last basic attack variant was the A-6E, which first flew in February 1970; total orders called for 318 A-6Es, including 119 converted from A-6As. Other conversions of the basic A-6A were the A-6C, with enhanced night attack capability, and the KA-6D flight refueling tanker.

SPECIFICATION: Type all-weather strike aircraft (data A-6A) • Crew 2 • Powerplant two 9,300-lb (4,218-kg) Pratt & Whitney J52-P-8A turbojets • Max speed 648mph (1,043km/h) at sea level • Service ceiling 47,500ft (14,480m) • Max range 1,011 miles (1,627km) with full weapon load • Wingspan 53ft (16.15m) • Length 54ft 7in (16.64m) • Height 16ft 2in (4.93m) • Weight 60,400lb (27,397kg) loaded • Armament five external hardpoints for up to 18,000lb (8,165kg) of ordnance

▲ With the TRAM turret prominent beneath their nose radomes, these A-6Es demonstrate the colors in which the type finished its active service.

▌Grumman E-1 Tracer

The Grumman E-1B Tracer was a specialized airborne warning and command-post aircraft developed from the versatile carrier-borne S-2 Tracker, featuring triple tail fins and a large lenticular radome mounted over the fuselage, housing an APS-82 radar scanner sweeping through 360 degrees six times a minute. The US Navy's S-2F was known as the "Stoof"—by analogy the Tracer gained the nickname "Stoof with a roof." The prototype flew in March 1957 and 80 were built for the US Navy, remaining in service from February 1958 to 1965.

SPECIFICATION: Type command and early warning aircraft • Crew 4 • Powerplant two 1,525hp Wright R-1820-82WA Cyclone radials • Max speed 290mph (466km/h) at 5,000ft (1,524m) • Service ceiling 23,000ft (7,010m) • Max range 900 miles (1,450km) • Wingspan 72ft 4in (22.05m) • Length 45ft 4in (13.82m) • Height 16ft 10in (5.13m) • Weight 27,000lb (12,247kg) loaded • Armament none

▲ *Grumman chose to house the large antenna of the WF-2's APS-82 radar in a fixed radome.*

▌Grumman E-2 Hawkeye

The US Navy's principal electronic surveillance aircraft in the Gulf War, and the mainstay of the USN's early warning capability for many years, was the Grumman E-2 Hawkeye, the prototype of which first flew on October 20, 1960. The first 20 E-2As were used for service evaluation and carrier trials, and the type was formally accepted into US Navy service in January 1964, when it began to equip Early Warning Squadron VAW-11 at San Diego. This unit went to sea with its Hawkeyes aboard the USS *Kitty Hawk* in 1966, by which time a second squadron, VAW-12, had also been formed.

Sixty-two E-2As were built, including the prototypes, and construction ended early in 1967. The E-2B, which flew in

February 1969, had a number of refinements including an L-304 microelectronic computer, and all operational E-2As were subsequently updated to E-2B standard. The early model Hawkeyes were equipped with the General Electric APS-96 search and tracking radar, which even in its original form was capable of automatic target detection and tracking over water. Trials and modifications to reject unwanted ground signals resulted in a new radar, the APS-120, which was capable of target detection and tracking over both sea and land. The system was fitted in a new model, the E-2C.

In 1962 Grumman proposed a carrier onboard delivery (COD) variant, which was accepted by the US Navy in 1964. This aircraft, without the radome and with a wider and deeper fuselage, was designated the C-2A Greyhound. As well as cargo, the C-2A can accommodate 39 troops, or 20 stretchers and four nursing staff.

◄ *The Grumman E-2 Hawkeye has been the subject of numerous upgrades during its long career, and remains a viable system in the 21st century.*

SPECIFICATION: Type airborne command and control/AEW aircraft (data E-2A) • Crew 5 • Powerplant two 4,050hp Allison T56-A-8A turboprops • Max speed 370mph (595km/h) at sea level • Service ceiling 31,700ft (9,660m) • Max range 1,900 miles (3,060km) • Wingspan 80ft 7in (24.56m) • Length 56ft 4in (17.17m) • Height 16ft 4in (4.88m) • Weight 49,500lb (22,453kg) • Armament none

Grumman FF-1 Series

USA

In 1931 a new name burst on to the scene of US naval aviation. On April 2nd that year, the US Navy signed its first contract with Grumman Aircraft, a company whose association with naval fighter aircraft would extend in an unbroken line into the 21st century. The contract involved the building of 27 fighter and 33 reconnaissance versions of the Grumman FF-1, the first military aircraft to be fitted with a retractable undercarriage, all for service on the USS *Lexington*. The prototype XFF-1 flew toward the end of 1931 and entered service in June 1933, followed by the SF-1 in March 1934. The success of the FF-1, which was a two-seater, encouraged the US Navy to order a more compact single-seat version; this was the XF2F-1, which first flew on October

▲ *The Grumman FF-1 was the first aircraft built by the firm for the US Navy, beginning a long association that continues today.*

SPECIFICATION: Type naval fighter biplane (data F3F-3) • Crew 1 • Powerplant one 950hp Wright R-1820-22 Cyclone 9-cylinder radial • Max speed 260mph (418km/h) • Service ceiling 32,300ft (9,845m) • Max range 1,130 miles (1,819km) • Wingspan 32ft (9.75m) • Length 23ft (7.01m) • Height 9ft 4in (2.84m) • Weight 4,750lb (2,155kg) • Armament one 0.50-in (12.7-mm) and one 0.30-in (7.62-mm) machine gun in upper forward fuselage; external bomb load of 232lb (105kg)

18, 1933. The order involved 54 production F-2F1s, deliveries beginning in 1935. In that year an improved model, the XF3F-1, made its appearance, and deliveries of 54 production F3F-1s began in 1936. The model built in the greatest numbers was the F3F-2, the first of 81 production aircraft going into service in 1938. The final variant was the F3F-3, 27 of which were produced. The F3F-3 had an uprated engine and was the last biplane fighter produced by Grumman; it was also the last biplane fighter to serve with the United States Navy.

Grumman F4F Wildcat

USA

In March 1936, the Grumman Aircraft Corporation was awarded a development contract to build an all-metal biplane fighter, the XF4F-1, for the US Navy. However, the biplane configuration was quickly shelved in favor of a monoplane design, the XF4F-2. This flew on September 2, 1937, powered by a 1,050hp Pratt & Whitney R-1830-66 Twin Wasp radial engine. The US Navy decided to develop the aircraft still further by installing a supercharged XR-1830-76 engine in a much redesigned airframe, the revamped machine, designated XF4F-3, flying for the first time on February 12, 1939. In August, the Navy issued its first pro-

duction contract for 53 Grumman F4F-3 Wildcats, as the fighter had been named. The first production aircraft flew in February 1940, but deliveries were slow and by the end of 1940 only 22 Wildcats had been handed over to Navy fighter squadrons VF-4 and VF-7, these units embarking on the USS *Ranger* and USS *Wasp* repectively.

In 1939, meanwhile, France—which had one aircraft carrier in commission and two more under construction—had expressed an interest in acquiring 100 Wildcats under the export designation G-36A. As the Twin Wasp

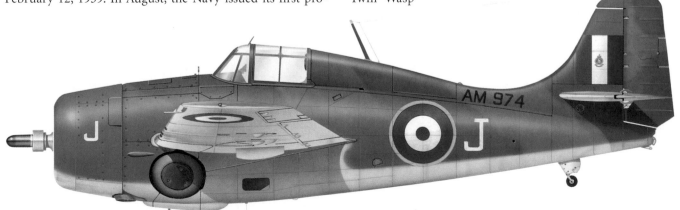

▲ *With its increased height vertical fin, this aircraft is easily recognizable as the more powerful General Motors-built FM-2 Wildcat.*

engine was in short supply, the French machines were to be powered by the 1,200hp R-1820-G205A Cyclone. The order was later reduced to 81, and flight testing of the first of these aircraft was still in progress when France was overrun, so the order was taken over by the British Purchasing Commission on behalf of the Royal Navy, in whose service the F4F-3 was named Martlet I. The first of these aircraft was delivered on July 27, 1940, a month before the US Navy received its first Wildcat. In October No. 804 Squadron began rearming with

SPECIFICATION: Type naval fighter (data F4F-3) • Crew 1 • Powerplant one 1,200hp Pratt & Whitney R-1830-66 radial engine • Max speed 318mph (512km/h) at 19,400ft (5,913m) • Service ceiling 34,900ft (10,638m) • Max range 770 miles (1,239km) • Wingspan 38ft (11.58m) • Length 28ft 9in (8.76m) • Height 11ft 10in (3.61m) • Weight 7,952lb (3,607kg) loaded • Armament six 0.50-in (12.7-mm) machine guns in wing; external bomb load up to 200lb (91kg)

the Martlet at Hatson, in the Orkney Islands, and scored an early success when two of its aircraft shot down a Junkers Ju 88 over the naval base at Scapa Flow. In April 1941 30 G-36As ordered by Greece were also diverted to Britain as Martlet IIIs, these aircraft having been offloaded at Gibraltar when the Germans invaded the Balkans. Neither the F4F-3 nor the Martlet I had folding wings, but these were incorporated in all but 10 of an order for 100 Martlet IIs (G-36As) placed by Britain in 1940. The total number of Martlets of all marks supplied to Britain eventually reached 1,191, the total including 220 Martlet IVs (F4F-4Bs with Cyclone engines), 311 as Martlet Vs, and 370 Wildcat VIs, the American name having by then been adopted by the Fleet Air Arm. This was the British equivalent of the F4F-8, with a 1,200hp R-1820-56 Cyclone engine and taller fin and rudder.

In American service, the Wildcat with folding wings received the designation F4F-4, the first example flying on April 14, 1941 and going to fighter squadron VF-42 in May for trials on the USS *Yorktown*. As 1941 drew to a close the Wildcat was rapidly replacing all other US carrier-borne fighters. Robust and capable of absorbing a large amount of battle damage, it nevertheless needed a highly experienced pilot to give the Wildcat a fighting chance in combat with Japanese fighters. As American pilots gained combat experience during 1942, their superior tactics and teamwork began to have a telling effect on the course of the Pacific air war. In US Marine Corps hands, the Wildcat will forever be remembered for its defense of Guadalcanal in the latter half of 1942. The total number of Wildcats built, including 21 examples of an unarmed reconnaissance version, the F4F-7, was 7,885.

▌Grumman F6F Hellcat

USA

▲ *This F6F-5 was photographed just after the cessation of hostilities in World War II. At its peak, F6F production reached 20 aircraft per day.*

On June 30, 1941, less than six months before the Japanese attack on Pearl Harbor, the US Navy placed an order with the Grumman Aircraft Engineering Corporation for a prototype shipboard fighter to be designated XF6F-1. Early combat experience against the Zero fighter led to some important

changes being made to the basic concept, and it was as the XF6F-3 that the definitive prototype was rolled out to make its first flight on June 26, 1942. First deliveries of the Grumman F6F-3 Hellcat, as the fighter was now known, were made to VF-9 aboard the USS *Essex* on January 16, 1943, and the aircraft saw its first combat over Marcus, one of the Caroline Islands, on August 31st. Starting in the summer of 1943 the replacement of the Wildcat by the Hellcat in the USN's fighter squadrons was rapid, and by the end of the year 2,545 F6F-3s had been delivered. Britain received 252 F6F-3s under the terms of Lend-Lease; the first examples entered service with No. 800 Squadron of the Fleet Air Arm in July 1943, and in the following December, operating from the light escort carrier HMS *Emperor*, the squadron carried out antishipping operations off the Norwegian coast.

In the Pacific, the Hellcat played a prominent role in all US naval operations, in particular the Battle of the Philippine

SPECIFICATION: Type naval fighter (data F6F-5) • Crew 1 • Powerplant one 2,000hp Pratt & Whitney R-2800-10W radial engine • Max speed 380mph (612km/h) at 23,400ft (7,132m) • Service ceiling 37,300ft (11,369m) • Max range 945 miles (1,521km) • Wingspan 42ft 10in (13.05m) • Length 33ft 7in (10.24m) • Height 13ft 1in (3.99m) • Weight 15,487lb (7,025kg) loaded • Armament six 0.50-in (12.7-mm) machine guns in wings, or two 0.79-in (20-mm) cannon and four 0.50-in (12.7-mm), plus provision for two 1,000-lb (453-kg) bombs or six 5-in (12.7-cm) RPs

Sea (June 19/20, 1944). In this action, naval aircraft from nine Japanese aircraft carriers, together with shore-based aircraft, launched a massive air attack against the US Task Force 58. In a battle that became known as the "Marianas Turkey Shoot," American combat air patrols and AA fire destroyed 325 enemy aircraft, including 220 of the 328 launched by the carriers. American losses were 16 Hellcats in combat, and seven other aircraft destroyed by Japanese fighters or ground fire.

Night fighter variants of the F6F-3 were the F6F-3E with APS4 radar housed in a pod beneath the starboard wing, and the F6F-3N with the APS-6. Eighteeen F6F-3Es and 205 F6F-3Ns were built, becoming part of the total number of F6F-3s manufactured before production switched to the improved F6F-5 in April 1944.

The F6F-5 was fitted with a Pratt & Whitney R-2800-10W engine, capable of developing an emergency power of 2,200hp by using water injection. The F6F-5 had a redesigned engine cowling, an improved windshield, additional armor behind the pilot (which increased the total armor weight to 242lb/110kg), new ailerons, a strengthened tail assembly, and provision for racks to take two 1,000lb (453kg) bombs beneath the center section. Provision was also made for six 5-in (12.7-cm) rocket projectiles, and late production F6F-5s had 0.79-in (20-mm) cannon in place of the two inboard 0.50-in (12.5-mm) guns.

The F6F-5 began to reach the Pacific task forces in the summer of 1944, and 6,436 examples of this variant had been built when production ended in November 1945, about one-sixth of the total being F6F-5N night fighters. The Royal Navy took delivery of 930 F6F-5s as Hellcat IIs, and two squadrons, Nos. 891 and 892, were armed with the night fighter version. Two examples of an experimental version, the XF6F-6, powered by a 2,100hp R-280018W engine, were built and flown, but no production was undertaken. Some Hellcats, designated F6F-5K, were converted for use as attack drones during the Korean War. In all, 12,272 Hellcats were built.

▌ Grumman F7F Tigercat

USA

▼ Too late to see operational service in WWII, Grumman's powerful Tigercat was used as a night intruder over Korea.

Although it appeared too late to see operational service in World War II, the Grumman F7F Tigercat was significant in that it was the first twin-engined carrier-borne aircraft with a tricycle undercarriage to enter series production. The prototype XF7F-1 flew on November 3, 1943 and 34 series aircraft were produced with the designation F7F-1D, these being intended for long-range escort and tactical support. The F7F-2N (64 built) was a night fighter version, while the F7F-3 was the major pro-

SPECIFICATION: Type night fighter (data F7F-3N) • Crew 2 • Powerplant two
2,100hp Pratt & Whitney R-2800-34W Double Wasp 18-cylinder radials •
Max speed 435mph (700km/h) at 22,200ft (6,766m) • Service ceiling 40,700ft
(12,405m) • Max range 1,200 miles (1,930km) • Wingspan 51ft 6in (15.69m) •
Length 46ft 10in (14.27m) • Height 16ft 7in (5.05m) • Weight 25,720lb
(11,666kg) loaded • Armament four 0.79-in (20-mm) cannon

duction version, 189 being built. The F7F-3N was another night fighter, while the F7F-3E carried ECM equipment.

The F7F-3P was a photoreconnaissance version, and the F7F-4N was the last night fighter variant, appearing in June 1946. Production of the F7F ended with the 364th aircraft. During the Korean War, Tigercats operated as night intruders, with limited success.

▌Grumman F8F Bearcat

USA

Designed to replace the F6F Hellcat, the F8F was the last of Grumman's "cats" and, like the Tigercat, came too late to see operational service in World War II. The prototype flew on August 21, 1944 and the first of 765 F8F-1s was delivered to the US Navy in May 1945, followed in 1946 by 100 F8F-1Bs and 36 F8F-1F night fighters. In 1948 the more powerful F8F-2 made its appearance; production of this variant totaled 305, of which 12 were F8F-2N night fighters and 30 F8F-2P photoreconnaissance aircraft. One hundred Bearcats were supplied to France for service in Indo-China (they were subsequently handed over to the embryo South Vietnamese

Air Force), and about 100 were also delivered to the Royal Thai Air Force. Production ended in May 1949, by which time Grumman had built 1,266 Bearcats.

SPECIFICATION: Type naval fighter (data F9F-2) • Crew 1 • Powerplant one
5,000-lb (2,270-kg) thrust Pratt & Whitney J-42-P-6 turbojet • Max speed
526mph (846km/h) at 22,000ft (6,700m) • Service ceiling 44,600ft (13,600m)
• Max range 1,353 miles (2,180km) • Wingspan 38ft (11.58m) • Length 37ft 3in
(11.35m) • Height 11ft 4in (3.45m) • Weight 19,452lb (8,842kg) loaded •
Armament four 0.79-in (20-mm) cannon; 2,000lb (907kg) of ordnance

▲ Many surplus Bearcats, like the one pictured here, were sold off and converted as racing aircraft, a use for which the aircraft's high power output made it ideal.

▌Grumman F11F Tiger

USA

▲ For several years, the Tiger was the mount of the Blue Angels, the US Navy's aerobatic team, seen here at Reading, Pennsylvania, in 1966.

To replace the Panther and its swept-wing version, the F9F-8 Cougar, Grumman conceived the F11F Tiger supersonic fighter, which first flew on July 30, 1954. The Tiger's design featured area ruling and other aerodynamic refinements which were then novel, and although the formulas used turned out to be correct, the type experienced some serious technical troubles during early flight testing. These were gradually eliminated, and the F11F-1 Tiger entered service with Navy Squadron VA-156 in March 1937. On September 21, 1956 an F11F-1F Tiger piloted by Grumman test pilot Tom Attridge was involved in an extraordinary incident when it shot itself down during test firings off Long Island, overtaking and colliding with 0.79-in (20-mm) cannon shells

SPECIFICATION: Type naval fighter (data F11F-1) • Crew 1 • Powerplant one 7,700-lb (3,488-kg) thrust Wright J65-W-18 turbojet • Max speed 890mph (1,432km/h) at 36,000ft (10,980m) • Service ceiling 55,000ft (16,775m) • Combat radius 380 miles (611km) • Wingspan 31ft 7in (9.66m) • Length 44ft 6in (13.57m) • Height 12ft 8in (3.90m) • Weight 21,146lb (9,592kg) loaded • Armament four 0.79-in (20-mm) Mk 12 cannon

it had fired only seconds earlier. Only 201 Tigers were built, but the type made its mark on aviation history. On April 18, 1958, an F11F-1F, a variant powered by an afterburning J79-GE-1 engine, broke the world altitude record for the second time in three days, reaching a height of 76,989ft (23,466.4m).

Grumman F-14 Tomcat

USA

Selected in January 1969 as the winner of a US Navy contest for a carrier-borne fighter (VFX) to replace the Phantom, the prototype F-14A flew for the first time on December 21, 1970 and was followed by 11 development aircraft. The variable-geometry fighter completed carrier trials in the summer of 1972 and deliveries to the US Navy began in October that year, the Tomcat forming the interceptor element of a carrier air wing. At the heart of the Tomcat's offensive capability is

SPECIFICATION: Type fleet defense interceptor (data F-14D) • Crew 2 • Powerplant two 27,000-lb (12,247-kg) thrust General Electric F110-GE-400 turbofans • Max speed 1,235mph (1,988km/h) at altitude • Service ceiling 53,000ft (16,150m) • Max range 1,239 miles (1,994km) with full weapons load • Wingspan 64ft 1in (19.55m) unswept, 38ft 2in (11.65m) swept • Length 62ft 8in (19.10m) • Height 16ft (4.88m) • Weight 74,349lb (33,724kg) loaded • Armament one 0.79-in (20-mm) M61A1 Vulcan rotary cannon, plus a combination of AIM-7 Sparrow medium-range AAMs, AIM-9 short-range AAMs, and AIM-54 Phoenix long-range AAMs

▲ *The Tomcat had a troubled development history before it became a superlative fighting machine. Seen here is a development aircraft.*

the Hughes AN/AWG-9 weapons control system, which enables the two-man crew to detect airborne targets at ranges of up to 170nm (315km), depending on their size, and cruise missiles at 65nm (120km). Development of the production F-14A was hampered by the loss of the prototype in December 1970, but 478 aircraft were supplied to the US Navy in total, and 80 more F-14As were exported to Iran in the later 1970s. The F-14B, a proposed version with Pratt & Whitney F401P400 turbofans, was canceled, but 32 F-14As were fitted with the General Electric F110-GE-400 and redesignated F-14B. The F-14D is an improved version with more powerful radar, enhanced avionics, a redesigned cockpit, and a tactical jamming system; 37 aircraft were built from new and 18 converted from F-14As. The Tomcat has seen action in the Gulf War, the Balkans, and Afghanistan, and in the 1980s was involved in several clashes with Libyan fighters.

▌Grumman J2F Duck

USA

The Grumman J2F was a small biplane amphibian with a center float, retractable undercarriage, and wing floats. The prototype, designated JF-1, flew in May 1943 and was followed by no fewer than 27 series models. The J2F-1 variant appeared in 1937, 20 being built, and this was succeeded by the J2F-2 (21), J2F-3 (20), J2F-4 (32), J2F-5 (144), and J2F-6 (330). The Duck was used by the US Navy throughout World War II as a utility transportation and communications aircraft.

SPECIFICATION: **Type** utility transportation/liaison (data J2F-5) • **Crew** 2 • **Powerplant** one 850hp Wright R-1820-50 Cyclone 9-cylinder radial • **Max speed** 188mph (302km/h) at sea level • **Service ceiling** 27,000ft (8,230m) • **Max range** 780 miles (1,255km) • **Wingspan** 39ft (11.89m) • **Length** 34ft (10.36m) • **Height** 15ft 1in (4.60m) • **Weight** 6,711lb (3,044kg) loaded • **Armament** none

▲ *A handful of Ducks have been restored to flying condition in the US, including this J2F-6.*

▌Grumman OV-1 Mohawk

USA

Designed to a US Army and Marine Corps requirement for a battlefield surveillance aircraft capable of operating around the clock in all weathers, the G-134 Mohawk was selected in 1957, nine aircraft being ordered for evaluation. The first YOV-1A flew on April 14, 1959 and all nine aircraft were completed by the end of the year, by which time the USMC had withdrawn from the project. The production OV-1A entered service with the US Army in 1961 and saw extensive service in Vietnam. The OV-1B and -1C, the principal variants, carried more advanced surveillance equipment than the earlier model, and the last Mohawk variant, the OV-1D,

SPECIFICATION: **Type** battlefield surveillance aircraft • **Crew** 2 • **Powerplant** two 1,005hp Lycoming T53-L-3 turboprops • **Max speed** 317mph (510km/h) at 5,000ft (1,525m) • **Service ceiling** 35,000ft (10,670m) • **Max range** 1,680 miles (2,700km) • **Wingspan** 42ft (12.80m) • **Length** 41ft (12.50m) • **Height** 12ft 8in (3.86m) • **Weight** 10,423lb (4,728kg) loaded • **Armament** none

could be readily converted from infrared to radar surveillance, combining the tasks of the -1B and -1C. In total, 375 Mohawks were delivered between 1961 and 1970.

▲ *In its day, the Mohawk was the ultimate in state-of-the-art battlefield surveillance aircraft, its sensors mounted in a long under-fuselage pod.*

Grumman S-2 Tracker

USA

SPECIFICATION: Type antisubmarine warfare aircraft (data S-2A) • Crew 4 • Powerplant two 1,525hp Wright R-1820-82WA Cyclone 9-cylinder radials • Max speed 287mph (461km/h) at 5,000ft (1,524m) • Service ceiling 23,000ft (7,010m) • Max range 900 miles (1,450km) • Wingspan 69ft 8in (21.23m) • Length 42ft 3in (12.87m) • Height 16ft 3in (4.95m) • Weight 26,300lb (11,930kg) loaded • Armament two homing torpedoes, two Mk 101 depth bombs or four depth charges internally; six 250-lb (113-kg) bombs, 5-in (11.25-cm) HVARS or Zuni rockets on external pylons

▶ *The S-2 Tracker represented a huge leap forward in terms of carrier-borne anti-submarine aircraft, and served with several naval air arms.*

One of the most important carrier-borne aircraft of the post-war years, the Grumman XS2F-1 Tracker prototype flew for the first time on December 4, 1952. The initial series production S2F-1 (later S-2A) was powered by two 1,525hp Wright R-1820-82 engines; 755 were built, first deliveries to the USN being made in February 1954. The type was also supplied to Argentina, Japan, Italy, Brazil, Taiwan, Thailand, Uruguay, and the Netherlands. Subsequent variants were the S-2C (60 built), which had an enlarged torpedo bay, the S-2D (120 built), which had a greater wingspan, improved avionics, and greater endurance, and the S-2E (241 produced), which carried more weaponry and ASW electronics.

Grumman TBF Avenger

USA

Destined to be the most successful torpedo-bomber of World War II, the Grumman Avenger was a prewar design, two XTBF-1 prototypes being ordered in April 1940. The first of these flew on August 1, 1941 and the first production deliveries were made in January 1942, the type making its combat debut at the Battle of Midway in June (when five out of six aircraft were shot down). Up to December 1943 Grumman built 2,290 TBF-1s, 402 being supplied to the Royal Navy as the Avenger Mk I and 63 to the RNZAF. Production was then transferred to the Eastern Division of General Motors, which built 2,882 as the TBM-1 and -1C; 334 of these went to the Royal Navy as the Avenger II. Following this, Eastern completed 4,664 TBM-3s, with uprated Cyclone engines and wings strengthened to support rocket projectiles or a radar pod; 222 were delivered to the Royal Navy as the Avenger III. The Avenger was retired from US Navy service in 1954. The TBM-3 Avenger also served with the French Aéronavale, and was used operationally during the Suez landings of 1956.

▶ *A prominent feature of the TBM-3E Avenger was the underwing radome for its AN/APS-4 radar.*

SPECIFICATION: Type torpedo-bomber (data TBF-1C) • Crew 3 • Powerplant one 1,700hp Wright R-2600-8 Cyclone 14-cylinder radial • Max speed 257mph (414km/h) at 10,000ft (3,050m) • Service ceiling 21,400ft (6,525m) • Max range 2,685 miles (4,321km) • Wingspan 54ft 2in (16.51m) • Length 40ft 9in (12.42m) • Height 13ft 9in (4.19m) • Weight 17,364lb (7,876kg) loaded • Armament two 0.50-in (12.7-mm) machine guns in wing leading edges, plus one in dorsal turret; one 0.30-in (7.62-mm) machine gun in ventral position; up to 2,500lb (1,134kg) of torpedoes, bombs, and rockets

▌Halberstadt C.V.

The Halberstadt C.V, which reached the front in 1918, was widely used for reconnaissance during the final months of the war. Derived from the C.III of 1917, it was fitted with a supercharged version of the Benz BzIV engine, which developed 220hp at altitude. The cameras were mounted in the floor of the observer's cockpit. Other reconnaissance models developed by Halberstadt included the C.VIII, which had an operational ceiling of 29,530ft (9,000m).

SPECIFICATION: Type reconnaissance biplane • Crew 2 • Powerplant one 220hp Benz BzIV 6-cylinder liquid-cooled in-line engine • Max speed 106mph (170km/h) • Service ceiling 16,405ft (5,000m) • Endurance 3hrs 30mins • Wingspan 44ft 8in (13.62m) • Length 22ft 8in (6.92m) • Height 11ft (3.36m) • Weight 2,730lb (1,238kg) loaded • Armament two LMG 08/15 machine guns

▌Halberstadt D.II

▲ *The Halberstadt D.II served only for a short time, proving to be structurally weak. It was soon replaced by Albatros types.*

The Halberstadt D.II appeared on the Western Front in the summer of 1916, but was soon replaced by the Albatros series. Two subsequent variants, the D.III and D.IV, were also developed. The D.II and D.III were the most widely used, reaching their in-service peak during the winter of 1916–17, after which they were relegated to training duties.

SPECIFICATION: Type scouting biplane • Crew 1 • Powerplant one 120hp Merc. D.II 6-cylinder liquid-cooled in-line engine • Max speed 90mph (145km/h) • Service ceiling 13,123ft (4,000m) • Endurance 1hr 30mins • Wingspan 28ft 10in (8.80m) • Length 23ft 11in (7.30m) • Height 8ft 9in (2.66m) • Weight 1,696lb (771kg) loaded • Armament one 0.31-in (7.92-mm) LMG 08/15 machine gun

▌Handley Page Halifax

The prototype HP.57 Halifax flew for the first time on August 25, 1939 quickly followed by a second aircraft in October 1939. In November 1940 L7244 was borrowed from the Ministry of Aircraft Production and flown to RAF Leeming in Yorkshire to be used for training by No. 35 Squadron, which was forming as the first Halifax Nk I squadron in Bomber

▲ *A Halifax Mk VI aircraft of No. 77 Squadron, RAF Bomber Command. Note the H2S navigational radar blister under the fuselage.*

Command. In December the squadron moved to Linton-on-Ouse, near York, and it was from there, on the night of March 10/11, 1941, that six of its Halifaxes made the type's first operational sortie. One Halifax was lost, shot down in error by an RAF night fighter while on its way home.

Early production aircraft became known as the Halifax Mk I Series I, which was followed by the Mk I Series II with a higher gross weight and the Series III, with increased fuel tankage. The first major modification appeared in the Mk II Series I, which had a two-gun dorsal turret and uprated 1,390hp Merlin XX engines. The Mk II Series I (Special) had a fairing in place of the nose turret, and the engine exhaust muffs were omitted, while the Mk II Series IA was the first variant to introduce the drag-reducing molded Perspex nose that was a feature of all subsequent Halifaxes, a four-gun dorsal turret, and Merlin 22 engines. The Mk II Series IA also had large, rectangular vertical tail surfaces, because serious control difficulties had been experienced with the original tail configuration. Variants of the Mk II Series I (Special) and

Series IA, with Dowty landing gear instead of the standard Messier gear, were designated Mk V Series I (Special) and Mk V Series IA. In 1943 the Merlin engines were replaced by four 1,615hp Bristol Hercules XVI radial engines in the Halifax Mk III, which remained in the front line up to the end of the war.

The Halifax Mk IV was a project only. The next operational variants were the Mks VI and VII, the former powered by the 1,675hp Hercules 100 and the latter using the MK III's Hercules XVI. These were the ultimate bomber versions, and were produced in relatively small numbers. Some Halifax IIIs, Vs, and VIIs were converted to paratroop dropping and glider towing; in fact, the Halifax was the only aircraft capable of towing the massive Hamilcar glider, used to deliver heavy vehicles to the battlefront. The Halifax MK VIII, which entered service just before the end of the war, was a transportation version with faired-over gun positions and a detachable 8,000-lb (3,624-kg) freight pannier under the fuselage, and the final version, produced after the war, was another transport, the Mk IX. Various marks of Halifax also served with some squadrons of RAF Coastal Command as a long-range maritime patrol aircraft, supplementing very long-range (VLR) aircraft such as the Liberator and Fortress.

Although overshadowed by the Lancaster, the Halifax proved to be a far more versatile aircraft in that it could be adapted to many different roles, including electronic countermeasures. The total Halifax production figure of 6,176 aircraft included 2,050 Mks I and II, 2,060 Mk III, 916 Mk V, 480 Mk VI, 395 Mk VII, 100 Mk VIII, and the rest Mk IX. During World War II, Halifaxes flew a total of 75,532 sorties, dropping 227,610 tons (231,263 tonnes) of bombs.

SPECIFICATION: Type heavy bomber/transport/maritime patrol (data Mk III) • Crew 7 • Powerplant four 1,615hp Bristol Hercules VI or XVI 14-cylinder two-row radial engines • Max speed 282mph (454km/h) • Service ceiling 24,000ft (7,315m) • Max range 1,985 miles (3,194km) • Wing span 98ft 8in (30.07m) • Length 71ft 7in (21.82m) • Height 20ft 9in(6.32m) • Weights 39,000lb (17,690kg) empty; max t/o 68,000lb (30,845kg) • Armament one 0.303-in (7.7-mm) machine gun in nose position, four 0.303-in (7.7-mm) machine guns each in dorsal and tail turrets, plus an internal bomb load of 14,500lb (6,577kg)

▲ An early development Halifax Mk I pictured on a test flight "somewhere over England" in 1940.

▌Handley Page Hampden

▲ *Widely used by the RAF in the early part of WWII, the Hampden was not built for crew comfort; its fuselage was only 3ft (0.9m) wide at its fattest point.*

One of the RAF's most important medium bombers at the outbreak of World War II, the highly maneuverable but badly underarmed Hampden first flew in June 1937, the first of 1,430 Hampden Mk Is being delivered in September 1938. The Hereford, 100 of which were built, was a variant with Napier Dagger engines. From 1942 about 140 Hampdens were converted to Hampden TB.Mk.I torpedo bombers, some of these being supplied to the Soviet Naval Air Arm.

SPECIFICATION: Type medium bomber • Crew 4 • Powerplant two 1,000hp Bristol Pegasus XVIII 9-cylinder radials • Max speed 265mph (426km/h) • Service ceiling 22,700ft (6,920m) • Max range 1,885 miles (3,034km) • Wingspan 69ft 2in (21.08m) • Length 53ft 7in (16.33m) • Height 14ft 11in (4.55m) • Weight 11,780lb (5,343kg) • Armament one 0.303-in (7.7-mm) machine gun in port side of forward fuselage, one in nose position, two in dorsal, and two in ventral positions (after upgrading)

▌Handley Page Hastings

First flown on May 7, 1946, the Handley Page Hastings was the mainstay of RAF Transport Command for a decade. The first of 14 squadrons to receive it, in October 1948, was No. 47, and this unit took part in the Berlin Airlift. Production totaled 100 C.1s and 42 C.2s, the latter powered by four Bristol Hercules 106 engines in place of the C.1's Hercules 101s. Some Hastings were later used for bombing training, radio/radar trials, and weather reconnaissance.

SPECIFICATION: Type transport aircraft • Crew 5 (plus 50 passengers) • Powerplant four 1,675hp Bristol Hercules 106 14-cylinder radials • Max speed 348mph (560km/h) at 22,200ft (6,770m) • Service ceiling 22,000ft (6,080m) • Max range 4,250 miles (6,840km) • Wingspan 113ft (34.44m) • Length 82ft 8in (25.19m) • Height 22ft 6in (6.85m) • Weight 80,000lb (36,288kg) loaded • Armament none

▲ *This RAF Hastings C.Mk 1A is fitted with the type's optional underwing fuel tanks. The type was retired from Transport Command service in 1968.*

Handley Page Heyford

GREAT BRITAIN

The Handley Page Heyford was the last biplane bomber to serve with the RAF. Designed in 1927, the aircraft was unusual in that it featured a high-set fuselage that was attached flush to the upper mainplane. The prototype flew in June 1930 and was followed by 122 production aircraft built in four series. The Heyford was first issued to No. 99 Squadron in July 1933 and subsequently equipped 11 more bomber squadrons, being relegated to second-line duties in 1937.

SPECIFICATION: Type heavy bomber (data Heyford Mk IA) • Crew 4 • Powerplant two 575hp Rolls-Royce Kestrel IIIS 12-cylinder V-type engines • Max speed 142mph (229km/h) • Service ceiling 21,000ft (6,400m) • Max range 920 miles (1,481km) • Wingspan 75ft (22.86m) • Length 58ft (17.68m) • Height 17ft 6in (5.33m) • Weight 16,900lb (7,666kg) loaded • Armament one 0.303-in (7.7-mm) Lewis machine gun in nose, dorsal, and ventral positions; bomb load up to 3,500lb (1,588kg)

◄ *The Heyford had a metal wing structure with fabric covering, a metal fuselage covered with light alloy and robust fixed tailwheel landing gear.*

Handley Page Hinaidi

GREAT BRITAIN

Between 1926 and 1933 the RAF's night bomber squadrons were partly armed with two twin-engined biplane types produced by Handley Page, the Hyderabad and the Hinaidi. The Hinaidi was an improved and more powerful version of the Hyderabad, which had appeared in prototype form in October 1923. The Hinaidi prototype flew on March 26, 1927 and the type went into production as the Mk II after major structural modifications had been implemented. The first of 33 aircraft entered service in 1929, the type being issued to No. 99, 10, and 503 Squadrons. Some Hinaidis were converted to the transportation role for use on the North-West Frontier of India.

SPECIFICATION: Type heavy bomber • Crew 4 • Powerplant two 440hp Bristol Jupiter VIII 9-cylinder radials • Max speed 122mph (197km/h) • Service ceiling 14,500ft (4,400m) • Max range 850 miles (1,370km) • Wingspan 75ft (22.86m) • Length 59ft 2in (18.03m) • Height 17ft (5.18m) • Weight 14,400lb (6,500kg) • Armament one 0.303-in (7.7-mm) Vickers machine gun in nose, dorsal, and ventral positions

▲ *The Hinaidi was widely used as a transport aircraft overseas. This example, belonging to No. 10 Squadron, Ambala, is seen on India's North-West Frontier.*

▌Handley Page Victor

The last in a long line of Handley Page bombers, and the last in the RAF's trio of V-bombers, the HP.80 Victor's design owed much to research into the crescent wing carried out by the German Arado and Blohm & Voss firms in World War II. The prototype flew on December 24, 1952, but was destroyed when the tailplane broke away during a low-level run. The second prototype flew on September 11, 1954, followed by the first production Victor B.Mk.1 on February 1, 1956. The

SPECIFICATION: Type strategic bomber/tanker (data Victor B.2) • Crew 5 • Powerplant four 20,600-lb (9,344-kg) thrust Rolls-Royce Conway Mk.201 turbofans • Max speed 640mph (1,040km/h) at 40,000ft (12,190m) • Service ceiling 47,000ft (14,335m) • Max range 4,600 miles (7,400km) • Wingspan 120ft (36.58m) • Length 114ft 11in (35.05m) • Height 30ft 1in (9.20m) • Weight 233,000lb (105,687kg) • Armament one HS Blue Steel ASM (Red Snow warhead)

first Victor squadron, No. 10, became operational in April 1958, and three more, Nos. 15, 55, and 57, had formed by 1960. The B.Mk.1A was an updated variant with more advanced equipment, including ECM in the tail, and the B.Mk.2 was a more powerful version with a larger span. The B.Mk.2 was designed to carry the canceled US Skybolt IRBM, and two squadrons (Nos. 100 and 139) were armed with the Avro Blue Steel standoff missile.

The Victor B.(PR).Mk.1 and B.(PR).Mk.2 were photo-reconnaissance variants, both serving with No. 543 Squadron. In 1964–65 the earlier Victors were converted to the flight refueling tanker role as B.(K).Mk 1s and 1As, and 27 Mk.2s were converted to K.Mk.2 tankers in 1973–74. These aircraft served with Nos. 55 and 57 Squadrons and were withdrawn from service in the early 1990s, after participating in the Gulf War. Victor production totaled 50 B.1s/1As and 34 B.2s.

▲ After its nuclear deterrent days, the Victor gave excellent service as a tanker. Here, a Victor K.2 of No. 55 Squadron refuels a Phantom FGR.2 of No. 56.

■ Handley Page O/100

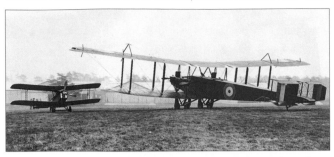

▲ *The Handley Page O/100 proved to be a splendid design, and was the mainstay of the British night bombing offensive from 1916.*

SPECIFICATION: **Type** heavy bomber biplane • **Crew** 3 • **Powerplant** two 250hp Rolls-Royce Eagle II V-12 engines • **Max speed** 76mph (122km/h) • **Service ceiling** 8,500ft (2,590m) • **Max range** 450 miles (724km) • **Wingspan** 100ft (30.48m) • **Length** 62ft 10in (19.16m) • **Height** 22ft (6.70m) • **Weight** 14,000lb (6,350kg) loaded • **Armament** two 0.303-in (7.7-mm) Lewis machine guns in nose cockpit; one each in dorsal and ventral positions; eight 250-lb (113-kg) or 16 112-lb (51-kg) bombs

The Handley Page O/100 owed its origins to a requirement, issued in December 1914, for a "bloody paralyser of an aeroplane" for the bombing of Germany. The nickname subsequently bestowed upon it by its crews was inevitable, but the "bloody paralyser" adequately met, and in some cases exceeded, its requirements in the role it was intended to perform.

The O/100 entered service with No. 3 Wing RNAS on the Western Front in November 1916, and from the spring of the following year its two squadrons, Nos. 14 and 16, concentrated on the night bombing of major German installations such as U-boat bases, railroad stations, and industrial centers. In September 1917 No. 16 Squadron was detached to form part of the 41st Wing RFC, and thereafter carried out many operations against strategic targets in the Saar. Fifty-six O/100s were delivered to the RNAS.

■ Handley Page O/400

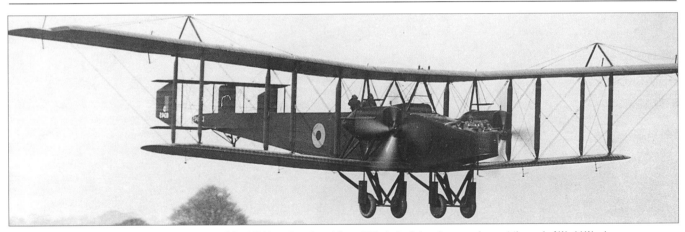

▲ *The Handley Page O/400 was a development of the O/100, and equipped three RAF strategic bomber squadrons at the end of World War I.*

A development of the O/100 with more powerful Eagle engines was designated the HP O/400, the numeral denoting the installed horsepower. The aircraft was fitted with a new

SPECIFICATION: **Type** heavy bomber • **Crew** 3 • **Powerplant** two 360hp Rolls-Royce Eagle VIII V-12 engines • **Max speed** 76mph (122km/h) • **Service ceiling** 8,500ft (2,590m) • **Max range** 450 miles (724km) • **Wingspan** 100ft (30.48m) • **Length** 62ft 10in (19.16m) • **Height** 22ft (6.70m) • **Weight** 14,000lb (6,350kg) loaded • **Armament** four 0.303-in (7.7-mm) Lewis machine guns; eight 250-lb (113-kg), or 16 112-lb (51-kg) bombs

bombsight designed by Lieutenant-Commander Wimperis; the Drift Sight Mk 1A took account of the aircraft's height above the target, its airspeed, wind velocity, and drift. It was far from efficient, but it was a vast improvement on the rudimentary equipment used previously.

In the summer of 1918 the O/400 was the backbone of the RAF's strategic bombing force, equipping Nos. 97, 115, and 215 Squadrons. The O/400 ultimately equipped 11 RAF squadrons at home and overseas; 550 were built in the UK and another 107 were assembled from parts manufactured in the US.

▌Handley Page V/1500

In September 1918, a new RAF Bomber Group, No. 27, formed at Bircham Newton in East Anglia for the purpose of launching strategic attacks on Germany, and in particular Berlin, from the UK with a new aircraft, the Handley Page V/1500. Its design based on the Vickers Vimy, the HP V/1500 was the RAF's first four-engined aircraft and, for the first time, featured a tail armament. Orders for 225 were placed, but only 35 were completed, the Armistice having inter-vened. Only three squadrons (Nos. 166, 167, and 274) were equipped with the type for a short period.

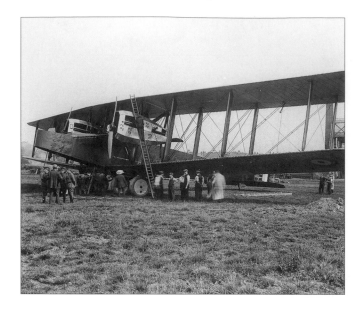

SPECIFICATION: Type heavy bomber biplane • Crew 4 • Powerplant four 375hp Rolls-Royce Eagle VIII 12-cylinder V-type • Max speed 97mph (156km/h) • Service ceiling 10,000ft (3,048m) • Endurance 6hrs • Wingspan 126ft (38.41m) • Length 62ft (18.90m) • Height 23ft (7.01m) • Weight 24,700lb (11,204kg) • Armament twin 0.303-in (7.7-mm) Lewis machine guns in nose and dorsal positions, one in ventral, and one in extreme tail positions; 7,500lb (3,402kg) of bombs

▶ *Groundcrew and the length of the ladder required for routine engine inspections serve to emphasize the huge size of the V/1500.*

▌Hannover CL.III

▲ *Having nosed-over on landing, this CL.III provides a useful demonstration of the type's unusual tail configuration.*

The Hannover CL.III, which was deployed on the Western Front early in 1918, was what would later be termed a multi-role aircraft, being used for reconnaissance, escort, and close support. One of the type's most notable features was its biplane tail, designed to cut out any blind spots for the observer. A total of 537 were built.

SPECIFICATION: Type multipurpose biplane • Crew 2 • Powerplant one 180hp Argus As III 9-cylinder liquid-cooled radial • Max speed 103mph (165km/h) at 16,400ft (5,000m) • Service ceiling 24,600ft (7,500m) • Endurance 3hrs • Wingspan 38ft 5in (11.70m) • Length 24ft 10in (7.58m) • Height 9ft 2in (2.80m) • Weight 2,378lb (1,081kg) loaded • Armament three 0.31-in (7.92-mm) LMG 08/15 machine guns, two in observer's cockpit

▌Hanriot HD.1

FRANCE

Designed by Pierre Dupont in 1916, the Hanriot HD.1 was a small and highly maneuverable scout which, although turned down by France's Aviation Militaire, was used with great success by the Italians and Belgians. The HD.1 went into service on the Italian front in the summer of 1917 and ultimately equipped 16 of the 18 operational Italian fighter squadrons, the initial batch of 100 aircraft being followed by a further 831, license-built by Macchi, before the war ended. On one occasion, on December 26, 1917, Hanriots of Grupo 6 shot down 11 German reconnaissance aircraft for no loss. In Belgium, the HD.1 went into service in August 1917 and remained first-line equipment until 1926.

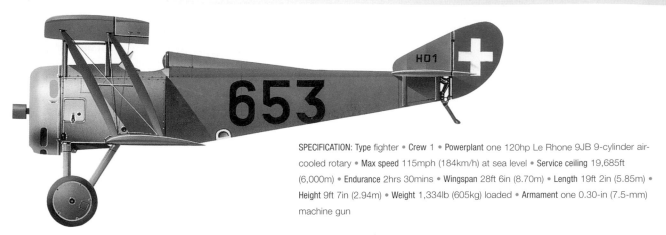

SPECIFICATION: Type fighter • Crew 1 • Powerplant one 120hp Le Rhone 9JB 9-cylinder air-cooled rotary • Max speed 115mph (184km/h) at sea level • Service ceiling 19,685ft (6,000m) • Endurance 2hrs 30mins • Wingspan 28ft 6in (8.70m) • Length 19ft 2in (5.85m) • Height 9ft 7in (2.94m) • Weight 1,334lb (605kg) loaded • Armament one 0.30-in (7.5-mm) machine gun

▌Hansa-Brandenburg KDW

GERMANY

Designed by Eernst Heinkel, the Hansa-Brandenburg KDW (Kampf Doppeldecker, Wasser—Fighting Biplane, Water) was adapted from the D.I landplane and was intended for coastal defense in the North Sea and Adriatic. Produced under license in Austria-Hungary by Phönix, about 60 were built in five production batches, starting in 1916, each batch having progressively more powerful engines. By 1918 they had become outclassed by the new Italian fighter designs.

◀ *The Hansa-Brandenburg KDW was the brainchild of Ernst Heinkel, whose bombers were to achieve notoriety in World War II.*

SPECIFICATION: Type floatplane fighter • Crew 1 • Powerplant one 150hp Benz Bz.III water-cooled in-line • Max speed 107mph (172km/h) at sea level • Service ceiling 13,123ft (4,000m) • Endurance 2hrs 30mins • Wingspan 30ft 4in (9.25m) • Length 26ft 3in (8m) • Height 11ft (3.35m) • Weight 2,293lb (1,040kg) loaded • Armament one or two fixed forward-firing machine guns (various types)

▌Hansa-Brandenburg W.12

GERMANY

The Hansa-Brandenburg W.12 was developed by Ernst Heinkel in an attempt to rectify the major weakness of the KDW, its vulnerability to attack from the rear. A rear cockpit was added to accommodate an observer/gunner, and the tail modified to provide him with an uninterrupted field of fire. The first W.12 flew early in 1917 and was followed by 146 production aircraft, one of which shot down the British airship C.27.

▲ *Suspended from a dockside crane, this W.12 shows the type's layout, including the unorthodox empennage, to advantage.*

SPECIFICATION: Type floatplane fighter • Crew 2 • Powerplant one 160hp Mercedes D.III 6-cylinder in-line • Max speed 99mph (160km/h) • Service ceiling 16,405ft (5,000m) • Endurance 3hrs 30mins • Wingspan 36ft 9in (11.20m) • Length 31ft 6in (9.60m) • Height 10ft 10in (3.30m) • Weight 3,206lb (1,454kg) loaded • Armament one or two fixed forward-firing 0.31-in (7.92-mm) LMG 08/15 machine guns; one 0.31-in (7.92-mm) Parabellum in rear cockpit

Hansa-Brandenburg W.29

GREAT BRITAIN / GERMANY

The Hansa-Brandenburg W.29 was one of the last German seaplane fighters, and was considered to be the best of Ernst Heinkel's naval warplane designs. A completely new aircraft, the W.29 was a monoplane, its impressive performance a result of eliminating the extra drag that was an inherent feature of biplane designs. This was in effect the only way Heinkel could have wrung greater performance from the type—better engines were simply not available. The 78 W.29s that were built for the German Navy served at their North Sea bases in the closing months of World War I.

▲ *Little more than a monoplane derivative of the W.12, the W.29 saw brief but useful service during World War I.*

SPECIFICATION: **Type** floatplane fighter • **Crew** 2 • **Powerplant** one 150hp Benz Bz III 6-cylinder liquid-cooled in-line • **Max speed** 109mph (175km/h) • **Service ceiling** not known • **Endurance** 4hrs • **Wingspan** 44ft 4in (13.50m) • **Length** 30ft 8in (9.38m) • **Height** 9ft 11in (3m) • **Weight** 3,285lb (1,494kg) • **Armament** one or two fixed forward-firing 0.31-in (7.92-mm) LMG 08/15 machine guns; one 0.31-in (7.92-mm) Parabellum in rear cockpit

Hawker Demon

GREAT BRITAIN

A development of the Hawker Hart light bomber, which had shown itself to be faster than contemporary fighters, the Hawker Demon two-seat fighter was intended as an interim measure until the Hawker Fury became available. Many aircraft were fitted or retrofitted with a hydraulically powered Frazer-Nash turret for the gunner. The type served with six regular and five auxiliary fighter squadrons, beginning with No. 23 Squadron in July 1931. Production ran to 244 aircraft.

SPECIFICATION: **Type** fighter biplane • **Crew** 2 • **Powerplant** one 584hp Rolls-Royce Kestrel IIS 12-cylinder V-type • **Max speed** 188mph (303km/h) • **Service ceiling** 21,320ft (6,500m) • **Max range** 470 miles (756km) • **Wingspan** 37ft 3in (11.35m) • **Length** 29ft 4in (8.94m) • **Height** 10ft 5in (3.17m) • **Weight** 4,554lb (2,066kg) • **Armament** two fixed forward-firing 0.303-in (7.7-mm) Vickers machine guns, plus one 0.303-in (7.7-mm) Lewis machine gun in rear cockpit

▲ *Fast for its time, and very maneuverable, the Hawker Demon was basically a Hawker Hart light bomber developed as a two-seat fighter.*

Hawker Fury

GREAT BRITAIN

The Hawker Fury was the epitome of British fighter biplane design and one of the most beautiful aircraft ever built. The first of 118 Fury Mk Is entered service with No. 43

Squadron at Tangmere in May 1931, and the type also served with Nos. 1 and 25 Squadrons. Further development of a version known as the High Speed Fury led to a pro-

◀ *Looking almost as though they were joined by an invisible thread, these Hawker Fury II fighter biplanes of No. 25 Squadron demonstrate a perfect echelon formation.*

duction order for 23 Fury Mk IIs, followed by another 75, and the first of these entered service with No. 25 Squadron in December 1936, also serving with four more squadrons of what was, by then, RAF Fighter Command. The Fury II was exported to Persia (22 aircraft), Spain, and Portugal (three each).

SPECIFICATION: **Type** fighter (data Fury Mk II) • **Crew** 1 • **Powerplant** one 700hp Rolls-Royce Kestrel VI 12-cylinder V-type • **Max speed** 223mph (359km/h) • **Service ceiling** 29,500ft (8,990m) • **Max range** 270 miles (435km) • **Wingspan** 30ft (9.14m) • **Length** 26ft 8in (8.13m) • **Height** 10ft 2in (3.10m) • **Weight** 3,609lb (1,637kg) loaded • **Armament** two fixed forward-firing 0.303-in (7.7-mm) Vickers machine guns

▌Hawker Hart

GREAT BRITAIN

The most widely used RAF light bomber of the 1930s was the Hawker Hart, designed by Sydney Camm. The prototype flew in June 1928 and deliveries of the first production aircraft began in January 1930, the recipient being No. 33 Squadron. A trainer version of the Hart was also produced, as was the Hart C general purpose aircraft, the Hart Special, and the Hart India, both of which were tropicalized versions. Eight Harts were exported to Estonia and four to Sweden, which built a further 24 Harts under license, these being powered by Pegasus radial engines. Faster than any contemporary RAF fighter, the Hart performed exceptionally well in the harsh climate of India's Northwestern Frontier.

▲ *This Hawker Hart, J9933, was used to test an experimental turret installation for the Hawker Demon two-seat fighter.*

SPECIFICATION: **Type** light bomber • **Crew** 2 • **Powerplant** one 525hp Rolls-Royce Kestrel IB 12-cylinder V-type • **Max speed** 184mph (298km/h) • **Service ceiling** 21,320ft (6,500m) • **Max range** 470 miles (756km) • **Wingspan** 37ft 3in (11.35m) • **Length** 29ft 4in (8.94m) • **Height** 10ft 5in (3.17m) • **Weight** 4,554lb (2,066kg) • **Armament** one fixed forward-firing 0.303-in (7.7-mm) Vickers machine gun, plus one 0.303-in (7.7-mm) Lewis machine gun in rear cockpit; up to 520lb (236kg) of bombs on underwing racks

▌Hawker Hind

GREAT BRITAIN

The Hawker Hind began to replace the Hart as the RAF's standard light bomber late in 1935. The prototype Hind first flew on September 12, 1934, and was essentially an improved Hart with a more powerful engine and refined aerodynam-ics. The Hind, 527 examples of which were produced, equipped no fewer than 47 RAF bomber squadrons between 1935 and 1939, when it was replaced by more modern types such as the Bristol Blenheim and Fairey Battle.

◀Showing the elegant lines of the Hawker biplane family, this Hind displays the pre-war markings of No. XV Squadron.

SPECIFICATION: Type light bomber • Crew 2 • Powerplant one 640hp Rolls-Royce Kestrel V 12-cylinder V-type • Max speed 184mph (298km/h) • Service ceiling 26,400ft (8,045m) • Max range 430 miles (692km) • Wingspan 37ft 3in (11.35m) • Length 29ft 7in (9.02m) • Height 10ft 7in (3.23m) • Weight 5,298lb (2,403kg) loaded • Armament one fixed forward-firing 0.303-in (7.7-mm) Vickers machine gun; one 0.303-in (7.7-mm) Lewis machine gun in rear cockpit

▌Hawker Horsley

GREAT BRITAIN

The Hawker Horsley was designed to be used either as a day bomber or torpedo-bomber. The prototype first flew in 1925, and was followed by 128 aircraft subdivided into two series, the all-wood Horsley Mk I and the Horsley Mk II, of mixed construction. The bomber version entered service in 1927, and the torpedo-bomber variant in the following year. The Horsley equipped five RAF squadrons, the TB version being deployed to India and Singapore.

SPECIFICATION: Type day bomber/torpedo-bomber • Crew 2 • Powerplant one 665hp Rolls-Royce Condor IIIA 12-cylinder V-type • Max speed 125mph (201km/h) • Service ceiling 14,000ft (4,265m) • Endurance 10hrs • Wingspan 56ft 6in (17.21m) • Length 38ft 10in (11.84m) • Height 13ft 8in (4.17m) • Weight 7,800lb (3,538kg) loaded • Armament one fixed forward-firing 0.303-in (7.7-mm) Vickers machine gun; one 0.303-in (7.7-mm) Lewis machine gun in rear cockpit; up to 1,500lb (680kg) of bombs or one 18-in (455-mm) torpedo

▶An unidentified civilian strikes a pose beside a Horsley Mk I. In trials, it beat three other types, the Handley Page Hardcross, Bristol Berkeley and Westland Yeovil, for an Air Ministry production contract.

▌Hawker Hunter

GREAT BRITAIN

The outbreak of the Korean War, together with fears that it might escalate into a wider conflict, led to the acceleration of combat aircraft reequipment programs in both east and west. In Britain, two new swept-wing fighter types, the Hawker Hunter and Supermarine Swift, were to replace the Meteor in the air defense role; their prototypes flew on July 20 and August 1, 1951 respectively and both types were ordered into "super-priority" production for RAF Fighter Command.

SPECIFICATION: Type fighter (data Hunter F.Mk.1) • Crew 1 • Powerplant one 6,500-lb (2,925-kg) thrust Rolls-Royce Avon 100 turbojet • Max speed 710mph (1,144km/h) at sea level • Service ceiling 50,000ft (15,240m) • Max range 490 miles (788km) • Wingspan 33ft 8in (10.26m) • Length 45ft 10in (13.98m) • Height 13ft 2in (4.02m) • Weight 16,200lb (7,347kg) loaded • Armament four 1.19-in (30-mm) Aden cannon; underwing pylons with provision for two 1,000lb (453kg) bombs and 24 3-in (76-mm) rockets

◀ *Hunters of No. 1 Tactical Weapons Unit breaking into the circuit at RAF Chivenor, Devon. The centre aircraft bears the markings of No. 72 Squadron, a so-called "shadow" unit.*

squadrons of the 2nd Tactical Air Force. The Hunter Mks 2 and 5 were variants powered by the Armstrong Siddeley Sapphire engine. In 1953 Hawker equipped the Hunter with the large 10,000-lb (4,536-kg) thrust Avon 203 engine, and this variant, designated Hunter F.MK.6, flew for the first time in January 1954. Deliveries began in 1956 and the F6 subsequently equipped 15 squadrons of RAF Fighter Command. The Hunter FGA.9 was a development of the F6 optimized for ground attack, as its designation implies. The Hunter Mks 7, 8, 12, T52, T62, T66, T67, and T69 were all two-seat trainer variants, while the FR.10 was a fighter-reconnaissance version, converted from the F.6. The GA.11 was an operational trainer for the Royal Navy.

In an illustrious career spanning a quarter of a century the Hunter equipped 30 RAF fighter squadrons, in addition to numerous units of foreign air forces. The aircraft was license-built in Holland and Belgium, and principal customers for British-built aircraft included India, Switzerland, and Sweden.

The grand total of Hunter production, including two-seat trainers, was 1972 aircraft; over 500 were subsequently rebuilt for sale overseas.

The Hunter F.Mk.1, which entered service early in 1954, suffered from engine surge problems during high-altitude gun firing trials, resulting in some modifications to its Rolls-Royce Avon turbojet, and this—together with increased fuel capacity and provision for underwing tanks—led to the Hunter F4, which gradually replaced the Canadair-built F-86E Sabre (which had been supplied to the RAF as an interim fighter) in the German-based

▌Hawker Hurricane

GREAT BRITAIN

The Hawker Hurricane was the first of Britain's new monoplane fighters, powered by the Rolls-Royce Merlin engine and given an armament of eight 0.303-in (7.7-mm) Colt-Browning machine guns. Developed from the Hawker Fury biplane (it was originally known as the Fury Monoplane) under the design leadership of Sydney Camm to meet Air Ministry Specification F.36/34, the prototype (K5083) flew on November 6, 1935, powered by a Merlin "C" engine of 990hp, and began Service trials at Martlesham Heath in March 1936. An order for 600 machines materialized in June 1936, and the first of these—after some delay caused by the

decision to install the 1,030hp Merlin II engine—flew on October 12, 1937, an initial batch being delivered to No. 111 Squadron at Northolt in November. In 1938 the first deliveries were made to foreign customers (Portugal, Yugoslavia, Persia, and Belgium); Hurricanes were also exported to Romania and Turkey.

Eventual production of the Hurricane Mk I, shared between the Hawker and Gloster factories in the UK and the Canadian Car and Foundry Co. of Montreal, amounted to 3,954. On June 11, 1940 Hurricane P3269 flew with a 1,185hp supercharged Merlin XX engine, serving as proto-

◄ *Previous pages: "The Last of the Many"; the very last Hurricane manufactured, now part of the RAF's Battle of Britain memorial flight.*

type for the Hurricane Mk II, and as more Mk IIs reached the squadrons many Mk Is were fitted with Vokes sand filters and sent to the Middle East. Early Mk IIs, which retained the eight-gun armament, were designated Mk IIAs; with 12 machine guns the designation became Mk IIB, while the Mk IIC had a wing armament of four 0.79-in (20-mm) Hispano cannon. The Mk IID was a special antitank version, armed with two underwing 1.58-in (40-mm) Vickers "S" guns and two 0.303-in (7.7-mm) Brownings in the wings. Both IIBs and IICs were fitted with cameras and used for reconnaissance as the Mks PR.IIB and PR.IIC. In 1942, Hurricane Is and IIAs operated in Singapore, the Netherlands East Indies, Ceylon, and Burma, and it was during the Burma Campaign that the Hurricane really came into its own as a tactical support aircraft, armed with a pair of 500-lb (226-kg) bombs. The only other British production model, the Mk IV, was also a ground attack type, armed principally with eight 60-lb (27-kg) rocket projectiles and fitted with a 1,620hp Merlin 24 or 27 engine. Alternative payloads included two 250- or 500-lb (113- or 226-kg) bombs, or two Vickers "S" guns. The Hurricane Mk V was designed to take the higher-powered Merlin 27 or 32.

In 1941 the Hurricane was adopted by the Royal Navy for fleet protection duties, the first Sea Hurricane Mk IAs being deployed on escort carriers (converted merchant vessels, known as Catapult Aircraft Merchantmen, or CAM ships, in 1941). As Hurricanes were progressively withdrawn from first-line RAF squadrons they were converted for naval use as Sea Hurricanes Mks IB, IIC, and XIIA.

One major user of the Hurricane was the Soviet Union, the first batch to be delivered comprising 24 Mk IIBs turned over to the Soviet Navy's 72nd Fighter Air Regiment by No. 141 Wing RAF, which operated in North Russia in the late summer of 1941. Altogether, 2,952 Hurricanes—over 20 percent of total UK production—were delivered to the USSR.

Overall Hurricane production in the UK was 13,080 by Hawker, Gloster, and Austin Motors; another 1,451 Mks X, XI, XII, and XIIA, fitted with various armament combinations and Packard-built Merlins, were produced by the Canadian Car and Foundry Company.

SPECIFICATION: Type antitank aircraft (data Hurricane Mk IID) • Crew 1 • Powerplant one 1,460hp Rolls-Royce Merlin XX 12-cylinder V-type • Max speed 322mph (518km/h) • Service ceiling 32,100ft (9,785m) • Max range 900 miles (1,448km) • Wingspan 40ft (12.19m) • Length 32ft 2in (9.81m) • Height 13ft 1in (3.98m) • Weight 8,100lb (3,674kg) loaded • Armament two fixed 1.58-in (40-mm) Vickers "S" guns under each wing; two Browning 0.303-in (7.7-mm) machine guns in each wing

▼ *A Hurricane Mk I of the Strathallan vintage aircraft collection, seen in the markings of No. 605 Squadron.*

Hawker Nimrod

GREAT BRITAIN

▲ *Derived from the Hawker Fury, the Nimrod was a third-generation post-WWI carrier-borne fighter. The last examples were retired in 1939.*

The Hawker Nimrod, which replaced the Fairey Flycatcher in Fleet Air Arm service, was a naval member of Sydney Camm's extensive Hart and Fury family. The prototype Nimrod flew on September 2, 1931, and an order was placed for an initial batch of 56 Nimrod Mk.Is. These were followed by 30 Nimrod Mk IIs, which featured some structural modifications.

SPECIFICATION: Type carrier-borne fighter biplane • Crew 1 • Powerplant one 608hp Rolls-Royce VFP 12-cylinder V-type • Max speed 193mph (311km/h) at sea level • Service ceiling 28,000ft (8,535m) • Endurance 1hr 40mins • Wingspan 33ft 7in (10.23m) • Length 26ft 6in (8.09m) • Height 9ft 10in (3m) • Weight 4,059lb (1,841kg) loaded • Armament two fixed forward-firing 0.303-in (7.7-mm) Vickers machine guns; provision for light bomb load on underwing racks

Hawker Osprey

GREAT BRITAIN

▶ *This aircraft was part of the first production batch of 20 Osprey Mk Is, which entered service in November 1932. It was delivered to No. 803 Sqn aboard HMS Eagle.*

SPECIFICATION: Type naval fighter-reconnaissance biplane • Crew 2 • Powerplant one 630hp Rolls-Royce Kestrel II 12-cylinder V-type • Max speed 168mph (270km/h) at 5,000ft (1,525m) • Service ceiling 23,500ft (7,160m) • Endurance 3hrs 15mins • Wingspan 37ft (11.28m) • Length 29ft 4in (8.94m) • Height 10ft 5in (3.17m) • Weight 4,950lb (2,245kg) • Armament one fixed forward-firing 0.303-in (7.7-mm) Vickers machine gun; one 0.303-in (7.7-mm) Lewis machine gun in rear cockpit

The Hawker Osprey was the naval version of the RAF's Hawker Hart light bomber. First flown in 1931, the Osprey was put into production in four versions; the Mk.I (37 built), Mk.II (14), Mk.III (52) with metal propellers and a dinghy stored in the starboard upper wing, and Mk.IV (26) with a more powerful engine. The advent of the Osprey, which remained in service until 1939, brought a new aircraft category—fighter reconnaissance—to the Fleet Air Arm.

▌Hawker Sea Fury

GREAT BRITAIN

▲ *The Hawker Sea Fury FB.Mk.11 represented the ultimate in piston-engined combat aircraft, and performed well in the Korean War.*

A naval version of the Centaurus-engined Hawker Fury, the Sea Fury came too late to see action in World War II, the prototype making its first flight on February 21, 1945. The first production Sea Fury F.Mk.X flew in September 1946 and deliveries to the Fleet Air Arm began in July 1947, the type eventually arming five squadrons. The second 50 aircraft of the first production batch were completed as FB.Mk.11 fighter-bombers, which performed very effectively in the Korean War and also claimed the destruction of at least two MiG-15s. Twenty-five FB.11s were operated by the Royal Canadian Navy. Sea Furies were exported to the Netherlands, Burma, Cuba, and Federal Germany, the latter being the TT.20 target-towing version. The type also equipped six squadrons of the Royal Naval Volunteer Reserve. Total Sea Fury production was 565 aircraft.

SPECIFICATION: Type naval fighter-bomber (data Sea Fury FB.11) • Crew 1 • Powerplant one 2,480hp Bristol Centaurus 18 18-cylinder radial • Max speed 460mph (740km/h) at 18,000ft (5,485m) • Service ceiling 36,000ft (10,970m) • Max range 700 miles (1,130km) • Wingspan 38ft 5in (11.71m) • Length 34ft 8in (10.56m) • Height 15ft 10in (4.82m) • Weight 12,500lb (5,670kg) loaded • Armament four 0.79-in (20-mm) Hispano cannon; 2,000lb (907kg) of bombs or rocket projectiles

Hawker Sea Hawk

The Hawker Sea Hawk started life as the P.1040, a prototype single-seat land-based interceptor. The Admiralty evaluated the design and found it suitable for naval operations, its "bifurcated trunk" jet exhaust system leaving the rear fuselage free to house a large fuel tank and so provide a wide combat radius. The first prototype Sea Hawk flew on

▲ Conventional in design, the Sea Hawk was an effective combat aircraft. It flew many ground attack missions during the Suez operations of 1956.

September 2, 1947, and the aircraft entered production as the Sea Hawk F.Mk.1, powered by a Rolls-Royce Nene turbojet. Hawkers were heavily committed to producing the Hunter day fighter for the RAF, so Sea Hawk production was handed over to Armstrong Whitworth Aircraft with the F.2, which had power-boosted ailerons. Later Sea Hawk variants, culminating in the FGA.6, had a strengthened wing to accommodate bombs, rockets, or drop tanks. Sea Hawks were issued to Fleet Air Arm squadrons in 1953, and three years later the type saw action with six squadrons during the Suez crisis, carrying out many ground attack operations against Egyptian airfields during the early days of the air campaign. Sea Hawks also served with the Royal Netherlands Navy, the Federal German Naval Air Arm, and the Indian Navy.

SPECIFICATION: Type naval fighter-bomber (data Sea Hawk FGA.Mk.6) • Crew 1 • Powerplant one 5,400lb (2,449kg) thrust Rolls-Royce Nene 103 turbojet • Max speed 602mph (969km/h) at sea level • Service ceiling 44,500ft (13,565m) • Max range 800 miles (1,287km) with external fuel tanks • Wingspan 39ft (11.89m) • Length 39ft 8in (12.09m) • Height 8ft 8in (2.64m) • Weight 16,200lb (7,348kg) • Armament four 0.79-in (20-mm) Hispano cannon; provision for four 500-lb (227-kg) bombs, or four 500-lb (227-kg) bombs and 20 3-in (10-cm) or 16 5-in (12.7-cm) rocket projectiles

Hawker Tempest II

SPECIFICATION: Type fighter-bomber • Crew 1 • Powerplant one 2,590hp Bristol Centaurus V 18-cylinder radial • Max speed 440mph (708km/h) • Service ceiling 37,000ft (11,285m) • Max range 1,700 miles (2,736km) • Wingspan 41ft (12.49m) • Length 34ft 5in (10.49m) • Height 14ft 6in (4.42m) • Weight 13,900lb (6,305kg) • Armament four 0.79-in (20-mm) Hispano cannon; external stores up to 2,000lb (907kg)

First flown in September 1943, the radial-engined Tempest II was intended primarily for operations in the Far East, but the war ended before the type made its operational debut. The Tempest II entered service with No. 54 Squadron RAF in November 1945. The type equipped eight squadrons in all, serving in India, Malaya, or with 2nd TAF in Germany. No. 33 Squadron used the Tempest II against terrorists in Malaya before converting to Hornets in 1951.

▌Hawker Tempest V

SPECIFICATION: Type fighter-bomber • Crew 1 • Powerplant one 2,260hp Napier Sabre IIA, IIB or IIC 24-cylinder H-type engine • Max speed 435mph (700km/h) • Service ceiling 36,000ft (10,975m) • Max range 1,300 miles (2,092km) • Wingspan 41ft (12.50m) • Length 33ft 8in (10.26m) • Height 16ft 1in (4.90m) • Weight 13,640lb (6,187kg) loaded • Armament four 0.79-in (20-mm) Hispano Mk V cannon; external stores up to 2,000lb (907kg)

Late in 1941 it became clear to the Hawker design team that a number of radical improvements to the basic design of the Hawker Typhoon would be necessary if the aircraft were to fulfill its primary role, which was still considered to be interception at all altitudes. Three main areas were isolated. First, cockpit visibility required drastic improvement; second, the wing would have to be redesigned to improve performance at altitudes above 20,000ft (6,100m) and in high-speed dives; and third, increased fuel tankage would have to be provided to improve the Typhoon's endurance, which was restricted to about an hour and a half.

The modified design, designated Hawker P.1012, was tendered to Air Ministry Specification F.10/41, and on November 18, 1941 Hawker Aircraft Ltd. received a contract to build two prototypes, to be known as the Typhoon Mk II. However, such were the differences, particularly in external appearance, between the Typhoon and the new design, that, before the prototype had flown, the type was renamed Tempest in August 1942. The prototype Tempest I flew on September 2, 1942 and an initial contract called for 400 Tempest Is, powered by the Napier Sabre IV engine, but this was canceled and the contract amended in favor of the Centaurus-powered Tempest Mk II. Delays in the production of this engine, however, and the cancelation of the projected Tempest Mks III and IV, meant that the first variant to enter production was the Tempest Mk V, powered by the Napier Sabre II. At the time it entered service with No. 3 Squadron RAF and No. 486 Squadron RNZAF (the two squadrons combining to form No. 150 Wing) in April 1944 the Tempest was the fastest and most powerful fighter in the world. After some early sorties across the English Channel the Tempest squadrons were assigned to the air defense of Great Britain, operating against the V-1 flying bombs that were now being launched against London. The Tempest's high speed made it the ideal interceptor in this new role; No. 3 Squadron was the top-scoring unit, with 258 V-1s destroyed, while No. 486 claimed 223. The Tempest squadrons subsequently moved to the Continent with 2nd TAF and became a potent addition to the Allies' striking power during the closing months of the war. Eleven squadrons were eventually armed with the Tempest Mk V and five with the Mk VI, which had a 2,700hp Sabre VA engine. Total Tempest V production was 805 aircraft.

▲ Hawker Tempest V EJ743 pictured on a test flight over southern England in 1944. The Tempest was rushed into service to combat the V1 flying bomb.

Hawker Typhoon

▲ In the ground-attack role, employing bombs and especially rockets, the Typhoon excelled. Note the chin radiator installation and prominent cannon-barrel fairings.

SPECIFICATION: Type low-level interceptor and ground attack aircraft • Crew 1 • Powerplant one 2,100 Napier Sabre I 24-cylinder in-line (Mk 1A); one 2,180hp Sabre IIA, 2,200 Sabre IIB, or 2,260hp Sabre IIC (Mk 1B) • Max speed 412mph (663km/h) • Service ceiling 35,200ft (10,730m) • Max range 980 miles (1,577km) with external tanks • Wingspan 41ft 7in (12.67m) • Length 31ft 11in (9.73m) • Height 15ft 4in (4.67m) • Weight 11,400lb (5,171kg) loaded • Armament 12 0.303-in (7.7-mm) fixed forward-firing machine guns with 500rpg in wing (Mk 1A); four 0.79-in (20-mm) fixed forward-firing cannon in wing, plus external bomb load up to 2,000lb (907kg) or eight 60-lb (27-kg) RPs

A cantilever low-wing monoplane of basically all-metal stressed-skin construction with a retractable tailwheel, the Hawker Typhoon was designed in response to a 1937 Air Staff requirement, leading to Air Ministry Specification F.18/37, for an aircraft capable of taking on heavily armed and armored escort fighters like the Messerschmitt Bf 110. In fact, two separate designs were submitted, the Type R and Type N. The Type R was powered by a Rolls-Royce Vulture engine; it flew in prototype form as the Tornado, but was abandoned when production of the Vulture was curtailed. The Type N, named Typhoon, was powered by a 2,100hp Napier Sabre H-type in-line engine and the first of two prototypes flew for the first time on February 24, 1940. The first production aircraft, however, did not fly until May 1941, and teething troubles with the type kept the first Typhoon squadron (No. 56) nonoperational until the end of May 1942. This unit, together with Nos. 609 and 266 Squadrons, formed the Duxford Wing, which was engaged in air defense duties against low-level intruders. The Typhoon MK 1A, which was armed with 12 0.303-in (7.7-mm) machine guns, was now giving way to the Mk 1B, whose four 0.79-in (20-mm) cannon proved highly effective in the ground attack role and which was powered by a somewhat more reliable 2,180hp Sabre IIA engine.

Mk I Typhoons had poor pilot visibility, and later variants had a clear bubble-type sliding canopy, which was a vast improvement. Although the Typhoon continued to have problems well into 1943 when they were finally rectified, and

its future still hung in the balance, its prowess against the Luftwaffe's low-level intruders tipped the scales in its favor. By the end of 1943, with the aircraft's technical problems cured and the growing number of Typhoon squadrons—now carrying a pair of 500-lb (226-kg) bombs or eight underwing rocket projectiles on their aircraft in addition to the built-in cannon armament—striking hard at the enemy's communications, shipping, and airfields, the Typhoon was heading for its place in history as the most potent Allied fighter-bomber of all. After the Allied landings in Normandy, the name of the rocket-armed Typhoon was synonymous with the breakup of an enemy counterattack at Mortain and the destruction of the retreating German army at Falaise. In the last days of the war, having supported the Canadian 1st and British 2nd Armies in their drive through northwestern Europe, its final actions were against enemy shipping in the Baltic.

In all, 3,330 Typhoons were built, all by Gloster except for the two prototypes, five Mk 1As and 10 Mk 1Bs. The Mk 1B was the major production version, over 3,000 being completed. About 60 percent of these had bubble-type canopies in place of the original frame-type cockpit hood and car-type access door.

▲ At an early stage in its development, the Typhoon had so many teething troubles that the Air Ministry considered canceling it and buying the Republic P-47 Thunderbolt instead.

▌Hawker Woodcock

▲ *Hawker Woodcock IIs of No 17 Squadron. Note the identifying pennant attached to the leading aircraft, denoting that it is the flight commander's.*

Although the Gloster Grebe replaced the Sopwith Snipe in some first-line RAF squadrons, the true successor to the Snipe was the Hawker Woodcock, the H.G. Hawker Engineering Company having reestablished Sopwith's for-

mer aviation enterprises. The Hawker Company's early activities involved refurbishing Snipes and Camels for sale overseas. The first of its own designs, the Duiker parasol monoplane, was unsuccessful, but the Woodcock single-seat fighter was accepted after lengthy trials and, as the Woodcock Mk.II, was delivered to No. 3 Squadron in May 1925, becoming the first new British fighter to enter production after the end of World War I. The Woodcock only equipped one other RAF squadron, No. 17, but a version of it known as the Danecock (or Dankok) served with the Danish Army and Naval Air Services until 1937.

SPECIFICATION: Type reconnaissance biplane • Crew 2 • Powerplant one 220hp Benz BzIV 6-cylinder liquid-cooled in-line engine • Max speed 106mph (170km/h) • Service ceiling 16,405ft (5,000m) • Endurance 3hrs 30mins • Wingspan 44ft 8in (13.62m) • Length 22ft 8in (6.92m) • Height 11ft (3.36m) • Weight 2,730lb (1,043kg) loaded • Armament two LMG 08/15 machine guns

▌Heinkel He 51

In Nazi Germany, the designer Ernst Heinkel—who had formed his own company in 1922—rapidly moved into a leading position, thanks to his willingness to design and build every type of aircraft required by the clandestine Luftwaffe's crash reequipment program. In 1933 he produced the He 51 fighter, which evolved through a series of small, streamlined biplane fighter prototypes (the He 37, He 38, He 49, and He 49a). The fourth He 49a, with modifications, became the prototype He 51A, which first flew in mid-

1933. First production deliveries of the He 51A-1 were made to JG 132 in April 1935, and the type was later allocated to JG

SPECIFICATION: Type fighter biplane • Crew 1 • Powerplant one 750hp BMW VI 12-cylinder V-type • Max speed 205mph (330km/h) • Service ceiling 25,260ft (7,700m) • Max range 354 miles (570km) • Wingspan 36ft 1in (11m) • Length 27ft 7in (8.40m) • Height 10ft 6in (3.20m) • Weight 4,178lb (1,895kg) • Armament two fixed forward-firing 0.31-in (7.92-mm) MG17 machine guns

▶ *Many of Germany's leading fighter aces of World War II sharpened their skills while flying He 51 fighters in the Spanish Civil War.*

131 and JG 134. In all, 700 He 51 production aircraft were built. Other variants were the He 51B, which replaced the He 51A on the production line; the He 51B-2 floatplane, which was fitted with catapult spools for service on board warships; and the C-1 and C-2 ground attack fighters, which saw action in Spain alongside the Condor Legion's He 51A-1s.

Heinkel He 100

The He 100 (originally He 113), one of two monoplane fighters designed by Ernst Heinkel's team in the 1930s, was developed as a potential successor to the Bf 109. The aircraft, which flew for the first time in January 1938, was very fast, with a top speed of 416mph (670km/h) at 13,000ft (4,000m), and the prototypes established a number of speed records, but the type did not go into service, the six prototypes and three preproduction aircraft being sold respectively to the USSR and Japan. It was, however, manipulated by the German propaganda machine, the 12 production He 100D-1s that were built being painted in a variety of spurious markings, with the result that in the first year of World War II many Allied pilots reported having encountered the "He 113" in combat. The 12 He 100D-1s were used for a while to provide defense for the Heinkel factory at Rostock. In many

SPECIFICATION: Type fighter • Crew 1 • Powerplant one 1,175hp Daimler-Benz DB 601M 12-cylinder inverted-Vee engine • Max speed 416mph (670km/h) at 13,120ft (4,000m) • Service ceiling 36,090ft (11,000m) • Max range 627 miles (1,010km) • Wingspan 30ft 10in (9.40m) • Length 26ft (8.20m) • Height 11ft 9in (3.60m) • Weight 5,511lb (2,500kg) loaded • Armament one 0.79-in (20-mm) cannon in engine installation, and either two 0.79-in (20-mm) cannon or two 0.31-in (7.92-mm) machine guns in the wing roots

respects the He 100 was a better aircraft than the Bf 109, but it was tailored very closely to the DB 601 engine, whose production was earmarked in full for the Messerschmitt fighter.

▼ *In many respects the Heinkel He 100 was a better aircraft than the Messerschmitt Bf 109, but was rejected due to internal politics.*

▌Heinkel He 162 Salamander

Developed as a last-ditch air defense fighter in the closing stages of World War II, the Heinkel He 162 Salamander, also known as the Volksjäger (People's Fighter), progressed from drawing board to first flight, on December 6, 1944, in a mere 10 weeks. Constructed mainly of wood, it was envisaged that the German aircraft industry was capable of turning out 2,000 of the turbojet-engined interceptors per month by May 1945. Despite the destruction of the first prototype in a fatal crash, another 30 prototypes were built, followed by 275

production He 162A-1s/2s, and following trials with Erprobungskommando 162 at Rechlin the type was issued to I/JG 1 at Leck in Schleswig-Holstein, but this unit did not become operational before the end of the war. Few contacts were made with Allied aircraft, but an unidentified aircraft claimed by a Hawker Tempest pilot of No. 222 Squadron RAF on April 19, 1945 was almost certainly an He 162.

SPECIFICATION: Type jet fighter • Crew 1 • Powerplant one 1,741-lb (790-kg) thrust BMW 109-003E turbojet • Max speed 562mph (905km/h) • Service ceiling 39,370ft (12,000m) • Max range 606 miles (975km) • Wingspan 23ft 7in (7.20m) • Length 29ft 8in (9.05m) • Height 8ft 6in (2.60m) • Weight 5,742lb (2,605kg) loaded • Armament two 0.79-in (20-mm) cannon in lower sides of forward fuselage

▲ *The He 162 Salamander was just becoming operational at the end of the war in Europe, and was encountered on rare occasions by Allied pilots.*

▌Heinkel He 177 Greif

The Heinkel He 177 Greif (Griffon) heavy bomber was plagued throughout its career by its engines. In an effort to reduce drag and enhance performance, the bomber's four Daimler-Benz engines were arranged in coupled pairs, each pair driving a single propeller, so that the aircraft had a twin-engined appearance. The He 177V-1 prototype flew on November 19, 1939, but continual engine overheating problems and a succession of structural failures delayed production, the first He 177A-1 being delivered to I/KG 40

SPECIFICATION: Type heavy bomber and antiship aircraft • Crew 6 • Powerplant two 3,100hp DB 610A 24-cylinder engines in coupled pairs • Max speed 303mph (488km/h) • Service ceiling 26,245ft (8,000m) • Max range 3,418 miles (5,500km) • Wingspan 103ft 1in (31.44m) • Length 72ft 2in (22m) • Height 20ft 11in (6.39m) • Weight 68,343lb (31,000kg) loaded • Armament one 0.31-in (7.92-mm) machine gun in nose position, one 0.79-in (20-mm) cannon and two 0.3-in (7.92-mm) machine guns in under-nose gondola; two 0.50-in (13-mm) machine guns in remotely controlled dorsal barbette; one 0.79-in (20-mm) cannon in tail; 13,228lb (6,000kg) of bombs

▼ *This He 177A-5/R6 was photographed just after its arrival in the UK for testing on September 10, 1944.*

for operational trials.

In all, 130 He 1877A-1s and 170 He 177A-3 production aircraft entered service. Subvariants of the latter were the He 177A-3/R3, which could carry three Hs 293 antiship missiles, the He 177A-3R/5, with a 2.95-in (75-mm) gun in a gondola under the nose, and the He 177A-3R/7 torpedo-bomber. The last variant was the He 177A-5 (there was no A-4), which was structurally strengthened; 565 were delivered.

▌Heinkel He 219

In the first half of 1943, General Josef Kammhuber, in charge of Germany's night defenses, pressed strongly for the production of new twin-engined types designed specifically for night fighting. At the forefront of these was the Heinkel He 219 Uhu

(Owl), the prototype of which had flown in November 1942 after months of delay caused by a lack of interest on the part of the German Air Ministry. By April 1943 300 examples had been ordered; Kammhuber wanted 2,000, but in the event only

294 were built before the end of the war. Formidably armed with six 1.19-in (30-mm) and two 0.79-in (20-mm) cannon and equipped with the latest AI radar, the He 219 would have

SPECIFICATION: Type night fighter • Crew 2 • Powerplant two 1,900hp DB 603G 12-cylinder inverted-Vee engines • Max speed 416mph (670km/h) • Service ceiling 41,665ft (12,700m) • Max range 1,243 miles (2,000km) • Wingspan 60ft 8in (18.50m) • Length 50ft 11in (15.54m) • Height 13ft 5in (4.10m) • Weight 33,730lb (15,300kg) loaded • Armament two 1.19-in (30-mm) cannon in wing roots; two 1.19-in (30-mm) and two 0.79-in (20-mm) cannon in ventral tray; two obliquely mounted 1.19-in (30-mm) cannon in upper part of rear fuselage

torn great gaps in Bomber Command's ranks had it been available in quantity. It also had a performance comparable to that of the Mosquito, which other German night fighters did not and therefore could have fought the RAF's intruders on equal terms. Admittedly, the He 219 suffered from a series of technical troubles in its early development career, but what it might have achieved in action was clearly shown on the night of June 11/12, 1943 by Major Werner Streib of I/NJG1. Flying a preproduction He 219 on operational trials from Venlo, he infiltrated an RAF bomber stream heading for Berlin and shot down five Lancasters in half an hour. The He 219 was the first fighter in the world to be fitted with ejection seats.

▮ Henschel Hs 123

GERMANY

The Henschel Hs 123—the Luftwaffe's last operational biplane—originated in a 1933 specification for a dive-bomber, although it was used operationally as a ground-attack aircraft. The prototype Hs 123V-1 flew for the first time in May 1935 and the type was ordered into production,

five Hs 123As being sent to Spain for operational evaluation with the Condor Legion in 1936. This resulted in the improved Hs 123B, which saw combat during the German invasions of Poland, France, and the USSR. The Hs 123C was a variant armed with 0.79-in (20-mm) cannon.

◀ The Henschel Hs 123 was an excellent ground attack aircraft, and was used to good effect during the campaign in Poland.

SPECIFICATION: Type close support biplane • Crew 1 • Powerplant one 880hp BMW 132Dc radial • Max speed 211mph (340km/h) at 6,560ft (2,000m) • Service ceiling 29,530ft (9,000m) • Max range 531 miles (855km) • Wingspan 34ft 5in (10.50m) upper wing • Length 27ft 4in (8.33m) • Height 10ft 6in (3.20m) • Weight 4,883lb (2,215kg) loaded • Armament two 0.31-in (7.92-mm) MG17 machine guns; up to 992lb (450kg) of bombs

▮ Henschel Hs 126

GERMANY

SPECIFICATION: Type army cooperation aircraft • Crew 2 • Powerplant one 850hp BMW Bramo 323A-1 9-cylinder radial • Max speed 221mph (356km/h) • Service ceiling 27,000ft (8,229m) • Max range 447 miles (720km) • Wingspan 47ft 7in (14.50m) • Length 35ft 7in (10.85m) • Height 12ft 3in (3.75m) • Weight 7,209lb (3,270kg) loaded • Armament two 0.31-in (7.9-mm) machine guns

▶ In addition to its primary role of observation, the Hs 126 was used as a ground attack aircraft during the German campaigns in Poland and France.

The Henschel Hs 126 was arguably the best medium-range observation aircraft of the early war years. A large, parasol-wing monoplane, the Hs 126A-1 entered service in 1938, having been evaluated in Spain. Large numbers were built to replace the obsolete Heinkel He 45 and He 46.

The Hs 126B-1, which had a more powerful 900 horse-power engine and better performance, first entered service with Aufklärungsgruppe 35 in 1939. It was quickly used to re-equip reconnaissance units and was in widespread use at the outbreak of war. More than 600 Hs 126s were built, including six used by the Spanish Air Force and 16 for the Greek Air Force.

The Hs 126 was progressively withdrawn from service during 1942, and was replaced by the Fw 189.

■ Henschel Hs 129

GERMANY

The Henschel Hs 129 was designed in response to a requirement of March 1937 calling for a compact heavily armored close support aircraft. The Henschel 129V-1 prototype flew in the spring of 1939, but poor performance and handling problems delayed deployment of Hs 129B-1 until April 1942, these aircraft being powered by captured French engines. The aircraft went into action on the Eastern Front, 843 Hs 129Bs being delivered. The Hs 129B-1 was followed by the more heavily armed Hs 129B-2, introduced in 1943. The final variant was the Hs 129B-3, of which about 25 were built and which carried an electropneumatically operated 2.95-in (75-mm) gun. The Hs 129 also saw action in North Africa, and in France after the D-Day landings. The Hs 129 units in

SPECIFICATION: Type close support and antitank aircraft • Crew 1 • Powerplant two 700hp Gnome-Rhone 14M-4/5 14-cylinder radials • Max speed 253mph (407km/h) • Service ceiling 29,530ft (9,000m) • Max range 429 miles (690km) • Wingspan 46ft 7in (14.20m) • Length 31ft 11in (9.75m) • Height 10ft 8in (3.25m) • Weight 8,862lb (4,020kg) • Armament two 0.79-in (20-mm) and two 0.51-in (13-mm) MG cannon, or one 1.19-in (30-mm) or 1.46-in (37-mm) cannon and two 0.79-in (20-mm) cannon in forward fuselage; up to 992lb (450kg) of bombs

Russia distinguished themselves during the battle of Kursk in July 1943, destroying hundreds of enemy tanks.

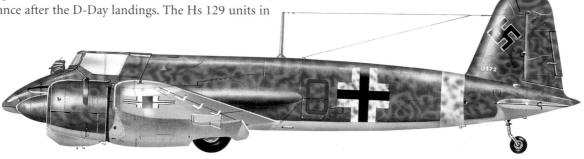

■ Hindustan HF-24 Marut

INDIA

Designed by a team under the leadership of Dr. Kurt Tank, architect of Germany's wartime Focke-Wulf fighters, the Hindustan Aviation Company HF-24 Marut (Wind Spirit) was the first supersonic fighter aircraft developed in Asia. The HF-24 underwent a protracted development history, over a decade elapsing between design work starting in 1956 and the first fully operational examples being delivered. The first series production Marut flew in November 1967 and the type eventually equipped three Indian Air Force squadrons, seeing combat in the ground attack role during the 1971 Indo-Pakistan war. Including a preproduction batch, 100 single-seat Marut Mk Is and 18 two-seat Mk IT trainers were delivered.

▲ *An interceptor configuration was originally proposed for the Marut, although the aircraft later saw service in the attack role.*

SPECIFICATION: Type fighter-bomber • Crew 1 • Powerplant two 4,850-lb (2,200-kg) thrust Rolls-Royce Orpheus 703 turbojets • Max speed 691mph (1,112km/h) at sea level • Service ceiling 40,000ft (12,200m) • Max range 620 miles (1,000km) • Wingspan 29ft 6in (9m) • Length 52ft 1in (15.87m) • Height 11ft 10in (3.60m) • Weight 24,048lb (10,908kg) loaded • Armament four 1.19-in (30-mm) cannon; 4,000lb (1,815kg) of bombs

∎ Hindustan HJT-16 Kiran

The Hindustan HJT-16 Kiran Mk I, which flew for the first time on September 4, 1964, was designed as a basic and advanced jet trainer, 190 aircraft being ordered for the Indian Air Force. In 1977, beginning with the 119th production air-craft, it was modified for light attack and weapons training as the Kiran Mk IA, the final derivative being the Kiran Mk II.

SPECIFICATION: Type basic and advanced jet trainer • Crew 2 • Powerplant one 2,500-lb (1,134-kg) thrust Rolls-Royce (Bristol Siddeley) Viper 11 turbojet • Max speed 432mph (695km/h) at sea level • Service ceiling 30,000ft (9,150m) • Max range 463 miles (745km) • Wingspan 35ft 1in (10.70m) • Length 34ft 9in (10.60m) • Height 11ft 11in (3.64m) • Weight 9,039lb (4,100kg) loaded • Armament 1,000lb (453kg) of bombs

▲ Illustrated in Mk I form, the Kiran featured unswept flying surfaces and was an all-metal monoplane powered by a simple turbojet engine.

∎ Hispano HA.200 Saeta

The HA.200 Saeta (Arrow) advanced jet trainer was the first jet aircraft to be produced by the Spanish aviation industry. Developed under the guidance of Willy Messerschmitt, the

SPECIFICATION: Type trainer • Crew 2 • Powerplant two 880-lb (400-kg) thrust Turbomeca Marbore IIA turbojets • Max speed 435mph (700km/h) at 29,500ft (9,000m) • Service ceiling 40,000ft (12,000m) • Max range 1,056 miles (1,700km) • Wingspan 34ft 2in (10.42m) • Length 29ft 2in (8.88m) • Height 10ft 8in (3.26m) • Weight 6,995lb (3,173kg) loaded • Armament two 0.50-in (12.7-mm) machine guns

▼ A sound design of Messerschmitt origins, the HA.200 is represented here by a preserved example in German civil markings.

prototype flew on August 12, 1955 and was followed by 35 production HA-200As. The HA-200D and E models were upgraded for the tactical support role. The aircraft was also built under license in Egypt as the Al Kahira (Cairo), 90 examples being produced.

∎ Hunting Percival (BAC) Jet Provost

The Jet Provost was designed as an *ab initio* jet trainer, replacing the piston-engined Provost from which it was developed, and served with the RAF in three versions, the Mks 3, 4, and 5, the latter having a redesigned nose and pres-surized cockpit. BAC went on to develop the type into a multirole aircraft, designated the Strikemaster. With a more powerful engine and provision for various underwing loads, the Strikemaster enjoyed considerable export success, seeing service with the air forces of Saudi Arabia, South Yemen, Oman, Kuwait, Botswana, Singapore, Kenya, New Zealand, Ecuador, and the Sudan.

▼ The Jet Provost brought a new dimension to the training of RAF pilots from the late 1950s, giving them "all-through" jet training facilities.

SPECIFICATION: Type jet trainer (data Jet Provost T.3) • Crew 2 • Powerplant one 1,750-lb (794-kg) thrust Armstrong Siddeley Viper ASV.8 turbojet • Max speed 330mph (530km/h) at 20,000ft (6,100m) • Service ceiling 31,000ft (9,450m) • Max range 493 miles (793km) • Wingspan 35ft 2in (10.72m) • Length 31ft 11in (9.73m) • Height 12ft 8in (3.86m) • Weight 5,850lb (2,654kg) loaded • Armament none

■ IAI Kfir

▲ *The marriage of a Mirage III airframe with a General Electric J79 turbojet proved successful. This Kfir was seen at the Paris Air Show in June 1977.*

The Israeli Aircraft Industries (IAI) Kfir (Lion Cub) was basically a Dassault Mirage III airframe married with a General Electric J79 turbojet, developed as an expedient when Israel was suffering from an arms embargo imposed by its traditional combat aircraft supplier, France. IAI produced 27 Kfir C.1s, which equipped two squadrons of the Israeli Air Force; after replacement by the improved C.2, all but two were leased to the US Navy for aggressor training, bearing the designation F-21A. The Kfir C.2, which appeared in 1976, was the major production version, 185 being delivered. Most C.2s were upgraded to C.7 standard between 1983–85, with improved engine thrust and avionics, and two extra stores pylons. The

Kfir saw a great deal of action in Lebanon's Bekaa Valley in the 1980s. Twelve were exported to Colombia.

SPECIFICATION: Type fighter/ground attack aircraft (data Kfir C.2) • Crew 1 •
Powerplant one 17,900-lb (8,119-kg) thrust General Electric J79-J1E turbojet
• Max speed 1,520mph (2,445km/h) at altitude • Service ceiling 58,000ft
(17,680m) • Combat radius 215 miles (346km) • Wingspan 26ft 11in (8.22m) •
Length 51ft 4in (15.65m) • Height 14ft 11in (4.55m) • Weight 35,715lb
(16,200kg) loaded • Armament one IAI (DEFA) 1.19-in (30-mm) cannon; nine
external hardpoints with provision for up to 12,732lb (5,775kg) of ordnance

IAR-80

ROMANIA

Bearing a number of design features copied from the PZL P.24 fighter, which the Industria Aeronautica Romana (IAR) had built under license in the 1930s, the IAR-80 was the only fighter of Romanian origin to be built in quantity during World War II. It became operational early in 1942 and about 125 were built, being used mainly in the defense of the Romanian oilfields. The IAR.81 was a fighter-bomber development, only a few being produced.

SPECIFICATION: Type fighter • Crew 1 • Powerplant one IAR-built Gnome-Rhone 14K 14-cylinder radial • Max speed 317mph (510km/h) at 13,000ft (4,000m) • Service ceiling 34,500ft (10,500m) • Max range 590 miles (950km) • Wingspan 32ft 10in (10m) • Length 26ft 9in (8.16m) • Height 11ft 10in (3.60m) • Weight 5,040lb (2,286kg) loaded • Armament two 0.79-in (20-mm) cannon and four 0.303-in (7.7-mm) machine guns

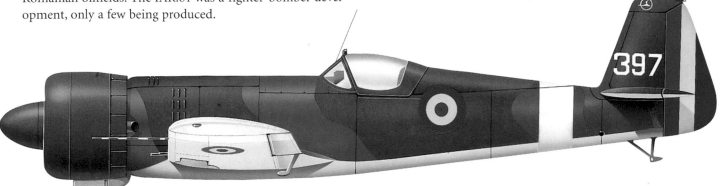

Ikarus S-49

YUGOSLAVIA

The first postwar fighter to be designed in Yugoslavia, the S-49 was a development of the prewar Ikarus IK-3, production of which had been halted by the German invasion after only a few evaluation aircraft had been completed. The prototype flew in 1948, powered by a Klimov VK-105PF-2 liquid-cooled engine, and the first examples entered service as the S-49A in 1951. Subsequent aircraft were powered by the Hispano-Suiza 12Z-11Y engine, purchased after Yugoslavia severed relations with the USSR. In this guise, and with other refinements, the aircraft emerged as the S-49C.

SPECIFICATION: Type fighter/ground attack (data S-49C) • Crew 1 • Powerplant one 1,500hp Hispano-Suiza 12Z-11Y in-line • Max speed 398mph (640km/h) at 5,000ft (1,525m) • Service ceiling 32,810ft (10,000m) • Max range 497 miles (799km) • Wingspan 33ft 9in (10.29m) • Length 29ft 8in (9.1m) • Height not known • Weight 7,646lb (3,463kg) loaded • Armament one 0.79-in (20-mm) Mauser MG.151 cannon and two 0.50-in (12.7-mm) machine guns; four 3.2-in (82-mm) or 4.3-in (110-mm) RPs; four 55-lb (24.9-kg) or 110lb (50kg) bombs on underwing racks

Ilyushin Il-2/Il-10

USSR

Based on a 1938 design for a single-engined assault aircraft, and much modified subsequently, the Ilyushin Il-2 (Company designation TsKB-57) successfully completed its State Acceptance Trials in March 1941 and was ordered into full production, 249 being produced before the German invasion of June 1941. Most of these were used for training, and it was a small batch of preproduction aircraft, completed even before the TsKB-57 had completed its trials, that was the first to see combat. The lack of a rear gun position (deleted during development) proved to be a serious drawback, and losses were heavy. Following urgent requests from operational units, early in 1942 the decision was taken in princi-

▲ Although an unsurpassed ground attack aircraft, the Ilyushin Il-2 was shot down in large numbers until a rear gun position was added.

SPECIFICATION: Type long-range maritime patrol aircraft • Crew 12–15 •
Powerplant four 4,000hp Ivchenko AI-20 turboprops • Max speed 400mph
(643km/h) at 26,260ft (8,006m) • Service ceiling 28,000ft (8,540m) • Max
range 4,500 miles (7,240km) • Wingspan 122ft 8in (37.48m) • Length 129ft
10in (39.61m) • Height 33ft 9in (10.29m) • Weight 134,922lb (61,200kg)
loaded • Armament variety of ASW stores

▶ *The Il-38 has proven effective in the ASW role, despite some reliability
problems with the Berkut submarine detection system.*

▪ Ilyushin Il-76 "Mainstay"

▲ *Ilyushin's "Mainstay" represents the first truly effective AWACS asset to
be employed by Russia, with around 25 examples operational.*

SPECIFICATION: Type military transportation (data Il-76M) • Crew 5 • Powerplant
four 26,455-lb (12,000-kg) thrust Soloviev D-30KP turbofans • Max speed
528mph (850km/h) at 29,500ft (9,000m) • Service ceiling 50,850ft (15,500m)
• Max range 3,100 miles (5,000km) • Wingspan 165ft 8in (50.5m) • Length
152ft 11in (46.59m) • Height 48ft 5in (14.76m) • Weight 374,785lb
(170,000kg) loaded • Armament none

The Ilyushin Il-76 was designed to meet an important
requirement for a replacement for the Antonov An-12BP.
Among the requirements was the ability to carry a 40-ton
cargo for 3,105 miles (5,000km) in less than six hours. The
aircraft also had to be able to operate from short unpaved
airstrips, maintain reliability in the extreme climatic conditions of the hot southern Steppes and deserts on the one
hand and the Arctic wastes of northern Siberia on the other,
and be easy to service.

The Il-76 first flew on March 25, 1971. During its operational career the Il-76 has had a number of applications other
than that of transportation. A three-point hose-and-drogue
tanker variant, the Il-78 (Midas) became operational in 1987
to replace the Soviet Air Force's aging Mya-4 Bison tankers,
and the type was also converted to the airborne early warning role (Mainstay) to replace the inadequate Tu-126 Moss,
which was little more than a stop-gap AEW aircraft. The military Il-76M also serves with the Indian Air Force and Iraq.

▪ IMAM (Meridionali) Ro.37-Ro.44

Although it made its first appearance in 1934, the Ro.37
reconnaissance biplane was still widely used during World
War II in Africa and the Mediterranean. The Ro.43 floatplane
was the naval equivalent. The Ro.44 was a single-seat fighter
version; its performance was greatly inferior to that of contemporary Allied fighters, and only a few were built.

SPECIFICATION: Type shipboard reconnaissance floatplane (data Ro.43) • Crew
2 • Powerplant one 700hp Piaggio PXR 9-cylinder radial engine • Max speed
186mph (299km/h) at 8,200ft (2,500m) • Service ceiling 21,600ft (6,583m) •
Max range 678 miles (1,092km) • Wingspan 37ft 11in (11.57m) • Length 31ft
10in (9.71m) • Height 11ft 6in (3.51m) • Weight 5,300lb (2,400kg) loaded •
Armament two 0.303-in (7.62-mm) machine guns

▲ *The Ro.44 floatplane fighter was the naval version of the Ro.37 reconnaissance biplane, which was widely used by the Regia Aeronautica.*

■ Junkers CL.I

An angular, low-wing all-metal monoplane that first flew on March 4, 1918, the Junkers CL.I was the best assault aircraft produced by Germany during World War I. Evolved via two all-metal ancestors, the J.I and D.I, its production was limited by the difficulties of construction by an industry used to working with wood and fabric, and only 47 were delivered. It was very well armed, having three machine guns and bomb racks along the fuselage for dispensing antipersonnel grenades.

SPECIFICATION: Type assault aircraft • Crew 2 • Powerplant one 180hp Mercedes D.IIIa 6-cylinder liquid-cooled in-line • Max speed 100mph (161km/h) • Service ceiling 19,685ft (6,000m) • Endurance 2hrs • Wingspan 39ft 6in (12.04m) • Length 25ft 11in (7.90m) • Height 7ft 8in (2.65m) • Weight 2,310lb (1,050kg) • Armament three LMG 08/15 0.31-in (7.92-mm) machine guns; antipersonnel grenades

■ Junkers Ju 52/3m

▲ Junkers Ju 52s pictured on an Axis airfield in North Africa. Aircraft were shot down in large numbers on re-supply missions over the Mediterranean.

In 1934 a military version of the Ju 52/3m civil airliner was produced for use by the still-secret Luftwaffe. Designated Ju 52/3mg3e, the aircraft was designed as a heavy bomber with a crew of four and armed with two MG 15 machine guns, one mounted in the dorsal position and the other in a retractable "trash can" suspended under the fuselage. In 1934–35 no fewer than 450 Ju 52/3ms were delivered to the Luftwaffe, the type entering service with KG 152 Hindenburg. In August 1936 20 aircraft were sent to Spain, where, flown by German volunteers, their first task was to transport 10,000 troops

SPECIFICATION: Type bomber/transport • Crew 2–3, plus 18 troops or 12 stretcher cases • Powerplant three 730hp BMW 132T-2 9-cylinder radial engines • Max speed 178mph (286km/h) • Service ceiling 19,360ft (5,900m) • Max range 811 miles (1,305km) • Wing span 95ft 10in (29.20m) • Length 62ft (19.90m) • Height 14ft 10in (4.52m) • Weight 24,317lb (11,030kg) loaded • Armament four 0.31-in (7.92-mm) machine guns, one each in forward and rear dorsal positions and one in each beam position

from Spanish Morocco. In the following November, about 50 Ju 52/3mg4e bombers were included in the equipment of the German Condor Legion, deployed to Spain in support of Franco's Nationalist forces. Operations included the bombing of Republican-held Mediterranean ports and the support of the land battle around Guernica, the destruction of which town brought the German bombers notoriety. In Luftwaffe service the Ju 52 bomber was soon replaced by types such as the Ju 86 and Do 17, and from then on it operated purely as a military transport. In April 1940 the Ju 52 was at the forefront of the invasions of Denmark and Norway, 160 transports dropping paratroops to capture key airfields while a further 340 aircraft flew in supplies and reinforcements. About 475 Ju 52s were available for the invasion of the Netherlands, and suffered serious losses (167 aircraft) in the opening stages of the operation.

The next large-scale airborne operation, the invasion of Crete in April/May 1941, was the last of its kind undertaken by the Luftwaffe. The force committed included 493 Ju 52s and over 80 DFS 230 gliders. The invasion—Operation Merkur—cost the Germans 7,000 men killed or wounded (including 25 percent of the paratroops dropped) and 271 Ju 52s. When the Germans invaded the Soviet Union in June 1941, their offensive was supported by six Ju 52 transport Gruppen. Later, 266 Ju 52s were lost in attempts to relieve the German Sixth Army at Stalingrad. Another 150 aircraft were assigned to support Rommel's offensives in North Africa, and by the end of the year around 300 Ju 52s were operating in the Mediterranean theater. In July, August, and September 1942, Ju 52s and other transport aircraft ferried 46,000 men and 4,000 tons of equipment to North Africa; but after the Battle of El Alamein in October, severe losses were inflicted on the Ju 52s by Desert Air Force fighters, 70 aircraft being destroyed between October 25th and December 1st. The real martyrdom of the Ju 52 Gruppen in the Mediterranean, however, came early in 1943, when the Germans and Italians made frantic efforts to resupply the Axis forces in Tunisia. On one day alone—April 7, 1943—American and British fighters destroyed 52 out of 77 Ju 52s near Cap Bon, most of the gasoline-laden transports exploding in spectacular fashion. Between April 5th and 22nd, no fewer than 432 German transport aircraft, mostly Ju 52s, were destroyed for the loss of 35 Allied fighters.

Total production of the Ju 52/3m between 1939 and 1944, including civil models, was 4,845 aircraft.

▲ *A Ju 52 pictured on a snowbound airfield in Russia. The number of Ju 52s available was inadequate to supply the German Sixth Army at Stalingrad.*

▌Junkers Ju 86

GERMANY

The Junkers Ju 86 was designed in 1934 to the same specification as the Heinkel He 111, calling for an aircraft capable of being developed both as a bomber and commercial transport. The first two production variants, the Ju 86D and Ju 86E, entered service in the first half of 1936. The aircraft proved to have a poor performance, so the type was further developed as a civil transport (Ju 86B, Ju 86F, and Ju 86Z), bomber trainer (Ju 86G), and export bomber (Ju 86K), the latter being sold to Sweden, Chile, Portugal, and Hungary. The Ju 86P and Ju 86R were high-altitude photoreconnaissance versions. Thirteen civilian Ju 86s were converted as bombers by the South African Air Force in 1939.

SPECIFICATION: Type bomber/transport • Crew 4 • Powerplant two 600hp Junkers Jumo 205C-4 Diesel engines • Max speed 202mph (325km/h) • Service ceiling 19,360ft (5,900m) • Max range 708 miles (1,140km) • Wingspan 73ft 9in (22.50m) • Length 58ft 7in (17.57m) • Height 16ft 7in (5.06m) • Weight 18,078lb (8,200kg) loaded • Armament one 0.31-in (7.92-mm) in nose, dorsal, and ventral "trash can" positions; internal bomb load of 2,205lb (1,000kg)

▌Junkers Ju 87

GERMANY

Although the word Stuka—an abbreviation of *Sturzkampfflugzeug*, which literally translates as "diving combat aircraft," was applied to all German bomber aircraft with a dive-bombing capability during World War II. It will forever be associated with the Junkers Ju 87, with its ugly lines, inverted-gull wing and, above all, the banshee howl of its wing-mounted sirens as it plummeted toward its target.

The first prototype Ju 87V-1 was flown for the first time in the late spring 1935 powered by a 640hp Rolls-Royce

SPECIFICATION: Type dive-bomber/assault aircraft • Crew 2 • Powerplant one 1,400hp Junkers Jumo 211J inverted-Vee piston engine • Max speed 255mph (410km/h) • Service ceiling 23,950ft (7,300m) • Max range 954 miles (1,535km) • Wingspan 45ft 3.33in (13.80m) • Length 37ft 8in (11.50m) • Height 12ft 9in (3.88m) • Weight 14,550lb (6,600kg) loaded • Armament two 0.31-in (7.92-mm) fixed forward-firing machine guns in wing leading edges; one 0.31-in (7.92-mm) trainable twin-barrel rearward-firing machine gun in rear cockpit; external bomb load of up to 3,968lb (1,800kg)

▲ *The Junkers Ju 87 served until the last days of the war on the Eastern Front, where it proved a very capable tank destroyer.*

▲ *A preserved Junkers Ju 87 seen at the RAF Museum, Hendon. The Ju 87 was a large aircraft, and remarkably agile for its size.*

Kestrel engine. This aircraft had twin fins and rudders, replaced by a single fin and rudder in the Ju 87V-2. Production began with the preseries Ju 87A-0, powered by the Jumo 210Da engine, and continued with the Ju 87A-1, first deliveries of which were made to I/St.G 162 Immelmann, the unit tasked with developing operational tactics, in 1937. In December 1937 three Ju 87A-1s were sent to Spain for operational trials with the Condor Legion, the German units flying in support of the Spanish Nationalists. The Ju 87A-2 subseries, the next to appear, differed only in the type of propeller used. The A model was succeeded on the production line in 1938 by an extensively modified version, the Ju 87B, which used the more powerful 1,100hp Jumo 211Da. The aircraft had a redesigned cockpit and a "spatted" undercarriage. An antishipping version of the Ju 87B-2 was known as the Ju 87R.

One of the more interesting and little-known versions of the Stuka was the Ju 87C, a shipboard dive-bomber intended for service on Germany's planned aircraft carrier, the *Graf Zeppelin*. It had hydraulically operated folding wings, deck arrester gear, and a jettisonable undercarriage. The Ju 87C-0 was a conversion of the Ju 87B-1 without wing folding mechanism. A small production batch of Ju 87C-1 aircraft was

built and a unit, 4(Stuka)186 formed, but the *Graf Zeppelin* was abandoned when it was virtually complete and the aircraft were converted to Ju 87B standard. 4/Stuka186 took part in the Polish campaign. *Graf Zeppelin's* air group was to have comprised 29 Stukas and 12 Bf 109 fighters.

The next production model was the Ju 87D, which was fitted with a 1,400hp Jump 211J-1 with induction cooling. Several subseries of the Ju 87D were produced in some quantity, incorporating modifications to suit the type for a variety of tasks. The Ju 87E and F were proposals only, and the last Stuka variant was the Ju 87G, a standard Ju 87D-5 converted to carry two BK 37 cannon (1.46-in (37-mm) Flak 18 guns) under the wing. No dive brakes were fitted, and the Ju 87G proved very adept at destroying Russian armor. Its chief exponent was Colonel Hans-Ulrich Rudel, who knocked out 500 tanks on the Eastern Front. The Ju 87H was the designation given to all dual control versions of the Du 87D-1, D-3, D-5, D-7, and D-8. In the final analysis, although the Stuka was a very effective weapon when under an umbrella of fighter superiority, when the latter was lacking—as was the case in the Battle of Britain, when the Stuka units suffered heavy losses—it was easy prey. Total Ju 87 production was 5,700 aircraft.

Junkers Ju 88

◀ A Junkers Ju 88 in flight. From certain angles the Ju 88 could be mistaken for the Bristol Blenheim, which led to some "friendly fire" incidents.

SPECIFICATION: Type medium/dive-bomber • Crew 4 • Powerplant two 1,340hp Junkers Jumo 211J inverted V-12 engines • Max speed 280mph (450km/h) at 19,685ft (6,000m) • Service ceiling 26,900ft (8,200m) • Max range 1,696 miles (2,730km) • Wingspan 65ft 7in (20.00m) • Length 47ft 3in (14.40m) • Height 15ft 11in (4.85m) • Weight 30,865lb (14,000kg) loaded • Armament up to seven 0.31-in (7.92-mm) MG15 or MG81 machine guns; maximum internal and external bomb load of 7,935lb (3,600kg).

One of the most versatile and effective combat aircraft ever produced, the Junkers Ju 88 remained of vital importance to the Luftwaffe throughout World War II, serving as a bomber, dive-bomber, night fighter, close support aircraft, long-range heavy fighter, reconnaissance aircraft, and torpedo-bomber. The prototype Ju 88 flew for the first time on December 21, 1936, powered by two 1,000hp DB 600A in-line engines; the second prototype was essentially similar, except that it was fitted with Jumo 211A radials, the engines that were mostly to power the aircraft throughout its career. A preseries batch of Ju 88A-0s was completed during the summer of 1939, the first production Ju 88A-1s being delivered to a test unit, Erprobungskommando 88. In August 1939 this unit was redesignated I/KG 25, and soon afterward it became I/KG 30, carrying out its first operational mission—an attack on British warships in the Firth of Forth—in September. About 60 operational aircraft were in service by the end of the year. The Ju 88A was built in 17 different variants up to the Ju 88A-17, with progressively uprated engines, enhanced defensive armament, and improved defensive capability. The most widely used variant was the Ju 88A-4, which served in both Europe and North Africa. This was the first version to incorporate technical inprovements resulting from the combat experience gained during the battles of France and Britain; it had extended-span wings, Jumo 211J engines, and a heavier defensive armament. Twenty Ju 88A-4s were supplied to Finland, and some were supplied to Italy, Romania, and Hungary. The Ju 88A-5 was generally similar, with some equipment changes.

The Ju 88A saw considerable action in the Balkans and the Mediterranean, and on the Eastern Front. Some of their most outstanding service, however, was in the Arctic, where aircraft of KG 26 and KG 30, based in northern Norway, carried out devastating attacks on Allied convoys to Russia.

The Ju 88B was the subject of a separate development program, and eventually evolved into the Ju 188, which made

its operational debut later in the war. Chronologically, the next major production model was the Ju 88C heavy fighter; the first version was the Ju 88C-2, which was a conversion of the Ju 88A1 with a "solid" nose housing three MG 17 machine guns and a 0.79-in (20-mm) MG FF cannon, plus a single rearward-firing MG 15. It entered service with NJG.1 in the late summer of 1940 and was used for intruder operations over the British Isles. It was followed by a relatively small number of Ju 88C-4s, using the same extended-span wing of the Ju 88A-4, and the C-5.

The next variant, the Ju 88C-6, had Jumo 211J engines and two 0.79-in (20-mm) cannon added to its forward armament, the rear MG 15 being replaced by an MG 131. The Ju 88C-6, and the last varient in this series, the C-7, were used as both day and night fighters. The last fighter variant of the Ju 88, which made its appearance in the spring of 1944, was the Ju 88G. This version, which used the angular tail unit of the Ju 188 and carried improved Lichtenstein AI radar, was a highly effective night fighter. Two more subvariants, the Ju 88H2 and the Ju 88R, brought the fighter Ju 88 line to an end.

A specialist version of the Ju 88, the Ju 88P, also made its appearance during World War II, armed with either a 2.95-in (75-mm) gun (Ju 88P-1) or two 1.46-in (37-mm) cannon (Ju 88P-2). Total production of the Junkers 88 was 14,676 aircraft, of which about 3,900 were fighter or ground attack variants.

▲ The Ju 88 was without doubt one of the finest combat aircraft to emerge from World War II, and one of the most versatile.

▌Junkers Ju 90

Designed in parallel with the abandoned Ju 89 bomber, and using the same wings, tail assembly, and undercarriage, the 40-passenger Ju 90 commercial transport began trials on August 28, 1937. The Ju 90V-1 prototype made several record flights, but suffered many teething troubles and was lost on a test flight when a wing failed. The Ju 90 did not see airline service, but 13 development aircraft were built, and seven of these were assigned as Ju 90B-1s to the Luftwaffe for transportation duties in 1943.

SPECIFICATION: Type transportation aircraft • Crew 4/5 • Powerplant four 1,550hp BMW 139 radial engines • Max speed 217mph (350km/h) at 8,202ft (2,500m) • Service ceiling 18,044ft (5,500m) • Max range 1,300 miles (2,092km) • Wingspan 114ft 10in (35.02m) • Length 86ft 3in (26.30m) • Height not known • Weight 50,706lb (23,000kg) loaded • Armament one 0.31-in (7.92-mm) machine gun in tail position

▲ *The Junkers Ju 90 was designed as a commercial airliner for Lufthansa's transatlantic routes, but was instead used for military purposes.*

▌Junkers Ju 188/388

Flown in prototype form in the latter half of 1940, the Junkers Ju 188 was a logical development of the Ju 88, characterized by its large, bulbous "glasshouse" nose and an extended wing with pointed tips. The first major version, the Ju 188E-1, entered production in 1941 and was operational in 1942, together with a reconnaissance variant, the Ju 188F. The first version into service was to have been Ju 188A, but its introduction was delayed pending the availability of its Junkers Jumo 213A engines. The Ju 188D was a fully armed reconnaissance counterpart to the Ju 188A; the Ju 188G, produced in small numbers, was another bomber variant. The last model was the Ju 188S, a fast, high-altitude bomber with an impressive performance. The Ju 388 was a progressive development of the Ju 188 and was intended to be a multirole aircraft, but only one version, the Ju 388L reconnaissance model, was produced in time to see service before the end of the war.

SPECIFICATION: Type bomber (Ju 188E-1) • Crew 4 • Powerplant two 1,600hp BMW 801ML radial engines • Max speed 310mph (500km/h) at 19,686ft (6,000m) • Service ceiling 30,513ft (9,300m) • Max range 1,541 miles (2,480km) • Wingspan 72ft 2in (22m) • Length 49ft 5in (15.06m) • Height 14ft 7in (4.46m) • Weight 32,121lb (14,570kg) loaded • Armament one 0.79-in (20-mm) cannon in nose position; one 0.51-in (13-mm) machine gun in dorsal turret, one 0.51-in (13-mm) machine gun in rear of cockpit, and one 0.31-in (7.92-mm) twin-barrel MG in gondola under nose; 6,614lb (3,000kg) of bombs

▲ *The Junkers Ju 388 was the last operational version of the famous Junkers bomber. Only the Ju 388L reconnaisance version saw service.*

▌ Junkers Ju 252/352

GERMANY

The three-engined Ju 252 was designed as a successor to the Ju 52/3m. Its drawback was that it was an all-metal design, conceived at a time when strategic materials were in short supply in Germany. Only 15 aircraft were produced, and interest switched to the Ju 352 Herkules, which was of a similar overall design but which used lower-priority materials. The first Ju 352 flew in October 1943, six more prototypes and 43 Ju 352A-1 production aircraft being completed. Most of the completed aircraft were employed on the Eastern Front.

SPECIFICATION: Type transportation aircraft (all data apply to Ju 352) • Crew 4 • Powerplant three 1,000hp BMW 323R-2 9-cylinder radial engines • Max speed 230mph (370km/h) at 16,404ft (5,000m) • Service ceiling 19,685ft (6,000m) • Max range 1,860 miles (2,993km) • Wingspan 112ft 3in (34.21m) • Length 80ft 8in (24.60m) • Height 18ft 10in (5.75m) • Weight 43,011lb (19,510kg) loaded • Armament one 0.79-in (20-mm) cannon in dorsal turret

▌ Junkers Ju 290

GERMANY

The Junkers Ju 290 was a progressive development of the Ju 90, the prototype—which flew in 1941—being the reengined Ju 90V-7. The first two production Ju 290A-1s were transportation aircraft, but in the spring of 1943 the basic design

SPECIFICATION: Type transportation and maritime reconnaissance aircraft • Crew 7–9 • Powerplant four 1,600hp BMW 801L 14-cylinder radial engines • Max speed 273mph (439km/h) at 19,030ft (5,800m) • Service ceiling 19,685ft (6,000m) • Max range 3,820 miles (6,150km) • Wingspan 137ft 9in (42.00m) • Length 93ft 11in (28.63m) • Height 22ft 5in (6.83m) • Weight 90,323lb (40,970kg) loaded • Armament six 0.79-in (20-mm) cannon; one 0.51-in (13-mm) machine gun

was adapted to the maritime reconnaissance role as a Focke-Wulf Fw 200 replacement. It also had an antiship capability, being able to carry a pair of Hs 293 or Fritz-X missiles. In the transportation role the Ju 290 could carry 40 troops. Modified Ju 290s with extra fuel tankage made several flights from the Ukraine to Japanese-occupied Manchuria early in 1944, carrying special cargoes. Fifty Ju 290s were delivered to the Luftwaffe; proposed variants, which were not completed, included the Ju 290B high-altitude bomber. A scaled-up version, designated the Ju 390, was planned for long-range bombing of North America. One prototype flew within 12 miles (19km) of New York before returning to its base in France.

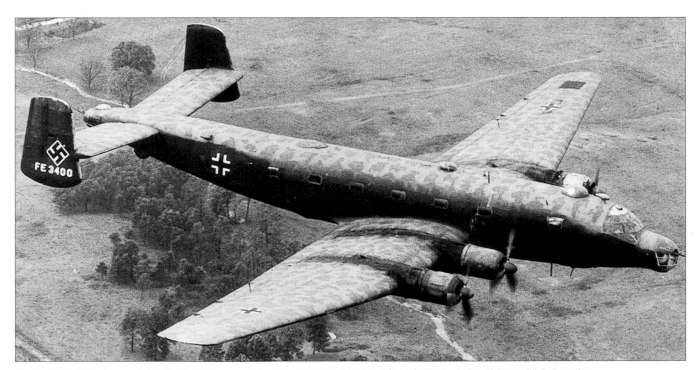

▲ In addition to its transport role, the Ju 290 was used for long-range special missions by KG 200, the Luftwaffe's special duties unit.

▌Kawanishi E15K-1 Shiun "Norm"

The Kawanishi E15K-1 Shiun (Violet Cloud) three-seat floatplane was designed specifically for reconnaissance missions in areas where the enemy had air superiority, and its central float could be jettisoned to increase speed while leaving the combat area. The float mechanism, however, failed to function, and six (out of the total of 15 built) E15K-1s which were sent to Palau island in the South Pacific for trials were destroyed by US fighters.

SPECIFICATION: Type reconnaissance floatplane • Crew 3 • Powerplant one 1,460hp Mitsubishi Kasei 24 radial engine • Max speed 291mph (468km/h) at 18,700ft (5,700m) • Service ceiling 32,270ft (9,836m) • Max range not known • Wingspan 45ft 11in (13.99m) • Length 45ft 11in (11.59m) • Height not known • Weight 10,787lb (4,893kg) loaded • Armament one 0.303-in (7.7-mm) machine gun in rear cockpit

▌Kawanishi H6K "Mavis"

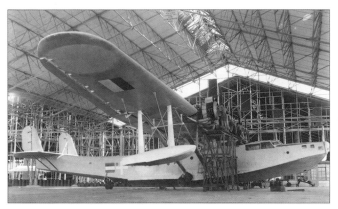

▲ *The Kawanishi H6K was a very effective long-range maritime reconnaissance flying boat, but its lack of armour made it easy prey for US fighters.*

Designed to meet a requirement of the Imperial Japanese Navy for a high-performance long-range reconnaissance flying boat, the prototype of the H6K flew for the first time on

SPECIFICATION: Type maritime reconnaissance flying boat (data H6K-5) • Crew 9 • Powerplant two 1,300hp Mitsubishi Kinsei 51/53 14-cylinder radials • Max speed 239mph (385km/h) at 16,405ft (5,000m) • Service ceiling 31,365ft (9,560m) • Max range 4,208 miles (6,772km) • Wingspan 131ft 2in (40m) • Length 84ft 0in (25.63m) • Height 20ft 6in (6.27m) • Weight 50,706lb (23,000kg) loaded • Armament one 0.79-in (20-mm) cannon in tail turret and four 0.303-in (7.7-mm) machine guns, one in bow and dorsal positions and two in blister positions; torpedo and bomb load of 3,527lb (1,600kg)

July 14, 1936, the first 10 production aircraft entering service as the H6K-2. An improved variant, the H6K-4, appeared in 1940; this was the major production model, 127 examples being produced. In 1941 production switched to an updated version, the H6K-5, of which 36 were built. The H6K proved extremely vulnerable to fighter attack, mainly because it lacked armor protection for the crew and its fuel tanks were not self-sealing, and from 1943 it was gradually assigned to the transportation role.

▌Kawanishi H8K "Emily"

SPECIFICATION: Type maritime reconnaissance flying boat • Crew 10 • Powerplant four 1,850hp Mitsubishi Kasei 22 14-cylinder radials • Max speed 290mph (467km/h) at 16,405ft (5,000m) • Service ceiling 28,740ft (8,760m) • Max range 4,460 miles (7,180km) • Wingspan 14ft 8in (38m) • Length 92ft 3in (28.13m) • Height 30ft (9.15m) • Weight 71,650lb (32,500kg) loaded • Armament five 0.79-in (20-mm) cannon, one each in bow, dorsal, and tail positions and two beam blisters; four 0.303-in (7.7-mm) machine guns in beam hatches; up to 4,409lb (2,000kg) of bombs or two 1,764-lb (800-kg) torpedoes

▶ *All aspects of Kawanashi's flying boat expertise were embodied in the H8K 'Emily'. It was a difficult aircraft to shoot down.*

Considered one of the finest military flying-boats ever produced, the large Kawanishi H8K was designed in 1938 in response to an Imperial Japanese Navy requirement for an H6K replacement, the latter having just entered production. The prototype flew in January 1941 and the first production model, the H8K-1, entered service early in 1942.

Only 14 H8K-1s were built before production switched to the H8K-2, 148 examples being delivered. These included a batch of 36 H8K-2L transports, known to the Japanese as Seiku (Clear Sky). The Emily carried a very heavy defensive armament, and was by no means an easy opponent for Allied fighters.

▌Kawanishi N1K Kyofu "Rex"

JAPAN

A first-class design with an excellent performance, the Kawanishi N1K Kyofu (Mighty Wind) made its appearance in August 1942, but within three months the decision was taken to convert the design to a landplane fighter configuration. Only 89 were built, the survivors being used in the defense of the Japanese homeland in the last months of the war.

SPECIFICATION: Type fighter floatplane • Crew 1 • Powerplant one 1,460hp Mitsubishi MK4C Kasai 13 radial • Max speed 304mph (489km/h) at 18,700ft (5,700m) • Service ceiling 34,775ft (10,600m) • Max range 652 miles (1,050km) • Wingspan 39ft 4in (12m) • Length 34ft 9in (10.59m) • Height 15ft 7in (4.75m) • Weight 8,184lb (3,712kg) loaded • Armament two fixed forward-firing 0.79-in (20-mm) cannon; two 0.303-in (7.7-mm) machine gun; provision for two 66-lb (30-kg) bomber under wings

▲ The Imperial Japanese Navy saw floatplane fighters like the Kyofu as an ideal means of defending the Pacific island garrisons.

▌Kawanishi N1K-J Shiden "George"

JAPAN

The land-based fighter developed from the Kyofu fighter floatplane was the Kawanishi N1K-J Shiden (Violet Lightning). The Shiden, production of which began in August 1943, was one of the finest fighter aircraft to serve in the Pacific, and was used extensively in the Philippines, around Formosa and in the defense of the Japanese home islands. Production totaled 1098 N1K1-Js.

▼ This N1K2-J Shiden Kai is preserved at the USAF Museum at Wright-Patterson AFB, Dayton, Ohio.

SPECIFICATION: Type fighter (data N1K1-J) • Crew 1 • Powerplant one 1,990hp Nakajima NK9H Homare 21 18-cylinder radial • Max speed 361mph (581km/h) at 19,685ft (6,000m) • Service ceiling 41,010ft (12,500m) • Max range 1,581 miles (2,544km) • Wingspan 39ft 4in (12m) • Length 29ft 1in (8.88m) • Height 13ft 3in (4.06m) • Weight 95,726lb (43,421kg) loaded • Armament two 0.79-in (20-mm) cannon in wing leading edges and two in underwing gondolas; two 0.303-in (7.7-mm) machine guns in upper forward fuselage; provision for external bomb load of 265lb (120kg)

Kawasaki C-1

JAPAN

SPECIFICATION: Type transportation • Crew 5, plus 60 passengers • Powerplant two 14,500-lb (6,577-kg) thrust Mitsubishi JT8D-M-9 turbojets • Max speed 501mph (806km/h) • Service ceiling 38,000ft (11,580m) • Max range 2,084 miles (3,353km) • Wingspan 100ft 5in (30.6m) • Length 95ft 2in (29m) • Height 32ft 9in (9.99m) • Weight 99,210lb (45,000kg) loaded • Armament none

Designed to replace the elderly Curtiss C-46Ds in service with the Japanese Air Self-Defense Force, the Kawasaki C-1 medium-range twin-jet military transport flew for the first time on November 12, 1970, the first of 36 aircraft being delivered in December 1974 and the last in March 1976. Some aircraft were converted to the ELINT role.

Kawasaki Ki.10 "Perry"

JAPAN

Designed by Takeo Doi in response to a Japanese Army requirement of September 1934, the Kawasaki Ki.10 (type 95) fighter was of all-metal construction, with alloy and fabric covering, and was an unequal-span biplane with N-form

▼ The Kawasaki Ki.10 saw a good deal of action during the Sino-Japanese conflict of 1937, but was obsolete by the outbreak of World War II.

SPECIFICATION: Type fighter biplane • Crew 1 • Powerplant one 850hp Kawasaki Ha9 11a 12-cylinder V-type • Max speed 250mph (400km/h) at 9,800ft (3,000m) • Service ceiling 32,800ft (10,000m) • Max range 3,680 miles (1,100m) • Wingspan 31ft 4in (9.55m) • Length 23ft 7in (7.2m) • Height 9ft 10in (3m) • Weight 3,640lb (1,650kg) loaded • Armament two fixed forward-firing 0.303-in (7.7-mm) machine guns

bracing struts. Production Ki.10s were operating in China shortly after hostilities broke out with that country in July 1937, and they saw action against Polikarpov I-15bis fighters supplied by the Soviet Union. By the summer of 1939 the Ki.10 was obsolescent, and shortly afterward the last of Japan's fighter biplanes was withdrawn from first-line service.

Kawasaki Ki.32 "Mary"

 JAPAN

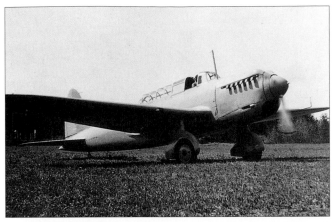

▲ Like the Ki.10 fighter, the Kawasaki Ki.32 light bomber was widely used in China from 1938, but was withdrawn soon after the outbreak of WWII.

An excellent single-engined light bomber design in the same class as the Fairey Battle, but a good deal more effective, the Kawasaki Ki.32 flew in prototype form in March 1937, the first of 854 production aircraft appearing in the second half of 1938. The Ki.32 was widely used in China, but was withdrawn from service shortly after the outbreak of World War II.

SPECIFICATION: Type light bomber • Crew 2 • Powerplant one 850hp Kawasaki Ha9 11b 12-cylinder V-type • Max speed 263mph (423km/h) at 12,598ft (3,840m) • Service ceiling 29,265ft (8,920m) • Max range 1,218 miles (1,965km) • Wingspan 49ft 2in (15m) • Length 38ft 2in (11.64m) • Height 9ft 6in (2.90m) • Weight 8,311lb (3,770kg) • Armament two 0.303-in (7.7-mm) machine guns; 992lb (450kg) of bombs

Kawasaki Ki.45 Toryu "Nick"

 JAPAN

The Kawasaki Ki.45 Toryu (Dragon Slayer) was designed in 1937 to meet a requirement for a twin-engined heavy fighter in the same class as Germany's Messerschmitt Bf 110. The prototype flew in January 1939, but development was protracted and the type did not enter service until the fall of 1942 as the Ki.45 Kai-a fighter and the Ki.45 Kai-b ground attack and antishipping strike aircraft. The Ki.45 Kai-c was a night fighter version, while the Kai-d was an improved ground attack/antishipping variant. Total production of the Toryu was 1,675 aircraft, of which 477 were night fighters.

SPECIFICATION: Type night fighter (data Ki.45 Kai-c) • Crew 2 • Powerplant two 1,080hp Mitsubishi Ha-102 14-cylinder radials • Max speed 336mph (540km/h) at 16,405ft (5,000m) • Service ceiling 32,810ft (10,000m) • Max range 1,243 miles (2,000km) • Wingspan 49ft 3in (15.02m) • Length 36ft 1in (11m) • Height 12ft 1in (3.70m) • Weight 12,125lb (5,500kg) loaded • Armament one 1.45-in (37-mm) fixed forward-firing cannon in underside of forward fuselage; two obliquely-mounted 0.79-in (20-mm) cannon in upper central fuselage; one 0.31-in (7.92-mm) machine gun in rear cockpit

▲ The Kawasaki Ki.45 Toryu, in its heavily armed night fighter guise, was a formidable opponent for the USAAF's B-29 bombers.

Kawasaki Ki.48 "Lily"

 JAPAN

Although it was built in considerable numbers, the Kawasaki Ki.48 light bomber, roughly in the same class as the Bristol Blenheim, was not a particularly successful aircraft. Although it was fast, its handling and general performance did not come up to expectation. The initial version, the Ki.48-Ia, entered service in 1940 and saw action in China. After 557

aircraft of this series had been built, production switched to the somewhat improved Ki.48-IIa in April 1942. Many Ki.48s were expended in kamikaze attacks at Okinawa, some being armed with an 1,764-lb (800-kg) bomb load detonated when a long nose-mounted rod made contact with the target. Total production of the Ki.48, all variants, was 1,997.

SPECIFICATION: Type light bomber (data Ki.48-IIa • Crew 4 • Powerplant two 1,130hp Nakajima Ha.115 radials • Max speed 314mph (505km/h) at 18,375ft (5,600m) • Service ceiling 33,135ft (10,100m) • Max range 1,491 miles (2,400km) • Wingspan 57ft 3in (17.45m) • Length 41ft 9in (12.75m) • Height 12ft 5in (3.8m) • Weight 14,350lb (6,500kg) loaded • Armament three 0.303-in (7.7-mm) machine guns, on each in nose, dorsal, and ventral positions; up to 1,764lb (800kg) of bombs

▲ The Kawasaki Ki.48 was widely used by the Japanese Army Air Force during its campaigns in China and South-East Asia.

▮ Kawasaki Ki.56 "Thalia"

 JAPAN

The Ki.56 was a military version of the Lockheed 14 trans-

SPECIFICATION: Type transportation • Crew 4 • Powerplant two 950hp Nakajima Ha.25 14-cylinder radials • Max speed 248mph (400km/h) at 11,480ft (3,500m) • Service ceiling 26,250ft (8,000m) • Max range 1,500 miles (2,413km) • Wingspan 65ft 6in (19.96m) • Length 48ft 10in (14.90m) • Height 11ft 9 in (3.60m) • Weight 17,692lb (8,025kg) loaded • Armament none

portation aircraft, which the Kawasaki firm was preparing to build under license in 1939. The type remained in production at the Kawasaki factory until September 1943 with the delivery of the 121st aircraft; a further 688 were produced by Tachikawa. The aircraft first saw action during the invasion of Sumatra, dropping paratroops on key objectives, and was often misidentified as a captured Lockheed Hudson.

▮ Kawasaki Ki.61 Hien "Tony"

 JAPAN

The Kawasaki Ki.61 was designed to replace the Nakajima Ki.43 Hayabusa (Oscar) in Japanese army service, and began to reach front-line air units in August 1942. Given the Japanese name Hien (Swallow), it was the only operational Japanese fighter to feature an inverted-V engine (a license-built DB 601), and until Allied pilots became familiar with it its appearance gave rise to erroneous reports that the Japanese were using Messerschmitt 109s. Between 1942 and the end of the Pacific war 3,028 examples were built, serving in all areas. The principal versions were the KI.61-I (1,380

aircraft built); the Ki.61 Kai, with a lengthened fuselage and different armament fits (1,274 built); and the Ki.61-II, optimised for high-altitude operation with a Kawasaki Ha.140 engine (374 built).

▲ This view of a Kawasaki Ki.61 Hien clearly shows the characteristic lines of the DB 601 inverted-V engine, produced under license by Kawasaki.

SPECIFICATION: Type fighter • Crew 1 • Powerplant one 1,175hp Kawasaki Ha.40 12-cylinder inverted-V • Max speed 368mph (592km/h) at 16,405ft (5,000m) • Service ceiling 38,057ft (11,600m) • Max range 684 miles (1,100km) • Wingspan 39ft 4in (12m) • Length 28ft 8in (8.75m) • Height 12ft 1in (3.70m) • Weight 7,165lb (3,250kg) loaded • Armament four 0.50-in (12.7-mm) machine guns, two in upper forward fuselage, and two in wings

Kawasaki Ki.100

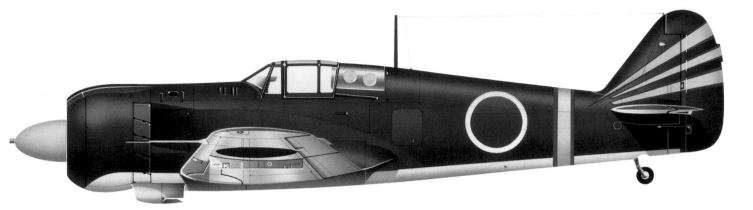

The Kawasaki Ki.100 was the Imperial Japanese Army's last fighter, and its development came about more or less by accident. In November 1944, a considerable number of Ki.61 Hien airframes were in storage, awaiting delivery of license-built DB601 engines. These had proved to be unreliable in any case, so it was decided to fit the airframes with the 1,500hp Mitsubishi Ha.112-II radial. The "new" aircraft flew for the first time on February 1, 1945 and conversion of 275 Ki.61-II airframes began immediately. The Ki.100 was produced in two principal series, the Ia and Ib, the latter being new-build aircraft; 396 examples of both versions were completed before production was halted. The Ki.100 showed itself to be a very effective high-altitude interceptor, and saw a great deal of action against the American B-29 formations in the closing months of the Pacific war. An upgraded variant, the Ki.100-II, flew in March 1945 but was produced in prototype form only.

▲ The Kawasaki Ki.100 was the last fighter to be produced for the Imperial Japanese Army, and proved to be a very effective high-altitude interceptor.

SPECIFICATION: Type interceptor • Crew 1 • Powerplant one 1,500hp Mitsubishi Ha.112-II 14-cylinder radial • Max speed 360mph (580km/h) at 16,405ft (5,000m) • Service ceiling 36,090ft (11,000m) • Max range 1,242 miles (2,000km) • Wingspan 39ft 4in (12m) • Length 28ft 11in (8.82m) • Height 12ft 3in (3.75m) • Weight 7,705lb (3,495kg) loaded • Armament two 0.79-in (20-mm) cannon in upper forward fuselage; two 0.50-in (12.7-mm) machine guns in wings

Kawasaki Ki.102 "Randy"

▶ The Kawasaki Ki.102 entered production in October 1944 as the Army Type 4 Assault Aircraft, and saw limited action at Okinawa.

SPECIFICATION: Type heavy assault fighter (data Ki.102b) • Crew 2 • Powerplant two 1,500hp Mitsubishi Ha.112-II 14-cylinder radials • Max speed 360mph (580km/h) at 16,405ft (5,000m) • Service ceiling 32,100ft (9,785m) • Max range 1,242 miles (2,000km) • Wingspan 51ft 1in (15.57m) • Length 37ft 7in (11.45m) • Height 12ft 2in (3.70m) • Weight 16,094lb (7,300kg) loaded • Armament one 1.46-in (37-mm) cannon in the nose; two 0.79-in (20-mm) cannon in fuselage belly; one 0.50-in (12.7-mm) machine gun in rear cockpit

Designed as a heavy assault fighter, the Ki.102 first flew in March 1944, and after some modifications went into production in October as the Army Type 4 Assault Aircraft (Ki.102b). Production was limited, only 238 aircraft being built; the total included 15 examples of a high-altitude interceptor variant, the Ki.102a. Production of a proposed night fighter version, the Ki.102c, was interrupted by the end of the war.

▌Keystone B-4A

USA

The most widely used USAAC bombers of the late 1920s and early 1930s were those built by the Keystone Aircraft Corporation, beginning with the LB-5 of 1927. The LB-5 fixed the basic configuration of the Keystone bombers, subsequent aircraft—250 being produced in total—differing only in minor structural alterations and engine detail. The last production models were the B-4A and B-6A, both appearing in 1932. As well as forming the backbone of the Army's offensive force, the Keystone bombers frequently took part in US national air races, carried air mail when the civil carriers had difficulties, and generally provided excellent publicity for the USAAC.

◀ *The Keystone bomber series formed the backbone of the USAAC's offensive force in the 1930s. A formation of B-3s is seen here over New York.*

SPECIFICATION: Type bomber • Crew 5 • Powerplant two 575hp Pratt & Whitney Hornet 9-cylinder radials • Max speed 121mph (195km/h) at sea level • Service ceiling 14,100ft (4,300m) • Max range 855 miles (1,376km) • Wingspan 74ft 9in (22.78m) • Length 48ft 10in (14.88m) • Height 15ft 9in (4.8m) • Weight 13,200lb (6,000kg) loaded • Armament three 0.30-in (7.62-mm) Browning machine guns; up to 2,500lb (1,130kg) of bombs

▌Kokusai Ki.76 "Stella"

JAPAN

SPECIFICATION: Type artillery spotter and liaison aircraft • Crew 2 • Powerplant one 310hp Hitachi Ha.42 9-cylinder radial • Max speed 111mph (178km/h) at sea level • Service ceiling 18,470ft (5,630m) • Max range 466 miles (750km) • Wingspan 49ft 2in (15m) • Length 31ft 4in (9.65m) • Height 9ft 6in (2.9m) • Weight 1,623kg (3,571lb) loaded • Armament one 0.303-in (7.7-mm) machine guns in rear cockpit

Similar to, and inspired by, the Luftwaffe's Fieseler Fi.156 Storch, the Kokusai Ki.76 high-wing monoplane entered production toward the end of 1942 and was widely used by the Imperial Japanese Army as an artillery spotter and liaison aircraft. In many ways the Ki.76 was a better aircraft than the Storch, having a much more powerful engine and a more efficient Fowler wing flap system that reduced its landing run.

▌Kyushu J7W Shinden

JAPAN

Although it never entered service, the Kyushu J7W Shinden (Magnificent Lightning) was noteworthy as the only aircraft of canard configuration to be ordered into quantity production anywhere in the world during World War II. Designed as a heavily armed high-performance fighter for the Imperial Japanese Navy, the type was ordered into full production even before the prototype made its first flight on August 3, 1944, just 12 days before Japan surrendered. A version powered by a 1,984-lb (900-kg) thrust Ne-130 turbojet was planned but not built.

SPECIFICATION: Type heavy interceptor • Crew 1 • Powerplant one 2130hp Mitsubishi MK9D 18-cylinder radial • Max speed 466mph (750km/h) at 28,545ft (8700m) • Service ceiling 39,370ft (12,000m) • Max range 529 miles (850km) • Wing span 36ft 5in (11.11m) • Length 31ft 8in (9.66m) • Height 12ft 10in (3.92m) • Weight 10,854lb (4928kg) loaded • Armament four nose-mounted 1.19in (30mm) Type 5 cannon

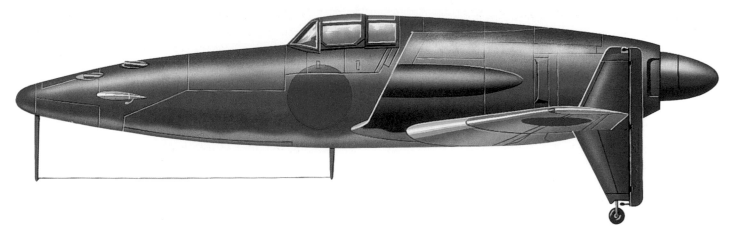

▌Kyushu K11W Shiragiku

The Kyushu Shiragiku (White Crysanthemum) single-engined crew trainer first flew in November 1942 and was widely used by the Imperial Japanese Navy from 1943 to the

end of the Pacific war, 798 being produced. Late in the war the aircraft was modified to carry a single 551-lb (250-kg) bomb for kamikaze missions. A two-seat utility transport and antisubmarine variant, the Q3W1 Nankai (South Sea) did not enter production.

◀ *This aircraft was photographed in China immediately after VJ-Day, wearing "surrender" colors – overall white with green crosses.*

SPECIFICATION: **Type** crew trainer • **Crew** 5 • **Powerplant** one 515hp Hitachi GK2B Amakaze 21 9-cylinder radial • **Max speed** 143mph (230km/h) at 5,580ft (1,700m) • **Service ceiling** 18,440ft (5,620m) • **Max range** 1,093 miles (1,760km) • **Wingspan** 49ft 2in (14.98m) • **Length** 33ft 7in (10.24m) • **Height** 12ft 10in (3.93m) • **Weight** 6,183lb (2,805kg) loaded • **Armament** one 0.303-in (7.7-mm) machine gun; 132lb (60kg) of bombs

▌Kyushu Q1W Tokai "Lorna"

Entering service in 1944, the Kyushu Q1W Tokai (Eastern Sea) was a shore-based reconnaissance and antisubmarine aircraft, the only one of its type produced by Japan in World

War II. The prototype flew in September 1943 and 153 examples of the only variant, the Q1W1, were produced, being mainly used for convoy escort.

SPECIFICATION: **Type** reconnaissance and antisubmarine aircraft • **Crew** 3 • **Powerplant** two 610hp Hitachi GK2C Amakaze 31 9-cylinder radials • **Max speed** 200mph (322km/h) at 4,395ft (1,340m) • **Service ceiling** 14,730ft (4,490m) • **Max range** 834 miles (1,342km) • **Wingspan** 52ft 6in (16m) • **Length** 39ft 8in (12.08m) • **Height** 13ft 6in (4.11m) • **Weight** 11,750lb (5,330kg) loaded • **Armament** one or two forward-firing 0.79-in (20-mm) cannon; one flexible rearward-firing 0.303-in (7.7-mm) machine gun; two 771-lb (350-kg) bombs or depth charges carried externally

▲ *Q1Ws were operated from bases in Japan, Formosa, and China, tasked with the protection of supply convoys from the Dutch East Indies and Malaya.*

▌Latécoère 298

The Laté 298 floatplane, which first flew in May 1936, was without doubt one of the most versatile Allied combat aircraft to take part in the Battle of France, serving in the surveillance, reconnaissance, bomber, and attack roles. Eighty

▲ *The Laté 298B differed from the 298A in having folding wings, dual controls, and an additional crew member.*

aircraft were delivered to the Aéronavale before the armistice; they were never used in their primary role of torpedo-bomber during the campaign, being mainly employed on ground attack work in support of the French Army. Thanks to the aircraft's rugged construction and high degree of maneuverability, combat losses were relatively light.

SPECIFICATION: Type torpedo-bomber/reconnaissance floatplane • Crew 2–3 • Powerplant one 880hp Hispano-Suiza 12Ycrs-1 12-cylinder V-type • Max speed 180mph (290km/h) • Service ceiling 21,325ft (6,500m) • Max range 1,367 miles (2,200km) • Wingspan 50ft 10in (15.50m) • Length 41ft 2in (12.56m) • Height 17ft 1in (5.23m) • Weights 6,750lb (3,062kg) empty; 10,582lb (4,800kg) loaded • Armament two wing-mounted 0.30-in (7.5-mm) machine guns and one in rear cockpit; external torpedo or bomb load of 1,477lb (670kg)

▌Latécoère 521

The famous Latécoère 521 "Lieutenant de Vaisseau Paris" stemmed from the Laté 520 commercial flying boat project of 1930 and was intended for the North Atlantic route, carrying 30 passengers and eight crew. In January 1936, during long-range trials, it was wrecked by a typhoon in Pensacola Bay. Dismantled and shipped back to France, it was rebuilt and handed over to the Aéronavale soon after the outbreak of

World War II for maritime reconnaissance use. It began operations in January 1940, flying patrols over the Atlantic, and was at Port Lyautey, Morocco, at the time of the armistice in June. Flown back to Berre in southern France, it was damaged beyond repair by retreating German forces in 1942.

SPECIFICATION: Type maritime patrol flying boat/commercial transportation • Crew 8 • Powerplant six 860hp Hispano-Suiza 12Ybrs liquid-cooled V-type • Max speed 130mph (210km/h) • Service ceiling 20,669ft (6,300m) • Max range 2,547 miles (4,100km) • Wingspan 161ft 9in (49.31m) • Length 103ft 9in (31.62m) • Height 29ft 9in (9.07m) • Weight 83,627lb (37,933kg) loaded • Armament four 0.30-in (7.5-mm) Darne machine gun behind hull hatches; eight GPU racks for 440-lb (200-kg) bombs

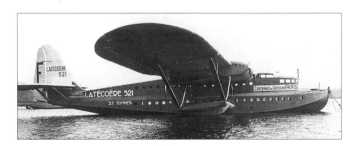

▲ *The six-engined Laté 521 "Lieutenant de Vaisseau Paris" was a huge aircraft for its time.*

▌Lavochkin LaGG-3

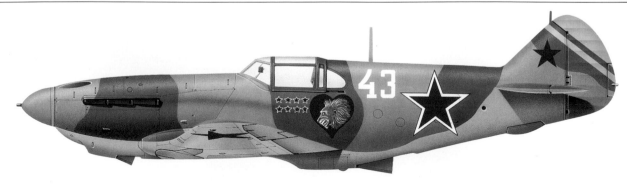

It was not until 1939–40 that the prototypes of three Soviet fighters that could really be classed as modern made their appearance. The first was the LaGG-1 (I-22), which took its name from the initials of the three engineers who conceived it Lavochkin, Gorbunov, and Gudkov. It was a remarkable little aircraft, built entirely of wood and bearing a strong resemblance to France's Dewoitine D.520. The LaGG-1 flew for the first time in March 1940 and was superseded by an improved variant, the LaGG-3, after 100 examples had been built. These still equipped two air regiments at the time of the German invasion of June 1941, but it was the LaGG-3 that held the line during the first critical months of the German onslaught. Production ended in 1942 after 6,427 had been built.

SPECIFICATION: Type fighter (data LaGG-3) • Crew 1 • Powerplant one 1,260hp Klimov VK-105PF-1 12-cylinder V-type • Max speed 357mph (575km/h) at 16,405ft (5,000m) • Service ceiling 31,825ft (9,700m) • Max range 621 miles (1,000km) • Wingspan 32ft 1in (9.80m) • Length 28ft 11in (8.81m) • Height 8ft 4in (2.54m) • Weight 7,032lb (3,190kg) • Armament one ShVAK 0.79-in (20-mm) cannon, two ShKAS 0.30-in (7.62-mm) machine guns and one 0.50-in (12.7-mm) BS (Beresin) machine gun

■ Lavochkin La-5 Series   USSR

SPECIFICATION: Type interceptor fighter (La-7) • Crew 1 • Powerplant one 1,850hp Shvetsov M-82FN (ASh-82FN) radial piston engine • Max speed 413mph (665km/h) • Service ceiling 35,435ft (10,800m) • Max range 395 miles (635km) • Wing span 32ft 1in (9.80m) • Length 28ft 2in (8.60m) • Height 8ft 4in (2.54m) • Weight 7496lb (3400kg) loaded • Armament two or three Beresin B-20 0.79-in (20-mm) cannon plus up to 400lb (200kg) of bombs on underwing racks

The Lavochkin La-5 was developed from the earlier LaGG-3 in response to a desperate requirement for the Soviet Air Force, which had suffered appalling casualties at the hands of the Luftwaffe in the second half of 1941, for a modern fighter that could hold its own with the Messerschmitt 109. Semyon Lavochkin retained the basic LaGG-3 airframe, which was lightweight, of wooden construction, and easy to assemble, and married it with a 1,330hp Shvetsov M-82F radial engine. Other modifications included a cut-down rear fuselage, providing much improved pilot visibility, and a heavier armament. The prototype La-5 completed its State Acceptance Trials in May 1942 and entered production two months later. By the end of the year, 1182 La-5s had been issued to front-line units, a remarkable achievement by any standard.

Early combats showed that the La-5 was a better all-round performer than the Messerschmitt 109G, although its rate of climb was inferior. Lavochkin therefore undertook some redesign work to reduce the fighter's weight, and re-engined it with the 1,510hp M-82FN direct-injection engine, which endowed the La-5 with better climbing characteristics and maneuverability than either the Bf 109G or the Focke-Wulf FW 190A-4. The modified aircraft, designated La-5FN, made its appearance at the front in the Battle of Stalingrad in late 1942. The aircraft soon began to make its presence felt in the hands of some very competent Soviet fighter pilots. Among them was Ivan Kozhedub, who made his combat debut just before the battle of Kursk in the summer of 1943 and who went on to score 62 kills while flying Lavochkin fighters, making him the top-scoring Allied air ace. In addition to Soviet Air Force units, the La-5FN also equipped the 1st Czech Fighter Regiment, whose pilots scored some notable successes. Refined progressively for the remainder of World War II, the La-5FN was built in numbers approaching 10,000.

A variant of the La-5, the La-7, had a similar engine to the La-5 and differed only in minor design detail. A two-seat trainer version, the La-5UTI, was also produced, bringing total production of the La-5/La-7 series to 21,975 examples by the end of the war.

The last of the Lavochkin piston-engined fighter line were the La-9 and La-11. Design work on the La-9 began in 1944 and development continued during the last months of the war, although it entered service too late to see action. It was slightly larger than the La-5/La-7, and differed from its predecessors in having all-metal construction, a redesigned cockpit canopy, and square-cut wingtips. The La-11 had a slightly smaller wing area than the La-9 and carried a reduced armament. Both types were supplied to Soviet satellite air forces, including China and North Korea, and were encountered in action during the Korean War. The La-11 remained in service with Communist forces into the 1960s.

▲ *These Lavochkin La-5FNs, operated by the 1st Czech Fighter Regiment, were photographed on September 11, 1944.*

▮ Letov Sm.1

CZECHOSLOVAKIA

The Sm.1 was the first aircraft produced by the Vojenská továrna na letadla Letov company —created from the former Czechoslovak Military Air Arsenal on November 1, 1918.

▲ *The S-1 and S-2 (pictured) were the first military aircraft to be wholly Czech designed and built.*

First flown in April 1920, it proved to be a robust design, armed with up to three machine guns and capable of carrying a reasonable bomb load. A variant with a Maybach engine, known as the S-2, was built by the Aero factory.

Ninety Sm.1 and S-2 aircraft were completed, and were the first military aircraft to be wholly designed and built in Czechoslovakia.

SPECIFICATION: **Type** light bomber • **Crew** 2 • **Powerplant** one 230hp Hiero L six-cylinder in-line engine • **Max speed** 120mph (194km/h) at 6,560ft (2,000m) • **Service ceiling** 19,685ft (6,000m) • **Max range** 445 miles (715km) • **Wingspan** 43ft 4in (13.20m) • **Length** 27ft 3in (8.30m) • **Height** 10ft 2in (3.10m) • **Weight** 2,987lb (1,355kg) empty • **Armament** two machine guns, 265lb (120kg) of bombs

▮ Lioré et Olivier LeO 20

FRANCE

First flown in 1926, the LeO 20 constituted the French night bomber force from 1927 to 1936, when it was replaced by the Bloch MB.200, although at the eve of war almost 100 aircraft were still in flying condition and used as target tugs or trainers. Typical of French bomber designs of the time, this large, ugly biplane was used for some interesting armament experiments, including the mounting of a 1.46-in (37-mm) cannon in the nose. The Armée de l'Air took delivery of 311 examples, the last in 1932; two were exported to Brazil and seven to Romania.

SPECIFICATION: **Type** night bomber • **Crew** 4 • **Powerplant** two 420hp Gnome-Rhone Jupiter 9 Ady 9-cylinder radials • **Max speed** 123mph (198km/h) • **Service ceiling** 18,865ft (5,750m) • **Max range** 620 miles (1,000km) • **Wingspan** 72ft 10in (22.20m) • **Length** 45ft 2in (13.77m) • **Height** 16ft 6in (5.05m) • **Weight** 12,037lb (5,460kg) loaded • **Armament** five 0.303-in (7.7-mm) machine guns, two each in nose and dorsal positions and one in ventral "trash can"; up to 1,102lb (500kg) of bombs internally and beneath fuselage and lower wings

▲ *Many LeO 20s went to the multi-engine training school of the Aéronautique Militaire at Etampes, as well as to front-line bomber units.*

▌Lioré et Olivier LeO 451

The first flight of the prototype LeO 45-01 on January 16, 1937 was followed by an initial order for 20 production LeO 451 medium bombers. In the following two years total orders reached 749, of which 449 were built before the armistice. The first unit to receive the new bomber was GB I/31. By May 10, 1940 110 LeO 451s were on Armée de l'Air charge, 59 of them operational. Seven groupes were equipped or partially equipped with the type during the Battle of France, in which about 130 LeO 451s were lost from all causes. At the armistice 183 LeO 451s remained in southern France and about 100 in North Africa. Like the Dewoitine D.520, the LeO 451 subsequently fought for and against the Allies, seeing action during the campaign in Syria (June 1941). Some

were used as transports and navigational trainers by the Luftwaffe, and at least one was employed by I/KG 200, the Luftwaffe's special duties unit.

SPECIFICATION: Type medium bomber • Crew 4 • Powerplant two 1,140hp Gnome-Rhone 14N-48/49 14-cylinder radials • Max speed 307mph (495km/h) • Service ceiling 29,530ft (9,000m) • Max range 1,429 miles (2,300km) • Wingspan 73ft 10in (22.52m) • Length 56ft 4in (17.17m) • Height 17ft 2in (5.24m) • Weights 5,820lb (2,640kg) empty; 17,229lb (7,815kg) loaded • Armament one 0.30-in (7.5-mm) machine gun in forward fuselage and one in ventral turret, and one 0.79-in (20-mm) cannon in dorsal turret; internal bomb load of 4,409lb (2,000kg)

▌Lockheed A-28 Hudson

The Lockheed Hudson was a military version of the Lockheed Model 14 twin-engined commercial airliner, one of the success stories of the late 1930s. The RAF placed an initial order for 200 aircraft, the first of which were delivered to No. 224 Squadron at Leuchars, Scotland, in May 1939. Lockheed supplied 350 Hudson Is and 20 Hudson IIs (the same as the Mk I except for different propellers) before introducing the Mk III, an improved version of the Mk I with 1,200hp Wright GR-1820-G205A Cyclone engines, ventral and beam gun positions. The RAF received 428 of this version, all purchased direct; subsequent aircraft, however, were supplied under Lend-Lease, the only other direct purchases being 309 Hudson Vs with 1,200hp Pratt & Whitney Twin Wasp engines. Lend-Lease aircraft included 382 Cyclone-engined Mk IIIAs, 30 Mk IVs and 450 Mk VIs with Twin Wasp engines.

In the North Atlantic, one of the Hudson's most famous actions occurred on August 27, 1941, when the German submarine U570 was attacked and damaged by an aircraft of No. 269 Squadron (Sqn. Ldr. J. Thompson) off Iceland. The Hudson circled the U-boat, which was unable to dive until its

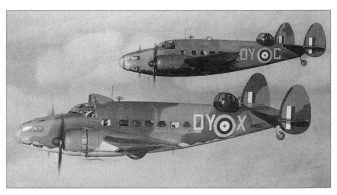

▲ Lockheed Hudsons of No. 48 Sqn, Coastal Command, pictured over the North Sea in 1942.

the PBO-1. On March 1, 1942, a PBO-1 Hudson of VP-82 (Ensign William Tepuni, USNR) attacked and sank the submarine U-656 southwest of Newfoundland; this was the first German U-boat sunk to US forces during World War II. In July 1942, a Hudson of the same squadron sank the U701 off the eastern coast of the United States. RAF Hudsons accounted for at least five U-boats in 1942–43, during the height of the Battle of the Atlantic.

Hudsons were also used for clandestine operations, landing parties of agents in France and bringing them out again. No. 161 (Special Duties) Squadron used several Hudsons in this capacity until the end of the war, latterly dropping supplies to agents in Germany itself. Three Hudsons were shot down on the night of March 20/21, 1945, possibly destroyed

in error by Allied night fighters. Hudsons were also used for similar missions over Burma by No. 357 (Special Duties) Squadron, which flew many successful sorties for comparatively small loss. The Hudsons operated mainly from Dum Dum, in India.

SPECIFICATION: Type maritime reconnaissance aircraft (data Hudson Mk.I) • Crew 6 • Powerplant two 1,100hp Wright GR-1820-G102A Cyclone radial engines • Max speed 222mph (357km/h) at sea level • Service ceiling 21,000ft (6,400m) • Max range 1,960 miles (3,154km) • Wingspan 65ft 6in (19.96m) • Length 44ft 3in (13.50m) • Height 10ft 10in (3.32m) • Weight 19,500lb (8,845kg) loaded • Armament two 0.303-in (7.7-mm) fixed forward-firing machine guns in upper part of forward fuselage, two 0.303-in (7.7-mm) machine guns in dorsal turret, two in beam positions, and one in ventral position; internal bomb load of 1,350lb (612kg)

▲ *Developed from the Lockheed Model 14 airliner, the A-28 Hudson proved very versatile as a military aircraft.*

Lockheed C-5A Galaxy

USA

The largest transportation aircraft in the world at the time of its appearance, the Lockheed C-5A Galaxy was first flown on June 30, 1968 and the first production aircraft was delivered to Military Airlift Command in December 1969. Although the Galaxy has provision for 270 troops on the lower deck and 75 on the upper, the lower deck is intended for freight and can accommodate complete tactical missile systems or

SPECIFICATION: Type heavy-lift strategic transportation • Crew 5 (plus up to 345 passengers) • Powerplant four 41,000-lb (18,642-kg) General Electric TF39 turbofans • Max speed 571mph (919km/h) • Service ceiling 34,000ft (10,360m) • Max range 3,749 miles (6,033km) with maximum payload • Wingspan 222ft 8in (68.88m) • Length 247ft 10in (75.54m) • Height 65ft 1in (19.85m) • Weight 769,000lb (348,810kg) • Armament none

▲ *This view of a Lockheed C-5A well illustrates the aircraft's massive cargo-carrying capacity, vital to the rapid deployment and resupply of US troops.*

M1 Abrams main battle tanks. Despite its large size the Galaxy can operate from rough airstrips. Eighty-one aircraft equipped four MAC squadrons. The C-5B is an improved version, with uprated engines, better avionics, and an extended-life wing. Total C-5A/C-5B production was 126 aircraft.

▌Lockheed Constellation/Super Constellation
USA

▲ *The Lockheed Constellation and its successor, the Super Constellation, brought about a revolution in long-range military air transport after WWII.*

The Lockheed C-69 Constellation was designed as a long-range military transport, but only 22 had been delivered by the end of World War II and it was in its commercial transport guise that the aircraft was to achieve fame. The "stretched" version, the L-1049 Super Constellation, proved to be an ideal platform for various military uses, from transportation to airborne early warning. The transport version was the C-121, while the WV-2 served with the US Navy as a high-altitude reconnaissance and early warning radar intelligence aircraft, carrying some five and a half tons of electronic equipment; the USAF's EC-121 variant served a similar purpose.

Between 1955–65 WV-2s and EC-121s carried out early warning coverage of the North Atlantic and Pacific and also carried out electronic intelligence missions; on April 14, 1969 an EC-121 was shot down by North Korean fighters over the Sea of Japan while carrying out one such surveillance mission, with the loss of all 31 crew members.

SPECIFICATION: Type long-range transportation (data C-69) • Crew 4 • Powerplant four 2,200hp Wright R-3350-35 radials • Max speed 327mph (526km/h) • Service ceiling 25,000ft (7,620m) • Max range 2,400 miles (3,860km) • Wingspan 123ft (37.49m) • Length 95ft 2in (29m) • Height 23ft 8in (7.21m) • Weight 72,500lb (32,860kg) loaded • Armament none

▌Lockheed C-130 Hercules
USA

Without doubt the most versatile tactical transportation aircraft ever built, the Lockheed C-130 Hercules flew for the first time on August 23, 1954. The Hercules has been in production for more than half a century, longer than any other aircraft type.

The initial production versions were the C-130A and -B, of which 461 were built, and these were followed by the major production variant, the C-130E, 510 of which were produced. Other versions include the AC-130E gunship, the WC-130E weather reconnaissance aircraft, the KC-130F assault transport for the USMC, the HC-130H for aerospace rescue and recovery, the C-130K for the RAF, and the LC-130R, which has wheel/ski landing gear. On order for the

▲ *The Lockheed Hercules, first flown in 1954, proved itself to be the most versatile tactical transport ever, and was also used in many other roles.*

USAF is a psychological warfare variant, the C-130J Commando Solo. Total production of the Hercules, all variants, was some 1,800 aircraft. As well as the US forces and the RAF, the Hercules was supplied to no fewer than 61 air forces around the world. The RAF is the second largest Hercules user, operating 80 aircraft (C.1s, C.3s, C.4s, and C.5s).

SPECIFICATION: Type tactical transport (data C-130E) • Crew 4 • Powerplant four 4,050hp Allison T56-A-7 turboprops • Max speed 340mph (547km/h) at 20,000ft (6,100m) • Service ceiling 33,000ft (10,060m) • Max range 3,820 miles (6,145km) • Wingspan 132ft 7in (40.41m) • Length 97ft 9in (29.79m) • Height 38ft 4in (11.68m) • Weight 155,000lb (70,308kg) loaded • Armament none

▌Lockheed C-141 StarLifter

USA

First flown on December 17, 1963, the C-141A StarLifter was designed to provide the USAF Military Air Transport Service with a high-speed global airlift and strategic deployment capability. Deliveries to the USAF began in April 1965 and the aircraft ultimately equipped 13 squadrons of Military Airlift Command, 277 being built. Starting in 1976, all surviving C-141A aircraft were upgraded to C-141B standard, the fuselage being stretched by 23ft 4in (7.11m).

SPECIFICATION: Type heavy-lift strategic transport (data C-141A) • Crew 4 • Powerplant four 21,000-lb (9,526-kg) thrust Pratt & Whitney TF33-7 turbofans • Max speed 567mph (912km/h) at altitude • Service ceiling 42,000ft (12,800m) • Max range 6,445 miles (10,370km) • Wingspan 159ft 11in (48.74m) • Length 168ft 3in (51.29m) • Height 39ft 3in (11.96m) • Weight 343,000lb (155,582kg) • Armament none

▲ In C-141A form the StarLifter was handicapped by its limited cabin volume, but nevertheless proved a highly capable airlifter.

▌Lockheed Martin F-22 Raptor

USA

Without doubt, the most exciting combat aircraft of the early 21st century is the Lockheed Martin F-22 Raptor. In the late 1970s, the USAF identified a requirement for 750 examples of an Advanced Tactical Fighter (ATF) to replace the F-15 Eagle. The goal was to produce a tactical aircraft that would remain viable for at least the first quarter of the 21st century; an aircraft that would have a range 50–100 percent greater than that of the F-15, be capable of short takeoff and landing on damaged airfields, and be able to engage multiple targets at once, beyond visual range. It had to incorporate stealth technology and supercruise (supersonic cruise without afterburning) and, operated by a single pilot, it must be able to survive in an environment filled with people, both in the air and on the ground, whose sole

▼ The Lockheed Martin F-22 Raptor was originally known as the USAF's Advanced Tactical Fighter.

purpose was to destroy it. To test the concepts that would eventually be combined in the ATF, the USAF initiated a series of parallel research programs. The first was the YF-16 control-configured vehicle (CCV) which flew in 1976–7 and demonstrated the decoupled control of aircraft flight path and attitude; in other words the machine could skid sideways, turn without banking, climb or descend without changing its attitude, and point its nose left or right or up or down without changing its flight path. Other test vehicles involved in the ATF program included the Grumman X-29, which flew for the first time in December 1984 and which was designed to investigate forward-sweep technology, and an F-111 fitted with a mission adaptive wing (MAW)—in other words, a wing capable of reconfiguring itself automatically to mission requirements. Flight testing of all these experimental aircraft came under the umbrella of the USAF's Advanced Fighter Technology Integration (AFTI) program. In September 1983, while the AFTI program was well under way, the USAF awarded ATF concept definition study contracts to six American aerospace companies, and of these two—Lockheed and Northrop—were selected to build demonstrator prototypes of their respective proposals. Each produced two prototypes, the Lockheed YF-22 and Northrop YF-23, and all four aircraft flew in 1990. Two different powerplants, the Pratt & Whitney YF119 and the General Electric YF120, were evaluated, and in April 1991 it was announced that the F-22 and F119 was the winning combination. The F119 advanced technology engine, two of which power the F-22, develops 35,000lb (15,872kg) and is fitted with two-dimensional convergent/divergent exhaust nozzles with thrust vectoring for enhanced performance and maneuverability.

The F-22 combines many stealth features. Its air-to-air weapons, for example, are stored internally; three internal bays house advanced short-range, medium-range, and beyond visual range air-to-air missiles. Following an assessment of the aircraft's combat role in 1993, it was decided to add a ground attack capability, and the internal weapons bay can also accommodate 1,000-lb (454-kg) GBU-32 precision guided missiles. The F-22 is designed for a high sortie rate, with a turnround time of less than 20 minutes, and its avionics are highly integrated to provide rapid reaction in air combat, much of its survivability depending on the pilot's ability to locate a target very early and kill it with a first shot. The

F-22 was designed to meet a specific threat, which at that time was presented by large numbers of highly agile Soviet combat aircraft, its task being to engage them in their own airspace with beyond visual range weaponry. The USAF requirement is for 438 aircraft.

▲ *The Lockheed Martin F-22 Raptor was the most exciting combat aircraft to be developed in the later years of the 20th century, but at vast expense.*

SPECIFICATION: **Type** air superiority fighter • **Crew** 1 • **Powerplant** two Pratt & Whitney F119-P-100 turbofans • **Max speed** 1,450mph (2,335km/h) at altitude • **Service ceiling** 65,000ft (19,812m) • **Combat radius** 800 miles (1,285km) • **Wingspan** 43ft (13.10m) • **Length** 64ft 2in (19.55m) • **Height** 17ft 8in (5.39m) • **Weight** 60,000lb (27,216kg) • **Armament** AIM-9X and AMRAAM AAMS; GBU-32 Joint Direct Attack Munition and other advanced weapons

▌Lockheed F-80 Shooting Star   USA

America's first fully operational jet fighter was the Lockheed P-80 Shooting Star, which like its British counterparts was of very conventional design and which was to become the workhorse of the American tactical fighter-bomber and fighter-interceptor squadrons for five years after World War II. The prototype XP-80 was designed around a de Havilland H-1 turbojet which was supplied to the United States in July 1943 and the aircraft was completed in just 143 days, making its first flight on January 9, 1944. In April 1945 two YP-80s

were sent to England, where they were attached to the Eighth Air Force, and two more went to Italy, but none experienced any operational flying in Europe before the war's end. Early production P-80As entered USAAF service late in 1945 with the 412th Fighter Group, which became the 1st Fighter Group in July 1946 and comprised the 27th, 71st, and 94th Fighter Squadrons. The P-80A was replaced by the P-80B in 1947; the major production version was the F-80C (the P for "pursuit" prefix having changed to the much more logical F for "fighter" in the meantime). The F-80C was the fighter-bomber workhorse of the Korean War, flying 15,000 sorties in the first four months alone, and aircraft of the 51st Fighter Wing took part in history's jet-versus-jet battle on November 7, 1950, shooting down a MiG-15. Total production of the Shooting Star was 1718, many being later converted to target drones.

SPECIFICATION: **Type** fighter-bomber (data F-80C-5) • **Crew** 1 • **Powerplant** one 5,400-lb (2,449-kg) thrust Allison J33-A-35 turbojet • **Max speed** 600mph (966km/h) at sea level • **Service ceiling** 46,800ft (14,265m) • **Max range** 825 miles (1,328km) • **Wingspan** 38ft 9in (11.81m) • **Length** 34ft 5in (10.49m) • **Height** 11ft 3in (3.43m) • **Weight** 16,856lb (7,646kg) • **Armament** six 0.50-in (12.7-mm) machine guns, plus two 1,000-lb (454-kg) bombs and eight rockets

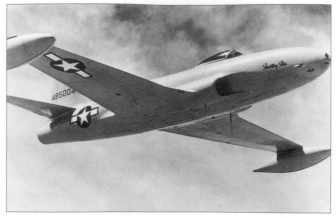

▲ Originally intended as an interceptor, the Lockheed Shooting Star, America's first operational jet, proved its worth in the Korean War.

∎ Lockheed F-94 Starfire

USA

The Lockheed F-94 Starfire was developed from the T-33A trainer, two production T-33 airframes being converted as YF-94s. The first of these flew on April 16, 1949, and four months later the USAF placed contracts for 17 F-94A-1-LO and 92 F-94A5-LO fighters, together with one YF-94B—the latter having centrally mounted wingtip tanks instead of underslung tanks.

The F-94A, which incorporated 75 percent of the components used in the T-33 and F-80 Shooting Star, had 940lb (426kg) of radar equipment in the nose and an armament of four 0.50-in (12.7-mm) Colt-Browning machine guns. The aircraft was powered by an Allison J33-A-33 centrifugal-type turbojet with reheat. The F-94A went into production in 1949; 200 were built, the first entering service in June 1950 with the 319th All-Weather Fighter Squadron.

SPECIFICATION: **Type** all-weather interceptor (data F-94A) • **Crew** 2 • **Powerplant** one 6,000-lb (2,742-kg) thrust Allison J33-A-33 turbojet • **Max speed** 580mph (933km/h) at 30,000ft (9,150m) • **Service ceiling** 48,000ft (14,630m) • **Max range** 1,150 miles (1,850km) • **Wingspan** 38ft 10in (11.85m) not including tip tanks • **Length** 40ft 1in (12.20m) • **Height** 12ft 8in (3.86m) • **Weight** 15,710lb (7,125kg) • **Armament** four 0.50-in (12.7-mm) machine guns

The YF-94B was converted from the 19th F-94A in 1950, and 357 F-94Bs were built. Apart from the revised wingtip tanks, they differed from the F-94A mainly in having a modified hydraulics system and avionics, including a Sperry Zero-Reader flight recorder. The next variant, the F-94C, differed so extensively from its predecessors that it was originally known as the YF-97A. This designation remained in force from the aircraft's maiden flight on January 16, 1950 until September 12th that year, when the designation YF-94C was officially adopted.

The F-94C was fitted with an afterburning Pratt & Whitney J48P-5, and other changes included an increase in wing dihedral and a reduction in thickness/chord ratio from 13 to 10 percent, the introduction of a swept tailplane, and the replacement of the gun armament by 24 unguided FFAR in a ring of tubes around the nose cone. Later, provision was made for a further 24 rockets in wing pods. The F-94C carried 1,200lb (543kg) of electronics, and two 1,000-lb (454-kg) thrust RATOG (rocket assisted takeoff gear) packs could be fitted under the fuselage. Total production of the F-94C came to 387 aircraft before the series was completed in 1954.

◀ Strictly speaking the F-94C was the only variant named Starfire. In this view the F-94C's swept tailplane, FFAR pods and tip tanks are clearly evident.

∎ Lockheed F-104 Starfighter

▲ *Photographed in the early 1960s, this pair of Fiat-built F-104Gs belongs to the 9º Gruppo/4º Stormo, the first Italian Starfighter user.*

SPECIFICATION: Type multimission strike fighter (data F-104G) • Crew 1 • Powerplant one 15,600-lb (7,076-kg) thrust General Electric J79-GE-11A turbojet • Max speed 1,146mph (1,845km/h) at 50,000ft (15,240m) • Service ceiling 50,000ft (15,240m) • Max range 1,081 miles (1,740km) • Wingspan 21ft 9in (6.62m) • Length 54ft 8in (16.66m) • Height 13ft 5in (4.09m) • Weight 29,035lb (13,170kg) • Armament one 0.79-in (20-mm) General Electric M61A1 cannon; Sidewinder AAMs on wing or fuselage stations; up to 4,000lb (1,814kg) of ordnance, including Bullpup ASMs

Development of the F-104 was begun in 1951, when the lessons of the Korean air war were starting to bring about profound changes in combat aircraft design. A contract for two XF-104 prototypes was placed in 1953 and the first of these flew on February 7, 1954, only 11 months later. The two XF-104s were followed by 15 YF-104s for USAF evaluation, most of these, like the prototypes, being powered by the Wright J65-W-6 turbojet. The aircraft was ordered into production as the F-104A, deliveries to the USAF Air Defense Command beginning in January 1958. Because of its lack of all-weather capability the F-104A saw only limited service with Air Defense Command, equipping only two fighter squadrons. F-104As were also supplied to Nationalist China and Pakistan, and saw combat during the Indo-Pakistan conflict of 1969.

The F-104B was a two-seat version, and the F-104C was a tactical fighter-bomber, the first of 77 examples being delivered to the 479th Tactical Fighter Wing (the only unit to use it) in October 1958. Two more two-seat Starfighters, the F-104D and F-104F, were followed by the F-104G, which was numerically the most important variant. A single-seat multimission aircraft based on the F-104C, the F-104G had a strengthened structure and many equipment changes. The first F-104G flew on October 5, 1960 and 1,266 examples were produced up to February 1966, 977 by the European Starfighter Consortium and the remainder by Lockheed. Of these, the Luftwaffe received 750, the Italian Air Force 154, the Royal Netherlands Air Force 120, and the Belgian Air Force 99. The basically similar CF-104 was a strike-reconnaissance aircraft, 200 of which were built by Canadair for the RCAF. Canadair also built 110 more F-104Gs for delivery to the air forces of Norway, Nationalist China, Spain, Denmark, Greece, and Turkey. Also similar to the F-104G was the F-104J for the Japan Air Self-Defense Force; the first one flew on 30 June 1961 and 207 were produced by Mitsubishi. The F-104S was an interceptor development of the F-104G, with provision for external stores, and was capable of Mach 2.4; 165 were license-built in Italy.

▲ *Lockheed F-104 Starfighters of the Italian Air Force, one of the last NATO air arms to operate the type in first-line service.*

❚ Lockheed F-117A Night Hawk

USA

SPECIFICATION: Type stealth interdictor • Crew 1 • Powerplant two 10,800-lb (4,899-kg) thrust General Electric F404-GE-F1D2 turbofans • Max speed 0.92M at altitude • Service ceiling classified • Max range classified • Wingspan 43ft 4in (13.20m) • Length 65ft 11in (20.08m) • Height 12ft 5in (3.78m) • Weight 52,500lb (23,814kg) • Armament provision for 5,000lb (2,268kg) of stores on rotary dispenser in weapons bay, including the AGM-88 HARM antiradiation missile, AGM-65 Maverick ASM, GBU-19, and GBU-27 optronically guided bomb, BLU-109 laser-guided bombs, and B61 free-fall nuclear bomb

▲ *The Lockheed F-117A, seen here on a test flight, uses many different design features and materials to achieve "stealth" capability. It has proved highly effective in action.*

Under development since 1978, the F-117A "stealth" strike aircraft made its first flight in June 1981 and entered service in October 1983. The F-117A is a single-seat, subsonic aircraft powered by two nonafterburning GE F404 turbofans with shielded slot exhausts designed to dissipate heat emissions (aided also by heat-shielding tiles), thus minimizing the infrared signature. The use of faceting (angled flat surfaces) scatters incoming radar energy; radar-absorbent materials and transparencies treated with conductive coating reduce the F-117A's radar signature still further. Armament is carried on swing-down trapezes in two internal bays. The F-117A has quadruple redundant fly-by-wire controls, steerable turrets for FLIR and laser designator, head-up and head-down displays, laser communications, and nav/attack system integrated with a digital avionics suite.

F-117As of the 37th Tactical Fighter Wing played a prominent part in the 1991 Gulf War, making first strikes on high priority targets; since then they have been used in the Balkans and Afghanistan. The last of 59 F-117As was delivered in July 1990.

▲ *The F-117 was cloaked in secrecy for years, and there was much speculation about its appearance – which was more bizarre than anything conjectured.*

▌Lockheed PV-1 Ventura/PV-2 Harpoon

USA

Produced originally to meet a British requirement for a Hudson and Blenheim successor, the PV-1 Ventura was a development of Lockheed's Model 18 Lodestar. The first Ventura Mk Is were delivered to No. 2 Group of RAF Bomber Command (188 aircraft) in October 1942, but suffered heavy losses in the daylight bombing role and were reassigned to Coastal Command. Other orders included 487 Ventura Mk IIs (235 of which were repossessed by the US) and 387 Ventura Mk.Vs. The Ventura served with all the British Commonwealth air forces, the Free French Air Force, and the

Brazilian Air Force. The repossessed Lend-Lease aircraft were pressed into US service as the B-34 Lexington bomber, and as bombing, gunnery, and navigational trainers. The principal version was the PV-1 patrol bomber for the US Navy; 1,800 were built, including the 387 transferred to the RAF as Ventura GR.5s. The PV-1 was used mostly in the Pacific theater, where it operated alongside a progressive development, the PV-2 Harpoon. The Harpoon featured redesigned wings of greater span, a new tail assembly, and had an increased range and payload. The USN took delivery of 535 Harpoons.

▶ *The Lockheed PV-2 Harpoon was a progressive development of the PV-1 Ventura, and was widely used in the Pacific theater.*

SPECIFICATION: **Type** maritime patrol bomber (data PV-1) • **Crew** 5 • **Powerplant** two 2,000hp Pratt & Whitney R-2800-31 Double Wasp 18-cylinder radials • **Max speed** 322mph (518km/h) at sea level • **Service ceiling** 26,300ft (8,015m) • **Max range** 1,660 miles (2,671km) • **Wingspan** 65ft 6in (19.96m) • **Length** 51ft 9in (15.77m) • **Height** 11ft 11in (3.63m) • **Weight** 34,000lb (15,422kg) • **Armament** two 0.50-in (12.7-mm) machine guns in upper forward fuselage, or three in under-nose gun pack; two in dorsal turret; and two 0.303-in (7.7-mm) machine guns in ventral position. Bomb load of up to 5,000lb (2,268kg)

▌Lockheed P2V Neptune

USA

The first land-based aircraft designed specifically for the long-range maritime reconnaissance role, the Lockheed Neptune was destined to be one of the longest-serving military aircraft ever built. The first of two XP2V-1 prototypes

flew on May 17, 1945, orders already having been placed for 15 preproduction and 151 production P2V-1s. Deliveries to the US Navy began in March 1947. The aircraft proved highly effective in its role and was used extensively in United

▲ *The RCAF's Lockheed P2V-7s were the only examples built without J34 booster jets, though these were retrofitted later.*

SPECIFICATION: Type long-range maritime patrol aircraft (data P2V-7) • Crew 10 • Powerplant 3,500hp R-3350-32W piston engines and two 3,400-lb (1,542kg) thrust Westinghouse K34-WE-36 auxiliary turbojets • Max speed 345mph (555km/h) • Service ceiling 22,000ft (6,700m) • Max range 2,200 miles (3,540km) • Wingspan 103ft 10in (31.65m) • Length 91ft 4in (27.83m) • Height 29ft 4in (8.94m) • Weight 75,000lb (34,246kg) loaded • Armament full range of maritime offensive stores internally; provision for air-to-surface missiles on underwing racks

States operations in Southeast Asia.

The P2V-2, which first flew in 1947, had a longer nose housing extra search radar equipment and a battery of six 0.79-in (20-mm) cannon, as well as uprated engines. Next variant was the P2V-3; 83 were built, including 30 P2V-3W early warning aircraft. Another engine change produced the P2V-4, which carried underwing fuel tanks. The P2V-5 Neptune, which flew in December 1950, was the first to be fitted with MAD equipment in an extended tail cone in place of the tail gun turret and was also the first variant to be supplied to foreign air arms, 36 P2V-5Fs being supplied to the RAF as Neptune MR.1s. The P2V-5F was fitted with two Westinghouse J34-WE-36 turbojets in underwing pods outboard of the main engine nacelles.

The P2V-6 (P2F) Neptune had a minelaying capability in addition to its ASW role; 83 were delivered to the US Navy and 12 to France's Aéronavale. The last production version was the P2V-7 (P2H), which, in addition to being delivered to the RCAF, RAAF, RNethAF, and Aéronavale, was built under license in Japan (48 aircraft). Excluding the Japanese-built aircraft, total Neptune production was 1,099, of which 838 went to the US Navy.

▌Lockheed P-3 Orion

USA

A development of the Lockheed Electra airliner, the P-3 (formerly P3V-1) Orion was Lockheed's winning submission in a 1958 US Navy contest for a new off-the-shelf ASW aircraft that could be brought into service very rapidly by modifying an existing type. The first of two YP3V-1 prototypes flew on August 19, 1958 and deliveries of production P-3As began in August 1962. The WP-3A was a weather reconnaissance version, the next patrol variant being the P-3A. Total P-3A/B production ran to 286 aircraft for the US Navy, plus five for the RNZAF, ten for the RAAF, and five for Norway. The P-3C, which appeared in 1969, was equipped with a Univac digital computer, the nerve center of a fully integrated search, analysis, and attack system. Further improvements were incorporated in 1974–75, and in addition to the 132 P-3Cs delivered to the USN, 10 aircraft were ordered by the RAF. Further variants of the Orion include the EP-3A electronic intelligence aircraft, the P-3F, six of which were delivered to the Imperial Iranian Air Force in 1975, and the CP-140 Aurora for the Canadian Armed Forces. The Orion was built under license in Japan (100 aircraft), and also serves with the Republic of Korea (8), the Netherlands (13), Pakistan (3), Portugal (6), and Spain (7). In US Navy service, the type has been continually upgraded.

▲ *No. 92 Wing of the RAAF maintains two operational squadrons and one training squadron of P-3Cs at RAAF Edinburgh.*

SPECIFICATION: Type long-range maritime patrol aircraft (data P-3C) • Crew 10 • Powerplant four 4,910hp Allison T56-A-14 turboprops • Max speed 473mph (761km/h) at 15,600ft (4,750m) • Service ceiling 28,300ft (8,625m) • Max range 2,383 miles (3,835km) • Wingspan 99ft 8in (30.37m) • Length 116ft 10in (35.61m) • Height 33ft 8in (10.29m) • Weight 135,000lb (61,235kg) loaded • Armament up to 19,250lb (8,735kg) of ASW stores

▌Lockheed P-38 Lightning

USA

Although it tended to be overshadowed by the Republic P-47 Thunderbolt and the North American P-51 Mustang, the Lockheed P-38 Lightning was a very effective long-range tactical fighter and played a vital part in winning air superiority for the Allies, particularly in the Pacific theater. Distinctive with its twin tail booms, the P-38 was designed to meet the exacting requirements of a 1937 USAAC specification, calling for a high-altitude interceptor capable of 360mph

SPECIFICATION: Type fighter-bomber (data P-38J) • Crew 1 • Powerplant two 1,425hp Allison V-1710-91 12-cylinder V-type • Max speed 414mph (666km/h) at 25,000ft (7,620m) • Service ceiling 44,000ft (13,400m) • Max range 2,240 miles (3,600km) • Wingspan 52ft (15.85m) • Length 37ft 10in (11.53m) • Height 9ft 10in (2.99m) • Weight 21,600lb (9,798kg) loaded • Armament one 0.79-in (20-mm) cannon and four 0.50-in (12.7-mm) machine guns in the nose; external bomb and rocket load of 4,000lb (1,814kg)

▲ A P-38J Lightning in the colors of the 55th Fighter Squadron, 20th Fighter Group, seen in 1992 after restoration, a process that took six years.

(580km/h) at 20,000ft (6,100m) and 290mph (467km/h) at sea level and of reaching optimum altitude at sea level. The sole XP-38 prototype flew on January 27, 1939 and was followed by 13 YP-38 evaluation aircraft with more powerful V-1710 engines and a nose armament of four machine guns and a 1.46-in (37-mm) cannon. An initial production batch of 30 P-38s was built, these being delivered from the summer of 1941; the next production model was the P-38D, 36 of which were produced. In November 1941 the P-38E appeared, with a more powerful armament; the RAF had by now taken an interest in the P-38 (in fact, it was the RAF who bestowed the name Lightning on the type) and ordered 143 P-38Es as the Lightning Mk.I, but after evaluating three of them the order was canceled, mainly because the Americans would not release aircraft with supercharged engines. The P-38F, appearing early in 1943, was the first variant to be used in large numbers, operating in Europe starting in the summer of 1942 and in North Africa from November; 527 were built. This was followed by the P-38G (1,082) and P-

38H (601), these variants featuring either armament or engine changes. The P-38G, of which 2,970 were produced, was one of the most widely used models; the RAF placed an order for 524 as the Lightning Mk.II, but this was subsequently canceled and the aircraft were taken over by the USAAF for its own use. The largest production quantity was achieved with the P-38L (3,923 built), which like the J was equipped with a glazed nose and used as a bomber. The last version was the P-38M, a two-seat variant designed as a night fighter and equipped with radar. Total Lightning production was 9,923, of which more than 1,000 were converted into photoreconnaissance aircraft as F-4s and F-5s. The P-38 carried out many notable missions during World War II, perhaps the most famous being the shooting down, in April 1943, of a G4M Betty bomber carrying the Japanese Naval C-in-C, Admiral Isoroku Yamamoto.

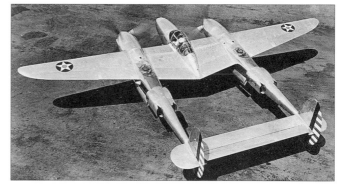
▲ First flown by Lieutenant B. S. Kelsey at March Field on January 27, 1939, the prototype XP-38 promised to be an outstanding fighter from the outset.

▮ Lockheed SR-71A

USA

The fastest air-breathing aircraft ever built, the Lockheed

SPECIFICATION: Type strategic reconnaissance aircraft • Crew 2 • Powerplant two 32,500-lb (14,742-kg) Pratt & Whitney JT11D-20B turbojets • Max speed 2,000mph (3,220km/h) at 80,000ft (24,385m) • Service ceiling 80,000ft (24,385m) • Max range 2,983 miles (4,800km) • Wingspan 55ft 7in (16.94m) • Length 107ft 5in (32.74m) • Height 18ft 6in (5.64m) • Weight 170,000lb (77,111kg) loaded • Armament none

SR-71A was developed from the YF-12A experimental aircraft, which in turn was derived from the A-11 strategic interceptor. The latter appeared as a prototype on April 26, 1962 and seven evaluation and development aircraft were built. The SR-71A flew for the first time on December 22, 1964 and 20 aircraft were built, deliveries beginning to the 4,200th Strategic Reconnaissance Wing in January 1966. The SR-71A's main operating unit was the 9th SRW, which deployed detachments of SR-71As worldwide, as required.

▲ *The advanced technology employed in the Lockheed SR-71A provided the US intelligence services with vital information throughout much of the Cold War era.*

▌Lockheed S-3A Viking

USA

▶ *The Lockheed S-3A Viking was the US Navy's first fully computerized anti-submarine warfare system.*

SPECIFICATION: Type carrier-borne ASV aircraft (data S-3A) • Crew 4 • Powerplant two 9,275-lb (4,207-kg) General Electric TF34-GE-2 turbofans • Max speed 506mph (814km/h) at sea level • Service ceiling 35,000ft (10,670m) • Max range 2,302 miles (3,705km) • Wingspan 68ft 8in (20.93m) • Length 53ft 4in (16.26m) • Height 22ft 9in (6.93m) • Weight 42,500lb (19,278kg) loaded • Armament internal weapons bay with provision for up to 2,000lb (907kg) of ASW stores; two underwing pylons for bombs, rockets, missiles etc.

The Lockheed S-3A Viking was designed in response to a 1969 US Navy requirement for a carrier-borne ASW system built around what was at the time a highly advanced piece of technology, the Univac digital computer. The prototype flew for the first time on January 21, 1972, and 93 production S-3As had been ordered by the end of 1973, deliveries beginning to VS-41, an operational training unit, in March 1974. The last of 187 Vikings was delivered to the USN in 1978. The Viking fleet was substantially updated to S-3B standard in the early 1990s, some aircraft being converted to the electronic warfare role as ES-3As.

▌Lockheed T-33/T-1A

The most widely used advanced trainer in the world, the Lockheed T-33 flew in 1948 and was developed from the F-80C Shooting Star airframe. It is estimated that some 90 percent of the West's military jet pilots trained on the T-33 during the 1950s and 1960s. T-33 production totaled 5,691 in the US alone, and many others were built under license in Canada and Japan. A version adapted to carry underwing offensive stores was offered to small air arms in the counter-insurgency role. About 700 T-2Vs were built for the US Navy/USMC, this variant being redesignated T-1A.

▶ *Never a "star" performer, the T-33 nevertheless carved its place in aviation history by virtue of its longevity and versatility.*

SPECIFICATION: **Type** jet trainer (data T-33A) • **Crew** 2 • **Powerplant** one 5,400-lb (2,449-kg) Allison J33-A-35 turbojet • **Max speed** 546mph (879km/h) at 25,000ft (7,620m) • **Service ceiling** 48,000ft (14,630m) • **Endurance** 3hrs 7mins • **Wingspan** 38ft 10in (11.85m) • **Length** 37ft 10in (11.51m) • **Height** 11ft 8in (3.56m) • **Weight** 14,442lb (6,551kg) loaded • **Armament** two 0.50-in (12.7-mm) machine guns

▌Lockheed TriStar K.Mk.I

The TriStar K.Mk.I is a tanker/passenger conversion of the well-known Lockheed airliner, operated by the Royal Air Force. Six series 500 aircraft were acquired from British Airways in the early 1980s and converted by Marshall of Cambridge for inflight refueling operations. Four retained passenger accommodation, these being designated K.Mk.I; the other two were configured as freighters and are designated KC.Mk.I. Three more were later acquired from Pan American in 1984/85 and are used as dedicated passenger transports (260 passengers) as C.Mk.2s.

SPECIFICATION: **Type** strategic transportation and flight refueling tanker (data K.Mk.I) • **Crew** 4 (plus 204 passengers) • **Powerplant** three 50,000-lb (22,680-kg) thrust Rolls-Royce RB-211-524B turbofans • **Max speed** 599mph (964km/h) at 35,000ft (10,670m) • **Service ceiling** 43,000ft (13,105m) • **Max range** 4,836 miles (7,783km) • **Wingspan** 164ft 4in (50.09m) • **Length** 164ft 2in (50.05m) • **Height** 55ft 4in (16.87m) • **Weight** 540,000lb (244,944kg) • **Armament** none

▲ *The Lockheed TriStar brought a new dimension to the RAF's long-range transport capability, filling a requirement stemming from the Falklands War.*

▌Lockheed U-2

Probably the most controversial and politically explosive aircraft of all time, the Lockheed U-2 originated in an urgent USAF requirement for a high-level, deep-penetration reconnaissance aircraft, the Korean War having shown that existing types had a low survival factor in hostile airspace. Essentially a glider powered by a jet engine, the U-2 made its

SPECIFICATION: **Type** high-altitude reconnaissance aircraft (data U-2R) • **Crew** 1 • **Powerplant** one 17,000-lb (7,711-kg) thrust Pratt & Whitney J75 P-13B turbojet • **Max speed** 495mph (796km/h) at 40,000ft (12,200m) • **Service ceiling** 90,000ft (27,430m) • **Max range** 2,600 miles (4,183km) with auxiliary tanks • **Wingspan** 103ft (31.39m) • **Length** 62ft 9in (19.13m) • **Height** 16ft (4.88m) • **Weight** 41,300lb (18,733kg) loaded • **Armament** none

first flight in August 1955, an order for 52 production aircraft following quickly. Overflights of the USSR and Warsaw Pact territories began in 1956, and continued until May 1, 1960, when a Central Intelligence Agency pilot, Francis G. Powers, was shot down near Sverdlovsk by a Soviet SA-2 missile battery. U-2s were used to overfly Cuba during the missile crisis of 1962, one being shot down, and the type was also used by the Chinese Nationalists to overfly mainland China, all four aircraft being subsequently lost. U-2s also operated over North Vietnam in 1965–66. The last U-2 variant was the U-2R, but in 1978 the production line was reopened for the building of 29 TR-1A battlefield surveillance aircraft, developed from the U-2R. All TR-1As were redesignated U-2R in the 1990s.

▲ The Lockheed U-2's overflights of the USSR ended on May 1, 1960 when one was shot down, but the type remains a viable reconnaissance system.

▌LTV (Vought) F-8 Crusader

USA

The first carrier-borne fighter capable of supersonic speed in level flight, the Crusader was the winner of a May 1953 US Navy competition for a new day fighter. The prototype XF8U-1 flew on March 25, 1955 and exceeded Mach One on its maiden flight, powered by a Pratt & Whitney J57 engine. The first production F8U-1 flew on September 30, 1955, and completed carrier trials in April 1956. The type was accepted into service as the F8U-1 in the following December, only 21 months after the prototype flew. Production of the F8U-1 (later F-8A) ended in 1958, by which time 218 had been built. The F8U1 was followed in September 1958 by the F8U-1E (F-8B). This version of which 130 were built, had a larger nose radome and limited all-weather capability. Meanwhile, a reconnaissance version, the F8U-1P (RF-8A), had flown in December 1956. This variant was capable of both day and night reconnaisance and was used extensively for surveillance during the Cuban crisis of 1962 and its aftermath. Of the 144 built, 53 were modernized in 1965–66 and redesig-

▲ An RF-8A Crusader of Light Photographic Squadron VFP-63 fires a salvo of high-velocity rockets over a US Navy range.

nated RF-8G; these were used for fast low-level reconnaissance over Vietnam. The F8U-2 (F-8C) was an improved version of the F-8A with a J57-P-16 turbojet, and flew in December 1967. Externally similar to the F-8A, it carried four Sidewinder AAMs as well as its cannon armament and had an improved fire control system. It entered service in April 1959 with VF-84, and 187 were built; 87 were later refurbished and designated F-8K. The F8U-2N (F-8D) Crusader, which first flew in February 1960, had an all-weather capability and was powered by a J57-P20 turbojet with reheat, giving it a maximum speed approaching Mach 2.0. This variant had no HVAR rocket belly pack, but retained its 0.79-in (20-mm) gun armament and four Sidewinders. Deliveries to the US Navy and Marine Corps were completed in January 1962 after 152 had been built; 89 were later refurbished, given an attack capability and designated F-8H. The last Crusader variant to carry the old US Service nomenclature was the F8U-2NE (F-8E), which was

basically similar to the F-8D but with more advanced search and fire control radar equipment. The F-8E was the first Crusader to be developed for the strike role, being fitted with underwing pylons to carry a wide variety of offensive loads. Over 250 F-8Es were built, and 136 were refurbished under the designation F-8J. The F-8E(FN) was a version for the French Navy; 42 were ordered in August 1963 and the last aircraft was delivered in January 1965, this being the final new Crusader to be built.

SPECIFICATION: Type carrier-borne fighter (data F-8E) • Crew 1 • Powerplant one 18,000-lb (8,165-kg) thrust Pratt & Whitney J57 P-20 turbojet • Max speed 1,120mph (1,800km/h) at 40,000ft (12,192m) • Service ceiling 60,000ft (17,983m) • Combat radius 600 miles (966km) at altitude • Wingspan 35ft 2in (10.72m) • Length 16.61m (54ft 6in) • Height 15ft 9in (4.80m) • Weight 34,000lb (15,422kg) loaded • Armament four 0.79-in (20-mm) Colt Mk 12 cannon; various underwing combinations of rockets, bombs, and ASMs

▌LTV (Vought) A-7 Corsair II   USA

Based on the design of the F-8 Crusader, but in reality a completely different aircraft, the Corsair II flew for the first time on September 27, 1965, and several versions were subsequently produced for the US Navy and USAF by the Vought Corporation, a subsidiary of Ling-Temco-Vought. The first attack variant was the A-7A, which made its combat debut in the Gulf of Tonkin in October 1966; 199 A-7As were delivered before production switched to the A-7B, which had an uprated engine. The USN took delivery of 198 examples. The next variant was the A-7D tactical fighter for the USAF,

▲ The A-7 Corsair II saw much action during the Vietnam War, and was also used in the April 1986 strikes on targets in Libya.

SPECIFICATION: Type attack aircraft (data A-7D) • Crew 1 • Powerplant one 14,250-lb (6,465-kg) thrust Allison TF41-1 (Rolls Royce Spey) turbofan • Max speed 698mph (1,123km/h) at sea level • Service ceiling 51,000ft (15,545m) • Max range 700 miles (1,127km) • Wingspan 38ft 9in (11.80m) • Length 46ft 1in (14.06m) • Height 16ft (4.90m) • Weight 42,000lb (19,050kg) • Armament one 0.79-in (20-mm) M61 Vulcan cannon; provision for up to 15,000lb (6,804kg) of external stores

which went into action in Vietnam in October 1972; 459 were built, many being allocated to Air National Guard units. Also deployed to Southeast Asia was the A-7E, a close support/interdiction variant developed for the US Navy. By the end of the conflict in Vietnam, A-7s had flown more than 100,000 combat missions. Corsair IIs were also operated by the Hellenic, Portuguese, and Thai air forces.

■ Loire 46

The Loire 43–46 series of single-seat fighters was designed at Saint Nazaire by the aircraft division of the shipbuilding firm Ateliers et Chantiers de la Loire. The last of the line, the Loire 46, flew for the first time on September 1, 1934, powered by a Gnome-Rhone 14Kes engine, and began official trials in January 1935. In the following month the Loire 46 was reengined with a Gnome-Rhone 14Kfs, and shortly afterward 60 production aircraft were ordered for the Armée de l'Air, the first of these flying in February 1936.

Deliveries began in the fall to the 6e Escadre, which operated the type until it received Morane-Saulnier MS.406 fighters in December 1938. The surviving Loire 46s were used as gunnery trainers. Four aircraft were delivered secretly to the Republican Air Arm during the Spanish Civil War (1936–39), but within a few months two had been lost in accidents and two shot down.

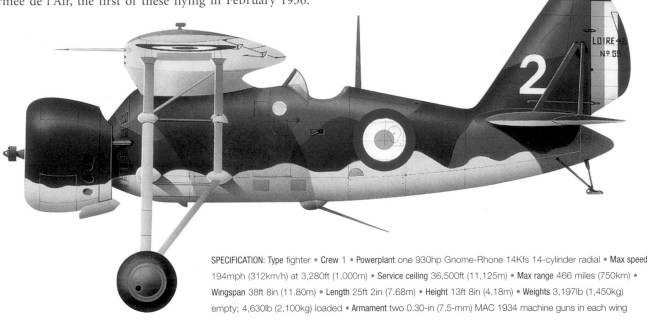

SPECIFICATION: Type fighter • Crew 1 • Powerplant one 930hp Gnome-Rhone 14Kfs 14-cylinder radial • Max speed 194mph (312km/h) at 3,280ft (1,000m) • Service ceiling 36,500ft (11,125m) • Max range 466 miles (750km) • Wingspan 38ft 8in (11.80m) • Length 25ft 2in (7.68m) • Height 13ft 8in (4.18m) • Weights 3,197lb (1,450kg) empty; 4,630lb (2,100kg) loaded • Armament two 0.30-in (7.5-mm) MAC 1934 machine guns in each wing

■ LVG C.II

Some of the best general-purpose aircraft produced in the early years of World War I were manufactured by the LVG (Luft Verkehrs Gesellschaft) company. The first was the C.I, which appeared at the front about the middle of 1915. At the end of the year it was joined by an improved version, the C.II, with a more powerful Mercedes D.III engine and a stronger structure. The two types remained in first-line service until the end of 1916, carrying out light bombing mis-

▲ *The LVG C.II was the first German heavier-than-air machine to attack London, on November 28, 1916.*

SPECIFICATION: Type reconnaissance/bomber biplane • Crew 2 • Powerplant one 160hp Mercedes D.III 6-cylinder liquid-cooled in-line • Max speed 81mph (130km/h) • Service ceiling 16,405ft (5,000m) • Endurance 4hrs • Wingspan 42ft 2in (12.85m) • Length 25ft 7in (7.79m) • Height 9ft 7in (2.93m) • Weight 3,097lb (1,405kg) loaded • Armament one or two 0.30-in (7.5-mm) Parabellum machine guns

sions as well as reconnaissance. On November 28, 1916 a lone C.II (sometimes described as a C.IV) penetrated as far as London and dropped six 22-lb (10-kg) bombs between Brompton Road and Victoria Station, causing much panic but little damage. The crew's target had been the Admiralty. Around 300 C.I/II aircraft were produced in total.

▌Macchi MC.200 Saetta

The MC.200 Saetta (Lightning), the second of Italy's monoplane fighters, was designed by Mario Castoldi, who had been responsible for some highly successful seaplane racers between the wars and who had drawn on experience gained with the M.39, winner of the 1926 Schneider Trophy, and the MC.72, holder of the world air speed record in its class. Powered by a Fiat A74 radial engine, whose bulk tended to spoil the aircraft's otherwise neat contours, the MC.200 first flew on December 24, 1937, deliveries to the Regia Aeronautica beginning in October 1939. About 150 aircraft were in service by June 1940. Production C.200s were C.200A-1 and A-2, the latter having a strengthened wing for the carriage of two small bombs. Early production C.200s had a fully enclosed cockpit, but this was later altered to an open and then a semienclosed type. About 1,000 MC.200s were built.

SPECIFICATION: Type fighter-bomber (data MC.200A-2) • Crew 1 • Powerplant one 870hp Fiat A.74 RC.38 14-cylinder radial • Max speed 312mph (503km/h) at 16,400ft (5,000m) • Service ceiling 29,200ft (8,900m) • Max range 541 miles (870km) • Wingspan 34ft 8in (10.58m) • Length 26ft 10in (8.19m) • Height 11ft 5in (3.51m) • Weight 4,867lb (2,208kg) loaded • Armament two 0.50-in (12.7-mm) machine guns in upper forward fuselage; external bomb load of 705lb (320kg)

▲ The Saetta was a nimble but ultimately underarmed fighter, and suffered accordingly.

▌Macchi MC.202 Folgore

Italian monoplane fighters of the late 1930s were handicapped by the lack of a suitable powerplant. A case in point was the Macchi MC.200. Attempts to improve its performance began in 1938, but it was not until early in 1940 that a suitable engine became available in the shape of the Daimler-Benz DB 601A-1 liquid cooled in-line engine. This was installed in a standard Saetta airframe and flown on August 10, 1940, producing excellent results, and the aircraft, designated MC.202 Folgore (Thunderbolt) was ordered into production fitted with the license-built DB 601. The type entered service with the 1° Stormo at Udine in the summer of 1941, moving to Sicily to take part in operations over Malta in November. The Folgore remained in production

SPECIFICATION: Type day fighter • Crew 1 • Powerplant one 1,075hp Alfa Romeo RA 1000 RC.411 12-cylinder inverted V-type • Max speed 373mph (600km/h) at 18,373ft (5,600m) • Service ceiling 37,730ft (11,500m) • Max range 379 miles (610km) • Wingspan 34ft 8in (10.58m) • Length 29ft (8.85m) • Height 11ft 6in (3.50m) • Weight 6,459lb (2,930kg) loaded • Armament two 0.5-in (12.7-mm) Breda-SAFAT machine guns in nose; two 0.303-in (7.7-mm) in wings; late production aircraft, two 0.79-in (20-mm) cannon in wings

until the Italian armistice of September 1943. Macchi built 392 MC.202s, and around 1,100 more were produced by other companies, mainly Breda.

■ Macchi MC.205 Veltro

The ultimate fighter of the MC.200 series was the MC 205 Veltro (Greyhound), which went into operational service in April 1943. When the Italian government concluded a separate armistice with the Allies on September 8, 1943 some 40 aircraft remustered with the Italian Co-Belligerent Air Force, which fought on the Allied side, and saw active service until the end of the war, mainly on the Yugoslav Front. About 30 more escaped to join the Aviazione della RSI, which continued to fight on the side of the Germans, and which also acquired 112 more Veltros built up to May 1944.

SPECIFICATION: Type fighter • Crew 1 • Powerplant one 1475hp Daimler-Benz DB605A 12-cylinder V-type • Max speed 403mph (650km/h) at 24,300ft (7,400m) • Service ceiling 37,200ft (11,350m) • Max range 646 miles (1,040km) • Wingspan 34ft 8in (10.59m) • Length 29ft 1in (8.85m) • Height 10ft (3.05m) • Weight 7,120lb (3,224kg) loaded • Armament two 0.79-in (20-mm) cannon; two 0.50-in (12.7-mm) machine guns

■ Macchi M.5-M.41

The Macchi M.5 and M.9, which made their appearance in 1918, were among the best of the small seaplanes produced during World War I. The M.5, which was a fighter (270 built) was fast and maneuverable, and a match for the opposing Austrian landplane fighters. The M.5mod had a more powerful 250hp engine. The M.9 was an armed reconnaissance variant. The final Macchi fighter flying boat was the M.41 of 1927, a few of which were still in service on the eve of World War II.

SPECIFICATION: Type fighter seaplane (data Macchi M.5mod) • Crew 1 • Powerplant one 250hp Isotta-Fraschini V6B liquid-cooled in-line • Max speed 130mph (209km/h) at sea level • Service ceiling 16,405ft (5,000m) • Endurance 3hrs 40mins • Wingspan 32ft 7in (9.95m) • Length 26ft 7in (8.10m) • Height 9ft 8in (2.95m) • Weight 2,381lb (1,080kg) loaded • Armament two 0.303-in (7.62-mm) fixed forward-firing machine guns

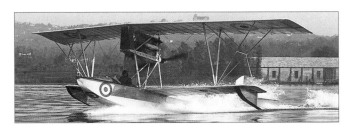

▲ The M.5 was flown by some US Navy and US Marine Corps pilots in the Adriatic.

■ Martin B-10

The Martin B-10 was a very advanced aircraft when it first made an appearance in 1932. It was the first American bomber of all-metal construction to enter large-scale production, the first US warplane with turreted armament, and the US Army Air Corps' first cantilever low-wing monoplane. The USAAC took delivery of 151 B-10s and a slightly improved version, the B-12, and although the type was retired from first-line US service by the outbreak of WWII the production line remained open to fulfill orders from Argentina (35), China (9), Thailand (26), Turkey (20), and the Netherlands East Indies (120).

SPECIFICATION: Type medium bomber (data B-10B) • Crew 4 • Powerplant two 775hp (Wright R-1820 G-102 Cyclone 9-cylinder radials • Max speed 200mph (322km/h) • Service ceiling 25,200ft (7,680m) • Max range 590 miles (950km) • Wingspan 70ft 10in (21.60m) • Length 44ft 2in (13.46m) • Height 11ft 7in (3.53m) • Weight 15,894lb (7,210kg) • Armament one 0.30-in (7.62-mm) machine gun in nose, dorsal, and ventral positions; up to 2,260lb (1,025kg) of bombs

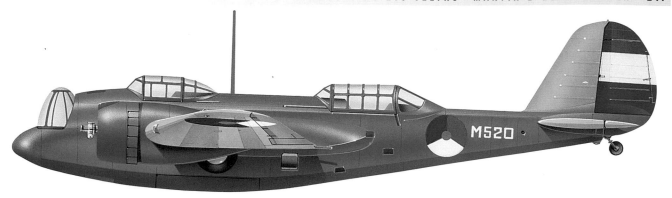

■ Martin B-26 Marauder

One of the most controversial Allied medium bombers of World War II, at least in the early stages of its career, the Glenn L. Martin 179 was entered in a US Army light and medium bomber competition of 1939. Its designer, Peyton M. Magruder, placed the emphasis on high speed, producing an aircraft with a torpedo-like fuselage, two massive radial engines, tricycle undercarriage, and stubby wings. The advanced nature of the aircraft's design proved so impressive that an immediate order was placed for 201 examples off the drawing board, without a prototype. The first B-26 flew on November 25, 1940, powered by two Pratt & Whitney R-2800-5 engines; by this time, orders for 1,131 B-26A and B-26B bombers had been received. The first unit to rearm with a mixture of B-26s and B-26As was the 22nd Bombardment Group at Langley Field in February 1941. Early in 1942 it moved to Australia, where it became part of the US Fifth Air Force, attacking enemy shipping, airfields, and installations in New Guinea and New Britain. It carried out its first attack, a raid on Rabaul, on April 5, 1942. During the Battle of Midway, four B-26As of the 22nd and 38th BG attacked units of the Japanese fleet with torpedoes. The 22nd BG used B-26s exclusively until October 1943, when some B-25s were added. In February 1944 it became a heavy bombardment group, equipped with B-24s.

The next variant, the B-26B, had uprated engines and increased armament. Of the 1,883 built, all but the first 641

▲ The Martin B-26 earned a fearsome reputation as a "widow maker" among its crews, who were unused to its high-speed handling characteris-

aircraft featured a new extended-span wing and taller tail fin. The B-26B made its debut in the European Theater with the 322nd BG in March 1943. After some disastrous low-level daylight attacks, all B-26 units in the European Theater were reassigned to the medium-level bombing role, which they fulfilled magnificently until the end of the war in both northwest Europe and Italy.

The B-26C, of which 1,210 were built, was essentially similar to the later B-26B models. These were succeeded by the B-26F (300 built), in which the angle of incidence (i.e. the angle at which the wing is married to the fuselage) was increased in order to improve takeoff performance. The final model was the B-26G, which differed from the F model in only minor detail; 950 were built.

The B-26 saw service in the Aleutians in 1942, and in the Western Desert, where it served with the RAF Middle East Command as the Marauder Mk I (B-26A), Marauder Mk IA (B-26B), Marauder Mk II (B-26F), and Marauder Mk III (B-26G). Only two RAF squadrons, Nos. 14 and 39, used the Marauder. The total number of Marauders delivered to the RAF included 52 Marauder Is and IAs, 250 Marauder IIs, and 150 Marauder IIIs. The Marauder was also used extensively by the Free French Air Force and the South African Air Force. Many were completed or converted as AT-23 or TB-26 trainers for the USAAF and JM-1s for the US Navy, some being used as target tugs. Total production was 4,708 aircraft.

SPECIFICATION: Type medium bomber • Crew 7 • Powerplant two 2,000hp Pratt & Whitney R-2800-41 radial engines • Max speed 317mph (510km/h) • Service ceiling 23,500ft (7,165m) • Max range 1,150 miles (1,850km) • Wingspan 65ft (19.81m) • Length 58ft 3in (17.75m) • Height 19ft 10in (6.04m) • Weight 34,200lb (15,513kg) loaded • Armament two 0.30-in (7.7-mm) machine guns (one each in nose and ventral positions, or two 0.50-in (12.7-mm) machine guns in beam positions instead of ventral gun; two 0.50-in (12.7-mm) machine guns in dorsal and two in tail turrets, plus a maximum bomb load of 5,200lb (2,359kg)

SPECIFICATION: Type medium bomber (data Martin 167 Maryland) • Crew 4 • Powerplant two 1,050hp Pratt & Whitney R-1830-S1C3-G • Max speed 304mph (489km/h) at 14,000ft (4,267m) • Service ceiling 29,500ft (8,992m) • Max range 1,300 miles (2,092km) • Wingspan 61ft 4in (18.69m) • Length 46ft 8in (14.22m) • Height 10ft 1in (3.07m) • Weight 15,297lb (6,939kg) loaded • Armament two 0.50-in (12.7-mm) machine guns in each wing and one each in dorsal and ventral positions; up to 1,250lb (567kg) of bombs

formed a useful reconnaissance role in the early part of World War II.

The Martin Baltimore, developed at the request of the British, was an improved version of the Maryland with a wider and deeper fuselage, flew in June 1941 and the entire production of 1,575 aircraft went to Britain. The type served exclusively in the Mediterranean theater with the RAF and Allied air forces under RAF command.

▌Martin B-57 Canberra

In 1953, the Glenn L. Martin company began license production of the English Electric Canberra B2 under the USAF designation B-57. First production model was the B-57A, but only eight were built before production switched to the RB-57A reconnaissance variant, the first of 67 aircraft being delivered in March 1954. The next US Canberra variant, the B-57B, incorporated much redesign, including a tandem two-seat cockpit under a one-piece canopy, a preloaded revolving bomb bay that rotated through 180 degrees, a wing-mounted armament of cannon and machine guns, and

SPECIFICATION: Type night interdictor (data B-57B) • Crew 2 • Powerplant two 7,100-lb (3,226-kg) thrust Wright J65-W5 turbojets • Max speed 582mph (937km/h) at 40,000ft (12,190m) • Service ceiling 48,000ft (14,630m) • Max range 2,300 miles (3,710km) • Wingspan 64ft (19.51m) • Length 65ft 6in (19.96m) • Height 15ft 7in (4.75m) • Weight 55,000lb (24,950kg) loaded • Armament eight 0.50-in (12.7-mm) machine guns or four 0.79-in (20-mm) cannon; 16 rocket projectiles on underwing rails and up to 6,000lb (2,722kg) of bombs in internal bomb bay

▲ The greatly enlarged wingspan of the RB-57D led to a number of structural problems, with at least three aircraft literally breaking.

underwing points for rockets or napalm tanks; 202 were delivered. The B-57C (38) was similar, but had dual controls for conversion training. Twenty-six B-57B/C aircraft were supplied to Pakistan, and saw combat during that country's conflicts with India in 1965 and 1971. The B-57E (68 produced) was a target-towing version, while the RB-57D (20 built) was a reconnaissance variant with an entirely new long-span wing, uprated engines, and a redesigned fuselage housing specialist equipment. The ultimate reconnaissance variant was the RB-57F, converted by General Dynamics; its span was extended to 122ft (37.21m), and power was supplied by two Pratt & Whitney TF-33 turbofans and two J-60 auxiliary turbojets. Only 21 were delivered. The last US Canberra variant was the B-57G, developed for night interdiction during the Vietnam War. Also used in Vietnam was the EB-57, an electronic warfare variant of the basic B-57.

▌Martinsyde F.4 Buzzard

▶ Although markedly superior to the contemporary Snipe, the F.4 was not adopted as a front-line RAF fighter.

SPECIFICATION: Type scouting biplane • Crew 1 • Powerplant one 300hp Hispano-Suiza 8-cylinder V-type • Max speed 145mph (233km/h) • Service ceiling 25,000ft (7,620m) • Endurance 2hrs 30mins • Wingspan 32ft 9in (10m) • Length 25ft 6in (7.77m) • Height 10ft 4in (3.15m) • Weight 2,289lb (1,038kg) loaded • Armament two fixed forward-firing 0.303-in (7.7-mm) Vickers machine guns

An outstanding fighter aircraft, the Buzzard was designed by George Handasysde and first flown in 1917. Orders were placed for 1,500, but only 52 had been delivered at the time of the Armistice. The aircraft was originally intended to have the Rolls-Royce Falcon engine, but as production was earmarked for the Bristol Fighter a 300hp Hispano engine was installed.

McDonnell FH-1 Phantom

The first jet aircraft designed to operate from carriers, the FH-1 originated in 1943. Initially designated XFD-1, it flew for the first time on January 25, 1945. Following carrier tri-

SPECIFICATION: Type carrier-borne fighter • Crew 1 • Powerplant two 1,600-lb (726-kg) thrust Westinghouse J30-WE-20 turbojets • Max speed 479mph (771km/h) at sea level • Service ceiling 41,000ft (12,525m) • Max range 695 miles (1,118km) • Wingspan 40ft 9in (12.42m) • Length 37ft 3in (11.35m) • Height 14ft 2in (4.32m) • Weight 12,035lb (5,459kg) loaded • Armament four 0.50-in (12.7-mm) machine guns

als, an order was placed for 100 production aircraft, but this was cut to 60. On May 5, 1948 Fighter Squadron 17-A, equipped with 16 FH-1s, became the first carrier-qualified jet squadron in the US Navy, operating from the USS Saipan. The type remained in first-line service until July 1950.

◄ *The prototype FH-1 was the first US jet aircraft to be flown on to and from an aircraft carrier, the USS* Franklin D. Roosevelt.

McDonnell F2H Banshee

SPECIFICATION: Type carrier-borne fighter (data F2H-2) • Crew 1 • Powerplant one 3,205-lb (1,474-kg) thrust Westinghouse J34-E-34 turbojet • Max speed 580mph (933km/h) at sea level • Service ceiling 46,600ft (14,205m) • Max range 1,170 miles (1,883km) • Wingspan 41ft 9in (12.73m) • Length 48ft 2in (14.68m) • Height 14ft 6in (4.42m) • Weight 25,214lb (11,437kg) loaded • Armament four 0.79-in (20-mm) cannon; underwing racks with provision for two 500-lb (227-kg) or four 250-lb (113-kg) bombs

The FH-1's successor, the F2H Banshee, stemmed from a 1945 contract for a jet fighter-bomber. The prototype flew for the first time on January 11, 1947, and the first series production F2H-1s were delivered in March 1949. The Banshee went into combat in Korea for the first time on August 23, 1951, when F2H-2s of VF-172 (USS *Essex*) struck at targets in northwestern Korea. The F2H-2P was a photoreconnaissance variant, 89 of which were built. The F2H-3 (redesignated F2-C in 1962) was a long-range limited all-weather development; 250 were built, and the type equipped two squadrons of the Royal Canadian Navy, operating from the carrier HMCS *Bonaventure*.

▼ *Similar in configuration to its predecessor the FH-1 Phantom, the Banshee was larger and fitted with more powerful turbojet engines.*

▪McDonnell F3H Demon

The McDonnell F3H Demon flew for the first time on August 7, 1951, powered by the new Westinghouse XJ40-WE-6 turbojet. This aircraft was subsequently destroyed, but the test program continued with the second prototype, and the US Navy placed substantial production orders. However, problems with the J40 engine, and the eventual decision to abandon it altogether, caused serious disruption to the whole Demon program, and production was held up until the Allison J71 turbojet became available. It was with this engine

▲ The McDonnell F3H Demon was plagued by problems with its Westinghouse J40 engine, which seriously disrupted development work.

SPECIFICATION: Type carrier-borne strike fighter (data F3H-2) • Crew 1 • Powerplant one 14,000-lb (6,350-kg) thrust Allison J71-A-2E turbojet • Max speed 647mph (1,041km/h) at sea level • Service ceiling 42,650ft (13,000m) • Max range 1,370 miles (2,200km) • Wingspan 35ft 4in (10.77m) • Length 58ft 11in (17.96m) • Height 14ft 7in (4.44m) • Weight 33,900lb (15,377kg) loaded • Armament four 0.79-in (20-mm) cannon; four underwing hardpoints with provision for up to 6,000lb (2,722kg) of ordnance

that the Demon became operational with VF-14 in March 1956. The first Demons to be assigned to the fleet were the F3H-2N night and all-weather fighter variant; further variants were the F3H-2M day fighter, armed with Sparrow missiles, and the F3H-2P photoreconnaissance aircraft. The first Sparrow-armed F3H-2Ms were deployed with the Seventh Fleet in the Pacific late in 1958. Production of the Demon ended in 1959, 119 aircraft being built, and the F2H-3M remained in service until 1961.

▪McDonnell F-4 Phantom II

One of the most potent and versatile combat aircraft ever built, the McDonnell F-4 Phantom stemmed from a 1954 project for an advanced naval fighter designated F3H-G/H. A mock-up was built, and in October 1954 the US Navy ordered two prototypes for evaluation under the designation YAH-1. This aircraft was to have been a single-seater, armed with four 0.79-in (20-mm) cannon and powered by two Wright J65 turbojets, but when the Navy finalized its requirement in April 1955 the design was changed substantially, the aircraft being fitted with two General Electric J79s, two seats, and an armament of four Sparrow AAMs instead of the cannon. The designation was changed to F4H-1, and the XF4H-1 prototype flew for the first time on May 27, 1958. Twenty-three development aircraft were procured, followed by 45 production machines for the US Navy. These were originally

designated F4H-1F, but this was later changed to F-4A.

The F-4B was a slightly improved version with J79-GE-8 engines, and between them the F-4A and F-4B captured many world records over a four-year period. Carrier trials were carried out in 1960, and in December that year the first Phantoms were delivered to training squadron VF-121. The first fully operational Phantom squadron, VF-114, commissioned with F-4Bs in October 1961, and in June 1962 the first USMC deliveries were made to VMF(AW)-314. Total F-4B production was 649 aircraft. Twenty-nine F-4Bs were loaned to the USAF for evaluation in 1962 and proved superior to any Air Force fighter-bomber. A production order was quickly placed for a USAF variant; this was originally designated F-110A, but later changed to F-4C. Deliveries to the USAF began in 1963, 583 aircraft being built. The RF-4B and RF-4C were unarmed reconnaissance variants for the USMC and USAF, while the F-4D was basically an F-4C with improved systems and redesigned radome. The major production version was the F-4E, 913 of which were delivered to the USAF between October 1967 and December 1976. F-4E export orders totaled 558. The RF-4E was the tactical reconnaissance version. The F-4F (175 built) was a version for the Luftwaffe, intended primarily for the air superiority

◀ Germany's F-4F ICE aircraft will remain in service until replaced by the far more capable Eurofighter Typhoon.

▲ *Although designed originally as a multi-role combat aircraft for the US Navy, the Phantom was quickly adopted by the US Air Force.*

role but retaining multirole capability, while the F-4G Wild Weasel was the F4E modified for the suppression of enemy defense systems. The successor to the F-4B in USN/USMC service was the F-4J, which possessed greater ground attack capability; the first of 522 production aircraft was delivered in June 1976.

The first foreign nation to order the Phantom was Great Britain, the British aircraft being powered by Rolls-Royce RB168-25R Spey 201 engines. Versions for the Royal Navy and the RAF were designated F-4K and F-4M respectively. Fifty-two F-4Ks were delivered to the Royal Navy in 1968–9 and these were progressively handed over to the RAF with the run-down of the RAF's fixed wing units, becoming the Phantom FG.1 in RAF service; the FG.1 was used in the air

defense role. The RAF's own version, the F-4M Phantom FGR.2, equipped 13 air defense, strike, and reconnaissance squadrons. By 1978 all the RAF's F-4M Phantoms, of which 118 were delivered, were assigned to air defense, replacing the Lightning in this role. Other foreign customers for the Phantom included the Imperial Iranian Air Force, which received some 200 F-4Es and 29 RF-4Es; the surviving aircraft, under new management, saw combat during the long-running war between Iran and Iraq in the 1980s. Israel also received over 200 F-4Es between 1969 and 1976, these aircraft seeing considerable action during the Yom Kippur war of 1973. F-4D Phantoms were delivered to the Republic of Korea Air Force as a temporary measure, pending the arrival of Northrop F-5As. The Japanese Air Self-Defense Force equipped five squadrons with 140 Phantom F-4EJs, most of which were built under license, and the RAAF leased 24 F-4Es in 1970. The Luftwaffe's F-4Fs, already mentioned, replaced the F-104 Starfighter in the air superiority role and the Fiat G.91 in the ground attack role; the Luftwaffe also received 88 F-4Es in 1971. Smaller numbers of Phantoms were delivered to Spain, Greece, and Turkey, so that by the mid-1970s several key NATO air forces were standardized on the type. By this time, the Phantom had proved its worth many times over in combat, in the hostile environment of Vietnam.

SPECIFICATION: Type fighter/attack aircraft (data F-4E) • Crew 2 • Powerplant two 17,900-lb (8,119-kg) thrust General Electric J79-GE-17 turbojets • Max speed 1,485mph (2,390km/h) at altitude • Service ceiling 58,000ft (26,308m) • Max range 1,750 miles (2,817km) on internal fuel • Wingspan 38ft 5in (11.70m) • Length 58ft 3in (17.76m) • Height 16ft 3in (4.96m) • Weight 58,000lb (26,308kg) loaded • Armament one 0.79-in (20-mm) M61A1 Vulcan cannon and four AIM-7 Sparrow AAMs recessed under fuselage; up to 12,980lb (5,888kg) of ordnance and stores on underwing pylons

∎ McDonnell F-101 Voodoo

USA

Second of the "century" fighters was the McDonnell F-101 Voodoo, which was based on the design of the canceled XF-88 heavy twin-engined escort fighter of 1948. The resurrected design was subjected to a number of changes, including the lengthening of the fuselage by more than 13ft (4m) to accommodate extra fuel tankage, and the remodeled aircraft was designated YF-101A. The prototype flew on December 29, 1954, and although Strategic Air Command had long since abandoned the long-range escort fighter idea, the pro-

▲ *In its two-seat F-101B form, the Voodoo was an interceptor of some capability, especially when armed with nuclear-tipped Genies.*

SPECIFICATION: Type tactical fighter-bomber (data F-101A) • Crew 1 • Powerplant two 14,880-lb (6,750-kg) thrust Pratt & Whitney J57-P-13 turbojets • Max speed 1,009mph (1,623km/h) at 35,000ft (10,675m) • Service ceiling 55,800ft (17,000m) • Max range 1,900 miles (3,057km) • Wingspan 39ft 8in (12.09m) • Length 67ft 4in (20.54m) • Height 18ft (5.49m) • Weight 52,400lb (23,768kg) loaded • Armament four 0.79-in (20-mm) cannon; one tactical nuclear weapon or up to 2,000lb (907kg) of conventional ordnance

gram was taken over by Tactical Air Command, which saw the F-101 as a potential replacement for the Northrop F-89 Scorpion. The aircraft went into production as the F-101A,

powered by two Pratt & Whitney J57-P-13 turbojets, and the 75 examples built equipped three squadrons of TAC. The next Voodoo variant, the two-seat F-101B, equipped 16 squadrons of Air Defense Command, and production ran to 359 aircraft. This version also equipped three Canadian air defense squadrons as the CF-101B.

The F-101C was a single-seat fighter bomber version for TAC, entering service with the 523rd Tactical Fighter Squadron of the 27th Fighter Bomber Wing in May 1957. It equipped nine squadrons, but its operational career was relatively short-lived because it was replaced by more modern combat types in the early 1960s.

■ McDonnell Douglas C-17

USA

▲ *Designed to replace the C-141 as the USAF's heavy transport, the C-17 has the ability to land on unprepared strips worldwide.*

SPECIFICATION: Type heavy-lift strategic transportation • Crew 4 • Powerplant four 40,100-lb (18,195-kg) thrust Pratt & Whitney F-117-P-100 turbofans • Max speed 515mph (829km/h) at 35,000ft (10,670m) • Service ceiling 45,000ft (13,715m) • Max range 3,225 miles (5,190km) • Wingspan 165ft (50.29m) • Length 174ft (53.04m) • Height 55ft 1in (16.79m) • Weight 580,000lb (263,083kg) • Armament none

Selected in 1981 as the USAF's CX long-range transport to replace the C-141 StarLifter, the C-17 Globemaster III made its first flight in September 1991 and entered service in 1994. The C-17 is similar in size to the C-141 but carries twice the payload; the aircraft has the fuselage diameter of the C-5 Galaxy, which enables it to carry the M-1 Abrams tank and other outsize cargo over strategic distances to land on unprepared strips. The 120th and last C-17 was due to be handed over in 2004. Four C-17s are used by the Royal Air Force, which operates the type under lease.

McDonnell Douglas F-15 Eagle

USA

▲ An F-15 Eagle of the USAF Tactical Fighter Weapons School at Nellis AFB, Nevada, home of the famous "Red Flag" air warfare exercises.

SPECIFICATION: Type air superiority fighter (data F-15A) • Crew 1 • Powerplant two 24,000-lb (10,885-kg) thrust Pratt & Whitney F100-PW-100 turbofans • Max speed 1,650mph (2,655km/h) at altitude • Service ceiling 100,000ft (30,500m) • Max range 1,200 miles (1,930km) on internal fuel • Wingspan 42ft 9in (13.05m) • Length 63ft 9in (19.43m) • Height 18ft 5in (5.63m) • Weight 56,000lb (25,424kg) loaded • Armament one 0.79-in (20-mm) M61A1 cannon; four AIM-7 and four AIM-9 AAMs; up to 16,800lb (7,620kg) of underwing stores

In 1969, it was announced that McDonnell Douglas had been selected as prime airframe contractor for a new air superiority fighter, then designated FX; as the F-15A Eagle, it flew for the first time on July 27, 1972, and first deliveries of operational aircraft were made to the USAF in 1975. Simply stated, the F-15 Eagle was designed to outperform, outfly, and outfight any opponent it might encounter in the foreseeable future, in engagements extending from beyond visual range (BVR) right down to close-in turning combat. The tandem-seat F-15B was developed alongside the F-15A, and the main production version was the F-15C. The latter was built under license in Japan as the F-15J. The F-15E was supplied to Israel as the F-15I and to Saudi Arabia as the F-15S. The F-15E Strike Eagle is a dedicated strike/attack variant and, while the F-15C established and maintained air superiority, was at the forefront of precision bombing operations in the 1991 Gulf War. The F-15E was supplied to Israel as the F-15I and to Saudi Arabia as the F-15S. In all, the USAF took delivery of 1286 F-15s (all versions), Japan 171, Saudi Arabia 98, and Israel 56.

▲ F-15E Strike Eagles from Luke AFB, Arizona, in formation over the desert. The F-15E is capable of extremely precise strike operations.

McDonnell Douglas F-18 Hornet

USA

While the F-14 replaced the Phantom in the naval air superiority role, the aircraft that replaced it in the tactical role (with both the USN and USMC) was the McDonnell Douglas F-18 Hornet. First flown on November 18, 1978, the prototype Hornet was followed by 11 development aircraft. The first production versions were the fighter/attack F-18A and the two-seat F-18B operational trainer; subsequent variants are the F-18C and F-18D, which have provision for AIM-120 AAMs and Maverick infrared missiles, as well as an airborne self-protection jamming system. The aircraft also serves with the Canadian Armed Forces as the CF-188 (138 aircraft). Other customers are Australia (75), Finland (64), Kuwait (40), Spain (72), and Switzerland (34). Total US deliveries, all variants, were 1,150 aircraft.

SPECIFICATION: Type fighter and strike aircraft (data F/A-18A) • Crew 1 • Powerplant two 16,000-lb (7,264-kg) thrust General Electric F404-GE-400 turbofans • Max speed 1,183mph (1,912km/h) at 40,000ft (12,190m) • Service ceiling 50,000ft (15,240m) • Combat radius 662 miles (1,065km) • Wingspan 37ft 6in (11.43m) • Length 56ft (17.07m) • Height 15ft 3in (4.66m) • Weight 56,000lb (25,401kg) • Armament one 0.79-in (20-mm) M61A1 Vulcan cannon; external hardpoints with provision for up to 17,000lb (7,711kg) of stores

▲ Two US Marine Corps F/A-18s on a training exercise near Naval Air Station Fallon, Nevada. The aircraft in the foreground is a two-seat D model.

▮ McDonnell Douglas/B.Ae AV-8B Harrier II

A key element in modern offensive battlefield support is the short takeoff, vertical landing (STOVL) aircraft, epitomized by the British Aerospace/McDonnell Douglas Harrier. Although it was the British who were responsible for the early development of this remarkable aircraft, it was the US Marine Corps who identified the need to upgrade their original version, the AV-8A. The Harrier used 1950s technology in airframe design and construction and in systems, and by the 1970s, despite systems updates, this was restricting the further development of the aircraft's potential. In developing the USMC's new Harrier variant the basic design concept was retained, but new technologies and avionics were fully

SPECIFICATION: Type V/STOL close support aircraft • Crew 1 • Powerplant one 23,800-lb (10,796-kg) thrust Rolls-Royce F402-RR-408 vectored thrust turbofan • Max speed 661mph (1,065km/h) at sea level • Service ceiling 50,000ft (15,240m) • Combat radius 172 miles (277km) with 6,000-lb (2,722-kg) payload • Wingspan 30ft 4in (9.25m) • Length 46ft 4in (14.12m) • Height 11ft 7in (3.55m) • Weight 31,000lb (14,061kg) loaded • Armament one 0.98-in (25-mm) GAU-12U cannon; six external hardpoints with provision for up to 17,000lb (7,711kg) or 7,000lb (3,175kg) of stores (short and vertical takeoff respectively)

▲ The two-seat TAV-8B has been more successful than its RAF counterpart, the T.Mk 10.

exploited. One of the major improvements was a new wing, with a carbon fiber composite structure, a supercritical aerofoil, and a greater area and span. The wing has large slotted flaps linked with nozzle deflection at short takeoff unstick to improve control precision and increase lift. Leading-edge root extensions (LERX) are fitted to enhance the aircraft's air combat agility by improving the turn rate, while longitudinal fences (LIDS, or Lift Improvement Devices) incorporated beneath the fuselage and on the gun pods to capture ground-reflected jets in vertical takeoff and landing, give a much bigger ground cushion and reduce hot gas recirculation.

A prototype AV-8B Harrier II first flew in November 1978, followed by the first development aircraft in November 1981, and production deliveries to the USMC began in 1983. Delivery of the RAF's equivalent, the Harrier GR5, began in 1987; production GR5s were later converted to GR7 standard. This version, general similar to the USMC's night-attack AV-8B, has FLIR, a digital moving map display, night vision goggles for the pilot and a modified head-up display.

▮ Messerschmitt Bf 109

Development of Willi Messerschmitt's famous Bf 109 began in 1933, when the Reichsluftministerium (RLM) issued a requirement for a new monoplane fighter. The prototype Bf 109V-1 flew for the first time in September 1935, powered by a 695hp Rolls-Royce Kestrel engine, as the 610hp Junkers Jumo 210A which was intended for it was not yet available. The Bf 109V-7, armed with two machine guns and a single MG FF (0.79-in (20-mm) Oerlikon cannon), became the prototype for the first series production model, the Bf 109B, powered by a 610hp Jumo 210 engine. Three of the Bf 109 prototypes were evaluated in Spain in February and March 1937 and were followed by 24 Bf 109B-2s, which immediately proved superior to any other fighter engaged in the civil war. It was the use of the Bf 109 in Spain that enabled the

▲ The Messerschmitt Bf 109G, an example of which is preserved here, was perhaps the best and most potent of the Bf 109 models.

SPECIFICATION: Type fighter (Bf 109G-6) • Crew 1 • Powerplant one 1,474hp Daimler-Benz DB 605AM 12-cylinder inverted-Vee engine • Max speed 386mph (621km/h) at 22,967ft (7,000m) • Service ceiling 37,890ft (11,550m) • Max range 620 miles (1,000km) • Wingspan 32ft 6in (9.92m) • Length 29ft (8.85m) • Height 8ft 2in (2.50m) • Weight 7,496lb (3,400kg) loaded • Armament one 0.79-in (20-mm) or 1.19-in (30-mm) fixed forward-firing cannon in an engine installation, and two 0.50-in (12.7-mm) fixed forward-firing machine guns in the upper part of the forward fuselage; external bomb load of 551lb (250kg)

Luftwaffe to develop the fighter tactics that would enable it to wreak havoc among its opponents in the early years of World War II.

By the time that conflict began in September 1939, 1,060 Bf 109s of various subspecies were in service with the Luftwaffe's fighter units. These included the Bf 109C and Bf 109D, which were already being replaced by the Bf 109E series; this model was to be the mainstay of the Luftwaffe's fighter units throughout 1940. The series extended to the E-9, including models built as fighters, fighter-bombers, and reconnaissance aircraft. Ten Bf 109Es were converted for operations from Germany's planned aircraft carrier, the *Graf Zeppelin*, under the designation Bf 109T. The best of all Bf 109 variants, the Bf 109F, began to reach Luftwaffe units in France in May 1941 and was superior in most respects to the principal RAF fighter of the time, the Spitfire Mk V. The Bf 109F differed from the Bf 109E in having a generally cleaned-up airframe, redesigned engine cowling, wing, radiators, and tail assembly. It was succeeded by the Bf 109G, which appeared late in 1942. Preproduction Bf 109G-0 aircraft retained the DB 601E of the F series, but the first production model, the Bf 109G-1, had the more powerful DB 605A engine. The G-1, G-3, and G-5 had provision for pressurized cockpits and were fitted with the GM-1 emergency power-boost system, which was lacking in the G-2 and G-4. Various

armament combinations were employed, and later aircraft were fitted with wooden tail units. The fastest G model, the Bf 109G-10, without wing armament and with MW 50 power-boost equipment, reached a maximum speed of 425mph (687km/h) at 24,278ft (7,400m), climbed to 20,000ft (6100m) in six minutes and had an endurance of 55 minutes.

The last operational versions of the Bf 109 were the K-4 and K-6, which both had DB 605D engines with MW 50 power boost. The Bf 109K-4 had two 0.58-in (15-mm) MG 151 guns semiexternally mounted above the engine cowling and a 0.79-in (20-mm) MK 108 or 1.19-in (30-mm) Mk 103 firing through the propeller hub. The Bf 109K-6 had the cowling-mounted MG 151s replaced by 0.50-in (12.7-mm) MG 131 machine guns and had two 1.19-in (30-mm) MK 103 cannon in under-wing gondolas. The last variant was the Bf 109K-14, with a DB 605L engine, but only two examples saw service with JG 52.

The Bf 109G was built in both Spain (as the Hispano Ha-1109) and Czechoslovakia (as the Avia S-199). Some of the Czech-built aircraft were acquired by Israel in 1948. Bf 109 production reached an approximate total of 35,000 aircraft.

▌Messerschmitt Bf 110

GERMANY

The Messerschmitt Bf 110 was designed in response to a 1934 specification for a long-range escort fighter and Zerstörer (destroyer) aircraft. Three prototypes were completed with DB 600 engines, the first of these flying on May 12, 1936. Four preseries Bf 110A-0s were ordered, powered by 610hp Jume 210B engines, while a small number of Bf 110B-0 trials aircraft were fitted with the 690hp DB 600A, but these were inadequate and the first production model, the Bf 110C-1,

used the more powerful (1,100hp) DB 601A. The aircraft also featured several aerodynamic improvements over the Bf 110A-0, such as square-cut wingtips (which increased speed but had an adverse effect on maneuverability) and an improved cockpit canopy.

Armament comprised four 0.31-in (7.9-mm) MG17 machine guns and two 0.79-in (20-mm) MGFF cannon, the former in the upper half of the nose and the latter in a detachable tray attached to the fuselage belly. In addition, a manually operated MG15 machine gun was provided in the rear cockpit. First deliveries were made in 1938. The Bf 110C was also produced in bomber and reconnaissance subvariants.

Despite suffering very serious losses during the Battle of Britain the aircraft continued in quantity production, and in 1940 the Messerschmitt factories turned out 1,008 Bf 110 fighters and 75 reconnaissance aircraft. The Bf 110D was originally intended as a long-range escort fighter, and the Bf 110D-0 preseries aircraft featured a large ventral fuel tank, but the drag this created impaired the aircraft's performance to the extent that it was deleted in the production Bf 110D-1 and replaced by external wing tanks. The D-2 could be used in either the fighter or bomber roles and could carry up to two 2,205-lb (1,000-kg) bombs, and the D-3 was a D-1 with bomb racks attached. The Bf 110E-1 and E-2 were able to carry four 110-lb (50-kg) bombs under the wing in addition to the larger bombs slung under the fuselage, while the E-3 was a special long-range reconnaissance model.

Earlier variants had 1,300hp DB 601F engines, but the final major production aircraft, the Bf 110G, produced in larger numbers than any other variant, adopted the 1,350hp DB 605 engine. The Bf 110G-4 was a night fighter, and it was in this role that the Bf 110 truly excelled, being responsible

▲ *This Messerschmitt Bf 110 bears the code markings of Aufklärungsgruppe 14, a reconnaissance unit.*

SPECIFICATION: Type night fighter (Bf 110G) • Crew 2–3 • Powerplant two 1,475hp Daimler-Benz DB 605B-1 12-cylinder inverted-Vee type engines • Max speed 550km/h (342mph) at 22,965ft (7,000m) • Service ceiling 26,245ft (8,000m) • Max range 808 miles (1,300km) • Wingspan 53ft 3in (16.25m) • Length 42ft 9in (13.05m) including SN-2 radar antenna • Height 13ft 8in (4.18m) • Weight 21,799lb (9,888kg) • Armament two 1.19-in (30-mm) fixed forward-firing cannon in the nose, two 0.79-in (20-mm) fixed forward-firing cannon in ventral tray, and one twin-barrel machine gun in the rear cockpit position; alternatively, two upward-firing 0.79-in (20-mm) cannon in rear fuselage dorsal position

for the majority of Bomber Command's night losses to fighter attack beginning in early 1943.

▲ *A Messerschmitt Bf 110D of ZG 26 over North Africa, pictured in 1942. The Bf 110D made its combat debut in the Battle of Britain.*

▌Messerschmitt Me 163 Komet

GERMANY

The remarkable Me 163 rocket-powered interceptor was based on the experimental DFS 194, designed in 1938 by Professor Alexander Lippisch and transferred, together with its design staff, to the Messerschmitt company for further development. The first two Me 163 prototypes were flown in

the spring of 1941 as unpowered gliders, the Me 163V-1 being transferred to Peenemunde later in the year to be fitted with its 1,653-lb (750-kg) thrust Walter HWK R.II rocket motor. The fuel used was a highly volatile mixture of T-Stoff (80 percent hydrogen peroxide and 20 percent water) and C-

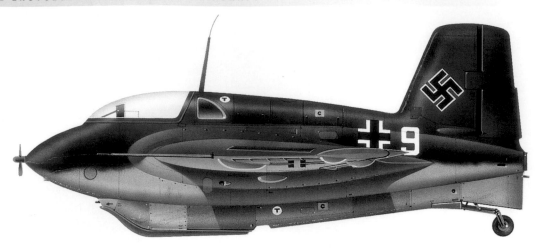

Stoff (hydrazine hydrate, methyl alcohol, and water). The first rocket-powered flight was made in August 1941, and during subsequent trials the Me 163 broke all existing world air speed records, reaching speeds of up to 620mph (1,000km/h). Because of the need for secrecy, these achievements remained unpublicized until after the war. Development of the Me 163 was accelerated, the first 70 pre-series airframes being allocated to various trials under the designation Me 163B-a1, but the program became protracted because of delays with the production version of the rocket motor, the HWK 509A. The program entered a new phase early in 1943, when some Me 163s powered by early examples of the HWK 509A were each fitted with two MG151 0.79-in (20-mm) cannon.

In May 1944, after operational trials with Erprobungkommando EK 16, whose principal function was to pioneer the Me 163B (the fully operational version) into Luftwaffe use, and to train a cadre of experienced pilots, an operational Komet unit, JG400, began forming at Wittmundhaven and Venlo, and in June all three Staffeln of this unit moved to Brandis near Leipzig, together with EK16. The task of the Komets at Brandis was to defend the Leuna oil refinery, which lay 55 miles (90km) to the south. Taking off on its jettisonable trolley, the Komet would climb initially at 11,800ft/min (3,600m/min), this rate rising to 33,470ft/min (10,200m/min) at 32,020ft (9,760m). Time to the Komet's operational ceiling of 39,698ft (12,100m) was a mere 3.35 minutes. Maximum powered endurance was eight minutes. With its fuel exhausted the Me 163 would make high-speed gliding attacks on its targets, using its two MK 108 1.19-in (30-mm) cannon and Revi 16B gunsight. With its 120 rounds of ammunition used up and its speed beginning to drop, the Komet would then dive steeply away from the combat area and glide back to base, landing on a skid. This in itself was a hazardous procedure, since there was always a risk of explosion if any unburned rocket fuel remained in the aircraft's tanks. Many Me 163s were lost in landing accidents. About 300 Komets were built, but JG400 remained the only operational unit and the rocket fighter recorded only nine kills during its brief career. The Me 163C, the last version to be built for operational use, had a pressurized cockpit, an improved Walter 109-509C motor, and featured a bubble canopy on a slightly lengthened fuselage. Only a few examples were produced, and these were not issued to units. The Me 163C was to have been fitted with a novel armament arrangement developed by Dr. Langweiler (inventor of the Panzerfaust one-man antitank weapon) comprising five vertically-mounted tubes in each wing, each tube containing a 1.95-in (50-mm) shell. The equipment was activated by a photoelectric cell as the rocket fighter passed under an enemy bomber.

The final development of the Komet was the Me 163D, which incorporated substantial redesign, including a retractable undercarriage. The aircraft was redesignated Me 263, a single prototype being built in 1944.

SPECIFICATION: **Type** rocket-powered fighter • **Crew** 1 • **Powerplant** one 3,748-lb (1,700-kg) thrust Walter 109-509A-2 rocket motor • **Max speed** 593mph (955km/h) normal operational • **Service ceiling** 39,370ft (12,000m) • **Max range** 22 miles (35.50km) combat radius • **Wingspan** 30ft 7in (9.33m) • **Length** 19ft 2in (5.85m) • **Height** 9ft (2.76m) • **Weight** 9,502lb (4,310kg) loaded • **Armament** two 1.19-in (30-mm) Mk 108 cannon in wing roots

▲ *The rocket-powered Me 163 Komet, seen here on display at Colerne, Wiltshire, in 1966, was a highly dangerous aircraft – to its pilots.*

Messerschmitt Me 210

GERMANY

The Messerschmitt Me 210 was planned as a replacement for the Bf 110, the Me 210V-1 prototype flying, initially with twin fins and rudders, on September 2, 1939. There were two major production subtypes, the Me 210A-1 heavily armed "destroyer" and the Me 210A-2 fighter-bomber. The latter became operational on the Eastern Front with II/ZG 1 in 1941 and subsequently operated over the British Isles, Tunisia, and Italy as a fast attack bomber. The type was also built under license in Hungary. The Me 210 had an appalling accident rate, mainly due to extreme instability, and despite constant attempts to improve its flight characteristics it was never a success.

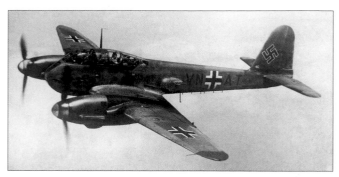

SPECIFICATION: Type fighter-bomber (Me 210A-2) • Crew 2 • Powerplant two 1,100hp Daimler-Benz DB 601Aa in-line engines • Max speed 385mph (620km/h) • Service ceiling 22,967ft (7,000m) • Max range 1,491 miles (2,400km) • Wingspan 53ft 7in (16.40m) • Length 36ft 8in (11.20m) • Height 14ft (4.30m) • Weight 17,857lb (8,100kg) loaded • Armament two 0.79-in (20-mm) cannon and two 0.31-in (7.92-mm) machine guns; internal load of two 1,102lb (500kg) bombs and external load of two 550lb (250kg) bombs

▲ Even in its A-1 production form as illustrated, the Me 210 offered poor performance by the standards of the time.

Messerschmitt Me 262

GERMANY

▲ The Messerschmitt Me 262 was a beautiful design from the aerodynamic point of view, but suffered from unreliable engines.

Design work on the Me 262, the world's first operational jet fighter, began in September 1939, a month after the successful flight of the world's first jet aircraft, the Heinkel He 178. Due to delays in the development of satisfactory engines, the massive damage caused by Allied air attacks and Hitler's later obsession with using the aircraft as a bomber rather than a fighter, six years elapsed between the 262 taking shape on Messerschmitt's drawing board and its entry into Luftwaffe service. Because of the lack of jet engines the prototype Me 262V-1 flew on April 18, 1941 under the power of a Jumo 210G piston engine, and it was not until July 18, 1942 that the Me 262V-3 made a flight under turbojet power. December 1943 saw the first flight of the Me 262V-8, the first of the type to carry a full armament of four 1.19-in (30-mm) MK 108 cannon. By the end of 1944 730 Me 262s had been completed, and a further 564 were built in the early months of 1945, making a total of 1,294 aircraft. The Me 262 initially went into production as a pure fighter, entering service in August 1944.

The Me 262 presented a serious threat to Allied air superiority during the closing weeks of 1944. Two versions were now being developed in parallel, the Me 262A-2a Sturmvogel (Stormbird) bomber variant and the Me 262A-1a fighter. The Sturmvogel was issued to Kampfgeschwader 51 "Edelweiss" in September 1944; other bomber units that armed with the type at a later date were KG 6, 27 and 54. There were also two reconnaissance versions, the Me 262A-1a/U3 and Me 262A-5a. The first Jagdgeschwader to arm with the Me 262 fighter was JG 7 Hindenburg. In the middle of February 1945 III/JG 7 took delivery of the first consignment of R4M 5cm air-to-air rockets; the Me 262 could carry 24 of these missiles mounted on simple wooden racks beneath the wings, and when the salvo was fired toward an enemy bomber formation it spread out rather like the charge from a shotgun, increasing the chances of hitting one

SPECIFICATION: Type jet fighter (data apply to the Me 262A-1a) • Crew 1 • Powerplant two 1,984lb (900kg) thrust Junkers Jumo 109-004B 4 turbojets • Max speed 541mph (870km/h) at 22,965ft (7,000m) • Service ceiling 37,565ft (11,450m) • Max range 652 miles (1,050km) • Wingspan 41ft (12.51m) • Length 34ft 9in (10.60m) • Height 11ft 6in (3.50m) • Weight 15,720lb (7,130kg) loaded • Armament four 1.19-in (30-mm) MK 108 cannon in nose

or more targets. During their first series of operations using a combination of R4Ms, 1.19-in (30-mm) cannon and Revi gunsight, in the last week of February 1945, the pilots of III/JG 7 destroyed no fewer than 45 four-engined American bombers and 15 of their escorting fighters for the loss of only four Me 262s. Meanwhile, authority had been given for the formation of a second Me 262 jet fighter unit. Known as Jagdverband 44, it comprised 45 highly experienced pilots, many of them Germany's top-scoring aces. Its main operating base was München-Riem, where its main targets were the bombers of the Fifteenth Army Air Force, coming up from

the south, while JG 7 continued to operate from bases in northern and central Germany before the jets were grounded through lack of fuel or engine spares, the Jumo 004 having a life of only 25 hours. Most of the 262s were destroyed by their ground crews shortly before the airfield was overrun by American tanks on May 3rd.

Several variants of the Me 262 were proposed, including the radar-equipped Me 262B-1a/U1 two-seat night fighter, which saw service briefly from March 1945 with 10/NJG11 under Leutnant Welter, who on the night of March 30/31 destroyed four RAF Mosquitoes on the approaches to Berlin.

Messerschmitt Me 323

The Messerschmitt Me 323 was a powered version of the massive Me 321 transport glider, which first flew in March 1941, towed into the air by a Junkers Ju 90. In addition to this aircraft, the glider could be towed by a trio of Bf 110Cs or a single Heinkel He 111Z; rocket-assisted takeoff was also used. About 200 Me 321s were built, and were mostly used to ferry material to the Eastern Front. Two versions of the powered

Me 323 were built, the four-engined Me 323V-1, which was underpowered, and the six-engined Me 323V-2. The production version of this aircraft was the Me 323D, the first units being used to ferry supplies and reinforcements from Sicily to North Africa in 1942–3. They suffered grievous losses, 21 Me 323s being destroyed in a single engagement with Allied fighters on April 22, 1943. The last version of the giant aircraft was the Me 323E, with increased armament and more powerful engines; other variants remained projects only.

▲ The Messerschmitt Me 323 transport was easy prey for Allied fighters, and suffered serious losses during attempts to supply Axis forces in Tunisia in 1943.

SPECIFICATION: Type transport aircraft (Me 323D-1) • Crew 5–7 • Powerplant six 1,140hp Gnome-Rhone 14N 14-cylinder radial engines • Max speed 144mph (232km/h) • Service ceiling 13,120ft (4,000m) • Max range 810 miles (1,300km) • Wingspan 180ft 5in (55m) • Length 93ft 6in (28.50m) • Height 31ft 6in (9.60m) • Weight 96,010lb (43,550kg) loaded • Armament five 0.51-in (13-mm) MG 131 machine guns and two 0.79-in (20-mm) cannon

Messerschmitt Me 410

The Messerschmitt Me 410 Hornisse (Hornet) was a development of the Me 210 twin-engine fighter, with revised aerodynamic and structural features and DB 603A engines.

It was flown in prototype form in the fall of 1942 and production ran to 1,913 aircraft. The principal subtypes were the A-1 fighter-bomber, the A-1/U2 and A-2 heavy fighters,

▲ A Messerschmitt Me 410 on display at the RAF Museum, Hendon. The Me 410 was used on intruder operations over the British Isles.

and the reconnaissance A-3. The Me 410 played a significant part in the so-called "Little Blitz" against Britain in the early weeks of 1944.

SPECIFICATION: Type heavy fighter (Me 410A-2/U4) • Crew 2 • Powerplant two 1,750hp DB 603A 12-cylinder inverted-Vee engines • Max speed 388mph (624km/h) • Service ceiling 32,808ft (10,000m) • Max range 1,037 miles (1,670km) • Wingspan 53ft 7in (16.35m) • Length 40ft 11in (12.48m) • Height 14ft (4.28m) • Weight 23,478lb (10,650kg) loaded • Armament one 1.97-in (50-mm) BK5 cannon and two 0.79-in (20-mm) cannon in nose; one rearward/lateral firing 0.50-in (13-mm) machine gun in each of two remotely-controlled barbettes on sides of fuselage

Mikoyan-Gurevich MiG-1/MiG-7 USSR

The MiG-1 was developed to meet a Soviet Air Force requirement, issued in 1938, for a high-altitude fighter, and although it was unstable and difficult to fly it was rushed into production because of its high performance. The prototype flew in April 1940. The MiG-1 was redesignated MiG-3 after the 100th machine had been produced, the main improvements being a fully enclosed cockpit and the addition of an auxiliary

▶ This aircraft was the first of the unarmed I-200 prototypes. These machines evolved into the MiG-1 following an extensive series of modifications.

SPECIFICATION: Type fighter (data MiG-3) • Crew 1 • Powerplant one 1,350hp Mikulin AM-35A 12-cylinder V-type • Max speed 398mph (640km/h) at 16,405ft (5,000m) • Service ceiling 39,370ft (12,000m) • Max range 742 miles (1,195km) • Wingspan 33ft 5in (10.20m) • Length 27ft (8.25m) • Height 8ft 3in (2.51m) • Weight 7,385lb (3,350kg) • Armament one 0.50-in(12.7-mm) and two 0.30-in (7.62-mm) machine guns in upper forward fuselage

fuel tank. Total MiG-3 production was 3,322 aircraft. The next MiG fighter design, the MiG-5, was basically a MiG-3 with a Shvetsov M-82A radial engine and was produced only in small numbers in 1943, the La-5 being preferred for mass production. The MiG-7, which featured an in-line engine, was developed as a high-altitude interceptor in 1944, but appeared only in small numbers.

Mikoyan-Gurevich MiG-9 "Fargo" USSR

Development of the MiG-9, the USSR's second jet fighter, was initiated in February 1945, the aircraft initially known as

SPECIFICATION: Type fighter • Crew 1 • Powerplant two 1,764-lb (800-kg) thrust RD-20 (BMW 003A) turbojets • Max speed 566mph (911km/h) at 16,400ft (5,000m) • Service ceiling 44,290ft (13,500m) • Max range 900 miles (1,448km) with underwing tanks • Wingspan 32ft 10in (10m) • Length 32ft (9.75m) • Height 13ft (3.96m) • Weight 11,177lb (5,070kg) loaded • Armament one 1.46-in (37-mm) and two 0.9-in (23-mm) cannon

the I-300. The prototype flew on April 24, 1946, powered by two BMW 003 turbojets. These were mounted side by side in the fuselage, with a 1.46-in (37-mm) cannon between them. A small series production batch was built with deliveries to the Soviet Air Force beginning in December 1946. Early in 1947, production MiG-9s were fitted with the uprated RD-21 engine and redesignated MiG-9F. The last batch of production aircraft had pressurized cockpits and carried the designation MiG-9FR. About 550 aircraft were built in total, including a two-seat trainer variant, the MiG-9UTI.

■ Mikoyan-Gurevich MiG-15 "Fagot"   USSR

▲ *An example of the quality of official images emerging from the USSR during the Cold War. The censor has erased details of the armament of these MiG 15Bs.*

One of the most famous jet fighters of all time, and certainly one of the most outstanding combat aircraft of the post-war years, the MiG-15 was designed by a Russo-German

SPECIFICATION: Type fighter (data MiG-15B) • Crew 1 • Powerplant one 5,952-lb (2,700-kg) Klimov VK-1 turbojet • Max speed 684mph (1,100km/h) at 25,000ft (7,625m) • Service ceiling 51,000ft (15,545m) • Max range 885 miles (1,424km) with slipper tanks • Wingspan 33ft (10.08m) • Length 36ft 3in (11.05m) • Height 11ft 1in (3.40m) • Weight 12,566lb (5,700kg) loaded • Armament one 1.46-in (37-mm) N-37 and two 0.9-in (23-mm) NS-23 cannon; up to 1,102lb (500kg) of underwing stores

team headed by Artem I. Mikoyan and Mikhail I. Gurevich. The type flew for the first time on December 30, 1947 and entered series production in the following year.

The first MiG-15s were powered by the Rolls-Royce Nene copy, designated RD-45. The prototype crashed during testing, killing its pilot, and the second aircraft was extensively modified, with a strengthened wing featuring slight anhedral and boundary layer fences. Many first-line fighter units of the Soviet Air Force had equipped with the type by the end of 1948, and a number of improvements were made to the basic design. Airframe design progress, in fact, proceeded in parallel with engine development, and starting in November 1948 the MiG-15's fuselage was modified to accommodate an uprated version of the Nene designated VK-1 (the engineer responsible being Vladimir Klimov). This engine had redesigned turbine blades, larger combustion chambers and developed 5,945-lb (2,697-kg) thrust (6750lb/3,058kg with water injection). The uprated aircraft was designated MiG-15B, and was serving in large numbers with the Soviet Air Force by the end of 1950. Production of the MiG-15 eventually reached some 18,000 aircraft, this figure including a tandem two-seat trainer version, the MiG-15UTI. The MiG-15 was built under license in the People's Republic of China as the Shenyang F-2, in Poland as the LIM-1, and in Czechoslovakia as the S-102.

The MiG-15 saw a great deal of action in its heyday, starting with the Korean war, where it fought the North American F-86 Sabre in history's first jet-versus-jet air battles. It also took part in the various Arab–Israeli conflicts, serving with the Syrian and Egyptian air forces, and was used operationally over North Vietnam and in the Nigerian civil war.

▌Mikoyan-Gurevich MiG-17 "Fresco"   USSR

When the MiG-17 first appeared in the early 1950s, western observers at first believed that it was an improved MiG-15, with new features that reflected the technical lessons learned during the Korean War. In fact, design of the MiG-17 had begun in 1949, the new type incorporating a number of aerodynamic refinements that included a new tail on a longer fuselage and a thinner wing with different section and platform and with three boundary layer fences to improve handling at high speed. The basic version, known to NATO as Fresco-A, entered service in 1952; this was followed by the MiG-17P all-weather interceptor (Fresco-B) and then the major production variant, the MiG-17F (Fresco-C) which had structural refinements and was fitted with an afterburner. The last variant, the MiG-17PFU, was armed with air-to-air missiles. About 9,000 MiG-17s were produced in total, and like the MiG-15 the type was widely exported to countries within the Soviet sphere of influence. Also like the MiG-15, the MiG-17 fought in the Middle East conflicts and over North Vietnam, where it proved a dangerous opponent in combat with much more advanced American types.

▲ During the war in Vietnam, the highly maneuverable MiG-17 caused serious problems for more advanced American jets like the F-4 Phantom.

SPECIFICATION: Type fighter (data Fresco-C) • Crew 1 • Powerplant one 7,458-lb (3,383-kg) thrust Klimov VK-1F turbojet • Max speed 711mph (1,145km/h) at 9,840ft (3,000m) • Service ceiling 54,460m (16,600m) • Max range 913 miles (1,470km) with slipper tanks • Wingspan 31ft (9.45m) • Length 36ft 3in (11.05m) • Height 11ft (3.35m) • Weight 13,300lb (6,000kg) loaded • Armament one 1.46-in (37-mm) N-37 and two 0.9-in (23-mm) NS-23 cannon; up to 1,102lb (500kg) of underwing stores

▌Mikoyan-Gurevich MiG-19 "Farmer"   USSR

Designed as a successor to the MiG-17, the MiG-19 was the first operational Soviet aircraft capable of exceeding Mach 1.0 in level flight. The first production model proved to have stability problems, and after modifications a second variant, the MiG-19S, went into service in 1956. Both were known to NATO as Farmer-A. In 1958 an all-weather fighter variant appeared, designated MiG-19P (Farmer-B), followed by the MiG-19C (Farmer-F) with more powerful engines. The MiG-19PF was a missile-armed all-weather variant, while the MiG-19PM was a night fighter. Like its predecessors, the MiG-19 was built under license in China, Poland, and Czechoslovakia. Despite manufacturing problems which resulted in an entire batch of aircraft being scrapped, Chinese-built aircraft (known as the Shenyang F-6) were exported to Pakistan and Vietnam, seeing combat with the air forces of both countries.

SPECIFICATION: Type interceptor (data MiG-19PM) • Crew 1 • Powerplant two 7,165-lb (3,250-kg) thrust Klimov RD-9B turbojets • Max speed 920mph (1,480km/h) at 29,800ft (9,080m) • Service ceiling 58,725ft (17,900m) • Max range 1,367 miles (2,200km) with external tanks • Wingspan 29ft 6in (9m) • Length 44ft 7in (13.58m) • Height 13ft 2in (4.02m) • Weight 20,944lb (9,500kg) • Armament four AA-1 Alkali or AA-2 Atoll air-to-air missiles on underwing pylons

▲ *The MiG-19 was produced in China as the Shenyang F-6, two examples of which are seen here, and was supplied to the Pakistan Air Force.*

▌Mikoyan-Gurevich MiG-21 "Fishbed"

USSR

The MiG-21 was a child of the Korean War, where Soviet air combat experience had identified a need for a light, single-seat target defense interceptor with high supersonic maneuverability. Two prototypes were ordered, both appearing early in 1956; one, code-named Faceplate, featured sharply swept wings and was not developed further. The initial production versions (Fishbed-A and -B) were built only in limited numbers, being short-range day fighters with a comparatively light armament of two 1.19-in (30-mm) NR-30 cannon, but the next variant, the MiG-21F Fishbed-C, carried two K-13 Atoll infrared homing AAMs, and had an uprated Tumansky R-11 turbojet as well as improved

avionics.

The MiG-21F was the first major production version; it entered service in 1960 and was progressively modified and updated over the years that followed. In the early 1970s the MiG-21 was virtually redesigned, reemerging as the MiG-21B (Fishbed-L) multirole air superiority fighter and ground attack version. The Fishbed-N, which appeared in 1971, introduced new advanced construction techniques, greater fuel capacity and updated avionics for multirole air combat and ground attack. In its several versions the MiG-21 became the most widely used jet fighter in the world, being license-built in India, Czechoslovakia, and China, where it was designated Shenyang F-8, and equipping some 25 Soviet-aligned air forces. In Vietnam, the MiG-21 was the Americans' deadliest opponent.

▲ *A line-up of MiG-21 Fishbed-J fighters at a Soviet air base. The MiG-21 proved a formidable opponent in the air war over Vietnam.*

SPECIFICATION: **Type** multirole combat aircraft (data MiG-21B) • **Crew** 1 • **Powerplant** one 16,535-lb (7,507-kg) thrust Tumanskii R-25 turbojet • **Max speed** 1,385mph (2,229km/h) at 36,090ft (11,000m) • **Service ceiling** 57,400ft (17,500m) • **Max range** 721 miles (1,160km) on internal fuel • **Wingspan** 23ft 5in (7.15m) • **Length** 51ft 8in (15.76m) • **Height** 13ft 5in (4.10m) • **Weight** 22,925lb (10,400kg) • **Armament** one 0.9-in (23-mm) GSh-23 twin-barrel cannon in pack under fuselage; four underwing pylons with provision for 3,307lb (1,500kg) of stores, including AAMs, rocket pods, napalm tanks, and drop tanks

▌Mikoyan-Gurevich MiG-23 "Flogger"

The MiG-23, which flew in prototype form in 1967 and entered service with the Frontal Aviation's attack units of the 16th Air Army in Germany in 1973, was a variable-geometry fighter-bomber with wings sweeping from 23 to 71 degrees, and was the Soviet Air Force's first true multirole combat aircraft. The MiG-23M Flogger-B was the first series production version and equipped all the major Warsaw Pact air forces; a simplified version for export to Libya and other Middle East air forces was designated MiG-23MS Flogger-E. The MiG-23UB Flogger-C was a two-seat trainer, retaining the combat capability of the single-seat variants, while the MiG-23BN/BM Flogger-F and -H were fighter-bomber versions for export. The MiG-27, which began to enter service in the late 1970s, was a dedicated battlefield support variant known to NATO as Flogger-D; the MiG-27D and -27K Flogger-J were improved versions, while the MiG-23P was a dedicated air defense variant. About 5,000 MiG-23/27s were built, and in the 1990s the type was in service with 20 air forces.

SPECIFICATION: Type fighter (data MiG-23MF) • Crew 1 • Powerplant one 22,046-lb (10,000-kg) thrust Tumanskii R-27F2M-300 turbojet • Max speed 1,520mph (2,445km/h) at altitude • Service ceiling 60,000ft (18,290m) • Combat radius 600 miles (966km) hi-lo-hi • Wingspan 45ft 10in (13.97m) spread; 25ft 6in (7.78m) swept • Length 54ft 10in (16.71m) • Height 15ft 9in (4.82m) • Weight 40,000lb (18,145kg) • Armament one 0.9-in (23-mm) GSh-23L cannon; underwing pylons for various combinations of AAM

▲ The MiG-23 Flogger was one of the Soviet military aviation industry's major success stories, being widely exported to many different air forces.

▌Mikoyan-Gurevich MiG-25 "Foxbat"

The prototype MiG-25 was flown as early as 1964 and was apparently designed to counter the projected North American B-70 bomber, with its Mach 3.0 speed and ceiling of 70,000ft (21,350m). The cancelation of the B-70 left the Foxbat in search of a role; it entered service as an interceptor in 1970 with the designation MiG-25P (Foxbat-A), but soon a MiG-25RB (Foxbat-B) variant appeared, equipped with

▶ The MiG-25 Foxbat was originally designed to intercept supersonic, high-altitude bombers, but found a new role as a reconnaissance aircraft.

SPECIFICATION: Type interceptor • Crew 1 • Powerplant two 22,487-lb (10,200-kg) thrust Tumanskii R-15B-300 turbojets • Max speed 1,848mph (2,974km/h) at altitude • Service ceiling 80,000ft (24,383m) • Combat radius 702 miles (1,130km) • Wingspan 45ft 11in (14.02m) • Length 78ft 1in (23.82m) • Height 20ft (6.10m) • Weight 82,508lb (37,425kg) • Armament four underwing pylons for various combinations of air-to-air missile

cameras and electronic surveillance equipment, and it was in this role that the type found its true value. The MiG-25RB produced several subvariants, all with modifications of a sufficiently obvious nature for them to receive the NATO appellation Foxbat-D. The MiG-25 in its various forms was also operated by Algeria, India, Iraq, Libya, and Syria.

Mikoyan MiG-29 "Fulcrum"

USSR

▲ *With the reunification of Germany, the Luftwaffe inherited 23 former East German MiG-29s, one of which is seen here alongside an ageing Phantom II.*

Just as the F-15 was developed to counter the MiG-25 Foxbat and the MiG-23 Flogger, both of which were unveiled in the late 1960s, the MiG-29 Fulcrum and another Russian fighter, the Sukhoi Su-27 Flanker, were designed in response to the F-15 and its naval counterpart, the Grumman F-14 Tomcat. Both Russian aircraft share a similar configuration, combining a wing swept at 40 degrees with highly swept wing root extensions, underslung engines with wedge intakes, and twin fins. The combination of modest wing sweep with highly swept root extensions, designed to enhance maneuverability, is also used on the Lockheed Martin F-16 Fighting Falcon and the McDonnell Douglas F-18 Hornet.

The MiG-29, the first of the new Russian air superiority fighters to enter service, is powered by two Klimov/Sarkisov RD-33 two-spool low bypass turbofan engines which, at the aircraft's normal takeoff weight of 15 tons, give a thrust-weight ratio of 1.1. Design emphasis from the start was on very high maneuverability and the ability to destroy targets at distances of between 660ft (200m) and 32nm (60km). Forty percent of the MiG-29's lift is provided by its lift-generating center fuselage and the aircraft is able to achieve angles of attack at least 70 percent higher than earlier fighters. The aircraft has an RP-29 pulse-Doppler radar capable of detecting targets at around 62 miles (100km) against a back-

SPECIFICATION: Type air superiority fighter (data MiG-29 Fulcrum-A) • Crew 1 • Powerplant two 18,298-lb (8,300-kg) thrust Sarkisov RD-33 turbofans • Max speed 1,518mph (2,443km/h) at 36,090ft (11,000m) • Service ceiling 55,775ft (17,000m) • Max range 932 miles (1,500km) on internal fuel • Wingspan 37ft 3in (11.36m) • Length 56ft 10in (17.32m) • Height 25ft 6in (7.78m) • Weight 40,785lb (18,500kg) • Armament one 1.19-in (30-mm) GSh-30 cannon; eight external hardpoints with provision for up to 9,921lb (4,500kg) of stores, including six AAMs rocket pods, bombs etc.

ground of ground clutter. Fire control and mission comput-
ers link the radar with a laser rangefinder and infrared
search/track sensor, in conjunction with a helmet-mounted
target designator. The radar can track ten targets simultaneously, and the system allows the MiG-29 to approach and
engage targets without emitting detectable radar or radio signals. The Fulcrum-A became operational in 1985. The
MiG-29K is a navalized version, the MiG-29M is a variant
with advanced fly-by-wire systems, and the MiG-29UB is a
two-seat operational trainer.

■ Mikoyan MiG-31 "Foxhound" USSR

Just as the MiG-29 and the Su-27/37 were
developed to take on the air superiority
role, the MiG-31, a greatly developed version of the MiG-25, was initiated to
counter the threat to the former Soviet
Union from B-52s and B-1s carrying air-
launched cruise missiles. The aircraft is a
two-seat, all-weather, all-altitude
interceptor designed to be guided

▲ The MiG-31 Foxhound was developed to counter the threat from US
strategic aircraft capable of launching cruise missiles.

SPECIFICATION: Type interceptor • Crew 2 • Powerplant two 34,171-lb (15,500-kg)
thrust Soloviev D-30F6 turbofans • Max speed 1,865mph (3,000km/h) at
57,400ft (17,500m) • Service ceiling 67,600ft (20,600m) • Combat radius 870
miles (1,400km) with weapons load • Wingspan 44ft 2in (13.46m) • Length 74ft
5in (22.68m) • Height 20ft 2in (6.15m) • Weight 101,850lb (46,200kg) •
Armament four AA-9 Amos semiactive radar homing long-range AAMs on
ejector pylons under the fuselage, plus two AA-6 Acrid medium-range infrared
AAMs, and four AA-8 Aphid short-range infrared AAMs on underwing pylons.

automatically to its targets and to engage them under ground
control. In a typical mission profile, an interception would be
made by a flight of four aircraft, the leader being linked to
the AK-RLDN ground radar guidance network and the other
three linked to the leader by APD-518 digital datalink. This
arrangement permits a line abreast radar sweep covering a
zone some 485-nm (900-km) wide.

■ Mitsubishi A5M "Claude" JAPAN

First flown in prototype form in January 1935, the
Mitsubishi A5M was Japan's first carrier-borne monoplane
fighter and its appearance was of great importance, for it
marked the end of Japanese dependence on foreign designs.
The prototype had an inverted gull wing, but subsequent aircraft featured a wing with a straight center section and dihedral on the outboard panels. The initial production model
was designated A5M1 Type 96 and had an enclosed cockpit,
the first to be used by a Japanese fighter. It was not popular
with the A5M's pilots and subsequent variants reverted to an
open cockpit. These were the A5M2a, with a more powerful
engine, and the A5M2b, with a three-blade propeller. The
A5M3 was an experimental model fitted with a 0.79-in
(20-mm) cannon firing through the propeller hub, and the
last production model was the A5M4, the A5M4-K being a
tandem two-seat trainer version. The A5M was widely used
in China, but with the exception of one attack on Davao in
the Philippines the type did not see combat against the Allies.
Production totaled 1,094 aircraft.

▲ The Mitsubishi A5M, known as Claude to the Allies, was the Japanese
Navy's first monoplane fighter, and was highly maneuverable.

SPECIFICATION: Type naval fighter (data A5M4) • Crew 1 • Powerplant one
785hp Nakajima Kotobjuki 41 9-cylinder radial • Max speed 270mph
(435km/h) at 9,845ft (3,000m) • Service ceiling 32,150ft (9,800m) • Max range
870 miles (1,400km) • Wingspan 36ft 1in (11m) • Length 24ft 9in (7.54m) •
Height 10ft 8in (3.27m) • Weight 4,016lb (1,822kg) • Armament two fixed
forward-firing 0.303-in (7.7-mm) machine guns in upper forward fuselage;
external bomb load of 132lb (60kg)

▌Mitsubishi A6M Reisen "Zeke", "Zero"

▲ *A captured Mitsubishi A6M2 Zero being test flown by an American pilot. The Zero was a light and robust design married to a powerful engine.*

The Imperial Japanese Navy bore the brunt of long-range operations against Chinese targets during the Sino-Japanese wars, the aircraft industry developing bombers for missions at extreme range and also a fighter capable of escorting them to the target and back. The result was one of the finest fighter aircraft of all time, the Mitsubishi A6M Reisen. Designed by Jiro Horikoshi to Specification 12-shi (1937), this superb fighter first flew on April 1, 1939, powered by a 780hp Zuisei 13 radial engine, and after 15 aircraft had been evaluated under combat conditions in China, the type was accepted for service with the Japanese Naval Air Force in July 1940, entering full production in November that year as the A6M2 Model 11. Sixty-four Model 11s were completed, these being powered by the more powerful Sakae 12 engine, and were followed by the Model 21 with folding wingtips. This was the major production version at the time of the attack on Pearl Harbor in December 1941.

The A6M2 soon showed itself to be clearly superior to any fighter the Allies could put into the air in the early stages of the Pacific war. Armed with two 0.79-in (20-mm) Type 99 cannon and two 0.303-in (7.7-mm) Type 97 machine guns, it was highly maneuverable and structurally very strong, despite being lightweight. Instead of being built in several separate units, it was constructed in two pieces. The engine, cockpit, and forward fuselage combined with the wings to form one rigid unit, the second unit comprising the rear

fuselage and the tail. The two units were joined together by a ring of 80 bolts. Its main drawback was that it had no armor plating for the pilot and no self-sealing fuel tanks, which meant that it could not absorb as much battle damage as Allied fighters. One well-placed burst of gunfire was usually enough to make the aircraft disintegrate.

In 1942 the Americans allocated the code name Zeke to the A6M, but as time went by the name "Zero" came into general use, due to its designation as the Navy's Type 0 Carrier Fighter. During the first months of the Pacific war the Zeros carved out an impressive combat record. In the battle for Java, which ended on March 8, 1942, they destroyed 550 Allied aircraft, including large numbers of fighters such as the Brewster Buffalo, Curtiss-Wright CW.21, Curtiss Hawk, Curtiss P-40, and Hawker Hurricane. Japanese losses were extremely light. In 1942 Japanese Navy fighter units began to receive the A6M3 Model 32, with a supercharged 1300 Sakae 21 engine. This model had its folding wingtips removed to improve performance, but this impaired the fighter's maneuverability and the full-span wing was restored in the A6M3 Model 22. By early 1943 it was becoming apparent that the A6M3 could no longer retain superiority over the latest Allied fighters, so the A6M5 Model 52 was developed, retaining the Sakae 21 engine but having a shorter-span wing (in essence, a Model 32 wing with rounded tips). Subtypes produced included the A6M5a Model 52A, with strengthened wings and increased ammunition, the A6M5b Model 52B with heavier armament and armor protection, and the A6M5c Model 52C, with more armor, two 0.79-in (20-mm) and three 0.51-in (13-mm) guns. The latter subtype had a Sakae 31 engine with methanol injection, bullet-proof fuel tanks, and underwing rocket rails. The A6M7 Model 63 was a special Kamikaze version, of which 465 were built; hundreds more Zeros were also expended in suicide attacks. Other versions were the A6M8c Model 54C, with a 1,500hp Mitsubishi Kinsei 62 engine and four wing guns, a twin-float seaplane, the A6M2-N, and the A6M2-K2 two-seat trainer. In all, 10,937 Zeros of all versions were built.

SPECIFICATION: Type naval fighter (data A6M2) • Crew 1 • Powerplant one 950hp Nakajima NK1C Sakae 12 14-cylinder radial • Max speed 332mph (534km/h) • Service ceiling 32,810ft (10,000m) • Max range 1,929 miles (3,104km) • Wingspan 39ft 4in (12m) • Length 29ft 8in (9.06m) • Height 10ft (3.05m) • Weight 6,164lb (2,796kg) loaded • Armament two 0.79-in (20-mm) Type 99 (Oerlikon) fixed forward-firing cannon in wing leading edges; two fixed forward-firing 0.303-in (7.7-mm) machine guns in forward fuselage; external bomb load of 265lb (120kg)

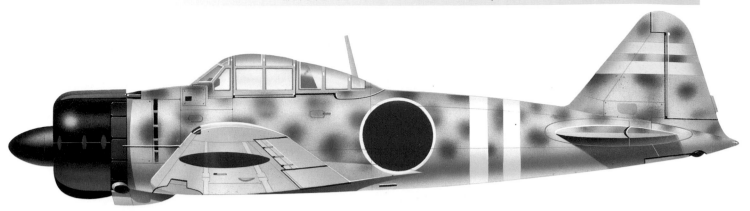

▌ Mitsubishi A7M Reppu "Sam"

Intended to replace the Zero as the Navy's standard carrier-borne fighter, the A7M Reppu (Hurricane) was ordered into production in 1940, but because of delays only nine proto-types and one production aircraft were built. The first proto-type flew for the first time on October 30, 1944, by which time most of the Japanese carrier force had been destroyed.

SPECIFICATION: **Type** naval fighter (data A7M2) • **Crew** 1 • **Powerplant** one 1,570hp Mitsubishi MK9A 18-cylinder radial • **Max speed** 390mph (627km/h) at 21,655ft (6,600m) • **Service ceiling** 35,760ft (10,900m) • **Endurance** 2hrs 30mins • **Wingspan** 45ft 11in (14m) • **Length** 36ft 1in (11m) • **Height** 14ft (4.28m) • **Weight** 10,406lb (4,720kg) loaded • **Armament** four wing-mounted 0.79-in (20mm) cannon

▲ *The A7M2 showed much promise as a fighter, especially when powered by the Mitsubishi MK9A engine, shown here.*

▌ Mitsubishi B2M

The Mitsubishi B2M was a metal structure torpedo-bomber and reconnaissance aircraft that was actually designed by Blackburn Aircraft Ltd. as the Navy Type 89. (The "type numbers" of Japanese aircraft indicated the year in which the air-craft was manufactured according to the Japanese calendar. "Type 89" meant that the B2M1 entered production in 1929, the Japanese year 2589). The type was constructed in two main series, the B2M1 and B2M2, a total of 104 being built.

▶ *The design for the B2M was subcontracted to other companies, and the British company Blackburn won the contest in 1928.*

SPECIFICATION: **Type** torpedo-bomber and reconnaissance aircraft • **Crew** 2 • **Powerplant** one 600hp Hispano-Mitsubishi 12-cylinder V-type • **Max speed** 132mph (213km/h) • **Service ceiling** 14,763ft (4,500m) • **Max range** 600 miles (960km) • **Wingspan** 49ft 11in (15.22m) • **Length** 33ft 8in (10.27m) • **Height** 12ft 2in (3.71m) • **Weight** 7,936lb (3,600kg) loaded • **Armament** two 0.303-in (7.7-mm) machine guns; 1,763lb (800kg) of bombs

▌ Mitsubishi F.1

JAPAN ●

Designed to replace the F-86 Sabre in the Japanese Air Self-Defense Force, the F.1 strike fighter was developed from the T.2 supersonic trainer. The second and third production T.2s were converted as prototypes and the first of 77 F.1s was delivered in September 1977, the last delivery being made in March 1987.

▼ *Remarkably similar to the SEPECAT Jaguar, the F.1 is used principally in what is known to the JASDF as the anti-landing craft role.*

SPECIFICATION: **Type** strike fighter • **Crew** 1 • **Powerplant** two 7,308-lb (3,315-kg) thrust Ishikawajima-Harima TF40 IHI-801A turbojets • **Max speed** 1,061mph (1,708km/h) at 35,000ft (10,675m) • **Service ceiling** 50,000ft (15,240m) • **Combat radius** 218 miles (350km) with 4,000-lb (1,816-kg) weapons load hi-lo-hi • **Wingspan** 25ft 10in (7.88m) • **Length** 58ft 7in (17.86m) • **Height** 14ft 4in (4.39m) • **Weight** 30,203lb (13,700kg) • **Armament** one 0.79-in (20-mm) JM61 Vulcan six-barrel cannon; five hardpoints with provision for up to 6,000lb (2,722kg) of external stores

▌ Mitsubishi F1M "Pete"

JAPAN

The Mitsubishi F1M biplane was developed in the mid-1930s as a catapult-launched floatplane to be carried on board the Imperial Japanese Navy's capital ships. Production reached a total of 1,118—the aircraft being used in a wide variety of roles that eventually encompassed fighter, close support, and dive-bombing.

◄ The Mitsubishi F1M was unique among Japanese naval aircraft in that it was the only observation seaplane to enter quantity production.

SPECIFICATION: Type general-purpose floatplane • Crew 2 • Powerplant one 875hp Mitsubishi Zuisei 14-cylinder radial • Max speed 230mph (370km/h) at 11,285ft (3,440m) • Service ceiling 30,970ft (9,440m) • Max range 460 miles (740km) • Wingspan 36ft 1in (11m) • Length 31ft 2in (9.50m) • Height 13ft 1in (4m) • Weight 6,926lb (3,141kg) loaded • Armament two fixed forward-firing 0.303-in (7.7mm) machine guns; one flexible 0.303-in (7.7mm) machine gun in rear cockpit

▮ Mitsubishi G3M "Nell"   JAPAN

The Imperial Japanese Naval Air Force's Mitsubishi G3M medium bomber was developed by way of a series of experimental designs in the early 1930s, the prototype making its first flight in July 1935. The initial version, the G3M1, went into production in June 1936, but only 34 examples were built before it was replaced on the production line by the improved G3M2. Some G3M1s were converted into passenger transports under the designation L3Y1. Total production of the G3M series, which reached 1048 aircraft, included the Kinsei

▲ Of limited value as a bomber in the later stages of the war, the G3M found new utility as the transport L3Y2.

42-powered G3M2b, the G3M2d (L3Y2) transport, which received the Allied code name Tina, and the final bomber version, the G3M3, with 1,300hp Kasei 51 engines. The G3M was widely used in China, and about 250 were still in service when Japan entered World War II. Some specially converted aircraft were used to photograph American installations in the Pacific in the months before the attack on Pearl Harbor. The G3M saw widespread service during the Pacific war, one of its first successful actions being the sinking of HM warships *Prince of Wales* and *Repulse* off Malaya on December 10, 1941.

SPECIFICATION: Type medium bomber (data G3M2) • Crew 7 • Powerplant two 1,075hp Mitsubishi Kinsei 41/42/45 14-cylinder radials • Max speed 232mph (373km/h) at 9,845ft (3,000m) • Service ceiling 29,950ft (9,130m) • Max range 2,722 miles (4,380km) • Wingspan 82ft (25m) • Length 53ft 11in (16.45m) • Height 12ft 1in (3.69m) • Weight 17,637lb (8,000kg) • Armament one 0.79-in (20-mm) cannon in dorsal turret; three 0.303-in (7.7-mm) machine guns, one each in retractable ventral turret and in two beam positions; bomb or torpedo load of 1,764lb (800kg)

▮ Mitsubishi G4M "Betty"   JAPAN

Although the G3M had an excellent performance, the Japanese Naval Staff was anxious to make improvements with special regard to speed and range, and in the second half of 1937 Mitsubishi developed the G4M, the prototype making its first flight on October 23, 1939 and the initial production G4M1 version coming off the assembly lines from April 1941. About 200 were in service at the time of the attack on Pearl Harbor and were used in the torpedo attack as well as the level-bombing role. In November 1942 the much improved G4M2 made its appearance, this variant gradually replacing the G4M1, which was assigned to transport, reconnaissance, and training duties. Subvariants of the G4M2 were the

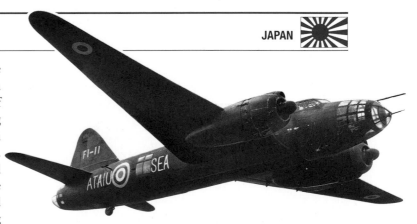

▲ A captured G4M seen in the markings of the Allied Tactical Air Intelligence Unit, South-East Asia Command, at the end of World War II.

SPECIFICATION: Type medium bomber (data G4M2) • Crew 7 • Powerplant two 1,800hp Mitsubishi MK4P Kasei 21 14-cylinder radials • Max speed 272mph (438km/h) at 26,245ft (8,000m) • Service ceiling 30,185ft (9,200m) • Max range 3,765 miles (6,059km) • Wingspan 82ft (25m) • Length 65ft 7in (20m) • Height 19ft 8in (6m) • Weight 27,557lb (12,500kg) • Armament two 0.303-in (7.7-mm) machine guns in nose position; four 0.79-in (20-mm) cannon, one each in dorsal, beam, and tail positions; bomb or torpedo load of 1,764lb (800kg)

G4M2a, with Kasei 25 engines, the high-altitude G4M2b, with Kasei 27s, the G4M2c (Kasei 25b engines), and the G4M2d, which was a turbojet engine test bed. The G4M2e was specially modified to carry the Ohka piloted suicide aircraft. One of the drawbacks in the design of the G4M was its lack of protective armor and self-sealing fuel tanks; these shortcomings were rectified in the last bomber version, the G4M3, but only 60 were completed out of a total production figure of 2,479.

▌Mitsubishi J2M Raiden "Jack"

JAPAN

Although the Mitsubishi A6M Zero remained the principal Japanese naval fighter throughout the Pacific war, two other types were produced which were more suited to meet the Hellcats and Corsairs of the US Navy on equal terms. The first was the Mitsubishi J2M Raiden (Thunderbolt), known to the Allies as Jack, which was the first Japanese naval fighter designed specifically as an interceptor. The first of three J2M prototypes flew on March 20, 1942, and after some necessary modifications the type was ordered into production in October that year.

The tubby, radial-engined Jack was used almost exclusively for home defense, although some were encountered during the Marianas campaign in September 1944. Probably the best variant was the J2M5, which had its armament reduced to two 0.79-in (20-mm) cannon. Its excellent rate of climb made it an ideal high-altitude interceptor, but supply shortages of its Kasei 26a engine resulted in only 35 being built out of a total of about 500. In fact, production of the Raiden was slowed down in the summer of 1944 because of the priority given to the Kawanishi N1K Shiden.

▲ The Mitsubishi J2M Raiden was a formidable interceptor, but its rate of production was hampered by shortages of components, notably engines.

SPECIFICATION: Type fighter (data J2M3) • Crew 1 • Powerplant one 1,870hp Mitsubishi MK4R Kasei 23a 14-cylinder radial • Max speed 365mph (587km/h) • Service ceiling 38,385ft (11,700m) • Max range 1,180 miles (1,899km) • Wingspan 35ft 5in (10.80m) • Length 31ft 10in (9.70m) • Height 12ft 11in (3.95m) • Weight 8,697lb (3,945kg) • Armament four wing-mounted 0.79-in (20-mm) cannon

▌Mitsubishi J8M Shusui

JAPAN

In late 1943 Japan acquired manufacturing rights to the Messerschmitt Me 163 rocket-powered interceptor, and despite the fact that one of the two submarines carrying the necessary technical data was sunk en route to Japan, Mitsubishi was given the task of designing and producing the aircraft. After tests with an unpowered glider, seven prototypes of the powered J8M1 Shusui (Sword Stroke) were built, and one was made ready for testing on July 7, 1945. The one and only test flight ended in disaster when the rocket motor failed after takeoff; the aircraft was destroyed and its pilot killed.

▲ This picture illustrates the similarities between the J8M and the Messerschmitt Me 163B Komet.

SPECIFICATION: Type rocket-powered interceptor • Crew 1 • Powerplant one 3,307-lb (1,500-kg) thrust Toko Ro2 bifuel rocket motor • Max speed 559mph (900km/h) at 32,810ft (10,000m) • Service ceiling 39,370ft (12,000m) • Powered endurance 5mins 30secs • Wingspan 31ft 2in (9.50m) • Length 19ft 10in (6.05m) • Height 8ft 10in (2.70m) • Weight 8,565lb (3,885kg) loaded • Armament one or two wing-mounted 1.19-in (30-mm) cannon (J8M1 and Ki.100 respectively)

▌Mitsubishi Ki.2

The Mitsubishi Ki.2 was a twin-engined bomber based on the design of the Junkers K.37, an example of which had been purchased for the Japanese Army by public subscription in 1931. The type was produced in two variants, the Ki.2-1 (113 built) and Ki.2-2 (61 built). The Ki.2 saw action in China, and was still in use as a trainer at the outbreak of World War II.

▶ *The Japanese had been most impressed with a Junkers K.37 imported and used in Manchuria in 1931, and designed the Ki.2 along similar lines.*

SPECIFICATION: Type bomber • Crew 3 • Powerplant two 570hp Nakajima Kotobuki 9-cylinder radials • Max speed 158mph (255km/h) at 9,842ft (3,000m) • Service ceiling 23,000ft (7,000m) • Max range 560 miles (900km) • Wingspan 65ft 6in (19.96m) • Length 41ft 4in (12.60m) • Height 15ft 2in (4.64m) • Weight 10,030lb (4,550kg) loaded • Armament two 0.303-in (7.7-mm) machine guns; 660lb (300kg) of bombs

▌Mitsubishi Ki.15 "Babs"

Development of the Mitsubishi Ki.15 long-range reconnaissance aircraft began in July 1935, the prototype flying in May 1936, and a year later the second prototype, bearing the civil registration J-BAAI and the name Kamikaze (Divine Wind) caused a sensation by flying from Tachikawa to London in a net flying time of 51 hours 17 minutes and 23 seconds at an average speed of 100mph (160km/h). The Ki.15 was evaluated in China and 435 examples were subsequently built for the Army. The Navy also adopted the type, procuring 50 aircraft under the designation C5M1 (20) and C5M2 (30). Both Army and Navy models were relegated to second-line duties in 1943.

◀ *J-BAAL* Kamikaze *(Divine Wind) was owned by* Asahi Shimbun, *Japan's leading newspaper.*

SPECIFICATION: Type reconnaissance aircraft (data C5M2) • Crew 2 • Powerplant one 900hp Mitsubishi Ha-26 14-cylinder radial • Max speed 317mph (510km/h) at 16,405ft (5,000m) • Service ceiling 31,430ft (9,580m) • Max range 690 miles (1,110km) • Wingspan 39ft 4in (12m) • Length 28ft 6in (8.70m) • Height 10ft 11in (3.34m) • Weight 5,470lb (2,481kg) • Armament one 0.303-in (7.7-mm) machine gun in rear cockpit

▌Mitsubishi Ki.21 "Sally"

The Mitsubishi Ki.21 (Army Type 97) heavy bomber first flew on December 18, 1936, and when deliveries to the JAAF began in August 1938 it had few equals anywhere in the world. In service from the beginning of the Sino-Japanese conflict of 1939 until the end of the Pacific war, it was at the forefront of the Japanese attacks on Hong Kong, Thailand, the Philippines, Malaya, the Dutch East Indies, and Myanmar, where it suffered badly in the face of determined fighter opposition because of inadequate defensive armament and lack of armor.

▲ Despite becoming increasingly obsolete, the "Sally" served in first-line service until the end of the war.

SPECIFICATION: Type heavy bomber • Crew 7 • Powerplant two 1,500hp Mitsubishi Ha-101 14-cylinder radials • Max speed 302mph (486km/h) at 19,685ft (6,000m) • Service ceiling 32,810ft (10,000m) • Max range 1,678 miles (2,700km) • Wingspan 73ft 9in (22.50m) • Length 52ft 6in (16m) • Height 15ft 11in (4.85m) • Weight 23,391lb (10,610kg) loaded • Armament five 0.303-in (7.7-mm) machine guns, one each in dorsal turret, nose, and ventral positions, and beam positions; bomb load of 2,205lb (1,000kg)

▌Mitsubishi Ki.30 "Ann"

JAPAN

First flown in 1937, the prototype Ki.30 light bomber was followed by 17 more prototypes and service trials aircraft and 686 production machines. It was used operationally in China against negligible opposition and had an undistinguished career, but it was noteworthy for being the JAAF's first operational aircraft featuring a double-row radial engine, internal weapons bay, variable pitch propeller, and split flaps. Surviving aircraft were used as crew trainers starting in 1942.

▶ The Ki.30 was the first Japanese light bomber to have an internal bomb-bay and split flaps.

SPECIFICATION: Type light bomber • Crew 2 • Powerplant one 950hp Nakajima Ha-5 14-cylinder radial • Max speed 263mph (423km/h) at 16,405ft (5,000m) • Service ceiling 28,120ft (8,570m) • Max range 1,056 miles (1,700km) • Wingspan 47ft 8in (14.55m) • Length 33ft 11in (10.34m) • Height 11ft 11in (3.64m) • Weight 7,324lb (3,322kg) loaded • Armament two 0.303-in (7.7-mm) machine guns, one in port wing and one in rear cockpit; 882lb (400kg) of bombs

▌Mitsubishi Ki.46 "Dinah"

JAPAN

One of the best reconnaissance aircraft of World War II, and aerodynamically one of the most perfect aircraft produced by any of the belligerents, the design of the Mitsubishi Ki.46 owed much to studies carried out by the Institute of Aeronautical Research at the University of Tokyo in 1938–39.

The prototype flew for the first time in November 1939 and was followed by a small production batch of 34 Ki.46-I aircraft with 900hp Mitsubishi Ha.26-I radial engines. Production then switched to the first fully operational model, the KI.46-II, 1,093 examples of which were built. Such was the success of this aircraft that at one point a technical mission from Germany seriously considered applying for a production license. A further version, the Ki.46-IIIa, appeared in 1943; this featured a redesigned all-glazed nose section, 654 being built. The Ki.46-III-Kai was an interceptor version with a "solid" nose, mounting a 1.45-in (37-mm) cannon and either two 0.79-in (20-mm) cannon or two 0.5-in (12.7-mm) machine guns, while the similarly armed Ki.46-IIIb was a ground attack aircraft. Production of all versions totaled 1,783 aircraft.

▲ The most obvious external change in the Ki.46-III interceptor was the distinctive redesign of the forward fuselage.

SPECIFICATION: Type high-altitude reconnaissance aircraft (data KI.46-II) • Crew 2 • Powerplant two 1,055hp Mitsubishi Ha.102 14-cylinder radials • Max speed 375mph (604km/h) at 26,245ft (8,000m) • Service ceiling 35,170ft (10,720m) • Max range 1,537 miles (2,474km) • Wingspan 48ft 2in (14.70m) • Length 36ft 1in (11m) • Height 12ft 8in (3.88m) • Weight 12,787lb (5,800kg) • Armament one 0.303-in (7.7-mm) machine gun in rear cockpit

▌Mitsubishi Ki.51 "Sonia"

JAPAN

First flown in 1939, the Ki.51 reconnaissance/dive-bomber was a development of the Ki.30 and remained one of the Japanese Army's most important close support aircraft throughout the war, being used in every theater. Such was the

demand for it that a new assembly line had to be opened at the Army's Tachikawa arsenal in 1944. The basic design remained substantially unaltered throughout the type's service, 2,385 examples were built.

▶ *The Ki.51 was a smaller ground attack version of the Ki.30, and was widely used during the war in the Pacific.*

SPECIFICATION: **Type** reconnaissance/dive-bomber • **Crew** 2 • **Powerplant** one 940hp Mitsubishi Ha.26-II 14-cylinder radial • **Max speed** 263mph (424km/h) at 9,840ft (3,000m) • **Service ceiling** 27,130ft (8,270m) • **Max range** 660 miles (1,060km) • **Wingspan** 39ft 8in (12.10m) • **Length** 30ft 2in (9.21m) • **Height** 8ft 11in (2.73m) • **Weight** 6,426lb (2,915kg) • **Armament** three 0.303-in (7.7-mm) machine guns; 441lb (200kg) of bombs

▌Mitsubishi Ki.57 "Topsy"

JAPAN

The Ki.57 was one of Japan's standard military transport types of World War II. The prototype flew in July 1940 and was followed by 101 examples of the KI.46-I initial produc-

tion version. The principal variant was the Ki.57-II, which had more powerful engines. The type remained in production until January 1945, the final total being 507 aircraft.

SPECIFICATION: **Type** transport (data Ki.57-II) • **Crew** 4 (plus 11 passengers) • **Powerplant** two 1,050hp Mitsubishi Ha.102 14-cylinder radials • **Max speed** 292mph (470km/h) at 19,028ft (5,800m) • **Service ceiling** 26,250ft (8,000m) • **Max range** 1,865 miles (3,000km) • **Wingspan** 74ft 2in (22.60m) • **Length** 52ft 10in (16.10m) • **Height** 15ft 8in (4.80m) • **Weight** 18,640lb (8,455kg) loaded • **Armament** none

◀ *This civil MC-20-II wears the livery of Dai Nippon Koku K.K. (Greater Japan Air Line Co. Ltd).*

▌Mitsubishi Ki.67 Hiryu "Peggy"

JAPAN

The Ki.67 Hiryu (Flying Dragon) was unquestionably the best bomber to see service with the Imperial Japanese Army, combining an excellent performance with good defensive firepower. The prototype flew in December 1942, but development was protracted and deliveries of fully operational Ki.67-I aircraft did not begin until the summer of 1944.

The initial Ki.67-Ia was quickly supplanted by the KI.67-Ib, which remained in production until the end of the war. As a result of attacks on manufacturing centers by allied bombers, production totaled only 698 aircraft. The type serving as a bomber, torpedo-bomber, reconnaissance aircraft, interceptor, ground attack aircraft, and suicide-bomber. The interceptor

version, armed with a 3-in (75-mm) cannon, was designated Ki.109, and was not a success, only 22 being completed.

SPECIFICATION: **Type** medium bomber • **Crew** 6 • **Powerplant** two 1,900hp Mitsubishi Ha.104 18-cylinder radials • **Max speed** 334mph (537km/h) at 19,685ft (6,000m) • **Service ceiling** 31,070ft (9,470m) • **Max range** 2,361 miles (3,800km) • **Wingspan** 73ft 9in (22.50m) • **Length** 61ft 4in (18.70m) • **Height** 25ft 3in (7.70m) • **Weight** 30,347lb (13,765kg) • **Armament** one 0.79-in (20-mm) cannon in dorsal turret and five 0.50-in (12.7-mm) machine guns, two in tail position, one in nose position and one in each beam position; bomb or torpedo load of 2,359lb (1,070kg)

▲ *Had the Hiryu not been flown mainly by inexperienced young crews, the story of the Pacific war may have been very different.*

▌Mitsubishi Ki.83

JAPAN

SPECIFICATION: **Type** long-range escort fighter • **Crew** 2 • **Powerplant** two 2,070hp Mitsubishi Ha.211 18-cylinder radials • **Max speed** 438mph (704km/h) at 29,530ft (9,000m) • **Service ceiling** 41,535ft (12,660m) • **Max range** 2,175 miles (3,500km) • **Wingspan** 50ft 10in (15.50m) • **Length** 41ft (12.50m) • **Height** 15ft 1in (4.60m) • **Weight** 20,790lb (9,430kg) loaded • **Armament** four 0.79-in (20-mm) cannon in lower forward fuselage

The Mitsubishi Ki.83, one of the most elegant Japanese combat aircraft, was designed to meet a 1943 specification for a long-range escort fighter and was in the same class as the Grumman F7F Tigercat and de Havilland Hornet. The prototype flew on November 18, 1944, but the war ended before the type entered production.

▌Mitsubishi K3M "Pine"

JAPAN

Making its appearance in 1931, the Mitsubishi K3M was an adaptation of the Fokker Universal monoplane and was widely used for crew training by the Imperial Japanese Navy, the principal version being the K3M2. The Watanabe firm also built the type as the K3M3, the two companies producing 624 aircraft between them. The K3M3-L was a light transport vari-

ant. The aircraft could carry a small bomb load and was often employed on "nuisance" raids at night over Allied positions.

▲ *K3Ms were used extensively as trainers and, to a smaller degree, utility transports during World War II.*

SPECIFICATION: **Type** general-purpose aircraft • **Crew** 1–5 • **Powerplant** one 580hp Nakajima Kotobuki 9-cylinder radial • **Max speed** 149mph (240km/h) • **Service ceiling** 20,965ft (6,390m) • **Max range** 497 miles (800km) • **Wingspan** 51ft 9in (15.78m) • **Length** 31ft 4in (9.56m) • **Height** 12ft 6in (3.82m) • **Weight** 4,850lb (2,200kg) loaded • **Armament** one 0.303-in (7.7-mm) machine gun

▌Mitsubishi 1MF

JAPAN

The early 1920s saw the establishment of Kawasaki, Mitsubishi, and Nakajima as the "big three" of Japan's embryo aircraft industry, whose early development work relied heavily on aid from Britain, the US, France, and Germany. The

◀ *The Type 10-2 or 1MF3 proved a tough, reliable fighter and remained in service for a number of years.*

SPECIFICATION: Type naval fighter (data 1MF-I) • Crew 1 • Powerplant one 300hp Hispano-Mitsubishi 8-cylinder V-type • Max speed 147mph (237km/h) at 6,560ft (2,000m) • Service ceiling 23,000ft (7,000m) • Endurance 2hrs 30mins • Wingspan 30ft 6in (9.30m) • Length 22ft (6.71m) • Height 9ft 8in (2.95m) • Weight 2,510lb (1,140kg) loaded • Armament two fixed forward-firing 0.303-in (7.7-mm) machine guns

Mitsubishi design team was led by Herbert Smith, formerly of

the Sopwith company, which in 1922 developed the Mitsubishi B1M, the first Japanese aircraft designed for the torpedo attack role. It remained in production until 1933, by which time 442 had been produced for the Navy and 48 for the Army. Herbert Smith's team also designed the Mitsubishi 1MF carrier-borne biplane fighter, which in February 1923 made the first successful takeoff by a Japanese-built aircraft from Japan's first aircraft carrier, the *Hosho*. Production of the 1MF ended in 1929, with the 138th machine.

▌Morane-Saulnier MS.A1

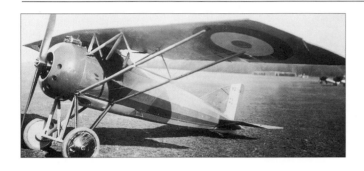

SPECIFICATION: Type fighter monoplane • Crew 1 • Powerplant one 150hp Gnome Monosoupape 9N nine-cylinder rotary • Max speed 137mph (220km/h) • Service ceiling 22,965ft (7,000m) • Endurance 2hrs 30mins • Wingspan 21ft 4in (6.51m) • Length 18ft 6in (5.65m) • Height 7ft 9in (2.40m) • Weight 1,486lb (674kg) loaded • Armament two 0.30-in (7.5-mm) machine guns

◀ *This MoS.27 variant of the Al was armed with a single Vickers machine gun.*

Designed around the middle of 1917 by Robert and Leon Morane and Raimond Saulnier, the MS.A1 was a high-wing monoplane with a very streamlined fuselage and modern lines. Three versions were developed, all with different armament and engine. The first of 1,210 examples was delivered

in September 1917, but after only two months the type was withdrawn from first-line service and relegated to training, the pretext being that it lacked power and was structurally unsound. The A1 proved a popular aircraft with amateur aviators in the postwar years.

▌Morane-Saulnier H

The Morane-Saulnier MS H of 1913 stemmed from the successful family of monoplanes designed by Leon Morane and Raimond Saulnier from 1911 onward, which French aviator

▶ *The Morane-Saulnier Type G, pictured here, was a larger two-seat version of the Type H. Both were used in small numbers.*

SPECIFICATION: Type reconnaissance monoplane • Crew 1 • Powerplant one 80hp Gnome rotary • Max speed 84mph (135km/h) • Service ceiling 3,280ft (1,000m) • Max range not known • Wingspan 29ft 11in (9.12m) • Length 20ft 7in (6.28m) • Height 7ft 6in (2.30m) • Weight 1,036lb (470kg) loaded • Armament none

Roland Garros had made famous through a series of long-distance flights in 1912. The model H was produced in parallel with a slightly larger two-seat version, the model G, and both types were used in small numbers by the Aviation Militaire.

▌Morane-Saulnier L

Known also by the military designation MS.3, the Type L was the first of Morane-Saulnier's parasol monoplane fighters, and was ordered in large numbers at the outbreak of World

War I. It was initially used for reconnaissance in a two-seater configuration, the observer armed with a cavalry carbine, but in March 1915 Roland Garros arrived at his unit (MS.23)

▶ *Similarly powered to the Type L, the Type LA had slightly improved performance and was normally armed with a single machine gun.*

SPECIFICATION: Type fighter/reconnaissance monoplane • Crew 1–2 • Powerplant one 80hp Gnope rotary • Max speed 71mph (115km/h) • Service ceiling 13,123ft (4,000m) • Endurance 2hrs 30mins • Wingspan 36ft 9in (11.20m) • Length 22ft 6in (6.88m) • Height 12ft 10in (3.93m) • Weight 1,441lb (655kg) loaded • Armament one 0.31-in (7.9-mm) Hotchkiss machine gun

with a Type L fitted with a forward-firing Hotchkiss 0.303-in (8-mm) machine gun and deflector plates on both propeller blades. With this combination he scored five victories in three weeks, before being forced down behind enemy lines. A Type L was also used to destroy the Zeppelin *LZ 37* by dropping bombs on the envelope and setting it on fire. Nearly 600 Type Ls were built, serving with the Aviation Militaire, the RFC, RNAS, and the Imperial Russian Air Service.

▌Morane-Saulnier Type N   FRANCE

The Type L was followed into service by two larger, more powerful, and better-armed variants, the Type LA and Type P. The latter was the more widely used of the two, being adopted by both the French and British; 565 were built. The next variant, the Type N, was by no means as successful. Of advanced design, with very clean lines, its high landing speed and extremely sensitive controls made it unpopular with all but the most expert pilots, and only 49 were built. Designated MS.5C.1 in French service, the type also equipped four squadrons of the RFC, in which it was known as the "Bullet." A few Type Ns were also supplied to the 19th Squadron of the Imperial Russian Air Service.

▶ *Among successful French exponents of the Type N were Jean Navarre of Escadrille MS.12 and pre-war aerobatic pilot Adolphe Pégoud of MS.49.*

SPECIFICATION: Type fighter • Crew 1 • Powerplant one 110hp Le Rhone 9J rotary • Max speed 102mph (165km/h) at 6,562ft (2,000m) • Service ceiling 13,123ft (4,000m) • Endurance 1hr 30mins • Wingspan 27ft 2in (8.30m) • Length 21ft 11in (6.70m) • Height 8ft 2in (2.50m) • Weight 1,124lb (510kg) loaded • Armament one 0.303-in (7.7-mm) Vickers machine gun

▌Morane-Saulnier MS.225   FRANCE

◀ *Although it was only a stopgap pending the arrival of monoplane fighters, the MS.225 was the first French service fighter with a supercharged engine.*

SPECIFICATION: Type fighter • Crew 1 • Powerplant one 500hp Gnome-Rhone 9Kbrs 9-cylinder radial • Max speed 207mph (333km/h) at 13,123ft (4,000m) • Service ceiling 34,448ft (10,500m) • Max range 590 miles (950km) • Wingspan 34ft 7in (10.55m) • Length 23ft 9in (7.25m) • Height 10ft 10in (3.30m) • Weight 3,484lb (1,581kg) loaded • Armament two 0.303-in (7.7-mm) Vickers machine guns in upper front fuselage

Developed from the earlier MS.121 and MS.224 designs, the MS.225, which first flew in 1932, retained the parasol wing configuration of its predecessors. A sturdy aircraft, it was constructed of duralumin and wood with fabric-covered surfaces. Fifty-five aircraft were built for the newly created Armée de l'Air, being delivered to the 7e Escadre de Chasse in the first half of 1933. Twelve examples were also built for the French Navy, and seven were exported to China.

■ Morane-Saulnier MS.406   FRANCE

A straightforward development of the MS.405 of 1935 (the first French fighter with a retractable undercarriage and enclosed cockpit), the MS.406 was numerically the most important fighter in French service in September 1939. The number eventually built reached 1,080, and although many were exported to Switzerland and Turkey, a number of export orders were never fulfilled due to the outbreak of war. The MS.406 equipped 16 Groupes de Chasse and three Escadrilles in France and overseas, and 12 of the Groupes saw action against the Luftwaffe.

The aircraft was very maneuverable and could withstand a tremendous amount of battle damage, but it was outclassed by the Bf 109 and losses were heavy (150 aircraft lost in action and 250–300 lost through other causes).

After the armistice only one Vichy unit, GC I/7, was equipped with the MS.406.

◄ Designed as a culmination of previous fighter experience translated into a monoplane, the MS.406 was an inelegant and underpowered fighter.

SPECIFICATION: Type fighter • Crew 1 • Powerplant one 860hp Hispano-Suiza 12Y-31 12-cylinder V-type • Max speed 304mph (490km/h) • Service ceiling 30,840ft (9,400m) • Max range 932 miles (1,500km) • Wingspan 34ft 5in (10.49m) • Length 26ft 9in (8.17m) • Height 10ft 8in (3.25m) • Weights 4,127lb (1,872kg) empty; 6,000lb (2,722kg) loaded • Armament one 0.79-in (20-mm) cannon or 0.29-in (7.5-mm) machine gun in an engine installation, and two 0.29-in (7.5-mm) machine guns in wing leading edges

■ Myasischchev Mya-4 "Bison"   USSR

The production of the Soviet Union's first strategic jet bombers was entrusted to the Tupolev and Myasischchev design bureaus. While Tupolev developed the Tu-16 "Badger," Myasischchev's efforts culminated in the four-engined Mya-4, which first appeared at Tushino in 1954.

Although never an outstanding success in the long-range strategic bombing role for which it was intended, the Mya-4 was nevertheless the Soviet Union's first operational four-engined jet bomber, and was roughly comparable with early versions of the Boeing B-52. Its main operational role in later years was maritime and electronic reconnaissance, and some were converted as flight refueling tankers.

▲ A Myasischchev M-4 "Bison" is shadowed by a US Navy F-4 Phantom during a routine reconnaissance flight over the Atlantic during the Cold War.

SPECIFICATION: Type strategic bomber/reconnaissance aircraft (data Bison-C ELINT aircraft • Crew 6-13, depending on mission • Powerplant four 28,660-lb (13,000-kg) thrust Soloviev D15 turbojets • Max speed 560mph (900km/h) at 30,000ft (9,150m) • Service ceiling 49,200ft (15,000m) • Max range 6,835 miles (11,000km) • Wingspan 165ft 7in (50.48m) • Length 154ft 10in (47.20m) • Height 46ft (14.10m) • Weight 375,000lb (170,000kg) loaded • Armament six 0.9-in (23-mm) cannon in two forward turrets and tail turret; 10,000lb (4,500kg) of ordnance or equipment in internal bay

■ Nakajima A2N/A4N

In 1931 Nakajima produced the A2N carrier-borne fighter, which was developed from the Navy Type 3 Carrier Fighter (this was a version of the British-designed Gloster Gambet, produced as a replacement for the Imperial Japanese Navy's aging Gloster Sparrowhawks). An extremely agile biplane

with tapered, staggered wings, the A2N was very popular with its pilots. It entered service in 1930 as the Navy Type 90 carrier fighter and production ended in 1936 with the 106th aircraft. Nakajima AN2s were used operationally in the Sino-Japanese war, operating from the carrier Kaga in the Shanghai area. The A2N's replacement was the Nakajima A4N1, which entered service as the Type 95 Carrier Fighter. It evolved in response to a Japanese Navy requirement for an interim fighter, 221 being produced between 1935 and 1938. It, too, participated in the Sino-Japanese conflict, carrying out ground attack operations in addition to establishing air superiority.

▲ Based on the design of the British Gloster Gambet, Nakajima's A2N also owed much to the Boeing Model 69B naval fighter.

SPECIFICATION: Type naval fighter (data A2N1) • Crew 1 • Powerplant one 450hp Nakajima-built Bristol Jupiter VI 9-cylinder radial • Max speed 182mph (293km/h) at 9,843ft (3,000m) • Service ceiling 29,528ft (9,000m) • Max range 270 miles (435km) • Wing span 30ft 9in (9.37m) • Length 20ft 3in (6.18m) • Height 9ft 11in (3.02m) • Weight 3,307lb (1,500kg) loaded • Armament two 0.303-in (7.7-mm) machine guns in upper front fuselage; two 66-lb (30-kg) bombs under lower wing

■ Nakajima A6M2-N "Rufe"

Intended for operations from water bases among the scattered Pacific atolls, the Nakajima A6M2-N was a floatplane fighter adaptation of the A6M2 Zero. The project was assigned to the Nakajima company, who completed 327 aircraft between April 1942 and September 1943. The A6M2-N was used mainly for home defense and reconnaissance, although it was occasionally encountered in its fighter role at the Aleutian Islands, Guadalcanal, and over the Bay of Bengal.

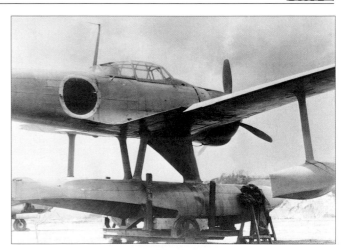

SPECIFICATION: Type floatplane fighter • Crew 1 • Powerplant one 950hp Nakajima NK1C Sakae 12 14-cylinder radial • Max speed 270mph (434km/h) at 16,400ft (5,000m) • Service ceiling 32,810ft (10,000m) • Max range 1,107 miles (1,780km) • Wing span 39ft 4in (12m) • Length 33ft 2in (10.10m) • Height 14ft 1in (4.30m) • Weight 6,382lb (2,895kg) • Armament two 0.79-in (20-mm) cannon, one 0.50-in (12.7-mm), and one 0.303-in (7.7-mm) machine gun

▲ The Nakajima A6M2-N fighter floatplane sometimes caused problems for the RAF's long-range Liberator bombers flying to targets in Burma.

■ Nakajima B5N "Kate"

Designed in 1936, the prototype B5N torpedo-bomber first flew in January 1937 and became operational as the B5N1 light bomber in China. Most of the B5N-1s were allocated to the training role as they were progressively replaced by the

B5N2 in 1939–40. The B5N2 featured prominently in the attack on Pearl Harbor, 144 aircraft taking part in the strike, and in the year that followed B5N2s delivered fatal blows to the US aircraft carriers Lexington, Yorktown, and Hornet, as well as supporting Japanese amphibious assaults. The B5N2 remained in production until 1943, by which time 1,149 examples of both variants had been built. Many B5Ns were later assigned to antisubmarine patrol work.

▼ *A captured Nakajima B5N "Kate" torpedo-bomber pictured during a test flight from the US Navy's test centre at Patuxent River.*

SPECIFICATION: Type torpedo-bomber • Crew 3 • Powerplant one 1,000hp Nakajima NK1B Sakae 11 14-cylinder radial • Max speed 235mph (378km/h) at 11,810ft (3,600m) • Service ceiling 27,100ft (8,260m) • Max range 1,242 miles (2,000km) • Wing span 50ft 11in (15.51m) • Length 33ft 9in (10.30m) • Height 12ft (3.70m) • Weight 9,056lb (4,108kg) loaded • Armament one 0.303-in (7.7-mm) machine gun; one 1,764-lb (800-kg) torpedo

▊ Nakajima B6N Tenzan "Jill"

JAPAN

The Nakajima B6N Tenzan (Heavenly Mountain) torpedo-bomber was developed as an urgent replacement for the B5N Kate, the prototype flying in March 1942. The engine selected for the first production model, the B6N1, was the 1,870hp Mamoru II radial, and although constant trouble was experienced with this powerplant, 133 B6N1s were completed, the first entering service in 1943. The next production version, the B6N2, had the much more reliable Kasei 25, and 1,135 examples were produced, bringing the total to 1,268. Operationally, the B6N suffered from a lack of aircraft carriers and a shortage of trained crews. A great many surviving

SPECIFICATION: Type naval torpedo-bomber • Crew 3 • Powerplant one 1,850hp Mitsubishi MK4T Kasei 25 14-cylinder radial • Max speed 299mph (481km/h) at 16,405ft (5,000m) • Service ceiling 29,660ft (9,040m) • Max range 1,892 miles (3,045km) • Wingspan 48ft 10in (14.89m) • Length 35ft 7in (10.87m) • Height 12ft 5in (3.80m) • Weight 12,456lb (5,650kg) loaded • Armament two 0.303-in (7.7-mm) machine guns, one in rear cockpit and one in ventral tunnel; one 1,764-lb (800-kg) torpedo

Tenzans were expended in kamikaze attacks at Okinawa and Iwo Jima.

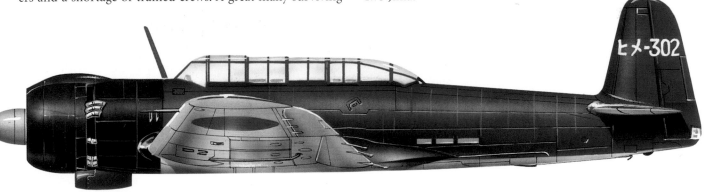

▊ Nakajima C6N Saiun "Myrt"

JAPAN

Designed primarily for the reconnaissance role, the first prototype of the Nakajima C6N Saiun (Painted Cloud) flew on May 15, 1943 and was followed by no fewer than 23 more prototypes in an effort to shorten the development period.

Deliveries of the series production C6N1 to the Imperial Japanese Navy began in August 1944, after lengthy delays caused by the problematical Homare engine. The reconnaissance variant of the Saiun was very fast and could outpace and outclimb most Allied fighters. The C6N1-B was a three-seat torpedo-bomber variant, and the C6N1-S was a night fighter conversion with a crew of two and two obliquely mounted 0.79-in (20-mm) cannon. The last aircraft to be

destroyed in WWII was a C6N1, shot down by a US Navy pilot, Lt Cdr Reidy, at 05:40 on August 15, 1945.

SPECIFICATION: Type reconnaissance/torpedo-bomber/night fighter (data C6N1) • Crew 3 • Powerplant one 1,780hp Nakajima NK9B Homare 18-cylinder radial • Max speed 403mph (648km/h) at 20,000ft (6,100m) • Service ceiling 34,350ft (10,470m) • Max range 2,855 miles (4,595km) • Wingspan 41ft (12.50m) • Length 36ft 5in (11.12m) • Height 13ft (3.96m) • Weight 11,596lb (5,260kg) • Armament one 0.303-in (7.7-mm) machine gun in rear cockpit

▲ *This C6N1 was tested in the US. A C6N1 shot down at 05.40 on August 15, 1945 was the last confirmed air-to-air kill of the war.*

▌ Nakajima E8N "Dave"

A small reconnaissance floatplane, the Nakajima E8N was designed to be catapult-launched from the Imperial Japanese Navy's capital ships and to operate from coastal

bases. The prototype flew in 1933 and 775 E8N1 aircraft were built up to 1940. Many were still in service in various roles at the end of the Pacific war.

◀ *Having seen widespread service aboard IJN ships in the immediate pre-war years, the E8N survived into the first stages of World War II.*

SPECIFICATION: Type reconnaissance floatplane • Crew 2 • Powerplant one 580hp Nakajima Kotobuki 9-cylinder radial • Max speed 186mph (300km/h) at sea level • Service ceiling 23,850ft (7,270m) • Max range 559 miles (900km) • Wingspan 36ft (10.98m) • Length 28ft 11in (8.81m) • Height 12ft 7in (3.84m) • Weight 4,189lb (1,900kg) loaded • Armament two 0.303-in (7.7-mm) machine guns; 132lb (60kg) of bombs

▌ Nakajima G8N Renzan "Rita"

The G8N Renzan (Mountain Range) was designed in response to a Japanese Imperial Navy specification of September 1943 calling for a high-performance four-engined heavy bomber. The first of four prototypes flew on

October 23, 1944 and plans were made to produce 48 G8N1s, including 16 prototypes including an all-steel variant, but in the event only four were completed before the Japanese surrender.

▶ *The G8N Renzan might have made a significant contribution to the air war in the Pacific, especially after Japan's carrier forces were destroyed.*

SPECIFICATION: Type long-range heavy bomber • Crew 10 • Powerplant four Nakajima NK9K-L Homare 18-cylinder radials • Max speed 368mph (592km/h) at 26,250ft (8,000m) • Service ceiling 33,465ft (10,200m) • Max range 4,639 miles (7,461km) • Wingspan 106ft 9in (32.54m) • Length 75ft 3in (22.93m) • Height 23ft 7in (7.20m) • Weight 70,879lb (32,150kg) • Armament twin 0.79-in (20-mm) cannon in dorsal, ventral, and tail turrets; two 0.303-in (7.7-mm) in nose and one in each beam position

Nakajima J1N Gekko "Irving"

Used in the roles of reconnaissance aircraft, night fighter, and light bomber, the Nakajima J1N Gekko (Moonlight) made its reconnaissance debut as the J1N1-C early in 1943, the prototype having flown in May 1941. Some aircraft were converted to emergency night fighters with the designation J1N1-R

and deployed to locations such as Rabaul, where they operated successfully against B-24 Liberator night bombers. The J1N1-S was built from the outset as a night fighter, armed with obliquely mounted 0.79-in (20-mm) cannon. Total J1N1 production, all variants, amounted to 479 aircraft.

▶ *Armed with upward-firing cannon, the Gekko proved moderately useful as a night fighter.*

SPECIFICATION: **Type** reconnaissance aircraft (data J1N1-C) • **Crew** 3 • **Powerplant** two 1,130hp Nakajima NK1F Sakae 14-cylinder radials • **Max speed** 329mph (530km/h) at 19,685ft (6,000m) • **Service ceiling** 33,795ft (10,300m) • **Max range** 1,678 miles (2,700km) • **Wingspan** 55ft 8in (16.98m) • **Length** 39ft 11in (12.18m) • **Height** 15ft (4.56m) • **Weight** 16,594lb (7,542kg) • **Armament** one 0.303-in (7.7-mm) machine gun in rear cockpit

Nakajima Kikka

The Kikka (Orange Blossom) was the only turbojet-powered aircraft built and flown in Japan during World War II. Resembling Germany's Me 262, but smaller, the Kikka was powered by a pair of underslung engines whose design was based on the BMW 003 axial-flow turbojet. The prototype flew for the first time on August 7, 1945 and 19 other prototypes and preproduction aircraft were in various stages of assembly when the war came to an end.

SPECIFICATION: **Type** attack bomber • **Crew** 1 • **Powerplant** two 1047-lb (475-kg) thrust Ne-20 axial-flow turbojets • **Max speed** 406mph (654km/h) at sea level • **Service ceiling** 39,370ft (12,000m) • **Max range** 586 miles (943km) • **Wingspan** 32ft 9in (10m) • **Length** 26ft 8in (8.12m) • **Height** 9ft 8in (2.95m) • **Weight** 7,716lb (3,500kg) loaded • **Armament** one 1,102-lb (500-kg) or 1,764-lb (800-kg) bomb

Nakajima Ki.27 "Nate"

SPECIFICATION: Type fighter-bomber (Ki.27b) • Crew 1 • Powerplant one Nakajima Ha-1b 9-cylinder radial • Max speed 292mph (470km/h) at 16,405ft (5,000m) • Service ceiling 40,190ft (12,250m) • Max range 1,063 miles (1,710km) • Wingspan 37ft 1in (11.31m) • Length 24ft 8in (7.53m) • Height 10ft 8in (3.25m) • Weight 3,946lb (1,790kg) loaded • Armament two fixed 0.303-in (7.7-mm) machine guns in upper forward fuselage; external bomb load of 220lb (100kg)

The Imperial Japanese Army Air Force's equivalent of the Navy's Mitsubishi A5M, the Ki.27 first flew in October 1936 and was the JAAF's standard fighter up to the middle of 1942, playing a prominent part in Japan's campaigns in China and Southeast Asia. Production totaled 3,495 aircraft, the main variants being the Ki.27a with an uprated engine and a metal-faired canopy, and the Ki.27b with a clear-view canopy and underwing bomb racks.

▌Nakajima Ki.43 Hayabusa "Oscar" JAPAN

Like its naval counterpart, the Mitsubishi Zero, the Nakajima Ki.43 Hayabusa (Peregrine Falcon) was in action from the first day of Japan's war until the last, by which time it was woefully outclassed by the latest Allied fighters. The prototype flew in early January 1939 and 716 early production models were produced. These were the Ki.43-I, K.43-Ia, Ki.43-Ib, and Ki.43-Ic, the last two having a better armament. They were followed in 1942 by a much improved model, the Ki.43-II; this appeared in three subvariants, the Ki.43-IIa and -IIb, and the Ki.43-KAI, which adopted all the refinements incorporated in the earlier models. The final model was the Ki.43-III, the only variant to include cannon in its armament. Production of all versions totaled 5,878 aircraft, including 3,200 by Nakajima and 2,629 by Tachikawa.

The Hayabusa was the Allies' principal opponent in Myanmar and was encountered in large numbers during the battle for Leyte, in the Philippines, and in the defense of the Kurile Islands north of Japan. An excellent and versatile fighter, the Hayabusa's main drawback was its lack of adequate armament.

▲ Entering the war in the Pacific at a very early stage, the Ki.43 came as a complete shock to the Allied powers and easily outclassed Allied fighters.

SPECIFICATION: Type fighter-bomber (data Ki.43-IIb) • Crew 1 • Powerplant one 1,150hp Nakajima Ha.115 14-cylinder radial • Max speed 329mph (530km/h) at 16,405ft (5,000m) • Service ceiling 36,750ft (11,200m) • Max range 1,990 miles (3,200km) • Wingspan 35ft 6in (10.84m) • Length 29ft 3in (8.92m) • Height 10ft 8in (3.27m) • Weight 6,450lb (2,925kg) loaded • Armament two 0.50-in (12.7-mm) machine guns in upper forward fuselage; external bomb load of 1,102lb (500kg)

▌Nakajima Ki.44 Shoki "Tojo" JAPAN

▶ The Nakajima Ki.44 Shoki had an excellent rate of climb and was a potent interceptor, but it was tricky to handle at low speeds.

The Nakajima Ki-44 Shoki (Demon), which entered service in the summer of 1942, was designed specifically as an interceptor. It proved to be outstanding in this role, due to its excellent speed and rate of climb, although its high takeoff and landing

SPECIFICATION: Type interceptor (data Ki.44-II) • Crew 1 • Powerplant one 1,520hp Nakajima Ha.109 14-cylinder radial • Max speed 376mph (605km/h) at 16,405ft (5,000m) • Service ceiling 36,745ft (11,200m) • Max range 1,056 miles (1,700km) • Wingspan 31ft (9.45m) • Length 28ft 10in (8.79m) • Height 10ft 8in (3.25m) • Weight 6,598lb (2,993kg) • Armament four 0.50-in (12.7-mm) machine guns

speeds made it unpopular with Japanese pilots. The most effective version of the Shoki was the heavily armed Ki-44-IIc, which was used in the air defense of Japan and which achieved some noteworthy successes against B-29 bombers.

Nakajima Ki.49 Donryu "Helen"

Japan's efforts to improve the effectiveness of its bomber force by introducing new types after the outbreak of World War II met with scant success; in fact, some of the new aircraft were inferior to those they were meant to replace. The Ki.49 Donryu (Storm Dragon) was a classic example. Designed in 1938 as a replacement for the Ki.21, its performance was so indifferent that it supplemented rather than replaced the older type. Deliveries of the Donryu to the JAAF began in the summer of 1941, and the aircraft was deployed in attacks on Australia and in the New Guinea campaign. Experience showed that the Ki.49 was underpowered, with either speed or bomb load suffering as a result.

The type was produced in two main versions, the Ki.49-I and Ki.49-II, the latter having uprated engines, more armor, and better defensive firepower. Total production was 819, including three prototypes of an "escort fighter" derivative, the Ki.58, which carried a trainable armament of five 0.79-in (20-mm) cannon and five 0.50-in (12.7-mm) machine guns.

SPECIFICATION: Type medium bomber (data Ki.49-IIa) • Crew 8 • Powerplant two 1,500hp Nakajima Ha.109 14-cylinder radials • Max speed 306mph (492km/h) at 16,405ft (5,000m) • Service ceiling 30,510ft (9,300m) • Max range 1,833 miles (2,950km) • Wingspan 67ft (20.42m) • Length 54ft 1in (16.50m) • Height 13ft 11in (4.25m) • Weight 25,133lb (11,400kg) loaded • Armament one 0.79-in (20-mm) cannon in dorsal turret; three 0.50-in (12.7-mm) machine guns, one each in nose, tail, and ventral positions; one 0.303-in (7.7-mm) machine gun in each beam position; bomb load of 2,205lb (1,000kg)

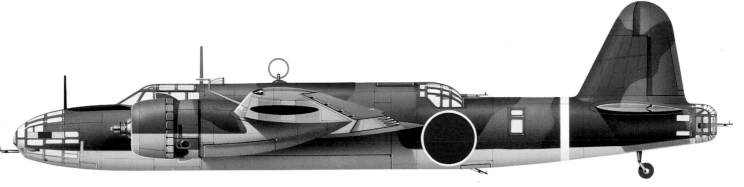

Nakajima Ki.84 Hayate "Frank"

Production of the Ki.44 Shoki was suspended at the end of 1944 in favor of another army fighter type, the Nakajima Ki-84 Hayate (Gale). The Hayate was more agile than the Shoki, and easier to handle; it was also a later design, originating in 1942. Service trials in the fall of 1943 produced promising results and the fighter was ordered into mass production, about 3,500 being completed in the 18 months before the end of hostilities. The Ki.84 proved to be more maneuverable and have a better rate of climb than the P-51 Mustangs and P-47N Thunderbolts of the Allies. The type was produced in two principal variants, the Ki.84-I (four subvariants, each

with increasingly powerful armament) and the Ki.84-II, which had a wooden rear fuselage and fittings in an effort to reduce the drain on Japan's dwindling reserves of strategic light alloys. The last version was the Ki.116, a converted Ki.84-Ia with a lighter engine.

SPECIFICATION: Type fighter-bomber (data Ki.84-Ia) • Crew 1 • Powerplant one 1,900hp Nakajima Ha.45 18-cylinder radial • Max speed 392mph (631km/h) at 16,405ft (5,000m) • Service ceiling 34,450ft (10,500m) • Max range 1,347 miles (2,168km) • Wingspan 36ft 10in (11.24m) • Length 32ft 6in (9.92m) • Height 11ft 1in (3.39m) • Weight 9,193lb (4,170kg) • Armament two 0.79-in (20-mm) cannon; two 0.50-in (12.7-mm) machine guns

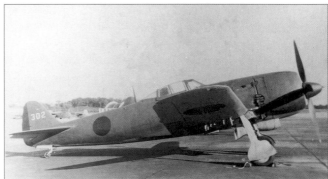

▲ *The Japanese were building underground production lines for the Ki.84 at the end of World War II.*

▌Nakajima Type 91

JAPAN

In 1927, the three leading Japanese aircraft manufacturers submitted prototypes in response to a Japanese Army requirement for a new single-seat fighter. All were parasol-wing machines, designed in Japan by teams led wholly or partly by European engineers. The winner was the Nakajima Type 91. (The Curtiss P-1C was also evaluated, but did not measure up to exacting Japanese performance requirements.) Deliveries of the Type 91 began in 1931, replacing the French-designed Nieuport-Delage NiD-29C, which was license-built by Nakajima, in Army service. The Type 91 first saw action with the 11th Air Battalion, operating with the Army Kanto Command in Manchuria in 1933. By then the Type 91 had become the standard Japanese Army fighter with the newly formed Air Wings (Hiko Rentai).

▶ *Introduced from 1932 onwards, Type 91s were deployed in action in Manchuria against the Chinese.*

SPECIFICATION: Type fighter • Crew 1 • Powerplant one 500hp Nakajima-built Bristol Jupiter 9-cylinder radial • Max speed 186mph (299km/h) • Service ceiling 29,500ft (9,000m) • Max range 370 miles (600km) • Wingspan 36ft 1in (10.99m) • Length 23ft 10in (7.26m) • Height 9ft 2in (2.79m) • Weight 3,370lb (1,530kg) loaded • Armament two fixed forward-firing 0.303-in (7.7-mm) machine guns

▌Nanchang Q-5 Fantan

CHINA

Design of the Nanchang Q-5, which began in 1958, was based on that of the MiG-19 fighter, the Chinese aircraft retaining a similar wing and rear fuselage configuration but featuring a new nose containing an attack radar and twin air intakes. Deliveries to the CPAF began in 1970, and about 100 were in service by 1980. Export customers have included Pakistan (52), Bangladesh (20), and North Korea (50) (approximate figures).

▲ *This Pakistani A-5 demonstrates both the type's distinctive airbrake configuration and the dedicated Sidewinder rails used on the PAF's Fantans.*

SPECIFICATION: Type close support fighter • Crew 1 • Powerplant two 7,165-lb (3,250-kg) thrust Shenyang WP-6 turbojets • Max speed 739mph (1,190km/h) at 36,090ft (11,000m) • Service ceiling 52,500ft (16,000m) • Combat radius with max load 249 miles (400km) • Wingspan 31ft 9in (9.68m) • Length 51ft 4in (15.65m) • Height 14ft 2in (4.33m) • Weights 14,054lb (6,375kg) empty; 26,080lb (11,830kg) loaded • Armament two 0.9-in (23-mm) Type 23-2K cannon; up to 4,409lb (2,000kg) of external stores

▌Nieuport 11

FRANCE

One of the most effective fighter aircraft of World War I, it was the Nieuport II, nicknamed Bébé (Baby), that was mainly responsible for restoring the air power balance during the "Fokker scourge" of 1915. Put into service in the summer of that year, it was fast, maneuverable and proved well able to stand up to the Fokker Monoplane. During the Battle of Verdun in February 1916, leading French pilots, flying the

▶ *The Nieuport 11 was one of the finest fighters of World War I. This example is seen on display at the Musée de l'Air, Paris.*

SPECIFICATION: Type fighter • Crew 1 • Powerplant one 80hp Le Rhone 9C 9-cylinder rotary engine • Max speed 97mph (155km/h) • Service ceiling 14,765ft (4,500m) • Endurance 2hrs 30mins • Wingspan 24ft 9in (7.55m) • Length 19ft (5.80m) • Height 8ft (2.45m) • Weights 772lb (350kg) empty; 1,058lb (480kg) loaded • Armament one forward-firing Vickers 0.303-in (7.7-mm) machine gun

Nieuport 11, inflicted such heavy losses on the enemy that the Germans were forced to alter their tactics. The Nieuport 11 served with both the RFC and the RNAS, and one of the RFC's leading aces, Captain Albert Ball (later to be awarded the VC) scored the first of his 43 victories in one.

■ Nieuport 17

The Nieuport 17 was without question one of the finest Allied combat aircraft of World War I. First flown in January 1916, deliveries to front-line units began in May. The type was highly maneuverable, with a good all-round performance and an excellent rate of climb. Its lower mainplane was strengthened to overcome the problem of wing-twist that had affected the Nieuport 11 at high speeds. Hundreds were built for the Aviation Militaire, the RFC, and RNAS, Belgiuim, Russia, Holland, Italy, Finland, and the US Army Air Service.

▲ *Hundreds of examples of the excellent Nieuport 17 were produced. This photograph shows a captured aircraft in German markings.*

SPECIFICATION: Type fighter • Crew 1 • Powerplant one 110hp Le Rhone 9J rotary engine • Max speed 106mph (170km/h) • Service ceiling 17,388ft (5,300m) • Endurance 2hrs • Wingspan 26ft 11in (8.20m) • Length 19ft 7in (5.96m) • Height 8ft (2.44m) • Weights 825lb (374kg) empty; 1,235lb (560kg) loaded • Armament one fixed forward-firing Vickers 0.303-in (7.7-mm) machine gun

■ Nieuport 27

The basic Nieuport 17 airframe yielded a number of variants. The most successful offshoot was the Type 21, with an 80hp engine and enlarged ailerons. The Type 23 was a slightly heavier version, with either an 80hp or 120hp engine, while the Type 24 was yet another variant, with improved streamlining,

a fixed vertical fin, and a circular-section fuselage. The Nieuport 27 had a modified tailplane and tail skid. Largest user of both the 24 and 27 was the American Expeditionary Force, which purchased 261 Nieuport 24s as fighter trainers and ordered 287 Nieuport 27s, although not all were delivered.

SPECIFICATION: Type fighter • Crew 1 • Powerplant one 120hp Le Rhone rotary engine • Max speed 115mph (185km/h) • Service ceiling 18,210ft (5,550m) • Max range 155 miles (250km) • Wingspan 26ft 11in (8.20m) • Length 19ft 2in (5.85m) • Height 7ft 11in (2.42m) • Weights 838lb (380kg) empty; 1,289lb (585kg) loaded • Armament one fixed forward-firing 0.303-in (7.7-mm) Vickers and one fixed forward-firing 0.303-in (7.7-mm) Lewis machine gun

▌Nieuport 28   FRANCE

The Nieuport 28, which entered service in March 1918, was an elegant design let down by an unreliable engine. The V-struts of earlier Nieuport models were eliminated and

replaced by parallel struts bracing wings of equal proportion. The Nieuport 28 had a number of idiosyncracies, including a tendency of the upper wing to shed its fabric during violent maneuvers at high speed. Despite these shortcomings, it was the only modern fighter available in sufficient numbers to equip the American Expeditionary Force in the spring of 1918, although these soon converted to Spads.

◀ *The Nieuport 28 was the first type to equip the fighter squadrons of the American Expeditionary Force when the latter reached France in 1918.*

SPECIFICATION: Type fighter • Crew 1 • Powerplant one 160hp Gnome-Le Rhone 9N rotary engine • Max speed 121mph (195km/h) • Service ceiling 17,060ft (5,200m) • Max range 248 miles (400km) • Wingspan 26ft 3in (8m) • Length 20ft 4in (6.20m) • Height 8ft 2in (2.48m) • Weights 1,172lb (532kg) empty; 1,631lb (740kg) loaded • Armament two fixed forward-firing Vickers 0.303-in (7.7-mm) machine guns

▌Nieuport-Delage NiD 29   FRANCE

SPECIFICATION: Type fighter • Crew 1 • Powerplant one 300hp Hispano-Suiza 8Fb 8-cylinder V-type • Max speed 146mph (235km/h) • Service ceiling 27,885ft (8,500m) • Max range 360 miles (580km) • Wingspan 31ft 10in (9.70m) • Length 21ft 3in (6.49m) • Height 8ft 5in (2.56m) • Weights 1,675lb (760kg) empty; 2,535lb (1,150kg) loaded • Armament two fixed forward-firing 0.303-in (7.7-mm) Vickers machine guns

One of the most widely used fighters of the post-World War I era, the NiD 29 had its origin in a requirement of September 1918, and was the first of Gustave Delage's designs for the Nieuport company to dispense with a rotary engine. Instead of opting for an air-cooled radial engine, as did most designers of the time, Delage designed his fighter around the V-type Hispano-Suiza motor, which had proved very successful in

◄ *This example of a Nieuport-Delage NiD 29 is on display among the many splendid exhibits at France's National Air Museum.*

the wartime Spad fighters. In its original form, the Nieuport 29 was capable of a maximum speed of 146mph (235km/h). The aircraft did not begin its acceptance trials until the end of 1918, and was therefore too late to see service in WWI; more-over, the original aircraft failed to meet the altitude require-ment of 29,930ft (9,129m), which was only achieved by a sec-ond prototype in June 1919. This aircraft was ordered into production as the NiD 29C1. Over 250 examples were built for the Aviation Militaire, equipping 25 escadrilles at their peak. The type also formed the main fighter element of the Belgian and Italian air arms in the 1920s; it was also produced under license by Nakajima under the designation Ko-4 for the Imperial Japanese Army Air Force, 602 being built. The NiD 29 was gradually replaced by the NiD 62C1, which began to enter squadron service in 1927 and which by 1932 equipped about two-thirds of the French fighter escadrilles.

■ Nieuport-Delage NiD 622   FRANCE

A further line of excellent fighter aircraft from Nieuport-Delage was the biplane Series 62, which emerged from various military aviation competitions of the early 1920s. The most important subvariant was the NiD 62C-1, 345 of which were built for the French Air Force. The follow-on NiD 622 had a more powerful engine, a metal propeller, and modified ailerons; it went into service in 1931, 330 being delivered. Fifty examples of the more powerful NiD 629 were also delivered.

▶ *When the German Blitzkrieg was launched in May 1940, 143 NiD 62 series aircraft were still in service, including the NiD 629, pictured.*

SPECIFICATION: Type fighter • Crew 1 • Powerplant one 500hp Hispano-Suiza 12Md 12-cylinder liquid-cooled V-type • Max speed 154mph (248km/h) at 16,400ft (5,000m) • Service ceiling 25,260ft (7,700m) • Max range 404 miles (650km) • Wingspan 39ft 5in (12m) • Length 25ft (7.63m) • Height 9ft 10in (3m) • Weight 4,052lb (1,838kg) loaded • Armament two fixed forward-firing 0.303-in (7.7-mm) Vickers machine guns

■ Nord Noratlas   FRANCE

First flown on September 10, 1949, the Nord 2501 Noratlas tactical transport was the mainstay of France's Military Air Transport Command throughout the Cold War era, with 120 aircraft (out of some 200 delivered in total) equipping four squadrons. The type was also used by the Federal German Luftwaffe. The Noratlas saw active service at Suez in 1956.

◄ *Greece augmented its C-47 force with the Noratlas and began to supplement and replace the type with the C-130H from 1975.*

SPECIFICATION: Type tactical transportation • Crew 5 • Powerplant two 2,040hp SNECMA Hercules 730 14-cylinder radials • Max speed 273mph (440km/h) • Service ceiling 23,000ft (7,000m) • Max range 1,553 miles (2,500km) • Wingspan 106ft 7in (32.50m) • Length 72ft (21.96m) • Height 19ft 8in (6m) • Weight 48,500lb (22,000kg) loaded • Payload 45 passengers or 18,646lb (8,458kg) of equipment

North American AT-6 Texan

One of the best-known training aircraft of all time, the AT-6 Texan was designed in the late 1930s as a low-cost advanced trainer with the handling characteristics of a high-speed fighter, and was developed from the fixed-undercarriage BC-1 combat trainer produced for the USAAC in 1937. The first production AT-6 appeared in 1940 and was followed in 1941 by the AT-6A (US Navy SNJ-3), 1,549 of which were built. The AT-6B was similar, but intended for gunnery training;

SPECIFICATION: Type advanced trainer (data AT-6A) • Crew 2 • Powerplant one 600hp Pratt & Whitney R-1340-49 Wasp 9-cylinder radial • Max speed 208mph (335km/h) at sea level • Service ceiling 24,000ft (7,325m) • Max range 750 miles (1,205km) • Wingspan 42ft (12.80m) • Length 29ft (8.84m) • Height 11ft 9in (3.55m) • Weight 5,300lb (2,404kg) loaded • Armament two 0.30-in (7.62-mm) machine guns

and the AT-6C (SNJ-4) had structural modifications to save on aluminum, 2,970 being built. The major production version was the AT-6D (SNJ-5), 4,388 of which were produced, and the last variant was the more powerful AT-6F (965 built). Around 15,000 Texans were produced in total, some 5,000 of which went to the RAF and Commonwealth air forces as the Harvard. (In fact, the first Harvards delivered to the RAF were BC-1s, which entered service in 1938. In all, the Harvard served with the RAF for 16 years.) The type was also produced under license in Australia, Canada, and Sweden. The Texan/Harvard was used for many tasks during its career, including counterinsurgency and forward air control.

◄ This AT-6A was photographed during its service with the Gunnery School at Harlingen, Texas, during 1942.

North American A-5/RA-5 Vigilante

USA

First flown as the YA-5A on August 31, 1958, the Vigilante completed its carrier trials in July 1960. The aircraft was designed to carry either conventional or nuclear weapons in a linear bomb bay consisting of a tunnel inside the fuselage, the bombs being ejected rearward between the two jet pipes. Fifty-seven A-5As were built, followed by 20 examples of the A-5B, an interim long-range variant.

The Vigilante's career as an attack bomber was relatively short-lived, the majority of A-5A and A-5B airframes being converted to RA-5C reconnaissance configuration. First service deliveries of the RA-5C were made in January 1964 to VAH-3, the training squadron for Heavy Attack Wing One, and Reconnaissance Attack Squadron 5 (RVAH-

▲ An RA-5C Vigilante of the US Navy's Heavy Reconnaissance Squadron 7. The Vigilante was originally designed as a nuclear attack bomber.

SPECIFICATION: Type carrier-borne reconnaissance aircraft • Crew 2 • Powerplant two 17,860-lb (8,101-kg) thrust General Electric J79-GE-10 turbojets • Max speed 1,385mph (2,230km/h) at altitude • Service ceiling 67,000ft (20,400m) • Max range 3,200 miles (5,150km) • Wingspan 53ft (16.15m) • Length 75ft 10in (23.11m) • Height 19ft 5in (5.92m) • Weight 80,000lb (36,285kg) loaded • Armament none

5) became operational on the USS Ranger in the South China Sea in June that year, the first of 10 RA-5C squadrons to be activated; of these, eight were to see service in Vietnam. The RA-5C proved so successful in action over Vietnam that the production line was reopened in 1969 and an additional 48 aircraft built. Eighteen aircraft were lost on operations.

North American B-25 Mitchell

USA

SPECIFICATION: Type medium bomber (data B-25D) • Crew 5 • Powerplant two 1,700hp Wright R-2600-13 18-cylinder two-row radial engines • Max speed 284mph (457km/h) • Service ceiling 21,200ft (6,460m) • Max range 1,525 miles (2,454km) with a 3,200-lb (1,452-kg) bomb load • Wingspan 67ft 7in (20.60m) • Length 67ft 7in (20.59m) • Height 15ft 10in (4.82m) • Weight 41,800lb (18,960kg) loaded • Armament two 0.50-in (12.7-mm) guns in nose position, dorsal, and tail turrets, plus an internal and external bomb/torpedo load of 3,000lb (1,361kg)

▲ The North American B-25 Mitchell served with all the Allied air forces during World War II, replacing the Douglas Boston in the medium bomber squadrons of No 2 Group RAF.

One of the most important US warplanes of World War II, the North American B-25 was designed as a tactical bomber, but found a valuable second role as a potent antishipping aircraft in the Pacific Theater. The prototype, bearing the company designation NA-40, flew for the first time in January 1939, and the first batch of production B-25s was delivered from February 1941, further deliveries comprising 40 B-25As and 120 B-25Bs, the former with self-sealing tanks and the latter with dorsal and ventral turrets but no tail gun position. On April 16, 1942, the Mitchell leapt into the headlines when the aircraft carrier USS *Hornet*, from a position at sea 668 miles (1,075km) from Tokyo, launched 16 B-25Bs of the 17th AAF Air Group, led by Lt Col J.H. Doolittle, for the first attack on the Japanese homeland.

The B-25B was followed into service by the virtually identical B-25C, 1,619 of which were built at North American's Inglewood plant, and B-25D, with uprated engines, an autopilot, external hardpoints for one 2,000-lb (907-kg) torpedo or eight 250-lb (113-kg) bombs, provision for forward-firing machine guns in packs attached to the sides of the forward fuselage and, in later aircraft, increased fuel capacity. North American's Kansas City factory produced 2,290 B-25Ds. The two variants were used in most theaters of war, and 533 B-25C/D aircraft were delivered to the RAF as Mitchell Mk IIs to supplement an earlier delivery of 23 Mitchell Mk I (B-25B) aircraft. Eight squadrons of the RAF's No. 2 Group, including two Dutch and one Free French, used the Mitchell. The dedicated antishipping version of the Mitchell was the B-25G, 405 of which (including five B-25C conversions) were produced. Developed for use in the Pacific Theater, the B-25G had a four-man crew and was fitted with a 2.95-in (75-mm) M4 gun in the nose, adding to its already powerful nose armament of four

0.50-in (12.7-mm) guns. The follow-on variant, the B-25H (1,000 built) had a lighter 2.95-in (75-mm) gun, eight 0.50-in (12.7-mm) fixed forward-firing machine guns, six 0.50-in (12.7-mm) machine guns (two each in the dorsal and tail positions and one in each of the two new beam positions), and provision for eight 5-in (127-mm) rockets under the wings. The 4,318 examples of the next variant, the B-25J featured either a glazed B-25D nose or, in later aircraft, a "solid" nose with eight 0.50-in (12.7-mm) machine guns. The RAF took delivery of 313 B-25Js as the Mitchell III, and 458 B-25Js were transferred to the US Navy starting in 1943, these aircraft being designated PBJ-1H. They were used primarily by the US Marine Corps, taking part in many air attacks on stubborn Japanese targets such as Rabaul, which held out until the end of the war. The Soviet Union also took delivery of 862 Mitchells under Lend-Lease. Total production of all Mitchell variants was 9,816 aircraft. Surplus B-25s were widely exported after World War II and the type continued to serve for many years.

▼ The B-25 first came to the attention of the American public after the historic raid on Tokyo of April 1942, led by Colonel Jimmy Doolittle.

▪ North American FJ-1 Fury

USA

On May 18, 1945, 100 NA-141s (production developments of the NA-134 naval jet fighter under development by North American) were ordered for the US Navy as FJ-1s, although this order was subsequently reduced to 30 aircraft. Known as the Fury, the FJ-1 flew for the first time on November 27, 1946 and went on to serve with Navy Fighter Squadron VF-51, remaining in service until 1949. The FJ-1 was the first US carrier jet fighter to be deployed in squadron strength.

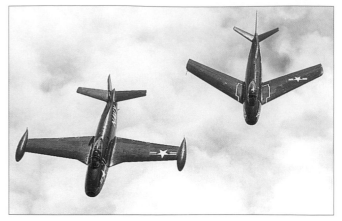

SPECIFICATION: Type carrier-borne jet fighter • Crew 1 • Powerplant one 4,000-lb (1,816-kg) thrust Allison J35-A-2 turbojet • Max speed 547mph (880km/h) at 9,000ft (2,743m) • Service ceiling 32,000ft (9,754m) • Max range 1,500 miles (2,414km) • Wingspan 38ft 2in (11.6m) • Length 34ft 5in (10.50m) • Height 14ft 10in (4.50m) • Weight 15,600lb (7,076kg) • Armament six 0.50-in (12.7-mm) machine guns

▲ *This image graphically shows the fundamental differences between the US Navy's FJ-1 Fury (left) and the later, Sabre-derived, FJ-2 Fury.*

▪ North American FJ-2/FJ-4 Fury

USA

▲ *A US Marine Corps FJ-2 Fury equipped with a pair of long-range fuel tanks. The Fury underwent a good deal of development during its career.*

In 1951, the US Navy Bureau of Aeronautics asked North American to "navalize" two F-86E Sabre airframes for carrier trials, and the first of these aircraft flew on February 19, 1952, designated XFJ-2, and the second aircraft carried an armament of four 0.79-in (20-mm) cannon in place of the F-86's 0.5-in (12.7-mm) machine guns. Carrier trials aboard the USS *Midway* were completed in August 1952 and the type entered full production for the US Navy as the FJ-2 Fury. The first unit to receive the FJ-2 was Marine Fighter Squadron

VMF-122, in January 1954. The FJ-2 gave way on the production line to the FJ-3, with a Wright J65-W-3 turbojet, and the last variant was the FJ-4, which incorporated so many new design features that it was virtually a new aircraft. The FJ-4 had provision for a wide variety of underwing stores, and a further variant, the FJ-4B, was developed specifically for low-level attack, featuring a good deal of structural strengthening and an altitude bombing system for the delivery of a tactical nuclear weapon. The last of 1,115 Furies was delivered in May 1958 and the FJ-4B remained in first-line service until September 1962, the last unit to use it being VA-216. In April 1959 an FJ-4B unit, VA-212 (USS *Lexington*) became the first to deploy overseas with Bullpup air-to-surface missiles.

SPECIFICATION: Type carrier-borne fighter-bomber (data FJ-3M) • Crew 1 • Powerplant one 8,000-lb (3,648-kg) thrust Wright J65-W-2 turbojet • Max speed 678mph (1,091km/h) at sea level • Service ceiling 54,600ft (16,640m) • Max range 835 miles (1,344km) • Wingspan 37ft 1in (11.3m) • Length 37ft 6in (11.43m) • Height 14ft 8in (4.47m) • Weight 20,611lb (9,350kg) loaded • Armament six 0.50-in (12.7-mm) Colt-Browning M-3 machine guns; up to 2,000lb (907kg) of underwing stores

▪ North American F-82 Twin Mustang

USA

The North American F-82 Twin Mustang, conceived in 1943 to meet a requirement for a long-range escort fighter for service in the Pacific theater, was destined to be the last piston-engined

fighter ordered by the USAAF. Design was begun in January 1944, the aircraft consisting basically of two F-51H Mustang fuselages joined together by a constant chord wing center section and a rectangular tailplane. The pilot was housed in the port fuselage, the second pilot/navigator in the starboard. The end of the Pacific war reduced an original order for 500 Twin Mustangs to a mere 20 aircraft, but in 1947 orders were placed for a night and all-weather fighter version of the F-82. In the night and all-weather fighter roles the F-82 replaced the Northrop P-61 Black Widow with the USAF Air Defense Command, and several squadrons were deployed to Japan for service with the Fifth Air Force.

SPECIFICATION: **Type** night fighter (data F-82G) • **Crew** 2 • **Powerplant** two 1,600hp Allison V-1710-145 V-type • **Max speed** 461mph (741km/h) at 21,000ft (6,400m) • **Service ceiling** 38,900ft (11,856m) • **Max range** 2,240 miles (3,600km) • **Wingspan** 51ft 3in (15.62m) • **Length** 42ft 5in (12.92m) • **Height** 13ft 10in (4.21m) • **Weight** 25,643lb (11,632kg) loaded • **Armament** six 0.50-in (12.7-mm) machine guns; 4,000lb (1,818kg) of bombs

▲ *The North American F-82 Twin Mustang filled a crucial USAF air defense gap until the deployment of jet equipment like the Lockheed F-94 Starfire.*

∎ North American F-86 Sabre

In 1944, before German advanced aeronautical research data became available, the USAAF issued specifications drawn up around four different fighter requirements, the first of which involved a medium-range day fighter that could also serve in the ground attack and bomber escort roles. This awakened the interest of North American Aviation, whose design team was then working on the NA-134, a projected carrier-borne jet fighter for the US Navy (which emerged as the FJ-1 Fury). The NA-134 was of conventional straight-wing design and was well advanced, so North American offered a land-based version to the USAAF under the company designation NA-140. On May 18, 1945, North American received a contract for the building of three NA-140 prototypes under the

USAAF designation XP-86. A mock-up of the XP-86 was built and, in June 1945, was approved by the USAAF. There was, however, one worrying factor. According to North American's estimates, the XP-86 would have a maximum speed of 574mph (924km/h) at sea level, which fell short of the USAAF specification. Fortunately, it was at this point that material on German research into high-speed flight, in particular swept-wing designs, became available. North American obtained a complete Me 262 wing assembly and, after carrying out more than 1,000 wind tunnel tests on it, decided that the swept wing was the answer to the XP-86's performance problems. The redesigned XP-86 airframe, featuring sweepback on all flying surfaces, was accepted by the

▲ *The North American F-86D Sabre was intended to be an interim all-weather fighter, bridging the gap until the arrival of purpose-built types.*

SPECIFICATION: Type fighter-bomber (data F-86F) • Crew 1 • Powerplant one 5,970-lb (2,710-kg) thrust General Electric J47-GE-27 turbojet • Max speed 678mph (1,091km/h) at sea level • Service ceiling 50,000ft (15,240m) • Max range 835 miles (1,344km) • Wingspan 37ft 1in (11.30m) • Length 37ft 6in (11.43m) • Height 14ft 8in (4.47m) • Weight 20,613lb (9,350kg) loaded • Armament six 0.50-in (12.7-mm) Colt-Browning machine guns; up to 2,000lb (907kg) of underwing stores, plus eight RPs

USAAF on November 1, 1945 and received final approval on February 28, 1946. In December 1946 the USAAF placed a contract for an initial batch of 33 P-86A production aircraft, and on August 8, 1947 the first of two flying prototypes was completed, making its first flight under the power of a General Electric J35 turbojet. The second prototype, designated XF-86A, made its first flight on May 18, 1948, fitted with the more powerful General Electric J-47-GE-1 engine, and deliveries of production F-86As began 10 days later. The first operational F-86As were delivered to the 1st Fighter Group early in 1949. As yet, the F-86A was an aircraft without a name, and one of the 1st Fighter Group's acts was to sponsor a competition to find a suitable one. Seventy-eight names were submitted, and one stood out above the rest. On March 4, 1949, the North American F-86 was officially named the Sabre.

Production of the F-86A ended with the 554th aircraft in December 1950, a date that coincided with the arrival of the first F-86As in Korea with the 4th Fighter Wing. During the next two and a half years, Sabres were to claim the destruction of 810 enemy aircraft, 792 of them MiG-15s. The next Sabre variants were the F-86C penetration fighter (which was redesignated YF-93A and which flew only as a prototype) and the F-86D all-weather fighter, which had a complex fire control system and a ventral rocket pack; 2,201 were built, the F-86L being an updated version. The F-86E was basically an F-86A with power-operated controls and an all-flying tail; 396 were built before the variant was replaced by the F-86F, the major production version with 2,247 examples being delivered. The F-86H was a specialized fighter-bomber armed with four 0.79-in (20-mm) cannon and capable of carrying a tactical nuclear weapon; the F-86K was essentially a simplified F-86D; and the designation F-86J was applied to the Canadair-built Sabre Mk.3. Most of the Sabres built by Canadair were destined for NATO air forces; the RAF, for example, received 427 Sabre Mk.4s. The Sabre Mk.6 was the last variant built by Canadair. The Sabre was also built under license in Australia as the Sabre Mk.30/32, powered by a Rolls-Royce Avon turbojet. The total number of Sabres built by North American, Fiat, and Mitsubishi was 6,208, with a further 1,815 produced by Canadair.

■ North American F-100 Super Sabre   USA

▲ *YQF-100D Super Sabre being checked out on a flight from Tyndall Air Force Base, Florida. Many F-100s were converted to QF-100 target drone configuration.*

SPECIFICATION: Type fighter-bomber • Crew 1 • Powerplant one 17,000-lb (7,711-kg) thrust Pratt & Whitney J57-P-21A turbojet • Max speed 864mph (1,390km/h) at 35,000ft (10,670m) • Service ceiling 46,000ft (14,020m) • Max range 600 miles (966km) on internal fuel • Wingspan 38ft 9in (11.82m) • Length 47ft 1in (14.36m) • Height 16ft 3in (4.95m) • Weight 34,832lb (15,800kg) loaded • Armament four 0.79-in (20-mm) cannon; eight external hardpoints with provision for up to 7,500lb (3,402kg) of stores

Originally known as the Sabre 45, the F-100 bore little resemblance to its predecessor, the F-86, having a contoured low-drag fuselage, and wings and tail surface swept at an angle of 45 degrees. On November 1, 1951 the USAF awarded a contract for two YF-100A prototypes and 110 F-100A production aircraft; the first prototype flew on May 25, 1953 and exceeded Mach One on its maiden flight. The first F-100A Super Sabres were delivered to the 479th Fighter Wing at George AFB, California, in September 1954, but were grounded in November following a series of unexplained crashes. It was established that the vertical tail surfaces were too small to maintain control during certain maneuvers, and so they were redesigned with 27 percent more area, the Wingspan also being slightly increased. With these modifications the F-100A began flying operationally again in February 1955 and 22 examples were built. The next series production variant was the F-100C, which was capable of carrying out both ground attack and interception missions. First deliveries to the USAF were made in July 1955 and total production was 451, of which 260 went to the Turkish Air Force. The F-100D differed from the F-100C in having an automatic pilot, jettisonable underwing pylons, and modified vertical tail surfaces; it was supplied to the USAF Tactical Air Command, Denmark, France, and Greece. The TF-100C was a two-seat trainer variant and served as the prototype of the TF-100F, which flew in July 1957. Total production of all Super Sabre variants was 2,294, many aircraft serving in Vietnam.

North American P-51 Mustang   USA

The North American P-51 Mustang was initially produced in response to a 1940 RAF requirement for a fast, heavily-armed fighter able to operate effectively at altitudes in excess of 20,000ft (6,100m). North American built the prototype in 117 days, and the aircraft, designated NA-73X, flew on October 26, 1940. The first of 320 production Mustang Is for the RAF flew on May 1, 1941, powered by an 1,100hp Allison V-1710-39 engine. The USAAF, somewhat belatedly, realized the fighter's potential and evaluated two early production Mustang Is under the designation P-51. The first two USAAF Mustang variants, both optimized for ground attack and designated A-36A and P-51A, were fitted with Allison engines. Trials with Mustangs fitted with Packard-built Rolls-Royce Merlin 61 engines showed a dramatic improvement in performance, maximum speed being raised from 390mph (627km/h) to 441mph (710km/h), and production of the

▲ This Mustang, 43-7116, was one of the first production batch of P-51Bs. The P-51B was the first to be fitted with the superb Packard-Merlin engine.

SPECIFICATION: Type long-range fighter (data: P-51D) • Crew 1 • Powerplant one 1,490hp Packard Rolls-Royce Merlin V-1650-7 • Max speed 437mph (704km/h) at 25,000ft (7,620m) • Service ceiling 41,900ft (12,770m) • Max range 2,080 miles (3,347km) • Wingspan 37ft (11.28m) • Length 32ft 3in (9.85m) • Height 12ft 2in (3.71m) • Weight 12,100lb (5,493kg) loaded • Armament six 0.50-in (12.7-mm) machine guns in the wings, plus provision for up to two 1,000-lb (454-kg) bombs or six 5-in (12.7-cm) rockets

Merlin-powered P-51B got under way in the fall of 1942. North American's Inglewood factory went on to build 1,988 P-51Bs, while the 1,750 aircraft built at the new Dallas plant were designated P-51C. P-51Bs of the 354th Fighter Group flew their first operational escort mission from England, escorting B-17s to Kiel and back, a round trip of 1,000 miles (1,600km), in December 1943.

The RAF, which had ordered 1,000 P-51Bs under the designation Mustang Mk III, began to receive its first aircraft early in 1944, the first 36 aircraft having been diverted to the US Eighth AAF to alleviate the critical shortage of escort fighters. Complaints about the poor visibility from the Mustang's cockpit led North American to test two P-51Bs with a one-piece sliding canopy and cut-down rear fuselage. Whereas the P-51B/C had been armed with four 0.50-in (12.7-mm) machine guns with 1,260rpg, the conversions, designated XP-51D-NA, had six 0.50 caliber Browning air-cooled machine guns with 1,880 rounds in a strengthened wing. The aircraft were

also later fitted with a dorsal fin to compensate for the loss of keel surface after the removal of the upper rear fuselage. Other refinements in the course of production included the addition of two sets of stub rocket launchers under each wing to carry 5-in (12.7-cm) rockets. The first production P-51Ds began to arrive in England in the late spring of 1944 and quickly became the standard equipment of the USAAF Eighth Fighter Command.

In the Pacific, Mustangs operating from the captured Japanese islands of Iwo Jima and Okinawa adopted similar tactics from April 1945, escorting B-29s to their targets and neutralizing the Japanese air force on the ground. Production totaled 7,956 P-51Ds and 1,337 basically similar P-51Ks (which had an Aeroproducts propeller instead of the Hamilton Standard unit); 876 became Mustang IVs with the RAF, and 299 became reconnaissance F-6Ds or F-6Ks. The fastest Mustang version, which saw service in the Pacific toward the end of the war, was the P-51H, with a top speed of 487mph (784km/h). The P-51H owed its origins to the XP-51F, XP-51G, and XP-51J, all of which were experimental lightweight versions of the Mustang with a laminar flow wing designed to a British requirement. The P-51H was the production lightweight Mustang, 555 being built.

The Mustang continued to serve with some 20 air forces around the world for years after the end of World War II, and gave valiant service during the early months of the Korean War with US, Australian, South African, and South Korean air units.

▪ North American B-45 Tornado

USA

Flown for the first time on March 17, 1947, the XB-45 Tornado was the first American multijet bomber to be ordered into production. The initial production version was the B-45A, of which 96 were built. The B-45C (10 built) was an updated version of the B-45A and the RB-45C (33

built), which was equipped for inflight refueling, was a high altitude photoreconnaissance variant equipped with stations for five cameras. Based at RAF bases in the UK, the USAFE's RB-45s took part in many hazardous clandestine photoreconnaissance flights over Eastern Europe during the 1950s, manned by RAF pilots. The first unit to equip with the Tornado was the 47th BW, which exchanged its B-26s for the new type in 1948.

▶ *A North American B-45 Tornado climbing away with the aid of rocket-assisted take-off gear (RATOG). The B-45 replaced the B-26 Invader.*

SPECIFICATION: Type photoreconnaissance aircraft (data RB-45C) • Crew 4 • Powerplant four 6,000-lb (2,721-kg) thrust General Electric J47-GE-13 turbojets • Max speed 570mph (917km/h) at 4,000ft (1,219m) • Service ceiling 40,250ft (12,270m) • Max range 2,530 miles (4,070km) • Wingspan 96ft (29.26m) • Length 75ft 11in (23.14m) • Height 25ft 2in (7.67m) • Weight 110,721lb (50,223kg) loaded • Armament two 0.50-in (12.7-mm) machine guns in tail position

▌North American T-2 Buckeye

USA

Designed to meet a requirement for a jet trainer for the US Navy, the T-2 (formerly T2J-1) Buckeye entered service in 1958, 217 production T-2As being built. These were followed by 100 T-2Bs and 144 T-2Cs. The T-2 Buckeye was a success on the export market, with orders for 12 T-2Ds for Venezuela and 30 T2Es for Greece.

SPECIFICATION: Type trainer • Crew 2 • Powerplant one 3,400-lb (1,542-kg) Westinghouse J34-WE-36 turbojet • Max speed 494mph (795km/h) at 25,000ft (7,625m) • Service ceiling 42,500ft (12,950m) • Max range 963miles (1,550km) • Wingspan 35ft 10in (10.92m) • Length 38ft 7in (11.78m) • Height 14ft 9in (4.50m) • Weight 10,000lb (4,536kg) • Armament none

▲ *The North American T-2 Buckeye, which entered service in 1958, gave many US Navy and foreign pilots their first taste of jet flying.*

■ North American T-28 Trojan

Designed to replace the T-6 Texan, the NAA Model 159 (XT-28) flew for the first time in September 1939. The T-28 was adopted by several air forces, including Argentina, South Korea, Cambodia, Ethiopia, Ecuador, Laos, the Philippines, and Mexico. France received 245 T-28s in 1960 for use as counterinsurgency aircraft in Algeria, where the type was known as the Fennec (Desert Fox). A dedicated single-seat counterinsurgency version, the T-28D, was produced in 1962 and this variant was exported to Bolivia, Thailand, Zaire, and South Vietnam.

▶ *The North American T-28 Trojan, apart from being a first-class training aircraft, proved effective in the counter-insurgency role.*

SPECIFICATION: Type trainer (data T-28A) • Crew 2 • Powerplant one 800hp Wright R-1300-1 Cyclone 7-cylinder radial • Max speed 283mph (455km/h) at 5,900ft (1,800m) • Service ceiling 24,000ft (7,300m) • Max range 1,000 miles (1,600km) • Wingspan 40ft 1in (12.21m) • Length 32ft (9.75m) • Height 12ft 8in (3.86m) • Weight 6,364lb (2,887kg) loaded • Armament provision for two 0.50-in (12.7-mm) machine guns

■ Northrop B-2 Spirit

▲ *The Northrop B-2 stealth bomber pictured after being rolled out for the first time. The USAF originally wanted 133 examples.*

The Northrop (Northrop Grumman) B-2 Spirit strategic penetration bomber may be said to be the embodiment of the "stealth" technology pioneered operationally by the Lockheed F-117A fighter-bomber. Development of the B-2 was begun in 1978 and the USAF originally wanted 133 examples, but by 1991 successive budget cuts had reduced this to twenty-one aircraft. The first B-2 (880329) was delivered to the 393rd Bomb Squadron of the 509th Bomb Wing at Whiteman AFB, Missouri, on December 17, 1993, with a second squadron, the 715th BS, equipping at a later date, bringing the 509th BW's establishment up to 16 aircraft. The B-2 has two weapons bays mounted side by side in the lower centerbody, each fitted with a Boeing rotary launcher assembly.

Undoubtedly the most expensive warplane ever built, each B-2 Spirit cost around $900 million.

SPECIFICATION: Type strategic bomber • Crew 4 • Powerplant four 19,000-lb (8,618-kg) thrust General Electric F118-GE-110 turbofans • Max speed 475mph (764km/h) at high altitude • Service ceiling 50,000ft (15,240m) • Max range 7,256 miles (11,675km) • Wingspan 172ft (52.43m) • Length 69ft (21.03m) • Height 17ft (5.18m) • Weight 400,000lb (181,437kg) loaded • Armament 16 AGM-129 Advanced Cruise Missiles, or alternatively sixteen B.61 or B.83 free-fall nuclear bombs, 80 Mk 82 500-lb (226-kg) bombs, 16 Joint Direct Attack Munitions, 16 Mk 84 2,000-lb (907-kg) bombs, 36 M117 750-lb (340-kg) fire bombs, 36 CBU-87/89/97/98 cluster bombs, and 80 Mk 36 560-lb (304-kg) or Mk 62 sea mines

▌Northrop F-5 Tiger

The Northrop N156 was conceived as a relatively inexpensive and simple aircraft capable of undertaking a variety of tasks. At the end of 1958, Northrop received a Department of Defense contract for three prototypes, the first of which flew on July 30, 1959, powered by two General Electric YJ85-GE-1 turbojets, and exceeded Mach One on its maiden flight. After nearly three years of intensive testing and evaluation, it was announced on April 25, 1962 that the N156 had been selected as the new all-purpose fighter for supply to friendly nations under the Mutual Aid Pact, and the aircraft entered production as the F-5A Freedom Fighter, the first example flying in October 1963.

The F-5A entered service with USAF Tactical Air Command in April 1964. The first overseas customer was the Imperial Iranian Air Force, which formed the first of seven F-5A squadrons in February 1965. The Royal Hellenic Air Force also received two squadrons in 1965, and Norway received 108 aircraft starting in 1967, these being fitted with arrester hooks and rocket-assisted takeoff for short field operations. Between 1965 and 1970 Canadair built 115 aircraft for the Canadian Armed Forces as CF-5A/Ds, these using Orenda-built J85-CAN-15 engines. Other nations using the type were Ethiopia, Morocco, South Korea, the Republic of Vietnam, Nationalist China, the Philippines, Libya, the Netherlands, Spain, Thailand, and Turkey.

An improved version, the F-5E Tiger II, was selected in November 1970 as a successor to the F-5A series. It served with a dozen overseas air forces, and also in the "aggressor" air combat training role with the USAF. The RF-5E TigerEye is a photoreconnaissance version. A wide range of update programs is available to ensure that the F-5 family will continue to be a viable warplane in the 21st century.

▲ The Northrop F-5A was extensively evaluated in Vietnam under a program called "Skoshi Tiger". The type was supplied to many US-aligned air forces.

SPECIFICATION: Type tactical fighter (data F-5A) • Crew 1 • Powerplant two 4,080-lb (1,850-kg) thrust General Electric J85-GE-13 turbojets • Max speed 924mph (1,487km/h) at 36,000ft (10,975m) • Service ceiling 50,500ft (15,390m) • Combat radius 195 miles (314km) with maximum warload • Wingspan 25ft 3in (7.70m) • Length 47ft 2in (14.38m) • Height 13ft 2in (4.01m) • Weight 20,667lb (9,374kg) loaded • Armament two 0.79-in (20-mm) M39 cannon; up to 4,400lb (1,996kg) of stores on external pylons

▌Northrop F-89 Scorpion

The first of two Northrop XF-89 prototypes flew on August 16, 1948, and after USAF evaluation Northrop received an order for an initial batch of 48 production aircraft, the first of these flying late in 1950. The first production model of the Scorpion, the F-89A, was powered by two Allison J35-A-21 turbojets with reheat and carried a nose armament of six 0.79-in (20-mm) cannon. The F-89B and F-89C were progressive

developments with uprated Allison engines, while the F-89D had its cannon deleted and carried an armament of 104 fold-

▲ The Northrop F-89 Scorpion, with its long range and abilty to carry nuclear air-to-air missiles, formed an important component of the US Air Defense Command.

SPECIFICATION: Type all-weather interceptor (data F-89H) • Crew 2 • Powerplant two 7,200-lb (3,266-kg) thrust Allison J35-A-35 turbojets • Max speed 636mph (1,023km/h) at 10,600ft (3,230m) • Service ceiling 49,200ft (14,995m) • Max range 1,370 miles (2,200km) • Wingspan 59ft 8in (18.18m) • Length 53ft 10in (16.40m) • Height 17ft 7in (5.36m) • Weight 42,241lb (19,160kg) loaded • Armament six Hughes GAR-1 Falcon missiles and 42 FFAR, or one MB-1 Genie nuclear AAM

ing-fin aircraft rockets (FFAR) in wingtip pods. Additional fuel tanks under the wings gave an eleven percent range increase over the F-89C and the aircraft was fitted with an automatic fire control system. The F-89H, which followed the F-89D into production, was armed with six Hughes GAR-1 Falcon missiles and 42 FFAR, and could also carry the MB-1 Genie nuclear AAM. The Falcons were housed in the wingtip pods and were extended prior to firing. The F-89H's armament was fired automatically, a sighting radar and fire control computer forming a fully integrated attack system.

■ Northrop N-3PB

USA

▲ *Manned by Norwegian crews, the Northrop N-3PB performed valuable service at a time when other maritime patrol aircraft were in short supply.*

In 1940, a Norwegian purchasing commission placed an order for 24 Northrop N-3PB floatplanes; however, Norway was overrun by the Germans in April that year. Nevertheless, all 24 aircraft were delivered to the exiled Royal Norwegian Naval Air Service in the first months of 1941, and these were operated by No. 330 Squadron as part of RAF Coastal Command from coastal sites in Iceland, flying antisubmarine patrols and convoy protection sorties. The N-3PBs flew their last sortie on December 30, 1942, being replaced by Catalinas.

SPECIFICATION: **Type** maritime patrol floatplane • **Crew** 3 • **Powerplant** one 1,100hp Wright GR-1820-G205A Cyclone 9-cylinder radial • **Max speed** 257mph (414km/h) at sea level • **Service ceiling** 24,000ft (7,315m) • **Max range** 1,000 miles (1,609km) • **Wingspan** 48ft 11in (14.91m) • **Length** 36ft (10.97m) • **Height** 12ft (3.66m) • **Weight** 10,600lb (4,808kg) loaded • **Armament** four 0.50-in (12.7-mm) fixed forward-firing machine guns in wings, plus one 0.30-in (7.62-mm) machine gun in rear cockpit and one in ventral position; bomb load of 2,000lb (907kg)

■ Northrop P-61 Black Widow

USA

▲ *Originally a P-61A, this P-61G Black Widow was one of a number stripped of all armament and converted to the weather reconnaissance role.*

SPECIFICATION: Type night fighter (data P-61B) • Crew 3 • Powerplant two 2,000hp Pratt & Whitney R-2800-65 18-cylinder radial engines • Max speed 366mph (589km/h) at 20,000ft (6,095m) • Service ceiling 33,100ft (10,090m) • Max range 2,800 miles (4,506km) • Wingspan 66ft (20.12m) • Length 49ft 7in (15.11m) • Height 14ft 8in (4.46m) • Weight 29,700lb (13,472kg) loaded • Armament four 0.79-in (20-mm) cannon in fuselage belly, fixed to fire forward; provision for four 1,600-lb (726-kg) bombs under wings; last 250 aircraft armed with four 0.50-in (12.7-mm) machine guns in remotely controlled dorsal turret

In January 1941 Northrop received a contract for the construction of two prototypes of a new night fighter, originally developed for possible service with the RAF, under the designation XP-61, and production contracts totaling 573 aircraft

were issued within the next 13 months. The first prototype flew on May 21, 1942, but it was another 18 months before the first production P-61A Black Widow aircraft appeared. The P-61 was fitted with a Westinghouse SCR-270 AI radar, which had a British magnetron. Early P-61A operations were plagued by lack of serviceability of the aircraft's Pratt & Whitney R-2800-65 engines, and after 200 P-61As had been built production switched to the P-61B, of which 450 were built. The last production version of the Black Widow was the P-61C, which had 2,800hp R-2800-73 engines; 41 were built. In the immediate postwar years P-61s were replaced by the North American P-82 Twin Mustang. The P-61 served in all theaters of war, and enjoyed particular success in the Pacific as a night intruder.

∎ Northrop T-38A Talon   USA

First flown in April 1959, the T-38A Talon jet trainer stemmed from the same program that produced the F-5. Three YF-38 prototypes were ordered, and after three years of development flight trials were undertaken to assess the performance of different powerplants before the type entered USAF service in 1961. The aircraft proved highly successful, with 1,139 examples completed. Some T-38s were used for astronaut training, while others simulated MiG-21s in various air combat schools.

▲ *The Northrop T-38 Talon, produced in large numbers during the 1960s, was a very successful design. Some were used to train astronauts.*

SPECIFICATION: Type trainer • Crew 2 • Powerplant two 3,850-lb (1,746-kg) General Electric J85-GE-5 turbojets • Max speed 858mph (1,381km/h) at 36,000ft (10,975m) • Service ceiling 53,600ft (16,340m) • Max range 1,093 miles (1,759km) on internal fuel • Wingspan 25ft 3in (7.70m) • Length 46ft 4in (14.14m) • Height 12ft 10in (3.92m) • Weight 11,820lb (5,361kg) • Armament none

Panavia Tornado

The development history of the Tornado goes back to 1969, when the British Aircraft Corporation, Messerschmitt-Bölkow-Blohm and Aeritalia joined forces to form the tri-national Panavia company. Development was complex; each of the three nations involved had different requirements, and the resolution of a design to meet the majority of these in a single airframe was a triumph of collaboration. Originally known as the Multirole Combat Aircraft, the prototype Tornado IDS (Interdictor/Strike) aircraft flew in August 1974, with deliveries of the Tornado GR.Mk.1 to the Tri-National Tornado Training Establishment at RAF Cottesmore beginning in 1981. The RAF received 229 GR.1 strike aircraft, the Luftwaffe 212, the German Naval Air Arm 112, and the Italian Air Force 100. RAF and Italian Tornados

▲ *A Tornado ECR of the Luftwaffe's Einsatzgeschwader 1, carrying a variety of anti-radar missiles. Only Germany uses the ECR version.*

SPECIFICATION: **Type** multirole combat aircraft (data Tornado GR.Mk.1) • **Crew** 2 • **Powerplant** two 16,075-lb (7,292-kg) thrust Turbo-Union RB.199-34R Mk 103 turbofans • **Max speed** 1,452mph (2,337km/h) at altitude • **Service ceiling** 50,000ft (15,240m) • **Combat radius** 864 miles (1,390km) hi-lo-hi • **Wingspan** 45ft 7in (13.91m) • **Length** 54ft 10in (16.72m) • **Height** 19ft 6in (5.95m) • **Weight** 60,000lb (27,216kg) loaded • **Armament** two 1-in (27-mm) IWKA-Mauser cannon; seven external hardpoints with provision for up to 19,840lb (9,000kg) of stores

saw action in the 1991 Gulf War. The Tornado GR.1A is a variant with a centerline reconnaissance pod, deliveries beginning in 1990, while the GR.4, armed with Sea Eagle missiles, is an antishipping version, the GR.4A being the tactical reconnaissance equivalent. The Tornado ADV (Air Defense Variant) was developed to fulfill a UK air defense requirement, delivery of 18 F.Mk.2s being followed by 155 F.Mk.3 aircraft. Forty-eight Tornado IDS and 24 ADV were supplied to the Royal Saudi Air Force.

Petlyakov Pe-2

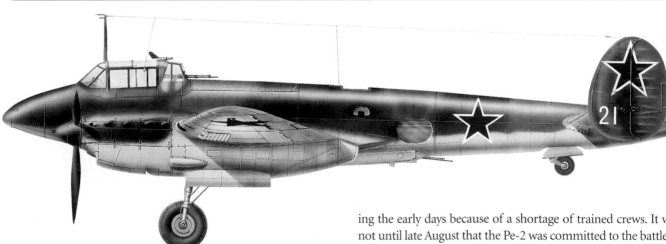

First flown as the PB-100 (the PB prefix denoting Pikiruyushchii Bombardirovshchik, or dive-bomber), the Pe-2 was ordered into production in February 1941. By June that year, when the Germans invaded the USSR, the total number of Pe-2s delivered had risen to 462, but comparatively few of these saw action dur-

ing the early days because of a shortage of trained crews. It was not until late August that the Pe-2 was committed to the battle in any numbers, making low-level attacks on German armored columns.

Production of the Pe-2 rapidly got into its stride, a further 1,405 aircraft being delivered to operational units in the second half of 1941. Pe-2 operations received a setback in the spring of 1942, when the Messerschmitt Bf 109F appeared on the

Russian Front, and late in 1942 the Pe-2FT appeared, this variant having two 1,260hp Klimov M-105PF engines and a 0.50-in (12.7-mm) UBT machine gun in a dorsal turret, replacing the flexible ShKAS machine gun at the rear of the cockpit. Numerous Pe-2 variants made their appearance during the aircraft's operational career. These included the P2-2M, a prototype with VK-105 engines and an enlarged bomb bay to carry a 1,100-lb (500-kg) bomb; the Pe-2FZ, a variant of the Pe-2FT with better cabin facilities; the Pe-2I, which had a mid- instead of a low-

SPECIFICATION: Type light bomber (data PE-2FT) • Crew 3 • Powerplant two 1,260hp Klimov VK-105PF 12-cylinder V-type • Max speed 360mph (580km/h) • Service ceiling 28,870 ft (8,800m) • Max range 817 miles (1,315km) with a 2,205-lb (1,000-kg) bomb load • Wingspan 56ft 1in (17.11m) • Length 41ft 11in (12.78m) • Height 11ft 2in (3.42m) • Weight 18,783lb (8,520kg) loaded • Armament two 0.303-in (7.62-mm) or one 0.303-in (7.62-mm) and one 0.50-in (12.7-mm) machine gun in nose, one 0.303-in (7.62-mm) machine gun in dorsal turret, one 0.303-in (7.62-mm) or 0.50-in (12.7-mm) machine gun in ventral position, aimed by a 120° vision periscope, and one 0.303-in (7.62-mm) or 0.50-in (12.7-mm) lateral-firing machine gun in window positions; 3,527lb (1,600kg) of bombs

▲ The Pe-2's radio operator/air gunner was provided with a roof hatch, two side windows and a ventral gun position.

wing configuration; the Pe-2RD, with an RD-1 auxiliary rocket engine in the tail (intended to give improved performance for takeoff and combat, the engine exploded during trials in 1944); and the Pe-2UT dual-control trainer. A multipurpose fighter version armed with cannon, machine guns, and underwing rockets, designated Pe-3, was also produced.

Total production of the Pe-2/3, including all variants, was 11,427 aircraft.

▌Petlyakov Pe-8 USSR

SPECIFICATION: Type heavy bomber • Crew 11 • Powerplant four 1,350hp Mikulin AM-35A V-type • Max speed 272mph (438km/h) at 24,935ft (7,600m) • Service ceiling 31,988ft (9,750m) • Max range 3,383 miles (5,445km) • Wingspan 131ft (39.94m) • Length 73ft 8in (22.47m) • Height 20ft (6.10m) • Weight 73,469lb (33,325kg) loaded • Armament one 0.79-in (20-mm) ShVAK cannon in each of the dorsal and tail turrets; one 0.50-in (12.7-mm) machine gun in the rear of each inboard engine nacelle; two 0.30-in (7.62-mm) machine guns in nose turret; bomb load of up to 8,818lb (4,000kg)

The Pe-8 (military designation TB-7) was the only Soviet heavy bomber to see service in World War II. First flown on December 27, 1936, it entered service in 1940, and in the summer of 1941 carried out the first major strategic attack of the war when a small force attacked Berlin. The Pe-8 was dogged by engine difficulties throughout its career and various powerplants were tried, including M-30B diesel engines. It nevertheless made some notable long-distance flights, including one of more than 11,000 miles (17,700km) from Moscow to Washington and back via Scotland, Iceland, and Canada.

▲ The Pe-8 was the only heavy bomber in the Soviet inventory during the Great Patriotic War, but was consistently troubled by unreliable powerplants.

▌Pfalz D.III GERMANY

The Pfalz D.III, which was issued to the Jagdstaffeln on the Western Front from August 1917, was somewhat inferior in performance to its contemporary Albatros and Fokker

scouts, although it was structurally stronger and more streamlined. About 600 examples were built, but only half a dozen Jastas were armed with the type. The installation of a more powerful engine resulted in the D.IIIa, which was a much more effective combat aircraft. The Pfalz Dr.I was an unsuccessful development of the D.III, only 10 being built. Pfalz also built an experimental triplane version of the D.III, with a third wing mounted between the existing biplane wings. Another Pfalz scout of this period, the D.XII, served in

small numbers for a short time, its performance failing to match that of other German fighters.

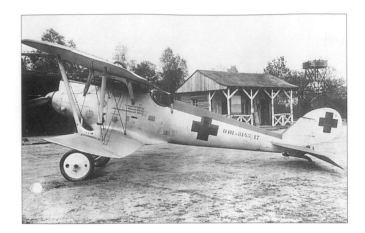

▶ *When production ended it was estimated that more than 600 D.IIIs and D.IIIas (illustrated) had been delivered.*

SPECIFICATION: **Type** scouting biplane • **Crew** 1 • **Powerplant** one 180hp Mercedes D.IIIa in-line engine • **Max speed** 103mph (165km/h) • **Service ceiling** 17,000ft (5,180m) • **Max range** 217 miles (350km) • **Wingspan** 30ft 10in (9.40m) • **Length** 22ft 9in (6.95m) • **Height** 8ft 9in (2.67m) • **Weight** 2,061lb (935kg) • **Armament** two nose-mounted 0.31-in (7.92-mm) LMG 08/15 machine guns

▌Piaggio P.108   ITALY

Designed by Giovanni Casiraghi, the Piaggio P.108 was the Regia Aeronautica's only four-engined bomber. The prototype made its first flight on November 24, 1939 and the first examples were delivered in May 1941, but the type did not become operational until June 1942. Active in the

Mediterranean during the last year of Italy's war, among other missions the aircraft was employed in attacks on Gibraltar, Mussolini's son Bruno being killed in one of these. The first version was the P.108A, only one of which was built; the remainder of the production aircraft were designated P.108B.

▲ *An excellent long-range bomber, the Piaggio P.108 entered service too late to influence the course of the Mediterranean Air War.*

SPECIFICATION: **Type** heavy bomber • **Crew** 6 • **Powerplant** four 1,350hp Piaggio P.XII RC35 18-cylinder radials • **Max speed** 261mph (420km/h) at 12,800ft (3,900m) • **Service ceiling** 26,400ft (8,050m) • **Max range** 2,190 miles (3,520km) • **Wingspan** 105ft (32m) • **Length** 75ft 2in (22.92m) • **Height** 17ft (5.18m) • **Weight** 65,884lb (29,885kg) loaded • **Armament** eight 0.50-in (12.7-mm) Breda-SAFAT machine guns; up to 7,700lb (3,500kg) of bombs or three torpedoes

▌Piper L-4 Grasshopper   USA

The military variant of the celebrated Piper Cub, which first appeared on the civil aviation market in 1938, the L-4 Grasshopper was selected for service in the USAAC in 1941, largely because of its impressive ability to operate from virtually any terrain and in very confined spaces. Over 5,500 were built, serving in all theaters of war.

SPECIFICATION: **Type** liaison aircraft • **Crew** 2 • **Powerplant** one 65hp Continental O-170-3 4-cylinder air-cooled • **Max speed** 85mph (137km/h) • **Service ceiling** 9,300ft (2,835m) • **Max range** 190 miles (305km) • **Wingspan** 35ft 3in (10.74m) • **Length** 22ft (6.70m) • **Height** 6ft 8in (2.03m) • **Weight** 1,220lb (553kg) loaded • **Armament** none

▲ *The Piper L-4 Grasshopper, the military version of the Piper Cub, gave tremendous service to the US forces in all theaters of war.*

▌Polikarpov I-5

In 1927 one of the most successful aircraft designers of the period, Nikolai N. Polikarpov, produced a single-seat fighter, the I-3. In 1929 he modified the basic design and produced the DI-2 two-seat fighter, which had an armament of three machine guns, one in the nose and two on a movable mount in the rear cockpit. In the spring of 1930 Polikarpov, in collaboration with Dmitri Grigorovitch, produced the I-5, a sin-

gle-seat biplane fighter with exceptional maneuverability. The prototype flew in April 1930, and about 800 I-5s were subsequently built.

SPECIFICATION: Type fighter biplane • Crew 1 • Powerplant one 480hp M-22 9-cylinder radial • Max speed 173mph (278km/h) at sea level • Service ceiling 23,950ft (7,300m) • Max range 410 miles (660km) • Wingspan 33ft 7in (10.24m) • Length 22ft 3in (6.78m) • Height 9ft 9in (2.98m) • Weight 2,767lb (1,254kg) • Armament two 0.303-in (7.7-mm) machine guns

▲ *Possessing exceptional maneuverability, the I-5 was the first really viable Russian-designed fighter type to see service with the Red Air Force.*

▌Polikarpov I-15/I-153

In 1933 Polikarpov designed the I-13 biplane, forerunner of the famous I-15, which made its first flight in October of that year. The I-15 was a biplane with a fixed undercarriage; the upper wing was gull-shaped, giving an excellent view forward and upward. It was fitted with a 750hp M-25 engine (the license-built version of the American Wright Cyclone), which gave it a top speed of 220 mph (354km/h). It was armed with four 0.30-in (7.62mm) machine guns and there was provision for light bombs in racks under the wings. In 1934, the I-15 was followed by the I-15bis, with an improved M-25V engine

that raised its top speed to 230mph (370km/h).

In a bid to raise the speed still further, Polikarpov then produced the I-153, which featured a retractable undercarriage, but the maximum speed of the early I-153s (240mph/386km/h) was still insufficient when compared with that of the new European fighter aircraft. The M-25V engine was consequently replaced by an M-62R developing 1,000hp, and then by a 1,000hp M-63, which raised the I-153's speed to its ultimate of 265mph (426km/h). The I-153, dubbed Chaika (Seagull) because of its distinctive wing shape, was a first-rate combat aircraft and was subsequently to prove its worth in air fighting, being able to out-turn almost every aircraft that opposed it in action. It was the last single-seat fighter biplane to be series-produced in the Soviet Union.

▲ *The I-15bis, with a more powerful engine and greater firepower, was also known as the I-152.*

SPECIFICATION: Type fighter biplane (data I-153) • Crew 1 • Powerplant one 1,000hp Shvetsov M-62 9-cylinder radial • Max speed 265mph (426km/h) at 9,845ft (3,000m) • Service ceiling 35,105ft (10,700m) • Max range 547 miles (880km) • Wingspan 32ft 9in (10m) • Length 20ft 3in (6.17m) • Height 9ft 2in (2.80m) • Weight 4,652lb (2,110kg) • Armament four ShKAS 0.30-in (7.62-mm) machine guns, plus a light bomb load or six RS-82 air-to-ground rockets

▌Polikarpov I-16

On December 31, 1933, two months after the appearance of the I-15 biplane, a new Polikarpov fighter made its first flight. This was the I-16 or TsKB-12, a low-wing monoplane with a retractable undercarriage, two wing-mounted 0.303-

in (7.62- mm) guns and a large 480hp M-22 engine. As the first production monoplane in the world to feature a retractable undercarriage, the I-16 attracted great interest among foreign observers when several flights of five aircraft

flew over Moscow's Red Square during the Air Parade of May 1, 1935. The I-16 was also the first Soviet fighter to incorporate armor plating around the pilot's cockpit.

The first production versions, the I-16 Types 4, 5, and 10, were fitted with a 750hp M-25B, increasing their top speed to around 290mph (466km/h). During the mid-1930s, the basic I-16 design was progressively modified to carry out a variety of different tasks. Among the variants produced was the TsKB-18, an assault version armed with four PV-1 synchronized machine guns, two wing-mounted machine guns, and 225lb (102kg) of bombs. The pilot was protected by armor plating in front, below, and behind. In 1938 the I-16 Type 17 was tested, armed with two wing-mounted cannon. This ver-

sion was produced in large numbers. Then Polikarpov produced the TsKB-12P, the first aircraft in the world to be armed with two synchronized cannon firing through the propeller arc. The last fighter version of the I-16 was the Type 24, fitted with a 1,000hp M-62R engine which gave it a top speed of 325mph (523km/h). Altogether, 6,555 I-16s were built before production ended in 1940. I-16s fought in Spain, against the Japanese in the Far East, and against the Luftwaffe.

▲ The Polikarpov I-16 was a very difficult aircraft to handle, but the fact that it was inherently unstable gave it a high degree of maneuverability.

SPECIFICATION: Type fighter • Crew 1 • Powerplant one 1,100hp Shvetsov M-63 9-cylinder radial • Max speed 304mph (489km/h) • Service ceiling 29,530ft (9,000m) • Max range 435 miles (700km) • Wingspan 29ft 6in (9m) • Length 20ft 1in (6.13m) • Height 8ft 5in (2.57m) • Weight 4,619lb (2,095kg) • Armament two 0.303-in (7.62-mm) machine guns in upper part of forward fuselage and two 0.303-in (7.62-mm) machine guns or two 0.79-in (20-mm) cannon in wing; external bomb and rocket load of 1,102lb (500kg)

▌Polikarpov Po-2   USSR

▶ Instructors, students and flight mechanics parade in front of their Po-2 biplanes during an inspection at a Soviet training school.

SPECIFICATION: Type training biplane • Crew 2 • Powerplant one 100hp M-11 5-cylinder radial • Max speed 93mph (149km/h) at sea level • Service ceiling 13,120ft (4,000m) • Max range 329 miles (530km) • Wingspan 37ft 5in (11.4m) • Length 26ft 9in (8.15m) • Height 9ft 6in (2.92m) • Weight 2,167lb (981kg) loaded • Armament one 0.30-in (7.62-mm) machine gun; up to 550lb (250kg) of bombs

Long-lived and produced in massive quantities, with over 20,000 leaving the assembly lines between 1928 and 1952, the Polikarpov Po-2 biplane carried out many duties over and above the training role for which it was intended. One of its key roles was "nuisance" night bombing, which it carried out in World War II and in Korea, sometimes with spectacular success.

Po-2 aircraft were also fitted with loudspeakers to broadcast propaganda to enemy troops, and equipped as an ambulance aircraft with containers for two stretchers.

Polikarpov R-5

USSR

Designed over a three-year period and first flown in 1928, the Polikarpov R-5 entered service in 1931 as a light reconnaissance bomber. Some 6,000 were subsequently built, including the R-Z ground-attack aircraft, armed with as many as seven machine guns, and the R-5T of 1935, a single-seat torpedo-bomber. The R-5 was used by the USSR while fighting the Japanese in the Far East, by the Republican Army in the Spanish Civil War, and against Finland in the Winter War.

▲ The Polikarpov R-5 "Natasha" light bomber and reconnaissance aircraft was used in huge quantities by the Red Air Force in the late 1930s.

SPECIFICATION: Type light reconnaissance bomber • Crew 2 • Powerplant one 680hp M17 12-cylinder V-type • Max speed 142mph (228km/h) at 9,800ft (3,000m) • Service ceiling 21,000ft (6,400m) • Max range 500 miles (800km) • Wingspan 50ft 10in (15.50m) • Length 34ft 8in (10.55m) • Height 10ft 8in (3.25m) • Weight 6,515lb (2,955kg) loaded • Armament two 0.30-in (7.62-mm) machine guns; 530lb (240kg) of bombs

Potez 25
FRANCE

Flown for the first time early in 1925, the Potez 25 army cooperation biplane saw widespread service throughout France's colonial empire, 1,948 examples of the TOE (Colonial) version being produced for that specific purpose. Another 322 were exported to 17 countries. In addition, 150 were built under license in Poland, over 200 in Yugoslavia, and 27 in Portugal. Total production of the Potez 25 in France alone exceeded 4,000 aircraft.

▲ An extremely rugged design, the Potez 25 army co-operation biplane saw widespread service on "aerial policing" duties throughout France's colonies.

SPECIFICATION: Type army cooperation biplane • Crew 2 • Powerplant one 450hp Lorraine-Dietrich 12-cylinder liquid-cooled V-type • Max speed 137mph (220km/h) • Service ceiling 23,620ft (7,200m) • Max range 410 miles (660km) • Wingspan 46ft 7in (14.19m) • Length 30ft 2in (9.19m) • Height 11ft 11in (3.65m) • Weights 3,329lb (1,510kg) empty; 5,512lb (2,500kg) loaded • Armament one fixed forward-firing 0.303-in (7.7-mm) Vickers machine gun; two 0.303-in (7.7-mm) Lewis guns in ring mounting in observer's cockpit; up to 441lb (200kg) of bombs on underwing racks

Potez 63.11

FRANCE

A modified version of the earlier Potez 637 reconnaissance aircraft, the Potez 63.11—which flew for the first time on December 31, 1938—featured a completely redesigned forward fuselage that included an angular glazed nose section. Between November 1939 and June 1940 the Armée de l'Air took delivery of 723 Potez 63.11s. To operate effectively the aircraft needed strong fighter cover, but this was rarely available and losses were very heavy. In all, 225 Potez 63.11s were destroyed or abandoned, more than any other type. After the armistice, the surviving aircraft saw extensive service with both the Free French and Vichy forces, and in 1942 many were adopted by the Luftwaffe for training and liaison duties.

▶ *Although possessing a good turn of speed, the Potez 63 could not survive in an environment dominated by Messerschmitts, and many were lost.*

SPECIFICATION: **Type** general reconnaissance aircraft • **Crew** 3 • **Powerplant** two 700hp Gnome-Rhone 14M-4 radial engines • **Max speed** 264mph (425km/h) • **Service ceiling** 27,885ft (8,500m) • **Max range** 932 miles (1,500km) • **Wingspan** 52ft 6in (16m) • **Length** 35ft 10in (10.93m) • **Height** 10ft 1in (3.08m) • **Weights** 6,911lb (3,135kg) empty; 9,987lb (4,530kg) loaded • **Armament** various; up to 12 0.30-in (7.5-mm) machine guns; external bomb load of 661lb (300kg)

■ Potez 540

The Potez 540, which appeared in prototype form as the Potez 54-01 on November 14, 1933, was developed as a private venture in time to take part in the competitions held under the French government's modernization plans of June 1934. The Portez 540 M4 was accepted at the end of its trials and entered production; the first of 185 aircraft was delivered in November 1934. Several variants were built, including the Potez 540 TOE for overseas colonial policing. Some aircraft, fitted with high-altitude Hispano-Suiza 12-Y engines, carried out clandestime reconnaissance missions over northern Italy and the Siegfried Line just before the outbreak of World War II. Substantial numbers of the 540 series were still in service in 1940, the majority in Africa, where they were used as transports.

▲ *The Potez 540 reconnaissance bomber was relegated to reserve units on the outbreak of WWII. Forty-five survived the German invasion.*

SPECIFICATION: **Type** reconnaissance/bomber/transport • **Crew** 5 • **Powerplant** two 690hp Hispano-Suiza 12Kirs 12-cylinder liquid-cooled V-type • **Max speed** 193mph (310km/h) at 13,125ft (4,000m) • **Service ceiling** 19,680ft (6,000m) • **Max range** 745 miles (1,200km) • **Wingspan** 72ft 6in (22.10m) • **Length** 53ft 2in (16.20m) • **Height** 12ft 9in (3.88m) • **Weight** 13,115lb (5,950kg) loaded • **Armament** three 0.30-in (7.5-mm) Darne machine guns; 1,984lb (900kg) of bombs

■ PZL P.7-P.24

Powered by a Bristol Jupiter radial engine, the gull-winged PZL P-7a was one of the leading fighter aircraft of the interwar years; deliveries had begun in the latter half of 1932, and by the end of 1933 all first-line fighter squadrons of the Polish Air Force's 1st, 2nd, 3rd, and 4th Air Regiments were equipped with it. Its successor, the PZL P-11, was basically a more powerful derivative that first flew in September 1931, with deliveries beginning in 1934. Most P-11s were powered by Bristol Mercury engines, built under license by Skoda; the definitive version of the fighter was the P-11c, of which 175 were built. The P-11 was to have been replaced by a low-wing fighter monoplane, the P-50 Jastrzeb (Hawk), as part of a major expansion scheme, but cuts in the military budget resulted in the cancelation of an order for 300 P-50s, and more P-11s were purchased instead.

They suffered heavy losses during the German invasion of Poland in September 1939. The P.11b was an export model

▲ *Well liked by its pilots, the PZL P.11 was an excellent fighter by the standards of the mid-1930s, but was outmoded by the outbreak of World War II.*

SPECIFICATION: Type fighter (data PZL P.11) • Crew 1 • Powerplant one 560hp Bristol Mercury VS2 radial • Max speed 230mph (370km/h) at 14,760ft (4,500m) • Service ceiling 31,170ft (9,500m) • Max range 503 miles (810km) • Wingspan 35ft 2in (10.72m) • Length 24ft 9in (7.55m) • Height 9ft 4in (2.85m) • Weight 3,505lb (1,590kg) loaded • Armament two 0.303-in (7.7-mm) machine guns

for Romania, which also built a small number of the type under license.

The P.24, which appeared in 1933, was basically similar but had a 770hp Gnome-Rhone 14K engine and featured an enclosed cockpit. The P.24 never served in the Polish Air Force, but was used by Turkey (40 P.24C), Romania (6 P.24E), Greece (36 P.24F and G), and Bulgaria (24 P.24G).

■ PZL P.23 Karas

POLAND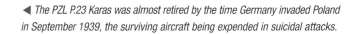

The PZL P.23 Karas (Carp) prototype flew for the first time in August 1934, and the initial production Karas-A entered service as an operational trainer in the following year. The major production version, appearing in 1936, was the P.23B Karas-B reconnaissance-bomber, 210 being completed to bring the total in Polish service to 250. A further 54 P.23Bs were built in

1937–39 for Bulgaria under the designation P-43. One Karas-B became a test bed for components of the PZL P-46 Sum (Swordfish) reconnaissance bomber, which was to have replaced the P.23 at the time of the German invasion. About 20 P.23s were still in service in September 1939, and suffered terrible losses in low-level attacks on enemy columns.

◀ The PZL P.23 Karas was almost retired by the time Germany invaded Poland in September 1939, the surviving aircraft being expended in suicidal attacks.

SPECIFICATION: Type reconnaissance-bomber (data P.23B) • Crew 3 • Powerplant one 680hp Bristol Pegasus VIII 9-cylinder radial • Max speed 198mph (319km/h) at 11,975ft (3,650m) • Service ceiling 23,950ft (7,300m) • Max range 782 miles (1,260km) • Wingspan 45ft 9in (13.95m) • Length 31ft 9in (9.68m) • Height 10ft 10in (3.30m) • Weight 7,178lb (3,256kg) loaded • Armament one forward-firing 0.303-in (7.7-mm) machine gun and one in ventral position; 2,200lb (1,000kg) of bombs

■ PZL P.37 Los

POLAND

The prototype PZL P.37 Los (Elk) medium bomber flew in 1936 and deliveries of the P.37A began in 1938, these aircraft having a single fin and rudder. The 30 Los-As were followed by 70 P.37Bs, with twin fins, but only 61 Los-B bombers were operational at the time of the German attack. Fifty escaped to Romania, some being used later against the Russians.

▶ The PZL Los was an excellent medium bomber design, but reached the front-line units too late to influence the course of the Polish campaign.

SPECIFICATION: Type medium bomber (data PZL P.37B) • Crew 4 • Powerplant two 873hp Bristol Pegasus XIIB 9-cylinder radials • Max speed 276mph (445km/h) at 11,154ft (3,400m) • Service ceiling 19,680ft (6,000m) • Max range 932 miles (1,500km) • Wingspan 58ft 10in (17.93m) • Length 42ft 5in (12.92m) • Height 16ft 8in (5.08m) • Weight 18,872lb (8,560kg) loaded • Armament three 0.303-in (7.7-mm) machine guns; 5,688lb (2,580kg) of bombs

▌PZL TS-11 Iskra

POLAND

The Polish aircraft industry produced some very worthwhile training aircraft during the 1950s and 1960s, including the PZL TS-8 Bies (Daredevil) basic trainer, which remained standard equipment from 1957 to 1962, when it was replaced by the TS-11 Iskra (Spark). First flown in 1961, the Iskra was Poland's first indigenous jet aircraft, and more than 600 were built up untill the late 1980s, the figure including a combat/reconnaissance version. The Indian Air Force also took delivery of 50 examples. The Iskra remains in service with both India and Poland.

SPECIFICATION: Type combat/reconnaissance trainer • Crew 2 • Powerplant one 2,425-lb (1,100-kg) thrust IL SO-3W turbojet • Max speed 478mph (770km/h) at 16,404ft (5,000m) • Service ceiling 36,090ft (11,000m) • Max range 783 miles (1,260km) • Wingspan 33ft (10.06m) • Length 36ft 7in (11.15m) • Height 11ft 7in (3.50m) • Weight 8,465lb (3,840kg) • Armament one 0.90-in (23-mm) cannon; four external hardpoints for stores up to 882lb (400kg)

▼ A cheap and effective trainer, the PZL TS-11 was Poland's first indigenous jet aircraft, and was widely used through three decades of the Cold War era.

▌PZL I-22 Iryda

POLAND

First flown in March 1985, the PZL I-22 Iryda was designed to replace the TS-11 as the primary jet trainer of the Polish Air Force. In the same class as the Dassault/Dornier Alpha Jet, it can undertake reconnaissance, ground attack, and air combat tasks. Deliveries to the Polish Air Force began in 1993, but were halted in 1995 by manufacturing disputes.

SPECIFICATION: Type multirole trainer and light close-support aircraft • Crew 2 • Powerplant two 2,425-lb (1,100-kg) thrust PZL-Rzeszow SO-3W22 turbojets • Max speed 522mph (840km/h) at 16,405ft (5,000m) • Service ceiling 36,090ft (11,000m) • Max range 261 miles (420km) with maximum warload • Wingspan 31ft 6in (9.60m) • Length 43ft 4in (13.22m) • Height 14ft 1in (4.30m) • Weight 15,211lb (6,900kg) loaded • Armament one 0.90-in (23-mm) GSh-23L cannon; four external hardpoints for up to 2,645lb (1,200kg) of stores

▲ First flown in 1985, the PZL I-22 Iryda tended to be overshadowed by the Aero L-39, which proved more popular with former Eastern Bloc countries.

■ Reggiane Re.2000 Series

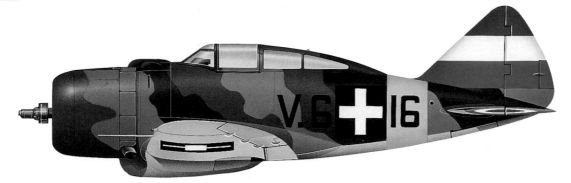

First flown in May 1939, the Re.2000 was the first fighter designed by Reggiane, a subsidiary of Caproni. Although it initially failed to win domestic orders it went into production as the Re.2000 Series I to meet export orders from Sweden (60 aircraft) and Hungary (70, plus 191 built under license). Of the 27 that remained in Italy, ten were converted as shipborne fighters (Series II) for service aboard Italy's aircraft carrier, the Aquila (which was practically complete at the time of the armistice) and the other 17 were converted to the long-range fighter-bomber role as Series III aircraft. The next variant, the Re.2001 Falco II, was fitted with a DB601 engine; 110 were produced as fighters and fighter-bombers (Series I and II),

SPECIFICATION: Type fighter (data Re.2000 Falco I) • Crew 1 • Powerplant one 985hp Piaggio P.XI RC40 14-cylinder radial • Max speed 329mph (530km/h) at 19,685ft (6,000m) • Service ceiling 34,450ft (10,500m) • Max range 870 miles (1,400km) • Wingspan 36ft 1in (11m) • Length 26ft 2in (7.99m) • Height 10ft 6in (3.20m) • Weight 6,349lb (2,880kg) loaded • Armament two 0.50-in (12.7-mm) fixed forward-firing machine guns in upper front fuselage

while 124 were given a heavier armament for the night-fighter role (Series III and IV). The Re.2002 Ariete (Ram), of which 227 were built, was a fighter-bomber version, as was the Re.2005 Sagittario (Archer), only 37 of which were completed.

■ Republic F-84 Thunderjet

The Republic F-84 Thunderjet, which was to provide many of NATO's air forces with their initial jet experience, began life in the summer of 1944, when Republic Aviation's design team investigated the possibility of adapting the airframe of the P-47 Thunderbolt to take an axial-flow turbojet. This proved impractical, and in November 1944 the design of an entirely new airframe was begun around the General Electric J35 engine. The first of three XP-84 prototypes was completed in December 1945 and made its first flight on February 28, 1946. Three prototypes were followed by 15 YP-84As for the USAF. Delivered in the spring of 1947, they were later converted to F-84B standard. Deliveries of the F-84B began in the summer of 1947 to the 14th

Fighter Group, and 226 were built. The F-84C, of which 191 were built, was externally similar to the F-84B, but incorporated an improved electrical system and an improved bomb release mechanism. The next model to appear, in November 1948, was the F-84D, which had a strengthened wing and a modified fuel system. It was followed, in May 1949, by the F-84E, which in addition to its six 0.50-in (12.7-mm) machine guns could carry two 1,000-lb (453-kg) bombs, or 32 rockets. The F-84G, which appeared in 1952, was the first Thunderjet variant to be equipped for flight refueling from the outset.

SPECIFICATION: Type fighter-bomber (data F-84G) • Crew 1 • Powerplant one 5,600lb (2,542kg) thrust Wright J65-A-29 turbojet • Max speed 605mph (973km/h) at 4,000ft (1,220m) • Service ceiling 40,500ft (12,353m) • Max range 1,000 miles (1,609km) • Wingspan 36ft 4in (11.05m) • Length 38ft 5in (11.71m) • Height 12ft 10in (3.90m) • Weight 28,000lb (12,701kg) loaded • Armament six 0.50-in (12.7-mm) Browning M3 machine guns; provision for up to 4,000lb (1,814kg) of external stores

▲ "Miss Jaque II" of the 136th Fighter-Bomber Wing, the first F-84 to complete 1,000 hours, taxies out on her 364th combat mission over Korea.

▌ Republic F-84F Thunderstreak

The XF-84F, which used about 60 percent of the F-84's components, flew for the first time on June 3, 1950, only 167 days after it was ordered. The first production F-84F flew on November 22, 1952 and the type was officially accepted by the USAF in the following month. The first USAF unit to arm with the swept-wing F-84F, in 1954, was the 407th Tactical Fighter Wing. The F-84F replaced the Thunderjet in several NATO air forces, giving many European pilots their first experience of modern, swept-wing jet aircraft. In French Air Force service, it saw action during the 1956 Anglo-French operation to secure the Suez Canal. The RF-84F Thunderflash was a low-level tactical reconnaissance variant.

SPECIFICATION: Type fighter-bomber • Crew 1 • Powerplant one 7,220-lb (3,278-kg) thrust Wright J65-W-3 turbojet • Max speed 695mph (1,118km/h) at sea level • Service ceiling 30,100ft (9,174m) • Combat radius 810 miles (1,304km) with drop tanks • Wingspan 33ft 7in (10.24m) • Length 43ft 4in (13.23m) • Height 14ft 4in (4.39m) • Weight 28,000lb (12,701kg) loaded • Armament six 0.50-in (12.7-mm) Browning M3 machine guns; provision for up to 6,000lb (2,722kg) of external stores

▼ *A Republic F-84F Thunderstreak, one of a formation heading for Europe from the USA, tops up from a KB-29 flight refueling tanker.*

▌ Republic F-105 Thunderchief

The Republic F-105 Thunderchief was conceived as a successor to the F-84F at a time when the USAF was building up its nuclear deterrent. Although beset by continual difficulties during development, the F-105 eventually emerged as the workhorse of Tactical Air Command during the early 1960s. The first of two YF-105 prototypes flew on October 22, 1955, and deliveries of operational F-105Bs began in May 1958 to the 4th Tactical Fighter Wing. Only 75 F-105Bs were built,

SPECIFICATION: Type fighter-bomber (data F-105D) • Crew 1 • Powerplant one 24,500-lb (11,113-kg) thrust Pratt & Whitney J75-19W turbojet • Max speed 1,480mph (2,382km/h) at altitude • Service ceiling 52,000ft (15,850m) • Combat radius 230 miles (370km) with full bomb load • Wingspan 34ft 11in (10.65m) • Length 64ft 3in (19.58m) • Height 19ft 8in (5.99m) • Weight 52,546lb (23,834kg) loaded • Armament one 0.79-in (20-mm) M61 cannon; provision for up to 8,000lb (3,629kg) of bombs internally and 6,000lb (2,722kg) externally

being replaced on the production line in 1959 by the all-weather ground-attack F-105D, of which 610 were produced. In its F-105D version the nuclear-capable Thunderchief served with 13 tactical fighter wings, and was widely used in strikes on north Vietnam. The F-105F two-seat trainer saw combat in the antiradar "Wild Weasel" role, as did the F-105G.

▲ *The Republic F-105 Thunderchief suffered very heavy losses over North Vietnam. Originally designed as a nuclear bomber, it was nicknamed the "Thud".*

▌Republic P-43 Lancer

 USA

The Republic P-43 Lancer was a development of the Seversky P-35, the first examples of which were supplied in 1937. Inadequate as a fighter, the P-43 was later converted to the photoreconnaissance role. Total production of the P-43 was 272 aircraft, of which 103 were sent to China; these were the only Lancers to see action.

SPECIFICATION: Type fighter • Crew 1 • Powerplant one 1,200hp Pratt & Whitney R-1830-49 Twin Wasp 14-cylinder radial • Max speed 356mph (570km/h) at 25,000ft (7,620m) • Service ceiling 36,000ft (11,000m) • Max range 800 miles (1,290km) • Wingspan 36ft (10.97m) • Length 28ft 6in (8.68m) • Height 14ft (4.27m) • Weight 7,935lb (3,600kg) loaded • Armament four 0.30-in (7.62-mm) machine guns

▌Republic P-47 Thunderbolt

 USA

One of the truly great fighter aircraft of all time, the Republic P-47 Thunderbolt represented the culmination of a line of aircraft which had its origin in two 1936 designs, the Seversky P-35 and P-43. The original XP-47 and XP-47A prototypes were designed around the Allison engine, but designer Alexander Kartveli realized that this powerplant, with its mediocre performance at high altitude, would not be suitable. He therefore drew up an alternative design around the most powerful engine then available, the new 2,000hp Pratt & Whitney Double Wasp radial. The new proposal was submitted to the USAAC in June 1940 as the XP-47B and was immediately accepted, orders being placed in September for 171 production P-47Bs and 602 P-47Cs. The two were basically similar, except that the P-47C had a slightly longer fuselage to improve stability. The XP-47B flew for the first time on May 6, 1941. In June 1942 the 56th Fighter Group began to rearm with the P-47, and in December 1942–January 1943 it

SPECIFICATION: Type single-seat fighter/fighter-bomber (data P-47D) • Crew 1 • Powerplant one 2,300hp Pratt & Whitney R-2800-59 radial engine • Max speed 428mph (689km/h) at 30,000ft (9,145m) • Service ceiling 42,000ft (12,800m) • Max range 1,260 miles (2,028km) • Wingspan 40ft 9in (12.43m) • Length 36ft 1in (11.01m) • Height 14ft 2in (4.32m) • Weight 19,400lb (8,800kg) loaded • Armament six or eight 12.7-mm (0.50-in) machine guns in the wings; two 1,000lb (454kg) bombs or 10 RPs

deployed to England, flying its first combat mission—a fighter sweep over St. Omer—on April 13, 1943. From that first operational sortie over Europe until the end of the fighting in the Pacific in August 1945, Thunderbolts flew 546,000 combat sorties, dropped 132,000 tons (134,000 tonnes) of bombs, launched 60,000 rockets, and expended more than 135 million rounds of ammunition. In the European Theater alone, from D-Day (June 6, 1944) to VE Day (May 8, 1945), the Thunderbolt was credited with destroying 9,000 locomotives, 86,000 railroad cars, and 6,000 armored vehicles. In all theaters of war, its pilots claimed the destruction of 3,752 enemy aircraft in the air and a further 3,315 on the ground. By the time the 56th Fighter Wing flew its first operational sortie in the spring of 1943, huge orders had been placed for the P-47D, which was at first externally almost identical to the P-47C. As time went by, however, so many changes were introduced in the P-47D that it differed as much from the original P-47D as did that fighter from the XP-47B prototype.

In all, 12,602 P-47Ds were built by Republic in four batches, a further 354 being built by Curtiss-Wright as P-47Gs. The RAF acquired 354 early-model P-47Ds as the Thunderbolt I, while a further 590 later model P-47Ds were supplied as the Thunderbolt II. All the RAF's Thunderbolts were assigned to squadrons in Southeast Asia Command (India and Myanmar), where they replaced the Hawker Hurricane in the ground attack role. The next production version was the P-47M, 130 being completed with the 2,800hp R-2800-57 engine. It was built specifically to help combat the V-1 flying bomb attacks on Britain. The last variant was the P-47N, a

▲ *P-47 Thunderbolts of No. 134 Squadron, RAF, at Ratnap, Burma, late 1944. This unit was renumbered No. 131 Squadron in July 1945.*

very long-range escort and fighter-bomber, of which Republic built 1816. Overall P-47 production, which ended in December 1945, was 15,660 aircraft. About two-thirds of these, almost all P-47Ds, survived the war and found their way into the air forces of Brazil, Chile, Colombia, Dominica, Ecuador, Mexico, Peru, Turkey, and Yugoslavia. France also used the P-47D in its operations against dissidents in Algeria during the 1950s, the Armée de l'Air having found jet aircraft unsuitable for close support in that particular environment. During World War II, the Soviet Union received 195 P-47s out of the 203 allocated, some having been lost en route.

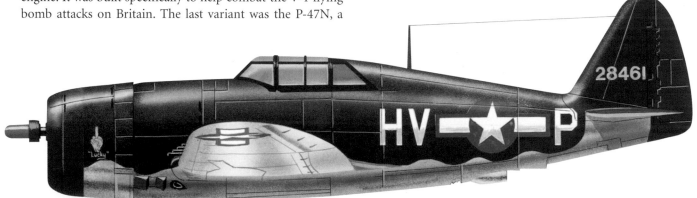

▋ Rockwell B-1B Lancer   USA

The Rockwell B-1 variable-geometry supersonic bomber was designed to replace the B-52 and FB-111 in the low-level penetration role. The B-1 prototype flew on December 23, 1974, and subsequent flight trials and evaluation progressed rapidly. On June 30, 1977, however, it was announced by President Carter that the B-1 would not be produced. Then, on October 2, 1981, President Ronald

Reagan's new administration took the decision to resurrect the Rockwell B-1 program. The operational designation of the supersonic bomber, 100 of which were to be built for SAC, was to be B-1B, the prototypes already built now being known as B-1As. The primary mission of the B-1B would be penetration with free-fall weapons, using SRAMS for defense suppression. The aircraft would also be modi-

▲ *A Rockwell B-1B supersonic bomber. This variable-geometry aircraft program was canceled, but later resurrected by President Reagan's administration.*

fied to carry the ALCM, being fitted with a movable bulkhead between the two forward bomb bays to make room for an eight-round ALCM launcher.

The first B-1B flew in October 1984 and was well ahead of schedule, despite the crash several weeks earlier of one of the two B-1A prototypes taking part in the test program, and the first operational B-1B (83-0065) was delivered to the 96th Bomb Wing at Dyess AFB on July 7, 1985.

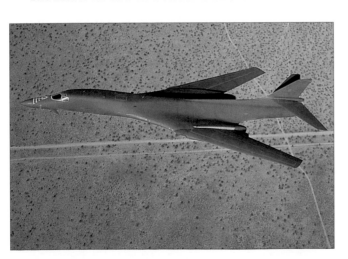

◄ *The primary mission of the B-1B is to penetrate enemy airspace at very low level with free-fall weapons, either nuclear or conventional.*

SPECIFICATION: Type strategic bomber • Crew 4 • Powerplant four 30,780-lb (13,962-kg) thrust General Electric F101-GE-102 turbofans • Max speed 825mph (1,328km/h) at high altitude • Service ceiling 50,000ft (15,240m) • Max range 7,455 miles (12,000km) on internal fuel • Wingspan 136ft 8in (41.67m) • Length 147ft (44.81m) • Height 34ft (10.36m) • Weight 477,000lb (216,634kg) loaded • Armament up to 84,500lb (38,320kg) of Mk 82 or 24,200lb (10,974kg) of Mk 84 iron bombs in the conventional role, 24 SRAMs, 12 B-28 and B-43 or 24 B-61 and B-83 free-fall nuclear bombs, eight ALCMs on internal rotary launchers and 14 more on underwing launchers, and various combinations of other underwing stores. Low-level operations are flown with internal stores only

▌Rockwell OV-10 Bronco

First flown in July 1965, the OV-10A battlefield support aircraft entered service with the US Marine Corps and USAF in 1968, 270 being built. Fifteen aircraft were modified for night forward air control, the OV-10B was a target-towing version supplied to Federal Germany (24), while the OV-10C was a version for the Royal Thai Air Force (36 delivered). Other variants were the OV-10E for Venezuela (16), and the OV-10F for Indonesia (6).

SPECIFICATION: Type battlefield support/COIN aircraft • Crew 2 • Powerplant two 715hp AiResearch T76-410/411 turboprops • Max speed 281mph (452km/h) at sea level • Service ceiling 30,000ft (9,150m) • Max range 600 miles (960km) • Wingspan 40ft (12.19m) • Length 41ft 7in (12.67m) • Height 15ft 2in (4.62m) • Weight 14,466lb (6,560kg) loaded • Armament two 0.30-in (7.62-mm) machine guns in sponsons on lower fuselage; up to 3,600lb (1,632kg) of bombs and/or rockets

▲ An OV-10 Bronco in US Navy colors. The Bronco was a viable battlefield support system and carried sophisticated sensors.

▌Roland D.II

Although produced in some quantity—around 300 aircraft in total—the Roland D.II of 1917 was inferior to the Albatros series of fighters, and did not remain in first-line service for long. Its successor, the Roland D.VI, was produced in limited numbers to make up for delays in the delivery of the Fokker D.VII.

◀ The Roland D.II scout was not one of Germany's success stories, and was inferior to the Albatros D.III, which soon replaced it.

SPECIFICATION: Type scouting biplane • Crew 1 • Powerplant one 160hp Mercedes D.III 6-cylinder liquid-cooled engine • Max speed 105mph (169km/h) • Service ceiling 16,400ft (5,000m) • Endurance 2hrs • Wingspan 29ft 3in (8.91m) • Length 22ft 8in (6.91m) • Height 9ft 3in (2.82m) • Weight 1,748lb (793kg) loaded • Armament two LMG 08/15 machine guns

▌Royal Aircraft Factory BE.2 Series

In 1909, HM Balloon Factory at Farnborough, which as its name implies had been involved in the production of lighter-than-air craft, began building airplanes, and changed its title to the Royal Aircraft Factory. Its first aircraft product, built in 1911, was the BE.1 (Bleriot Experimental) tractor biplane; the BE.2 that followed it used the same basic airframe and was the first military machine to be built as such in Britain. By mid-1913 it equipped 13 squadrons of the recently formed Royal Flying Corps. Production gave way to the BE.2a with wing of unequal span, and the BE.2b with revised decking around the cockpits and ailerons instead of wing-warping controls. The BE.2c introduced the 80hp RAF 1a engine and was the first to be armed with a machine gun. In the night-fighter role, it was used with success against

SPECIFICATION: Type reconnaissance/bomber/night fighter biplane (data BE.2c) • Crew 2 • Powerplant one 80hp RAF 1a in-line engine • Max speed 90mph (145km/h) • Service ceiling 9,000ft (2,745m) • Endurance 4hrs • Wingspan 40ft 9in (12.42m) • Length 27ft 3in (8.31m) • Height 12ft (3.66m) • Weight 2,100lb (953kg) loaded • Armament one 0.303-in (7.7-mm) Vickers machine gun mounted on upper wing center section or in observer's cockpit

German Zeppelin airships in 1916. The last variant was the BE.2e. In wartime service the BE.2 variants performed well in the reconnaissance role, but a great many were lost during the time of the "Fokker Scourge" of 1915–16. According to extant records, 3,535 BE.2s of all types were built, but the real figure is certainly much higher.

▲ An early example of the BE.2, apparently lost. Its pilot (bottom right) is studying a map and enjoying a cigarette dangerously close to a haystack.

▌Royal Aircraft Factory BE.8

GREAT BRITAIN

Making its appearance in 1912, the BE.8 was issued in small numbers to various RFC squadrons from May 1914. The BE.8a, at least 38 of which were delivered from March 1915, had shorter span wings with aileron control. The BE.8 had an unspectacular career in France and was withdrawn by the spring of 1915; the BE.8a was used solely as a training aircraft.

SPECIFICATION: Type general-purpose biplane • Crew 2 • Powerplant one 80hp Gnome rotary • Max speed 70mph (113km/h) • Service ceiling not known • Max range not known • Wingspan 39ft 6in (12.03m) • Length 27ft 3in (8.30m) • Height 9ft 4in (2.84m) • Weight not known • Armament 100lb (45kg) of bombs

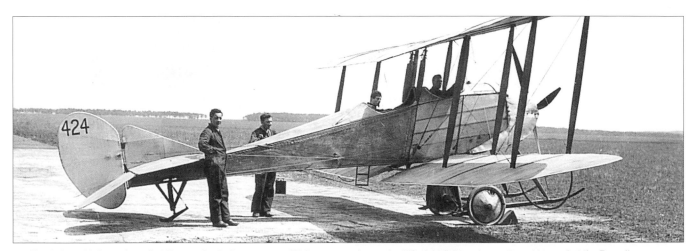

▲ After being withdrawn from first-line service in France, some BE.8s were used as makeshift night fighters in an attempt to combat the Zeppelin menace.

▌ Royal Aircraft Factory BE.12

Originally designed as a fighter to counter the threat of the Fokker Monoplane, the BE.12 proved to be a disappointment in its intended role, and after only a few weeks in service it was relegated to light bombing in September 1916, serving in Palestine and Macedonia as well as France. BE.12s also served with Home Defence squadrons, and one shot down Zeppelin L.48 in June 1917. Total orders for the BE.12 amounted to 600 aircraft.

SPECIFICATION: **Type** light bomber/night fighter • **Crew** 1 • **Powerplant** one 150hp RAF 4a 12-cylinder in-line V type • **Max speed** 102mph (164km/h) at sea level • **Service ceiling** 12,500ft (3,810m) • **Endurance** 3hrs • **Wingspan** 37ft (11.28m) • **Length** 27ft 3in (8.31m) • **Height** 11ft 1in (3.39m) • **Weight** 2,352lb (1,067kg) loaded • **Armament** one or two 0.303-in (7.7-mm) machine guns

▲ *The BE.12 was unable to fulfill the fighter role for which it had been designed, having the same inherent stability drawbacks as the BE.2.*

▌ Royal Aircraft Factory FE.2b

The Nieuport 11 virtually held the line against the Fokker Monoplane until the introduction of two British fighter types, the FE.2b and DH.2. The original FE.2a was completed in August 1913, but it was a year before the first 12 aircraft were ordered, the first of these flying in January 1915. Had matters moved more quickly, and production of the FE.2 been given priority, it is possible that the Fokker Monoplane would never have achieved the supremacy that it did. The first FE.2b flew in March 1915, and in May a few production examples arrived in France for service with No. 6 Squadron

RFC at Abeele, Belgium, but it was not until January 1916 that the first squadron to be fully equipped with the FE, No. 20, deployed to France. A two-seat "pusher" type powered by a 120hp Beardmore engine and armed with one Lewis gun in the front cockpit and a second on a telescopic mounting firing upward over the wing center section, the FE.2b was slightly slower than the Fokker E.III but a match for it in maneuverability. Later in the war the FE was used in the light night-bombing role. The FE.2d was a variant with a longer span. Total FE.2 production was 2,325 aircraft.

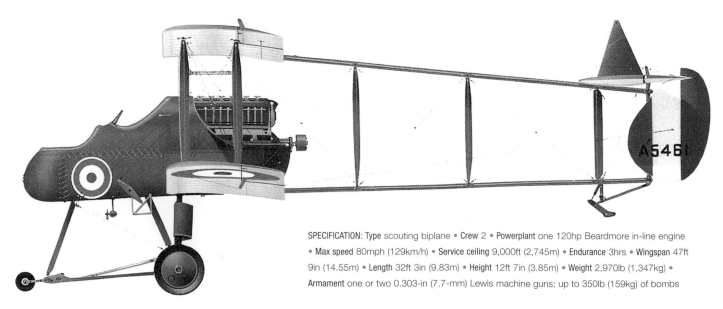

SPECIFICATION: **Type** scouting biplane • **Crew** 2 • **Powerplant** one 120hp Beardmore in-line engine • **Max speed** 80mph (129km/h) • **Service ceiling** 9,000ft (2,745m) • **Endurance** 3hrs • **Wingspan** 47ft 9in (14.55m) • **Length** 32ft 3in (9.83m) • **Height** 12ft 7in (3.85m) • **Weight** 2,970lb (1,347kg) • **Armament** one or two 0.303-in (7.7-mm) Lewis machine guns; up to 350lb (159kg) of bombs

Royal Aircraft Factory FE.8

GREAT BRITAIN

Similar in appearance to the Airco DH.2, the FE.8, first flown in October 1915, enjoyed none of the Airco biplane's success. Serious flight stability and engine problems delayed its entry into service until August 1916, by which time it was obsolescent. The FE.8 was withdrawn from first-line service in mid-1917.

▶ *Owing to the lack of an interrupter gear, the FE.8 fighter was designed as a pusher, but gave poor service.*

SPECIFICATION: **Type** scouting biplane • **Crew** 1 • **Powerplant** one 100hp Gnome Monosoupape 9-cylinder rotary • **Max speed** 94mph (151km/h) at sea level • **Service ceiling** 14,500ft (4,420m) • **Endurance** 2hrs 30mins • **Wingspan** 31ft 6in (9.60m) • **Length** 23ft 8in (7.21m) • **Height** 9ft 2in (2.79m) • **Weight** 1,346lb (610.5kg) • **Armament** one 0.303-in (7.7-mm) Lewis machine gun

Royal Aircraft Factory RE.5

GREAT BRITAIN

The RE.5 was an unarmed reconnaissance biplane that made its appearance in 1914. It did not have the maneuverability to survive in combat with the new types of German aircraft, and was soon withdrawn. Some were used for experimental purposes; one single-seat aircraft, given a longer span, reached an altitude of 17,000ft (5,182m) in July 1914.

◀ *The RE.5 was the first of the Royal Aircraft Factory's "Reconnaissance Experimental" (RE) biplanes to be put into production, 24 being built.*

SPECIFICATION: **Type** reconnaissance biplane • **Crew** 2 • **Powerplant** one 120hp Beardmore 6-cylinder in-line engine • **Max speed** 78mph (126km/h) at sea level • **Service ceiling** not known • **Max range** not known • **Wingspan** 44ft 6in (13.56m) • **Length** 26ft 2in (7.98m) • **Height** 9ft 8in (2.95m) • **Weight** not known • **Armament** 60lb (27.2kg) of bombs

Royal Aircraft Factory RE.7

GREAT BRITAIN

Deployed to France with the RFC from the beginning of 1916, the RE.7, derived from the RE.5 reconnaissance aircraft, was designed to carry a new 336-lb (152.4-kg) bomb which had been tested by its predecessor in 1915. No. 21 Squadron was the only unit to be completely equipped with the RE.7, but its aircraft were used for escort and reconnaissance, and no bombing operations were undertaken until July 1916. By that time, the RE.7 was already being replaced by the BE.12.

▶ *The RE.7 was intended to carry a single 336lb (152kg) bomb, designed by Royal Aircraft Factory experts.*

SPECIFICATION: **Type** bomber • **Crew** 2 • **Powerplant** one 150hp RAF 4a 12-cylinder in-line V-type • **Max speed** 85mph (137km/h) at sea level • **Service ceiling** 6,500ft (1,981m) • **Endurance** 6hrs • **Wingspan** 57ft (17.37m) • **Length** 31ft 10in (9.72m) • **Height** 12ft 7in (3.84m) • **Weight** 3,449lb (1,564kg) • **Armament** one 0.303-in (7.7-mm) Lewis gun in front cockpit; one 336lb (152.4kg) bomb

▌Royal Aircraft Factory RE.8

GREAT BRITAIN

Nicknamed "Harry Tate" after the Cockney comedian, the RE.8 reconnaissance and artillery spotting aircraft resembled a scaled-up BE.2, but it had a much sturdier fuselage and a far better armament. The first aircraft were delivered in the autumn of 1916 but were grounded after a series of accidents that led to the redesign of the tail unit. The RE.8 was subse-

quently very widely used, equipping 33 RFC squadrons. Like the BE.2, it was far too stable to be agile in combat and suffered serious losses, usually having to operate under heavy escort. Production totaled 4,077 aircraft.

SPECIFICATION: Type reconnaissance and artillery observation biplane • Crew 2 • Powerplant one 150hp RAF 4a 12-cylinder in-line V-type • Max speed 102mph (164km/h) • Service ceiling 13,500ft (4,115m) • Endurance 4hrs 15mins • Wingspan 42ft 7in (12.98m) • Length 20ft 11in (6.38m) • Height 9ft 6in (2.90m) • Weight 2,869lb (1,301kg) • Armament one fixed forward-firing 0.303-in (7.7-mm) Vickers machine gun; one 0.303-in (7.7-mm) Lewis machine gun in rear cockpit; up to 224lb (102kg) of bombs

▲ *In September 1917 RE.8s flew missions in support of the Ypres offensive, flying 260 bomb sorties in 90 days.*

▌Royal Aircraft Factory SE.5

GREAT BRITAIN

The SE.5 single-seat scout entered RFC service in the spring of 1917, being delivered to No. 56 Squadron in March. Although less maneuverable than the French-built Nieuports

and Spads, the SE.5 was faster and had an excellent rate of climb, enabling it to hold its own in combat with the latest German fighter types. The SE.5s of No. 56 Squadron flew

▲ *A replica of the SE.5a is put through its paces at a Shuttleworth Collection vintage aircraft flying display in 1972. The SE.5a entered service in June 1917.*

SPECIFICATION: Type scouting biplane • Crew 1 • Powerplant one 200hp
Wolseley (license-built Hispano-Suiza 8a eight-cylinder V-type • Max speed
138mph (222km/h) • Service ceiling 17,000ft (5,185m) • Max range 300 miles
(483km) • Wingspan 26ft 7in (8.11m) • Length 20ft 11in (6.38m) • Height 9ft
6in (2.89m) • Weight 1,988lb (902kg) • Armament one fixed forward-firing
0.303-in (7.7-mm) Vickers machine gun, plus one similar caliber Lewis
machine gun on Foster mounting on upper wing

their first operational patrol on April 22, 1917. The original
SE.5 was followed into service, in June 1917, by the SE.5a,

with a 200hp Hispano-Suiza engine. The type was first issued
to Nos. 56, 40, and 60 Squadrons, in that order, and by the end
of the year had been delivered to Nos. 24, 41, 68, and 84.
Deliveries were slowed by an acute shortage of engines, but
the pilots of the units that did receive the SE.5a were full of
praise for the aircraft's fine flying qualities, physical strength,
and performance. It is probably no exaggeration to say that,
in most respects, the S.E.5a was the Spitfire of World War I. At
the end of World War I some 2,700 SE.5as were on RAF
charge, the type having served with 24 British, two American,
and one Australian squadrons.

Rumpler C.I

The Rumpler C.I armed reconnaissance aircraft, which made
its appearance at the beginning of 1915 and remained in service until February 1918, was one of the best of its type.
Tough, fast, well-armed, and very difficult to shoot down, it

made an enormous contribution to the German war effort.
Its successor was the C.IV, a long-range reconnaissance and
intruder aircraft which proved equally as efficient and which
was built in large quantities.

◀ *The Rumpler C.I was an excellent machine, serving on the Eastern and
Western fronts, in Macedonia, Palestine, and Salonika, until February 1918.*

SPECIFICATION: Type reconnaissance biplane • Crew 2 • Powerplant one 160hp
Mercedes D.III liquid-cooled in-line engine • Max speed 95mph (152km/h) •
Service ceiling 16,400ft (5,000m) • Endurance 4hrs • Wingspan 39ft 10in
(12.15m) • Length 25ft 9in (7.85m) • Height 10ft (3.06m) • Weight 2,938lb
(1,333kg) • Armament two machine guns; 220lb (100kg) of bombs

Ryan FR-1 Fireball

Design work on the Ryan Model 28, or FR-1, was initiated in
1943, and the aircraft was in production before the end of the
war in the Pacific. It was the first operational aircraft in
which a piston engine was combined with a turbojet, using
both powerplants for takeoff, climb, and combat and having
the ability to fly and land with either engine shut down. The

prototype XFR-1 flew on June 25, 1944 and the type entered
service with Navy Fighter Squadron VF-66 in March 1945,
too late to see service in World War II. Only 69 aircraft were
built, the last examples being delivered to VF-1E in June
1947. One FR-1 was converted as a test bed for the first US-
built turboprop engine, and designated XF2R-1.

▶ *At the time Ryan was authorized to proceed with the XFR-1, the company
had no experience in building either Navy aircraft or combat airplanes.*

SPECIFICATION: Type carrier-borne fighter • Crew 1 • Powerplant one 1,350hp
Wright R-1820-72W radial engine in the nose, and one 1,600-lb (726-kg)
thrust General Electric J31-GE-3 turbojet in the tail • Max speed 404mph
(650km/h) at sea level • Service ceiling 43,100ft (13,136m) • Max range 1,620
miles (2,606km) • Wingspan 40ft (12.19m) • Length 32ft 4in (9.85m) • Height
13ft 11in (4.24m) • Weight 11,652lb (5284kg) loaded • Armament four 0.50-in
(12.7-mm) machine guns

■ Saab AJ-37 Viggen

The Saab 37 Viggen (Thunderbolt) was designed to carry out the four roles of attack, interception, reconnaissance, and training. Part of the requirement was that it should be capable of operating from sections of Swedish highways. The first of seven prototypes flew for the first time on February 8, 1967, followed by the first production AJ-37 single-seat all-weather attack variant in February 1971. Deliveries of the first of 110 AJ-37s to the Royal Swedish Air Force began in June that year.

The JA-37 interceptor version of the Viggen, 149 of which were built, replaced the J35F Draken; the SF-37 (26 delivered) was a single-seat armed photoreconnaissance

▲ *The SAAB AJ-37 Viggen multi-role combat aircraft was one of the most potent designs of the 1970s, and could operate from motorways.*

SPECIFICATION: Type all-weather attack aircraft (data Saab AJ-37) • Crew 1 • Powerplant one 26,232-lb (11,899-kg) thrust Volvo Flygmotor RM8 turbofan • Max speed 1,320mph (2,124km/h) at altitude • Service ceiling 60,000ft (18,290m) • Combat radius 621 miles (1,000km) hi-lo-hi, full weapons load • Wingspan 34ft 9in (10.60m) • Length 53ft 5in (16.30m) • Height 18ft 4in (5.60m) • Weight 45,194lb (20,500kg) • Armament seven external hardpoints with provision for 13,228lb (6,000kg) of stores, including 1.19-in (30-mm) Aden cannon pods, 5.30-in (135-mm) rocket pods, AAMs, and ASMs

variant; and the SH-37 (26 delivered) was an all-weather maritime reconnaissance version, replacing the S-32C Lansen. The SK-37 (18 delivered) was a tandem two-seat trainer, retaining a secondary attack role. Some Viggens were expected to remain in service until 2010.

■ Saab J-21A/R

Although Sweden had been mostly reliant on foreign combat types before and during World War II, the Swedish aircraft manufacturer, SAAB, had produced an indigenous fighter aircraft, the J-21A. A twin-boom pusher design, powered by a DB605B liquid-cooled engine, the J-21A made its first flight on July 13, 1943, and during trials it reached a respectable top speed of 398mph (640 km/h) at 15,000ft (4,575m). The J-21A's advanced all-metal flush-riveted stressed-skin wing employed a new high-speed aerofoil section, and other innovations included a cartridge-type ejection seat for the pilot, enabling him to clear

▲ *The SAAB J-21A was a novel design, entering service in 1945. It was followed by a jet-powered variant, the J-21R.*

SPECIFICATION: Type fighter/attack aircraft (data J-21R) • Crew 1 • Powerplant one 3,000-lb (1,361-kg) thrust de Havilland Goblin turbojet • Max speed 497mph (800km/h) • Service ceiling 39,400ft (12,000m) • Max range 450 miles (720km) • Wingspan 37ft 4in (11.37m) • Length 34ft 3in (10.45m) • Height 9ft 6in (2.90m) • Weight 11,023lb (5,000kg) loaded • Armament one 0.79-in (20-mm) Bofors cannon and four 0.51-in (13.2-mm) M/39A machine guns; centreline pod housing eight 0.51-in (13.2-mm) guns; wing racks for rocket projectiles

the propeller blades and tail unit. The new aircraft entered service with the Royal Swedish Air Force late in 1945, 298 production aircraft being delivered. By this time SAAB was working on a jet-powered version, the J-21R. This flew on March 10, 1947, but because of many modifications that had to be made to the airframe production deliveries did not take place until 1949, and an order for 120 aircraft was cut back to 60. After a short career as a fighter the J.21 was converted to the attack role as the A-21R. The type was the only aircraft ever to see first-line service with both piston and jet power.

▌Saab J-29

SPECIFICATION: Type fighter (data J-29F) • Crew 1 • Powerplant one 6,170-lb (2,800-kg) license-built DH Ghost 50 turbojet • **Max speed** 659mph (1,060km/h) • Service ceiling 50,850ft (15,500m) • **Max range** 1,060 miles (1,700km) • **Wingspan** 36ft 1in (11m) • Length 33ft 2in (10.10m) • Height 12ft 3in (3.73m) • Weight 17,637lb (8,000kg) loaded • Armament four 0.79-in (20-mm) Hispano cannon; 1,000lb (453kg) of underwing stores

▶ *The SAAB J-29 was the first swept-wing fighter of western European design to enter service after World War II, following the wartime Me 262.*

The Saab J-29 was the first swept-wing fighter of western European design to enter service after World War II. The first of three prototypes flew on September 1, 1948 and the first production model, the J-29A, entered service in 1951. Other variants of the basic design were the J-29B, with increased fuel tankage; the A-29 ground-attack version, identical to the J-29 except for underwing ordnance racks; and the S-29C reconnaissance version. The J-29D was an experimental version with an afterburner, while the J-29E interceptor had a modified "saw-tooth" wing. The last production variant was the J-29F, which combined the refinements of the J-29D and -E and began to enter service in 1954. The J-29 saw limited action in support of UN forces during the Congo crisis of 1962–63. It was the first Swedish aircraft to be exported, several being delivered to the small Austrian Air Force.

▌Saab J-32 Lansen

In the fall of 1946, SAAB began design studies of a new turbojet-powered attack aircraft for the Swedish Air Force, and two years later the Swedish Air Board authorized the construction of a prototype under the designation P1150. This aircraft, now known as the A-32 Lansen (Lance), flew for the first time on November 3, 1952, powered by a Rolls-Royce Avon RA7R turbojet. Three more prototypes were built, and one of these exceeded Mach One in a shallow dive on October 25, 1953. The A-32A attack variant was followed by the J-32B all-weather fighter, which first flew in January 1957. A two-seater, the J-32B was powered by an RM6 (license-built RA28) turbojet and carried an improved armament, navigation equipment, and fire control system.

The J-37B was very much an interim aircraft, filling a gap until the advent of a much more potent system, the SAAB J-35 Draken. The S-32C was a reconnaissance version, with a modified nose containing cameras and radar equipment.

The Lansen remained in service with the Flygvapen for more than 40 years, equipping seven squadrons at its peak. It served in many other roles, including target tug and trials aircraft, well into the 1990s.

▶ *The J-32D target tug was a special version of the J-32B. Later the aircraft was used in the ECM training role.*

SPECIFICATION: Type all-weather and night fighter (data Saab J-32B) • Crew 2 • Powerplant one 15,190-lb (6,890-kg) thrust license-built Rolls-Royce Avon turbojet • Max speed 692mph (1,114km/h) • Service ceiling 52,500ft (16,013m) • Max range 2,000 miles (3,220km) with external fuel • Wingspan 42ft 7in (13m) • Length 47ft 6in (14.50m) • Height 15ft 3in (4.65m) • Weight 29,800lb (13,529kg) • Armament four 1.19-in (30-mm) Aden cannon; AAMs or folding-fin aircraft rockets

Saab J-35 Draken

▲ A Saab J-35 Draken of the Austrian Air Force. The type's unique planform was first tested on an experimental aircraft, the Saab 210.

SPECIFICATION: Type interceptor (data J-35F) • Crew 1 • Powerplant one 17,110-lb (7,761-kg) license-built Rolls-Royce Avon 300 series turbojet • Max speed 1,320mph (2,125km/h) at altitude • Service ceiling 65,000ft (20,000m) • Max range 2,020 miles (3,250km) with maximum fuel •Wingspan 30ft 10in (9.40m) • Length 50ft 6in (15.40m) • Height 12ft 9in (3.90m) • Weight 35,274lb (16,000kg) • Armament one 1.19-in (30-mm) Aden cannon; four AAMs

Designed from the outset to intercept transonic bombers at all altitudes and in all weathers, the Draken (Dragon) was probably, at the time of its service debut, the finest fully integrated air defense system in western Europe. The Swedish government's requirement was for an aircraft with a performance 50 percent greater than that of fighters currently in service with other nations' air forces. The first of three prototypes of Saab's unique "double delta" fighter flew for the first time on October 25, 1955, and the initial production version, the J-35A, entered service early in 1960.

The major production version of the Draken was the J-35F, which was virtually designed around the Hughes HM-55 Falcon radar-guided air-to-air missile and was fitted with an improved S7B collision-course fire control system, a high capacity datalink system integrating the aircraft with the STRIL 60 air defense environment, an infrared sensor under the nose, and PS-01A search and ranging radar. The J-35F also featured increased fuel capacity, giving it a very good operational range. Total production of the Draken was around 600 aircraft, equipping 17 RSAF squadrons.

In the mid-1960s, Saab turned its attention to the export market, and received orders for 46 aircraft for Denmark and 12 for Finland, which also purchased another 20 ex-Swedish J-35s. In 1985 Austria acquired 24 surplus Swedish J-35Ds, which were redesignated J-35Ö. These aircraft continue to serve with the Austrian air force in 2002.

The Draken was the first fully supersonic aircraft in western Europe to be deployed operationally.

▲ The SAAB J-35 Draken employed a unique double-delta configuration, and had a very advanced computerized weapons system.

Saab J-39 Gripen

The Saab JAS-39 Gripen (Griffon) lightweight multirole fighter was conceived in the 1970s as a replacement for the attack, reconnaissance, and interceptor versions of the Viggen. The

prototype Gripen was rolled out on April 26, 1987 and made its first flight on December 9, 1988. The loss of this aircraft in a landing accident on February 2, 1989 led to a revision of the Gripen's advanced fly-by-wire control system.

Orders for the Gripen totaled 140 aircraft, all for the

▲ *This JAS-39A is armed with a maritime attack load of two Rb 75 Mavericks and two Rb 15F anti-ship missiles, plus a pair of AIM-9L self-*

Royal Swedish Air Force. The type entered service in 1995. The JAS-39 is a canard delta design with triplex digital fly-by-wire controls, a multimode Ericsson pulse-Doppler radar, laser inertial navigation system, wide-angle head-up display, and three monochrome head-down displays. The aircraft's Volvo Flygmotor RM.12 turbofan (a license-built General Electric GE F404) is hardened against birdstrike.

SPECIFICATION: Type multirole combat aircraft • Crew 1 • Powerplant one 18,100-lb (8,210-kg) thrust Volvo Flygmotor RM12 turbofan • Max speed Mach 2 plus • Service ceiling classified • Max range 2,020 miles (3,250km) • Wingspan 26ft 3in (8m) • Length 46ft 3in (14.10m) • Height 15ft 5in (4.70m) • Weight 27,500lb (12,473kg) • Armament one 1-in (27-mm) Mauser BK27 cannon; six external hardpoints for Sky Flash and Sidewinder AAMs, Maverick ASMs, antiship missiles, bombs, cluster bombs, reconnaissance pods, drop tanks, ECM pods etc.

▌Saab B.18　　　　SWEDEN 🇩🇰

The Saab B.18 originated in a 1930 Swedish Air Force requirement for a reconnaissance aircraft, this being altered later to dive-bomber. The first prototype flew on June 19, 1942 and was followed by 60 production Saab B.18As, these entering service in 1944. A few were later converted to the reconnaissance role as the S.18A. The B.18A was powered by two Pratt & Whitney Twin Wasp engines, but the next variant, the Saab B.18B, had Daimler-Benz DB.605s, bringing about a marked improvement in performance. This model

entered service in 1946 and 120 examples were built.

The final variant, the T.18B, was originally intended as a torpedo-bomber, but the 62 aircraft produced were modified for the attack role with a 2.24-in (57-mm) Bofors and two 0.79-in (20-mm) cannon in the nose. One of the fastest twin piston-engined bombers ever built, the Saab 18 remained in first-line service until 1956.

SPECIFICATION: Type bomber (data B.18A) • Crew 3 • Powerplant two 1,065hp Pratt & Whitney Twin Wasp 14-cylinder radials • Max speed 289mph (465km/h) at 19,685ft (6,000m) • Service ceiling 26,250ft (8,000m) • Max range 1,367 miles (2,200km) • Wingspan 55ft 9in (17m) • Length 43ft 5in (13.23m) • Height 14ft 3in (4.35m) • Weight 17,946lb (8,140kg) loaded • Armament two 0.51-in (13.2-mm) and one 0.31-in (7.92-mm) machine guns; 3,307lb (1,500kg) of bombs; rocket projectiles on underwing racks

▲ *The last B.18 variant, the T.18B, was intended as a torpedo-bomber, but was later modified for the attack role.*

▌Salmson 2　　　　FRANCE 🇫🇷

One of the most widely used reconnaissance aircraft in the last year of World War I was the Salmson 2, which entered service at the beginning of 1918. In fact it was a true multi-purpose aircraft, being able to carry out day bombing and ground attack missions in addition to its primary role. Production ran to 3,200 aircraft, of which 705 went to the Americans. The Salmson 2 was also built under license in Japan, where it equipped one air battalion.

SPECIFICATION: Type reconnaissance biplane • Crew 2 • Powerplant one 260hp Salmson (Canton-Unné) 9-cylinder radial • Max speed 115mph (185km/h) • Service ceiling 20,505ft (6,250m) • Endurance 3hrs • Wingspan 38ft 8in (11.80m) • Length 27ft 10in (8.50m) • Height 9ft 6in (2.90m) • Weight 2,954lb (1,340kg) loaded • Armament two to three 0.30-in (7.5-mm) machine guns

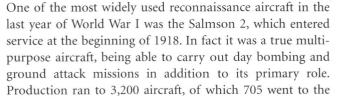

▐ Saunders-Roe (Saro) London

The Saro A.27 London was produced to Air Ministry Specification R.24/31, the first of 10 Mk.I aircraft being delivered in 1936. The next 20 aircraft, with uprated engines, were designated Mk.II, and all Mk.Is were upgraded to Mk II standard. The London equipped seven Coastal Command squadrons, and was operational in the early months of WWII.

SPECIFICATION: Type coastal patrol flying boat • Crew 5 • Powerplant two 1,055hp Bristol Pegasus X radial engines • Max speed 155mph (249km/h) • Service ceiling 19,900ft (6,065m) • Max range 1,100 miles (1,770km) • Wingspan 80ft (24.38m) • Length 56ft 9in (17.31m) • Height 18ft 9in (5.72m) • Weight 18,400lb (8,346kg) loaded • Armament one 0.303-in (7.7-mm) Lewis machine gun in bow and one in each of two midships positions; up to 2,000lb (907kg) of bombs or depth charges on underwing racks

▲ The Saro London was still operational at the outbreak of World War II, serving mostly with overseas squadrons.

▐ Savoia-Marchetti SM.75 Marsupiale

▲ The SM.75 Marsupiale set up a number of international records during its career as a civil airliner. The principal operator was Ala Littoria.

Designed in 1937, the SM.75 Marsupiale was a three-engined civil airliner. The 34 aircraft in service at the time of Italy's entry into the war in June 1940 were requisitioned as military transports and were eventually joined by 56 more newly built machines. Some of the survivors remained in service until 1949.

SPECIFICATION: Type transport • Crew 4–5 (plus 18 passengers) • Powerplant three 750hp Alfa Romeo AR.126 RC34 radials • Max speed 225mph (363km/h) at 13,120ft (4,000m) • Service ceiling 20,500ft (6,250m) • Max range 1,070 miles (1,720km) • Wingspan 97ft 5in (29.68m) • Length 70ft 10in (21.60m) • Height 16ft 9in (5.10m) • Weight 28,700lb (13,000kg) loaded • Armament one 0.303-in (7.62-mm) machine gun

▐ Savoia-Marchetti SM.79 Sparviero

The SM.79 was a completely new design, its prototype being an eight-seater airliner built specifically to take part in the prestigious London–Melbourne air race. The second prototype was completed as a bomber, and did not differ a great deal from the airliner, the only variations being the addition of a ventral gondola and of a raised cockpit which gave the aircraft its characteristic hunchbacked appearance. Production of the military SM.79 Sparviero (Sparrowhawk) began in October 1936 and was to have an uninterrupted run until June 1943, by which time 1,217 aircraft had been built.

The Regia Aeronautica lost no time in testing the SM.79

operationally in Spain, where the type was used with considerable success by the 8° and 111° Stormi Bombardamento Veloce (High Speed Bomber Groups). The initial production version, the SM.79-I, was powered by three 780hp Alfa Romeo 126 radial engines and had a range of 1,180 miles (1,898km).

In 1937 an SM.79-I underwent trials with a 17.7-in (450-mm) torpedo, and later two, beneath the fuselage, and these indicated that the aircraft could easily carry two of these weapons if it were fitted with more powerful engines. In October 1939 production began of the SM.79-II, equipped with 1,000hp Piaggio P.XI radial engines (apart from one

SPECIFICATION: Type bomber/torpedo-bomber • Crew five • Powerplant three 1,000hp Piaggio P.XI RC 40 radial engines • Max speed 270mph (435km/h) at 11,975ft (3,650m) • Service ceiling 21,325ft (6,500m) • Max range 1,181 miles (1,900km) with a 2,756lb (1,250kg) bomb load • Wingspan 69ft 2in (21.08m) • Length 51ft 3in (15.62m) • Height 14ft 5in (4.40m) • Weight 24,912lb (11,300kg) • Armament three 0.50-in (12.7-mm) Breda-SAFAT machine guns in two dorsal and one ventral positions, one 0.303-in (7.62-mm) Lewis gun on a sliding mount in the rear fuselage; two 17.7-in (450-mm) torpedoes or 2,756lb (1,250kg) of bombs

▶ The SM.79 Sparviero played a major part in the Axis air offensive against the island of Malta, the key to strategic control of the Mediterranean.

batch with 1,030hp Fiat A.80 RC 41s) for the torpedo-bomber squadrons of the Regia Aeronautica, and it was in this role that the aircraft was to excel during World War II. When Italy entered that conflict in June 1940, SM.79s of both variants accounted for well over half the Italian Air Force's total bomber strength. SM.79s saw continual action in the air campaign against Malta and in North Africa, becoming renowned for their high-level precision bombing, while the torpedo-bomber version was active against British shipping in the Aegean during the German invasion of Crete and against naval forces and convoys in the central Mediterranean. Despite the obvious value of the SM.79 to the Axis war effort in the Mediterranean, the aircraft (like most Italian types) suffered from poor servicing arrangements, with the result that only about half the total force was available for operations at any given time.

After the Italian surrender in September 1943 SM.79s continued to fly with the Co-Belligerent Air Force, while the pro-German Aviazione della RSI employed several SM.79-IIIs.

The SM.79B, first flown in 1936, was a twin-engined export model, the middle engine being replaced by an extensively glazed nose. Brazil took delivery of three, Iraq four, and Romania 48, each version with a different powerplant. The Romanian IAR factories also produced the SM.79B under license, equipped with Junkers Jumo 211D in-line engines, and used the aircraft in both bomber and transportation roles on the Eastern Front. Including the export models, total production of all SM.79 variants reached 1,330 aircraft before output ceased in 1944.

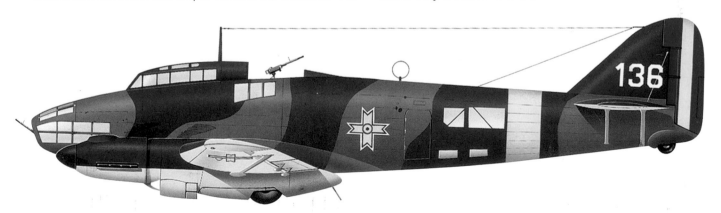

∎ Savoia-Marchetti SM.81 Pipistrello

ITALY

Although it was effective in the limited wars in which Italy was involved in the 1930s, the bomber force of the Regia Aeronautica never equaled, either in the quality of the aircraft types it used or in numbers, that of the allied air forces that opposed it during World War II. The three-engined

machines produced by Savoia-Marchetti, a firm with considerable experience in the field of commercial aircraft design, were typical examples of the bombers that formed the backbone of the Regia Aeronautica. One such design was the SM.73, an 18-passenger airliner with a tapered cantilever low wing and a fixed undercarriage; the military version was the SM.81 Pipistrello (Bat), which, when it made its service debut in 1935, represented a considerable advance over the Regia Aeronautica's existing bomber types.

Fast, well-armed and with a good range, it was used to good effect during the Italian campaign in Abyssinia, which began in October 1935, and from August 1936 it was also used operationally during the Spanish Civil War. In World War II most were employed in East Africa and on the Russian Front, latterly in the transportation role.

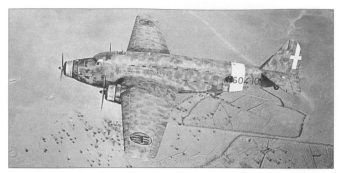

SPECIFICATION: **Type** bomber/transportation • **Crew** 5 • **Powerplant** three 670hp Piaggio P.X RC35 9-cylinder radials • **Max speed** 211mph (340km/h) at 9,845ft (3,000m) • **Service ceiling** 22,965ft (7,000m) • **Max range** 1,243 miles (2,000km) • **Wingspan** 78ft 9in (24m) • **Length** 58ft 4in (17.80m) • **Height** 19ft 8in (6m) • **Weight** 22,167lb (10,055kg) loaded • **Armament** two 0.303-in (7.62-mm) machine guns in dorsal turret, two in ventral position, and one each in beam positions; 4,409lb (2,000kg) of bombs

▲ *145° Gruppo T was the most active North African transport unit, carrying 11,600 men to and from Sicily from June 1940 until 1941.*

▎Savoia-Marchetti SM.82 Canguro

Developed from the SM.75, the SM.82 Canguro (Kangaroo) was the largest transport aircraft in use by the Regia Aeronautica during World War II. It could carry a wide variety of payloads, including fuel supplies, dismantled single-engined fighters, and 40 troops. Some were used by the Luftwaffe after the Italian surrender in September 1943.

SPECIFICATION: **Type** transportation • **Crew** 4–5 • **Powerplant** three 860hp Alfa Romeo AR.126 RC.18 14-cylinder radials • **Max speed** 230mph (370km/h) at sea level • **Service ceiling** 19,600ft (6,000m) • **Max range** 1,865 miles (3,000km) • **Wingspan** 97ft 5in (29.68m) • **Length** 75ft 4in (22.95m) • **Height** 19ft 8in (6m) • **Weight** 39,340lb (17,840kg) loaded • **Armament** four 0.303-in (7.62-mm) machine guns; up to 8,800lb (4,000kg) of bombs

▎SEPECAT Jaguar

Developed jointly by the British Aircraft Corporation and Breguet (later Dassault-Breguet) under the banner of SEPECAT (Société Européenne de Production de l'Avion Ecole de Combat et Appui Tactique), the Jaguar emerged from protracted development as a much more powerful and effective aircraft than originally envisaged. The first French version to fly, in September 1968, was the two-seat E model, 40 being ordered by the French Air Force, followed in March 1969 by the single-seat Jaguar A tactical support aircraft.

▶ *RAF Germany's Jaguar force formed a major element of Britain's tactical nuclear striking power.*

SPECIFICATION: **Type** fighter • **Crew** 1 • **Powerplant** one 120hp Le Rhone 9JB 9-cylinder air-cooled rotary • **Max speed** 115mph (184km/h) at sea level • **Service ceiling** 19,685ft (6,000m) • **Endurance** 2hrs 30mins • **Wingspan** 28ft 6in (8.70m) • **Length** 19ft 2in (5.85m) • **Height** 9ft 7in (2.94m) • **Weight** 1,334lb (605kg) loaded • **Armament** one 0.30-in (7.5-mm) machine gun

Service deliveries of the E began in May 1972, the first of 160 Jaguar As following in 1973. The British versions, known as the Jaguar S (strike) and Jaguar B (trainer), flew on October 12, 1969 and August 30, 1971 respectively, being delivered to the RAF as the Jaguar GR.Mk.1 (165 examples) and Jaguar T.Mk.2/2A (38). The Jaguar GR.1A/3A are upgrades.

The Jaguar International, first flown in August 1976, was a version developed for the export market. It was purchased by Ecuador (12), Nigeria (18), and Oman (24) and was license-built in India by HAL (98, including 40 delivered by B.Ae).

▲ The SEPECAT Jaguar was one of the first collaborative ventures to be undertaken in Europe, and over the years has proved to be a very viable combat aircraft.

▌Seversky P-35

USA

The Army Air Corps' first modern fighter aircraft was the Seversky P-35, development of which originated in 1935.

▲ In spring 1938 the 17th, 27th and 94th Squadrons of the 1st Pursuit Group received their first P-35s. This example served with the 27th Squadron.

Designed by Alexander Kartveli, it flew for the first time in August 1935 and an order for 76 production models was placed by the Air Corps in June 1936, delivery taking place between July 1937 and August 1938. Of the 177 P-35s built, 40 were exported to Sweden and 60 were used in the Philippines at the time of the Japanese attack at the end of 1941. After two days of fighting only eight remained airworthy; the P-35 was soon retired from front-line service.

SPECIFICATION: Type fighter • Crew 1 • Powerplant one 950hp Pratt & Whitney R-1830-9 14-cylinder radial • Max speed 281mph (452km/h) at 500ft (1,525m) • Service ceiling 30,600ft (9,325m) • Max range 1,150 miles (1,851km) • Wingspan 36ft (10.97m) • Length 25ft 2in (7.67m) • Height 9ft 1in (2.77m) • Weight 6,295lb (2,855kg) loaded • Armament one 0.50-in (12.7-mm) and one 0.30-in (7.62-mm) machine gun in upper forward fuselage

▌Shin Meiwa PS-1

JAPAN

First flown on October 5, 1967 as the PX-S, this long-range STOL amphibian entered service in 1973 in its PS-1 anti-submarine form, 20 examples being built. The US-1, which flew in prototype form in October 1974, was an air-sea res-cue variant. Both examples of this unusual modern flying-boat were eventually replaced by helicopters.

▶ Operated by the 71st Koku-tai at Iwakuni since 1976, the US-1 can cover a vast area of the Pacific using seaborne refueling bases.

SPECIFICATION: Type antisubmarine warfare amphibian (data PS-1) • Crew 10 • Powerplant four 2,850hp Ishikawajima-built General Electric T64-1H1-10 turboprops • Max speed 340mph (547km/h) at 4,900ft (1,500m) • Service ceiling 29,500ft (9,000m) • Max range 1,347 miles (2,168km) • Wingspan 107ft 3in (32.68m) • Length 109ft 11in (33.50m) • Height 31ft 10in (9.70m) • Weight 86,862lb (39,400kg) loaded • Armament various ASW stores in upper deck weapons bay aft of tactical compartment

▌Short Belfast

GREAT BRITAIN

Designed to carry heavy loads such as missiles (specifically the Blue Streak IRBM, which was canceled), as well as artillery and vehicles, the Short Belfast heavy-lift freighter flew for the first time on May 1, 1964 and ten Belfast C.Mk.1s were subsequently delivered to No. 53 Squadron, RAF Air

Support Command. The type was retired in 1976 and sold for commercial use, although two aircraft held in reserve by the RAF were used during the Falklands conflict of 1982.

▶ *The Short Belfast long-range strategic transport suffered from an inadequate altitude performance. It was in service for less than a decade.*

SPECIFICATION: **Type** heavy-lift transport • **Crew** 5 (plus 150 passengers) • **Powerplant** four 5,730hp Rolls-Royce Tyne RTy.12 turboprops • **Max speed** 352mph (566km/h) • **Service ceiling** 30,000ft (9,145m) • **Max range** 5,300 miles (8,530km) • **Wingspan** 158ft 9in (48.42m) • **Length** 136ft 5in (41.57m) • **Height** 47ft (14.30m) • **Weight** 230,000lb (104,300kg) loaded • **Armament** none

▌Short Singapore

GREAT BRITAIN

The Singapore series of flying boats began with the Singapore I of 1926, famous for its circumnavigation of Africa in the hands of Sir Alan Cobham. It was followed in 1930 by the Singapore II, which did not go into production

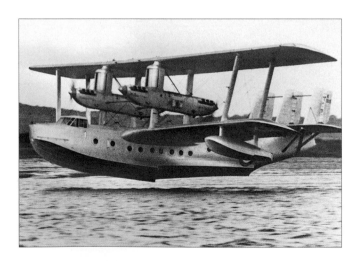

but which provided the basis for the Singapore III—ordered into series production for delivery from 1935. The first of four development aircraft flew in July 1934 and these were followed by 37 production Singapore IIIs, all of which had been delivered by mid-1937. Singapores equipped seven RAF squadrons at home and overseas; a few were still in service at the outbreak of World War II, and some were acquired by the Royal New Zealand Air Force.

◀ *Early production Singapore IIIs entered service with No. 230 Squadron RAF in April 1935. They were mostly replaced by the Short Sunderland.*

SPECIFICATION: **Type** maritime patrol flying boat • **Crew** 6 • **Powerplant** four 560hp Rolls-Royce Kestrel VIII 12-cylinder V-type • **Max speed** 145mph (233km/h) • **Service ceiling** 15,000ft (4,570m) • **Max range** 1,000 miles (1,609km) • **Wingspan** 90ft (27.43m) • **Length** 76ft (23.16m) • **Height** 23ft 7in (7.19m) • **Weight** 27,500lb (12,474kg) • **Armament** one 0.303-in (7.7-mm) Lewis gun in nose, dorsal, and tail positions; up to 2,000lb (907kg) of bombs

▌Short Stirling

GREAT BRITAIN

The first of the RAF's trio of four-engined heavy bombers, the Short Stirling was designed to a 1936 specification and was first flown as a half-scale prototype in 1938. The full-scale prototype flew in May 1939 and was damaged beyond repair on its first flight when its undercarriage collapsed. Production deliveries of the Stirling Mk I were made to No. 7

Squadron in August 1940, the squadron flying its first operational sortie on February 10/11, 1941. The Stirling Mk II, powered by Wright Cyclone engines, did not progress beyond the prototype stage; the main bomber variant was the Mk III, which had Hercules XVI engines and which introduced the two-gun dorsal turret. Stirlings flew their last bombing mission in September 1944, having equipped 15 squadrons of RAF Bomber Command. By this time the aircraft had found a new role as a transport and glider tug

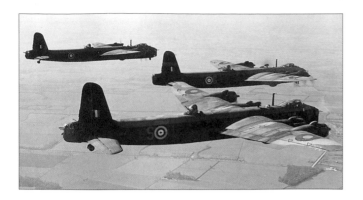

(Stirling Mk IV). The last variant was the Mk V transport, which entered service in January 1945 and was unarmed. Stirling production, all variants, was 2,375 aircraft.

◀ *Stirling production was severely disrupted by an attack on the Shorts factory at Rochester, Kent, in 1940.*

SPECIFICATION: **Type** heavy bomber (data Stirling Mk III) • **Crew** 7 • **Powerplant** four 1,650hp Bristol Hercules XVI 14-cylinder radials • **Max speed** 270mph (434km/h) • **Service ceiling** 17,000ft (5,180m) • **Max range** 2,010 miles (3,235km) • **Wingspan** 99ft 1in (30.20m) • **Length** 87ft 3in (26.59m) • **Height** 22ft 9in (6.93m) • **Weight** 70,000lb (31,752kg) loaded • **Armament** two 0.303-in (7.7-mm) Browning machine guns in nose and dorsal turrets, plus four in tail turret; internal bomb load of 14,000lb (6,350kg)

■ Short Sunderland

The design of the Short Sunderland, which eventually was to become one of the RAF's longest-serving operational aircraft, was based on that of the stately Short C Class "Empire" flying boats, operated by Imperial Airways in the 1930s. The maiden flight of the Sunderland prototype took place on October 16, 1937, and the first production Sunderland Mk Is were delivered to No. 230 Squadron in Singapore early in June 1938, and by the outbreak of World War II in September

SPECIFICATION: **Type** long-range maritime patrol aircraft (data Sunderland Mk.V) • **Crew** 10 • **Powerplant** four 1,200hp Pratt & Whitney R-1830-90 Twin Wasp 14 cylinder air-cooled radial engines • **Max speed** 217mph (349km/h) at 5,000ft (1,525m) • **Service ceiling** 17,900ft (5,445m) • **Max range** 2,980 miles (4,796km) • **Wingspan** 112ft 9in (34.36m) • **Length** 85ft 3in (26m) • **Height** 34ft 6in (10.52m) • **Weight** 60,000lb (27,216kg) loaded • **Armament** two fixed forward-firing 0.303-in (7.7-mm) machine guns, two 0.303-in (7.7-mm) machine guns each in bow and dorsal turrets, and four 0.303-in (7.7-mm) machine guns in tail turret; war load of up to 4,960lb (2,250kg) of bombs, mines, or depth charges on retractable racks in hull sides

1939 three more squadrons were equipped with the type. The Sunderland Mk I, of which 90 were built, was followed by 55 Mk IIs; these were fitted with Pegasus XVIII engines with two-stage superchargers, a twin-gun dorsal turret, an improved rear turret, and ASV Mk II radar. Production of the Sunderland Mk II reached 55 aircraft. The major production version was the Mk III, with a modified hull; the first Short-built Sunderland Mk III flew on December 15, 1941 and the parent company eventually produced 286 Mk IIIs, a further 170 being built by Blackburn Aircraft. (The latter company had already built 15 Mk Is and five Mk IIs.)

The Sunderland III equipped 11 RAF squadrons (including one Polish and one Free French), and was followed by the Sunderland IV, a larger and heavier development with 1,700hp Bristol Hercules engines, eight 0.50-in (12.7-mm)

machine guns and two 0.79-in (20-mm) cannon. In fact, only two prototypes and eight production aircraft were built and given the name Seaford, but after evaluation by Coastal and Transport Commands the Sunderland IV/Seaford was abandoned and the aircraft later converted for commercial use as the Short Solent. The last operational Sunderland, therefore, was the Mk V, 100 of which were built by Shorts and 50 by Blackburn. The MK V, powered by four 1,200hp Pratt & Whitney R-1830-90 Twin Wasps and carrying the ASV Mk VIc radar, made its appearance late in 1943 and continued to serve for many years after WWII, the last RAF Sunderland Vs retiring from No. 205 Squadron at Changi, Singapore, in 1959. Nineteen Sunderland Mk Vs were exported to France's Aéronavale, retiring in 1960, and 16 to the RNZAF, where they served until 1966.

◀ *A Sunderland GR.5 of No. 201 Squadron, Pembroke Dock, moored on the Thames by Tower Bridge in the early 1950s.*

▌Siemens-Schuckert SSW D.III

Early in 1918 the Siemens-Schuckert Werke (SSW), were contracted to build 60 examples of their D.III scout, which had taken part in the same contest as the Fokker D.VII. Believed by some German pilots to be the best fighter at the front in the summer of 1918, the SSW D.III was a stubby, compact little biplane of wooden construction powered by a 160hp Siemens-Halske rotary engine. During flight trials in October 1917, the prototype D.III had reached a level speed of 112mph (180km/h) and climbed to 19,600ft (5,978m) in less than 20 minutes, a performance which justified its being ordered into immediate production. At the same time, the IDFLIEG—Inspektion der Fliegertruppen—placed small orders for two further developments, the D.IV and D.V.

▲ *The D.III was built by a branch of the Siemens electrical firm, which also developed airships and "Grossflugzeuge" (Giant aircraft) bombers.*

SPECIFICATION: Type scouting biplane • Crew 1 • Powerplant one 200hp Siemens-Halske Sh.IIIa rotary engine • Max speed 112mph (180km/h) • Service ceiling 26,245ft (8,000m) • Endurance 2hrs • Wingspan 27ft 8in (8.43m) • Length 18ft 8in (5.68m) • Height 9ft 2in (2.80m) • Weight 1,598lb (725kg) loaded • Armament two fixed forward-firing 0.31-in (7.92-mm) LMG 08/15 machine guns

The first batch of 30 SSW D.III scouts was delivered for operational trials in January 1918, and in February the IDFLIEG ordered 30 more aircraft. Beginning in late April, 41 examples were allocated to operational units on the Western Front; most of these went to JG.2, which equipped its Jasta 15 with the type. The pilots were delighted with the new aircraft, but the engine gave constant problems, and the whole fleet was withdrawn to be reengined. By the time deliveries were resumed, the war was virtually over.

▌Sikorsky Ilya Murometz

Designed by a talented young engineer whose name was to make its mark on the history of aviation, the Ilya Murometz—named after a legendary Russian hero—was the world's first four-engined airplane. Igor Sikorsky was chief designer of the Russo-Baltic Railroad Factories, and in 1912

he launched an ambitious program for the production of a large multiengined transportation aircraft. This resulted in a machine unofficially named the Bolshoi Bal'tisky (Great Baltic) Type B, which made a 10-minute flight on May 13, 1913. Sikorsky used the basic design to build a larger aircraft, the Ilya Murometz, 10 of which were ordered for military use after some very successful proving flights, including one in which the aircraft lifted 16 people and a dog to an altitude of 6,560ft (2,000m) and flew for five hours at 62mph (100km/h) over Moscow. With the outbreak of World War I the order was increased to 80 aircraft. The first series model was the Ilya Murometz A, which was purchased by the Imperial Navy and equipped with floats; this was followed by the Type B, four of which were built, the Type V (32 built), the first to be conceived from the outset as a bomber, the Type G (30 built), and the Type E (12), the last and most powerful variant. The bombers were concentrated into a special unit named the Eskadra Vozdushnykh Korablei (Squadron of Flying Ships) which became operational in February 1915.

Between then and the October Revolution of 1917 the huge machines made over 400 raids on targets in Germany and Lithuania, operating from Vinnitza in Poland. Only one aircraft was lost to enemy action; most others were destroyed on the ground to prevent their capture by the Germans in the wake of the armistice concluded with the Bolsheviks in 1918.

▼ *The Sikorsky Ilya Murometz was the world's first four-engined bomber, the type carrying out over 400 attacks on enemy targets from 1915–17.*

SPECIFICATION: **Type** heavy bomber (data Type V) • **Crew** 4–7 • **Powerplant** four 150hp Sunbeam 8-cylinder in-line engines • **Max speed** 75mph (121km/h) • **Service ceiling** 9,840ft (3,000m) • **Endurance** 5hrs • **Wingspan** 97ft 9in (29.80m) • **Length** 56ft 1in (17.10m) • **Height** 15ft 6in (4.72m) • **Weight** 10,117lb (4,589kg) loaded • **Armament** three–seven 0.30-in (7.62-mm) machine guns; 1,150lb (522kg) of bombs

▮ SOKO Galeb/Super Galeb

YUGOSLAVIA

First flown in May 1961, the SOKO G-2A Galeb (Seagull) jet trainer entered service with the Yugoslav Air Force in 1963. The G-4 Super Galeb, although based on the earlier aircraft, was in fact a completely new design, with swept flying surfaces and updated systems. A ground attack variant, designated the G-4M, was also developed.

▼ *The Soko Galeb and Super Galeb series of trainers served the Yugoslav Air Force well through three decades, and could also be used in the strike role.*

SPECIFICATION: **Type** jet trainer (data G-2A Galeb) • **Crew** 2 • **Powerplant** one 2,500-lb (1,134-kg) thrust Rolls-Royce Viper 11 Mk 226 turbojet • **Max speed** 454mph (730km/h) at 19,685ft (6,000m) • **Service ceiling** 39,370ft (12,000m) • **Max range** 771 miles (1,240km) • **Wingspan** 31ft 11in (9.73m) • **Length** 33ft 11in (10.34m) • **Height** 10ft 9in (3.28m) • **Weight** 9,480lb (4,300kg) • **Armament** two 0.50-in (12.7-mm) machine guns; underwing racks for bombs, rockets, and bomblet containers

SOKO Jastreb

SPECIFICATION: Type light attack aircraft • Crew 1 • Powerplant one 3,000-lb (1,361-kg) thrust Rolls-Royce Viper Mk 531 turbojet • Max speed 510mph (820km/h) at 19,685ft (6,000m) • Service ceiling 39,370ft (12,000m) • Max range 944 miles (1,520km) • Wingspan 38ft 3in (11.68m) • Length 38ft 8in (11.78m) • Height 11ft 11in (3.64m) • Weight 11,244lb (5,100kg) loaded • Armament three 0.50-in (12.7-mm) machine guns; up to 1,102lb (500kg) of stores on underwing racks

The SOKO J-1 Jastreb (Hawk) was a light attack version of the G-2A Galeb, featuring an uprated Viper engine to enhance payload capacity. The RJ-1 was a photoreconnaissance version. Some Jastrebs were also supplied to the air forces of Libya and Zambia. Production of the Jastreb ended in 1983.

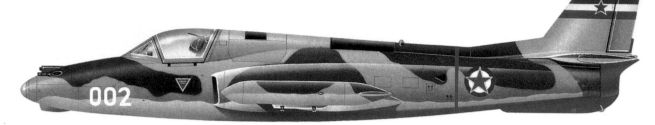

SOKO/Avioane J-22 Orao

The J-22 Orao (Hawk) was the result of a collaborative effort between SOKO of Yugoslavia and the Romanian IAv (Intrepinderea De Avione Bucaresti) company.

Each country built prototypes, which flew simultaneously in 1974, and production of an initial batch of 20 Romanian aircraft, designated IAR-93A, began in 1979, with SOKO starting production of the similar J-22 in 1980. An improved version with afterburning engines, the J-22M Orao 2 (IAR-93B), went into production in 1984, with orders

totaling 165 in both countries.

Only a fraction of this number was delivered, production being seriously disrupted following the collapse of the communist regime in Romania and the civil war in Yugoslavia.

SPECIFICATION: Type ground attack aircraft (data IAR-93A) • Crew 1 • Powerplant two 5,000lb (2,268kg) Turbomecanica (Rolls-Royce Viper Mk 633-47) turbojets • Max speed 721mph (1,160km/h) at sea level • Service ceiling 41,010ft (12,500m) • Combat radius 329 miles (530km) • Wingspan 31ft 6in (9.62m) • Length 48ft 10in (14.90m) • Height 14ft 7in (4.45m) • Weight 22,267lb (10,100kg) • Armament two 0.90-in (23-mm) GSh-23L cannon; up to 6,173lb (2,800kg) of stores on five external hardpoints

▲ The IAR-93A/B continues to provide Romania with five squadrons of strike/ground-attack aircraft.

Sopwith Baby

The little Sopwith Baby floatplane was derived from the Sopwith Tabloid, which had won the Schneider Trophy contest in 1914. The Royal Naval Air Service ordered 136 Tabloids for short-range maritime patrol, these being followed by 457 examples of the Baby. The Baby operated in all theaters of war, from seaplane carriers as well as shore bases, and was built under license by the Italian firm Ansaldo.

SPECIFICATION: Type reconnaissance/light bomber floatplane • Crew 1 • Powerplant one 130hp Clergét 9-cylinder rotary • Max speed 100mph (161km/h) • Service ceiling 7,600ft (2,317m) • Endurance 2hrs 15mins • Wingspan 25ft 8in (7.82m) • Length 23ft (7.01m) • Height 10ft (3.05m) • Weight 1,715lb (778kg) • Armament one machine gun (various types); 130lb (59kg) of bombs

▮ Sopwith Camel

GREATBRITAIN

Although it had a number of vicious tendencies, the Sopwith Camel—first issued to No. 4 Squadron RNAS and No. 70 Squadron RFC on the Western Front in July 1917—was a superb fighting machine in the hands of a skilled pilot, and by November 1918 the many squadrons operating it had claimed the destruction of at least 3,000 enemy aircraft, more than any other type.

Total production reached 5,490, many serving with foreign air arms. Early production Camel F.1s were powered either by the 130hp Clerget 9B or the 150hp Bentley BR.1 rotary engine, but subsequent aircraft were fitted with either the Clerget or the 110hp Le Rhone 9J. In addition to serving overseas, the Camel F.1 also equipped a number of Home Defence squadrons, the night-fighter version being equipped

SPECIFICATION: Type scouting biplane (data Camel F.1) • Crew 1 • Powerplant one 130hp Clerget rotary engine • Max speed 115mph (185km/h) • Service ceiling 19,000ft (5,790m) • Endurance 2hrs 30mins • Wingspan 28ft (8.53m) • Length 18ft 9in (5.72m) • Height 8ft 6in (2.59m) • Weight 1,453lb (659kg) loaded • Armament two fixed forward-firing 0.303-in (7.7-mm) Vickers machine guns; up to four 25lb (11.3kg) bombs

with a pair of Lewis guns. The final production version was the Camel 2F.1, designed for shipboard operation. As well as being flown from the aircraft carriers HMS *Furious* and HMS *Pegasus*, the 2F.1 could also be catapulted from platforms erected on the gun turrets and forecastles of other capital ships, or launched from a lighter towed behind a destroyer.

▲ *Although the Sopwith Camel had some vicious tendencies, it was a superb fighter aircraft in the hands of a skilled pilot.*

▮ Sopwith Pup

GREAT BRITAIN

SPECIFICATION: Type scouting biplane • Crew 1 • Powerplant one 80hp Le Rhone rotary engine • Max speed 112mph (179km/h) • Service ceiling 17,500ft (5,334m) • Max range 310 miles (500km) • Wingspan 26ft 6in (8.08m) • Length 19ft 4in (5.89m) • Height 9ft 5in (2.87m) • Weight 1,225lb (556kg) • Armament one fixed forward-firing obliquely mounted 0.303-in (7.7-mm) Vickers or Lewis machine gun

A delightful aircraft to fly, and possessing an exceptionally good rate of climb, the Sopwith Pup first flew in February 1916, powered by an 80hp Le Rhone rotary engine. It was very small, simple, and reliable, and its large wing area gave it a good performance at altitude. The Pup was initially ordered for the Royal Naval Air Service, 170 being delivered, and a further 1,600 were built for the RFC.

The Pup was superior to many German first-line scouts, thanks mainly to its small radius of turn, and it could still hold its own at the time of its withdrawal early in 1918. Many Pups subsequently served on Home Defence duties, some being armed with eight Le Prieur anti-Zeppelin rockets mounted on the interplane struts, and in various training roles.

▲ The Sopwith Pup was a delightful aircraft to fly, and had an extremely good rate of climb. Very reliable, it was also highly maneuverable.

▌Sopwith Cuckoo

GREAT BRITAIN

In 1918 Britain led the field in naval aviation, particularly in torpedo-bomber design. One such aircraft was the Sopwith T.1 Cuckoo, which first flew in June 1917; 350 were eventually ordered, but the first batch was not delivered until September 1918.

At the time of the Armistice 150 Cuckoos had been built, but only 61 had been taken on charge by the RAF, these equipping Nos. 185, 186, and 210 Squadrons. The latter, in fact, formed from No. 186 Squadron in 1920 and retained its Cuckoos until April 1923.

▲ The Sopwith Cuckoo was scheduled to be built in considerable numbers, but production was severely curtailed at the end of World War I.

SPECIFICATION: Type torpedo-bomber • Crew 1 • Powerplant one 200hp Hispano-Suiza water-cooled V-type • Max speed 103mph (166km/h) • Service ceiling 15,600ft (4,755m) • Endurance 3hrs 15mins • Wingspan 46ft 9in (14.25m) • Length 28ft 6in (8.69m) • Height 11ft (3.35m) • Weight 3,572lb (1,620kg) loaded • Armament one 18-in (45.7-cm) torpedo

▌Sopwith Snipe

Designed as a replacement for the Sopwith Camel, the Snipe was built around the new 230hp Bentley BR.2 rotary engine and was considered to be the best Allied fighter in service at the time of the Armistice. Ordered into production at the beginning of 1918 after a somewhat protracted development program, the Snipe was issued to No. 43 Squadron in France in September, followed by No. 208 Squadron, and No. 4 (Australian) Squadron. By September 30, 161 Snipe Mk Is had been delivered, together with two long-range Mk.IAs. Over 4,500 examples of this very effective fighter were ordered, but there were heavy cancelations and only 497 were

SPECIFICATION: Type scouting biplane • Crew 1 • Powerplant one 230hp Bentley BR.2 rotary engine • Max speed 121mph (195km/h) • Service ceiling 19,500ft (5,945m) • Endurance 3hrs • Wingspan 30ft 1in (9.17m) • Length 19ft 9in (6.02m) • Height 8ft 9in (2.67m) • Weight 2,020lb (916kg) • Armament two fixed forward-firing 0.303-in (7.7-mm) Vickers machine guns; up to four 25-lb (11.3-kg) bombs on external racks

built. The Snipe became the RAF's standard postwar fighter, equipping 21 squadrons; some remained in service until 1926.

▲ The Sopwith Snipe was considered to be the best Allied fighter of WWI, and formed the basis of the RAF's post-war fighter strength.

▌Sopwith Tabloid

The Sopwith Tabloid originated as a small racing seaplane with an astonishing performance for its time. It won the Schneider Trophy in 1914. Four were sent to France shortly after the outbreak of war, and 36 were subsequently built for the RNAS and RFC. In October 1914 RNAS Tabloids operat-

▶ A Sopwith Tabloid flown by Howard Pixton, who swept the board at the 1914 Schneider Trophy contest with an average speed of 87mph (140km/h).

SPECIFICATION: Type general-purpose seaplane • Crew 1 • Powerplant one 100hp Gnome Monosoupape 9-cylinder rotary • Max speed 92mph (148km/h) • Service ceiling 15,000ft (4,600m) • Max range 315 miles (510km) • Wingspan 25ft 6in (7.77m) • Length 23ft (7.02m) • Height 10ft (3.05m) • Weight 1,580lb (717kg) loaded • Armament one 0.303-in (7.7-mm) Lewis machine gun (RNAS aircraft only)

ing from Antwerp attacked Zeppelin sheds at Düsseldorf and Cologne, destroying the former with small bombs and damaging Cologne's central railroad station.

▌ Sopwith Triplane

The Sopwith Triplane was a successful attempt by Sopwith's talented designer, Herbert Smith, to produce yet more

▲ When the Triplane made its first flight in June 1916, the Pup from which it was derived was yet to enter service.

maneuverability from the basic design that had produced the Pup. The Triplane had superlative agility and rate of climb, so much so that it had still not been outclassed when the Sopwith Camel began to replace it in the summer of 1917. So impressed were the enemy that no fewer than 14 German and Austrian manufacturers, including Anthony Fokker, produced triplane designs of their own, but never quite succeeded in matching the Sopwith aircraft.

SPECIFICATION: Type scouting triplane • Crew 1 • Powerplant one 130hp Clerget 9B 9-cylinder rotary engine • Max speed 117mph (188km/h) • Service ceiling 20,500ft (6,250m) • Endurance 2hrs 45mins • Wingspan 26ft 6in (8.08m) • Length 18ft 10in (5.74m) • Height 10ft 6in (3.20m) • Weight 1,541lb (699kg) • Armament one or two fixed forward-firing 0.303-in (7.7-mm) Vickers machine guns

▌ Sopwith 1½ Strutter

SPECIFICATION: Type multipurpose biplane (data bomber variant) • Crew 2 • Powerplant one 130hp Clerget rotary engine • Max speed 102mph (164km/h) • Service ceiling 13,000ft (3,960m) • Max range 350 miles (565km) • Wingspan 33ft 6in (10.21m) • Length 25ft 3in (7.70m) • Height 10ft 3in (3.12m) • Weight 2,149lb (975kg) • Armament one fixed forward-firing 0.303-in (7.7-mm) Vickers machine gun; up to four 56lb (25kg) of bombs

The spring and summer battles of 1917 saw Royal Naval Air Service fighters employed in growing numbers on the Western Front. The first really effective combat aircraft to serve with the RNAS was the Sopwith 1½-Strutter, so called because of its unusual wing bracing. Originally designed as a high-performance two-seat fighter, with a 110hp Clerget 9Z engine, this aircraft went into production for the RNAS at the beginning of 1916 and was the first British aircraft to feature

an efficient synchronized forward-firing armament. Early aircraft were armed with a forward-firing Vickers machine gun and a Lewis gun in the rear cockpit, later aircraft having a Scarff ring for the observer's gun in place of the original Nieuport mounting. The 1½-Strutter was first deployed to France with No. 5 Wing RNAS in April 1916, being used initially for bomber escort, but it later switched to the bombing role, as did aircraft issued to Nos. 43, 45, and 70 Squadrons RFC. About 1,500 1½-Strutters were built in Britain, and it is worth noting that some 4,500 were completed by French manufacturers, some being supplied to Belgium and Russia. Many, after being replaced by Sopwith Camels on the Western Front, served in the United Kingdom's home defense squadrons, while others went to sea aboard the Royal Navy's early aircraft carriers and other major warships, flying from specially constructed platforms in the latter case.

▲ The Sopwith 1½ Strutter was the first really effective combat aircraft to serve with the Royal Naval Air Service.

▌SPAD A2

The Société Pour l'Aviation et ses Derivées (SPAD) A2 was the first fighter designed by Louis Béchereau, who had also designed Deperdussin's single-seat racing monoplanes of

SPECIFICATION: **Type** scout • **Crew** 2 • **Powerplant** one 80hp Le Rhone rotary • **Max speed** 80mph (130km/h) • **Service ceiling** 10,827ft (3,300m) • **Max range** 155 miles (250km) • **Wingspan** 31ft 4in (9.55m) • **Length** 23ft 11in (7.29m) • **Height** 8ft 6in (2.60m) • **Weight** 1,561lb (708kg) loaded • **Armament** one 0.303-in (7.7-mm) Hotchkiss machine gun

1912. The A2, the first SPAD fighter was not a particular success, but it was unusual in that it had a nacelle forward of the engine in which a machine gun was mounted, a wire mesh protecting the gunner's back from the propeller, which was mounted in a large cut-out section forward of the pilot's cockpit. The gunner's nacelle allowed him access to the engine, being attached to the upper wing framework by steel tubes. One hundred were built in 1915, seeing service with the Aviation Militaire and the Imperial Russian Air Service.

▌SPAD VII

In the fall of 1916 many Escadrilles began to equip with a new fighter type, the SPAD VII. Although less maneuverable than the Nieuport types, the SPAD VII was a strong, stable gun platform with a top speed of 119mph (191km/h) and an excellent rate of climb. The SPAD VII was also used by the

RFC and RNAS, and filled a crucial gap at a time when many units were still equipped with aging and vulnerable aircraft. Others were supplied to Italy and to the United States. Ultimately, 5,600 SPAD VIIs were built in France by eight manufacturers.

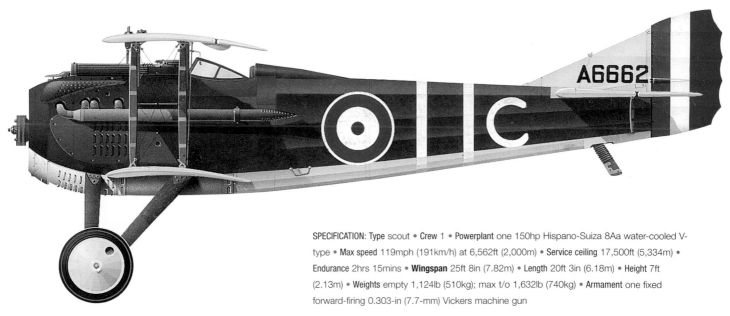

SPECIFICATION: **Type** scout • **Crew** 1 • **Powerplant** one 150hp Hispano-Suiza 8Aa water-cooled V-type • **Max speed** 119mph (191km/h) at 6,562ft (2,000m) • **Service ceiling** 17,500ft (5,334m) • **Endurance** 2hrs 15mins • **Wingspan** 25ft 8in (7.82m) • **Length** 20ft 3in (6.18m) • **Height** 7ft (2.13m) • **Weights** empty 1,124lb (510kg); max t/o 1,632lb (740kg) • **Armament** one fixed forward-firing 0.303-in (7.7-mm) Vickers machine gun

▌SPAD XIII

In May 1917, the French Escadrilles de Chasse began to standardize on a new type, the SPAD XIII. Like its predecessor, it was an excellent gun platform and was extremely strong, although it was tricky to fly at low speeds. Powered by a Hispano-Suiza 8Ba engine and armed with two forward-firing Vickers guns, it had a maximum speed of nearly 140mph

SPECIFICATION: **Type** scout • **Crew** 1 • **Powerplant** one 220hp Hispano-Suiza 8BEc 8-cylinder V-type • **Max speed** 139mph (224km/h) • **Service ceiling** 21,815ft (6,650m) • **Endurance** 2hrs • **Wingspan** 26ft 7in (8.10m) • **Length** 20ft 8in (6.30m) • **Height** 7ft 8in (2.35m) • **Weight** 1,863lb (845kg) loaded • **Armament** two fixed forward-firing 0.303-in (7.7-mm) Vickers machine guns

(225km/h)—quite exceptional for that time—and could climb to 22,000ft (6,710m). The SPAD XIII subsequently equipped more than 80 Escadrilles, and 8,472 were built. The type also equipped 16 squadrons of the American Expeditionary Force, which purchased 893 examples, and was supplied to Italy, which still had 100 in service in 1923. After World War I, surplus French SPAD XIIIs were sold to Belgium (37), Czechoslovakia, Japan, and Poland (40).

▲ A Spad XIII bearing the insignia of the Escadrille des Cigognes, the famous Stork Squadron, which achieved fame in both world wars.

▌Stinson L-5 Sentinel

USA

The Stinson L-5 Sentinel, which shared the US army liaison task with the L-4 Grasshopper in World War II, was a militarized version of the civil Voyager, having a slightly enlarged fuselage for use as an air ambulance and casevac aircraft. In service from 1942, over 3,000 were built, and the type continued in active service up to the end of the Korean War.

▲ The Stinson L-5 Sentinel served the US forces throughout World War II and was also used for liaison and artillery spotting in Korea.

SPECIFICATION: Type liaison aircraft • Crew 2 • Powerplant one 185hp Lycoming O-435-1 4-cylinder air-cooled • Max speed 130mph (209km/h) at sea level • Service ceiling 20,000ft (6,100m) • Max range 500 miles (805km) • Wingspan 34ft (10.36m) • Length 24ft 1in (7.34m) • Height 7ft 11in (2.41m) • Weight 2,000lb (916kg) loaded • Armament none

▌Sud-Ouest SO4050 Vautour

FRANCE

Designed from the outset to carry out three tasks—all-weather interception, close support, and high-altitude bombing—the Vautour (Vulture) flew for the first time on October 16, 1952. Two production versions were ordered, the Vautour IIB light bomber and the IIN all-weather interceptor. The first of 70 Vautour IINs entered service in 1956 with the 6e Escadre de Chasse, followed by EC 30 in the following year, while the first of 40 Vautour IIBs entered service in December 1957 with 1/92 "Bourgogne" and 2/92 "Aquitaine" at Bordeaux.

The final version of the Vautour was the IIBR, a bomber-reconnaissance variant. The close-support version of the Vautour, the IIA, was not used by the French Air Force, but

SPECIFICATION: Type assault aircraft • Crew 2 • Powerplant one 1,000hp Tumanskii M-88B 14-cylinder radial • Max speed 286mph (460km/h) at 13,125ft (4,000m) • Service ceiling 28,870ft (8,800m) • Max range 746 miles (1,200km) • Wingspan 46ft 11in (14.30m) • Length 34ft 3in (10.46m) • Height 12ft 3in (3.75m) • Weight 9,645lb (4,375kg) loaded • Armament up to eight 0.30-in (7.62-mm) wing-mounted machine guns, plus one in the rear cockpit; max bomb load 1,984lb (900kg)

20 examples were supplied to Israel, together with four IINs, and saw action in the six-day war of 1967.

▌Sukhoi Su-7/17/22 "Fitter"

USSR

First seen in public in 1956, the Su-7, designed for close air support with the Frontal Aviation, remained the Soviet Air Force's standard tactical fighter-bomber throughout the 1960s. Later, the Sukhoi bureau redesigned the Su-7, giving it a more powerful engine, variable-geometry wings, and increased fuel tankage. In this guise it became the Su-17/20 Fitter C, which was unique among combat aircraft in being a variable-geometry derivative of a fixed-wing machine.

The development of the Fitter-C was an excellent example of a remarkable Russian talent for developing existing designs to their fullest extent. It was a facet of the Russians' practice of constant development, enabling them to keep one basic design of combat aircraft in service for 30 or 40 years and foster long-term standardization. Also, the use of the

same production facilities over a long period of time helped greatly to reduce costs, which is why the USSR was able to offer combat types on the international market at far more competitive rates than the West.

The Su-22 was an updated version with terrain-avoidance radar and other improved avionics. The Su-7U, code-named Moujik, was a two-seat trainer version.

SPECIFICATION: Type tactical fighter-bomber (data Su-20 Fitter-C) • Crew 1 • Powerplant one 24,802-lb (11,250-kg) thrust Lyulka AL-21F-3 turbojet • Max speed 1,380mph (2,220km/h) at altitude • Service ceiling 49,865ft (15,200m) • Combat radius 419 miles (675km) hi-lo-hi with 50 percent load • Wingspan 45ft 3in (13.80m) spread; 32ft 10in (10m) swept • Length 61ft 6in (18.75m) • Height 16ft 5in (5m) • Weight 42,990lb (19,500kg) loaded • Armament two 1.19-in (30-mm) NR-30 cannon; nine external pylons with provision for up to 9,370lb (4,250kg) of stores

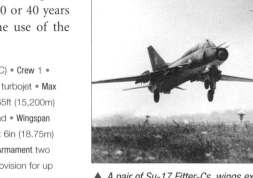

▲ *A pair of Su-17 Fitter-Cs, wings extended, taking off from a Soviet air base. The Fitter-C was a variable-geometry version of the Su-7.*

▌Sukhoi Su-9/Su-11 "Fishpot"

Contemporary with the Su-7, the Su-9 Fishpot-A was a single-seat interceptor; to some extent, an Su-7 with a delta wing. It was armed with the first Soviet AAM, the semiactive radar homing Alkali, four of which were carried under the wings. In 1961 a new model, the Su-11 Fishpot-B, was developed from the Su-9, and was followed into service by the Fishpot-C, which had an uprated engine. A tandem two-seat trainer variant of the Su-9 was given the NATO reporting name Maiden.

SPECIFICATION: Type all-weather interceptor (data Su-9) • Crew 1 • Powerplant one 22,045-lb (10,000-kg) thrust Lyulka AL-7F TRD31 turbojet • Max speed 1,190mph (1,915km/h) at altitude • Service ceiling 55,000ft (16,765m) • Max range 900 miles (1,450km) • Wingspan 27ft (8.23m) • Length 58ft (17.68m) • Height 16ft (4.88m) • Weight 30,000lb (13,610kg) loaded • Armament four Alkali radar-homing or two Anab infrared homing AAMs

▲ The Sukhoi Su-11 utilized the Su-9's airframe, but coupled this with an uprated engine and an Uragan-5B radar complex.

▌Sukhoi Su-15 "Flagon"

The follow-on from the Su-11 aircraft was the Su-15 Flagon, a twin-engined delta-wing interceptor that first flew in 1965 and was in Soviet Air Force service by 1969. Capable of carrying two AAMs, the Flagon was Russia's most important all-weather interceptor by the mid-1970s. The prototype from which the Su-15 was developed was basically an enlarged version of the Su-11, but the T-58 that followed had a "solid" nose housing AI radar equipment and intakes on the fuselage sides. A number of Flagon variants were produced, culminating in the definitive Su-15TM Flagon-F of 1971.

▶ The Sukhoi Su-15 "Flagon" achieved notoriety as the fighter that shot down a Korean Airlines Boeing 747 over the Sea of Japan.

SPECIFICATION: Type all-weather interceptor • Crew 1 • Powerplant two 13,680-lb (6,205-kg) thrust Tumanskii R-11F2S turbojets • Max speed 1,386mph (2,230km/h) at high altitude • Service ceiling 65,615ft (20,000m) • Combat radius 450 miles (725km) • Wingspan 28ft 3in (8.61m) • Length 70ft (21.33m) • Height 16ft 8in (5.10m) • Weight 39,680lb (18,000kg) loaded • Armament four external pylons for two R8M medium-range AAMs outboard and two AA-8 Aphid short-range AAMs inboard; two 0.90-in (23-mm) cannon pods under fuselage

■ Sukhoi Su-24 "Fencer"

USSR

In 1965, the Soviet government instructed the Sukhoi design bureau to begin design studies of a new variable-geometry strike aircraft in the same class as the General Dynamics F-111. The resulting aircraft, the Su-24, made its first flight in 1970 and deliveries of the first production version, the Fencer-A, began in 1974. Several variants of the Fencer were produced, culminating in the Su-24M Fencer-D, which entered service in 1986. This variant has inflight refueling equipment, upgraded navigational/attack systems, and laser/TV designators. The Su-24MR is a tactical reconnaissance version.

SPECIFICATION: Type strike/attack aircraft • Crew 2 • Powerplant two 24,802lb (11,250kg) thrust Lyulka AL-21F3A turbojets • Max speed 1,439mph (2,316km/h) at high altitude • Service ceiling 57,415ft (17,500m) • Combat radius 650 miles (1,050km) hi-lo-hi with 6,614-lb (3,000-kg) load • Wingspan 57ft 10in (17.63m) spread; 34ft (10.36m) swept • Length 80ft 5in (24.53m) • Height 16ft (4.97m) • Weight 87,520lb (39,700kg) loaded • Armament one 1.19-in (23-mm) GSh-23-6 six-barreled cannon; nine external pylons with provision for up to 17,635lb (8,000kg) of stores

▲ The Sukhoi Su-24 "Fencer" was roughly the equivalent of the General Dynamics F-111, and was intended to perform much the same tasks.

■ Sukhoi Su-25 "Frogfoot"

USSR

A Russian requirement for an attack aircraft in the A-10 class materialized in the Sukhoi Su-25 Frogfoot, which was selected in preference to a rival design, the Ilyushin Il-102. Deployment of the single-seat close-support Su-25K began in 1978, and the aircraft saw considerable operational service during the Soviet Union's involvement in Afghanistan. As a result of lessons learned during that conflict an upgraded version known as the Su-25T was produced, with an external cannon and improved defensive systems to counter weapons like the infamous shoulder-launched Stinger surface-to-air missile.

The Su-25UBK is a two-seat export variant, while the Su-25UBT is a navalized version with a strengthened undercarriage and arrestor gear.

SPECIFICATION: Type close support aircraft (data Su-25 Frogfoot-A) • Crew 1 • Powerplant two 9,921-lb (4,500-kg) Tumanskii R-195 turbojets • Max speed 606mph (975km/h) at sea level • Service ceiling 22,965ft (7,000m) • Combat radius 466 miles (750km) lo-lo-lo with 9,700-lb (4,400-kg) war load • Wingspan 47ft 1in (14.36m) • Length 50ft 11in (15.53m) • Height 15ft 9in (4.80m) • Weight 38,800lb (17,600kg) loaded • Armament one 1.19-in (30-mm) GSh-30-2 cannon; eight external pylons with provision for up to 9,700lb (4,400kg) of stores

▲ This Akhtunbinsk-based Su-25 is pictured over the Volga during weapons trials.

▌Sukhoi Su-27/Su-35 "Flanker"

▲ *The Su-27 "Flanker" was designed as an air superiority aircraft, its aerodynamic configuration producing an extraordinary degree of maneuverability.*

The Sukhoi Su-27, like the F-15, is a dual-role aircraft; in addition to its primary air superiority task it was designed to escort Su-24 Fencer strike aircraft on deep penetration missions. Full-scale production of the Su-27P Flanker-B air defense fighter began in 1980, but the aircraft did not become fully operational until 1984.

Like its contemporary, the MiG-29 Fulcrum, the Su-27 combines a wing swept at 40 degrees with highly-swept wing root extensions, underslung engines with wedge intakes, and twin fins. The combination of modest wing sweep with highly swept root extensions is designed to enhance maneuverability and generate lift, making it possible to achieve extreme angles of attack. The Su-27UB Flanker-C is a two-seat training version. The Sukhoi Su-35 derived from the Flanker-B and originally designated Su-27M, is a second-generation version with improved agility and enhanced operational capability.

SPECIFICATION: **Type** air superiority fighter (data Su-35) • **Crew** 1 • **Powerplant** two 27,557-lb (12,500-kg) thrust Lyulka AL-31M turbofans • **Max speed** 1,500mph (2,500km) at high altitude • **Service ceiling** 59,055ft (18,000m) • **Combat radius** 930 miles (1,500km) • **Wingspan** 48ft 2in (14.70m) • **Length** 71ft 11in (21.94m) • **Height** 20ft 10in (6.36m) • **Weight** 66,138lb (30,000kg) loaded • **Armament** one 1.19-in (30-mm) GSh-3101 cannon; 10 external hardpoints with provision for various combinations of AAMs

▌Supermarine Attacker

The Attacker, the Royal Navy's first jet fighter, was based on the Vickers-Supermarine E.10/44, which had originally been proposed as a land-based fighter for the RAF. The RAF, however, had decided to adopt the Meteor and Vampire, both of which had a better performance, and so Supermarine offered a navalized version to the Admiralty, who wrote Specification E.1/45 around it.

The prototype first flew in its navalized form on June 17, 1947, and, as the Vickers-Supermarine Attacker F.Mk.1, the aircraft went into production for the Royal Navy, entering service in 1951.

Sixty Attackers were ordered and served with two Fleet Air Arm squadrons; a further 36 aircraft were supplied to the Pakistan Air Force in 1952–53.

SPECIFICATION: **Type** naval jet fighter • **Crew** 1 • **Powerplant** one 5,100-lb (2,313-kg) thrust Rolls-Royce Nene 3 turbojet • **Max speed** 590mph (949km/h) at sea level • **Service ceiling** 45,000ft (13,715m) • **Max range** 1,190 miles (1,915km) • **Wingspan** 36ft 11in (11.25m) • **Length** 37ft 6in (11.43m) • **Height** 9ft 11in (3.02m) • **Weight** 11,500lb (5,216kg) loaded • **Armament** four 0.79-in (20-mm) Hispano cannon

◄ *The Supermarine Attacker, seen here about to touch down on an aircraft carrier, was the Royal Navy's first jet fighter.*

▌Supermarine Scimitar

GREAT BRITAIN

The Supermarine Scimitar was the end product of a lengthy evolutionary process dating back to 1945 and the Supermarine 505, a carrier-based fighter project which was revised several times, its design becoming successively the Types 508, 525, and 529. The design finally crystallized in the Type 544, the first of three prototypes flying on January 20, 1956. The type was ordered into production for the Fleet Air Arm as the Scimitar F.1 and the first production aircraft flew on January 11, 1957, powered by two Rolls-Royce Avon 202 turbojets. The Scimitar became operational with No. 803 Squadron in June 1958 and three other squadrons later received the type, an original order for 100 aircraft having

been cut back to 76 in the meantime. In 1962 the Scimitar was modified to carry the Bullpup ASM, and its striking power was further extended by provision for four Sidewinder AAMs in addition to its four 1.19-in (30-mm) cannon. The Scimitar was replaced in FAA service by the Blackburn Buccaneer and was withdrawn from first-line units by the end of 1966.

SPECIFICATION: **Type** naval strike fighter • **Crew** 1 • **Powerplant** two 11,250-lb (5,105-kg) thrust Rolls-Royce Avon 202 turbojets • **Max speed** 710mph (1,143km/h) at sea level • **Service ceiling** 50,000ft (15,240m) • **Max range** 600 miles (966km) • **Wingspan** 37ft 2in (11.33m) • **Length** 55ft 4in (16.87m) • **Height** 15ft 3in (4.65m) • **Weight** 34,200lb (15,513kg) loaded • **Armament** four 1.19-in (30-mm) Aden cannon; four 1,000-lb (454-kg) bombs, or four Bullpup ASMs, or four Sidewinder AAMs

▲ *A Supermarine Scimitar (Type 544) seen taking off from the aircraft carrier HMS Ark Royal during proving trials in 1956.*

▌Supermarine Seafire

GREAT BRITAIN

Between the two world wars, the Royal Navy's carrier-borne aircraft evolved at a much slower pace than did their land-based counterparts. With the outbreak of World War II the Royal Navy found a partial solution to the problem of its outdated fighters by adapting land-based aircraft like the Hawker Hurricane for carrier operations, and in late 1941 it was decided to adapt the Spitfire in similar fashion under the name of Seafire. The main variants were the Seafire Mk IB (166 conversions from Spitfire VB airframes); Mk IIC (372 intended for low- and medium-altitude air combat and air reconnaissance); 30 Mk III (Hybrid) aircraft with fixed wings, followed by 1,220 examples of the definitive Seafire

Mk III with folding wings; and the Seafire Mks XV, XVII, 45, 46, and 47, these being Griffon-engined variants. The Seafire saw much action in the Mediterranean in the summer of

SPECIFICATION: **Type** naval fighter (data Seafire Mk III) • **Crew** 1 • **Powerplant** one 1,600hp Rolls-Royce Merlin 55m 12-cylinder V-type • **Max speed** 348mph (560km/h) • **Service ceiling** 24,000ft (7,315m) • **Max range** 553 miles (890km) • **Wingspan** 36ft 10in (11.23m) • **Length** 30ft 2in (9.21m) • **Height** 11ft 2in (3.42m) • **Weight** 7,640lb (3,465kg) • **Armament** two 0.79-in (20-mm) Hispano cannon and four 0.303-in (7.7-mm) Browning machine guns; external bomb or rocket load of 500lb (227kg)

1943 and in the Pacific in 1945. The Seafire 47, operating from HMS *Triumph*, took part in air strikes against terrorists in Malaya and against North Korean forces in the early weeks of the Korean War. Although far from suitable for carrier operations because of its narrow-track undercarriage and long nose, the Seafire performed well and was used by RN Reserve Air Squadrons until 1954.

■ Supermarine Southampton

GREAT BRITAIN

First flown in March 1925, the elegant Supermarine Southampton flying boat was designed by Reginald Mitchell and was selected for service with the RAF's coastal reconnaissance flights. The Mk I had a wooden hull, but the Mk II's hull was of duralumin, which represented a considerable weight saving. A variant (the Southampton IV) with Rolls-Royce Kestrel engines was renamed the Scapa, while the Southampton V was named the Stranraer.

SPECIFICATION: **Type** coastal reconnaissance flying boat • **Crew** 5 • **Powerplant** two 500hp Napier Lion VA W-12 in-line engines • **Max speed** 108mph (174km/h) • **Service ceiling** 14,000ft (4,265m) • **Max range** 930 miles (1,497km) • **Wingspan** 75ft (22.86m) • **Length** 51ft 1in (15.58m) • **Height** 22ft 4in (6.82m) • **Weight** 15,200lb (6,895kg) loaded • **Armament** one 0.303-in (7.7-mm) Lewis machine gun in nose and two midships positions; up to 1,100lb (499kg) of bombs

▲ *Six Southamptons were ordered straight off the drawing board in August 1924, with a seventh – N218, seen here – ordered for experimental purposes.*

■ Supermarine Spitfire

GREAT BRITAIN

The legendary Supermarine Spitfire was designed by a team under the direction of Reginald Mitchell, and traced its ancestry to Supermarine's racing floatplanes developed for the Schneider Trophy contest. The design was so evidently superior to the original Air Ministry Specification to which it had been submitted, F.5/34, that a new one, F.37/34, was drafted to cover the production of a prototype. This aircraft, K5054, made its first flight on March 5, 1936 and, like the Hawker Hurricane, with which it was to share so much fame, was powered by a Rolls-Royce Merlin "C" engine. A contract for the production of 310 Spitfires was issued by the Air Ministry in June 1936, at the same time as the Hurricane contract, and the first examples were delivered to No. 19 Squadron at Duxford in August 1938. Eight other squadrons had equipped with Spitfires by September 1939, and two Auxiliary Air Force units, Nos. 603 and 609, were undergoing operational training. Production of the Spitfire Mk I, which was powered by a 1030 Merlin II or III engine, eventually reached 1,566 aircraft. It was this variant that saw the most combat in the Battle of Britain, the Mk II with the 1,175hp Merlin XII engine being

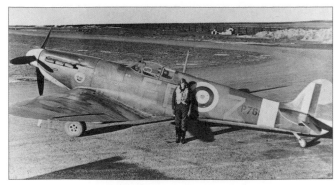

▲ *This Spitfire II, as the legend on its nose shows, was presented to the RAF with funds raised by the Observer Corps.*

SPECIFICATION: Type fighter (data Spitfire Mk.VB) • Crew 1 • Powerplant one 1,440hp Rolls-Royce Merlin 45/46/50 V-12 engine • Max speed 374mph (602km/h) at 13,000ft (3,960m) • Service ceiling 37,000ft (11,280m) • Max range 470 miles (756km) • Wingspan 36ft 10in (11.23m) • Length 29ft 11in (9.11m) • Height 11ft 5in (3.48m) • Weight 6,785lb (3,078kg) loaded • Armament two 0.79-in (20-mm) cannon and four 0.303-in (7.7-mm) machine guns in the wings

issued to the squadrons of Fighter Command in September 1940. Mk II production, including the Mk IIB, which mounted two 0.79-in (20-mm) cannon and four 0.303-in (7.7-mm) machine guns in place of the standard eight 0.303-in (7.7-mm), totaled 920 aircraft. During the battle, from July 1–31 October 1940, 361 of the 747 Spitfires delivered to Fighter Command were destroyed, not all in combat.

The Spitfire Mk III was an experimental "one-shot" aircraft, while the Mk IV (229 built) was a photoreconnaissance version. It was actually produced after the next variant, the Mk V, which began to reach the squadrons in March 1941. Converted from Mk I and II airframes, the Mk V was to be the major Spitfire production version, with 6,479 examples completed. The Spitfire V, however, failed to provide the overall superiority Fighter Command needed so badly. At high altitude, where many combats took place, it was found to be inferior to the Bf 109F, and several squadrons equipped with the Mk V took a severe mauling during that summer.

To counter the activities of high-flying German reconnaissance aircraft the Spitfire Mk VI was produced, with a long, tapered wing and a pressurized cockpit. The Mk VII, also with a pressurized cockpit, was powered by a Rolls-Royce

Merlin 60 engine, a two-stage, two-speed, intercooled powerplant which was to take development of the Merlin to its ultimate. The answer to the problems experienced with the Spitfire V was to marry a Mk V airframe with a Merlin 61 engine. The resulting combination was the Spitfire Mk IX, which for a stopgap aircraft turned out to be a resounding success. Deliveries to the RAF began in June 1942 and 5,665 were built, more than any other mark except the Mk V.

The Spitfire Mk X and XII were unarmed PR variants, while the Mk XII, powered by a 1,735hp Rolls-Royce Griffon engine, was developed specifically to counter the low-level attacks by Focke-Wulf 190s. Only 100 MK XII Spitfires were built, but they were followed by the more numerous Mk XIV. The latter, based on a Mk VIII airframe, was the first Griffon-engined Spitfire variant to go into large-scale production, and the first examples were issued to No. 322 (Netherlands) and No. 610 Squadrons in March and April 1944. The next variant, the Mk XIV, was based on the Mk VIII, with an airframe strengthened to take a 2,050hp Griffon 65 engine. The Spitfire XVI, which entered service in 1944, was a ground attack version similar to the Mk IX, but with a Packard-built Merlin 266 engine. The Spitfire XVIII was a fighter-reconnaissance variant, just beginning to enter service at the end of WWII, as was the PR Mk XIX. The last variants of the Spitfire, produced until 1947, were the Mks 21, 22, and 24. They bore very little resemblance to the prototype Mk I of a decade earlier. Total production of the Spitfire was 20,351 plus 2,334 examples of the naval version, the Seafire.

▪ Supermarine Swift

◀ Previous pages: With the late Mark Hannah at the controls, this Spitfire Mk VIII bears the markings of No. 222 Squadron.

Together with the Hawker Hunter, the Supermarine Swift was intended to replace the Meteor in the air defense role within RAF Fighter Command. Their prototypes flew on July 20, and August 1, 1951 respectively and both types were ordered into "super-priority" production for RAF Fighter Command. The Swift F.Mk.1, however, was found to be unsuitable for its primary role of high-level interception, being prone to tightening in turns and suffering frequent high-altitude flameouts as a result of shock waves entering the air intakes when the cannon were fired. The Swift was adapted to the low-level fighter/reconnaissance role, three cameras being installed in a lengthened nose, and as the Swift FR.5 equipped Nos. 2 and

▶ The Supermarine Swift fighter was ordered into "super-priority" production for the RAF, but was unsuitable for high-level interception.

SPECIFICATION: **Type** tactical reconnaissance aircraft (data Swift FR.Mk.5) • **Crew** 1 • **Powerplant** one 9,450-lb (4,287-kg) thrust Rolls-Royce Avon 114 turbojet • **Max speed** 685mph (1,100km/h) at sea level • **Service ceiling** 45,800ft (13,959m) • **Max range** 630 miles (1,014km) • **Wingspan** 32ft 4in (9.85m) • **Length** 42ft 3in (12.88m) • **Height** 12ft 6in (3.80m) • **Weight** 21,400lb (9,706kg) • **Armament** two 1.19-in (30-mm) Aden cannon

79 Squadrons of the 2nd Allied Tactical Air Force in Germany. Sixty-two Swift FR.Mk.5s were produced, 35 being converted from Swift F.Mk.4 airframes.

▪ Supermarine Walrus

The Supermarine Walrus began life as the Supermarine Seagull, a three-seat amphibian designed as a fleet spotter.

▲ After the end of World War II many Walrus aircraft were sold to civilian companies. The example seen here bears a Netherlands registration.

The prototype Mk V version of the Seagull was fitted with a Bristol Pegasus engine in a pusher configuration, and was ordered for service with the Fleet Air Arm as the Walrus Mk.I. Production began in 1936 and 746 aircraft were eventually produced. The Walrus was stressed for catapult launching and saw service in almost every theater of war on capital ships and cruisers. It was also used by the RAF as an air-sea rescue aircraft.

SPECIFICATION: **Type** fleet reconnaissance amphibian • **Crew** 4 • **Powerplant** one 750hp Bristol Pegasus VI radial engine • **Max speed** 135mph (217km/h) • **Service ceiling** 17,100ft (5,210m) • **Max range** 600 miles (966km) • **Wingspan** 45ft 10in (13.97m) • **Length** 37ft 3in (11.35m) • **Height** 15ft 3in (4.65m) • **Weight** 7,200lb (3,266kg) • **Armament** one 0.303-in (7.7-mm) Vickers K machine gun in nose position, and one or two Vickers K machine guns in beam positions; up to 600lb (272kg) of bombs or two Mk VIII depth charges on underwing racks

▌Tachikawa Ki.54 "Hickory"

SPECIFICATION: Type bombing trainer and light transport • Crew 5–9 •
Powerplant two 450hp Hitachi Ha-13a radials • Max speed 234mph (376km/h)
at 6560ft (2000m) • Service ceiling 22,555ft (7180m) • Max range 597 miles
(960km) • Wing span 58ft 9in (17.90m)• Length 39ft 2in (11.94m) • Height 11ft
9in (3.58m) • Weight 8591lb (3897kg) loaded • Armament four flexible 0.303in
(7.7mm) machine guns; practice bombs; depth charges.

One of the more versatile aircraft types produced by Japan during the war years, the Tachikawa Ki.54 made its appearance in 1940 and served as a crew trainer, light transport, and antisubmarine patrol aircraft, 1,368 examples being built. The initial production version, the Ki.54a, was purely a pilot trainer, but the Ki.54b had facilities for full multiengine crew training, including four gunnery stations. The Ki.54c was the transport variant, which was also produced as a civil variant designated Y-59. The ASW aircraft carried eight depth charges and was designated Ki.54.

▲ *The Tachikawa Ki.54 was used both as a bomber trainer and a transport. A few examples of an anti-submarine patrol version were also produced.*

▌Tchetverikov ARK-3

A contemporary of the Beriev Be-2, the ARK-3 was a small reconnaissance flying boat intended for service in Arctic waters. The aircraft proved ideally suited for the tasks assigned to it, and its principal mission during World War II was to provide convoy protection in the far north. The ARK-3 first appeared in 1935; both prototypes broke up in midair as a result of a design fault. Most of the design and construction work took place at Sevastopol in the Crimea.

SPECIFICATION: Type reconnaissance flying boat • Crew 5 • Powerplant two
tandem-mounted 730hp M-24V 9-cylinder radials • Max speed 199mph
(320km/h) at 4,920ft (1,500m) • Service ceiling 27,890ft (8,500m) • Max range
932 miles (1,500km) • Wingspan 65ft 3in (19.90m) • Length 47ft 7in (14.50m)
• Height not known • Weight 11,558lb (5,243kg) loaded • Armament two
0.30-in (7.62-mm) machine guns

▌Tchetverikov MDR-6 "Mule"

Igor V. Tchetverikov followed his successful ARK-3 with another excellent design, the MDR-6, which entered service with the Soviet Navy in 1939. Larger and more powerful than its predecessor, the original MDR-6 was succeeded by the MDR-6A of 1941 and the MDR-6B of 1944 each with improved engines and payload capacity. The MDR-6 remained in operational use until 1955. Throughout the aircraft's development career Tchetverikov strove to improve its overall performance by refining the design, but it grew progressively heavier and performance suffered accordingly.

SPECIFICATION: Type maritime reconnaissance flying boat • Crew 5 • Powerplant
two 1,100hp M-63 9-cylinder radials • Max speed 224mph (360km/h) at
16,400ft (5,000m) • Service ceiling 29,500ft (9,000m) • Max range 746 miles
(1,200km) • Wingspan 64ft 11in (19.78m) • Length 48ft 3in (14.70m) • Height
not known • Weight 14,969lb (6,790kg) loaded • Armament two 0.30-in
(7.62-mm) machine guns; 1,320lb (600kg) of bombs

▊Thomas Morse MB-3

Founded in 1912 in Bath, New York State to license-build foreign aircraft types for the US Army Air Service, the Thomas Morse Company's first indigenous fighter design was the S-4, but this was modified into a single-seat advanced trainer. In 1919 the company produced a second fighter, the MB-3; 250 of these biplanes were built, mostly by the Boeing Company. The MB-3A remained in first-line service until the late 1920s.

▲ Experience in building the MB-3, seen here, gave Boeing the knowledge to design its own fighter type, the PW-9, starting the company along a path of fighter production lasting until the 1930s.

SPECIFICATION: Type fighter biplane • Crew 1 • Powerplant one 300hp Wright (Hispano-Suiza) V-type • Max speed 140mph (225km/h) • Service ceiling 19,510ft (5,947m) • Max range 300 miles (482km) • Wingspan 26ft (7.93m) • Length 20ft (6.10m) • Height 8ft 7in (2.62m) • Weight 2,535lb (1,150kg) loaded • Armament two 0.30-in (7.62-mm) machine guns; later two 0.50-in (12.7-mm)

▊Transall C-160

▲ Developed as a joint venture between France and Federal Germany, the Transall C-160 proved to be a very effective tactical transport.

SPECIFICATION: Type tactical transport (data Transall C-160T) • Crew 4 • Powerplant two 6,100hp Rolls-Royce Tyne RTy.20 Mk.22 turboprops • Max speed 333mph (536km/h) • Service ceiling 27,900ft (8,500m) • Max range 2,832 miles (4,558km) • Wingspan 131ft 3in (40m) • Length 106ft 3in (32.40m) • Height 38ft 5in (11.65m) • Weight 35,270lb (16,000kg) loaded • Armament none

The Transall 160 tactical transport was designed and produced as a joint venture between France and Federal Germany, Transall being an abbreviation of the specially formed consortium, Transporter Allianz, comprising the companies of MBB, Aérospatiale, and VFW-Fokker. The prototype flew for the first time on February 25, 1963, and series production began four years later. The principal variants were the C-160A, consisting of six preseries aircraft; the C-160D for the Luftwaffe (90 built); the C-160F for France (60 built); the C-160T (20 built for export to Turkey); and the C-160Z (nine built for South Africa). An upgraded Transall C-160 Series II was produced in limited numbers.

▌ Tupolev ANT-5   USSR

The ANT-5 was an all-metal sesquiplane fighter conceived by Tupolev, Pavel O. Sukhoi, and Vladimir Petlyakov. By this time, Tupolev had established a firm reputation as a pioneer in all-metal construction, and the ANT-5, known as the I-4 in Air Fleet service, was the first Russian fighter built in this way. A single-seater with a fixed undercarriage, the I-4 was built of Kolchugalumin, a type of duralumin produced by the Kolchuga factories. The I-4 was superior to all other contemporary Russian fighter designs, and quantity production continued for several years after 1928, the total number built being around 370. Several different versions of the I-4 were produced, including a twin-cannon variant, a seaplane variant, and a version fitted with six solid fuel rockets for short takeoff.

SPECIFICATION: Type fighter • Crew 1 • Powerplant one 460hp M-22 (Bristol Jupiter) radial • Max speed 160mph (257km/h) • Service ceiling 25,100ft (7,655m) • Max range 466 miles (750km) • Wingspan 37ft 5in (11.42m) • Length 23ft 10in (7.27m) • Height 9ft 2in (2.82m) • Weight 3,000lb (1,359kg) loaded • Armament two 0.30-in (7.62-mm) fixed forward-firing machine guns

▌ Tupolev SB-2   USSR

The Tupolev SB-2 was almost certainly the most capable light bomber in service anywhere in the world in the mid-1930s. It was the first aircraft of modern stressed-skin construction to be produced in the USSR, and in numerical terms was also the most important bomber of its day. The SB-2 entered service in 1935, and 6,967 aircraft were built before production ended in 1941. The type saw action in the Spanish Civil War and in the "Winter War" against Finland in 1939–40. Among the principal variants were the SB-2bis of 1938, with uprated engines and greater fuel capacity, and the SB-2RK dive-bomber version of 1940. By the time of the German invasion of Russia in 1941 the SB-2 was obsolescent, and heavy losses sustained in daylight attacks led to the type being assigned to the night bombing role. Later, many SB-2s were used as target tugs, crew trainers, and transports. The bomber was license-built in Czechoslovakia as the B-71, being produced.

SPECIFICATION: Type light bomber (data SB-2bis) • Crew 3 • Powerplant two 960hp Klimov M-103 12-cylinder V-type • Max speed 280mph (450km/h) at 3,280ft (1,000m) • Service ceiling 29,530ft (9,000m) • Max range 1,429 miles (2,300km) • Wingspan 66ft 8in (20.33m) • Length 41ft 2in (12.57m) • Height 10ft 8in (3.25m) • Weight 17,372lb (7,880kg) loaded • Armament two 0.30-in (7.62-mm) machine guns in nose position, one in dorsal turret, and one in ventral position; bomb load of 1,323lb (600kg)

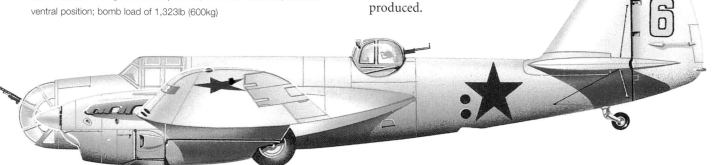

▌Tupolev TB-3

One of the more veteran bombers in service with the Soviet Air Force at the time of the German invasion was the TB-3 (ANT-6), a massive four-engined type which had entered service in 1931. The aircraft had a troubled development, and did not appear in its definitive form until 1935. Production ended in 1937 after 800 had been built. In 1941, the TB-3 was rele-

gated to the freight and paratroop transport roles, its designation being changed to G-2. The type was withdrawn in 1944.

▶ *The TB-3 also took part in parasite fighter experiments, a fighter being attached to the underside of the fuselage by a trapeze.*

SPECIFICATION: Type heavy bomber • Crew 8 • Powerplant four 715hp M-17F (BMW) 12-cylinder V-type • Max speed 179mph (288km/h) at sea level • Service ceiling 12,470ft (3,800m) • Max range 2,004 miles (3,225km) • Wingspan 132ft 10in (40.48m) • Length 83ft (25.54m) • Height 27ft 9in (8.47m) • Weight 38,360lb (17,400kg) loaded • Armament six 0.30-in (7.62-mm) machine guns; 4,800lb (2,200kg) of bombs

▌Tupolev Tu-2 "Bat"

SPECIFICATION: Type light bomber (data Tu-2S) • Crew 4 • Powerplant two 1,850hp Shvetsov Ash-82FN radial engines • Max speed 340mph (547km/h) at 17,715ft (5,400m) • Service ceiling 31,170ft (9,500m) • Max range 1,243 miles (2,000km) • Wingspan 61ft 10in (18.86m) • Length 45ft 3in (13.80m) • Height 14ft 11in (4.56m) • Weight 28,219lb (12,800kg) loaded • Armament two 0.79-in (20-mm) ShVAK cannon in wing roots and three 0.50-in (12.7-mm) UBT machine guns (two in dorsal and one in ventral positions), plus a maximum bomb load of 6,614lb (3,000kg)

▲ *As late as 1945, the Tu-2 still had plenty of design potential, and was the principal light bomber in service with post-war Soviet Bloc air forces.*

An all-metal, midwing monoplane with a crew of three and powered by two 1,400hp Mikulin AM-37 V-12 in-line engines, the prototype Tu-2 (ANT-58) flew for the first time on January 29, 1941 and subsequent flight testing showed that the aircraft had an outstanding performance. Because of shortages, it was decided to replace the AM-37s with a pair of

▲ *A Tupolev Tu-2 preserved at the Russian Air Force Museum, Morino. The tail of a Lend-Lease Martin B-26 can be seen on the extreme right.*

1,330hp Shvetsov Ash-82 radial engines, and production at last got under way at the beginning of 1942, the bomber now being designated Tu-2. Because of the technical problems, however, series production of the Tu-2 did not start until 1943, and combat units did not begin to rearm with the bomber until the spring of 1944. Although total wartime production was only 1,111 aircraft, the Tu-2 proved to be of immense value to the Soviet tactical bomber forces, and also saw service in a number of other roles. One of these was as a carrier for the GAZ-67B cross-country vehicle, which was widely used by Soviet paratroop units. The vehicle was carried partially recessed in the aircraft's bomb bay and dropped by parachute. In October 1944 a long-range variant, the Tu-2D (ANT-62), made its appearance; this had an increased span and a crew of five. A torpedo-bomber variant, the Tu-2T (ANT-62T), was tested between January and March

1945 and issued to units of the Soviet Naval Aviation. The Tu-2R, also designated Tu-6, carried a battery of cameras in the bomb bay and featured an extended wing for high-altitude operations, a redesigned and lengthened nose section, an enlarged tail assembly, and modified engine nacelles. An experimental ground attack version, the Tu-2Sh, was tested with various armament combinations; these included a 0.303-in (7.7-mm) gun mounted in a "solid" nose, and a battery of 48 7.62 submachine guns mounted in the bomb bay and directed to fire downward on unprotected personnel.

After World War II, the Tu-2 proved to be an ideal test vehicle for various powerplants, including the first generation of Soviet jet engines. Production continued after 1945, some 3,000 aircraft eventually being delivered to various Soviet Bloc air forces. The last Tu-2 model was the ANT-68, a high-altitude version that saw limited service as the Tu-10.

∎ Tupolev Tu-14 "Bosun"   USSR

Like Ilyushin's Il-28, the Tu-14 was designed to meet a Soviet Air Force requirement for a light jet attack bomber to replace the Tu-2. The prototype flew for the first time in 1949. The Il-28 was selected in preference, but the Tu-14's greater endurance, together with a longer weapons bay

capable of housing torpedoes, made it suitable for the naval attack role, and it went into production for the light attack squadrons of the Soviet Navy. The two principal versions were the Tu-14T torpedo-bomber and the Tu-14R maritime reconnaissance aircraft.

SPECIFICATION: Type naval attack/reconnaissance aircraft • Crew 4 • Powerplant two 5,952-lb (2,700-kg) thrust Klimov VK-1 turbojets • Max speed 525mph (845km/h) at sea level • Service ceiling 36,745ft (11,200m) • Max range 1,870 miles (3,010km) • Wingspan 71ft 1in (21.68m) • Length 72ft (21.95m) • Height 21ft 11in (6.68m) • Weight 51,477lb (23,350kg) loaded • Armament four forward-firing 0.50-in (12.7-mm) machine guns plus two 0.90-in (23-mm) cannon in tail position; up to 6,614lb (3,000kg) of bombs, torpedoes, or mines

▲ *The Tupolev Tu-14 proved to be a versatile and reliable aircraft, and was used for maritime reconnaissance after it had relinquished its attack role.*

▌Tupolev Tu-16 "Badger" USSR

The Tu-16 strategic jet bomber flew for the first time in 1952 under the manufacturer's designation Tu-88, and was destined to become the most important bomber type on the inventories of the Soviet Air Force and Naval Air Arm. The first production version was the Badger-A, which was also supplied to Iraq (9) and Egypt (30). The Badger-B was similar, but was equipped to carry two antishipping missiles (NATO reporting name Kennel) on underwing pylons. Twenty-five Badger-Bs were supplied to Indonesia.

The Badger-C, identified in 1961, was equipped to carry a very large ASM (NATO reporting name Kipper), while the Badger-D was a maritime reconnaissance version. The Badger-E was basically an -A with a battery of cameras in the bomb bay for high-altitude maritime reconnaissance. The last variant, the Badger-G, was armed with two AS-5 Kelt or AS-6 Kingfish ASMs. Some Badgers were converted to flight refueling tankers.

The Tu-16, over 2,000 examples of which are thought to have been produced, was also license-built in China as the Xian H-6.

SPECIFICATION: Type medium bomber (data Badger-A) • Crew 7 • Powerplant two 20,944-lb (9,500-kg) thrust Mikulin RD-3M turbojets • Max speed 597mph (960km/h) at 19,685ft (6,000m) • Service ceiling 49,200ft (15,000m) • Max range 2,983 miles (4,800km) • Wingspan 108ft 3in (32.99m) • Length 114ft 2in (34.80m) • Height 34ft 2in (10.36m) • Weight 167,110lb (75,800kg) loaded • Armament one forward and one rear ventral barbette each with two 0.90-in (23-mm) NR-23 cannon; two 0.90-in (23-mm) cannon in radar-controlled tail position; up to 19,842lb (9,000kg) of bombs

▲ *An atmospheric photograph of the versatile Tupolev Tu-16 "Badger", pictured by a NATO aircraft during a routine surveillance flight.*

▌Tupolev Tu-22 "Blinder" USSR

The Tupolev Tu-22 Blinder, designed as a supersonic successor to the Badger, was first seen publicly at the Tushino air display in 1961. The Tu-22s seen at Tushino were preseries trials aircraft, and first deliveries of the type to the Dalnaya Aviatsiya (Soviet Strategic Air Force) were not made until the following year. The first operational version, code-named Blinder-A, was produced in limited numbers only, its range of

about 1,926 miles (3,100km) falling short of planned strategic requirements. The second variant, the Tu-22K Blinder-B, was equipped with a flight refueling probe; 12 aircraft were supplied to Iraq and 24 to Libya. The Tu-22R Blinder-C was a dedicated maritime reconnaissance variant.

SPECIFICATION: Type medium bomber (data Blinder-A) • Crew 3 • Powerplant two 35,273lb (16,000kg) thrust Koliesov VD-7M turbojets • Max speed 924mph (1,487km/h) at 19,685ft (6,000m) • Service ceiling 60,040m (18,300m) • Max range 1,926 miles (3,100km) • Wingspan 77ft 11in (23.75m) • Length 132ft 11in (40.53m) • Height 35ft (10.67m) • Weight 185,188lb (84,000kg) • Armament one 0.90-in (23-mm) NR-23 cannon in tail position; up to 26,455lb (12,000kg) of bombs, or one AS-4 Kitchen ASM semirecessed under fuselage

▲ *In Soviet service, the rakish Tu-22 was nicknamed "Shilo" (awl). Post-USSR, the Tu-22 was taken into Russian and Ukrainian service.*

▌Tupolev Tu-22M "Backfire"

USSR

In 1969, American satellite reconnaissance identified the prototype of a new variable-geometry bomber at Tupolev's manufacturing plant at Kazan in central Asia. Designated Tu-22M, the aircraft reached initial operational capability (IOC) in 1973 and, during the years that followed, replaced

the Tu-16 Badger in Soviet service. Contrary to previously held beliefs, the Backfire is not a derivative of the Tu-22 Blinder, although the Tupolev Bureau deliberately fostered the impression that it was in order to avoid having to obtain the approval of the Communist Party Central Committee to start a new aircraft development program. The original design (Backfire-A) underwent major modifications and re-emerged as the Tu-22M-2 Backfire-B. About 400 Tu-22Ms were produced, 240 of them M-2s/3s. The M-3 is the latest version, with reduced defensive armament and the flight refueling probe deleted.

SPECIFICATION: Type bomber/maritime strike aircraft (data Backfire-A) • Crew 4 • Powerplant two 44,092-lb (20,000-kg) thrust Kuznetsov NK-144 turbofans • Max speed 1,321mph (2,125km/h) at altitude • Service ceiling 59,055ft (18,000m) • Max range 2,485 miles (4,000km) • Wingspan 112ft 6in (34.30m) spread; 76ft 9in (23.40m) swept • Length 129ft 11in (39.59m) • Height 35ft 5in (10.80m) • Weight 286,596lb (130,000kg) loaded • Armament two 23-mm (0.90-in) GSh-23 twin-barrel cannon in radar controlled tail barbette; up to 26,455lb (12,000kg) of stores in weapons bay, or one S-4 missile, or three AS-16 missiles

▌Tupolev Tu-28 "Fiddler"

USSR

The advent of bomber aircraft armed with stand-off weapons gave urgent impetus to the development of Soviet strategic fighters in the early 1960s, and resulted in the appearance in 1961 of the Tupolev Tu-28, a long-range, missile-armed all-weather interceptor. The Tu-28 was the largest interceptor to see service anywhere, and Western intelligence experts noted with interest that its designation carried the suffix "P" for Perekhvachnik (interceptor). The interesting point was that this suffix was only applied to the designations of Soviet aircraft which had been adapted to the fighter role, indicating that the Tu-28 had originally been designed as a low-level strike aircraft, possibly in the antishipping role, and that its adaptation as a fighter was the the result of an urgent Soviet Air Defense Forces requirement for an aircraft capable of intercepting Strategic Air Command B-52s while the latter

were still outside missile launch range. The major production version was the Tu-28P Fiddler-B.

SPECIFICATION: Type interceptor • Crew 2 • Powerplant two 24,690-lb (11,200-kg) thrust Lyulka AL-21F turbojets • Max speed 1,150mph (1,850km/h) at 36,090ft (11,000m) • Service ceiling 65,615ft (20,000m) • Max range 3,105 miles (5,000km) • Wingspan 59ft 4in (18.10m) • Length 89ft 3in (27.20m) • Height 23ft (7m) • Weight 88,185lb (40,000kg) loaded • Armament four AA-5 Ash long-range AAMs

▲ A Tu-28 "Fiddler" at the Morino air museum, Moscow. The aircraft is fitted with AA-5 "Ash" long-range air-to-air missiles.

∎ Tupolev Tu-95 "Bear"

USSR

Flight testing of the Tu-95 turboprop-powered strategic bomber began in the summer of 1954. The type entered service with the Soviet strategic forces in 1957, some early examples having played a prominent part in Soviet nuclear weapons trials. The initial Bear-A was followed by the Bear-B of 1961, a maritime reconnaissance variant with a large radome under the nose and armed with a Kangaroo ASM; the Bear-C and -D

▲ The ultimate maritime "Bear" variant is the Tu-142MZ, the most obvious feature of which is its nose ECM thimble radome.

of 1964–65, both specialized maritime reconnaissance and ELINT variants; and the Bear-E and -F, which were earlier models with upgraded equipment and avionics; these and later aircraft are designated Tu-142. Later models include the Bear-H, equipped to carry up to four cruise missiles, and the Bear-J, a VLF communications platform based on the Bear-F.

SPECIFICATION: Type strategic bomber (data Bear-A) • Crew 10 • Powerplant four 15,000hp Kuznetsov NK-12MV turboprops • Max speed 500mph (805km/h) at 41,000ft (12,500m) • Service ceiling 44,000ft (13,400m) • Max range 7,800 miles (12,550km) • Wingspan 159ft (48.50m) • Length 155ft 10in (47.50m) • Height 38ft 8in (11.78m) • Weight 340,000lb (154,000kg) • Armament six 0.90-in (23-mm) cannon; bomb load of up to 25,000lb (11,340kg)

∎ Tupolev Tu-126 "Moss"

USSR

First identified in 1968, the Tu-126 was a military development of the Tu-114 civil airliner, fitted with a large lenticular

▲ Despite operational shortcomings, the spacious Tu-126 was popular in service. One example was operational during the 1971 Indo-Pakistan War.

early warning scanner above the fuselage. The Tu-126 was intended to work with advanced interceptors such as the MiG-25 Foxbat, and could also operate as an airborne command post. About 20 Tu-126 AWACS aircraft were produced.

SPECIFICATION: Type AWACS aircraft • Crew 10–15 • Powerplant four 14,795hp Kuznetsov NK-12MV turboprops • Max speed 478mph (770km/h) at 29,500ft (8,995m) • Service ceiling 39,370ft (12,000m) • Max range 5,560 miles (8,950km) • Wingspan 168ft (51.20m) • Length 181ft 1in (55.20m) • Height 50ft 10in (15.50m) • Weight 374,800lb (170,000kg) loaded • Armament none

∎ Tupolev Tu-160 "Blackjack"

USSR

SPECIFICATION: Type strategic bomber • Crew 4 • Powerplant four 55,115-lb (25,000-kg) thrust Kuznetsov NK-321 turbofans • Max speed 1,243mph (2,000km/h) at 36,090ft (11,000m) • Service ceiling 60,040ft (18,300m) • Max range 8,700 miles (14,000km) • Wingspan 182ft 9in (55.70m) spread; 116ft 9in (35.60m) swept • Length 177ft 6in (54.10m) • Height 43ft (13.10m) • Weight 606,261lb (275,000kg) loaded • Armament provision for up to 36,376lb (16,500kg) of stores in two internal weapons bays and on underwing hardpoints, including up to 12 RK-55 (AS-15 Kent) cruise missiles or 24 RKV-500B AS-16 Kickback short-range attack missiles

The Tu-160 supersonic bomber, comparable to but much larger than the Rockwell B-1B, began test flights in 1982 and became operational in 1989. About 20 aircraft (out of a planned total of 100, reduced after the collapse of the USSR) are in service with the Russian Air Force. These aircraft have experienced flight control system and servicing problems.

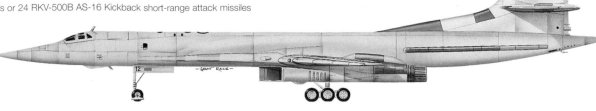

▌ Vickers FB.5

At the 1913 Aero Show at Olympia, London, the engineering firm Vickers Ltd. exhibited its Type 18 "Destroyer," a two-seat biplane with a water-cooled Wolseley pusher engine and a free-firing, belt-fed Maxim gun mounted in the nose. The aircraft was later redesignated EFB.1 (Experimental Fighting Biplane No. 1) and was the progenitor of the FB.5 "Gunbus," first delivered to No. 5 Squadron RFC in February 1915.

The two-seat FB (Fighting Biplane) 5 was armed with a drum-fed Lewis gun mounted in the front cockpit and powered by a Gnome Monosoupape "pusher" engine. No. 11 Squadron, the first to be fully armed with the type, became the first specialized fighter squadron ever to form. The squadron deployed to Villers-Brettoneux, France, in July 1915 and for several months carried out offensive patrols and

ground attack work. No. 18 Squadron, also armed with FB.5s, also arrived in France in November 1915. However, the FB.5 was no match in combat for the aircraft the Germans now had in the air fighting arena.

The FB.9 was an improved version with rounded wingtips, rounded tailplane, and a more streamlined nacelle. Production (both variants) totaled 210 aircraft built in the UK, with 99 more being built under license in France.

SPECIFICATION: Type scouting biplane • Crew 2 • Powerplant one 100hp Gnome Monosoupape 9-cylinder rotary • Max speed 70mph (113km/h) at 5,000ft (1,524m) • Service ceiling 9,000ft (2,743m) • Endurance 4hrs 30mins • Wingspan 36ft 6in (11.13m) • Length 27ft 2in (8.28m) • Height 11ft 6in (3.51m) • Weight 2,050lb (930kg) loaded • Armament one or two 0.303-in (7.7-mm) machine guns in front cockpit

▲ *This production FB.5 displays the spigot mounting on the nose for a Lewis gun, situated directly ahead of the observer's cockpit.*

▌ Vickers Valiant

▲ *Resplendent in its white anti-flash paintwork, Valiant B.1 XD823 is pictured prior to delivery to RAF Bomber Command.*

The Vickers Valiant was the first of the RAF's trio of "V-Bombers," and played a vital part in Britain's strategic nuclear deterrent. The first Vickers Type 660 Valiant flew on May 18, 1951 and production Valiant B.Mk.Is were delivered

in January 1955. No. 138 Squadron was the first to equip with the type, and No. 49 Squadron was the nuclear weapons trials unit, its aircraft participating in nuclear tests in Australia (1956) and Christmas Island (1957–58). Valiants

SPECIFICATION: Type strategic bomber • Crew 5 • Powerplant four 10,050lb (4,559kg) Rolls-Royce Avon 204 turbojets • Max speed 567mph (912km/h) at altitude • Service ceiling 54,000ft (16,460m) • Max range 4,600 miles (7,424km) • Wingspan 114ft 4in (34.85m) • Length 108ft 3in (33m) • Height 32ft 2in (9.80m) • Weight 175,000lb (79,378kg) • Armament one 10,000-lb (4,530-kg) MC Mk 1 Blue Danube nuclear bomb; four 2,000-lb (906-kg) Red Beard tactical nuclear bombs; one 6,000-lb (2,721-kg) Mk 5 (US) nuclear bomb; four Mk 28 or Mk 43 (US) thermonuclear bombs; or 21 x 1,000-lb (453-kg) conventional bombs

saw action in the Anglo-French Suez operation of October–November 1956, attacking Egyptian airfields with conventional bombs. In 1963 the Valiant force was assigned to the tactical bombing role, but was withdrawn prematurely because of fatigue cracks in the main spar. The Valiant BK.1 was a flight refueling tanker conversion, and the Valiant B.MK.2 was a one-shot prototype stressed for low-level, high speed penetration. Valiant production amounted to 108 aircraft, plus two prototypes and the solitary B.Mk.2. Of this total, 14 were B.(PR)K.1s and 45 were BK.1s.

◾ Vickers Valetta and Varsity

GREAT BRITAIN

Developed from the Vickers Viking civil airliner, the Valetta C.1 medium-range transport was widely used by the RAF in the 1950s, equipping 14 squadrons (including one Auxiliary, No. 622 and one aerial survey, No. 683). Valettas also took part in the British air drops in the Suez Canal Zone in

November 1956. The Vickers Varsity crew trainer, which appeared in 1951, was based on the design of the Valetta, but with a tricycle undercarriage; it served with the RAF's multi-engine training squadrons for 20 years until replaced by more modern types such as the HS125 Dominie and HP Jetstream.

◀ *The Vickers Varsity, seen here with the yellow band of RAF Flying Training Command around the rear fuselage, was based on the earlier Valetta.*

SPECIFICATION: Type crew trainer (data Varsity T.Mk.1) • Crew 4 • Powerplant two 1,950hp Bristol Hercules 264 14-cylinder radials • Max speed 288mph (463km/h) at 10,000ft (3,050m) • Service ceiling 28,700m (8,750m) • Max range 2,648 miles (4,260km) • Wingspan 95ft 7in (29.13m) • Length 67ft 6in (20.57m) • Height 23ft 11in (7.29m) • Weight 37,500lb (17,010kg) loaded • Armament 600lb (272kg) of practice bombs in pannier

◾ Vickers Vildebeest

GREAT BRITAIN

The Vickers Vildebeest, first flown in April 1928, was designed to replace the Hawker Horsley in the day/torpedo-bomber role. The Vildebeest Mks I and II had different variants of the Bristol Pegasus engine, while the Mk III had a revised cockpit to accommodate a third crew member. The production run for the first three series amounted to 152 aircraft, these being followed by 57 Mk IVs. The Vildebeest

equipped five RAF squadrons, and about 100 aircraft were still operational in the Far East at the outbreak of World War II. In December 1941, Nos. 36 and 100 Squadrons, based on Singapore Island, suffered nearly 100 percent casualties in attempting to attack Japanese invasion shipping.

SPECIFICATION: Type day/torpedo-bomber (data Vildebeest Mk III) • Crew 3 • Powerplant one 660hp Bristol Pegasus IIM3 sleeve-valve radial • Max speed 142mph (230km/h) • Service ceiling 17,000ft (5,182m) • Max range 1,553 miles (2,500km) • Wingspan 49ft (14.94m) • Length 36ft 8in (11.17m) • Height 17ft 9in (5.42m) • Weight 8,100lb (3,673kg) loaded • Armament one fixed forward-firing 0.303-in (7.7-mm) Vickers machine gun; one 0.303-in (7.7-mm) Lewis gun in rear cockpit; one 18-in (45.7-cm) torpedo or 1,100-lb (499-kg) of bombs under fuselage

▲ *The Vildebeest was still in first-line service at Singapore in December 1941, and took terrible casualties in attempting to attack Japanese shipping.*

▌Vickers Vimy

▲ *Instead of the original Rolls-Royce Eagle engines, this Vickers Vimy replica, pictured over English fields, is powered by a pair of BMW V12s.*

In the closing stages of World War I Vickers produced a large biplane bomber, the FB.27 Vimy, with the object of attacking Berlin. Ordered into large-scale production for the newly-formed Independent Force, (the RAF's strategic bombing force), the Vimy showed exceptional handling qualities and proved capable of lifting a greater load than the Handley Page O/400 on half the power. Production of the Vimy Mk I, which really got under way after the end of World War I, totaled 158 aircraft, deliveries to RAF bomber squadrons beginning in July 1919. The type began to be withdrawn from the bomber role in 1924, but many served on with various training establishments and parachute schools, the last

military Vimy being retired from No. 4 Flying Training School at Abu Sueir, Egypt, in 1933. Many variants of the basic Vimy were produced, both military and civil; the last two were the Vimy Ambulance and the Vernon bomber/transport. The aircraft is best remembered for its long-range pioneering flights, including the crossing of the Atlantic by Alcock and Brown in 1919.

SPECIFICATION: **Type** heavy bomber (data Vimy Mk.II) • **Crew** 3 • **Powerplant** two 360hp Rolls-Royce Eagle VIII 12-cylinder V-type • **Max speed** 103mph (166km/h) • **Service ceiling** 7,000ft (2,135m) • **Max range** 910 miles (1,464km) • **Wingspan** 68ft 1in (20.75m) • **Length** 43ft 6in (13.27m) • **Height** 15ft 7in (4.76m) • **Weight** 12,500lb (5670kg) • **Armament** one 0.303-in (7.7-mm) Lewis machine gun in nose, dorsal, and ventral positions; up to 4,804lb (2,179kg) of bombs in internal bomb cell and on underwing racks

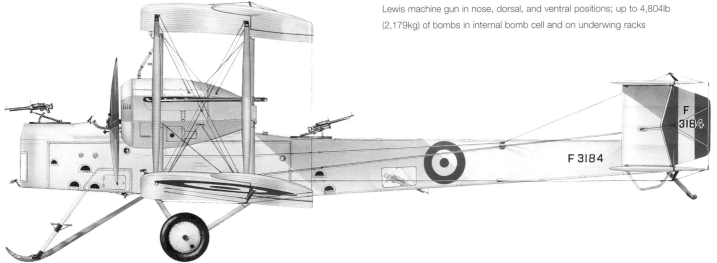

F 3184

▌Vickers Virginia

The Vickers Virginia was the standard heavy bomber of the Royal Air Force between 1924 and 1937. The aircraft appeared in many different variations, the first major pro-

duction version being the Mk V. Total production of the Virginia (Mks I to X) was only 126 aircraft, these equipping seven first-line and two Auxiliary RAF squadrons.

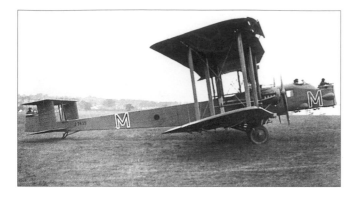

◀ *Virginia Mk Xs were used by Nos 7, 9 (pictured), 10, 51, 58, 214, 215, 500, and 502 (Bomber) Sqns, RAF, until late 1927.*

SPECIFICATION: **Type** heavy bomber • **Crew** 4 • **Powerplant** two 580hp Napier Lion VB 12-cylinder in-line engines • **Max speed** 108mph (174km/h) • **Service ceiling** 15,500ft (4,725m) • **Max range** 985 miles (1,585km) • **Wingspan** 87ft 8in (26.72m) • **Length** 62ft 3in (18.97m) • **Height** 18ft 2in (5.54m) • **Weight** 17,600lb (7,983kg) • **Armament** one 0.303-in (7.7-mm) Lewis machine gun in nose position, twin Lewis machine guns in dorsal position; up to 3,000lb (1,361kg) of bombs

▌Vickers Wellesley

Designed in 1933 as a private venture in response to a requirement for a general-purpose and torpedo-bomber, the Wellesley featured the novel geodetic construction devised by Barnes Wallis. The prototype of this high aspect ratio, cantilever monoplane first flew in June 1945, and the design showed such promise that the Air Ministry placed an order for 96 Wellesley Mk I aircraft, the first of these entering service in April 1937. Production up to May 1938 came to 176 aircraft, most of the later machines being completed with a long "glasshouse" canopy linking the front and rear cockpits. The Wellesley, which equipped 12 RAF squadrons, gave useful service in East and North Africa in the early campaigns against the Italians, and was also notable for several very long

range flights before the war. The Wellesley's bomb load was carried in underwing panniers.

▲ *Flying over mountainous terrain, this Vickers Wellesley is on its way to attack Italian positions in East Africa during the 1941 campaign.*

SPECIFICATION: **Type** general-purpose bomber • **Crew** 3 • **Powerplant** one 835hp Bristol Pegasus XX 9-cylinder radial • **Max speed** 228mph (367km/h) • **Service ceiling** 25,500ft (7,770m) • **Max range** 2,880 miles (4,635km) • **Wingspan** 74ft 7in (22.73m) • **Length** 39ft 3in (11.66m) • **Height** 15ft 3in (4.67m) • **Weight** 12,500lb (5,670kg) loaded • **Armament** one fixed forward-firing 0.303-in (7.7-mm) in leading edge of port wing, and one in rear cockpit; bomb load of 2,000lb (907kg) in underwing panniers

▌Vickers Wellington

The Vickers Wellington was designed by Barnes Wallis to Specification B.9/32. Like its predecessor, the Vickers Wellesley, the aircraft featured geodetic construction. In

December 1933 Vickers was awarded a contract for the construction of a single prototype under the designation Type 271, this aircraft flying on June 15, 1936. This aircraft was lost

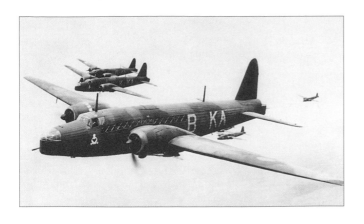

▲ *Wellingtons of No.9 Squadron RAF pictured in 1939. The Squadron's badge featured the motto "Per Noctem Volamus" (We Fly By Night).*

SPECIFICATION: Type medium bomber • **Crew** six • **Powerplant** two 1,500hp Bristol Hercules XI radial engines • **Max speed** 255mph (411km/h) at 12,500ft (3,810m) • **Service ceiling** 19,000ft (5,790m) • **Max range** 1,540 miles (2,478km) with 4,500lb (2,041kg) bomb load • **Wingspan** 86ft 2in (26.26m) • **Length** 64ft 7in (19.68m) • **Height** 17ft 5in (5.30m) • **Weight** 34,000lb (15,422kg) loaded • **Armament** two 0.303-in (7.7-mm) machine guns in nose turret, four in tail turret, and two in beam positions; up to 4,500lb (2,041kg) of bombs

on April 19, 1937 when it broke up during an involuntary high-speed dive, the cause being determined as elevator imbalance. As a result, the production prototype Wellington Mk I and subsequent aircraft were fitted with a revised fin, rudder, and elevator adapted from a parallel project, the Vickers B.1/35, which would enter service later as the Warwick. The fuselage also underwent considerable modification, so that production Wellingtons, ordered to Specification 29/36, bore little resemblance to the ill-fated prototype. The first Mk I, flew on December 23, 1937, powered by two Pegasus XX engines, and the first Bomber Command squadron to rearm, No, 9, began receiving its aircraft in December 1938.

The Wellingtons in RAF service at the outbreak of World War II were the Pegasus-engined Mks I and IA, the latter having a very slight increase in wing span and length. Prototypes of the Mk II and the Mk III were fitted with Bristol Hercules engines, and it was this powerplant that would be generally adopted. The most numerous early model, however, was the Mk IC, which had Pegasus XVIII engines. Differing little from the IA, the fuselage of the Wellington IC was slightly cut down behind the nose turret and reshaped in order to allow the turret a greater traverse. The aircraft was also fitted with beam

gun positions in place of the ventral gun turret, which caused too much drag, and self-sealing fuel tanks. In all, 2,685 Wellington Mk 1C aircraft were built.

The Wellington made its appearance in the Middle East in September 1940 and in the Far East early in 1942. By this time the principal version in service with Bomber Command was the Mk III (1,519 built), with two 1,500hp Bristol Hercules engines replacing the much less reliable Pegasus, although four squadrons used the Mk IV, which was powered by American Pratt & Whitney Twin Wasps. Coastal Command also found its uses for the versatile Wellington. The first general reconnaissance version of the aircraft, which made its appearance in the spring of 1942, was the GR.III, 271 being converted from standard Mk IC airframes. The aircraft were fitted with ASV Mk II radar and adapted to carry torpedoes. Use of the GR.III torpedo-bomber was mainly confined to the Mediterranean, where squadrons operating from the island of Malta preyed on the Axis convoys plying between Europe and North Africa. Fifty-eight more GR.IIIs were equipped as antisubmarine aircraft, being fitted with a powerful Leigh Light searchlight to illuminate U-boats traveling on the surface.

The last bomber version of the Wellington was the Mk X, of which 3,803 were built, accounting for more than 30 percent of all Wellington production. Its career with Bomber Command was brief, but it was used in the Far East until the end of the war. The GR.XI and GR.XIII were specifically intended for the torpedo-bomber role, while the GR.XII and GR.XIV were antisubmarine aircraft.

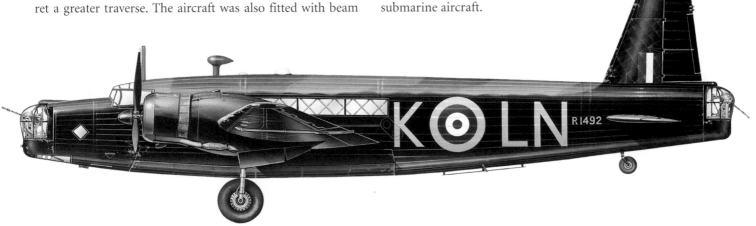

■ Voisin 3

Also designated Model LA, the Voisin 3 of 1914 was the standard French day and night bomber during the early part of

SPECIFICATION: **Type** light bomber • **Crew** 2 • **Powerplant** one 150hp Canton-Unné 9-cylinder liquid-cooled radial • **Max speed** 74mph (120km/h) at sea level • **Service ceiling** 11,485ft (3,500m) • **Max range** 310 miles (500km) • **Wingspan** 48ft 3in (14.75m) • **Length** 31ft 2in (9.50m) • **Height** 12ft 6in (3.8m) • **Weight** 3,020lb (1,370kg) loaded • **Armament** one machine gun; hand-dropped bombs, grenades, or darts

World War I. The Aviation Militaire took delivery of 800, Belgium about 30, and a few were supplied to the Russians. The Royal Flying Corps also received about 100 Voisin 3s, of which 50 were built under license. In Italy, 112 were also license-built and served with five squadrons of the Italian Air Corps. On October 5, 1914, the crew of a Voisin 3 of Escadrille VB24, Lt. Frantz and Cpl. Quénault, became the first Frenchmen to bring down an enemy aircraft, shooting down an Aviatik in flames near Reims with 47 rounds from Quénault's Hotchkiss machine gun.

■ Voisin 5

SPECIFICATION: **Type** bomber • **Crew** 2 • **Powerplant** one 150hp Canton-Unné 9-cylinder liquid-cooled radial • **Max speed** 65mph (105km/h) • **Service ceiling** 11,485ft (3,500m) • **Endurance** 3hrs 30mins • **Wingspan** 48ft 4in (14.75m) • **Length** 31ft 3in (9.53m) • **Height** 11ft 11in (3.63m) • **Weight** 2,516lb (1,140kg) loaded • **Armament** one 0.303-in (7.7-mm) machine gun or one 1.45- or 1.85-in (37- or 47-mm) cannon; 132lb (60kg) of bombs

◄ *In spite of their frail appearance, the Voisin pusher biplanes were extremely battleworthy, and were in continuous use throughout World War I.*

In 1915, the Voisin 3 was followed into service by the Voisin 4 and 5, which differed from the earlier model in small structural alterations, the adoption of more powerful engines, and the option of installing Hotchkiss 1.45-in (37-mm) or 1.85-in (47-

mm) cannon in place of the nose-mounted machine gun. This armament, although useless in aerial combat, was very effective against ground targets. These aircraft were not produced in large numbers; 200 Voisin Type 4s and 350 Type 5s were built.

■ Voisin 8

SPECIFICATION: **Type** bomber • **Crew** 2 • **Powerplant** one 220hp Peugeot 8-cylinder liquid-cooled in-line • **Max speed** 82mph (132km/h) • **Service ceiling** 14,110ft (4,300m) • **Endurance** 4hrs • **Wingspan** 61ft 8in (18.20m) • **Length** 36ft 2in (11.02m) • **Height** 11ft 5in (3.50m) • **Weight** 4,100lb (1,860kg) • **Armament** one or two 0.30-in (7.5-mm) machine guns; 400lb (180kg) of bombs

Although basically a good design, the Voisin 8 bomber, which made its appearance in 1916, was plagued by problems with its Peugeot engine. About 1,100 were built, but the snags were never completely eliminated and as a result the operational use of the aircraft was severely restricted. The troublesome Peugeot was eventually replaced by a 300hp Renault and the aircraft redesignated Type 10, which had a better performance and could carry almost double the bomb load.

■ Vought-Sikorsky OS2U Kingfisher

Designed in 1937, the prototype OS2U Kingfisher flew in prototype form in July 1938. The major variant was the OS2U-3, over 1,000 of which were built. The OS2U was an

extremely versatile aircraft, being used for dive-bombing, coastal patrol, and air-sea rescue as well as reconnaissance. One hundred examples of the OS2U-3 were supplied to the

Royal Navy, in whose service the type was named Kingfisher, and 300 examples of a landplane version, which were designated the OS2N-1, were built by the Naval Aircraft Factory.

▼ *The Vought-Sikorsky OS2U Kingfisher was the US Navy's first catapult-launched monoplane, entering service in August 1940.*

SPECIFICATION: Type naval reconnaissance floatplane • Crew 2 • Powerplant one 450hp Pratt & Whitney Wasp 9-cylinder radial Max speed 164mph (264km/h) at 5,500ft (1,680m) • Service ceiling 19,500ft (5,950m) • Max range 805 miles (1,300km) • Wingspan 35ft 11in (10.94m) • Length 33ft 7in (10.23m) • Height 15ft 1in (4.59m) • Weight 4,000lb (1,815kg) loaded • Armament two 0.30-in (7.62-mm) machine guns

▌Vought-Sikorsky SB2U Vindicator

USA

Ordered in October 1934, the SB2U was the US Navy's first monoplane scout and dive-bomber. The XSB2U-1 prototype flew for the first time in January 1936 and deliveries of SB2U-1 production aircraft began in 1937. The SB2U-2 had updated equipment, and the SB2U-3 had heavier armament and fuel tankage. France purchased 39 SB2U-2s under the designation V-156F, while 50 went to the Royal Navy as the Chesapeake Mk I, these being used for training and target towing.

SPECIFICATION: Type carrier-borne scout and dive-bomber (data SB2U-3) • Crew 2 • Powerplant one 825hp Pratt & Whitney R-1535-2 Twin Wasp 14-cylinder radial • Max speed 243mph (391km/h) at sea level • Service ceiling 23,600ft (7,195m) • Max range 1,120 miles (1,802km) • Wingspan 41ft 11in (12.77m) • Length 33ft 11in (10.36m) • Height 14ft 3in (4.34m) • Weight 9,421lb (4,273kg) loaded • Armament one fixed forward-firing 0.50-in (12.7-mm) machine gun in upper forward fuselage, and one in rear cockpit; external bomb load of up to 1,000lb (454kg)

▲ *This SB2U-3 served with VMS-1 in June 1941. Most aircraft were issued to Marine units.*

▌Vultee A-35 Vengeance

▲ *Although mostly used as a trainer, the Vultee Vengeance performed well when used as a dive-bomber by the RAF and the Indian Air Force in Burma.*

SPECIFICATION: **Type** dive-bomber • **Crew** 2 • **Powerplant** one 1,700hp Wright R-2600-13 14-cylinder radial • **Max speed** 279mph (449km/h) at 15,000ft (4,570m) • **Service ceiling** 22,300ft (6,795m) • **Max range** 1,400 miles (2,253km) • **Wingspan** 48ft (14.63m) • **Length** 39ft 9in (12.12m) • **Height** 15ft 4in (4.67m) • **Weight** 16,400lb (7,439kg) loaded • **Armament** six 0.50-in (12.7-mm) machine guns in wing leading edges, plus one in rear cockpit; internal and external bomb load of 2,000lb (907kg)

The Vultee Vengeance had its origins in a French order for a dive-bomber, the V-72, 300 of which were to be delivered by September 1941. The fall of France effectively terminated the contract, but the program was revived by the British, who placed orders for 700 V-72s with the designations Vengeance Mks I and II. The US also purchased 200 aircraft as Vengeance Mk IIIs (A-31s) for Lend-Lease transfer to the UK, then provided funds for 100 A-35s and 99 A-35A conversions, the latter having revised forward-firing armament. The Vengeance Mk IV (A-35B) comprised 563 further improved aircraft. The Vengeance was mostly used as a target tug by the RAF, but some were used operationally as dive-bombers by the RAF and the Indian Air Force in the Burma campaign and by the Free French in North Africa.

131 270

▌Vultee BT-13 Valiant

The Vultee BT-13 Valiant, which made its appearance in 1939, was one of the outstanding training aircraft of World War II. By the time production ended in 1944, 11,537 aircraft

had been built for the USAAF and USN. The type was produced in several subvariants, the principal ones being the BT-13A and BT-13B, which were respectively designated SNV-1 and SNV-2 in the USN. The final variant was the BT-15, which had a Wright R-975 radial engine.

▲ *Lovingly restored, this Vultee Valiant was photographed at Abbotsford in Western Canada in 1970. It carries a civilian registration and 1941 tail stripes.*

SPECIFICATION: **Type** trainer (data BT-13A) • **Crew** 2 • **Powerplant** one 450hp Pratt & Whitney R-985-AN-1 9-cylinder radial • **Max speed** 183mph (295km/h) at sea level • **Service ceiling** 16,500ft (5,030m) • **Max range** 513 miles (826km) • **Wingspan** 42ft 2in (12.86m) • **Length** 28ft 9in (8.76m) • **Height** 12ft 5in (3.75m) • **Weight** 4,360lb (1,980kg) loaded • **Armament** none

■ Westland Lysander

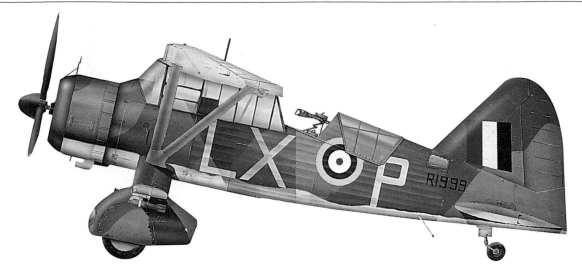

Originating in a 1934 requirement for a battlefield army coop-eration and reconnaissance aircraft, the Westland Lysander prototype first flew in June 1936, and entered service in June 1938. The Lysander Mk II had a 905hp Bristol Perseus engine, while the Mk III was fitted with the Mercury XX.

The type was in widespread use in the early years of WWII, particularly in France and North Africa, but was pro-gressively replaced by the Curtiss Tomahawk starting in 1941. Seventy Mk IIIs were converted to Mk IIIA standard for tar-get towing and air-sea rescue, 100 new aircraft being built, and the type was used to infiltrate Allied agents into enemy-occupied territory and bring them out again. Total produc-tion was 1,593 aircraft, comprising 131 Mk Is, 433 Mk IIs, and 804 Mk IIIs built in Great Britain, and 225 built in Canada.

SPECIFICATION: Type army cooperation aircraft (data Lysander Mk I) • Crew 2 • Powerplant one 890hp Bristol Mercury XII 9-cylinder radial • Max speed 229mph (369km/h) • Service ceiling 26,000ft (7,925m) • Max range 600 miles (966km) • Wingspan 50ft (15.24m) • Length 30ft 6in (9.30m) • Height 11ft (3.35m) • Weight 7,500lb (3,402kg) • Armament one 0.303-in (7.7-mm) machine gun in each wheel fairing and one in rear cockpit; external bomb load of 500lb (227kg)

■ Westland Wapiti

The Westland Wapiti was designed to replace the DH.9A, the prototype flying in March 1927. As first flown, the Wapiti had DH.9A wings and tail assembly, but the production Wapiti I had an enlarged tailplane and a 420hp Bristol Jupiter VI engine. Ten Wapiti IIs with uprated Jupiter VI engines were followed by the Wapiti IIA with the 550hp Jupiter VIII, this variant appearing in 1931. In all, Westland built 565 Wapitis.

▶ *Westland Wapiti J9719 of No. 39 Squadron, Risalpur, India, lets go its bomb load over a target on the infamous North-West Frontier in the 1920s.*

SPECIFICATION: Type general-purpose biplane (data Wapiti Mk III) • Crew 2 • Powerplant one 490hp Armstrong Siddeley Jaguar VI 14-cylinder radial • Max speed 140mph (225km/h) • Service ceiling 20,600ft (6,280m) • Max range 660 miles (1,062km) • Wingspan 46ft 5in (14.15m) • Length 32ft 6in (9.91m) • Height 11ft 10in (3.61m) • Weight 5,400lb (2,449kg) loaded • Armament one 0.303-in (7.7-mm) machine gun in upper forward fuselage, plus one in rear cockpit; external bomb load of 580lb (263kg)

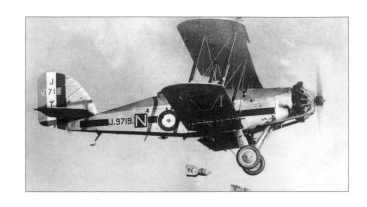

Westland Welkin

SPECIFICATION: Type high-altitude interceptor • Crew 1 • Powerplant two 1,290hp Rolls-Royce Merlin 61 in-line engines • Max speed 330mph (529km/h) at 30,000ft (9,150m) • Service ceiling 44,000ft (13,420m) • Max range 1,200 miles (1,930km) • Wingspan 70ft (21.35m) • Length 41ft 6in (12.65m) • Height 15ft (4.57m) • Weight 21,892lb (9,928kg) loaded • Armament four 0.79-in (20-mm) cannon

▶ The Westland Welkin interceptor was designed to counter German high-altitude reconnaissance aircraft like the Junkers Ju 86P, but only a few prototypes were built.

The Westland Welkin was designed to meet a requirement for a cannon-armed fighter capable of operating at over 40,000ft (12,200m). The prototype flew on November 1, 1942 and plans were made to place the aircraft in series production, but the development program was beset by many technical diffi-culties and only a few prototypes were completed. The Welkin, which had a long-span high aspect ratio wing, was one of the first RAF fighters to have a pressurized cockpit.

Westland Whirlwind

SPECIFICATION: Type long-range fighter-bomber (data Whirlwind Mk IA) • Crew 1 • Powerplant two 765hp Rolls-Royce Peregrine 12-cylinder V-type • Max speed 360mph (579km/h) • Service ceiling 30,000ft (9,150m) • Max range 800 miles (1,287km) • Wingspan 45ft (13.72m) • Length 32ft 3in (9.83m) • Height 10ft 6in (3.20m) • Weight 11,388lb (5,166kg) • Armament four 0.79-in (20-mm) cannon; external bomb load of 1,000lb (454kg)

◀ The Whirlwind would have made a superlative long-range escort fighter had it been fitted with Rolls-Royce Merlin engines instead of Peregrines.

Designed originally as a long-range escort fighter, the Westland Whirlwind first flew on October 11, 1938 but did not enter RAF service until June 1940. Its intended power-plant was the Rolls-Royce Merlin, but as this was earmarked for the Spitfire and Hurricane, the Rolls-Royce Peregrine—an upgraded version of the Kestrel—was selected instead. The Whirlwind was highly maneuverable, faster than a Spitfire at low altitude, and its armament of four closely grouped 0.79-in (20-mm) cannon in the nose made it a match for any German fighter of the day, but continual prob-lems with the Peregrine engine delayed its service debut and only two squadrons (Nos. 137 and 263) were equipped with it. The aircraft was later converted to the fighter-bomber role as the Whirlwind Mk IA, being replaced by the Typhoon at the end of 1943.

Westland Wyvern

▲ *The powerful Westland Wyvern was the only turboprop-powered naval fighter ever to see operational service. It saw combat in the 1956 Suez operations.*

The world's first turboprop-powered combat aircraft, the Westland Wyvern was originally fitted with the Rolls-Royce Eagle piston engine, but further development was concentrated around the Armstrong Siddeley Python turboprop. The first Python-engined aircraft flew on March 22, 1949 and the type was fully operational by September 1953. Vulnerable to ground fire due to its size, the aircraft had been withdrawn from first-line service by mid-1958.

SPECIFICATION: Type naval strike fighter • Crew 1 • Powerplant one Armstrong Siddeley Python ASP.3 turboprop • Max speed 383mph (616km/h) at sea level • Service ceiling 28,000ft (8,535m) • Max range 904 miles (1,455km) • Wingspan 44ft (13.41m) • Length 42ft 3in (12.87m) • Height 15ft 9in (4.80m) • Weight 24,500lb (11,113kg) loaded • Armament four 0.79-in (20-mm) cannon; 3,000lb (1,360kg) of bombs, 16 RPs, or one torpedo

▌Wibault 72C-1

In 1923 the French designer Michel Wibault, whose first fighter aircraft had been a 1917 prototype biplane, produced the Wibault 7, a strut-braced parasol-wing monoplane with a radial engine. Designed for high-altitude interception, it was a metal-framed aircraft with fabric-covered surfaces. The Wibault 7 had an excellent rate of climb, being able to reach 13,123ft (4,000m) in just under 11 minutes. Sixty pro-

duction Wibault 72s were ordered by the Aviation Militaire, the first entering service in 1926. The Wibault 74 and 75 were navalized versions of the 72, being fitted with deck arrester gear for service aboard the aircraft carrier Béarn. Eighteen of each version were completed, and served until 1934.

▲ *The parasol-winged Wib.7, with its metal-strip-reinforced wings, was an advance over its fabric-covered contemporaries.*

SPECIFICATION: Type fighter • Crew 1 • Powerplant one 420hp Gnome-Rhone Jupiter 9Ac 9-cylinder radial • Max speed 141mph (227km/h) at 16,400ft (5,000m) • Service ceiling 26,575ft (8,100m) • Max range 373 miles (600km) • Wingspan 35ft 11in (10.95m) • Length 24ft 5in (7.45m) • Height 9ft 8in (2.96m) • Weight 3,183lb (1,444kg) loaded • Armament two 0.303-in (7.7-mm) Vickers and two 0.30-in (7.5-mm) Darne machine guns

▌Yakovlev Yak-1/Yak-3

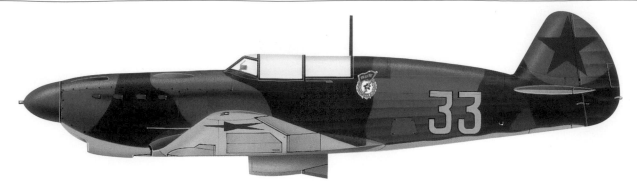

The Yak-1 Krasavyets (Beauty) made its first public appearance during an air display on November 7, 1940. It was Aleksandr S. Yakovlev's first fighter design, and it earned him the Order of Lenin, the gift of a Zis car, and a prize of 100,000 rubles. The fighter was powered by a 100hp M-105PA engine and carried an armament of one 0.79-in (20-mm) ShVAK cannon, two 0.30-in (7.62-mm) ShKAS machine guns, and sometimes six RS-82 rockets. The Yak-1 was of mixed construction, fabric and plywood covered; it was simple to build and service, and a delight to fly. Maximum speed was 360mph (580km/h).

Production was slow because of the need to relocate factories following the German invasion, and so it was decided to convert a trainer variant of the Yak-1, the Yak-7V, into a single-seat fighter by covering the second cockpit with metal sheeting and arming the aircraft with one ShVAK cannon and two ShKAS machine guns. In this new guise the aircraft was designated Yak-7A. In 1942 the basic Yak-1 evolved into the Yak-1M, which had a smaller wing area, a revised rear fuselage, and a three-piece sliding cockpit hood; it was also slightly faster than the Yak-1. Similar modifications to the Yak-7A led to the improved Yak-7B, of which 6,399 were built. Further

refinements to the Yak-1M were introduced before the aircraft entered quantity production in the spring of 1943, resulting in the production fighter being redesignated Yak-3. The first Yak-3s reached the front line during the early summer months of 1943, in time to take part in the battle of Kursk.

The Yak-3 quickly proved itself in combat; it rarely operated above 11,500ft (3,500m), below which it was markedly more maneuverable than either the FW 190A or Bf 109G; in fact, it was probably the most maneuverable fighter aircraft to see service during World War II. At a relatively early stage in the production life of the Yak-3 the wooden wing spars were replaced by spars of light alloy, first introduced in the Yak-9, and the VK-105 engine was replaced by the more powerful 1,620hp VK-107. During trials with the new engine the aircraft reached a speed of 447mph (720km/h) at 18,865ft (5,750m), faster than either the FW 190A-4 or Me 109G-2. The Soviet Air Force received a total of 4,848 Yak-3s.

▼ *The Yak-1B, pictured during state tests, offered an improved pilot's view, as a result of a lower aft fuselage and all-round canopy.*

SPECIFICATION: **Type** fighter • **Crew** 1 • **Powerplant** one 1,222hp VK-105PF-2 or 1,620hp VK-107 engine • **Max speed** 409mph (658km/h) at 11,482ft (3,500m) • **Service ceiling** 35,475ft (10,800m) • **Max range** 560 miles (900km) • **Wingspan** 30ft 2in (9.20m) • **Length** 28ft (8.55m) • **Height** 9ft 10in (3m) • **Weight** 5,863lb (2,660kg) loaded • **Armament** one 0.79-in (20-mm) ShVAK cannon with 120 rounds firing through the propeller shaft, and two 0.50-in (12.7-mm) Beresin BS machine guns in the forward fuselage decking.

▌Yakovlev Yak-9 "Frank"

The Yakovlev Yak-9 was a progressive development of the Yak-1, as was the Yak-3, but its evolution followed a separate path. From the basic Yak-1, Yakovlev developed the Yak-7B

and the Yak-7DI, both of which appeared in action in the summer of 1942. The Yak-7B had the same performance, engine and armament as the Yak-1, but it differed in having a redesigned cockpit, which afforded a better view to the rear, and a retractable tailwheel. The Yak-7DI was a long-range fighter version of the Yak-7B, and it was a slightly modified version of this type that served as the prototype Yak-9. The main difference between the Yak-9 and the Yak-7B was that the former had additional fuel tanks to extend its range, and the wing structure was modified to accommodate them. The type was initially built in two versions the Yak-9D armed with a ShVAK 0.79-in (20-mm) cannon and a synchronized 0.5-in (12.7-mm) machine gun, and the Yak-9T, with a 1.46-in

(37-mm) NS cannon in place of the 0.79-in (20-mm) weapon.

The Yak-9T was used as an antishipping aircraft, with some success. Later variants, differing in armament and equipment detail, included the Yak-9L and Yak-9M. The Yak-9U, an improved and more streamlined variant, was in production before the end of World War II, and the final version, the Yak-9P, remained in service with the Soviet and satellite air forces for some years after the war, seeing combat in Korea.

SPECIFICATION: Type fighter (data Yak-9U) • Crew 1 • Powerplant one 1,650hp Klimov VK-107A V-type • Max speed 435mph (700km/h) at 16,405ft (5,000m) • Service ceiling 39,040ft (11,900m) • Max range 540 miles (870km) • Wingspan 32ft (9.77m) • Length 28ft (8.55m) • Height 8ft (2.44m) • Weight 6,760lb (3,068kg) loaded • Armament one 0.90-in (23-mm) hub-firing VYa-23V cannon and two 0.50-in (12.7-mm) UBS machine guns

▲ Developed from the Yak-9T, primary armament of the Yak-9K anti-tank aircraft was a 45-mm cannon with 29 rounds.

■ Yakovlev Yak-15/17 "Feather"
USSR

Of all the aviation booty uncovered by the Russians during their advance into Germany, the most important haul was a large quantity of BMW 003A and Junkers Jumo 004A turbojets, which were distributed among the various aircraft designers for experimental use while the engine manufacturers geared up to produce them in series. One of the designers involved was Aleksandr S. Yakovlev, who set about adapting a standard Yak-3 airframe to accommodate a Jumo 004B. The resulting aircraft, designated Yak-15, flew for the first time on April 24, 1946. Deliveries to Soviet Air Force fighter squadrons began early in 1947, production aircraft retaining a tailwheel undercarriage and being powered by the RD-10 engine, as the Jumo 004B copy was known. At the time of its introduction the Yak-15 was the lightest jet fighter in the world, the lightweight structure of the Yak-3's airframe compensating for the relatively

▲ Seen here in Czech Air Force markings, the Yakovlev Yak-17 was a development of the much more rudimentary Yak-15.

low power of the RD-10 engine. In 1948 the Yak-15 was replaced on the production line by the Yak-17, an uprated variant with an RD-10A turbojet, tricycle undercarriage, and redesigned vertical tail surfaces. A two-seat variant, the Yak-17UTI, was the Soviet Air Force's first jet conversion trainer.

SPECIFICATION: Type fighter (data Yak-15) • Crew 1 • Powerplant 1,984lb (900kg) thrust RD-10 (Jumo 004) turbojet • Max speed 488mph (785km/h) at 16,400ft (5,000m) • Service ceiling 43,800ft (13,350m) • Max range 460 miles (740km) • Wingspan 30ft 2in (9.20m) • Length 28ft 10in (8.78m) • Height 7ft 3in (2.20m) • Weight 6,045lb (2,742kg) loaded • Armament two 0.90-in (23-mm) NS-23 cannon

▲ The Yak-17 differed from the Yak-15 mainly in its internal structure, but also benefited from retractable tricycle landing gear.

▌Yakovlev Yak-18 "Max"

USSR

The Yakovlev Bureau produced two main training types in the immediate postwar years. The first was the Yak-11, which was supplied in large numbers to the Soviet Bloc air forces in the late 1940s and built under license in Czechoslovakia as the C.11; the second was the Yak-18, which entered service with the Soviet Air Force in 1946 and which was subsequently used in large numbers throughout the communist-aligned world.

▶ *The Yak-18 was supplied to Soviet-aligned air forces in large numbers during the post-war years, and was also built under license in Czechoslovakia.*

SPECIFICATION: **Type** trainer (data Yak-18A) • **Crew** 2 • **Powerplant** one 260hp Ivchenko AI-14R 9-cylinder radial • **Max speed** 163mph (263km/h) at sea level • **Service ceiling** 16,600ft (5,060m) • **Max range** 441 miles (710km) • **Wingspan** 34ft 9in (10.60m) • **Length** 27ft 5in (8.35m) • **Height** 10ft 8in (3.25m) • **Weight** 2,923lb (1,326kg) loaded • **Armament** none

▌Yakovlev Yak-23 "Flora"

USSR

Developed from the Yak-15/17 series, the Yak-23 was produced as an insurance against the failure of the more advanced MiG-15 and flew for the first time in 1947. When the MiG-15 proved a success, it was decided to produce the Yak-23 in limited quantities for delivery to Russia's satellite air forces. A midwing monoplane of all-metal construction, the type was used by the air forces of Bulgaria, Poland, and Czechoslovakia. Although produced in far smaller numbers than the F-84 Thunderjet, the Yak-23 was its equivalent to the Warsaw Pact nations, introducing many pilots to jet fighter operation.

◀ *The unpressurized Yak-23 was simple to maintain and relatively easy to fly.*

SPECIFICATION: **Type** fighter • **Crew** 1 • **Powerplant** one 3,530-lb (1,600-kg) thrust RD-500 (Rolls-Royce Derwent 5) turbojet • **Max speed** 590mph (950km/h) at sea level • **Service ceiling** 51,840ft (15,800m) • **Max range** 745 miles (1,200km) • **Wingspan** 28ft 6in (8.69m) • **Length** 26ft 9in (8.16m) • **Height** 9ft 10in (3m) • **Weight** 7,460lb (3,384kg) loaded • **Armament** two 0.90-in (23-mm) NS-23 cannon

▌Yakovlev Yak-25 "Flashlight"

USSR

A midwing monoplane with 45 degrees of sweep, the Yak-25 was a tandem two-seater and featured a bicycle undercarriage with outriggers under the wings. It was fitted with an improved version of the Izumrud AI radar under a large plastic radome and was armed with two 1.19-in (30-mm) cannon mounted under the fuselage. The Yak-25 prototypes had two Mikulin AM-5 engines, but production aircraft had the more powerful AM-5F, the F denoting Forsazh, or reheat. Several prototypes were flying by the summer of 1952 and the aircraft

▶ *The Yak-25, dubbed "Flashlight" by NATO, gave the Soviet Air Force a true all-weather capability. It became fully operational in 1956.*

(Flashlight-A) entered service with a Soviet Air Force development unit in 1955, becoming fully operational in the following year. The Flashlight-B (MiG-25R) was a reconnaissance variant with a radome under the nose, while the Yak-27 (Flashlight-C) had longer engine nacelles, housing VK-9 afterburning turbojets, a pointed nose radome, and extended wing root chord. A further development, the Yak-26 (NATO reporting name Mangrove) reconnaissance aircraft was basically a Yak-27 with a glazed nose, and was built in quantity for the Soviet tactical air forces. The Yak-25RV (NATO

SPECIFICATION: Type all-weather fighter (data Yak-25A) • Crew 2 • Powerplant two 5730lb (2600kg) thrust Mikulin AM-5 turbojets • Max speed 630mph (1015km/h) at 25,000ft (7625m) • Service ceiling 46,000ft (14,000m) • Max range 1250 miles (2000km) • Wingspan 36ft 1in (11m) • Length 51ft 5in (15.67m) • Height 12ft 6in (3.80m) • Weight 21,826lb (9900kg) loaded • Armament two 1.46in (37mm) cannon; 50x 1.99in (50mm) air-to-air rockets

reporting name Mandrake) was a high-altitude reconnaissance aircraft, the Soviet equivalent of the RB-57F Canberra.

▌ Yakovlev Yak-28 "Brewer"   USSR

Although bearing a strong resemblance to the Yak-25/26/27

SPECIFICATION: Type all-weather interceptor (data Yak-28P) • Crew 2 • Powerplant two 13,681-lb (6,206-kg) thrust Tumanskii R-11 turbojets • Max speed 733mph (1,180km/h) at altitude • Service ceiling 52,495ft (16,000m) • Combat radius 575 miles (925km) • Wingspan 42ft 6in (12.95m) • Length 75ft 7in (23m) • Height 12ft 11in (3.95m) • Weight 41,890lb (19,000kg) • Armament four underwing pylons for two AA-2 or AA-3 air-to-air missiles

series, the Yak-28, first revealed at Tushino in 1961, was a completely new design. The two-seat tactical strike version, Brewer-A, entered service with the Soviet Frontal Aviation in 1961, replacing the Il-28. The Brewer-B and -C displayed minor changes from the early production version, while the Brewer-D (Yak-28R) was a reconnaissance version. The Brewer-E was an ECM version, with an active ECM pack partially recessed in the bomb bay, while the Yak-28P (Firebar) was a two-seat all-weather fighter variant.

▲ *The Yak-28P prototype, pictured here with dummy R-8 "Anab" AAMs, could be equipped with RATO gear, and entered production in 1961.*

▌ Yakovlev Yak-38 "Forger"   USSR

Apart from the Harrier family, the Yak-38 is the only other operational V/STOL aircraft in the world. Development of the Yak-36MP prototype began in the late 1960s and the type became operational on the Soviet carrier Kiev in 1976. All four Kiev-class carriers subsequently equipped with the type. Only about 90 aircraft are believed to have been built in two versions, the single-seat Forger-A and the two-seat Forger-B, and about one-third of these have been lost in accidents. The Yak-38 was to have been replaced by a more advanced V/STOL type, the Yak-141 (Freestyle), but only prototypes of this were built and the aircraft, its development affected by

economic restraints and accidents, did not enter production.

SPECIFICATION: Type carrier-borne fighter-bomber (data Forger-A) • Crew 1 • Powerplant two 6,724-lb (3,050-kg) thrust Rybinsk RD-36-35VFR turbojets and one 15,322-lb (6,950-kg) thrust Tumanskii R-27V-300 vectored-thrust turbojet • Max speed 627mph (1,009km/h) at altitude • Service ceiling 39,370ft (12,000m) at altitude • Combat radius 230 miles (370km) max load, hi-lo-hi • Wingspan 24ft (7.32m) • Length 50ft 8in (15.43m) • Height 14ft 4in (4.37m) • Weight 25,795lb (11,700kg) loaded • Armament four external hardpoints with provision for up to 4,409lb (2,000kg) of stores

▲ This Yak-38 "Forger" was seen at Farnborough in September 1992, after the end of the Cold War. The "Forger" was designed to operate from Kiev-class carriers.

▌Yokosuka D4Y Susei "Judy"

JAPAN

First flown in December 1940, the Yokosuka D4Y Susei (Comet) was widely used by the Imperial Japanese Navy and, in its D4Y2 version, was the fastest carrier-borne dive-bomber in service during World War II. The first production models, the D4Y1 and D4Y2, were respectively powered by the 1,185hp Aichi Atsuta 21 and 1,400hp Atsuta 32 in-line engines, which were virtual replicas of the German DB601 series, and constant trouble was experienced with them. The D4Y3 model was consequently refitted with a Mitsubishi Kinsei radial engine. The Susei was developed as a replace-

ment for the Aichi D3A1 Val, and it was the Aichi company that built most of the 2,319 aircraft completed. The Susei went into service in March 1943, and in June the following year the type suffered savage losses while attempting to attack US carrier task forces in the battle for the Mariana Islands, most of the 170 aircraft committed being destroyed by the American fighter screen before reaching their targets in what became known as the "Marianas Turkey Shoot."

SPECIFICATION: Type dive-bomber (data D4Y1) • Crew 2 • Powerplant one 1,185hp Aichi Atsuta 21 12-cylinder V-type • Max speed 343mph (552km/h) at 15,585ft (4,750m) • Service ceiling 32,480ft (9,900m) • Max range 978 miles (1,575km) • Wingspan 37ft 9in (11.50m) • Length 33ft 6in (10.22m) • Height 12ft 1in (3.67m) • Weight 9,390lb (4,260kg) loaded • Armament three 0.303-in (7.7-mm) machine guns; 683lb (310kg) of bombs

▲ Inspired by the design of the He 118, the D4Y was smaller, lighter, and aerodynamically superior.

▌Yokosuka E14Y "Glen"

JAPAN

Designed by the Yokosuka Naval Air Arsenal as a small reconnaissance aircraft capable of being stowed away aboard an ocean-going submarine, the E14Y replaced an earlier type, the Watanabe E9W1. On December 17, 1941 a Glen from the submarine I-7 made a reconnaissance of Pearl Harbor prior

to the Japanese attack, and in June 1942 an aircraft from the I-25 flown by Lt Fujita dropped four 168-lb (76-kg) incendiary bombs on woodland in the State of Oregon, this being the only time that the US mainland came under aircraft attack in World War II. Including the prototype, 126 E14Ys were built.

▶ *The E14Y's claim to fame was its attack on the US mainland in June 1942, when an aircraft dropped four incendiary bombs on the state of Oregon.*

SPECIFICATION: **Type** reconnaissance floatplane • **Crew** 2 • **Powerplant** one 340hp Hitachi Tempu 12 12-cylinder radial • **Max speed** 153mph (246km/h) at sea level • **Service ceiling** 17,780ft (5,420m) • **Max range** 548 miles (880km) • **Wingspan** 36ft 1in (11m) • **Length** 28ft (8.54m) • **Height** 12ft 6in (3.82m) • **Weight** 3,533lb (1,603kg) loaded • **Armament** one 0.303-in (7.7-mm) machine gun in observer's position

▌Yokosuka K5Y "Willow"

JAPAN

Yokosuka was the location of the Imperial Japanese Navy's First Naval Air Technical Arsenal. A tough and sturdy biplane, the K5Y was Japan's most widely used trainer during World War II. The type remained in continuous production from 1933–45 and 5,770 examples were built in two principal variants, the K5Y1 land-based trainer and the K5Y2 seaplane.

SPECIFICATION: **Type** basic trainer • **Crew** 2 • **Powerplant** one 340hp Hitachi Amakaze 11 9-cylinder radial • **Max speed** 132mph (212km/h) • **Service ceiling** 18,700ft (5,700m) • **Max range** 633 miles (1,020km) • **Wingspan** 36ft 1in (11m) • **Length** 26ft 5in (8.05m) • **Height** 10ft 6in (3.20m) • **Weight** 3,307lb (1,500kg) loaded • **Armament** one fixed forward-firing 0.303-in (7.7-mm) machine gun; one flexible 0.303-in (7.7-mm) in rear cockpit

▌Yokosuka MXY7 Ohka "Baka"

JAPAN

▲ *One of the more sinister weapons developed in World War II, this MXY7 Ohka suicide aircraft has been captured by US forces in the Pacific.*

The unpowered prototype MXY7 Ohka (Cherry Blossom) suicide aircraft flew in October 1944. The production model was the Ohka Model 11, of which 755 were built between

SPECIFICATION: **Type** suicide aircraft • **Crew** 1 • **Powerplant** three solid-fuel Type 4 Mk 1 Model 20 rockets with total thrust of 1,764lb (800kg) • **Max speed** 576mph (927km/h) in terminal dive • **Service ceiling** not applicable • **Max range** 23 miles (37km) • **Wingspan** 16ft 9in (5.12m) • **Length** 19ft 10in (6.07m) • **Height** 3ft 9in (1.16m) • **Weight** 4,718lb (2,140kg) loaded • **Armament** one 2,646lb (1,200kg) warhead

September 1944 and March 1945. The Ohka went into action for the first time on March 21, 1945, but the 16 Mitsubishi G4M2e parent aircraft (which carried the Ohkas shackled under the open bomb bay) were intercepted and forced to release their bombs short of the target. The first success came on April 1st, when Ohkas damaged the battleship USS *West Virginia* and three transport vessels. The first ship to be destroyed by an Ohka was the destroyer *Mannert L. Abele*, lost at Okinawa on April 12th. Several versions of the Ohka were proposed, including the turbojet-powered Model 33, but none saw operational service before the end of the war.

▌Yokosuka P1Y Ginga "Frances"

▲ *The third prototype P1Y1 Ginga was later experimentally fitted with a Tsu-11 jet engine beneath the rear fuselage.*

SPECIFICATION: Type medium bomber (data P1Y1) • Crew 3 • Powerplant two 1,650hp Nakajima NK9B Homare 11 18-cylinder radials • Max speed 340mph (547km/h) at 20,026ft (6,104m) • Service ceiling 30,840ft (9,400m) • Max range 3,338 miles (5,370km) • Wingspan 65ft 7in (20m) • Length 14ft 2in (4.32m) • Height 14ft 1in (4.29m) • Weight 23,149lb (10,500kg) • Armament one flexible 0.79-in (20-mm) cannon in nose and one in rear cockpit; one 1,764-lb (800-kg) torpedo or up to 2,205lb (1,000kg) of bombs

The Yokosuka P1Y Ginga (Milky Way) was roughly the Japanese equivalent of the de Havilland Mosquito and the Junkers Ju 88. An extremely versatile aircraft, the type entered service in 1943 as a fast bomber, 1,002 examples of the initial P1Y1 version being built. Later in the war, with increasing priority being given to the defense of the Japanese homeland, a night fighter version, the P1Y2-S Kyokko (Aurora) was produced by Kawasaki. Only 97 were built, powered by 1,850hp Kasei 25 engines, fitted with rudimentary AI radar, and carrying an armament of three 0.79-in (20-mm) cannon. However, performance at altitude proved disappointing, so most of these aircraft were operated as bombers.

▌Zeppelin-Staaken R.VI

The largest aircraft used in World War I were the sluggish but effective Riesenflugzeug (giant aircraft) series designed by the Zeppelin Werke Staaken, the design team responsible having previously worked for the former organization. After several "one-shot" bombers had been built, production standardized on the R.VI; one was built by the Staaken works, six by Aviatik, four by OAW, and seven by Schütte-Lanz. All the bombers were used in attacks on England or on the Eastern Front. During their combat career only two R.VIs were lost in action, but eight were destroyed in accidents.

SPECIFICATION: Type heavy bomber • Crew 7 • Powerplant four 245hp Maybach Mb.IV 6-cylinder in-line engines • Max speed 81mph (130km/h) • Service ceiling 12,467ft (3,800m) • Max range 500 miles (800km) • Wingspan 138ft 6in (42.20m) • Length 72ft 6in (22.10m) • Height 20ft 8in (6.30m) • Weight 25,265lb (11,460kg) loaded • Armament one or two 0.31-in (7.92-mm) machine guns in nose and dorsal positions, and one in rear position; provision for up to eighteen 220-lb (100-kg) or one 2,205lb (1,000kg) bomb carried in semirecessed position; maximum load 4,409lb (2,000kg)

▲ *The Zeppelin-Staaken R.IV was the first of the German Riesenflugzeug (Giant Aircraft) to enter service. It was powered by four Benz Bz.IV engines.*

IINDEX

IPICTURE CREDITS